W9-BBD-297

ENVIRONMENTAL POLICY

NEW DIRECTIONS FOR THE TWENTY-FIRST CENTURY

Sixth Edition

Edited by

Norman J. Vig
Carleton College

Michael E. Kraft
University of Wisconsin–Green Bay

CQ PRESS

A Division of Congressional Quarterly Inc.
Washington, D.C.

CQ Press
1255 22nd Street, NW, Suite 400
Washington, DC 20037

Phone, 202-729-1900; toll-free, 1-866-427-7737 (1-866-4CQ-PRESS)

Web: www.cqpress.com

Copyright © 2006 by CQ Press, a division of Congressional Quarterly Inc.

All rights reserved. No part of this publication may be reproduced or transmitted in any form or by any means, electronic or mechanical, including photocopy, recording, or any information storage and retrieval system, without permission in writing from the publisher.

Cover design by McGaughy Design, Centreville, Virginia

♾ The paper used in this publication exceeds the requirements of the American National Standard for Information Sciences—Permanence of Paper for Printed Library Materials, ANSI Z39.48-1992.

Printed and bound in the United States of America

09   08   07   06   05   1   2   3   4   5

Library of Congress Cataloging-in-Publication Data

Environmental policy : new directions for the twenty-first century / edited by Norman J. Vig, Michael E. Kraft.— 6th ed.
    p. cm.
  Includes bibliographical references and indexes.
  ISBN 1-933116-01-3 (pbk. : alk. paper)
  1. Environmental policy—United States. I. Vig, Norman J. II. Kraft, Michael E. III. Title.

GE180.E586 2006
363.7'056'0973—dc22

2005013438

Contents

Tables, Figures, and Boxes

Preface

In the early twenty-first century, environmental policy is being challenged as never before. New demands worldwide for dealing with the risks of climate change, threats to biological diversity, and similar issues will force governments everywhere to rethink policy strategies and find new ways to reconcile environmental and economic goals. In the United States the new century began on an ominous note when President George W. Bush announced that the U.S. government would abandon the Kyoto Protocol (1997), which for the first time established binding national limits on greenhouse gas emissions. Conservative Republican members of Congress, as well as the Bush White House, continued to voice strong concerns about environmental policies and programs, and they pushed for new approaches that favored economic development and imposed fewer restrictions on business activities. One consequence of the ongoing debate over the direction of environmental policy is that too little consensus exists in Congress to revise the nation's major environmental laws, which most scholars and specialists in the field believe must be changed to address contemporary challenges. As much as the debate over the environment shifted in important ways during the 1990s and early 2000s, it remains clear that government and politics will continue to play crucial roles in shaping our environmental future.

When the first environmental decade was launched in the early 1970s, protecting our air, water, and other natural resources seemed a relatively simple proposition. The polluters and exploiters of nature would be brought to heel by tough laws requiring them to clean up or get out of business within five or ten years. But preserving the life support systems of the planet now appears a more daunting task than anyone imagined back then. Not only are problems such as global climate change more complex than controlling earlier sources of pollution, but also the success of U.S. policies is tied, now more than ever, to the actions of other nations.

This book seeks to explain the most important developments in environmental policy and politics since the 1960s and to analyze the central issues that face us now. Like the previous editions, it focuses on the underlying trends, institutional strengths and shortcomings, and policy dilemmas that all policy actors face in attempting to resolve environmental controversies. All of the chapters have been thoroughly revised and updated. We have also attempted to place George W. Bush's administration and the congressional agenda in the context of the ongoing debate over the cost and effectiveness of past environmental policies, as well as the search for ways to reconcile and integrate economic, environmental, and social goals through sustainable development. As such, the book has broad relevance for the environmental community and for all concerned with the difficulties and complexities of finding solutions to environmental problems.

Part I provides a retrospective view of policy development as well as a framework for analyzing policy change in the United States. Chapter 1 serves as an introduction to the book by outlining the basic issues in U.S. environmental policy since the early 1970s, the development of institutional capabilities for addressing them, and the successes and failures in implementing policies and achieving results. In chapter 2 Barry G. Rabe considers the evolving role of the states in environmental policy at a time when continuing devolution of responsibilities is favored by both the White House and Congress. He focuses on innovative policy approaches used by the states and the promise of—as well as the constraints on—state action on the environment. In chapter 3 Robert C. Paehlke examines the intriguing efforts by communities throughout the nation to integrate environmental sustainability into policy decisions in areas as diverse as transportation, land use, and urban social life. Part I ends with a chapter by Christopher J. Bosso and Deborah Lynn Guber that analyzes trends in public opinion and the changing strategies of the environmental movement. They find that public support for environmental policies is not as strong or reliable as often assumed and that environmental groups continue to suffer from persistent conflicts over the most suitable political strategies to embrace.

Part II analyzes the role of federal institutions in environmental policy-making. Chapter 5, by Norman J. Vig, discusses the role of recent presidents as environmental actors, evaluating their leadership on the basis of several common criteria. In chapter 6 Michael E. Kraft examines the role of Congress in environmental policy, with special attention to the causes and consequences of policy gridlock. In chapter 7 Rosemary O'Leary uses several in-depth case studies of judicial action to explore how the courts shape environmental policy. In chapter 8 Walter A. Rosenbaum takes a hard and critical look at the Environmental Protection Agency, the nation's chief environmental institution. In particular, he examines controversies over the agency's use of science in regulatory standard setting and the role the White House plays in agency decision making.

Some of the broader dilemmas in environmental policy formulation and implementation are examined in Part III. The first two chapters focus on approaches that are increasingly being advocated to improve the efficiency and effectiveness of environmental regulation. In chapter 9 economist A. Myrick Freeman III discusses the potential for more rational economic decision making, including the use of cost-benefit analysis. He also asks how market incentives such as pollution taxes and tradable discharge permits could be introduced to achieve better results at less cost. Chapter 10, by Richard N. L. Andrews, takes up a parallel set of questions regarding scientific risk assessment: How well can environmental risks be measured and compared given the technical obstacles and human judgments involved, and to what extent is White House oversight of agency risk decisions becoming politicized?

The chapters in Part III also consider social responsibilities that are becoming recognized as central to environmental health and progress. In chapter 11 Evan J. Ringquist analyzes the emergence of the environmental justice movement in response to growing awareness of racial and social inequities in the distribution of environmental burdens. He presents new empirical evidence regarding these inequities and discusses potential remedies. Chapter 12 moves the spotlight to evolving business practices. In that chapter Daniel Press and Daniel A. Mazmanian examine the "greening of industry," particularly the increasing use of market-based initiatives such as voluntary pollution prevention, information disclosure, and environmental management systems. They find that a creative combination of voluntary actions and government regulation offers the best promise of success.

Part IV shifts attention to selected issues and controversies, both global and domestic. In chapter 13 Lamont C. Hempel surveys the key scientific evidence and major disputes over climate change, as well as the evolution of the issue, especially since the late 1980s. He also assesses government responses to the problem of climate change and the outlook for public policy actions in the twenty-first century. In chapter 14 William R. Lowry examines the return to traditional natural resource priorities under the Bush administration. He reviews the history of U.S. natural resource policies and agencies, the lively debates that have arisen over them in recent years, and a range of proposals for institutional change—from privatization and devolution to ecosystem management and collaborative planning—within the context of Bush administration policy shifts. In chapter 15 Richard J. Tobin examines the plight of developing nations that are struggling with a formidable array of threats brought about by rapid population growth and resource exploitation. He surveys the pertinent evidence, recounts cases of policy success and failure, and indicates the remaining barriers (including insufficient commitment by rich countries) to achieving sustainable development in these nations. The last chapter in Part IV, by David Vogel, discusses the effects, actual and potential, of new international trade agreements on national policies for resource preservation and environmental protection.

In the final chapter we summarize the arguments for integrating the concept of sustainable development more fully into policymaking at all levels of government. Moreover, we review the agenda of outstanding environmental problems facing the nation and the world, and we discuss a series of innovative policy instruments that might help us to better address these issues in the future.

We thank the contributing authors for their generosity, cooperative spirit, and patience in response to our seemingly ruthless editorial requests. It is a pleasure to work with such a conscientious and punctual group of scholars. Special thanks are also due to the staff of CQ Press, including Brenda Carter, Charisse Kiino, Colleen Ganey, Gwenda Larsen, Ann Davies, and Steve Pazdan, and to freelance copy editor Amy Marks for their customarily splendid editorial work. We also gratefully acknowledge support from the Department of Political Science and the Environmental and Technology Studies Program at Carleton College and the Department of Public and Environmental Affairs at the University of Wisconsin–Green Bay. Finally, we thank our students at Carleton and UW–Green Bay for forcing us to rethink our assumptions about what really matters. As always, any remaining errors and omissions are our own responsibility.

Norman J. Vig
Michael E. Kraft

Contributors

About the Editors

Michael E. Kraft is professor of political science and public affairs and Herbert Fisk Johnson Professor of Environmental Studies at the University of Wisconsin–Green Bay. He is the author of *Environmental Policy and Politics*, 3rd ed. (2004); coauthor of *Public Policy: Politics, Analysis, and Alternatives* (2004); and coeditor of *Public Reactions to Nuclear Waste* (1993); *Toward Sustainable Communities: Transition and Transformations in Environmental Policy* (1999); *Environmental Policy*, 5th ed. (2003); and *Business and Environmental Policy* (forthcoming, 2006).

Norman J. Vig is the Winifred and Atherton Bean Professor of Science, Technology, and Society, Emeritus, at Carleton College. He has written extensively on environmental policy, science and technology policy, and comparative politics, and is the coeditor (with Michael E. Kraft) of *Technology and Politics* (1988) and *Environmental Policy*, 5th ed. (2003). His most recent books are *Green Giants? Environmental Policies of the United States and the European Union* (2004), coedited with Michael Faure, and *The Global Environment: Institutions, Law, and Policy*, 2nd ed. (2005), coedited with Regina Axelrod and David Downie.

About the Contributors

Richard N. L. Andrews is the Thomas Willis Lambeth Distinguished Professor of Public Policy at the University of North Carolina at Chapel Hill. He has served on advisory panels of the U.S. Environmental Protection Agency Science Advisory Board, the National Research Council, and the National Academy of Public Administration on environmental risk management and regulatory innovation. He is the author of *Environmental Policy and Administrative Reform: Implementation of the National Environmental Policy Act* (1976); *Managing the Environment, Managing Ourselves: A History of American Environmental Policy* (1999); and many articles and other publications on environmental policy.

Christopher J. Bosso is associate professor of political science at Northeastern University. He writes on environmental politics, the tactics and strategies pursued by environmental groups, and public policymaking dynamics. He is the author of *Pesticides and Politics: The Life Cycle of a Public Issue* (1987) and coauthor of a textbook, *American Government: Conflict, Compromise, and Citizenship* (2000). His most recent work is *Environment, Inc.: From Grassroots to Beltway* (2005).

A. Myrick Freeman III is Research Professor of Economics at Bowdoin College. He also has held appointments as Senior Fellow at Resources for the

Future, Visiting College Professor at the University of Washington, and Robert M. La Follette Visiting Distinguished Professor at the University of Wisconsin –Madison. He is the author of several books, including *Air and Water Pollution Control: A Benefit-Cost Assessment* (1982) and *The Measurement of Environmental and Resource Values: Theory and Methods,* 2nd ed. (2003). He has served as director of Bowdoin's Environmental Studies Program and is presently a member of the U.S. Environmental Protection Agency Science Advisory Board.

Deborah Lynn Guber is associate professor of political science at the University of Vermont, where she specializes in public opinion, U.S. electoral politics, and environmental policy. Her work has appeared in journals such as *Social Science Quarterly, Society and Natural Resources,* and *State and Local Government Review.* She is the author of *The Grassroots of a Green Revolution: Polling America on the Environment* (2003).

Lamont C. Hempel is Hedco Professor of Environmental Studies and director of the Center for Environmental Studies at the University of Redlands. He specializes in U.S. and international environmental policy, with an emphasis on issues of climate change, sustainable community development, and coral reef protection. His publications include *Environmental Governance: The Global Challenge* (1996) and *Sustainable Communities: From Vision to Action* (1998).

William R. Lowry is professor of political science at Washington University in St. Louis. He has published numerous articles and four books: *The Dimensions of Federalism: State Governments and Pollution Control Policies* (1992), *The Capacity for Wonder: Preserving National Parks* (1994), *Preserving Public Lands for the Future: The Politics of Intergenerational Goods* (1998), and *Dam Politics: Restoring America's Rivers* (2003).

Daniel A. Mazmanian is the Bedrosian Chair of Governance, and director of the Judith and John Bedrosian Center on Governance and the Public Enterprise, in the School of Policy, Planning, and Development (SPPD) at the University of Southern California. From 2000 to 2005 he served as C. Erwin and Ione Piper Dean and Professor of SPPD and prior to that as dean of the School of Natural Resources and Environment at the University of Michigan. Among his several books are *Can Organizations Change? Environmental Protection, Citizen Participation, and the Corps of Engineers* (1979); *Implementation and Public Policy* (1989); *Beyond Superfailure: America's Toxics Policy for the 1990s* (1992); and *Toward Sustainable Communities* (1999).

Rosemary O'Leary is an environmental lawyer and a distinguished professor of public administration, with additional appointments in political science and law, at the Maxwell School of Syracuse University. She has written extensively on the courts and environmental policy. She is the winner of nine national research awards, including two "best book" awards for *Managing for the Environment,* written with Robert Durant, Daniel Fiorino, and Paul Weiland (1999). Her most recent book, *The Promise and Performance of Environmental Conflict Resolution,* coedited with Lisa Bingham, won the 2005 award for "Best Book in Environmental and Natural Resources Administration," given by the American Society for Public Administration.

Robert C. Paehlke is professor in the Environmental and Resource Studies Program at Trent University, Peterborough, Ontario. He is the author of *Environmentalism and the Future of Progressive Politics* (1989) and *Democracy's Dilemma: Environment, Social Equity, and the Global Economy* (2003); coeditor of *Managing Leviathan: Environmental Politics and the Administrative State*, 2nd ed. (2005); and editor of *Conservation and Environmentalism: An Encyclopedia* (1995). He is a founding editor of the Canadian journal *Alternatives: Perspectives on Society, Technology, and Environment.*

Daniel Press is professor and chair of environmental studies at the University of California, Santa Cruz, where he teaches environmental politics and policy. He is the author of *Democratic Dilemmas in the Age of Ecology* (1994) and *Saving Open Space: The Politics of Local Preservation in California* (2002).

Barry G. Rabe is a professor of public policy in the Gerald R. Ford School of Public Policy and a professor of environmental policy in the School of Natural Resources and Environment at the University of Michigan. He recently served as director of the university's Program in the Environment. Rabe is the author of, among other works, *When Federalism Works* (1986), *Fragmentation and Integration in State Environmental Management* (1986), and *Beyond NIMBY: Hazardous Waste Siting in Canada and the United States* (1994). His most recent book is *Statehouse and Greenhouse: The Emerging Politics of American Climate Change Policy* (2004). His current research examines the capacity of multilevel governance systems in North America and the European Union to develop and implement policies to reduce greenhouse gas emissions.

Evan J. Ringquist is professor of environmental policy in the School of Public and Environmental Affairs at Indiana University. He is the author of *Environmental Protection at the State Level* (1993) and *Contemporary Regulatory Policy* (2000), among other works. He is also completing a new book on environmental justice. Ringquist has served as a consultant for the U.S. Environmental Protection Agency, National Park Service, and several state and municipal governments.

Walter A. Rosenbaum is professor of political science emeritus at the University of Florida in Gainesville and visiting professor, Program in the Environment, at the University of Michigan, where he specializes in environmental and energy policy. He also served as a senior consultant to the Assistant Administrator for Policy, Planning, and Evaluation at the U.S. Environmental Protection Agency and is currently a consultant to the Federal Emergency Management Agency. Among his many published works is *Environmental Politics and Policy*, 6th ed. (2004).

Richard J. Tobin directs the Evaluation Group at the World Bank Institute in Washington, D.C. He formerly provided technical assistance to governments in developing countries through the U.S. Agency for International Development.

His book *The Expendable Future: U.S. Politics and the Protection of Biological Diversity* received the Policy Studies Organization's Outstanding Book Award.

David Vogel is a professor in the Haas School of Business and the Department of Political Science at the University of California, Berkeley. He has written extensively on business-government relations and government regulation in the United States, the European Union, and Japan. His books include *National Styles of Regulation: Environmental Policy in Great Britain and the United States* (1986), *Trading Up: Consumer and Environmental Regulation in a Global Economy* (1995), and *The Market for Virtue: The Potential and Limits of Corporate Social Responsibility* (2005).

1

Environmental Policy from the 1970s to the Twenty-First Century

Michael E. Kraft and Norman J. Vig

Environmental issues soared to a prominent place on the political agenda in the United States and other industrial nations in the early 1970s. The new visibility was accompanied by abundant evidence domestically and internationally of heightened public concern over environmental threats.[1] By the 1990s policymakers around the world pledged to deal with a range of important environmental challenges, from protection of biological diversity to air and water pollution control. Such commitments were particularly manifest at the 1992 UN Conference on Environment and Development (the Earth Summit) held in Rio de Janeiro, Brazil, where an ambitious agenda for redirecting the world's economies toward sustainable development was approved, and at the December 1997 Conference of the Parties in Kyoto, Japan, where delegates agreed to a landmark treaty on global warming. Although it received less media coverage, the World Summit on Sustainable Development, held in Johannesburg, South Africa, in September 2002, reaffirmed the commitments made a decade earlier at the Earth Summit, with particular attention to the challenge of alleviating global poverty.

Rising criticism of established environmental programs also was evident throughout the 1990s and into the early twenty-first century, as were a multiplicity of efforts to chart new policy directions. For instance, intense opposition to environmental and natural resource policies arose in the 104th Congress (1995–1997), when the Republican Party took control of both the House and Senate for the first time in forty years. Ultimately, much like the earlier effort in Ronald Reagan's administration, the antiregulatory campaign on Capitol Hill failed to gain public support.[2] Nonetheless, battles over environmental policy continued through the 108th Congress (2003–2005), with environmentalists pointing as well to a determined effort by the Bush White House to rewrite environmental rules and regulations to favor industry.[3] Increasing dissatisfaction with the effectiveness, efficiency, and equity of environmental policies was by no means confined to congressional conservatives and the Bush administration. It could be found among a broad array of interests, including the business community, environmental policy analysts, environmental justice groups, and state and local government officials.[4]

Since 1992, governments at all levels have struggled to redesign environmental policy for the twenty-first century. Under Presidents Bill Clinton and George W. Bush, the U.S. Environmental Protection Agency (EPA) tried to "reinvent" environmental regulation through the use of collaborative decision making involving multiple stakeholders, public-private partnerships, market-based incentives, information disclosure, and enhanced flexibility in rulemaking and enforcement (see chapters 9, 10, and 12).[5] Particularly during the Clinton administration, new emphases within the EPA and other federal agencies and departments on ecosystem management and sustainable development sought to foster comprehensive and long-term strategies for environmental protection (see chapter 14).[6] Many state and local governments have pursued similar goals, with adoption of a wide range of innovative policies that promise to address some of the most important criticisms directed at contemporary environmental policy (see chapter 2).

The precise way in which Congress, the states, and local governments will change environmental policies remains unclear, in part because the previous bipartisan consensus on policy goals and means has been replaced by heightened partisan conflict. Policy changes are likely to depend on how the various policy actors stake out and defend their positions on the issues, the way the media cover these disputes, the relative influence of opposing interests, and even the state of the economy. Political leadership will also play a role, especially in reconciling deep divisions between the major political parties on environmental protection and natural resource issues. Political conflict over the environment is not going to vanish any time soon. Indeed, it will likely increase as the United States and other nations struggle to define how they will respond to the latest generation of environmental problems.

Another conclusion is inescapable. The heightened antienvironmental rhetoric and political backlash that has been so evident since the early 1990s—in the states as well as at the national level of government—plainly indicate that environmental policy is at an important crossroads. More than ever, analysts, the public, and policymakers need to learn what works and what does not, and how best to refashion environmental policy for the demands of the twenty-first century. They also need to separate genuine efforts to reform environmental policies and programs by improving their effectiveness and efficiency from actions that would compromise the broadly supported commitment to environmental protection goals that the public and policymakers have made since 1970.

In this chapter we examine the continuities and changes in environmental politics and policy since 1970 and discuss their implications for the early twenty-first century. We review the policymaking process in the United States, and we assess the performance of government institutions and political leadership. We give special attention to the major programs adopted in the 1970s, their achievements to date, and the need for policy redesign and priority setting for the years ahead. The chapters that follow address in greater detail many of the questions explored in this introduction.

The Role of Government and Politics

The elevated political conflict over environmental protection efforts during recent years underscores the important role government plays in devising solutions to the nation's and the world's mounting environmental ills. Global climate change, population growth, the spread of toxic and hazardous chemicals, loss of biological diversity, and air and water pollution all require diverse actions by individuals and institutions at all levels of society and in both the public and private sectors. These actions range from scientific research and technological innovation to improved environmental education and significant changes in corporate and consumer behavior. As political scientists we believe government has an indispensable role to play in environmental protection and improvement. The chapters in this volume thus focus on environmental policies and the government institutions and political processes that affect them. Our goal is to illuminate that role and to suggest needed changes and strategies.

The government plays a preeminent role in this policy arena primarily because environmental threats represent public or collective goods problems. They cannot be resolved through purely private actions. There is no question that individuals and nongovernmental organizations, such as environmental groups and research institutes, can do much to protect environmental quality and promote public health. The potential for such action is demonstrated by the impressive growth of sustainable community efforts during the 1990s and early 2000s and the diversified efforts by business and industry to prevent pollution through development of greener products and services (see chapters 3 and 12).

Yet such actions are often insufficient without the backing of public policy, for example, laws mandating control of toxic chemicals that are supported by the authority of government. The justification for government intervention lies partly in the inherent limitations of the market system and the nature of human behavior. Self-interested individuals and a relatively unfettered economic marketplace guided mainly by a concern for short-term profits tend to create spillover effects, or externalities; pollution and other kinds of environmental degradation are examples. Collective action is needed to correct such market failures. In addition, the scope and urgency of environmental problems typically exceed the capacity of private markets and individual efforts to deal with them effectively. For these reasons, among others, the United States and other nations have relied on government policies—at local, state, national, and international levels—to address environmental and resource challenges.

Adopting public policies does not imply that voluntary and cooperative actions by citizens in their communities or various environmental initiatives by businesses cannot be the primary vehicle of change in many instances. Nor does it suggest that governments should not consider a full range of policy approaches—including market-based incentives, new forms of collaborative decision making, and information provision strategies—to supplement or even replace conventional regulatory policies where needed. The guiding principle should be to use the approaches that work best—those that bring about the desired improvements in environmental quality, minimize health and ecological risks, and help to integrate and balance environmental and economic goals.

Political Institutions and Public Policy

Public policy is a course of government action or inaction in response to social problems. It is expressed in goals articulated by political leaders; in formal statutes, rules, and regulations; and in the practices of administrative agencies and courts charged with implementing or overseeing programs. Policy states an intent to achieve certain goals and objectives through a conscious choice of means, usually within a specified period of time. In a constitutional democracy like the United States, policymaking is distinctive in several respects: It must take place through constitutional processes, it requires the sanction of law, and it is binding on all members of society. Usually the process is open to public scrutiny and debate, although secrecy may be justified in matters involving national security and diplomatic relations.

The constitutional requirements for policymaking were established well over two hundred years ago, and they remain much the same today. The U.S. political system is based on a division of authority among three branches of government and between the federal government and the states. Originally intended to limit government power and to protect individual liberty, today this division of power may impede the ability of government to adopt timely and coherent environmental policy. Dedication to principles of federalism means that environmental policy responsibilities are distributed among the federal government, the fifty states, and thousands of local governments (see chapter 2).

Responsibility for the environment is divided within the branches of the federal government as well, most notably in the U.S. Congress, with power shared between the House and Senate, and jurisdiction over environmental policies scattered among dozens of committees and subcommittees (Table 1-1). One study, for example, found that thirteen committees and thirty-one subcommittees in Congress had some jurisdiction over EPA activities.[7] The executive branch is also institutionally fragmented, with at least some responsibility for the environment and natural resources located in twelve cabinet departments and in the EPA, the Nuclear Regulatory Commission, and other agencies (Figure 1-1). Although most environmental policies are concentrated in the EPA and in the Interior and Agriculture Departments, the Departments of Energy, Defense, and State are increasingly important actors as well. Finally, the more than 100 federal trial and appellate courts play key roles in interpreting environmental legislation and adjudicating disputes over administrative and regulatory actions (see chapter 7).

The implications of this constitutional arrangement for policymaking were evident in the early 1980s as Congress and the courts checked and

Table 1-1   Major Congressional Committees with Environmental
Responsibilities

Committee	Environmental Policy Jurisdiction
House	
Agriculture	Agriculture generally; forestry in general and private forest reserves; agricultural and industrial chemistry; pesticides; soil conservation; food safety and human nutrition; rural development; water conservation related to activities of the Department of Agriculture
Appropriations[a]	Appropriations for all programs
Energy and Commerce	Measures related to the exploration, production, storage, marketing, pricing, and regulation of energy sources, including all fossil fuels, solar, and renewable energy; energy conservation and information; measures related to general management of the Department of Energy and the Federal Energy Regulatory Commission; regulation of the domestic nuclear energy industry; research and development of nuclear power and nuclear waste; air pollution; safe drinking water; pesticide control; Superfund and hazardous waste disposal; toxic substances control; health and the environment
Resources	Public lands and natural resources in general; irrigation and reclamation; water and power; mineral resources on public lands and mining; grazing; national parks, forests, and wilderness areas; fisheries and wildlife, including research, restoration, refuges, and conservation; oceanography, international fishing agreements, and coastal zone management; Geological Survey
Science	Environmental research and development; marine research; energy research and development in all federally owned nonmilitary energy laboratories; research in national laboratories; NASA, National Weather Service, and National Science Foundation
Transportation and Infrastructure	Transportation, including civil aviation, railroads, water transportation, and transportation infrastructure; Coast Guard and marine transportation; federal management of emergencies and natural disasters; flood control and improvement of waterways; water resources and the environment; pollution of navigable waters; bridges and dams
Senate	
Agriculture, Nutrition and Forestry	Agriculture in general; food from fresh waters; soil conservation and groundwater; forestry in general; human nutrition; rural development and watersheds; pests and pesticides; food inspection and safety
Appropriations[a]	Appropriations for all programs

(Continued on next page)

Table 1-1   *(Continued)*

Committee	Environmental Policy Jurisdiction
Commerce, Science and Transportation	Interstate commerce and transportation generally; coastal zone management; inland waterways; marine fisheries; oceans, weather, and atmospheric activities; transportation and commerce aspects of outer continental shelf lands; science, engineering, and technology research and development; surface transportation
Energy and Natural Resources	Energy policy, regulation, conservation, research and development; coal; oil, and gas production and distribution; civilian nuclear energy; solar energy systems; mines, mining, and minerals; irrigation and reclamation; water and power; national parks and recreation areas; wilderness areas; wild and scenic rivers; public lands and forests; historic sites
Environment and Public Works	Environmental policy, research, and development; air, water, and noise pollution; climate change; construction and maintenance of highways; safe drinking water; environmental aspects of outer continental shelf lands and ocean dumping; environmental effects of toxic substances other than pesticides; fisheries and wildlife; Superfund and hazardous wastes; solid waste disposal and recycling; nonmilitary environmental regulation and control of nuclear energy; water resources, flood control, and improvements of rivers and harbors; public works, bridges, and dams

Sources: Compiled from descriptions of committee jurisdictions reported in Congressional Quarterly, *Players, Politics, and Turf of the 105th Congress* (Washington, D.C.: Congressional Quarterly, March 22, 1997, vol. 55, supplement to no. 12); and "CQ Guide to the Committees," *CQ Weekly Report*, March 27, 2004, c1–c36.

[a] Both the House and Senate appropriations committees have interior and environment subcommittees that handle all Interior Department agencies as well as the Forest Service. As of 2005, EPA appropriations were added to their jurisdictions. The Energy Department, Army Corps of Engineers, and Nuclear Regulatory Commission fall under the jurisdiction of the subcommittees on Energy and Water Development. Tax policy affects many environmental, energy, and natural resources policies and is governed by the Senate Finance Committee and the House Ways and Means Committee.

balanced the Reagan administration's efforts to reverse environmental policies of the previous decade. They were equally clear during the 1990s when the Clinton administration vigorously opposed actions in the 104th, 105th, and 106th Congresses (1995 to 2001) to weaken environmental programs. They could be seen again early in the presidency of George W. Bush, when a Democratic Senate challenged the president's proposed national energy policy and other environmental initiatives.

By 2005, with Republican majorities in both houses of Congress and the Bush administration asserting that the 2004 presidential election gave it a clear mandate for the president's environmental policies, many

Figure 1-1 Executive Branch Agencies with Environmental Responsibilities

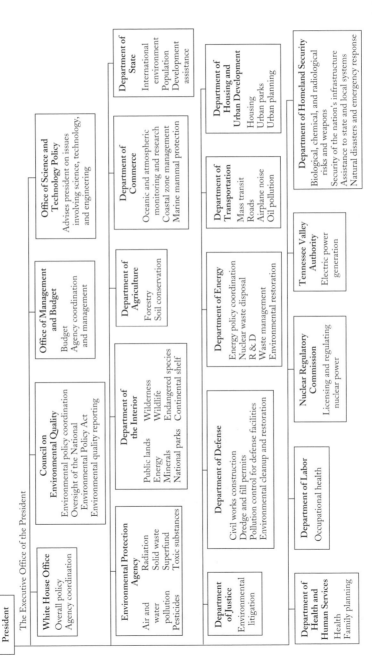

President

The Executive Office of the President

White House Office
Overall policy
Agency coordination

Council on Environmental Quality
Environmental policy coordination
Oversight of the National Environmental Policy Act
Environmental quality reporting

Office of Management and Budget
Budget
Agency coordination and management

Office of Science and Technology Policy
Advises president on issues involving science, technology, and engineering

Environmental Protection Agency
Air and water pollution
Pesticides
Radiation
Solid waste
Superfund
Toxic substances

Department of the Interior
Public lands
Energy
Minerals
National parks
Wilderness
Wildlife
Endangered species
Continental shelf

Department of Agriculture
Forestry
Soil conservation

Department of Commerce
Oceanic and atmospheric monitoring and research
Coastal zone management
Marine mammal protection

Department of State
International environment
Population
Development assistance

Department of Justice
Environmental litigation

Department of Defense
Civil works construction
Dredge and fill permits
Pollution control for defense facilities
Environmental cleanup and restoration

Department of Energy
Energy policy coordination
Nuclear waste disposal
R & D
Waste management
Environmental restoration

Department of Transportation
Mass transit
Roads
Airplane noise
Oil pollution

Department of Housing and Urban Development
Housing
Urban parks
Urban planning

Department of Health and Human Services
Health
Family planning

Department of Labor
Occupational health

Nuclear Regulatory Commission
Licensing and regulating nuclear power

Tennessee Valley Authority
Electric power generation

Department of Homeland Security
Biological, chemical, and radiological risks and weapons
Security of the nation's infrastructure
Assistance to state and local systems
Natural disasters and emergency response

Sources: Council on Environmental Quality, *Environmental Quality: Sixteenth Annual Report of the Council on Environmental Quality* (Washington, D.C.: U.S. Government Printing Office, 1987); *United States Government Manual 1997/98* (Washington, D.C.: U.S. Government Printing Office, 1997), and authors.

environmentalists feared for the worst. Yet if their access to policymakers at the national level was diminished, they could turn to state and local governments, where actions often have been more favorable to environmental interests (see chapter 2). A case in point was California's decision in late 2004 to adopt tough new regulations on greenhouse gas emissions from automobiles.[8]

More generally, divided authority produces slow and incremental alterations in public policy, typically after broad consultation and agreement among diverse interests both within and outside of government. Such political interaction and accommodation of interests enhance the overall legitimacy of the resulting public policies. Over time, however, the cumulative effect has been disjointed policies that fall short of the ecological or holistic principles of policy design so often touted by environmental scientists, planners, and activists.

Nonetheless, when issues are highly visible, the public is supportive, and political leaders act cohesively, the U.S. political system has proved flexible enough to permit substantial policy innovation.[9] As we shall see, this was the case in the early to mid-1970s, when Congress enacted major changes in U.S. environmental policy, and in the mid-1980s, when Congress overrode objections of the Reagan administration and greatly strengthened policies on hazardous waste and water quality, among others. Passage of the monumental Clean Air Act Amendments of 1990 is a more recent example of the same alignment of forces. With bipartisan support, Congress adopted the act by a margin of 401 to 25 in the House and 89 to 10 in the Senate. Comparable bipartisanship during the mid-1990s produced major changes in the Safe Drinking Water Act and in regulation of pesticide residues in food (see chapter 6).

Policy Processes: Agendas, Streams, and Cycles

Students of public policy have proposed several models for analyzing how issues get on the political agenda and move through the policy processes of government. These theoretical frameworks help us to understand both long-term policy trends and short-term cycles of progressive action and political reaction. One set of essential questions concerns *agenda setting*: How do new problems emerge as political issues that demand the government's attention, if they do achieve such recognition? For example, why did the federal government initiate controls on industrial pollution in the 1960s and early 1970s but do little about national energy issues until well into the 1970s, and even then only to a limited extent?

In an issue's rise to prominence, hurdles almost always must be overcome. The issue must first gain societal recognition as a problem, often in response to demographic, technological, or other social changes. Then it must get on the docket of government institutions, usually through the exercise of organized group pressure. Finally it must receive enough attention by government policymakers to reach the stage of decisional or policy action. An issue is not likely to reach this latter stage unless conditions are ripe—for example, a triggering event that focuses public opinion sharply, as occurred with the Exxon *Valdez* oil spill in 1989.[10] One model analyzes agenda setting according to the convergence of three streams that can be said to flow through the political system at any time: (1) evidence of the existence of problems, (2) available policies to deal with them, and (3) the political climate or willingness to act. Although largely independent of one another, these problem, policy, and political streams can be brought together at critical times when so-called policy entrepreneurs are able to take advantage of the moment and make the case for policy action.[11]

Once an issue is on the agenda, it must pass through several more stages in the policy process. These stages are often referred to as the *policy cycle*. Although terminology varies, most students of public policy delineate at least five stages of policy development beyond agenda setting. These are (1) *policy formulation* (designing and drafting policy goals and strategies for achieving them, which may involve extensive use of environmental science and policy analysis), (2) *policy legitimation* (mobilizing political support and formal enactment by law or other means), (3) *policy implementation* (putting programs into effect through provision of institutional resources and administrative decisions), (4) *policy evaluation* (measuring results in relation to goals and costs), and (5) *policy change* (modifying goals or means, including termination of programs).[12]

The policy cycle model is useful because it emphasizes all phases of policymaking. For example, how well a law is implemented is as important as the goals and motivations of those who designed and enacted the legislation. The model also suggests the continuous nature of the policy process. No policy decision or solution is final because changing conditions, new information, and shifting opinions will require policy reevaluation and revision. Other short-term forces and events, such as presidential or congressional elections or environmental accidents, can profoundly affect the course of policy over its life-cycle. Thus policy at any given time is shaped by the interaction of long-term social, economic, technological, and political forces and short-term fluctuations in the political climate. All of these factors are manifest in the development of environmental policy.

The Development of Environmental Policy from the 1970s to the Twenty-First Century

As implied in the policy cycle model, the history of environmental policy in the United States is not one of steady improvement in human relations with the natural environment. Rather, it has been highly uneven, with significant discontinuities, particularly since the late 1960s. It can be understood, to borrow from the concept of agenda setting, as the product of the convergence or divergence of two political currents, one that is deep and long term and the other shallow and short term.

Social Values and Environmental Policy Commitments

The deep political current consists of fundamental changes in American values that began after World War II and accelerated as the nation shifted from an industrial to a postindustrial (or postmaterialist) society. Preoccupation with the economy (and national security) has gradually given way to a new set of concerns that includes quality-of-life issues such as the environment.[13] These changes suggest that in the coming decades ecological issues will replace, or be integrated with, many traditional political, economic, and social issues, both domestically and internationally. This integration was evident at the 1992 Earth Summit and in its concern about sustainable development. It was also championed in *Our Common Future,* an influential report by the World Commission on Environment and Development that helped to shape the Earth Summit's agenda.[14] It is equally clear in the surge of interest in recent years in building sustainable communities (see chapter 3). Historian Samuel Hays describes these changes as a social evolutionary process affecting all segments of U.S. society. Political scientist Robert Paehlke, the author of chapter 3 in this volume, has characterized environmentalism as a new ideology with the potential to alter conventional political alignments.[15] These long-term social forces are setting a new direction for the political agenda.

The shallow political current consists of shorter-term political and economic forces—elections, economic cycles, and energy supply shocks—that may alter the salience of environmental issues. These short-term developments may either reinforce or weaken the long-term trends in society that support environmental protection. For example, in the early 1970s the deep and shallow currents converged to produce an enormous outpouring of federal environmental legislation. Yet later in the decade, energy shortages and high inflation rates led the Carter administration to pull back from some of its environmental commitments. Reagan's election in 1980 shifted the environmental policy agenda sharply to the right for much of the 1980s. The two currents joined once again in the early 1990s at the beginning of the Clinton administration. However, the 1994 congressional election, and several that followed, blunted that particular convergence (see chapter 6). At the same time, these elections and comparable developments at the state level reinforced the search for new directions in environmental policy to which we referred earlier.

The election of George W. Bush as president in 2000 brought a quite different environmental agenda to the fore than was evident in the Clinton administration. More striking yet was the abrupt shift downward in the salience of environmental issues following the terrorist attacks of September 11, 2001. Environmental challenges that had been prominent before September 11, such as global climate change, virtually disappeared from the political agenda for the remainder of 2001 and early 2002 (see chapter 4).

The interaction of these two currents helps to explain the fluctuations in environmental policy commitments from one year, or decade, to the next.

Over time, however, one can see the continuity of strong public support for environmental protection and expanding government authority. The near-term discontinuities, such as environmental policy opposition in the 104th Congress and the rollback of environmental regulations during George W. Bush's presidency, capture our attention, yet they can be misleading. The longer-term transition and transformations in American values and environmental behavior arguably are more important if not as visible.[16] We focus here on the major changes from 1970 to the early twenty-first century. We discuss the future agenda for environmental politics and policy in the concluding chapter of the book.

Policy Actions prior to 1970

Until about 1970 the federal government played a sharply limited role in environmental policymaking—public land management being a major exception. For nearly a century, Congress had set aside portions of the public domain for preservation as national parks, forests, grazing lands, recreation areas, and wildlife refuges. The multiple use and sustained yield doctrines that grew out of the conservation movement at the beginning of the twentieth century ensured that this national trust would contribute to economic growth under the stewardship of the Interior and Agriculture Departments. Steady progress was also made, however, in managing the lands in the public interest and protecting them from development.[17] After several years of debate, Congress passed the Wilderness Act of 1964 to preserve some of the remaining forest lands in pristine condition, "untrammeled by man's presence." At the same time, it approved the Land and Water Conservation Fund Act of 1964 to fund federal purchases of land for conservation purposes, and the Wild and Scenic Rivers Act of 1968 to protect selected rivers with "outstandingly remarkable features," including biological, scenic, and cultural value.[18]

During the mid-1960s the United States also began a major effort to reduce world population growth in developing nations through financial aid for foreign population programs, chiefly family planning and population research. President Lyndon B. Johnson and congressional sponsors of the programs tied them explicitly to a concern for "growing scarcity in world resources."[19]

Despite this longtime concern for resource conservation and land management, and the new interest in population issues, federal environmental policy was only slowly extended to control of industrial pollution and human waste. Air and water pollution were long considered to be a strictly local or state matter, and they were not high on the national agenda until around 1970. In a very early federal action, the Refuse Act of 1899 required individuals who wanted to dump refuse into navigable waters to obtain a permit from the Army Corps of Engineers; however, the agency largely ignored the pollution aspects of the act.[20] After World War II, policies to control the most obvious forms of pollution were gradually developed at the local, state, and federal levels. For example, the federal government began assisting local authorities in building sewage treatment plants and initiated a limited program for air pollution research. Following the Clean Air Act of 1963 and amendments to the Water Pollution Control Act of 1948, Washington began prodding the states to set pollution abatement standards and to formulate implementation plans based on federal guidelines.[21]

Agenda Setting for the 1970s

The first Earth Day was April 22, 1970. Nationwide "teach-ins" about environmental problems demonstrated ecology's new place on the nation's social and political agendas. With an increasingly affluent and well-educated society placing new emphasis on the quality of life, concern for environmental protection grew apace and was evident across the population, if not necessarily to the same degree among all groups.[22] The effect was a broadly based public demand for more vigorous and comprehensive federal action to prevent environmental degradation. In an almost unprecedented fashion, a new environmental policy agenda rapidly emerged. Policymakers viewed the newly visible environmental issues as politically attractive, and they eagerly supported tough new measures, even when the full impacts and costs of these measures were unknown. As a result, laws were quickly enacted and implemented throughout the 1970s but with a growing concern over their costs and effects on the economy and an increasing realization that administrative agencies at all levels of government often lacked the capacity to assume their new responsibilities.

Congress set the stage for the spurt in policy innovation at the end of 1969 when it passed the National Environmental Policy Act (NEPA). The act declared that

> it is the continuing policy of the Federal Government, in cooperation with State and local governments, and other concerned public and private organizations, to use all practicable means and measures, including financial and technical assistance, in a manner calculated to foster and promote the general welfare, to create and maintain conditions under which man and nature can exist in productive harmony, and fulfill the social, economic, and other requirements of present and future generations of Americans.[23]

The law required detailed environmental impact statements for all major federal actions and established the Council on Environmental Quality (CEQ) to advise the president and Congress on environmental issues. President Richard Nixon then seized the initiative by signing NEPA as his first official act of 1970 and proclaiming the 1970s as the "environmental decade." In February 1970 he sent a special message to Congress calling for a new law to control air pollution. The race was on as the White House and congressional leaders vied for environmentalists' support.

Policy Escalation in the 1970s

By the spring of 1970, rising public concern about the environment galvanized the Ninety-first Congress to action. Sen. Edmund Muskie, D-Maine, then the leading Democratic hopeful for the presidential nomination in 1972, emerged as the dominant policy entrepreneur for environmental protection issues. As chair of the Senate Public Works Committee, he formulated proposals that went well beyond those favored by the president. Following a process of policy escalation, both houses of Congress approved the stronger measures and set the tone for environmental policymaking for much of the 1970s. Congress had frequently played a more dominant role than the president in initiating environmental policies, and that pattern continued in the 1970s. This was particularly so when the Democratic Party controlled Congress during the Nixon and Ford presidencies. Although support for environmental protection was bipartisan, Democrats provided more leadership on the issue in Congress and were more likely to vote for strong environmental policy provisions than were Republicans.[24]

The increase in new federal legislation in the next decade was truly remarkable, especially since, as we noted earlier, policymaking in U.S. politics is usually incremental. Appendix 1 lists the major environmental protection and natural resource policies enacted between 1969 and 2004. They are arranged by presidential administration primarily to show a pattern of significant policy development throughout the period, not to attribute chief responsibility for the various laws to the particular presidents. These landmark measures covered air and water pollution control (the latter enacted in 1972 over a presidential veto), pesticide regulation, endangered species protection, control of hazardous and toxic chemicals, ocean and coastline protection, better stewardship of public lands, requirements for restoration of strip-mined lands, the setting aside of more than 100 million acres of Alaskan wilderness for varying degrees of protection, and the creation of a "Superfund" (in the Comprehensive Environmental Response, Compensation, and Liability Act, or CERCLA) for cleaning up toxic waste sites. Nearly all of these policies reflected a conviction that the federal government must have sufficient authority to compel polluters and resource users to adhere to demanding national pollution control standards and new decision-making procedures that ensure responsible use of natural resources.

There were other signs of commitment to environmental policy goals as Congress and a succession of presidential administrations through Jimmy Carter's cooperated on conservation issues. For example, the area designated as national wilderness (excluding Alaska) more than doubled, from 10 million acres in 1970 to more than 23 million acres in 1980. Seventy-five units, totaling some 2.5 million acres, were added to the national park system in the same period. The national wildlife refuge system grew similarly. Throughout the 1970s the Land and Water Conservation Fund, financed primarily through royalties from offshore oil and gas leasing, was used to purchase additional private land for park development, wildlife refuges, and national forests.

The government's enthusiasm for environmental and conservation policy did not extend to all issues on the environmentalists' agenda. Two noteworthy cases are population policy and energy policy. The Commission on Population Growth and the American Future recommended in 1972 that the nation should "welcome and plan for a stabilized population," but its advice was ignored. Birth rates in the United States were declining, and population issues were politically controversial. Despite occasional reports that highlighted the effect of population growth on the environment, such as the *Global 2000 Report to the President* in 1980, the issue remained more or less dormant over the next two decades.[25]

For energy issues the dominant pattern was not neglect but policy gridlock. Here the connection to environmental policy was clearer to policymakers than it had been on population growth. Indeed, opposition to pollution control programs as well as land preservation came primarily from conflicting demands for energy production in the aftermath of the Arab oil embargo in 1973. The Nixon, Ford, and Carter administrations all attempted to formulate national policies for achieving energy independence by increasing energy supplies, with Carter's efforts by far the most sustained and comprehensive. Carter also emphasized conservation and environmental safeguards. For the most part, however, these efforts were unsuccessful. No consensus on national energy policy emerged among the public or in Congress, and presidential leadership was insufficient to overcome these political constraints.[26]

Congress maintained its strong commitment to environmental policy throughout the 1970s, even as the salience of these issues for the public seemed to wane. For example, it revised the Clean Air Act of 1970 and the Clean Water Act of 1972 through amendments approved in 1977. Yet concerns over the impact of environmental regulation on the economy and specific objections to implementation of the new laws, particularly the Clean Air Act, began creating a backlash by the end of the Carter administration.

Political Reaction in the 1980s

The Reagan presidency brought to the federal government a markedly different environmental policy agenda (see chapter 5). Virtually all environmental protection and resource policies enacted during the 1970s were reevaluated in light of the president's desire to reduce the scope of government regulation, shift responsibilities to the states, and rely more on the private sector. Whatever the merits of Reagan's new policy agenda, it was put into effect through a risky strategy that relied on ideologically committed presidential appointees to the EPA and the Agriculture, Interior, and Energy Departments and on sharp cutbacks in budgets for environmental programs.[27]

Congress initially cooperated with Reagan, particularly in approving budget cuts, but it soon reverted to its accustomed defense of existing environmental policy, frequently criticizing the president's management of the EPA and the Interior Department under Anne Gorsuch (later Burford) and James Watt, respectively; both Burford and Watt were forced to resign by the end of 1983. Among Congress's most notable achievements of the 1980s were its strengthening of the Resource Conservation and Recovery Act (1984) and enactment of the Superfund Amendments and Reauthorization Act (1986), the Safe Drinking Water Act (1986), and the Clean Water Act (1987) (see appendix 1).

As we discuss later in this chapter, budget cuts and loss of capacity in environmental institutions took a serious toll during the 1980s. Yet even the determined efforts of a popular president could not halt the advance of environmental policy. Public support for environmental improvement, the driving force for policy development in the 1970s, increased markedly during Reagan's presidency and represented the public's stunning rejection of the president's agenda.[28]

Paradoxically, Reagan actually strengthened environmental forces in the nation. Through his lax enforcement of pollution laws and prodevelopment resource policies, he created political issues around which national and grassroots environmental groups could organize. These groups appealed successfully to a public that was increasingly disturbed by the health and environmental risks of industrial society and by threats to ecological stability. As a result, membership in national environmental groups soared and new grassroots organizations developed, creating further political incentives for environmental activism at all levels of government (see chapter 4).[29]

By the fall of 1989 there was little mistaking congressional receptivity to continuing the advance of environmental policy into the 1990s. Especially in his first two years as president, George H. W. Bush was eager to adopt a more positive environmental policy agenda than his predecessor, particularly evident in his support for the demanding Clean Air Act Amendments of 1990. Bush's White House, however, was deeply divided on environmental issues for both ideological and economic reasons (see chapter 5).

Seeking New Policy Directions: From the 1990s to the Twenty-First Century

Environmental issues received considerable attention during the 1992 presidential election campaign. Bush, running for reelection, criticized environmentalists as extremists who were putting Americans out of work. The Democratic candidate, Bill Clinton, took a far more supportive stance on the environment, symbolized by his selection of Sen. Al Gore, D-Tenn., as his running mate. Gore was the author of a best-selling book, *Earth in the Balance,* and had one of the strongest environmental records in Congress.

Much to the disappointment of environmentalists, Clinton exerted only sporadic leadership on the environment throughout his two terms in office.

However, he and Gore quietly pushed an extensive agenda of environmental policy reform as part of their broader effort to "reinvent government," making it more efficient and responsive to public concerns. Clinton was also generally praised for his environmental appointments and for his administration's support for initiatives such as restoration of the Florida Everglades and other actions based on new approaches to ecosystem management. Clinton reversed many of the Reagan- and Bush-era executive actions that were widely criticized by environmentalists, and he favored increased spending on environmental programs, alternative energy and conservation research, and international population policy.

Clinton also earned praise from environmental groups when he began speaking out forcefully against antienvironmental policy decisions of Republican Congresses (see chapters 5 and 6), for his efforts through the President's Council on Sustainable Development to encourage new ways to reconcile environmental protection and economic development, and for his "lands legacy" initiatives.[30] Still, Clinton displeased environmentalists as often as he gratified them.

The environmental policy agenda of George W. Bush's presidency is addressed in chapter 5 and throughout the rest of the book. As widely expected from statements Bush made on the campaign trail and from his record as governor of Texas, he and his cabinet departed significantly from the positions of the Clinton administration. The economic impact of environmental policy emerged as a major concern, and the president gave far more emphasis to economic development than he did to environmental protection or resource conservation.

Like his father, Bush recognized the political reality of popular support for environmental protection and resource conservation. Yet as a conservative Republican he was also inclined to represent the views of the party's core constituencies, particularly industrial corporations and timber, mining, agriculture, and oil interests. He drew heavily from those constituencies, as well as conservative ideological groups, to staff the EPA and the Interior, Agriculture, and Energy Departments, filling positions with what the press termed industry insiders.[31] In addition, he sought to further reduce the burden of environmental protection through the use of voluntary, flexible, and cooperative programs and to transfer to the states more responsibility for enforcement of federal laws.

The Bush administration's posture on environmental protection was evident across a range of policy actions, both domestic and international. Perhaps the most remarkable decision was the administration's unilateral withdrawal of the United States from the Kyoto Protocol on global climate change. The administration's tendency to minimize environmental concerns was equally clear in its proposed national energy policy (which concentrated on increased production of fossil fuels) and in many decisions throughout Bush's first term on clean air rules, water quality standards, mining regulations, and protection of national forests and parks that were widely denounced by environmentalists.[32]

Many of these decisions received considerably less media coverage than might have been expected. In part, this appeared to reflect the administration's strategy of keeping a low profile on potentially unpopular environmental policy actions. But the president benefited further from the sharply altered political agenda after the terrorist attacks of September 11 as well as the decision in 2003 to invade Iraq.[33]

Institutional Development and Policy Implementation

In this review of environmental policy development since 1970 we have highlighted the adoption of landmark policies and the political conflicts that shaped them. Yet another aspect of this history is institutional developments that affected implementation of those policies and in many ways inspired conservative reaction to them. A brief review of the most important of these developments is instructive, particularly in light of continuing opposition in Congress, the White House, and the states to many environmental programs from this era.

Institutionalizing Environmental Protection in the 1970s

The most notable institutional development in the 1970s was the establishment of the EPA by President Nixon in December 1970. Created as an independent agency that would report directly to the president, it brought together environmental responsibilities that had previously been scattered among dozens of offices and programs. Under its first administrator, William Ruckelshaus, the agency's legislative mandate grew rapidly as a consequence of the policy process summarized earlier, and it acquired many new programs, offices, and staffs. The EPA's operating budget grew from about $500 million in 1973 to $1.3 billion in 1980. Full-time employees increased from about 7,000 in 1971 to nearly 13,000 by 1980 (see appendixes 2 and 3), with two-thirds of them in the agency's ten regional offices and other facilities outside of Washington, D.C. Even with its expanded budget and staff, however, the nation's leading environmental agency found it increasingly difficult by 1980 to meet new program obligations.

During the 1970s virtually every federal agency was forced to develop some capabilities for environmental analysis under NEPA, which required that environmental impact statements be prepared for all "major federal actions significantly affecting the quality of the human environment." Detailed requirements for the statements were set out by the CEQ and enforced in the courts. Provisions for public hearings and citizen participation allowed environmental and community groups to challenge administrative decisions, often by filing legal suits questioning the adequacy of the impact statements. In response to these potential objections, agencies changed their project designs—sometimes dramatically. Although the impact statement process was roundly criticized (indeed, it was revised in 1979 to focus more sharply on crucial issues), most studies show that it forced greater environmental awareness and more careful planning in many agencies; moreover, such success led to the extension of this kind of impact analysis to other policy areas.[34]

Established natural resource agencies, such as Agriculture's Forest Service and Interior's Bureau of Land Management, generally made the transition to better environmental analysis and planning more easily. Long-standing doctrines of multiple use and strong professional norms of land management were gradually adapted to serve new environmental goals and interests. Wilderness preservation, never a dominant purpose of these agencies, came to be accepted as part of their mission, as did the new and comprehensive approach called ecosystem management (see chapter 14).[35]

Both in their compliance with new environmental laws and in their adjustment to democratic norms of open decision making and citizen participation in the 1970s, some agencies and departments lagged seriously behind others. Perhaps the most striking case is the Department of Energy, which for years had neglected changing standards and demands with respect to environmental protection, safety, and health. The price the nation pays for such environmental neglect and mismanagement can be seen in the enormous cost of cleaning up the department's seventeen principal weapons plants and laboratories—likely to be more than $200 billion by 2030.[36]

Successive administrations also gave modest support to the development of international environmental institutions. The United States played an active role in convening the UN Conference on the Human Environment held in Stockholm, Sweden, in June 1972. This conference, attended by delegations from 113 countries and 400 other organizations, addressed for the first time the environmental problems of developing nations. The result was the creation of the UN Environment Programme (UNEP), headquartered in Nairobi, Kenya. Although it disagreed with some of UNEP's initiatives, the United States provided the largest share (36 percent) of its budget between 1972 and 1980.[37]

Challenges to Environmental Institutions in the 1980s

By the time Reagan assumed the presidency in 1981, the effort to improve environmental quality at federal and state levels had been institutionalized, though not without a good many problems that required both statutory change and administrative reform. Implementation often lagged years behind schedule because much of the legislation of the 1970s overestimated the speed with which new technologies could be developed and applied. The laws also underestimated compliance costs and the difficulty of writing standards for hundreds of major industries. As regulated industries sought to block implementation and environmental organizations tried to speed it up, frequent legal challenges compounded the backlog. Other delays were caused by personnel and budgetary shortages; scientific and technical uncertainties; and the need for extensive consultation with other federal agencies, Congress, and state governments.[38]

As a result of these difficulties, an extensive agenda for reforming environmental policies and improving administrative capabilities emerged by 1980. Rather than address them directly, however, the Reagan administration chose to emphasize short-term regulatory relief to industry.[39] It did so by using an administrative strategy that J. Clarence Davies describes as "designed largely to reverse the institutionalization process" begun in the 1970s. This was accomplished through sharp budgetary reductions, weakening of the authority of experienced professionals in environmental agencies, and elimination or restructuring of many offices, particularly at the EPA.[40] Staff morale and EPA credibility suffered substantially under the leadership of Anne Burford, although both improved to some extent under administrators William Ruckelshaus and Lee Thomas in the Reagan administration and William Reilly in the Bush administration. Nevertheless, the damage done to administrative capacity in the early 1980s was considerable and long lasting.[41]

The administrative reform agenda that the Reagan administration largely failed to address reappeared regularly throughout the 1990s and into the 2000s. Critics of environmental policy continued to express concern about the costs and burdens of environmental protection and the need to develop a new generation of policy tools. Business leaders in particular remained dissatisfied with what they believed was still an unnecessarily expensive and rigid system of federal environmental regulation. Policy analysts proposed alternatives to regulation, such as the use of market-based incentives and information disclosure, and policy tools such as risk assessment and cost-benefit analysis continued to be widely discussed. These approaches often emerged as major issues in both federal and state debates over environmental policy, and they are discussed at some length in chapters 6, 8, 9, 10, and 12.

Institutional Capacity: Environmental Agency Budgets and Policy Implementation

Agency budgets are an important part of institutional capacity, which in turn affects the degree to which present laws might help to improve environmental quality. Although spending more public money does not guarantee policy success, substantial cuts can severely undermine established programs. For example, the massive reductions in environmental funding during the 1980s had long-term adverse effects on the government's ability to implement environmental policies. Equally sharp budget cuts proposed by Congress in 1995 and 1996 raised the same prospect, although they failed to win approval in the face of opposition by the U.S. public and the Clinton White House. Changes in budgetary support for environmental protection since the 1980s merit brief comment here. More detail is provided in the appendixes.

In constant dollars (that is, adjusting for inflation), the total spending authorized by the federal government for all natural resource and environmental programs was virtually unchanged between 1980 and 2000, and then rose nearly 21 percent by 2004 (see appendix 4). However, in some program areas, such as pollution control and abatement, spending actually declined from 1980 to 2004; in this instance, spending decreased by about 8 percent. In contrast, spending on conservation and land management rose appreciably between 1980 and 2004, by about 240 percent. For most budget categories, spending decreased during the 1980s before recovering under the administrations of George H. W. Bush and Bill Clinton, and to some extent under George W. Bush. An exception is spending on water resources, where the phase-out of federal grant programs resulted in a sharp decline in expenditures between 1980 and 2004 (31 percent). Even when the budget picture was improving, most agencies faced important fiscal challenges. Their responsibilities rose under environmental policies approved during the 1970s and 1980s, and they often found themselves with insufficient resources to implement those new policies fully and to achieve the environmental quality goals they embodied.

These constraints can be seen in the budgets and staffs of selected environmental and natural resource agencies (see appendixes 2 and 3). For example, in constant dollars, the EPA's operating budget as we calculate it (the EPA determines it somewhat differently) grew by only about 5.7 percent between fiscal years 1980 and 2000, despite the many new duties Congress gave the agency during this period. However, Congress increased the EPA's budget substantially between 2000 and 2004 even though the White House repeatedly called for cuts (see chapter 6). The EPA's staff grew by a greater percentage than its budget, rising from a little less than 13,000 in 1980, the last year of the Carter administration, to just short of 17,500 by 2000; it reached just over 17,700 by 2005. Some agencies saw a decrease in staff over the same period, and others remained at about the same level.

Improvements in Environmental Quality and Their Cost

It is difficult, both conceptually and empirically, to measure the success or failure of environmental policies.[42] Yet one of the most important tests of any public policy is whether it achieves its stated objectives. For environmental policies, we should ask if air and water quality are improving, hazardous waste sites are being cleaned up, and biological diversity is protected adequately. There is no simple way to answer those questions, and it is important to understand why that is so even if some limited responses are possible.[43]

Measuring Environmental Conditions and Trends

Environmental policies entail long-term commitments to broad social values and goals that are not easily quantified. Short-term and highly visible costs are easier to measure than long-term, diffuse, and intangible benefits, and these differences often lead to intense debates over the value of environmental programs.

Variable and often unreliable monitoring of environmental conditions and inconsistent collection of data over time also make it difficult to assess environmental trends. The time period selected for a given analysis also can affect the results, and many scholars discount some data collected prior to the mid-1970s as unreliable. One thing is certain, however. Evaluation of environmental policies depends on significant improvements in monitoring and data collection at both state and federal levels. With better and more appropriate data, we will be able to speak more confidently of policy successes and failures in the future.[44]

In the meantime, scientists and pundits continue to debate whether particular environmental conditions are deteriorating or improving. Many state-of-the-environment reports that address such conditions and trends are issued by government agencies and environmental research institutes.[45] For the United States, EPA and other agency reports, discussed below, are available on-line and offer authoritative data.[46] Not surprisingly, interpretations of the data may differ. For instance, critics of environmental policy tend to cite statistics that show rather benign conditions and trends (and therefore little reason to favor public policies directed at them), whereas most environmentalists focus on what they believe to be indicators of serious environmental decline and thus a justification for government intervention. The differences sometimes become the object of extensive media coverage.[47]

Despite the many limitations on measuring environmental conditions and trends accurately, it is nevertheless useful to examine selected indicators of environmental quality. They tell us at least something about what we have achieved or failed to achieve after more than three decades of national environmental protection policy. We focus here on a brief overview of trends in air quality, water quality, toxic chemicals and hazardous wastes, and natural resources.[48]

Air Quality. Perhaps the best data on changes in the environment can be found for air quality, even if disagreement exists over which measures and time periods are most appropriate. The EPA estimates that, between 1970 and 2003, aggregate emissions of the six principal, or criteria, air pollutants decreased by 51 percent even while the nation's population grew by 39 percent, the gross domestic product (GDP) rose by 176 percent, vehicle-miles traveled increased by 155 percent, and energy consumption grew by 45 percent.[49]

We can examine a more recent period, for which data are firmer, and focus on changes in ambient levels (concentrations in the air) rather than emissions. Between 1983 and 2002 the nation experienced a reduction in ambient levels of 94 percent for lead, 65 percent for carbon monoxide, 54 percent for sulfur dioxide, 21 percent for nitrogen dioxide, 22 percent for ozone (using the less stringent one-hour standard), and 13 percent for particulate matter (PM_{10}, covering only the period 1993–2002).[50]

Despite these impressive gains in air quality, as of fall 2002, approximately 146 million people (half of the U.S. population) lived in counties with pollution levels above the standards set for at least one of these criteria pollutants, typically for ozone and fine particulates. These figures vary from year to year, reflecting changing economic activity and weather patterns. The EPA reports that the severity of air pollution episodes in nonattainment areas has decreased in recent years, yet 34 of the 263 metropolitan statistical areas in the nation exhibited upward trends in air pollution, mostly for ground-level ozone, using the new and more stringent eight-hour standard. About 160 million tons of pollutants continue to be emitted into the air each year.[51]

One of most significant remaining problems is toxic or hazardous air pollutants, which have been associated with cancer, respiratory diseases, and other chronic and acute illnesses. The EPA was extremely slow to regulate these pollutants, and it had set federal standards for only seven of them by mid-1989. Public and congressional concern over toxic emissions led Congress to mandate more aggressive action in the 1986 Superfund amendments as well as in the 1990 Clean Air Act Amendments. The former required manufacturers of more than 300 different chemicals (later increased by the EPA to over 650) to report annually to the agency and the states in which they operate the amounts of those substances released to the air, water, or land. The EPA's Toxics Release Inventory (TRI) indicates that for the core chemicals from industry that have been reported in a consistent manner over time, total releases on- and off-site decreased by 49 percent between 1988 and 2002. Most of those decreases, however, occurred during the first five years after the TRI reporting requirements took effect, and the total volume of chemicals disposed of or otherwise released to the environment is still substantial, at over 4.8 billion pounds per year (see chapter 12 for further TRI data).[52]

The TRI numbers are difficult to assess for many reasons. For instance, many chemicals and industries were added to TRI reporting requirements during the 1990s and 2000s, complicating the determination of change over time. In addition to the TRI, under the 1990 Clean Air Act Amendments, the EPA regulates 188 listed air toxics, but nationwide monitoring of emissions is not standard.

Water Quality. The nation's water quality has improved since passage of the Clean Water Act of 1972, although more slowly and more unevenly than has air quality. Monitoring data are less adequate for water quality than for air quality. For example, the best evidence for the present state of water quality can be found in the EPA's biennial National Water Quality Inventory, which compiles data reported by each state. In 2000 (the most recent report), the states surveyed only 19 percent of all the nation's rivers and streams; 43 percent of lakes, ponds, and reservoirs; and 36 percent of estuaries.

Based on those inventories, 61 percent of the surveyed river and stream miles fully support the water quality standards set by states and tribes, and

39 percent were found to be impaired to some degree. Some 45 percent of lakes, ponds, and reservoirs also were found to be impaired. A classification as impaired means that water bodies are not meeting or fully meeting the national minimum water quality criteria for "designated beneficial uses" such as swimming, fishing, drinking-water supply, and support of aquatic life. These numbers indicate some improvement over previous years, yet they also tell us that many problems remain. The same survey found that 51 percent of the nation's estuaries were impaired, as were 78 percent of Great Lakes nearshore waters (generally because of persistent toxic pollutants in the food web and habitat degradation and destruction).[53] Prevention of further degradation of water quality in the face of a growing population and strong economic growth could be considered an important achievement. At the same time, water quality clearly falls short of the goals of federal clean water acts.

Further evidence can be seen in the data on wetlands loss. The EPA estimates that the nation currently experiences an average net loss each year of about 58,000 acres of marshes, swamps, and other ecologically important wetlands to commercial and residential development, agriculture, road construction, and modification of hydrologic conditions. This ongoing loss was well below the estimated 458,000 acres lost annually from the mid-1950s to the mid-1970s. Yet the loss remains unacceptably high, particularly in light of the valuable ecological functions contributed by wetlands. Moreover, the EPA reports that in 2000 the states and tribes assessed only 8 percent of remaining wetlands, providing scant data on their quality.[54]

To date, little progress has been made in halting groundwater contamination despite passage of the Safe Drinking Water Act of 1974 and the Resource Conservation and Recovery Act of 1976 and their later amendments. In its 2000 Water Quality Inventory, the EPA reported that groundwater quality can be adversely affected by human actions that introduce contaminants and that "problems caused by elevated levels of petroleum hydrocarbon compounds, volatile organic compounds (VOCs), nitrate, pesticides, and metals have been detected in ground water across the nation." The agency also noted that measuring groundwater quality is a complex task and data collection "is still too immature to provide comprehensive national assessments." Heading the list of contaminant sources are leaking underground storage tanks, septic systems, landfills, spills, fertilizer applications, and large industrial facilities. With some 46 percent of the nation's population relying on groundwater for drinking water (99 percent in rural areas), far more remains to be done.[55]

Toxic and Hazardous Wastes. Progress in dealing with hazardous wastes and other toxic chemicals has been the least satisfactory of all pollution control programs. Implementation of the major laws has been extraordinarily slow due to the extent and complexity of the problems, scientific uncertainty, litigation by industry, public fear of siting treatment and storage facilities nearby, budgetary limitations, and poor management and lax enforcement by the EPA. As a result, gains have been modest when judged by the most common measures. Some key trends reported in the EPA's TRI on the production and release of toxic chemicals to the environment were noted earlier in this chapter, and others are addressed in chapter 12.

One of the most carefully watched measures of government actions to reduce the risk of toxic and hazardous chemicals pertains to the federal Superfund program. For years it made painfully slow progress in cleaning up the nation's worst hazardous waste sites. By the late 1990s, however, the pace of action improved. The EPA reported that, as of September 2000, 757 Superfund sites had been fully cleaned up and construction (remediation or removal of material) was taking place at another 417 sites. By the end of fiscal year 2004, the agency said the number of cleaned-up sites had risen to 926, or about 61 percent of the 1,500 sites on the National Priorities List.[56] These achievements often come at a high price, with much dispute over the costs and benefits.

Historically the EPA has set a sluggish pace in the related area of testing toxic chemicals, including pesticides. For example, under a 1972 law mandating control of pesticides and herbicides, only a handful of chemicals used to manufacture the 50,000 pesticides in use in the United States had been fully tested or retested. The Food Quality Protection Act of 1996 required the EPA to undertake extensive assessment of the risks posed by new and existing pesticides. Following a lawsuit, the EPA apparently is moving more quickly toward meeting the act's goal of protecting human health and the environment from these risks.[57]

Natural Resources. Comparable indicators of environmental progress can be cited for natural resource use. As is the case with pollution control, however, interpretation of the data is problematic. We have few good measures of ecosystem health or ways to value ecosystem services, and much of the usual information in government reports concerns land set aside for recreational and aesthetic purposes rather than for protection of ecosystem functions.[58] Nonetheless, the trends in land conservation and wilderness protection suggest important progress over more than three decades of modern environmental and natural resource policies.

For example, the national park system grew from about 26 million acres in 1960 to over 84 million acres by 2003, and the number of units in the system doubled. Since adoption of the 1964 Wilderness Act, Congress has set aside 106 million acres of wilderness through the national wilderness preservation system. Since 1968 it has designated over 150 wild and scenic rivers with nearly 11,000 protected miles. The Fish and Wildlife Service manages more than 93 million acres in about 500 units of the national wildlife refuge system—triple the land area managed in 1970.[59]

Protection of biological diversity through the Endangered Species Act has produced some success as well, although far less than its supporters believe essential. By early 2005, over thirty years after passage of the act, more than 1,200 U.S. plant and animal species had been listed as either endangered or threatened. Over 470 critical habitats have been designated, nearly 500 habitat conservation plans have been approved, and about 1,000 recovery plans have been put into effect. Yet only a few endangered species have recovered fully. The Fish and Wildlife Service reported that 30 percent of listed species were stable, 6 percent were improving, 21 percent were declining, and the status of another 39 percent was uncertain.[60]

Assessing Environmental Progress

As the data reviewed in the preceding sections suggest, the nation made impressive gains between 1970 and 2005 in controlling many conventional pollutants and in expanding parks, wilderness areas, and other protected public lands. Despite some setbacks in the 1980s, progress on environmental quality continues, even if it is highly uneven from one period to the next. In the future, however, further advances will be more difficult, costly, and controversial. This is largely because the easy problems have already been addressed. At this point, marginal gains—for example, in air and water quality—will cost more per unit of improvement than in the past (see chapter 9). Moreover, second-generation environmental threats such as toxic chemicals, hazardous wastes, and nuclear wastes are proving even more difficult to regulate than the "bulk" air and water pollutants that were the main targets in the 1970s. In these cases, substantial progress may not be evident for years to come, and it will be expensive.

The same is true for the third generation of ecological problems, such as global climate change and protection of biodiversity. Solutions require an unprecedented degree of cooperation among nations and substantial improvement in institutional capacity for research, data collection, and analysis as well as policy development and implementation. Hence, success is likely to come slowly as national and international commitments to environmental protection grow and capabilities improve.

Some long-standing problems, such as population growth, will continue to be addressed primarily within nation-states, even though the staggering effects on natural resources and environmental quality are felt worldwide. By early 2005 the Earth's population of 6.4 billion people was increasing at an estimated 1.3 percent (or about 83 million people) each year, with continued growth expected for perhaps another 100 years. The U.S. population was growing at only a slightly slower rate of 1.1 percent a year, with the Census Bureau forecasting a rise to 414 million people by 2050, up from 295 million in 2005 (see chapter 15).

The Costs and Benefits of Environmental Protection

The costs and benefits of environmental protection have been vigorously debated since the 1980s. Critics argue that the kinds of improvements cited in the preceding sections are often not worth the considerable costs, particularly if they believe regulations adversely affect economic growth and employment or unduly restrict technological development. Environmentalists and other policy supporters point, however, to the improvements in public health, the protection of priceless natural amenities such as wilderness areas and clean lakes, and the preservation of biological diversity. They remain convinced that these benefits are well worth the investment of government and private funds. They also question assertions about adverse economic impacts of such policies, for which evidence is slim.[61] Some business leaders agree, and the evidence can be found in their determination to promote greening of their enterprises both for the economic gains they anticipate and to appeal to an environmentally concerned public (see chapter 12).

Skepticism about environmental policies led to several attempts in the 1980s and early 1990s under Presidents Reagan and Bush to impose regulatory oversight by the White House. It was hoped that costs could be limited by subjecting proposed regulations to cost-benefit analysis (see chapter 5). The imposition of these controls, particularly by Bush's White House Council on Competitiveness, sharpened debate over the costs and benefits of environmental policies. In January 1993 Clinton replaced the Reagan-Bush executive order with one of his own that reflected a more flexible use of economic studies in regulatory policy decisions. In a telling move, George W. Bush named a noted critic of regulation, John Graham, to head his administration's regulatory oversight office. Graham's actions tended to favor industry interests (see chapter 10).[62] Yet his Office of Information and Regulatory Affairs also issued a report to Congress in late 2003 that documented the substantial benefits of environmental rules and regulations, which often exceeded the costs they impose on industry and consumers.[63]

The impetus for these kinds of centralized control efforts, and the intensity of the conflict over them, can be seen in the amount of money spent on environmental protection by the federal government, as well as by state and local governments and the private sector. By 2005 the federal government was spending about $32.2 billion per year for all environmental and natural resource programs as calculated in the official budget category for these programs, or about 1.2 percent of total federal outlays (see appendix 4). This money is only a small part of the country's annual investment in environmental protection. It is difficult to find reliable data on those expenditures. The EPA estimated in 1994 that the nation's overall spending on the agency's environmental programs was about $140 billion per year, or about 2.2 percent of the GDP.[64] But such estimates are highly uncertain, and the costs could well decline in the future, depending on development of new technologies and pollution prevention initiatives. By one calculation, private industry bears about 57 percent of that amount, local governments 24 percent, the federal government 15 percent, and state governments 4 percent.[65]

The benefits of environmental programs are more difficult to calculate and are often omitted entirely from reports on the costs or burdens of environmental policies. Should we count only those benefits that are measurable in dollars? Should we include public health benefits of pollution control, but not aesthetic values? What about including the value of conserving ecosystems—water, soil, forests, wetlands—or of preventing disastrous climate change? Environmental scientists increasingly have made the case for including such estimates, and since the 1990s there has been a broad reex-amination of the way in which nations account for the value of natural resources.[66]

Making rough comparisons of the benefits and costs of environmental policies, one could fairly conclude that many programs can be justified through standard economic analysis. That is, they produce measurable ben-efits that exceed the costs. EPA studies make clear, for instance, that the Clean Air Act has produced benefits that greatly exceeded compliance costs, chiefly because of reduction in lead and particulate matter (see chapter 9). Energy conservation also makes good economic sense given the costs and environmental impacts of building and operating new power plants. Some environmental programs, such as thorough cleanup of all hazardous waste sites, however, are so expensive that they would be far more difficult to jus-tify on economic grounds alone (see chapter 9).[67]

Debates over the costs and benefits of environmental policies are likely to continue over the near term but with several new twists. Government spending on natural resources and the environment, which rose sharply in the 1970s, is unlikely to increase much over the next few years. Among the most important reasons for that outlook are persistent concern in Congress and the White House about growth in federal spending and substantial deficits in the years ahead; widespread resistance to raising taxes; competing budgetary priorities, particularly from national defense programs; and oppo-sition to regulatory programs by powerful interest groups and elected offi-cials.

The burden of raising additional funds for environmental programs may be shouldered by the states. Yet some of them are more able and willing to do so than others (see chapter 2). Thus the additional cost of environ-mental protection is likely to be borne by the private sector: by industry and, eventually, by the consumer. These fiscal conditions also suggest that both federal and state governments will focus on innovative policies that promise improvements in environmental quality without adding substantially to their budgets.

Also, government agencies will likely embrace some form of risk-based priority setting that allows scarce resources to be spent where they will do the most good in reducing risks to public health and the environment. This argument was advanced regularly by EPA administrator William Reilly in the early 1990s and by his successor under Clinton, Carol Browner. It is widely endorsed by students of environmental policy as well (see chapter 10).[68]

Policy developments over the past two decades reflect these concerns— for example, the passage of the Pollution Prevention Act of 1990, which puts a premium on preventing, rather than cleaning up, pollution. Industry is already actively seeking ways to reduce the generation of waste and to pro-mote sustainable development (see chapter 12). A parallel development among environmental groups, particularly the Nature Conservancy, is a suc-cessful venture into private purchase of ecologically important land for preservation. Private efforts to save endangered lands have been extended as well to financially strapped developing nations in so-called debt-for-nature swaps.

At another level the question of whether environmental programs are worth it must be answered with another question: What are the costs of inaction? In some cases the risks to the environment and to society's well-being are so great that it would be imprudent to delay development of public policy. This is particularly so when modest measures taken at an early enough date might forestall the enormous costs of remedial efforts in the future, whether paid for by governments or the private sector. That was clearly the lesson of environmental contamination at nuclear weapons facilities, as noted earlier in this chapter. It is also apparent that such a precautionary policy response is called for in the cases of global climate change and deterioration of the ozone layer, where the potential exists for significant adverse impacts on the environment, human health, and the economy. Much the same argument could be made for preserving biological diversity, investing in family planning programs, and responding to other compelling global environmental problems likely to be high on the agenda in the early twenty-first century.

Conclusion

Since the 1970s public concern and support for environmental protection have risen significantly, spurring the development of an expansive array of policies that substantially increased the government's responsibilities for the environment and natural resources, both domestically and internationally.

The implementation of these policies, however, has been far more difficult and controversial than their supporters ever imagined. Moreover, the policies have not been entirely successful, particularly when measured by tangible improvements in environmental quality. Further progress will likely require the United States to search for more efficient and effective ways to achieve these goals, including the use of alternatives to conventional command-and-control regulation.[69] Despite these qualifications, the record since the 1970s demonstrates convincingly that the U.S. government is able to produce significant environmental gains through public policies. Unquestionably the environment would be worse today if the policies enacted during the 1970s and 1980s had not been in place.

Emerging environmental threats on the national and international agenda are even more formidable than the first generation of problems addressed by government in the 1970s and the second generation that dominated political debate in the 1980s. Responding to these threats will require creative new efforts to improve the performance of government and other social institutions, and effective leadership to design appropriate strategies both within government and in society itself. We discuss this new policy agenda in chapter 17.

Government is an important player in the environmental arena, but it cannot pursue forceful initiatives unless the public supports such action. Ultimately, society's values will fuel the government's response to a rapidly changing world environment that, in all probability, will involve severe economic and social dislocations over the coming decades.

Notes

1. See survey data reviewed in chap. 4; Riley E. Dunlap, "Public Opinion and Environmental Policy," in *Environmental Politics and Policy: Theories and Evidence*, 2nd ed., ed. James P. Lester (Durham: Duke University Press, 1995); Riley E. Dunlap, George H. Gallup Jr., and Alec M. Gallup, "Of Global Concern: Results of the Health of the Planet Survey," *Environment* 35(9) (1993): 7–15, 33–40.
2. Norman J. Vig and Michael E. Kraft, eds., *Environmental Policy in the 1980s: Reagan's New Agenda* (Washington, D.C.: CQ Press, 1984).
3. See, for example, Natural Resources Defense Council, *Rewriting the Rules (2005 Special Edition): The Bush Administration's First Term Environmental Record*, January 19, 2005, www.nrdc.org/legislation/rollbacks/rollbacksinx.asp.
4. J. Clarence Davies and Jan Mazurek, *Pollution Control in the United States: Evaluating the System* (Washington, D.C.: Resources for the Future, 1998); National Academy of Public Administration (NAPA), *Setting Priorities, Getting Results: A New Direction for EPA* (Washington, D.C.: NAPA, 1995), and *Environment.gov: Transforming Environmental Protection for the 21st Century* (Washington, D.C.: NAPA, November 2000); Ken Sexton, Alfred A. Marcus, K. William Easter, and Timothy D. Burkhardt, eds., *Better Environmental Decisions: Strategies for Governments, Businesses and Communities* (Washington, D.C.: Island Press, 1998); Robert Durant, Rosemary O'Leary, and Daniel Fiorino, eds., *Environmental Governance Reconsidered: Challenges, Choices, and Opportunities* (Cambridge: MIT Press, 2004).
5. Daniel A. Mazmanian and Michael E. Kraft, eds., *Toward Sustainable Communities: Transition and Transformations in Environmental Policy* (Cambridge: MIT Press, 1999); Durant, O'Leary, and Fiorino, *Environmental Governance Reconsidered*.
6. Hanna J. Cortner and Margaret A. Moote, *The Politics of Ecosystem Management* (Washington, D.C.: Island Press, 1998); Marian R. Chertow and Daniel C. Esty, eds., *Thinking Ecologically: The Next Generation of Environmental Policy* (New Haven: Yale University Press, 1997); President's Council on Sustainable Development, *Sustainable America: A New Consensus for Prosperity, Opportunity, and a Healthy Environment* (Washington, D.C.: President's Council on Sustainable Development, 1996).
7. NAPA, *Setting Priorities*, 124–125.
8. Danny Hakim, "California Backs Plan for Big Cut in Car Emissions," *New York Times*, September 25, 2004, 1, B3.
9. John W. Kingdon, *Agendas, Alternatives, and Public Policies*, 2nd ed. (New York: HarperCollins, 1995); Frank R. Baumgartner and Bryan D. Jones, *Agendas and Instability in American Politics* (Chicago: University of Chicago Press, 1993).
10. Roger W. Cobb and Charles D. Elder, *Participation in American Politics: The Dynamics of Agenda-Building* (Boston: Allyn & Bacon, 1972). See also Thomas A. Birkland, *After Disaster: Agenda Setting, Public Policy, and Focusing Events* (Washington, D.C.: Georgetown University Press, 1997).
11. Kingdon, *Agendas*.
12. For a more thorough discussion of how the policy cycle model applies to environmental issues, see Michael E. Kraft, *Environmental Policy and Politics*, 3rd ed. (New York: Pearson Longman, 2003), chap. 3. The general model is discussed at length in James E. Anderson, *Public Policymaking: An Introduction*, 5th ed. (Boston: Houghton Mifflin, 2003).

13. Ronald Inglehart, *The Silent Revolution: Changing Values and Political Styles among Western Publics* (Princeton: Princeton University Press, 1977); and *Culture Shift in Advanced Industrial Society* (Princeton: Princeton University Press, 1990).
14. World Commission on Environment and Development, *Our Common Future* (New York: Oxford University Press, 1987). See also Regina S. Axelrod, David Leonard Downie, and Norman J. Vig, eds., *The Global Environment: Institutions, Law, and Policy*, 2nd ed. (Washington, D.C.: CQ Press, 2005).
15. Samuel P. Hays, *Beauty, Health, and Permanence: Environmental Politics in the United States, 1955–1985* (New York: Cambridge University Press, 1987); Robert C. Paehlke, *Environmentalism and the Future of Progressive Politics* (New Haven: Yale University Press, 1989). For a comprehensive review of public opinion surveys on the environment and the evolution of the environmental movement, see Riley E. Dunlap and Angela G. Mertig, eds., *American Environmentalism: The U.S. Environmental Movement, 1970–1990* (Philadelphia: Taylor & Francis, 1992); Dunlap, "Public Opinion and Environmental Policy"; and Deborah Lynn Guber, *The Grassroots of a Green Revolution: Polling America on the Environment* (Cambridge: MIT Press, 2003).
16. Mazmanian and Kraft, *Toward Sustainable Communities*.
17. Paul J. Culhane, *Public Lands Politics: Interest Group Influence on the Forest Service and the Bureau of Land Management* (Baltimore: Johns Hopkins University Press, 1981), esp. chap. 1. See also Richard N. L. Andrews, *Managing the Environment, Managing Ourselves: A History of American Environmental Policy* (New Haven: Yale University Press, 1999).
18. Andrews, *Managing the Environment*; Kraft, *Environmental Policy and Politics*, chap. 4.
19. Michael E. Kraft, "Population Policy," in *Encyclopedia of Policy Studies*, 2nd ed., ed. Stuart S. Nagel (New York: Marcel Dekker, 1994).
20. J. Clarence Davies III and Barbara S. Davies, *The Politics of Pollution*, 2nd ed. (Indianapolis, Ind.: Bobbs-Merrill, 1975).
21. Evan J. Ringquist, *Environmental Protection at the State Level: Politics and Progress in Controlling Pollution* (Armonk, N.Y.: M. E. Sharpe, 1993), chap. 2; Davies and Davies, *Politics of Pollution*, chap. 2. A much fuller history of the origins and development of modern environmental policy than is provided here can be found in Andrews, *Managing the Environment*, and Michael J. Lacey, ed., *Government and Environmental Politics: Essays on Historical Developments since World War Two* (Baltimore: Johns Hopkins University Press, 1989).
22. Hays, *Beauty, Health, and Permanence*. See also Dunlap, "Public Opinion and Environmental Policy," and Robert Cameron Mitchell, "Public Opinion and Environmental Politics in the 1970s and 1980s," in *Environmental Policy in the 1980s*, ed. Vig and Kraft.
23. Public Law 91-90 (42 USC 4321–4347), sec. 101. See Lynton Keith Caldwell, *The National Environmental Policy Act: An Agenda for the Future* (Bloomington: Indiana University Press, 1998).
24. Michael E. Kraft, "Congress and Environmental Policy"; Sheldon Kamieniecki, "Political Parties and Environmental Policy," in *Environmental Politics and Policy*, ed. Lester; Charles R. Shipan and William R. Lowry, "Environmental Policy and Party Divergence in Congress," *Political Research Quarterly* 54 (June 2001): 245–263.
25. Kraft, "Population Policy"; Council on Environmental Quality (CEQ) and Department of State, *The Global 2000 Report to the President* (Washington, D.C.: U.S. Government Printing Office, 1980).
26. James Everett Katz, *Congress and National Energy Policy* (New Brunswick, N.J.: Transaction, 1984).
27. Vig and Kraft, *Environmental Policy in the 1980s*.
28. See Riley E. Dunlap, "Public Opinion on the Environment in the Reagan Era," *Environment* 29 (July–August 1987): 6–11, 32–37; Mitchell, "Public Opinion and Environmental Politics."

29. The changing membership numbers can be found in Kraft, *Environmental Policy and Politics*, chap. 4. See also Christopher J. Bosso, *Environment, Inc.: From Grassroots to Beltway* (Lawrence: University Press of Kansas, 2005).
30. President's Council on Sustainable Development, *Sustainable America*.
31. Katharine Q. Seelye, "Bush Picks Industry Insiders to Fill Environmental Posts," *New York Times*, May 12, 2001, 1.
32. See Natural Resources Defense Council, "Rewriting the Rules"; Bruce Barcott, "Changing All the Rules," *New York Times Magazine*, April 4, 2004, 39–44, 66, 73, 76–77; Felicity Barringer, "Bush Record: New Priorities In Environment," *New York Times*, September 14, 2004, 1, A18; and Joby Warrick and Juliet Eilperin, "Big Energy in the Wild West: The Bush Administration's Land-Use Decisions Favor Oil and Gas," *Washington Post National Weekly Edition*, October 4–10, 2004.
33. Eric Pianin, "War Is Hell: The Environmental Agenda Takes a Back Seat to Fighting Terrorism," *Washington Post National Weekly Edition*, October 29–November 4, 2001, 12–13. See also Barcott, "Changing All the Rules"; and Joel Brinkley, "Out of the Spotlight, Bush Overhauls U.S. Regulations," *New York Times*, August 14, 2004, 1, A10.
34. Richard N. L. Andrews, *Environmental Policy and Administrative Change: Implementation of the National Environmental Policy Act* (Lexington, Mass.: Lexington, 1976); Robert V. Bartlett, *Policy through Impact Assessment: Institutionalized Analysis as a Policy Strategy* (New York: Greenwood, 1989).
35. See Jeanne Nienaber Clarke and Daniel C. McCool, *Staking Out the Terrain: Power and Performance among Natural Resource Agencies*, 2nd ed. (Albany: State University of New York Press, 1996); Cortner and Moote, *The Politics of Ecosystem Management*.
36. Michael E. Kraft, "Searching for Policy Success: Reinventing the Politics of Site Remediation," *Environmental Professional* 16 (September 1994): 245–253; Milton E. Russell, William Colglazier, and Bruce E. Tonn, "The U.S. Hazardous Waste Legacy," *Environment* 34 (1992): 12–15, 34–39.
37. John McCormick, *Reclaiming Paradise: The Global Environmental Movement* (Bloomington: Indiana University Press, 1989), 110. See also Axelrod et al., *The Global Environment*.
38. Alfred A. Marcus, *Promise and Performance: Choosing and Implementing Environmental Policy* (Westport, Conn.: Greenwood, 1980); Marc K. Landy, Marc J. Roberts, and Stephen R. Thomas, *The Environmental Protection Agency: Asking the Wrong Questions*, 2nd ed. (New York: Oxford University Press, 1994).
39. George C. Eads and Michael Fix, *Relief or Reform? Reagan's Regulatory Dilemma* (Washington, D.C.: Urban Institute Press, 1984).
40. J. Clarence Davies III, "Environmental Institutions and the Reagan Administration," and Richard N. L. Andrews, "Deregulation: The Failure at EPA," in *Environmental Policy in the 1980s*, ed. Vig and Kraft.
41. See Philip Shabecoff, "Reagan and Environment: To Many a Stalemate," *New York Times*, January 2, 1989, 1, 8.
42. Robert V. Bartlett, "Evaluating Environmental Policy," in *Environmental Policy in the 1990s*, 2nd ed., ed. Vig and Kraft; Evan J. Ringquist, "Evaluating Environmental Policy Outcomes," in *Environmental Politics and Policy*, ed. Lester; Gerrit J. Knaap and Tschangho John Kim, eds., *Environmental Program Evaluation: A Primer* (Champaign: University of Illinois Press, 1998).
43. One of the most thorough evaluations of environmental protection policies of this kind can be found in Davies and Mazurek, *Pollution Control in the United States*.
44. See NAPA, *Environment.gov*.
45. See, for example, UN Development Programme, UN Environment Programme, World Bank, and World Resources Institute, *World Resources 2002–2004* (Washington, D.C.: World Resources Institute, 2003), available at www.wri.org.
46. In previous years, the annual report of the Council on Environmental Quality consolidated data on environmental conditions and trends reported from the executive

agencies. However, current information can now be found at specific agency Web sites. For a guide to on-line state-of-the-environment reports for all levels of government, see *Environment* 42 (April 2000): 3–4.

47. One recent media fracas followed publication of Bjørn Lomborg's *The Skeptical Environmentalist: Measuring the Real State of the World* (Cambridge: Cambridge University Press, 2001). Lomborg argues that most environmental trends are far more positive than portrayed by environmentalists in what he calls "the Litany," and that many of their concerns are "phantom problems." Political conservatives and antienvironmental writers praised the book, but it was predictably challenged by environmentalists as the latest example of flawed "eco-optimism." Many leading environmental scientists also criticized Lomborg's highly selective use of data. See the collection of commentaries in "Misleading Math about the Earth," *Scientific American* 286 (January 2002): 61–71.

48. For a fuller account, see Kraft, *Environmental Policy and Politics,* chap. 2.

49. U.S. Environmental Protection Agency (EPA), "Air Emissions Trends—Continued Progress through 2003" (Washington, D.C.: EPA), January 2005, www.epa.gov/airtrends/econ-emissions.html.

50. EPA, *National Air Quality and Emissions Trends Report, 2003* (Washington, D.C.: EPA), September 2003, www.epa.gov/airtrends/reports.html.

51. Ibid.

52. EPA, *U.S. EPA Toxics Release Inventory—2002 Data Release* (Washington, D.C.: EPA), 2004, www.epa.gov/tri/tridata/tri02/pdr/index.htm. The volume of releases refers only to TRI facilities that reported to the EPA that year. Facilities falling below a threshold level are not required to report, nor are many smaller facilities. Environmental Defense makes TRI data available in many different formats, including as maps of polluting facilities in cities and neighborhoods; see www.scorecard.org.

53. EPA, *National Water Quality Inventory: 2000 Report* (Washington, D.C.: Office of Water), August 2002, www.epa.gov/305b/02report/index.html.

54. Ibid.

55. Ibid.

56. EPA, "Superfund Cleanup Figures," November 17, 2003, www.epa.gov/superfund/action/process/mgmtrpt.htm; and "Superfund National Accomplishments Summary Fiscal Year 2004," November 22, 2004, www.epa.gov/superfund/action/process/numbers04.htm.

57. The pertinent documents can be found at the EPA's Web site for pesticide programs, www.epa.gov/pesticides/index.htm.

58. Hallett J. Harris and Denise Scheberle, "Ode to the Miner's Canary: The Search for Environmental Indicators," in *Environmental Program Evaluation,* ed. Knaap and Kim. See also Gretchen C. Daily, ed., *Nature's Services: Societal Dependence on Natural Ecosystems* (Washington, D.C.: Island Press, 1997); and Water Science and Technology Board, *Valuing Ecosystem Services: Toward Better Environmental Decision-Making* (Washington, D.C.: National Academies Press, 2004).

59. The numbers come from the various agency Web sites and from Kraft, *Environmental Policy and Politics,* chaps. 6 and 7.

60. The Fish and Wildlife Service Web site (www.fws.gov) provides extensive data on threatened and endangered species and habitat recovery plans. The figures on improving and declining species come from the U.S. Fish and Wildlife Service, *2001–2002 Recovery Report to Congress,* August 9, 2004, http://endangered.fws.gov/recovery/reports_to_congress/2001-2002.

61. See, for example, Paul R. Portney and Robert N. Stavins, eds., *Public Policies for Environmental Protection,* 2nd ed. (Washington, D.C.: Resources for the Future, 2000); Tom Tietenberg, *Environmental Economics and Policy,* 4th ed. (Reading, Mass.: Addison-Wesley, 2004). Estimates of economic impacts show a wide variance, depending on the methods and models used and on the economic indicators selected, but generally they are small. A number of studies indicate that at the state level environmental protection and economic prosperity go hand in hand. See Richard C.

Feiock and Christopher Stream, "Environmental Protection versus Economic Development: A False Trade-Off?" *Public Administration Review* 61 (May–June 2001): 313–321.

62. Jocelyn Kaiser, "New Regulatory Czar Takes Charge," *Science,* October 9, 2001, 32–33; Rebecca Adams, "Regulating the Rule-Makers: John Graham at OIRA," *CQ Weekly,* February 23, 2002, 520–526; Adams, "GOP Adds New Tactics to War on Regulations," *CQ Weekly,* January 31, 2005, 224–226. See also Rick Weiss, " 'Data Quality' Law Is Nemesis of Regulation," *Washington Post,* August 16, 2004, A1.

63. Office of Information and Regulatory Affairs, *Informing Regulatory Decisions: 2003 Report to Congress on the Costs and Benefits of Federal Regulations and Unfunded Mandates on State, Local, and Tribal Entities* (Washington, D.C.: Office of Management and Budget), 2003, www.whitehouse.gov/omb/inforeg/2003_cost-ben_final_rpt.pdf.

64. See EPA, *Environmental Investments: The Cost of a Clean Environment* (Washington, D.C.: EPA, 1990).

65. See the budget tables in appendixes 2 and 4. For the estimates of who pays for these amounts, see Paul Portney and Katherine N. Probst, "Cleaning Up Superfund," *Resources* 114 (winter 1994): 2–5.

66. See, for example, Water Science and Technology Board, *Valuing Ecosystem Services.*

67. Portney and Stavins, *Public Policies for Environmental Protection.* See also Office of Information and Regulatory Affairs, *Informing Environmental Decisions.*

68. See NAPA, *Setting Priorities.*

69. See Mazmanian and Kraft, *Toward Sustainable Communities*; Sexton et al., *Making Better Environmental Decisions*; NAPA, *Environment.gov.*; and Durant, O'Leary, and Fiorino, *Environmental Governance Reconsidered.*

2

Power to the States:
The Promise and Pitfalls of Decentralization

Barry G. Rabe

The problem which all federalized nations have to solve is how to secure an efficient central government and preserve national unity, while allowing free scope for the diversities, and free play to the . . . members of the federation. It is . . . to keep the centrifugal and centripetal forces in equilibrium, so that neither the planet States shall fly off into space, nor the sun of the Central government draw them into its consuming fires.

Lord James Bryce,
The American Commonwealth

Before the 1970s the conventional wisdom on federalism viewed "the planet States" as sufficiently lethargic to require a powerful "Central government" in many areas of environmental policy. States were widely derided as mired in corruption, hostile to innovation, and unable to take a serious role in environmental policy out of fear of alienating key economic constituencies. In more recent years the tables have turned—so much so that the conventional wisdom now berates an overheated federal government that squelches state creativity and capability to tailor environmental policies to local realities. Even the past three administrators of the U.S. Environmental Protection Agency assumed their Washington duties after extensive stints in state government, including two governorships, and have proclaimed states as central players in environmental policy. The decentralization mantra of the 1990s called for the extended transfer of environmental policy resources and regulatory authority from Washington, D.C., to states and localities. Such a transfer would pose a potentially formidable test of the thesis that more localized units know best.

What accounts for this sea change in our understanding of the role of states in environmental policy? How have states evolved in recent decades and what sorts of functions do they assume most comfortably and effectively? Despite state resurgence, are there areas in which states fall short? Looking ahead, should regulatory authority devolve to the states, or are there better ways to sort out federal and state responsibilities? Furthermore, will the George W. Bush presidency and its controversial approach to environmental issues change our understanding of the proper distribution of federal and state authority?

This chapter addresses these questions, relying heavily on evidence of state performance in environmental policy. The chapter provides both an overview of state evolution and a set of brief case studies that explore state strengths and limitations. These state-specific accounts are interwoven with assessments of the federal government's role, for good or ill, in the development of state environmental policy.

The States as "New Heroes" of American Federalism

Policy analysts are generally most adept at analyzing institutional foibles and policy failures. Indeed, much of the literature on environmental policy follows this pattern, with criticism particularly voluminous and potent when directed toward federal efforts in this area. By contrast, states have received much more favorable treatment. Many influential books and reports on state government and federalism portray states as highly dynamic and effective. Environmental policy is often depicted as a prime example of this general pattern of state effectiveness. Some analysts routinely characterize states as the "new heroes" of American federalism, having long since eclipsed a doddering federal government. According to this line of argument, states are consistently at the cutting edge of policy innovation, eager to find creative solutions to environmental problems. When the states fall short, an overzealous federal partner is often said to be at fault.

Such commentary has considerable empirical support. The vast majority of state governments have undergone fundamental changes since the first Earth Day, in 1970. Many states have drafted new constitutions and gained access to unprecedented revenues through expanded taxing powers. Substantial amounts of federal transfer dollars have further swelled state coffers, allowing them to pursue policy commitments that previously would have been unthinkable. In turn, state bureaucracies have expanded and become more professionalized, as have the staffs serving governors and legislatures.[1] This activity has been stimulated by increasingly competitive two-party systems in many regions, intensifying pressure on elected officials to deliver desired services. Expanded use of direct democracy provisions, such as the initiative and referendum, and increasing activism by state courts and state attorneys general have further contributed to this new era. Studies of this resurgent "statehouse democracy" show that policymaking at the state level has proven highly responsive to dominant public opinion within each state.[2] On the whole, citizens are thought to be a good deal more satisfied with the package of public services and regulations dispensed from their state capitals than with those from Washington.

This transformed state role is evident in virtually every area of environmental policy. States directly regulate approximately 20 percent of the total U.S. economy, including many areas in which environmental concerns come into play.[3] They collectively issue more than 90 percent of all environmental permits, complete more than 75 percent of all environmental enforcement actions, and rely on the federal government for less than 25 percent of their total funding on environmental and natural resource concerns. Many areas of environmental policy are clearly dominated by states, including most aspects of waste management, groundwater protection, land use management, transportation, and electricity regulation. Even in policy areas that bear a firm federal imprint, such as air pollution control and pesticides regulation, states have considerable opportunity to oversee implementation and move beyond federal standards if they so choose. The Environmental Council of the States (ECOS) has estimated that the U.S. Environmental Protection Agency (EPA) had given states authority over 757 federal environmental programs by 1998, up from 434 in 1993, including 82 percent of all programs related to the Clean Air Act. Political scientist DeWitt John speaks for a wide range of policy analysts in noting that "states are willing to spend their own dollars and enact their own policies, without being forced by the federal government to do so. Virtually all states have taken some steps to go beyond federally imposed requirements, and some have taken the lead in several areas." [4] A study completed by Resources for the Future, an environmental think tank, confirms that a "basic tenet of correct thinking about current environmental policy is the desirability of decentralization" from the federal government to the states and that "hundreds of other reports over the past decade" have reached this conclusion. [5]

That growing commitment is further reflected in the institutional arrangements established by states to address environmental problems. Many states have long since moved beyond their traditional placement of environmental programs in public health departments in favor of comprehensive agencies that gather most environmental responsibilities under a single organizational umbrella. [6] These agencies have sweeping, cross-programmatic responsibilities and have continually grown in staff and complexity since 1970. Ironically many of these agencies mirror the organizational framework of the much-maligned EPA, dividing regulatory activity by environmental media of air, land, and water and thereby increasing the likelihood of shifting environmental contamination back and forth across medium boundaries. Despite this fragmentation, such institutions provide states with a firm institutional foundation for addressing a variety of environmental concerns.

This expanded state commitment to environmental policy may be accelerated not only by the broader factors introduced above but also by features somewhat unique to this policy area. First, a growing number of scholars contend that broad public support for environmental protection provides much impetus for bottom-up policy development. Such "civic environmentalism" stimulates numerous state and local stakeholders to take creative collective action independent of federal intervention. [7] In turn, game-theoretic analyses of efforts to protect so-called common-pool resources such as river basins side decisively with local or regional approaches to resource protection as opposed to top-down controls. Many such analyses go so far as to argue that any central government intervention in such settings is often unnecessary at best and downright destructive at worst.[8]

Second, the proliferation of environmental policy professionals, representing industry, advocacy groups, and particularly state agencies, has created a sizable base of talent and ideas for policy innovation. Contrary to conventional depictions of agency officials as shackled by elected "principals," an alternative view finds considerable policy entrepreneurship—or "bureaucratic autonomy"—in state and local policymaking circles.[9] This pattern is especially evident in environmental policy, where numerous areas of specialization place a premium on expert ideas and allow for considerable innovation within agencies.[10] Networks of professionals, working in similar capacities but in different states, have become increasingly influential in recent years. These networks facilitate information exchange, foster the diffusion of innovation, and pool resources to pursue joint initiatives. Specialized groups, such as ECOS and the National Association of State Energy Officials, also band together to influence federal policy. Other entities, such as the Northeast States for Coordinated Air Use Management and the Western Governors' Association, represent the interests of states in certain regions.

Third, environmental policy in many states is stimulated by direct democracy, facilitating initiatives, referendums, and recall of elected officials not allowed at the federal level. In every state except Delaware, state constitutional amendments must be approved by voters via referendum. Thirty-one states and Washington, D.C., also have some form of direct democracy for approving legislation, representing well over half the U.S. population. Use of this policy tool has grown at an exponential rate to consider a wide array of state environmental policy options, including nuclear plant closure, mandatory disclosure of commercial product toxicity, and public land acquisition. In November 2004, for example, Colorado voters decided that all electric utilities operating in the state must steadily increase the amount of energy they provide from renewable sources, reaching a level of at least 10 percent by 2015. At the same time, Montana citizens voted to ban the use of cyanide in gold and silver mining, establish a state fund to control noxious weeds, and recognize and preserve the right of its citizens to fish and hunt.

The Cutting Edge of Policy:
Cases of State Innovation

The convergence of these various political forces has unleashed substantial new environmental policy at the state level. A variety of scholars have attempted to analyze some of this activity through ranking schemes that determine which states are most active and innovative. They consistently conclude that certain states tend to take the lead in most areas of policy innovation, followed by an often uneven pattern of innovation diffusion across state and regional boundaries. One of the most thorough efforts to evaluate state "green capacity" involved a 100-point, 65-factor index completed in 2001 by the Resource Renewal Institute. This analysis considered

measures of state commitment to environmental protection, the strength of
state environmental agencies and management systems, and performance in
environmental policy innovation. The rankings, summarized in Table 2-1,
suggest considerable variation among states in each area that was examined.
Of course, any such ranking system has many limitations, particularly in
moving beyond measures of activity toward evaluation of actual pollution
reduction and environmental quality.

Somewhat related studies attempt to examine which economic and political factors are most likely to influence the rigor of state policy or the level of
resources devoted to it.[11] An important but less-examined question concerns
recent developments in state environmental policy and whether these developments constitute a marked improvement over conventional approaches in

Table 2-1   State Index of Environmental Protection Capacity and
Commitment, 2001

Rank	State	Total Points	Rank	State	Total Points
1	Oregon	73	26	Iowa	34
2	New Jersey	71	27	Idaho	31
3	Minnesota	64	28	New Hampshire	31
4	Maine	59	29	Montana	30
5	Washington	57	30	Virginia	29
6	Massachusetts	57	31	Arizona	29
7	Vermont	55	32	Rhode Island	28
8	Connecticut	45	33	Tennessee	28
9	Illinois	45	34	Hawaii	28
10	Florida	43	35	Ohio	26
11	Maryland	43	36	Colorado	25
12	California	42	37	Kansas	24
13	Georgia	42	38	Mississippi	23
14	Pennsylvania	42	39	South Dakota	22
15	Indiana	41	40	Louisiana	22
16	Delaware	40	41	Nebraska	20
17	Texas	40	42	Nevada	18
18	New York	39	43	Alaska	17
19	Utah	39	44	West Virginia	17
20	North Carolina	38	45	North Dakota	17
21	Wisconsin	37	46	Oklahoma	15
22	South Carolina	37	47	Arkansas	15
23	Kentucky	36	48	New Mexico	11
24	Missouri	36	49	Wyoming	10
25	Michigan	36	50	Alabama	8

Source: Resource Renewal Institute, *State of the States* (San Francisco: Resource Renewal Institute,
2001), chap. 2. The index consists of 100 possible points established through an evaluation of 56 measures that include various aspects of state environmental commitment, environmental policy innovation, and the strength of state environmental agencies and management systems.

Note: Total points have been rounded to the nearest whole number. States are ranked by their original
point value.

terms of environmental performance. Evidence from select states suggests that a number of state innovations offer worthy alternatives to prevailing approaches. Indeed, many of these innovations constituted direct responses to shortcomings in existing regulatory design. The brief case studies that follow indicate the breadth and potential effectiveness of state innovation.

Pollution Prevention

One of the greatest challenges facing U.S. environmental policy is the need to shift from a pollution control mode to one of prevention. Growing evidence suggests that some states are pursuing prevention in an increasingly systematic and effective way. All fifty states have at least one pollution prevention program, thirty-six of which are backed by state legislation. The oldest and most common of these involve technical assistance to industries and networking services that link potential collaborators. A smaller but growing set of state programs is redefining pollution prevention in larger terms, cutting across conventional programmatic boundaries with a series of mandates and incentives to pursue prevention opportunities. Fifteen states have established reporting requirements for state-based industries, and many states now use these data to guide pollution prevention planning.[12]

Among the more active states, Minnesota has one of the most comprehensive programs. The 1990 Minnesota Toxic Pollution Prevention Act requires approximately 350 Minnesota firms to submit annual toxic pollution prevention plans. These plans must outline each firm's current use and release of a long list of toxic pollutants and establish formal goals for their reduction or elimination over a specified period of time. Firms have considerable latitude in determining how to attain these goals, contrary to the technology-forcing character of much federal regulation. But they must meet state-established reduction timetables and pay fees on releases. Overall releases of these substances have dropped markedly and consistently since 1990.

Minnesota has continued to build on its early experience in pollution prevention and has made pollution prevention central to its expansion efforts to foster sustainable development and sustainable communities.[13] In addition, the Minnesota legislature and then-Governor Arne Carlson provided formal support for future innovation through the 1996 Environmental Regulatory Innovations Act. This legislation formally endorsed recent state initiatives and authorized state officials to continue to pursue intrastate or interstate innovation opportunities. It has served as a basis for ongoing state experimentation, including extended negotiation with industry and federal authorities in attempting to attain "superior environmental outcomes."[14]

Economic Incentives

Economists have long lamented the penchant for command-and-control rules and regulations in U.S. environmental policy. They would prefer to see a more economically sensitive set of policies, such as fees on emissions and incentives to reward good environmental performance. Neither federal nor state governments have escaped such critical scrutiny, although a number of states have attempted to respond in recent years. In all, the states have enacted more than 250 measures that can be characterized as "green taxes," including environmentally related charges and tax incentives.[15] Many states have become increasingly reliant on emissions or waste fees to provide both an economic disincentive to environmental degradation and a source of funds for program management.

A growing number of states are also revising their tax policies for environmental purposes. For example, Iowa exempts from taxation all pollution-control equipment purchased for use in the state, whereas Maryland offers major tax incentives to purchasers of low-emission vehicles. Numerous states offer a series of tax credits or low-interest loans for the purchase of recycling equipment or capital investments necessary to facilitate recycling or reuse of a particular product. Minnesota began to levy sizable sales taxes on nonrecycled municipal solid waste in 1989, which may well have contributed to the increase in the state's solid waste recycling rate from 9 percent in 1989 to 45.6 percent in 2002. The scope of this tax was expanded through legislation approved in 1997. New Jersey's campaign to deter sprawl and attempt to purchase nearly half of remaining undeveloped land to thwart potential development has been funded directly by new taxes on gasoline and rental car use.

Perhaps the most visible economic incentive programs involve refundable taxes on beverage containers. Ten states—covering 30 percent of the population—have such programs in place, and several others were actively considering adopting such programs or increasing their fees during 2004. Provisions of these programs vary somewhat, although most operate with limited direct involvement by state officials. Deposits pass along through a system that includes consumers, container redemption facilities such as grocery stores, and firms that reuse or recycle the containers. Michigan's program is widely regarded as among the most successful of these state efforts and, like a number of others, is a product of direct democracy. Michigan's program stands alone in placing a dime deposit on containers—double the more conventional nickel—which may contribute to its unusually high compliance rate.

This type of policy has diffused to other products, including tires, where the federal government has no current policy involvement. A few states began to experiment in the mid-1980s with fees on new tire purchases that could be used to launch a recycling market for old tires. More than 40 states now have some version of this policy, which has increased the national recycling rate for scrap tires from 25 percent in 1990 to 78 percent in 2001.[16] Once-familiar mountains of tires have essentially disappeared in these states, along with related environmental problems such as noxious fires and breeding grounds for disease-carrying insects. In recent years a growing number of states have applied this same approach to other items such as lead-acid batteries, motor oil, pesticide containers, and appliances with ozone-depleting substances.

Yet another area for state innovation based on economic incentives may be the literal use of state fiscal clout to attempt to leverage environmental change. States preside over substantial funds set aside for investment to support the future retirement of their officials and have increasingly experimented with ways to direct these investments toward socially productive ends while honoring their fiduciary responsibilities. In 2004, California state treasurer Phil Angelides announced the creation of the Green Wave Environmental Investment Initiative. He called upon the state's two largest public pension funds, with an estimated combined value of over $250 billion, to direct their investments toward "cutting-edge clean technologies and environmentally responsible companies." The directors of both pension funds responded favorably and pledged hundreds of million of dollars as an initial investment.[17]

Anticipating Future Challenges: Reducing Greenhouse Gases

Global climate change and the challenge of reducing the release of greenhouse gases such as carbon dioxide and methane have been characterized almost exclusively as the responsibility of national governments and international regimes. The world's largest source of greenhouse gases, the United States, is commonly depicted as disengaged on climate policy, reflected in its 2001 withdrawal from the Kyoto Protocol and failure during the Clinton administration and, thus far, during the Bush administration to enact policies to reduce these emissions (see chapter 13). States, however, have quietly begun to fill the "policy gap" created by federal inaction, with an increasingly diverse set of policies that address every sector of activity that generates greenhouse gases.

Many states are responsible for substantial amounts of greenhouse gas emissions, even by global standards. If all states were to secede and become independent nations, eighteen of them would rank among the top fifty nations in the world in terms of releases. Texas, for example, exceeds the United Kingdom in emissions, just as Ohio surpasses Turkey. In response, more than half of the states have enacted at least one piece of climate legislation or issued at least one executive order that sets formal requirements for reducing greenhouse gases. Nineteen states representing over 45 percent of the U.S. population have enacted "renewable portfolio standards," which mandate that a certain level of state electricity must come from renewable sources such as wind and solar; fifteen have used economic tools and established "social benefit charges," which tax energy use and allocate the funds for renewable energy or energy efficiency projects; and seven states formally regulate carbon dioxide emissions from power plants, through either regulations or more flexible market mechanisms. Some states, such as New Jersey, have developed policies in virtually every area that generates greenhouse gases, establishing a statewide goal that has put it on track to meet its share of reductions under the Kyoto Protocol.[18]

California also has been particularly active in this arena, including 2002 legislation that established the first carbon dioxide emissions standards for motor vehicles in North America or Europe. Under federal law, California can either adhere to existing air regulatory standards or elevate the regulatory bar. Once California has taken such steps, other states are free to embrace its policies, creating the potential for a competitive "race to the top" among states.[19] This pattern has occurred frequently in past decades, with carbon dioxide regulations adding a new twist. Signed into law by former Democratic governor Gray Davis and supported by his Republican successor, Arnold Schwarzenegger, California's Air Resources Board is required to establish carbon dioxide reduction requirements for all vehicles sold in California for the 2009 model year. A number of eastern states and the state of Washington have already decided to emulate the California program, although motor vehicle manufacturers and the Bush administration have alleged that California is exceeding its constitutional authority, moving beyond air quality emissions into fuel economy regulation, which is controlled by Washington.

Challenging the Federal Government

At the same time that states have eclipsed the federal government through new policies, they have also made increasingly aggressive use of litigation to attempt to force the federal government to take new steps or reconsider previous ones. This approach is largely attributable to strong reactions in some state capitals to actions of the Bush administration. But it has been further triggered by an increasingly active set of state attorneys general who have begun to develop joint litigation strategies to influence federal policy. Unlike their federal counterpart, most state attorneys general are elected officials and their powers have expanded significantly since the mid-1970s. They frequently represent a political party different than that of the sitting governor and often use their powers as a base to seek higher office. Forty percent of state attorneys general ultimately seek the governorship of their state, and it is no coincidence that prominent national officials such as former president Bill Clinton, Democratic senator Joseph Lieberman, and Bush administration interior secretary Gale Norton were all attorneys general of their respective home states.[20]

Collectively these officials have increasingly become a force to be reckoned with, not only in their home states but also as they expand their engagement through challenges brought into the federal courts. Indeed, one of the most common tactics in recent years has been for coalitions of respective attorneys general to join forces against the federal government and challenge some policy or interpretation. In some instances, state organizations such as ECOS or the National Conference of State Legislatures have joined in support of these challenges. During the Bush years, for example, different clusters of attorneys general have successfully challenged a variety of administration decisions. In 2003 and 2004 these challenges resulted in U.S. Court of Appeals decisions to reverse or delay Bush plans to weaken energy efficiency standards for air conditioners and to give far more latitude to electric power plants in making facility upgrades without incorporating new pollution controls.[21] States have also begun to explore litigable challenges to federal inaction on climate change, including a multistate suit against the Bush administration for failure to regulate carbon dioxide under the Clean Air Act.[22]

State Limits

Such a promising set of innovations would seem to augur well for the states' involvement in environmental policy. Any such enthusiasm must be tempered, however, by a continuing concern over how evenly that innovative vigor extends over the entire nation. One enduring rationale for giving the federal government so much authority in environmental policy is that states face inherent limitations in environmental policy. Rather than a consistent, across-the-board pattern of dynamism, we shall see a more uneven pattern of performance than conventional wisdom might anticipate. This imbalance becomes particularly evident when environmental problems are not confined to a specific state's boundaries. Many environmental issues are by definition transboundary, raising important questions of interstate and interregional equity in allocating responsibility for the burden of environmental protection.

Uneven State Performance

Many efforts to rank states according to their environmental regulatory rigor, institutional capacity, or general innovativeness find the same subset of states at the top of the list year after year. By contrast, a significant number of states consistently tend to fall much farther down the list, raising questions as to their overall regulatory capacity and commitment. As political scientist William Lowry has noted, "Not all states are responding appropriately to policy needs within their borders. . . . If matching between need and response were always high and weak programs existed only where pollution was low, this would not be a problem. However, this is not the case."[23] Given all the hoopla surrounding the newfound dynamism of states in environmental policy, and public policy more generally, there has been remarkably little analysis of the performance of states that not only fail to crack top-ten rankings but also consistently lag below the median.

What we do know about such states should surely give one pause over the extent to which state dynamism is truly cross-cutting. Despite considerable economic growth in formerly poor regions, such as the Southeast, substantial variation endures among state governments in their rates of public expenditure, with no demonstrable change in the amount of interstate expenditure variation since 1970.[24] Similar fiscal patterns are evident in environmental and natural resource spending. State expenditures in fiscal year 2003 ranged from $100 or more per capita in ten states to $50 or less per capita in fifteen others. Similar variation is evident when viewing such spending as a percentage of total state expenditures, in dollars per manufacturer, or as number of state environmental officials per capita, and it has remained relatively stable over time.[25] Cost-of-living differences among states account for only a small portion of this variation in state expenditure levels, and some states have either frozen or cut environmental expenditures since 2001 amid significant fiscal shortfalls. In turn, efforts to classify states by other measures reveal similarly discordant patterns. Such disparities are consistent with studies of state political culture and social capital, which indicate vast differences in likely state receptivity to governmental efforts to foster environmental improvement.[26]

Although many states are unveiling exciting new programs, there is growing reason to worry about how effectively states in general handle core functions either delegated to them under federal programs or left exclusively to their oversight. Studies of water quality program implementation during the 1990s found enormous variation in the methods used by states to determine water quality and in the willingness of states to take enforcement actions when violations were discovered.[27] States also use highly variable water quality standards in areas such as sewage contamination, groundwater protection, nonpoint water pollution, wetland preservation, fish advisories, and beach closures. Inconsistencies abound in reporting accuracy, suggesting that national assessments of water quality trends that rely on data from state reports may be highly suspect.

Comparable problems have emerged in state enforcement of air quality and waste management programs, where officially reported numbers on regulatory actions, emissions levels, waste disposal capacity, and waste reduction levels are of similarly questionable utility.[28] Despite efforts in some states to integrate and streamline permitting, many states have extensive backlogs in the permit programs they operate and thereby have no real indication of facility compliance with various regulatory standards. States have particularly struggled in issuance of Title V air quality permits.

A series of studies over the past decade have raised serious questions about basic program implementation in a number of states, including a scathing 1998 assessment by the EPA inspector general.[29] These analyses concluded that, in many states, major violations of federal environmental laws often go unreported, permit deadlines are routinely ignored, and mandatory emissions tests frequently are not conducted. These problems appear particularly extensive in certain states, many with significant concentrations of large industry. In 2004, for example, twenty-nine states were found to have created "legal loopholes" that allow major air emissions "spikes" from facility malfunctions and start-ups to be ignored and thereby keep regulated firms in compliance with federal law.[30]

Measurement of the impact of state programs on environmental outcomes remains imprecise in many areas. However, existing fifty-state indicators confirm the pattern of enormous state-by-state variation. State governments—alongside their local counterparts—have understandably claimed much of the credit for increasing solid waste recycling rates from a national average of 10 percent in 1990 to 26.7 percent in 2002. At the same time, state performance varies markedly. In 2002, five states—California, Iowa, Maine, Minnesota, and Oregon—had recycling rates of at least 40 percent, whereas twelve states, including Colorado, Georgia, Louisiana, New Mexico, and West Virginia, had rates of 18 percent or less. Other indicators of state environmental performance, such as per-capita rates of toxic waste generation or greenhouse gas release, also continue to vary markedly and often reflect varying degrees of policy engagement.

Enduring Federal Dependency

More sweeping assertions of state resurgence are undermined further by the penchant of many states to cling to organizational designs and program priorities set in Washington, D.C. Although some states have demonstrated that far-reaching agency reorganization and other integrative policies can be pursued without significant opposition—or grant reduction—from the federal government, the vast majority of states continue to adhere to a medium-based pollution control framework for agency organization that contributes to enduring programmatic fragmentation. Although a growing number of state officials speak favorably about shifting toward integrative approaches, many remain hard-pressed to demonstrate how their states have begun to move in that direction. Many Clinton-era federal initiatives to give states more freedom to innovate were used to streamline operations rather than foster prevention or integration.[31]

In fact, a good deal of the most innovative state-level activity has been at least partially stimulated—and underwritten—through federal grants. Indeed, in Canada, where central government grant assistance—and regulatory presence—is extremely limited, provinces have proven far less innovative than their American state counterparts.[32] Although a number of states have developed fee systems to cover a growing portion of their costs, many states rely heavily on federal grants to fund pollution prevention activities. In the 1990s more than one-third of all state pollution prevention expenditures came from federal sources, with some states reliant on federal dollars for up to one-half of their prevention efforts. States have continued to receive other important types of federal support, including grants and technical assistance to complete "state-of-the-state" environment reports, undertake comparative risk assessment projects, and launch inventories and action plans for greenhouse gas reductions. On the whole, states have received between one-quarter and one-third of their total environmental and natural resource program funding from federal grants in recent years, although a few states rely on the federal government for as much as 40 to 50 percent of their total funding.[33]

Furthermore, for all the opprobrium heaped on the federal government in environmental policy, it has provided states with at least four other forms of valuable assistance, some of which has contributed directly to the resurgence and innovation of state environmental policy. First, federal development in 1986 of a Toxics Release Inventory, modeled after programs initially attempted in Maryland and New Jersey, has emerged as a vital component of many of the most promising state policy initiatives. This program has generated unprecedented information concerning toxic releases and has provided states with an essential data source for exploring alternative regulatory approaches.[34] Current pollution prevention programs in New Jersey, Minnesota, and New York, for example, would be unthinkable without such an annual information source. Second, states remain almost totally dependent on the federal government for essential insights gained through research and development. Each year the federal government outspends the states in environmental research and development by more than twenty to one, and states have shown little inclination to assume this burden by funding research programs tailored to their particular technological and informational needs.

Third, the most successful efforts to coordinate environmental protection on a multistate, regional basis have received a great deal of federal input and support. A series of initiatives in the Chesapeake Bay, the Great Lakes basin, and New England have received much acclaim for tackling difficult issues and forging regional partnerships; federal participation—through grants, technical assistance, coordination, and efforts to unify regional standards—has proven useful in these cases.[35] By contrast, other major bioregions, including Puget Sound, the Gulf of Mexico, the Columbia River system, and the Mississippi River basin, have lacked comparable federal participation and have generally not experienced creative interstate partnerships.[36] Their experience contradicts the popular thesis that regional coordination improves when central authority is minimal or nonexistent.

Fourth, the EPA's ham-handedness is legendary, but its role in overseeing state-level program implementation looks far more constructive when examining the role played by the agency's ten regional offices. Most state-level interaction with the EPA involves such regional offices, which employ approximately two-thirds of the total EPA workforce. Relations between state and regional officials are generally more cordial and constructive than those between state and central EPA officials, and such relations may even be, in some instances, characterized by high levels of mutual involvement and trust.[37] Regional offices have played a central role in many of the most promising state-level innovations, including those in Minnesota and New Jersey. Their involvement may include formal advocacy on behalf of the state with central headquarters, direct collaboration on meshing state initiatives with federal requirements, and special grant support or technical assistance.

The Interstate Environmental Balance of Trade

States may be structurally ill-equipped to handle a large range of environmental concerns. In particular, states may be reluctant to invest significant energies to tackle problems that might literally migrate to another state in the absence of intervention. The days of state agencies being captured securely in the hip pockets of major industries are probably long gone, reflecting fundamental changes in state government.[38] Nonetheless, state regulatory dynamism does appear to diminish when faced with such cross-boundary issues.

The state imperative of economic development clearly contributes to this phenomenon. As states increasingly devise development strategies that resemble the industrial policies of Western European nations, a range of scholars have concluded they are far more deeply committed to strategies that promote investment or development than to those that involve social service provision or public health promotion.[39] A number of states now offer incentives in excess of $50,000 per new job to prospective developers and have intensified efforts to retain jobs in the struggling manufacturing sector. Environmental protection can be eminently compatible with economic development goals, promoting overall quality of life and general environmental attractiveness that entices private investment. In many states, the tourism industry has played an active role in seeking strong environmental programs designed to maintain natural assets.

But much of what a state might undertake in environmental policy may largely benefit other states or regions, thereby reducing an individual state's incentive to take meaningful action. In fact, in many instances, states continue to pursue a "we make it, you take it" strategy. As political scientist William Gormley Jr. has noted, sometimes "states can readily export their problems to other states," resulting in potentially serious environmental "balance of trade" problems.[40] In such situations, states may be inclined to export environmental contaminants to other states while enjoying any economic benefits to be derived from the activity that generated the contamination.

Such cross-boundary transfer takes many forms and may be particularly prevalent in environmental policy areas in which long-distance migration of pollutants is most likely. Air quality policy has long fit this pattern. States such as Ohio and Pennsylvania, for example, have depended heavily on burning massive quantities of high-sulfur coal to meet energy demands. Prevailing winds invariably transfer pollutants from this activity to other regions, particularly New England, leading to serious concern about acid deposition and related contamination threats. In turn, states throughout the nation have relied heavily on so-called dispersion enhancement to improve local air quality. Average industrial stack height in the United States soared from 243 feet in 1960 to 730 feet in 1980.[41] Although this increase resulted in significant air quality improvement in many areas near elevated stacks, it generally served to disperse air pollution problems elsewhere. It has also contributed to the growing problem of airborne toxics that ultimately pollute water or land in other regions. Between 80 and 90 percent of many of the most dangerous toxic substances found in Lake Superior, for example, stem from air deposition, much of which is generated outside of the Great Lakes basin.

Growing interstate conflicts, often becoming protracted battles in the federal courts, have emerged in recent decades as states allege they are recipients of such unwanted "imports." Midwestern and eastern states continue to be mired in a number of these disputes. Even a multiyear effort funded by the EPA to encourage all thirty-seven states east of the Rocky Mountains to find a collective solution to the transport of ground-level ozone failed to produce agreements on core recommendations. The so-called Ozone Transport Assessment Group (OTAG) received considerable national attention as a possible model of intergovernmental problem solving and did reach some important initial agreements among most of its members. But the participating states ultimately broke into warring camps, largely along regional lines, after OTAG issued its recommendations to the EPA in 1997. What has resulted is a series of interstate lawsuits by northeastern states against their midwestern counterparts for alleged unwillingness to reduce their emissions.

Perhaps nowhere is the problem of interstate transfer more evident than in the disposal of solid, hazardous, and nuclear wastes. In many respects states have been given enormous latitude to devise their own systems of waste management and facility siting, working either independently or in concert with other states. Many states, including a number of those usually deemed among the most innovative and committed environmentally, continue to generate massive quantities of waste and have been hugely unsuccessful in siting modern treatment, storage, and disposal facilities. Instead, out-of-state (and region) export has been an increasingly common pattern, with wastes often shipped to facilities opened before concern over waste and facility siting became widespread. At its worst, the system resembles a shell game in which waste is ultimately deposited in the least resistant state or facility at a given moment. In Michigan, a proactive effort to develop long-term capacity for solid waste management in previous decades has backfired, with the state serving as a magnet of sorts for waste from other jurisdictions. Approximately one-quarter of the waste deposited in state landfills comes from other states and the neighboring Canadian province of Ontario.[42] In response, the state enacted eleven new laws in 2004 that are designed to erect every conceivable barrier to these unwanted imports, although their constitutionality remains suspect.

Rethinking Environmental Federalism

The presidency of George W. Bush has raised a new set of questions concerning the future of state and federal government roles in environmental policy. Bush's record as Texas governor and his 2000 campaign rhetoric suggested considerable sympathy for decentralization strategies in environmental protection and other areas. During the 2000 campaign, Bush called for increased transfer of environmental program enforcement to state governments. He also relied heavily on former state officials to assume leadership roles in federal regulatory agencies with environmental jurisdiction.

This was perhaps most notable at the EPA, where Bush tapped New Jersey governor Christine Todd Whitman to serve as administrator. Whitman, in turn, stocked the top ranks of her staff with senior officials of agencies from Republican-controlled states. Once Whitman resigned in 2003, Bush replaced her with another governor, Utah's Mike Leavitt, who also espoused strong support for state-based approaches. Early Bush administration steps suggested a possible shift toward state authority. Initial administration budget proposals called for cuts of approximately 10 percent in areas such as environmental enforcement, coupled with plans to transfer some authority and resources to states. These factors suggested a less-active federal role and more autonomy for states in establishing and enforcing environmental policy. This environmental federalism did not emerge, however, as a major administration priority or lead to any formal plan to reallocate functions in a more decentralized manner.

Any possible Bush administration initiatives on environmental federalism, of course, were overshadowed by the September 11, 2001, terrorist attacks and elevation of antiterrorism and homeland security to top agenda items. These developments have resulted in a fundamental recalculation of the capacity of states and localities to continue to assume the bulk of responsibility for core public health functions, many of which involve environmental health and containment of communicable disease. Many state public health laws are more than a century old and many state health departments are antiquated, yet they guide state policy in responding to public health threats such as environmentally borne diseases. The federal government has increased financial and technical support for state and local environmental health responsibilities, but it remains unclear how effective these entities are likely to be in facing new challenges or whether states have had to transfer resources from other environmental protection functions to address possible bioterrorist threats.

A Failed Attempt at Accountable Decentralization

It has been difficult for any recent administration to achieve major shifts in federal and state authority in environmental policy. The Clinton administration learned this lesson through the limited impact of its National Environmental Performance Partnership System (NEPPS), launched in May 1995. NEPPS was linked to Clinton efforts to reinvent government and was heralded as a way to give states substantially greater flexibility in the management of many federal environmental programs if they could demonstrate innovation and actual performance in improving environmental quality. NEPPS also offered Performance Partnership Grants that would allow participating states to concentrate resources on innovative projects that promised environmental performance improvements.

More than forty states elected to participate in the NEPPS program, which required extensive negotiations between state and federal agency counterparts. Although a few promising examples of innovation can be noted, this initiative has failed to approach its ambitious goals. NEPPS stemmed from an administrative action and thereby lacked the clout of legislation. In response, federal authorities at the EPA often resisted altering established practices and thereby did not demonstrate the creativity or flexibility anticipated by NEPPS proponents. In turn, states proved far less amenable to innovation than expected. They tended to balk at any possibility that the federal government would establish—and publicize—serious performance measures that would evaluate their effectiveness and determine their ability to deviate from federal controls.[43]

Ultimately many NEPPS agreements were signed and continue to be implemented. Perhaps the most important impact of NEPPS has involved new projects funded under the Performance Partnership Grants. However, NEPPS cannot be considered a serious test of accountable decentralization, whereby state autonomy is increased formally in exchange for demonstrable performance. The Bush administration continued to honor existing NEPPS agreements but did not use them to more fully pursue reallocation of state and federal authority.

Challenges to State Routines

The future role of states in environmental policy may be further shaped by four additional developments. First, it remains increasingly unclear whether states will have sufficient fiscal resources to maintain core environmental protection functions and continue to consider new initiatives. Most states enjoyed generally robust fiscal health through the latter half of the 1990s, with overall tax revenues growing and swelling both annual surpluses and rainy-day funds. However, state fiscal conditions became increasingly gloomy in more recent years, as the onset of recession shrunk state coffers and prompted serious consideration of major program cuts in many statehouses. State expenditure growth in fiscal 2003, for example, was the lowest of any year in the preceding two decades. Given political pressures on states to sustain funding in areas such as education and health care, some observers contend that "smaller agencies such as environmental protection are taking disproportionate hits."[44] This picture began to brighten somewhat in fiscal 2004 and 2005 but with tremendous variation between states and regions.[45] In turn, there was no indication that states could rely increasingly on federal transfer dollars in the years ahead, because the federal budget surpluses disappeared rapidly after 2001 and nonenvironmental spending priorities took precedence.

This fiscal pinch may be particularly evident in states with elected leaders who lack a strong commitment to environmental policy. In Michigan, for example, three-term Republican governor John Engler used a series of executive orders in the 1990s to fragment existing agencies into separate units and restrict opportunities for public input by abolishing nineteen environmental boards or commissions, including the influential Air Pollution and Water Resources Commission. He also supported legislation to reverse earlier state polluter-pays laws and to eliminate a series of energy efficiency programs. Engler appointees to top environmental posts were often highly controversial, known for their eagerness to work cooperatively with regulated parties and for their ability to alienate state agency staff.[46] His 2003 successor, Democrat Jennifer Granholm, has toned down the antiregulatory rhetoric, but Granholm's primary focus has been on streamlining environmental regulatory decisions, such as permitting, to minimize disruption for industry. This theme has been increasingly evident in states with large manufacturing sectors that have faced serious job losses in recent years.

Second, the era of term limits has begun to unfold.[47] As of 2002, thirty-nine states had imposed some form of term limits on governors, and seventeen states had placed them on legislators. Many of these restrictions were established during the 1990s and are only just beginning to take effect. Legislative term limits were repealed in Idaho and Oregon in early 2002, and some remain under constitutional challenge in the state courts. Gubernatorial term limits most commonly involve a pair of four-year terms, whereas legislative term limits range from six to twelve years. Even before they formally took hold, the threat of these limits accelerated legislative turnover.[48] In many states, veteran legislators who championed the environmental programs that have given states such a dynamic image either have left office in recent years or will soon be forced to step down.[49] The long-term impact on environmental policy of the arrival of cascades of new elected officials, all allowed to stay in specific offices for limited periods, is anyone's guess.

Third, the 2004 election further assured a continuing pattern of divided, joint-party control of state government. Contrary to trends at the federal level, Democrats achieved some net gains in the total number of state legislative seats that they hold, leaving the nation's total number of legislative posts almost equally divided between the two main political parties.[50] In thirty states, including a number of large ones such as California and New York, control of state government is formally shared by the parties. In many instances, this pattern contributes to gridlock analogous to that long lamented in Washington, D.C. Under such circumstances, environmental policy will require the constructive engagement of both parties in a great many states in order to move forward productively.

Fourth, many states have begun to encounter a significant new force in environmental policy formation. The American Legislative Exchange Council (ALEC), a nonprofit organization based in Washington, D.C., was founded in the early 1970s but has dramatically expanded its activity and influence since the mid-1990s. ALEC perceives the vast majority of state environmental policy initiatives as a fundamental threat to the tenets of American democracy and seeks to either repeal existing laws or write more industry-friendly ones. Its membership includes more than 2,400 state legislators, nearly one-third of whom hold leadership positions.[51] Through conferences, retreats, and a large body of "model legislation" that can be modified and adopted by individual states, ALEC has attempted to redefine the boundaries of state environmental policy in numerous areas, including air quality, electricity, and mining regulation, as well as on broader issues such as the use of science in environmental policy proceedings and the content of environmental education materials used in the public schools. ALEC proposals are increasingly being enacted into law in various states, "at a rate of 1,500 bills a year," according to one assessment.[52]

Looking Ahead

Amid the continued squabbling over the proper role of the federal government vis-à-vis the states in environmental policy, remarkably little effort has been made to sort out which functions might best be concentrated in Washington and which transferred to state capitals. Some current and retired federal legislators of both parties offered useful proposals during the 1990s that might allocate such responsibilities more reasonably than at present. These proposals have been supplemented by thoughtful scholarly works by think tanks, political scientists, economists, and other policy analysts. Interestingly, many of these experts concur that environmental protection policy defies easy designation as warranting extreme centralization or decentralization. Instead, many observers endorse a process of selective decentralization, one leading to an appropriately balanced set of responsibilities across governmental levels.

In moving toward a more functional environmental federalism, certain broad design principles might be useful to consider. The Clinton administration experiment with NEPPS was billed as a major attempt at such reallocation, but a more serious effort would require establishment of state environmental performance measures that were publicized and utilized to determine a more appropriate allocation of functions. This would, in all likelihood, require legislation rather than managerial experimentation that can be wiped away as political leadership changes. It would also demand new flexibility from the EPA as well as a newfound willingness of states to be held accountable for their performance and treated accordingly.

A more discerning environmental federalism might also begin by concentrating federal regulatory energies on problems that are clearly national in character. Many air and water pollution problems, for example, are by definition cross-boundary concerns unlikely to be resolved by a series of unilateral state actions. In contrast, problems such as protecting indoor air quality and cleanup of abandoned hazardous waste dumps may present more geographically confinable challenges; they are perhaps best handled through substantial delegation of authority to states. As policy analyst John Donahue notes, "most waste sites are situated within a single state, and stay there," yet are governed by highly centralized Superfund legislation, in direct contrast to more decentralized programs in environmental areas in which cross-boundary transfers are prevalent.[53] Under a more rational system, the federal regulatory presence might intensify as the likelihood of cross-boundary contaminant transfer escalates. Such an initial attempt to sort out functions might be reinforced by federal policy efforts to encourage states or regions to take responsibility for internally generated environmental problems rather than tacitly allow exportation to occur. In the area of waste management, for example, federal per-mile fees on waste shipment might provide a disincentive for long-distance transfer, instead encouraging states, regions, and waste generators to either develop their own capacity or pursue waste reduction options more aggressively. In the rapidly evolving area of climate change, federal and state governments might assess fees for each ton of released greenhouse gases, thereby providing an incentive to reduce emissions and a pool of funds for mitigation strategies. The growing use of economic approaches to environmental policy at both state and federal levels provides numerous models that might be used to encourage states to be more responsible environmental citizens in the federal system.

In many areas, some shared federal and state role remains appropriate, reflecting the inherent complexity of many environmental problems. Effective intergovernmental partnerships may already be well established in certain areas. Even a 1995 National Academy of Public Administration study that excoriated many aspects of federal environmental policy conceded that the existing partnership between federal and state governments "is basically sound, and major structural changes are not warranted. The system has worked."[54] But even if essentially sound, the partnership could clearly benefit from further maturation. Alongside the sorting-out activities discussed earlier in this section, both federal and state governments could do much more to promote creative sharing of policy ideas and environmental data. There is remarkably limited dissemination of such information across state and regional boundaries, and potentially considerable advantage is to be gained from increasing such activity. More broadly, the federal government might explore other ways to encourage states to work cooperatively, especially on common-boundary problems. State capacity to find creative solutions to pressing environmental problems is on the ascendance, as we have seen. But as Lord Bryce concluded many decades ago, cooperation among states does not arise automatically.

Suggested Web Sites

Environmental Council of the States (www.ecos.org) The Environmental Council of the States represents the lead environmental protection agencies of all fifty states. The site contains access to state environmental data as well as the organization's quarterly publication, *ECOStates*.

National Conference of State Legislatures (www.ncsl.org) The National Conference of State Legislatures conducts extensive research on a wide range of environmental, energy, and natural resource issues for its primary constituency, state legislators, as well as the general citizenry. The organization offers an extensive set of publications, including specialized reports and books.

National Caucus of Environmental Legislators (www.ncel.net) The National Caucus of Environmental Legislators represents state legislators with a strong interest in environmental policy. It provides summaries of new and proposed state environmental legislation as well as related press releases and media accounts.

Initiative and Referendum Institute (www.iandrinstitute.org) The Initiative and Referendum Institute is affiliated with the Law School of the University of Southern California and provides detailed analysis of state-based direct democracy activities, including a special focus on environmental ballot propositions.

Notes

1. David M. Hedge, *Governance and the Changing American States* (Boulder: Westview Press, 1998).
2. Robert S. Erikson, Gerald C. Wright, and John P. McIver, *Statehouse Democracy: Public Opinion and Policy in the American States* (New York: Cambridge University Press, 1993).
3. Paul Teske, *Regulation in the States* (Washington, D.C.: Brookings Institution Press, 2004), 9.
4. DeWitt John, *Civic Environmentalism: Alternatives to Regulation in States and Communities* (Washington, D.C.: CQ Press, 1994), 80; John and Marian Mlay, "Community-Based Environmental Protection: Encouraging Civic Environmentalism," in *Better Environmental Decisions: Strategies for Governments, Businesses, and Communities,* ed. Ken Sexton et al. (Washington, D.C.: Island Press, 1999), 353–376.
5. J. Clarence Davies et al., *Reforming Permitting* (Washington, D.C.: Resources for the Future, 2001), 58.
6. Deborah Hitchcock Jessup, *Guide to State Environmental Programs,* 3rd ed. (Washington, D.C.: Bureau of National Affairs, 1994).
7. John, *Civic Environmentalism.*
8. Elinor Ostrom, *Governing the Commons: The Evolution of Institutions for Collective Action* (New York: Cambridge University Press, 1990); Elinor Ostrom, Roy Gardner, and James Walker, *Rules, Games, and Common-Pool Resources* (Ann Arbor: University of Michigan Press, 1994). For a contrary view, see Edward P. Schwartz and Michael R. Tomz, "The Long-Run Advantages of Centralization for Collective Action," *American Political Science Review* 91 (September 1997): 685–694.
9. Daniel P. Carpenter, *The Forging of Bureaucratic Autonomy* (Princeton: Princeton University Press, 2001); Michael Mintrom, *Policy Entrepreneurs and School Choice* (Washington, D.C.: Georgetown University Press, 2000).
10. Sandford Borins, *Innovating with Integrity* (Washington, D.C.: Georgetown University Press, 1998); Barry G. Rabe, "Permitting, Prevention, and Integration: Lessons from the States," in *Environmental Governance: A Report on the Next Generation of Environmental Policy,* ed. Donald F. Kettl (Washington, D.C.: Brookings Institution Press, 2002), 14–57.
11. Evan J. Ringquist, *Environmental Protection at the State Level: Politics and Progress in Controlling Pollution* (Armonk, N.Y.: M. E. Sharpe, 1993); James P. Lester, "A New Federalism? Environmental Policy in the States," in *Environmental Policy in the 1990s,* ed. Norman J. Vig and Michael E. Kraft (Washington, D.C.: CQ Press, 1994), 51–68.
12. Susan Hearn, "Reducing Toxics: Is Coercion or Encouragement the Best Policy Approach?," Ph.D. diss., University of Michigan, 2002; David H. Folz and Jean M. Peretz, "Evaluating State Hazardous Waste Reduction Policy," *State and Local Government Review* 29 (fall 1997): 134–146.
13. Barry G. Rabe, "Sustainability in a Regional Context: The Case of the Great Lakes Basin," in *Toward Sustainable Communities: Transition and Transformations in Environ-*

mental Policy, ed. Daniel A. Mazmanian and Michael E. Kraft (Cambridge: MIT Press, 1999), 266–269.

14. Alfred A. Marcus, Donald A. Geffen, and Ken Sexton, *Reinventing Environmental Regulation: Lessons from Project XL* (Washington, D.C.: Resources for the Future, 2002).

15. J. Andrew Hoerner, "Life and Taxes," *The Amicus Journal* (summer 1995): 14–17.

16. John J. Fialka, "States' Fee Programs for Tires Yield Big Gains in Recycling Rate," *Wall Street Journal,* December 5, 2002, A5.

17. News Release from California State Treasurer Phil Angelides, "State Treasurer Phil Angelides Launches 'Green Wave' Environmental Investment Initiative to Bolster Financial Returns, Create Jobs and Clean Up the Environment," Office of the State Treasury, Sacramento, February 3, 2004.

18. Barry G. Rabe, *Statehouse and Greenhouse: The Emerging Politics of American Climate Change Policy* (Washington, D.C.: Brookings Institution Press, 2004).

19. Matthew Weinbaum, "Implications of Automotive Emission Restrictions in California," *Federalism-E* 4 (February 2004): 1–32; John Pendergrass, "California Takes on Detroit Once Again," *The Environmental Forum* 21 (July/August 2004): 6.

20. Colin Provost, "State Attorneys General, Entrepreneurship, and Consumer Protection in the New Federalism," *Publius: The Journal of Federalism* 33 (spring 2003): 37–53.

21. Stephen R. Dujack, "Prosecutor on a Mission," *The Environmental Forum* (May/June 2004): 38–41; Donald F. Kettl, "Unreliable Source," *Governing* (June 2003): 14.

22. News release from the Office of New York Attorney General Eliot Spitzer et al., "States to Sue Bush Administration on Global Warming," February 20, 2003.

23. William R. Lowry, *The Dimensions of Federalism: State Governments and Pollution Control Policies* (Durham: Duke University Press, 1992), 125.

24. Paul E. Peterson, *The Price of Federalism* (Washington, D.C.: Brookings Institution Press, 1995), chap. 4.

25. Council of State Governments, *Resource Guide to State Environmental Management,* 5th ed. (Lexington, Ky.: Council of State Governments, 1999); "Environmental Spending," *Governing State and Local Sourcebook 2004* (Washington, D.C.: Congressional Quarterly, 2004), 21.

26. Robert D. Putnam, *Bowling Alone: The Collapse and Revival of American Community* (New York: Simon and Schuster, 2000), sect. 4; Tom W. Rice and Alexander F. Sumberg, "Civic Culture and Government Performance in the American States," *Publius: The Journal of Federalism* 27 (winter 1997): 99–114.

27. U.S. General Accounting Office (GAO, renamed the Government Accountability Office), "Water Pollution: Differences among the States in Issuing Permits Limiting the Discharge of Pollutants" (Washington, D.C.: GAO, 1996); Robert W. Adler, Jessica C. Landman, and Diane M. Cameron, *The Clean Water Act 20 Years Later* (Washington, D.C.: Island Press, 1993).

28. Ringquist, *Environmental Protection at the State Level*; Daniel A. Mazmanian and David Morell, *Beyond Superfailure: America's Toxics Policy for the 1990s* (Boulder: Westview Press, 1992), 107–110.

29. U.S. Environmental Protection Agency (EPA), *Office of Inspector General Semiannual Report to Congress* (Washington, D.C.: EPA, May 1998); John H. Cushman Jr., "E.P.A. and States Found to Be Lax on Pollution Law," *New York Times,* June 7, 1998, 1.

30. Kelly Haragan, *Gaming the System* (Washington, D.C.: Environmental Integrity Project, 2004).

31. J. Clarence Davies and Jan Mazurek, *Pollution Control in the United States: Evaluating the System* (Washington, D.C.: Resources for the Future, 1998), 41–42.

32. David R. Boyd, *Unnatural Law: Rethinking Canadian Environmental Law and Policy* (Vancouver: University of British Columbia Press, 2003); Barry G. Rabe, "Federalism and Entrepreneurship: Explaining American and Canadian Innovation in Pollution

Prevention and Regulatory Integration," *Policy Studies Journal* 27 (spring 1999): 288–306.

33. R. Steven Brown and Michael J. Kiefer, "Budgets Are Bruised, But Still Strong," *ECOStates* (summer 2003), 10–15.

34. Mary Graham, *Democracy by Disclosure* (Washington, D.C.: Brookings Institution Press, 2002).

35. Tom Horton and William M. Eichbaum, *Turning the Tide: Saving the Chesapeake Bay* (Washington, D.C.: Island Press, 1991); Rabe, "Sustainability in a Regional Context."

36. Adler, Landman, and Cameron, *The Clean Water Act 20 Years Later*, 221–224, 251.

37. Denise Scheberle, *Federalism and Environmental Policy: Trust and the Politics of Implementation*, revised ed. (Washington, D.C.: Georgetown University Press, 2004), chap. 7.

38. Teske, *Regulation in the States*.

39. John D. Donahue, *Disunited States: What's at Stake as Washington Fades and the States Take the Lead* (New York: Basic Books, 1997); Peterson, *The Price of Federalism*; Frank R. Baumgartner and Bryan D. Jones, *Agendas and Instability in American Politics* (Chicago: University of Chicago Press, 1993), chap. 11.

40. William T. Gormley Jr., "Intergovernmental Conflict on Environmental Policy: The Attitudinal Connection," *Western Political Quarterly* 40 (1987): 298–299.

41. Lowry, *The Dimensions of Federalism*, 45.

42. Thomas M. Fletcher, *From Love Canal to Environmental Justice: The Politics of Hazardous Waste on the Canada–U.S. Border* (Toronto: Broadview Press, 2003), 27–33.

43. GAO, "Collaborative EPA-State Effort Needed to Improve New Performance Partnership System" (Washington, D.C.: GAO, 1999); National Academy of Public Administration (NAPA), *Environment.gov: Transforming Environmental Protection for the 21st Century* (Washington, D.C.: NAPA, 2000), chap. 5.

44. Alan Greenblatt, "Making Do," *Governing* (December 2003): 32.

45. National Governors Association (NGA) and National Association of State Budget Officers (NASBO), *The Fiscal Survey of the States* (Washington, D.C.: NGA and NASBO, 2004).

46. Dave Dempsey, *Ruin and Recovery: Michigan's Rise as a Conservation Leader* (Ann Arbor: University of Michigan Press, 2001), chap. 15.

47. John M. Carey, Richard G. Niemi, and Lynda W. Powell, *Term Limits in the State Legislatures* (Ann Arbor: University of Michigan Press, 2000).

48. Alan Rosenthal, *The Decline of Representative Democracy: Process, Participation, and Power in State Legislatures* (Washington, D.C.: CQ Press, 1998), 72–74.

49. Rosenthal, *Heavy Lifting: The Job of the American Legislature* (Washington, D.C.: CQ Press, 2004), 244–245.

50. National Conference of State Legislatures, "2005 Partisan Composition of State Legislatures," February 11, 2005, www.ncsl.org/ncsldb/elect98/partcomp.cfm?yearsel =2005, February 21, 2005.

51. American Legislative Exchange Council (ALEC), *Energy, Environment, and Economics: A Guide for State Legislators* (Washington, D.C.: ALEC, 2003).

52. Alan Greenblatt, "What Makes ALEC Smart?" *Governing* (October 2003): 30.

53. Donahue, *Disunited States*, 65.

54. NAPA, *Setting Priorities, Getting Results: A New Direction for EPA*, (Washington, D.C.: NAPA, 1995), 71.

3

Environmental Sustainability and Urban Life in America

Robert C. Paehlke

Because most Americans live in or near large cities, the physical environment most of us experience every day is urban or suburban in character. This chapter considers how cities affect, and are affected by, environmental sustainability. In its broadest sense, sustainability is about the capacity of nature to support human well-being over the long term. Viewed the other way around, it is about the efficiency with which we utilize what nature offers by meeting human needs at the least cost to nature. Some European theorists call this relationship societal metabolism, analogous to the metabolism of the human body that guides the rate at which all living beings eat, drink, breathe, and excrete. The character of our economies and activities determines the "metabolic" rate of extractions from and returns to nature and, thereby, the number of humans that can survive comfortably for the long term within the earth's carrying capacity.

Since the late 1980s, especially since the publication of the report of the World Commission on Environment and Development, the concept of sustainability has become increasingly central to environmental policy.[1] Daniel Mazmanian and Michael Kraft see this emphasis on sustainability to be at the core of recent environmental policy.[2] Whereas earlier periods were characterized by policy formulations that treated the pollution of air, water, and land separately, sustainability analysis considers all material flows into and out of human economies in an integrated way. Recent policy has also witnessed a shift in the jurisdictional focus of environmental decisions away from national governments, in some cases to the global level through environmental treaties and, at the same time and especially, to state and local governments. This chapter considers how the quality and design of urban spaces, a key responsibility of state and local governments, strongly influences the sustainability of nature, as well as the sustainability of economic prosperity and our quality of life.

Defining and Measuring Sustainability

Sustainability can be defined either broadly or narrowly. Broadly, *environmental* sustainability is the capacity to continuously produce the necessities of a quality human existence within the bounds of a natural world of undiminished quality. Sustainability in this sense is a long-term societal objective rather than something achieved once and for all at any given time. Environmental sustainability encompasses high performance levels within three measurable sets of environmental values: (1) human health (especially as affected by environmental quality), (2) ecosystem health (the protection of habitat, wilderness, and biodiversity), and (3) resource sustainability. *Resource* sustainability, the narrower sense of sustainability, is achieved through the effective management of society's total material and energy requirements (TMR). Sustainable TMR implies a continuous reduction in the materials and energy extracted from nature per unit of economic output and, if possible, absolutely. In other words, resource sustainability seeks to minimize extraction; maximize materials reuse and recycling; and limit the use of renewable resources such as water, fish, and fiber to amounts well within nature's capacity to supply them perpetually.

Sustainability involves thinking about society in terms of a triple bottom line—economic prosperity, social well-being, and environmental quality (including resource sustainability).[3] In this view, economic prosperity is more a means than an end, and human well-being—rather than "mere" prosperity—is the primary goal of society and public policy. In analytic terms, at any given level of prosperity, individuals, communities, or nations experience widely varying levels of health, happiness, fairness, and education. Some minimum of prosperity is obviously necessary for comfortable survival, but beyond that considerable variability is found in the quality of society—and the quality of life within each society—obtained for each increment of wealth. There is also considerable variability in the degree of prosperity that can be obtained from any given rate of energy and materials use.

In the simplest of examples, given that highly energy-efficient refrigerators can preserve food using only 10–20 percent of the energy of inefficient refrigerators, significantly more prosperity and well-being would be obtained per unit of energy were all refrigeration so efficient. The sum total of thousands upon thousands of such changes in product design and production techniques is called *eco-efficiency*. The hope regarding eco-efficiency is that adequate environmental protection can be achieved through such efficiency gains rather than through actions that might limit prosperity. As important as eco-efficiency are the differences in the efficiency with which prosperity results in well-being. For example, one community might invest its prosperity gains in health and education and arguably thereby obtain greater societal well-being than a jurisdiction that spends its increments of wealth on junk food, military weapons, and "toys" for the rich. Thus there is a so-called double efficiency built into the triple bottom line of sustainability theory. Societies can produce wealth from nature more, or less, efficiently and can produce well-being from prosperity more, or less, effectively.

Eco-efficiency and Well-being

Using environmental indicators (including the measurement of TMR and other indicators such as combined pollution indices or the proportion of relatively undisturbed natural habitat), analysts can estimate how efficiently wealth is generated in environmental terms. The good news is that industrial economies are probably becoming more efficient in terms of resource use per dollar of GDP (gross domestic product, the sum of all goods and services produced) per capita. The bad news is that human numbers and prosperity are advancing more rapidly than this type of efficiency is improving; thus we are slowly imposing upon nature more and more. The challenge of sustainability is to accelerate eco-efficiency and to find ways to get more health and happiness out of each increment of prosperity.

There are, of course, disagreements about the urgency of eco-efficiency improvements in particular cases. How important, some would argue, is the existence of tropical insect and amphibian species? Are they more important than the continued export of tropical woods from a desperately poor country? Is the risk of climate change more important than the, sometimes assumed, right of each person to drive whenever and wherever he or she wishes? Any economy that replaces scarce tropical woods with other materials and provides high-quality public transit will be more eco-efficient. With some effort we can get fairly wide agreement on how to measure environmental quality and thereby eco-efficiency (in terms of air and water quality, habitat protection, and the efficient use of scarce and essential resources). These measures can be used to compare community or national performances over time.

However challenging questions regarding environmental quality sometimes are, the matter of getting more well-being from prosperity is almost always highly controversial. To begin with, well-being is affected by the proportion of societal wealth that is expended collectively rather than by individuals, and by the overall pattern of wealth distribution. How, indeed, do we decide these questions? Beyond distributional questions, little agreement exists about what expenditures produce greater well-being, or indeed what *is* well-being and what is not. Mercifully, although everyone's priorities are different, we do not have to agree on everything. I may listen to opera and you to hip-hop, but we can still agree that low infant mortality is a priority, that less crime is good, and that improving literacy is important. It is not, then, an impossible task to collectively develop a definition of well-being that is independent of (though likely related to) prosperity and that will still make sense to most people, however much they might disagree about what constitutes overall quality of life.

Sustainability and Public Policy

Sustainability analysis clearly has implications for virtually every aspect of public policy. In one analysis of these implications, John Robinson and Jon Tinker advocate two forms of "decoupling" as essential to moving toward sustainability.[4] One is the decoupling of economic output (as measured by GDP) from the increased use of energy and materials. The other is the partial decoupling of social well-being from GDP per capita (that is, improving quality of life faster than increases in wealth, getting more for our money).

The first of these decouplings might be advanced by taxing raw materials (instead of income, for example) to encourage expenditures on sustainable production innovations and altered consumer behavior. Environmentalists call such a strategy a tax-shift approach to environmental protection, or eco-taxation. The second decoupling (of prosperity and well-being) might be achieved through increased public expenditures on (or just better) health care or education, or even—arguably—through reductions in work time (freeing time for family and community life even with some loss in family income). Well-being improvements can result from increased prosperity especially if that added prosperity includes more equitable economic distribution.

Both the logic for, and the means of, advancing sustainability become clearer within a three-dimensional evaluation of societal performance in terms of economic prosperity, social well-being, and societal metabolism.[5] Recall that in this perspective social well-being (as measured by health, education, comfort, happiness, social cohesion, or any of a number of other indicators) is the primary objective and is achieved through prosperity that in turn depends on the long-term availability of sufficient materials and energy from nature. These causal links are the points at which partial decoupling can be achieved and at which an economy can become more *sustainably* productive, rather than just more productive in the everyday sense of that term—labor input per unit of economic output. From the perspective of sustainability analysis it is a mistake to think that the only way to improve well-being is through greater prosperity or to assume that the only way to enhance prosperity is to increase the use of energy and raw materials.

This perspective distinguishes sustainability from a common-sense model that takes prosperity (as measured by GDP) to be the overwhelmingly dominant goal of society and public policy. This common-sense model might be called *economism*. From the perspective of sustainability analysis this view consistently misdirects public policy by misconceiving fundamental objectives. There are three bottom lines, not one; economism, as a perspective, is unduly one-dimensional. The fact that greater prosperity *could be* channeled to environmental and social improvements is, in a sense, irrelevant; sustainability analysis measures performance within each of the three dimensions independently. Increased wealth may turn out to be better in terms of all three dimensions, but two other questions need to be answered first. Is social well-being rising both absolutely and per unit of prosperity? And, are we increasing materials and energy efficiency at least as fast as we are expanding GDP? Many environmentalists would argue that such a rate of improvement is insufficient for the achievement of sustainability, but all would agree that it is a necessary interim goal.[6]

Sustainability and the Economy

Achieving sustainability involves all aspects of the economy. Both production and consumption decisions play important roles. Many manufacturers are oriented to sustainability concerns within their own operations because using less energy and materials usually reduces costs. Sustainability initiatives, however, can hurt some industries. For example, if consumers opt for more durable products or greater energy efficiency, some businesses could lose sales. Even though other businesses might gain, sustainability carries much potential for political and policy conflict.

Within what might be called the political economy of sustainability decisions, the character and design of cities and urban transportation systems are especially important. Our choice of transportation mode and the amount that we travel daily are greatly affected by urban planning decisions, housing prices, municipal tax rates, the location of employment opportunities, and even crime rates and patterns. Transportation decisions have a large influence on sustainability—automobiles require more energy, metal, concrete, and land per passenger-mile than do most other forms of transportation. It is not just a matter of creating good public transportation; it is a matter of designing cities where people find it easier to walk or to take a streetcar than it is to drive, at least some of the time. We choose to drive only in part because it is (sometimes) an enjoyable experience. We also drive because the distances we must go often exclude walking and because low-density, suburban-style neighborhoods may all but preclude convenient and affordable public transit.

Sustainability in Cities

One of the best places to begin to understand the overall environmental sustainability impacts of today's cities is with the work of Peter Newman and Jeffrey Kenworthy, whose study of thirty-six cities demonstrated that choice of transportation mode, transportation fuel use, and air quality are primarily a function of residential density and land use configuration (both of which are a function of urban planning).[7] That is, more compact cities and mixed-use zoning (combining residential and commercial development in proximity to one another) result in reduced automobile use and increased use of public transit, cycling, and walking (Table 3-1). Low-density, suburban-style configurations, with segregated residential and commercial uses, subtly discourage the use of most means of mobility other than automobiles. In those settings, getting to work, school, or a store or visiting friends usually requires a car or makes people wish they had one.

Even a modest increase in overall residential density, however, changes that reality to one that can offer a real choice of transportation modes. As Table 3-1 illustrates, typical western North American cities (whose streetscapes and functional arrays were established after 1945) are dominated by automobile use, as is (not surprisingly) Detroit. Many large cities in eastern North America (Toronto, Chicago, and New York, for example) are more compact and have viable public transit systems. Some smaller cities (Portland, Oregon, for example) have worked hard and successfully at becoming exceptions to this overall pattern. European cities are typically

Table 3-1   Density and Transportation

City	Car Use (km per capita)	Population and Job Density	Transit Use (km per capita)
Houston	13,016	15	215
Phoenix	11,608	16	124
Detroit	11,239	21	171
Chicago	9,525	25	805
New York	8,317	30	1,334
Toronto	5,019	65	2,173
Munich	4,202	91	2,463
Paris	3,459	68	2,405
London	3,892	66	2,121

Source: Peter Newman and Jeffrey Kenworthy, *Sustainability and Cities: Overcoming Automobile Dependence* (Washington, D.C.: Island Press, 1999).

Note: All figures are for 1990; population and job density is a combined index.

very different. Their downtown streets were developed long before the automobile and are not easily altered (one simply does not replace cathedrals in which Charlemagne spoke). Moreover, Europeans have consciously invested in high-quality, well-integrated public transit systems, partly because they historically have faced higher gasoline prices. In Vienna, for example, the air, rail, subway, and light rail (streetcar) systems are seamlessly interconnected and sufficiently frequent and inexpensive that they are often faster and cheaper than driving.

Thus moderate density levels (as in, for example, a mix of commercial development, low-rise apartments, townhouses, and single-family dwellings on relatively compact lots) encourage frequent transit service as well as more walking and cycling. Many other aspects of sustainability also follow from these moderate density levels and mixed-use configurations. For example, farmland and wilderness nearer to urban and suburban residents are preserved, a possibility recognized by the American Farmland Trust and the U.S. Conference of Mayors in their 2002 joint list of "Ten Actions for Rural/Urban Leaders."[8]

In more compact cities fewer materials are needed per capita for the construction of infrastructure because existing infrastructure is more fully utilized—more people use each segment of sidewalk, water pipe, or fiber-optic cable. And, less energy is used because distances are shorter, transit delivers more passenger-miles per unit of energy, and multiple-family dwellings use less heating and cooling per person (because fewer walls are exterior walls and there is less roof per square foot of floor space). Also, compact mixed-use settings open the possibility for co-generation (using waste process heat for commercial and residential heating) or even technological innovations such as Toronto's massive new Deep Lake Water Cooling

System, which uses water from Lake Ontario to cool much of the downtown, saving enough electricity to power 12,000 air-conditioned homes.[9] Some cities in Spain and Sweden have even eliminated garbage and recycling trucks in favor of vacuum tube systems hooked to a central processing facility.

In contrast, urban sprawl leads to greater climate change emissions. In the United States, hundreds of millions of tons of carbon dioxide are emitted by motor vehicles each year. Overall, 30 percent of greenhouse gases come from transportation, and this proportion is rising even though automobiles have on average become 1 percent more fuel efficient per year since 1970. In this same period, however, per-vehicle emissions from light trucks, sport-utility vehicles, and vans have risen 30 to 50 percent, and the number of these vehicles has increased as a proportion of all vehicles.[10] Moreover, average distances driven per vehicle per year have increased in large part because cities continue to develop in distant low-density arrays. The overall result is a continuous increase in transportation-sector carbon emissions (and a concomitant political reluctance for the United States to join the Kyoto agreement on climate change).

Many proponents of sustainable cities, however, advocate a radically different approach: reduced automobile dependency. In *Winning Back the Cities,* Newman and Kenworthy suggest an interconnected three-part solution: light rail, urban villages, and traffic calming. Light rail is fuel efficient, clean, quiet, land efficient, and cost effective. It is used extensively in Portland, Toronto, and throughout continental Europe. Urban villages are small-scale neighborhoods that "combine medium and high density housing with diverse commercial facilities, in car-free environments."[11] Arterial roads lead to parking at the edges of these transit-serviced urban arrays where internal access is limited to emergency and delivery vehicles. The village-scale neighborhoods are pedestrian friendly with small parks and outdoor cafés replacing most roadways. In other urban residential neighborhoods, traffic-calming measures restrain the speed of auto traffic and in effect guide through-traffic onto nearby arterial roads. The three initiatives together, especially with an added emphasis on safe and easy pedestrian and cycling corridors, make for vastly more livable (and sustainable) urban spaces.

This urban-oriented environmental vision is very different from the early days of environmentalism in the late 1960s and early 1970s. At that time many environmentalists responded to urban pollution with ideas about getting "back to the land" and closer to nature, and in some cases advocated dispersing people to rural communities. They also often questioned many aspects of technology and industrial society. Today's approach is diametrically different—the emphasis is on reconfiguring settlement into more compact and transit-friendly cities and on the technological redesign of both products and production processes. This latter undertaking is variously called sustainable production, eco-efficiency, or industrial ecology. The notion that more and more people should live their everyday lives closer to nature may require more energy and materials and also runs the risk of "loving nature to death" through human overpopulation within scenic regions and once-wild spaces.

In their recent work, Newman and Kenworthy discuss the process of transforming existing urban regions into more sustainable and livable cities. Their proposals are in keeping with the new spirit of smart growth that is now taking hold in many North American cities, sometimes, as in Massachusetts, as part of comprehensive state-level climate change initiatives.[12] In *Sustainability and Cities,* Newman and Kenworthy envision a sustainable city as one that is multicentered, with each node incorporating walking and cycling access to work, shops, and local services. They describe a transition strategy in this way:

> How can this future "Sustainable" City be achieved in stages? The stages are considered to be: (1) revitalizing the central and inner cities, (2) focusing development on transit-oriented locations that already exist and are underutilized, (3) discouraging urban sprawl by growth management strategies, and (4) extending transit systems, particularly rail systems, and building associated urban villages to provide a sub-center for all suburbs.[13]

Frequently used services are easily accessible by short walking or cycling trips, and travel to other urban nodes by public transit is as convenient and affordable as by automobile. Cars remain for the uses to which they are best suited—for weekends in the country, for carpools, or for moving larger loads.

Within sustainable cities, then, automobiles are one transportation choice among many, rather than the only viable option. In many European cities, even when automobile ownership is widespread, about 40 percent of trips to work are by public transit and 20 percent by walking or cycling. In contrast, in Detroit, less than 1 percent of all trips are by public transit.[14] In many other North American cities, only poor, young, and elderly people ever use public transit. There are many reasons for this difference, not the least of which is habit—but the "driving" reasons are the twin factors of historic gasoline prices and sprawl syndrome. If cities are configured on the assumption that nearly everyone has a car, indeed everyone will need a car and will either use it for almost every purpose or experience considerable inconvenience. Moreover, when there are no separate pathways for bicycles used for transportation (rather than recreation), the risk of car-bicycle accidents is far higher. When too few people use transit, service is infrequent and systems lose money. Few will opt for transit if service is infrequent or if residences, employment, and commerce are highly dispersed. There are also a number of less apparent reasons why sprawl and automobile-dominated transportation continue to flourish seemingly by popular choice.

The Social Psychology of Urban Sprawl in America

Sprawl has many causes, including the general stress of contemporary urban life and, for many, a search, perhaps not fully conscious, for an increased sense of community or a reconnection with nature. Advertising for automobiles and suburban housing plays on such desires. In ads, automobiles travel on winding, empty roads through stunning natural scenery or miraculously sit alone on mountaintops. Or they are used to get busy parents to soccer games or school plays—metaphors for family and community life. New suburban developments have bucolic names like Meadowbrook Estates. The quest itself—for nature or community via a freeway—is, in part, an illusion. The ads are even greater illusions: few people ever drive to the top of craggy outlooks or park their vehicles on ocean beaches. Most driving is on congested roads from one vast suburban parking lot to another, and many of the stresses of urban life are associated with automobile traffic itself. Sprawl begets traffic and air pollution that in turn encourages more people to attempt to distance themselves from traffic congestion.

Driving becomes the most convenient way to travel only after buildings and activities are arrayed in low-density patterns. That is perhaps the point. Once a majority opts for single-family dwellings on large lots distant from nonresidential activities, heavy automobile use seems necessary to everyone physically and financially able to drive. City planning too often is driven solely by traffic congestion considerations, and more roads result in yet more traffic. The resulting total fossil fuel use is proving to be unsustainable in the long term, but our urban arrays—both buildings and infrastructure—are built to last for a century or more.[15] Indeed, given the environmental price paid to extract the materials to build cities, sustainability analysis indicates that most buildings and infrastructure *should* last for centuries. Over and above these concerns is the matter of climate warming. On all counts, urban sprawl is simply bad planning, planning with too short a time horizon. Unfortunately, other considerations affect the everyday decisions that produce this result.

In general, inner cities in North America have a higher concentration of social problems and related public costs, and suburbs avoid some of these costs through zoning and planning rules that exclude everyone without substantial income or wealth. This concentration of social problems has encouraged a flight from inner cities, undermining the property tax base and exacerbating the deterioration of inner city infrastructure and social problems. This familiar tale has, however, been slowed or even reversed in many U.S. cities in recent years. Sprawling land use patterns are still with us, but cities like Portland and Pittsburgh have created a large supply of new residential housing downtown and other cities such as New Orleans and even sprawl-famous Los Angeles are now adding popular streetcar systems that may help to promote more compact development patterns.[16]

It is important, nonetheless, to understand that urban sprawl has deep historic roots as well as contemporary social and economic causes. One historic root cause lies in the response by urban planners to the ugly and unhealthy industrial cities of the late nineteenth and early twentieth centuries—the notion of a "garden city" far removed from industry and squalor. Planners of that era rendered people's dreams—separating family life from work in steel mills and slaughterhouses as soon as, and as far as, transportation options allowed. These patterns have continued, out of habit and owing to the ease of travel by automobile, even though most people now work in benign or even attractive workplaces. Most new residences are still at a distance from both work and shopping, many designed and constructed in an era of cheap and seemingly limitless oil but continuing in that mode even today.

Sprawl is also advanced by the comparatively low cost of land at the urban fringe where the competing land uses are agriculture or gravel pits rather than higher cost uses such as hotels or office buildings. Moreover, many people choose to distance their residence from locally unwanted land uses including environmentally contaminated former industrial lands, from transportation and transmission corridors, and from rundown neighborhoods. These latter areas are often badly serviced commercially and may be perceived negatively even by those who live in them. Typically, educational quality and infrastructure maintenance are low and crime and unemployment are high. All of these factors contribute to the erosion of urban life and ultimately lie at the root of accelerated sprawl. Thus enhanced environmental sustainability requires social expenditure to improve the quality of life in U.S. inner cities. Deteriorating inner city infrastructure and poor building maintenance also carry high sustainability costs.

The quality of urban life is a subtle thing that depends on a widespread sense of trust and safety that has been lost within the core of many U.S. cities. Urban crime rates are often lower within the active streetscapes of areas with a mix of commercial and residential buildings. This is why the urban renewal attempts of the 1950s and 1960s failed so singularly despite good intentions and massive public expenditures.[17] Once a sense of safety was lost, urban streets were feared, and many people moved to protected buildings and gated suburban neighborhoods. People were, and are, willing to drive many miles on a daily basis in order to reside within single-class, originally largely white, residential areas where there is rarely anyone on the street who is not in a vehicle. In a search for security and community we settled for the former and often lost much of the latter, save for select friends in "neighborhoods" that are wholly residential. Work is physically separated from family life, and shopping takes place in increasingly large, distant, and anonymous locations.

Public social life, as Robert Putnam has documented, is in decline in both urban and suburban settings.[18] One reason for this decline is the scarcity of spaces, settings, and opportunities in which people can establish a sense of community life. Whether in urban or suburban settings we typically no longer live near the people with whom we work. Nor do we often happen upon friends on downtown streets; rather, our business is conducted by driving, alone or with family, to distant malls. Moreover, in many suburban settings there are few drop-in community spaces. Civic life is increasingly minimal, in part because everyone works long hours and almost everyone commutes a considerable distance. That, combined with the pervasiveness of television, leaves less time for participatory citizen activities. The suburban life chosen in the expectation of a greater sense of community is friendly enough but often much less actively community oriented than the old urban neighborhoods of an earlier era.

From this perspective we can better understand the multidimensional potential of Newman and Kenworthy's urban villages. These intraurban islands can be both green (creating usable public space on lands that might have been used for roadways) and mixed use, with high potential for the natural evolution of a sense of community. Given proximity, more everyday activities can be conducted on foot. This approach, with transit availability and a high proportion of multiple-family dwellings (mixed with single-family options), will also result in reduced per-capita energy and materials use and greater environmental sustainability. Also contributing to sustainability would be an emphasis on the restoration, adaptation, and incorporation of existing buildings into the new urban communities. Additional social and economic gains are possible if in this process the relatively low land and building prices of some poorer urban communities are seen as opportunities for simultaneous social and sustainability gains. Recent restoration and development efforts in parts of New York City's Harlem serve as an inspiration in this regard. Finally, it must be remembered that better land utilization within the urban core will free land at the city's periphery for agriculture, recreation, and habitat preservation.

Protecting Wilderness through Inner City Restoration

As early as the 1970s, some civil rights leaders were concerned that money spent on environmental protection was money that would not be spent on urban quality-of-life improvements. In the 1990s this same pattern of tension sometimes found voice in debates between wilderness protection advocates and environmental justice activists, with the latter oriented primarily toward urban environmental issues. (For a more comprehensive discussion of environmental justice, see chapter 11.) In broad terms, this dispute is an example of the generalization put forward by Andrew Dobson, that "it is just possible that a society would be prepared to sanction buying environmental sustainability at the cost of declining social justice, as it is also possible that it would be prepared to sanction increasing social justice at the cost of a deteriorating environment."[19] It is only rarely the case, he argues, that society will advance the two simultaneously.

Does this mean that social justice and environmentalism are inherently incompatible? Not necessarily, one might argue, because some policy initiatives could serve both ends simultaneously. Fixing our city cores and their social problems, for example, would advance social justice *and* environmental sustainability. As we have seen, improvements to residential neighborhoods, especially within urban cores, would help to make public transit more viable and cities as a whole more sustainable. Moreover, improved public transit helps poor and middle-income people the most (because they cannot so easily afford to operate automobiles within a city, where insurance, parking, and repairs usually cost more).

Improved city cores might well also slow urban sprawl. The restoration of the United States's inner cities and the reconfiguration of its urban regions have lately been called *smart growth*. The vast potential of smart growth, however, has not been fully seen even by all of its advocates. It is a truly rare opportunity to advance all three dimensions of the triple bottom line simultaneously. Sustainable urban growth has the potential to protect wilderness and habitat by reducing urban sprawl and thereby to appeal to wilderness defenders and environmental justice advocates simultaneously.[20]

Sprawl threatens wilderness and habitat in at least five ways: (1) sprawl disperses what are called urban shadow functions (gravel pits and waste disposal sites, for example) into the countryside, (2) sprawl, as we have seen, encourages transportation options that are themselves more land intensive, (3) energy-inefficient transportation adds urgency to energy extraction activities within wilderness regions, (4) sprawl may contribute to a pattern of deteriorating urban cores and building everything anew at the periphery, thereby encouraging additional extraction of raw materials in wilderness areas, and (5) sprawl displaces near-urban agriculture often to lands of lesser quality, thereby requiring more land per unit of agricultural output.

Existing buildings and infrastructure are, in effect, embedded energy and previously lost wildlife habitat. Urban core restoration avoids imposing those costs a second time. In sum, both social justice and the protection of wilderness, as well as environmental sustainability, are bound up with both architectural preservation and the restoration of North America's inner cities. Preservation, urban core restoration, the creation of urban villages (islands of mixed-use, medium-density development within the larger urban setting), and smart growth (which seeks limits to sprawl) are all potentially part of the evolution toward more sustainable cities.

Examples of imaginative and sensitive urban redevelopment in the form of urban villages abound. Urban villages emphasize quality urban walking spaces where commercial and residential uses are close to one another, lessening the need for extensive transportation. Examples include River Place and the Pearl district in Portland; False Creek in Vancouver, British Columbia; River Walk in San Antonio, Texas; Fisherman's Wharf and many other neighborhoods in downtown San Francisco. Thus effective mixed-use urban planning is at the heart of sustainable cities. So, too, are imaginative state, regional, and municipal policy initiatives of all kinds; it is to these and the trends that lie behind them that we now turn.

Smart Growth, the Big Box Syndrome, and Sustainability

Recently the smart growth concept has gained considerable public attention, but this concept has deep roots. It is in part a response to the urban growth control measures of the 1960s and 1970s that, as Lamont Hempel has noted, rarely succeeded because "the overall pattern has been to shift development to nearby communities."[21] The American Planning Association's Growing Smart guidelines specifically emphasize regional planning, the control of sprawl, environmental protection, and fiscal responsibility rather than growth at all costs. Smart growth does not oppose development so much as seek to create more sustainable communities. Sustainable community planning emphasizes a highly participatory process seeking to create livable urban areas and restore local democracy, community, and civic life. Hempel, for example, sees sustainable communities and Putnam's sense of urgency regarding social capital as closely linked.[22]

Several cases demonstrating this linkage are reported by Alex Farrell and Maureen Hart.[23] Beginning in 1990, for example, citizens in the organization Sustainable Seattle systematically measured and reported their community's progress toward sustainability using a set of indicators chosen with extensive community involvement. Interestingly, many participatory sustainable community and smart growth initiatives have arisen following periods of local economic decline. In Pittsburgh, once characterized as a Rustbelt city, manufacturing fell from 50 percent of total employment to 11 percent between 1970 and 1990, and the city's population fell from 700,000 to 360,000 between 1950 and 1990. As Franklin Tugwell and colleagues put it, "Outside the former Soviet Union, few places on earth have undergone such profound economic change in times of peace. The result transformed the city. Prime riverfront lands became contaminated brownfields, often with rusted hulks of mills still present on-site."[24] The initial impetus for change in Pittsburgh came from an urgent need for a more sustainable economy; an emphasis on incorporating greener forms of development evolved through extensive public participation processes.

Timothy O'Riordan has observed that in general the interest in sustainability and sustainability indicators at the community level coincides with global economic integration and a search for new democratic forms.[25] In this search, process is as important as product in the sense that learning to act together communally over very long periods of time is essential to achieving sustainability. Smart growth and sustainable community initiatives may have the potential to fulfill this aspiration to renewed democracy and civic life, at least in part. The first steps in the U.S. Department of Energy's *Ten Steps to Sustainability* are to involve the community in conducting a participatory local sustainability assessment.[26] The Sustainable Seattle initiative, which was founded in 1991, has involved hundreds of people at a time. Sometimes it is even possible to achieve wide consensus, as in the case of the 1997 comprehensive regional conservation plan developed under the U.S. Endangered Species Act for a large region near San Diego.[27]

At the same time, unsustainable development tendencies continue to advance within a pattern that might be called the big box syndrome. Many of the most successful retailers of the 1990s (including motel chains) have opted for a marketing strategy that emphasizes rapid expansion of very large outlets at the periphery of urban regions, even in rural locations likely to attract future development or shoppers willing to take a long drive "in the country" (but near a freeway off-ramp). Urban locations are generally avoided because land and labor costs, as well as property taxes, are lower in the locations selected. Taxes are lower because the municipal jurisdiction has few social problems or, for that matter, residents. This strategy helps to keep the price of goods low. In effect, these companies benefit from the many public services provided within other municipal jurisdictions through local property taxes (rather than, for example, through state or federal taxes on profits or incomes). The big box marketing strategy is thus effective from the point of view of the firm, though not from the point of view of the wider society or—because the strategy accelerates sprawl—sustainability.

The net effect of these pressures, combined with extensive "exurban" residential developments (distant gated communities on golf courses, for example), is to remove land from agricultural use and to diminish wild habitat.[28] An Environmental Law Institute study of new development in Virginia came to this conclusion: "Land use patterns in Virginia follow a national trend of rings of new residential developments around existing community centers. These new residential developments typically are bedroom communities from which residents must drive long distances to work, school, and other activities. This type of land use consumes farm land and open space, damaging Virginia's rural economy and natural heritage."[29] The overall result throughout the United States is a pattern whereby lands under development are expanding much more rapidly than is the population in state after state and metropolitan region after metropolitan region.

From 1970 to 1990 the population of the Chicago metropolitan area expanded by 4 percent, but the area of developed land expanded by 46 percent. The population of the Los Angeles region expanded by 45 percent, whereas developed land expanded by 300 percent. This trend has continued and has been accompanied by a sharp increase in vehicle-miles traveled, by 68 percent nationwide between 1980 and 1997, for example.[30] In another example, between 1970 and 1994 the population of the Chesapeake Bay region increased by 26 percent, and as the Environmental Law Institute puts it, the "demand for new development, often low density and single-use, has led to a significant loss of open land and new pollution concerns. . . . [O]pen land (consisting of farms and forests) now disappears at a rate of 90,000 acres annually—including 50,000 acres per year in Virginia. . .and. . .the region has now lost 60 percent of its wetlands."[31] Again, these losses result less from population increases than from sprawl that has outpaced population growth by a considerable measure over an extended period of time.

The clear alternative is to establish initiatives that guide a higher proportion of new development within existing urban configurations, more fully utilizing already urbanized spaces. A coordinated effort involving land use controls, incentives, and transit development is essential. Notable success stories in this regard include any number of European cities but also Portland; Boulder, Colorado; Boston; Toronto; and Vancouver.[32] In the 1970s Portland rejected the Mt. Hood freeway that would have eliminated 3,000 homes through the downtown of the city. In its place the city built a light rail system in the face of much scoffing from traditional traffic experts and others. The initiative has been a stunning success. Boulder is notable for the extensive greenbelt surrounding the city and for encouraging residential development within its boundaries. Portland and Boulder initiated traffic-calming measures within residential areas, bicycle routes, and restraints on downtown parking. Boulder has also developed urban villages with restrictions on cars and a variety of transit-use incentive schemes.

Boston uses gas taxes to fund transit and has kept fares exceptionally low. It has also frozen the downtown parking supply for twenty years. The result of these and other measures was in the 1980s a 34-percent increase in transit use (compared with a 6-percent average increase in all U.S. cities) with 22 percent of trips to work occurring via walking, cycling, or transit, well above the national average. Moreover, automobile use has declined by even more than transit use increases would explain. The main reason for these shifts is a reversal in the trend of declining downtown residential population. This is the best evidence that the changes have made the core of the city increasingly vital and attractive. Toronto and Vancouver have strongly encouraged residential development within their downtown cores and at the same time have achieved a high proportion of transit use. The two patterns are, clearly, mutually supportive.

Other especially innovative initiatives to enhance sustainability undertaken by state, regional, and local jurisdictions include land trusts and transferable development rights to protect open spaces within an overall development plan. Advocates of urban sustainability have also advanced ideas such as location-efficient mortgages (which provide preferred rates to those living closer to public transit, where housing prices are typically higher) and land value taxation (which taxes land more heavily than buildings, thereby promoting somewhat more compact urban development and discouraging the speculative purchase of open land). Some progressive U.S. banks, such as ShoreBank, permit buyers of homes in transit-friendly locations to carry larger mortgages because their transportation costs are likely to be lower.[33]

Several municipal jurisdictions—such as Santa Monica, California; Austin, Texas; and Boulder—have undertaken green building initiatives including in some cases tax advantages to builders for using green building materials. Many cities—including Chicago and Syracuse, New York—have provided financing or tax incentives to creative urban core preservation and restoration initiatives. And, within the private sector, the U.S. Green Building Council has developed LEED (Leadership in Energy and Environmental Design), a voluntary standard for the construction of high-performance, sustainable buildings that has resulted in numerous examples throughout the country.[34] Most of these green (LEED) buildings thus far are new, but some, including the 112-year-old Security Building in St. Louis, involve substantial (in this case, $14.5 million) renovations of historically important buildings.[35]

Cities and states can encourage green home construction with subsidies and policies that provide financial incentives for building green. In New York

City, developer Les Bluestone interspersed seventy green homes (some triplexes) in vacant lots and around public housing towers. Energy-efficient boilers and appliances added $8,000 to the cost of each house, but some of that was refunded by the state of New York and a bank foundation that together promote reduced energy costs and other green features. Harlem developer Carleton Brown builds condominiums with cleaner indoor air and geothermal heating and cooling systems that save residents $1,000 per year through reduced energy use. The state of New Jersey offers builders up to $7,500 toward more efficient heating systems, triple-glazed windows, and other features.[36]

On other sustainability fronts at the municipal level, Seattle has had great success with waste reduction by using per-unit charges for municipal solid waste combined with no-cost pick up of recycling. Equally important, since the early 1990s, utilities in New England, New York state, and (since the power shortages of 2000–2001) California have achieved considerable success with promoting the more efficient use of electrical energy, in part through the imaginative use of regulated prices. California utilities, for example, gave customers who reduced consumption by 20 percent from the previous year a rebate on their utility bills. It is important to learn from all of these innovative policy initiatives.

The Complex Politics of Sustainable Cities

The politics of sustainable cities and smart growth involves a complex array of conflicting political and economic interests. Considerable potential exists for easing environmental and social problems while simultaneously stimulating economic activity and local employment. In many urban jurisdictions, as we have seen, significant sustainability initiatives have been undertaken. In other jurisdictions, however, sprawl continues somehow to seem the only "natural" way that development can go forward. Linked to this situation, sometimes, is a corresponding view that modest global-scale sustainability initiatives, such as the Kyoto Protocol, threaten the so-called American way of life. One underlying difference between these two views is that individual consumer decisions typically focus on the present, whereas our urban configurations as a whole built to last for many decades or longer and the world of tomorrow in terms of energy (and other factors) is not likely to be the same as it is today. Somehow these two realities must be reconciled.

Even urban planners often do not fully appreciate the fact that the demand for transportation energy is driven upward by sprawl even when automobiles become, on average, more fuel efficient. As noted earlier, natural habitat is being consumed much more rapidly than the human population is growing. There are several reasons for this lack of foresight. Planners do not often enough adopt a systems perspective—one that utilizes geographic information systems and other tools that incorporate the effects of sprawl on water quality and quantity, air quality, the protection of near-urban wildlife habitat and agricultural land, and numerous other sustainability variables.

Moreover, developers, home buyers, and local officials alike make their decisions in terms of present, not possible future, energy prices, traffic patterns, and access to nature. Homebuilders and buyers simply do not consider the effect of tens of thousands of developments similar to theirs.

Although some governments of inner cities are encouraging smart growth by promoting residential and commercial development downtown, jurisdictions at the urban periphery are promoting (or at least accepting) development patterns that have the opposite effect on the overall region. Arguably then, sustainability and smart growth may well require effective regional-scale urban governance. Both inside and outside local government, a wider appreciation of the notion of redefining progress is needed. For example, although having millions of people sitting in traffic jams in expensive new cars does add to GDP, it is not necessarily evidence of economic health.[37] Triple bottom-line analysis and any prudent study of present trends and timelines make it clear that it is not too soon to undertake major urban redesign efforts. We must continue to look to those cities that have had notable successes to determine the elements of success that can be taken up elsewhere.

Elements of successful smart growth initiatives include (1) a participatory and inclusive urban planning process with a focus on sustainability, (2) improved public transit, (3) special attention to residential development and the affordability of housing within urban cores, (4) efforts to preserve existing historic buildings and architectural gems, and (5) diverse innovative policy initiatives that help to change habits (including transportation habits, investment habits, and the bureaucratic rules of the urban game). The first two elements were discussed earlier in this chapter, and their importance cannot be overestimated. In recent years the number of participatory sustainable city planning initiatives has been remarkable, and excellent Web sites that provide guidance for such initiatives are numerous.[38] The other three elements, however, warrant further attention.

Some cities have extensive and expanding downtown residential opportunities and others do not. Toronto, Chicago, and New York, for example, all have both residential opportunities and commercial development in proximity to one another within the urban core, although many such residences are priced beyond all but the wealthy. The effect of this mixed-use pattern is, nonetheless, remarkable in terms of the overall quality of urban life and greater use of public transit. The noted urban analyst Jane Jacobs makes clear how important mixed residential and commercial use is to quality urban life: neighborhoods and streets that are used both day and night, she argues, are more interesting, economically successful, and safer.[39] In terms of transportation, in Detroit—where the urban core is dominated by commercial uses and quality residential opportunities are rare—public transit accounts for some 1 percent of motorized travel, whereas in the metropolitan Toronto area, which has a more balanced commercial-residential mix, public transit provides 24 percent.[40] Overall, Detroit's residential density is about half that of Toronto.

Architectural preservation efforts are often at the heart of urban revitalization. This was true in Pittsburgh, where there has been a considerable emphasis on rehabilitating existing housing stock and on improving residential energy efficiency.[41] Also especially notable in this regard are Savannah, Georgia, and Charleston, South Carolina—cities with an abundance of architectural history. Savannah's unique downtown streetscape design dating to the 1730s incorporates tree-lined boulevards and parks in the form of squares every two blocks, with residential neighborhoods predominating. Savannah miraculously survived the Civil War only to suffer the dual threats of decline and redevelopment a century later. Since the 1950s, however, preservation and restoration have taken hold and have transformed the residential and commercial core of the city, revitalizing it to the point where tourism emphasizing architecture and history is a leading local industry. Most residential buildings in the downtown are now restored to exacting historic specifications, and the overall effect is a highly livable and pedestrian-oriented city. This is equally true of nearby Charleston, which has the added benefit of an especially attractive seascape. In both cities the downtown commercial areas are booming, with numerous limited-scale hotels, inns, and condominiums under construction and the entire region benefiting economically from the historically oriented urban restoration efforts.

Nevertheless, Pittsburgh, Savannah, and Charleston are not immune to sprawl within adjacent municipalities and countryside, but the restraint of sprawl begins with a viable urban core as an attractive residential alternative. The worst effects of existing sprawl can also be diminished through imaginative initiatives, both public and private. For example, one study showed that, in Los Angeles and Ottawa, Ontario, charging employees for parking (even when the same amount was added to employees' paychecks) significantly reduced single-passenger trips to work (by as much as 81 percent).[42] The charges applied were equal to the cost of providing the parking. In other words, if driving is not subsidized there is likely to be less of it, even where (as in Los Angeles) public transit is not extensive. Toll roads would presumably have a comparable effect. Currently most studies show the transit-driving playing field (in terms of public subsidies) to be tilted in favor of driving.[43] One particularly imaginative approach to this problem was implemented in Paris, France, where public transit is free on air pollution alert days.

Conclusion

Some immediate steps can be taken to change everyday habits, short of reconfiguring settlement arrays. Making cities more transit, pedestrian, and cycling friendly is an ongoing process that will take many years of active initiatives at the municipal level. Building sustainable cities has both long- and short-term aspects, and the overall effort may ultimately require policy initiatives in political jurisdictions at all levels and technological innovations as well (such as increased use of telecommunications in the place of travel within everyday life).

In the end, however, sustainability is inevitably the result of thousands of collective and personal decisions. People acting politically at the local level can affect sustainability within the civic life of each community, just as each of us can do so in our choices about where to live and work and how to travel on an everyday basis. Important changes do not require that we change the whole world all at once, but they do require that we learn to understand the complex connections between sustainability and our everyday habits and behaviors.

Suggested Web Sites

Apollo Alliance (www.apolloalliance.org) Web site of a coalition of environmental, labor, and political leaders working to reduce U.S. oil dependence and create millions of new jobs by investing in energy alternatives and energy efficiency.

Environmental Law Institute (www.eli.org) Web site includes extensive information on sustainable land use, green buildings, urban brownfield sites, and other topics.

GreenClips (www.greenclips.com) An extensive archive of news items on sustainable building design.

Greenlining Institute (www.greenlining.org) A California-based multiethnic public policy and advocacy organization focused on the full range of urban issues.

Natural Step (www.naturalstep.org) Presents principles for achieving ecological and economic sustainability for corporations, entrepreneurs, and communities.

Smart Communities Network (www.sustainable.doe.gov) Offers a wide variety of information for sustainability initiatives.

Sustainable Communities Network (www.sustainability.org) Presents numerous links and research sources.

Sustainable Measures (www.sustainablemeasures.com) Information on what goes into sustainability indicators.

U.S. Green Building Council (www.usgbc.org) Site with extensive information on green building examples, techniques, and standards.

Notes

1. World Commission on Environment and Development, *Our Common Future* (New York: Oxford, 1987).
2. Daniel A. Mazmanian and Michael E. Kraft, eds., *Toward Sustainable Communities: Transition and Transformations in Environmental Policy* (Cambridge: MIT Press, 1999).
3. John Elkington, *Cannibals with Forks: The Triple Bottom Line of 21st Century Business* (Stony Creek, Conn.: New Society Publishers, 1998).

4. John Robinson and Jon Tinker, "Reconciling Ecological, Economic and Social Imperatives: A New Conceptual Framework," in *Surviving Globalism: The Social and Environmental Challenges*, ed. Ted Schrecker (London: Macmillan, 1997).

5. Marina Fischer-Kowalski and Helmut Haberl, "Sustainable Development: Socio-Economic Metabolism and Colonization of Nature," *International Social Science Journal* (1998): 573–587.

6. See, for example, discussion in Michael Carley and Philippe Spapens, *Sharing the World* (London: Earthscan, 1998), and Ernst von Weizsäcker, Amory B. Lovins, and L. Hunter Lovins, *Factor Four: Doubling Wealth, Halving Resource Use* (London: Earthscan, 1998).

7. The study is detailed in Peter Newman and Jeffrey Kenworthy, *Sustainability and Cities: Overcoming Automobile Dependence* (Washington, D.C.: Island Press, 1999).

8. American Farmland Trust, "Ten Things Urban and Rural Leaders Can Do Together to Promote Smart Growth," April 2002, www.farmland.org/farm_city_forum/ten_things.htm, January 31, 2005. The American Farmland Trust Web site (www.farmland.org) also offers a discussion of farm-city forums.

9. For details on the Toronto project see www.enwave.com.

10. James J. MacKenzie, "Driving the Road to Sustainable Transportation," in *Frontiers of Sustainability*, ed. Roger C. Dower et al. (Washington, D.C.: Island Press, 1997), 121–190.

11. Peter Newman and Jeffrey Kenworthy, *Winning Back the Cities* (Marrickville, New South Wales: Australian Consumers' Association, 1992).

12. New England Climate Change Coalition, "Coalition Welcomes Release of Climate Change Plan in Massachusetts," press release, May 6, 2004, www.newenglandclimate.org/massgovernmentrelease.htm, March 10, 2005.

13. Newman and Kenworthy, *Sustainability and Cities*, 338.

14. Ibid., 213.

15. Colin J. Campbell and Jean Laherrére, "The End of Cheap Oil," *Scientific American* 278 (March 1998): 78–83.

16. Regarding Pittsburgh and many other sustainable city initiatives, see Kent E. Portney, *Taking Sustainable Cities Seriously: Economic Development, the Environment, and Quality of Life in American Cities* (Cambridge: MIT Press, 2003). Regarding the rapid growth of streetcar transit, see American Public Transportation Association, "Rail Organization Web Sites," www.apta.com/links/railorg.cfm#A1, January 31, 2005.

17. These particular renewal efforts were typically high-rise residential structures set apart from commercial development and available only to those with very low incomes. Thus they were segregated by both function and class, and often by race.

18. Robert D. Putnam, *Bowling Alone: The Collapse and Revival of American Community* (New York: Simon and Schuster, 2000).

19. Andrew Dobson, *Justice and the Environment* (New York: Oxford University Press, 1998), 3.

20. Robert Bullard and Glenn Johnson, eds., *Just Transportation: Dismantling Race and Class Barriers to Mobility* (Philadelphia: New Society Publishers, 1997).

21. Lamont C. Hempel, "Conceptual and Analytical Challenges in Building Sustainable Communities," in *Toward Sustainable Communities*, ed. Mazmanian and Kraft, 52.

22. Ibid., 50.

23. Alex Farrell and Maureen Hart, "What Does Sustainability Really Mean? The Search for Useful Indicators," *Environment* 40 (November 1998): 4–9, 26–31.

24. Franklin Tugwell, Andrew S. McElwaine, and Michele Kanche Fetting, "The Challenge of the Environmental City: A Pittsburgh Case Study," in *Toward Sustainable Communities*, ed. Mazmanian and Kraft, 197.

25. Timothy O'Riordan, "Sustainability Indicators and the New Democracy," *Environment* 40 (November 1998): 1. For a detailed guide for participatory sustainability ini-

tiatives, see Gwendolyn Hallsmith, *The Key to Sustainable Cities* (Philadelphia: New Society Publishers, 2003).

26. For details regarding such initiatives and regarding many aspects of sustainable cities, see Smart Communities Network, www.sustainable.doe.gov, January 31, 2005.

27. Michael E. Kraft and Daniel A. Mazmanian, "Conclusions: Toward Sustainable Communities," in *Toward Sustainable Communities,* ed. Mazmanian and Kraft, 298.

28. Golf courses almost always contribute to water problems if there is heavy pesticide and fertilizer use but can—if designed with ecological protection in mind—add to protected habitat compared with more intensive development alternatives.

29. Quoted from the Web site of the Environmental Law Institute of Washington, D.C. (www.eli.org), from materials available on May 13, 2001, and on file with the author.

30. Bennet Heart and Jennifer Biringer, "The Smart Growth-Climate Change Connection," retrieved from www.clf.org/transportation, January 31, 2005.

31. Quoted from the Web site of the Environmental Law Institute of Washington, D.C. (www.eli.org), from materials available on May 13, 2001, and on file with the author.

32. Newman and Kenworthy, *Sustainability and Cities,* chap. 4, provided data for this and the next paragraph.

33. See ShoreBank Web site (www.sbk.com).

34. See U.S. Green Building Council Web site at www.usgbc.org/leed.

35. Charlene Prost, "Rehab Brings 'Green' to Old Finance Hub," *St. Louis Post-Dispatch,* June 12, 2004, available from the U.S. Green Building Council at www.usgbc.org/news.

36. Motoko Rich, "Green Gets Real with Affordable Housing and Affordable Rents," *New York Times,* May 6, 2004, www.nytimes.com, January 31, 2005.

37. See especially Clifford Cobb, Ted Halstead, and Jonathan Rowe, *The Genuine Progress Indicator* (San Francisco: Redefining Progress, 1995).

38. See, for example, Web sites such as www.cfpa.org (Center for Policy Alternatives), www.sprawlwatch.org, and www.lgc.org (Local Government Commission). For a discussion of the use of indicators in several U.S. sustainable city initiatives, see Portney, *Taking Sustainable Cities Seriously,* chap. 7.

39. Jane Jacobs, *The Death and Life of Great American Cities* (New York: Vintage, 1961).

40. Newman and Kenworthy, *Sustainability and Cities,* 213.

41. Tugwell et al., "The Challenge of the Environmental City," 187–215.

42. Richard W. Willson and Donald C. Shoup, "Parking Subsidies and Travel Choices: Assessing the Evidence," *Transportation: An International Journal Devoted to the Improvement of Transportation Planning and Practice* 17 (1990): 141–157.

43. See, for example, David Malin Roodman, *Paying the Piper: Subsidies, Politics, and the Environment* (Washington, D.C.: Worldwatch Institute, 1996).

4

Maintaining Presence: Environmental Advocacy and the Permanent Campaign

Christopher J. Bosso and Deborah Lynn Guber

Earth Day 2004 (April 22) was a busy one for President George W. Bush. That morning, clad in appropriate outdoor apparel, he appeared before the assembled national press at an estuarine preserve in southern Maine to promote his commitment to wetlands protection and to extol his administration's environmental achievements. "My administration has put in place some of the most important anti-pollution policies in a decade," the president proclaimed, "policies that have reduced harmful emissions, reclaimed brownfields, cut phosphorus releases into our rivers and streams. Since 2001, the condition of America's land, air and water has improved."[1]

Later that day, back in his usual business suit, the president hosted a White House ceremony honoring winners of the President's Environmental Youth Awards—young people from around the nation recognized by the ten regional offices of the U.S. Environmental Protection Agency (EPA).[2] The next day, once more in casual attire, he appeared at an estuarine preserve in Florida to again promote his wetlands plan and, by extension, his overall environmental record with the approaching presidential election in mind. "I know there's a lot of politics when it comes to the environment," the president said before taking a few minutes to prune some nonnative plants. "But what I like to do is focus on results, and you've got yourself a results-oriented governor when it comes to protecting this environment."[3]

Each of these carefully staged events attracted the desired local and national media coverage and sent the intended message: President Bush cares about the environment. That he felt compelled to take time away from such pressing matters as the conflict in Iraq to make Earth Day–related appearances also said volumes about the centrality of environmental issues in U.S. politics. As every occupant of the Oval Office has understood since the first Earth Day in 1970, no president can afford to appear hostile to environmental protection.

Despite the president's public appearances that week, environmental groups were intent on using their own Earth Day events to take aim at the Bush administration's record on the environment. Three in particular, joined under the banner of the Environmental Victory Project, announced a multimillion-dollar ad campaign to target voters in swing states such as Florida, Oregon, New Mexico, and Wisconsin.[4] The Natural Resources Defense Council (NRDC) released a report lamenting the president's "unambiguous" assault on the environment,[5] and the Sierra Club promoted its director's new book, *Strategic Ignorance: Why the Bush Administration Is Recklessly Destroying a Century of Environmental Progress.*[6] The League of Conservation Voters, in a fit of whimsy, topped them all. Having previously awarded the president its first-ever "F" for his environmental record on its annual report card, League staffers sent a "nice lunch of tuna fish sandwiches" to Bush-Cheney campaign headquarters in Arlington, Virginia, with a wry note attesting to its safety.[7] They had asked the deli to "hold the mercury."[8]

The rhetoric used by environmental advocates may have appeared harsh, even vitriolic at times, but to environmentalists George W. Bush had become, unquestionably, the "archenemy."[9] In their view, he had taken every opportunity to roll back policies that safeguard air and water from harmful pollutants. He had pushed to open public lands in the West to commercial logging, and encouraged oil exploration in the Arctic National Wildlife Refuge (ANWR). They believed that he wanted to weaken key provisions of laws such as the Endangered Species Act[10] and the National Environmental Policy Act,[11] while offering slight initiatives of his own under the guise of "Clear Skies" and "Healthy Forests." That only some of those plans had succeeded politically was in their view a testament to how far out-of-step with mainstream America Bush had become.

Environmentalists were outraged, in particular, at the president's use of the Earth Day stage to claim credit for achievements that were (like progress on brownfields) the culmination of years of work by previous administrations, or (like the rule on wetlands) little more than a strategic retreat from original intentions.[12] Months earlier the EPA had proposed to loosen federal protection of wetlands, only to backtrack under White House orders when it became clear that the plan faced major legal hurdles, as well as political opposition from state governments and moderate Republicans in Congress. They also knew that what the administration gave with one hand it might take away with the other. Even as the president talked of protecting a million acres of wetlands, his administration was accused of considering the exclusion of twenty million more from protection under the Clean Water Act, and of failing to fund a program that encouraged farmers to preserve wetlands on their property.[13]

The tussle over wetlands was just one episode in what had become, for environmentalists, an endless struggle with an administration that had pursued a far more ideological tack on environmental and energy issues than many had thought possible given the president's narrow victory in 2000. It had been a bitter time: seemingly endless legal battles to force the administration to enforce existing law,[14] rear-guard actions in Congress to stave off undesirable statutory and appropriations actions, and efforts to blunt the policy influence of federal officials recruited from the industries they were supposed to regulate.

But none of this was publicly apparent that Earth Day as the cameras captured a president at ease in nature and not, as was the view of his critics, more consistently hostile to environmental values than any president in

memory. Environmentalists may have wanted to expose "the Bush campaign's photo ops as cynical attempts to disguise his dirty environmental
record," but the capacity of the presidency to command the symbolic and
rhetorical stage was on full display. If only for a moment, there was little
environmentalists could do about it.[15]

This chapter examines the opportunities and constraints facing environmentalists in the early twenty-first century. We look first at trends in
public opinion on environmental issues and at how a sagging economy at
home and the war on terrorism abroad have insulated the president from
public disapproval of his environmental record. By emphasizing the importance of agenda setting and issue framing, we then discuss the challenges
environmentalists face in translating environmental concern into concrete
support for political candidates and their policies. In doing so, we look at factors that influence the electoral behavior of voters but also at the larger constraints of party politics, where environmentalists have long debated whether
they should promote their agenda within the existing two-party system or
promote Green Party candidates instead. Between elections, of course, environmental groups are like any other organized interest, and so we evaluate
also the strategies used by major organizations that comprise the national
environmental advocacy community. Granted little access to decision
making under the Bush administration, they face more difficult political terrain than any other in a generation.

Public Opinion on the Environment

Despite the president's assurance on Earth Day that the environment
had improved under his stewardship, few Americans seemed willing to
agree. When asked by the Gallup Organization in March 2004 how they
would rate the "overall quality of the environment in this country today," a
majority of those polled described it as "only fair" (46 percent) or even "poor"
(11 percent). When pressed further, 58 percent feared that things were "getting worse." Granted, that appraisal was no more negative than it had been
at the start of Bush's term, but it was no better either.

In early 2001 the public had appeared eager to support and fund efforts
to improve environmental quality. Within months of Bush assuming the presidency, 61 percent of those polled by Gallup said they were either active in or
sympathetic to the environmental movement. Some 57 percent thought that
environmental protection should be given priority, "even at the risk of curbing
economic growth." Most important of all, despite long-standing concerns
about the size and scope of government, 55 percent believed that the United
States was doing "too little" to address environmental problems; just 11 percent said it was doing "too much."[16] In the political arena, where issues rise
and fall on the public agenda according to both chance and circumstance,
each of those measures stood at its highest level in a decade, creating a
window of opportunity for the new president to seize or ignore. By the
summer of 2001, the latter seemed more likely. In light of what they saw as a

disconnect between public demands on the one hand and presidential obsti-
nacy on issues such as global warming and arsenic on the other, the editorial
desk at the *New York Times* warned that Bush was "alarmingly out of touch
with what Americans are thinking," and that his aggressive tactics on the
environment reflected a "grievous misreading of the public temper."[17]

Ultimately, however, the president's environmental record did little to
harm his image, and even less to impede his reelection in the fall of 2004.
During a heated campaign season, few respondents polled by Gallup were
willing to credit Bush with strengthening the "nation's environmental protection policies" (6 percent), but many supposed that his administration had
kept things "about the same" (53 percent). A more pointed question about
the president's handling of environmental issues tracked a 10-percentage-
point decline over three years in the number of respondents who felt he was
doing a "good job," but for a president embattled by a war on terrorism
abroad and economic concerns at home, it was a trend overshadowed in
magnitude by growing doubts about his leadership in other areas.[18]

Why did support for the president's environmental record stay relatively
stable despite negative publicity in the news media? Why did voters and taxpayers, many of whom believed that the state of the environment was "only
fair" and "getting worse," not blame the president more directly for the conditions they observed? As the editors of the *New York Times* noted, "President Bush's critics have watched with mounting frustration as his
administration has compiled one of the worst environmental records in
recent history without paying any real political price."[19] In the eyes of some
scholars, simultaneous support for the president and for an environmental
agenda he opposed is an "anomaly" that demands explanation.[20] Five factors,
closely intertwined, seem to be at play.

Declining Concern

First, public concern about the environment experienced a slow but
steady decline throughout Bush's first term in office, weakening potential
opposition to his agenda. In March 2004 the Gallup Organization asked a
national sample of 1,008 adults how much they personally worried about "a list
of problems facing the country." When prompted to consider "the quality of
the environment" as an issue, nearly two-thirds said that it upset them "a great
deal" (35 percent) or at least "a fair amount" (27 percent). Only 7 percent worried "not at all." When pressed further, it became clear that the targets of their
concern stretched along a wide array of environmental problems: air and water
pollution, the extinction of plant and animal species, ozone depletion, and
global warming. Even the subject lowest on the list—acid rain—generated significant concern among nearly half of those polled (46 percent).[21] The cumulative results seemed to confirm what scholars and political pundits have long
recognized: Americans care deeply about the environment.

Those data, however, deserve a broader context. Concern for the quality
of the environment in general may have appeared high to the untrained eye

but had in fact declined by 15 percentage points over the previous three years.[22] The "personal worry" respondents felt for specific environmental problems had likewise fallen on every item. When averaged across the eleven topics included on the questionnaire, the 2004 results marked their lowest point since Gallup introduced that battery of questions in 1989.

The Gallup study published in the spring of 2004 held still more bad news for environmentalists.[23] First, the percentage of Americans who labeled themselves as either "active in" or "sympathetic to" the environmental movement had dropped to its lowest combined total since April 2000. Even more telling was that the proportion of those who believed that environmental protection should be given priority, "even at the risk of curbing economic growth," had eroded by a staggering 20 percentage points over the same period of time. The number of Americans willing to "prioritize protection of the environment" over the economy (49 percent) was now the lowest on record, extending back a full twenty years to Gallup's first query on the subject in 1984 (Figure 4-1). Within the span of three short years, environmental concern had somehow tumbled from decade highs to all-time lows.

The decline in environmental concern was the product of an unfortunate and quite extraordinary confluence of events. It coincided roughly with the terrorist attacks of September 11, 2001, but also with energy shortages and blackouts, soaring gasoline prices, and rising unemployment. Under conditions of crisis, and ultimately war, issue displacement came as no surprise. In a new frame of mind, Americans worried less not only about the environment but also, according to Gallup, about other issues: hunger and homelessness, crime and violence, drug use, and race relations. Whereas in the past, efforts to expand environmental policies had benefited from well-publicized disasters—such as those that occurred at Love Canal, Three Mile Island, Chernobyl, or Prince William Sound, where massive quantities of oil were spilled by the *Exxon Valdez*—the terrorist attacks on New York and Washington had a contrasting, even debilitating, effect. Those constraints may loosen in the near future, depending on perceived success in waging the war on terror, but they create rocky terrain for environmental advocates in the meantime, as well as leeway for the president's agenda.

Low Issue Salience

Second, public reaction to the president's environmental record was muted by low salience, as economic unease and terrorist concerns dominated public energy and attention. When prompted by eager pollsters, Americans may say they worry about a great many things, but not all issues generate an intensity of feeling strong enough to motivate action and consequence.

To measure just how prominent an issue is in an individual's mind, pollsters often record unprompted, open-ended answers to questions that ask people to name the nation's "most important problem." Under those conditions, the environment fares badly indeed, mentioned by just 2 percent of those polled in the fall of 2004—a figure not appreciably higher or lower

Figure 4-1   Trends in Willingness to Prioritize Protection of the Environment over Economic Growth, 1984–2004

"With which one of these statements about the environment and the economy do you most agree: Protection of the environment should be given priority, even at the risk of curbing economic growth (or) Economic growth should be given priority, even if the environment suffers to some extent."

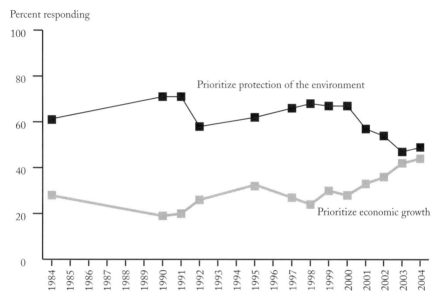

Source: The Gallup Organization (September 1984; April 1990; April 1991; January 5–March 31, 1992; April 17–19, 1995; July 25–27, 1997; April 17–19, 1998; April 13–14, 1999; April 3–9, 2000; March 5–7, 2001; March 4–7, 2002; March 3–5, 2003; March 8–11, 2004). Data retrieved from www.gallup.com/poll/content/default.aspx?ci=1615.

than that found by most other surveys over the past thirty years.[24] Because the concept of salience lends itself to comparison, however, an alternative (and more useful) approach uses lists of questions compiled by survey companies like Gallup to determine the implied rank of social priorities. If respondents express concern for an issue like the environment, it may be difficult to gauge interest by reference to the environment alone. Batteries of questions that prompt them to consider a wider range of issues allows researchers to form a frame of reference that uses those measures to speak in terms of "more" or "less."

The issue of global climate change offers an instructive example. A majority of Americans polled by Gallup in March 2004 believed that the problem was real and that human activities were its dominant cause. Most were also persuaded that the long-term effects of global warming were serious. Some 38 percent thought that the threat was "exaggerated," but a majority felt that news of the problem was either "generally correct" (25 percent) or "underestimated" (33 percent). A total of 51 percent feared that warming trends had "already begun."[25]

Yet even though respondents were aware of the dangers of global warming, few seemed to feel a great sense of anxiety or alarm. When asked how much they worried about each of eleven environmental problems, respondents ranked the "greenhouse effect" second to last.[26] The environment itself, meanwhile, placed ninth out of eleven issues in the number of respondents who reacted with intense concern. Only illegal immigration and race relations placed lower. In the end, a fair interpretation of the poll would need to note that global warming ranked near the bottom of a list of environmental problems, which themselves ranked near the bottom of a broader list of social priorities. Those results, of course, identify a nagging problem for environmental advocates but an opportune outcome for an administration whose priorities lay elsewhere. The environment as an issue had failed once again to generate the intensity it needed to muscle its way into the top-tier of the public agenda.

Selective Attention

Third, declining concern combined with low issue salience meant that distracted voters had little interest, and even less incentive, to pay attention to President Bush's record on the environment. Just 28 percent of those polled by the Pew Research Center for the People and the Press in April 2001 knew that the president had decided not to place limits on carbon dioxide emissions from power plants. Fewer still were aware that he delayed tighter standards on arsenic in drinking water (20 percent), or that he opposed the Kyoto Protocol (20 percent)—all largely unpopular decisions when presented to respondents.[27] Those conditions created, in the words of V. O. Key, a "permissive consensus," in which the administration could enjoy latitude to pursue its environmental agenda free from a watchful public eye.[28]

Three years later the issues had changed, but again in Bush's favor. According to the Pew Center, "the high price of gasoline" dominated public attention in the summer of 2004. Legal sovereignty had been transferred to a new Iraqi government just weeks before, and violent conflict involving U.S. soldiers stationed in the region continued, but far more respondents said they followed news stories on gasoline prices "very closely."[29] President Bush used the opportunity to press to open more federal lands to oil drilling to reduce American dependence on reserves abroad. "These measures have been repeatedly blocked by members of the Senate," he said, "and American consumers are paying the price."[30]

Ambivalence

Fourth, popular opinion on environmental issues is ambivalent and ill informed under the best of conditions. When the environment collides with other desirable goals, as it did beginning in 2001 with energy and national security, the signals citizens send to policymakers grow even more confused. In early March, prior to the president's rejection of the Kyoto Protocol and the release of the administration's energy plan, respondents in a Gallup survey were asked with which statement about energy and the environment they most agreed: "Protection of the environment should be given priority, even at the risk of limiting the amount of energy supplies—such as oil, gas and coal—which the United States produces," or the "development of U.S. energy supplies—such as oil, gas, and coal—should be given priority, even if the environment suffers to some extent?" The results seemed impressive: When prompted to consider the costs associated with protective environmental policies, 52 percent of those responding prioritized environmental protection, whereas 36 percent opted for the development of energy.[31]

That choice, however, was neither static nor indisputable. With talk of an impending recession and a growing "energy crisis" permeating the news media in the months that followed, respondents by late spring were inclined to believe that the energy situation had become "very serious"—more serious, in fact, according to poll trends, than at any time since 1977.[32] Although a steady majority in the Gallup study continued to oppose drilling in ANWR, impressive numbers by May supported the broader goals of "drilling for natural gas on public lands," and "investing in more gas pipelines." More than half were willing to go so far as to offer tax breaks to corporations to provide incentives for drilling to be done.[33] In the end, despite a firm belief in the value of energy efficiency and conservation, a combined 70 percent warned Gallup that it was either "very important" or "extremely important" that the president and Congress *increase* oil and gas production—something the Bush administration had intended regardless.[34] To argue, then, that the president ignored the public will in dealing with the environment is to fail to recognize that more than one "public will" often operates at the same time.

Issue Framing

Finally, as the energy issue demonstrates, President Bush diffused opposition to his environmental record by defining the terms of debate in ways sympathetic to his cause. As one team of scholars writes, "which general attitudes influence policy preferences partly depends on the particular symbols that become associated with a proposal—that is, on how the issue is symbolically framed."[35] Facing a valence issue they could not win, the administration directed public attention to a broader set of concerns by reference to a weakening U.S. economy and an emerging "energy crisis," reminding voters of soaring gasoline prices and electrical blackouts, both of which provided defensible ground for a rollback of environmental regulations.

The Bush administration's strategy was crafted, in part, on the advice of Republican pollster Frank Luntz. In a lengthy memo to party leaders, Luntz advised them to assure voters that they were committed to "preserving and protecting" the environment, but it could be done "more wisely and effectively."[36] He instructed Republicans to emphasize "sound science" and "common sense" in the debate over global warming, and to put the cost of environmental regulation in human terms by demanding on behalf of taxpayers "a fair balance" between the environment and the economy. Luntz's talking points soon defined the core message of the administration and helped Republicans in Congress to neutralize attacks on their own environmental records in key 2002 Senate races, which enabled them to regain control of the chamber.[37]

Critics were quick to dismiss the strategy as little more than misdirection, but it resonated with voters' emotions nevertheless by promoting simple goals with accessible language such as "safer," "cleaner," and "healthier." The *New York Times* may have mocked the president for playing an environmental word game that "underestimates the public and its capacity to distinguish rhetoric from reality," but given the public's slender knowledge of environmental problems, much less the science and policy behind them, the *Times* was almost certainly wrong.[38]

Issue Voting and the Environment

Activists watching President Bush's approval ratings on Iraq and the economy tumble throughout the spring and summer of 2004 began to believe that his environmental record would become a similar liability at the ballot box—not a large one, perhaps, but one strong enough to sway voters at the margins in key battleground states. Ever since 1994, when the new Republican majority in Congress began scaling back wildlife protection and pollution control laws, environmentalists had waited in vain for the environment to emerge as a potent wedge issue to attract young, socially moderate voters away from the Republican party.[39] Aside from the few voters who backed Green Party candidates, the environment had not been a factor in the 1996 or 2000 presidential campaigns. Given the generally negative reviews of President Bush's environmental record, however, the likelihood of a green revolt looked more promising in 2004.

The willingness of voters to cast ballots on the basis of candidates' environmental records and positions is crucial, not just to Democrats who want to win elections but also to those who place faith in public opinion as an engine of democracy. Issue voting would seem to ensure an active link between the views of citizens and those of elected officials in a way that ultimately enhances popular sovereignty and collective responsibility.[40] By nearly every account, however, that link fails to function well on the environment, where the subject has been so weak that scholars and political pundits seem ready to dismiss it as a political paper tiger, long on talk but short on action.[41]

The 2004 campaign forced no one to reconsider that position. Environmentalists may have found solace in the results of several congressional races, in which the group's "more aggressive and comprehensive approach can and did produce proenvironment results," according to League of Conservation Voters president Deb Callahan. But the presidential race, admittedly, left them "deeply disappointed."[42] As a campaign issue the environment generated just one question from a moderator across a span of three ninety-minute debates, and the candidates' tepid responses to it did little to ignite enthusiasm. Ultimately the Democratic Party was unable to create a political advantage out of its environmental agenda because comparatively few voters saw differences between the parties on environmental issues, and because those concerns failed to matter to them personally with enough intensity to override long-standing partisan commitments.[43]

Issue Salience

In an August 2004 poll administered for the Pew Research Center, respondents were asked to rate the importance of various issues when making a decision about who to vote for in the upcoming presidential election. A majority (55 percent) predicted that the candidates' positions on the environment would be a "very important" consideration for them. When compared with other topics, however, the subject settled toward the middle of a long list, above abortion and same-sex marriage, but well below health care, education, and the economy, not to mention national security concerns involving the conflict in Iraq and the broader war on terrorism.[44] Among those asked to explain their vote after the election, only 1 percent said the environment was the "one issue" that "mattered most."[45]

Quite simply, although Americans place genuine value on environmental quality, that concern is forced to compete for room on a crowded political agenda. Cross-pressured in many different ways, most voters have neither the time nor the inclination to view elections as a referendum on the president's environmental record.

Perceptions about Candidate Differences

Even if the salience of environmental issues were to rise suddenly due to media attention, ecological catastrophe, or politicians intent on using the bully pulpit to heighten awareness of environmental problems, voting green requires more. It is contingent on the ability of citizens to distinguish accurately between the policy positions of the candidates.[46] Clarity about political issues, in this sense, depends on clarity of choice, without which voters are left by default to decide based on other issues and considerations.[47]

Polling data routinely show that the environment is a strong issue for the Democratic Party and its candidates, but in the heat of a presidential campaign that advantage is often less significant than it appears. In a September 2004 NBC/*Wall Street Journal* poll, respondents preferred the Democratic candidate, Sen. John Kerry of Massachusetts (50 percent) by a wide margin over incumbent president George W. Bush (25 percent) as the "better" candidate on that issue. Yet when asked four months earlier if there were "real and important" differences between the candidates on the subject,

or only "small and unimportant" ones, the environment ranked comparatively low, below the war in Iraq, jobs and unemployment, taxes, and health
care. Some 20 percent conceded that they were simply "not sure" where the
candidates stood. Only on the topics of education and moral values were the
candidates' positions any less distinct in the eyes of voters, a result that pulls
the environment into a distinct disadvantage.[48]

Partisan Loyalty

Finally, the weight of partisanship also plays a role in muting the impact
of environmental concern in elections. Survey data show that judgments
about a candidate's record on the environment change slowly in response to
new information and are filtered through long-standing party loyalties.[49]
Because voting green often demands that Republicans cross party lines to
vote for liberal political candidates or strict regulatory policies, voters psy-
chologically anchored to their party may be reluctant to make those decisions
on principled grounds. Voters also tend to adhere to well-established patterns and traditions that consider ballots cast for a third-party candidate to
be wasted votes, leading many of those who are sympathetic to Green Party
candidates, like Ralph Nader, to abandon them in the end because of the
"cold-feet factor."[50]

In short, elections are imperfect vehicles for representing the environmental views of the electorate, much less selecting environmentally friendly
officeholders. Environmentalists, like so many other issue advocates, must
look for other ways to influence policy agendas and hold elected officials
accountable. For the most part, that task is left to environmental groups.

The Bumpy Terrain for Environmental Advocacy

The organizational roster of environmental advocacy in the United
States is dominated by household names: Sierra Club, Audubon Society,
National Wildlife Federation, The Nature Conservancy, and Greenpeace, to
name but a few (Table 4-1). So permanent are these organizations as fixtures
in national politics that their presence elicits little comment. Only their failures appear noteworthy. Indeed, organized environmentalism has been found
wanting almost continuously since environmental issues first climbed the
nation's agenda in the late 1960s.[51] National environmental organizations, in
particular, *always* seem to have less influence than imagined by their foes or
hoped by their friends, and they *always* seem to veer between their desire to
push the cause and the more prosaic dictates of organizational survival. Mark
Dowie, a trenchant critic of the major organizations, makes such an argument:

> American land, air, and water are certainly in better shape than they would
> have been had the movement never existed, but they would be in far better
> condition had environmental leaders been bolder; more diverse in class,
> race, and gender; less compromising in battle; and less gentlemanly in the

Table 4-1   Snapshot of National Environmental Organizations, 2004

Organization	Year Founded	Members[a]	2003 Revenue (in millions)	Web Site
Sierra Club	1892	736,000	$83.7[b]	www.sierraclub.org
National Audubon Society	1905	550,000	$78.6	www.audubon.org
National Parks Conservation Association	1919	375,000	$20.9	www.npca.org
Izaak Walton League	1922	45,000	$4.3	www.iwla.org
The Wilderness Society	1935	225,000	$18.8	www.tws.org
National Wildlife Federation	1936	650,000	$102.1	www.nwf.org
Ducks Unlimited	1937	656,000	$125.1	www.ducks.org
Defenders of Wildlife	1947	463,000	$21.8	www.defenders.org
The Nature Conservancy	1951	972,000	$972.4	www.nature.org
World Wildlife Fund—U.S.	1961	1,200,000	$93.3	www.worldwildlife.org
Environmental Defense	1967	350,000	$43.8	www.environmentaldefense.org
Friends of the Earth	1969	35,000	$3.8	www.foe.org
Natural Resources Defense Council	1970	450,000	$46.4	www.nrdc.org
League of Conservation Voters	1970	60,000	$7.0[b]	www.lcv.org
Earthjustice	1971	70,000	$17.9	www.earthjustice.org
Clean Water Action	1971	300,000	$14.5[b]	www.cleanwateraction.org
Greenpeace USA	1971	250,000	$25.9[b]	www.greenpeaceusa.org
Trust for Public Land	1972	45,000	$126.5	www.tpl.org
Ocean Conservancy	1972	100,000	$8.9	www.oceanconservancy.org
American Rivers	1973	30,000	$5.5	www.amrivers.org
Sea Shepherd Conservation Society	1977	35,000	$1.0	www.seashepherd.org
Center for Health, Environment and Justice	1981	28,000	$1.0	www.chej.org
Earth Island Institute	1982	20,000	$4.9	www.earthisland.org
National Park Trust	1983	33,000	$1.2	www.parktrust.org
Conservation Fund	1985	16,000	$60.1	www.conservationfund.org
Rainforest Action Network	1985	35,000	$2.2	www.ran.org
Conservation International	1987	70,000	$222.7	www.conservation.org
Earth Share	1988	n/a	$7.9	www.earthshare.org
Environmental Working Group	1993	n/a	$1.8	www.ewg.org
National Environmental Trust	1994	n/a	$10.7	www.net.org

Source: Annual reports, IRS form 990. See also Christopher J. Bosso, *Environment, Inc.: From Grassroots to Beltway* (Lawrence: University Press of Kansas, 2005).

Note: n/a indicates no membership in the classic sense.

[a] Includes "members" or "supporters," where known or possible to estimate.

[b] Indicates combined revenues of related entities, or for tax-exempt affiliate.

day-to-day dealings with adversaries. Over the past 30 years environmentalism has certainly risen close to the top of the American political agenda, but it has not prevailed as a movement, or as a paradigm.[52]

Not bold enough; not diverse enough; too willing to compromise; too gentlemanly: Dowie's disappointment with mainstream environmentalism is widely shared among activists. Yet any assessment about success or failure must take into account the profound changes in the political terrain on which environmentalists operate. Taken together, these changes have forced environmental groups to reconfigure their tactics and, indeed, their very role in the political system. As they well understand, the potential cost of not adapting is at best policy failure and at worst irrelevance.[53]

Conservatives Ascendant

The big story of the past thirty years is the ascendance of the conservative wing of the Republican Party at the expense of the more liberal wing once key to bipartisan agreement on environmental policy matters.[54] The result is a more homogenous Republican majority, now rooted in growing southern, southwestern, and Rocky Mountain states. The parallel leftward movement of the Democrats, despite the centrist tendencies of Jimmy Carter and Bill Clinton, by the 1990s had produced a partisan polarization that gives the nation more clearly demarcated—even "responsible"—parties but which affords environmental activists remarkably little room to maneuver. Despite campaign contributions to moderate Republican candidates and efforts to include Republicans on the boards of directors of environmental organizations, it seems clear that environmentalists must depend on the Democratic Party if their goal is to work through the existing two-party system.[55] Partisan polarization has, ironically, narrowed environmentalists' tactical options.

One need only recall the 2000 election to understand this reality and, for environmentalists, the strategic dilemma it poses. On one hand, most major environmental groups looked beyond their disappointment with the Clinton administration to back Al Gore as the only alternative to Republican nominee Bush. Such pragmatism was rooted in their realization that holding onto the White House was their sole bulwark against an ideologically hostile one-party government. That choice was unacceptable for activists on the left, however, because for them the parties are barely distinguishable defenders of corporate capitalism and unfettered global trade. The "greens" who fought the North American Free Trade Agreement (NAFTA) marched in Seattle against the World Trade Organization, and boycotted Shell Oil for its support of the military regime in Nigeria saw Democrats like Gore as only too willing to accept half measures that still favored corporate interests. Ultimately that discontent found a repository in Ralph Nader, whose decision to stand as the candidate of the Association of State Green Parties (ASGP) reflected his own belief that a third party alone could force a profound change in national discourse. To the Naderites, the Democratic Party itself was the problem.[56]

This was an old debate to be sure, but its effects in 2000 were significant and lasting. Votes for Green Party congressional candidates arguably cost Democrats several House seats that year.[57] Given the narrow majority by which Republicans held onto the House when Congress convened in

2001, it was no wonder that Democrats and their allies in the environmental community were bitter about the Green Party challenge. More important, Nader's small fraction of the vote as a presidential candidate—just 2.7 percent nationwide—may well have contributed to Gore's hairbreadth loss. Indeed, a shift of just one-half of one percent of Nader's support in Florida alone could have given Gore the state's twenty-five electoral college votes, and with it the presidency itself.[58] From the standpoint of the mainstream environmental movement, then, it is not hard to imagine why many Greens refused to back Nader's renewed efforts in 2004.[59]

The probability that conservatives will continue to dominate the Republican Party for years to come forces environmentalists to think hard about how close they can get to the Democrats. For those in old-line organizations like the National Wildlife Federation and the National Audubon Society, in particular, overt partisanship is unacceptable to their cultural orientations and membership base. Yet at the national level at least, Democrats may be the only option for groups that want to make policy, not just make a statement. In short, current conditions have forced environmentalists into an ideological and partisan box. With more at stake, and considerably more to lose, it makes the dilemma of *how* to participate in electoral politics even more acute.[60]

Counter-Mobilization

This recent surge of political conservatism has steeled opposition to the environmental movement from business and industry nationwide. The mobilization of business beginning in the late 1970s was in many ways a reaction to the growth of environmental and other public interest advocates in the previous decade.[61] By the early 1980s the explosion in the number of business lobbyists based in Washington was but one indicator that corporate America no longer was content to rely on its "privileged position" to defend its interests.[62]

The development of a powerful business lobby at the same time that Ronald Reagan entered office forced most environmental organizations to establish or expand their presence in the nation's capital. But such moves proved unpopular with grassroots activists for whom "Washington politics" meant succumbing to, in the words of Kirkpatrick Sale, "the inherently conservatizing pressure to play by the 'rules of the game' in the compromise world of Washington, D.C."[63] This balancing act became more difficult when many environmental organizations were hit with shrinking membership rolls and softening revenues during the recession of the early 1990s, but their need to be in Washington to counteract the greater physical presence of industry interests arrayed along K Street offered little choice.

At the same time, environmentalists increasingly encountered well-organized and well-funded opposition at the state and local levels from a variety of property rights and "wise use" groups.[64] Although the true size and grassroots nature of these groups were always hard to gauge, their activists undoubtedly helped to elect fellow conservatives to local, state, and federal office; shaped public debates on land use and resource issues; won lawsuits in federal courts populated by Reagan and George H. W. Bush appointees; and exploited their access to more sympathetic parts of the federal bureaucracy. Even with the apparent ebbing in their fervor by the late 1990s, their ties to conservative House Republicans, in particular, continued to give them a degree of influence in setting the agenda and crafting legislation, privileges enjoyed by environmentalists when Democrats ruled the Hill.

Conservative mobilization at the state and local levels also grew in importance as more authority over environmental implementation and enforcement was shifted to the states.[65] Greater state responsibility now meant that environmentalists had to extend their attention (and scarce resources) to many more venues at more levels of government.[66] As Sierra Club executive director Michael Fischer put it in 1990 in arguing about the need to shift Club resources from Washington to the states, "we'll have to be covering our opponents because the Wise Use movement and other folks are going to the statehouses. But look, we've just won the Clean Air Act. The next step is implementing the Clean Air Act at the state level. We've got Superfund problems. There are problems at the state level."[67]

In short, mobilization by business in Washington forced environmentalists to strengthen their presence there even as they were compelled to pay more attention to the grassroots in response to mobilization by property rights and wise use groups. Chapter-based organizations such as the Sierra Club, National Audubon Society, and National Wildlife Federation first felt the cross-pressures as activists became entangled in battles over land use and wilderness protection, often prompting accusations that national leaders were placing undue emphasis on national and international politics over local needs.[68] By the mid-1990s almost every national organization had gone through identical and often traumatic strategic planning exercises, in each instance deciding how to allocate their energies and budgets to cover more ground at all levels of government, if only to keep their opponents from solidifying their gains.

A Less Congenial Congress

In the past, whatever else was happening, environmentalists could depend on access and support in the legislative branch. Democratic control of Congress had been essential to the passage of major environmental laws under Republican presidents Nixon and Ford. Their control over the House enabled Democrats to blunt Reagan's initial efforts to remake environmental policy, and under George H. W. Bush their renewed dominance in both chambers enabled Democrats to convene committee investigations into the actions of the executive branch and enact the 1990 amendments to the Clean Air Act. If conservative southern Democrats wrangled often with their liberal colleagues over the scope of federal action, their shared desire to maintain party control led to compromises that served to advance environmental protection.[69]

That access and leverage has since evaporated, starting with the shift of congressional control to Republicans in 1995. In the decade that followed, environmentalists found themselves essentially excluded from the innermost circles of House decision making, and watched as their legislative proposals virtually disappeared from the agenda. The situation in the Senate was marginally better given the relatively even balance between the two parties and the chamber's strong norms of collegiality, but even there the slim majority won by Republicans affected the chamber's agenda and the access it granted to outside advocates. Republican gains in 2004, particularly an additional four Senate seats obtained at the expense of southern Democrats, further solidified their control over both chambers. Consequently, environmental groups must spend their time fighting attempts to roll back existing laws or to tuck antienvironmental riders into appropriations bills.[70] It is an essentially defensive stance imposed by the realities of the moment.

Presidential Power

As of January 2005 Republicans have controlled the presidency for twenty-four of the previous thirty-six years—or about two-thirds of the contemporary environmental era. President Bush's reelection extends that dominance and underscores the point that, since 1970, Republican presidents have shaped most of federal environmental policy, whether through legislative proposals, budget allocations, clearing regulations through the Office of Management and Budget, or appointments to federal agencies and the judiciary.[71] More important, as Bush underscored in reversing Clinton's support for the Kyoto Protocol and pushing for drilling in ANWR, presidents set the national agenda.

Presidents also decide who gets access. Whatever their disappointment about the Clinton administration, environmentalists knew that their views were heard at the highest levels, that the top layers of the bureaucracy were in friendly hands, and that Clinton would fight off most of the antienvironmental initiatives pursued by congressional conservatives. None of this has been true with Bush, save for an occasional meeting with "hook-and-bullet" organizations such as Ducks Unlimited and the National Wildlife Federation.[72] As far as the executive branch was concerned, under the Bush administration environmental organizations were on the outside looking in. They could still file Freedom of Information requests, offer comments on proposed regulatory actions, and even get invited to participate in the odd forum run by a marginalized EPA, but they had less access to and influence on executive decision making than even under Reagan. Their prospects are unlikely to improve in Bush's second term.

A More Restrictive Federal Judiciary

Republican dominance of the presidency has contributed to the increasingly conservative orientation of the federal judiciary on environmental and related regulatory matters. Federal judges in the early 2000s are more reluctant to extend standing to environmental claimants, more willing to give priority to property rights over environmental goods, and less likely to grant discretion to federal regulatory agencies and, even, to Congress with respect to the constitutional powers of the states.[73] The expectation that Bush will appoint at least two Supreme Court justices, not to mention uncounted lower federal court judges, will solidify these trends.

As a result, lawsuits that once shaped environmental policy are increasingly little more than narrow-gauge tools for forcing overburdened regulatory agencies to adhere to the letter of existing law. So low has the lawsuit fallen in favor that the two major "science and law" organizations, Environmental Defense and NRDC, now use it as a minor part of their tactical toolbox, below lobbying, research, and public communication. "We concentrate more on the promotion of ideas and programs dreamed up by economists and scientists," one Environmental Defense official commented. "Rather than go to court, we lobby, write reports, court the media."[74] Only Earthjustice, a "boutique" shop by comparison, continues to use lawsuits as a core tactic, augmented by lobbying and public communications.[75]

Outsiders, Again?

In May 2004 a federal district judge in Miami dismissed criminal charges brought against Greenpeace stemming from the arrest of two of its activists after they climbed aboard and displayed a protest banner on a ship thought to be carrying illegally harvested Brazilian mahogany. The activists originally were charged with misdemeanor trespass, but federal prosecutors later relied on an 1872 law, intended to deter brothel keepers from boarding ships to lure sailors to their establishments, to levy felony charges against the organization as an entity. The federal government's novel application of a law that had not been used in over a century was widely interpreted among activists as an effort to "chill" the use of civil disobedience.[76]

This episode underscores the contextual basis of advocacy. We tend to believe that organizations are free to select whatever tactics they deem optimal to meet their goals. To some degree they are—Greenpeace chooses to engage in civil disobedience, just as the apolitical Nature Conservancy does not—but the context in which issue advocacy occurs also imposes constraints. Not all environmental organizations want to use the same tactics, but the tactics *any* of them can use are affected by the political opportunities of the moment as much as, if not more than, they are shaped by the values of their members or the attitudes of political leaders.

Consequently, changes in that opportunity structure—such as how one administration interprets the current applicability of an old law—affect what tactics are available and, more important, deemed effective. In the 1970s, Jeffrey Berry suggested, environmental organizations and other citizen groups of the time "succeeded precisely because they quickly emerged as well-functioning bureaucracies. The watchword of these organizations was not 'power to the people' but 'policy expertise.' "[77] Environmentalists developed professional lobbying operations and legal teams because they needed to do so.

But strategies appropriate thirty years ago no longer suffice, particularly when access to decision making is shut off or otherwise limited by those in power. As a result, Robert Duffy notes, "environmental groups are devoting unprecedented resources and energy to framing issues and perceptions of candidates, in the hope that their preferred policies will be adopted and their preferred candidates will be elected."[78] Tactics such as lobbying and lawsuits no longer suffice in a time when everyone professes to support environmental goals. Defining those goals, and ranking them against other needs, makes tactics such as agenda setting and issue framing more nakedly imperative than ever.

In pursuit of these objectives, two trends are worth particular attention. One is use of the Internet to communicate directly with the public and supporters. The other is the greater attention being paid to members, not simply as financial backers but as elements of a real grassroots force. These trends are intertwined and must be understood in light of a general recognition that, in Robert Putnam's blunt assessment, the national environmental community had become a "defensive light air force, not a massed infantry for change." What is missing, he argues, is a "deep, active, and growing environmental grassroots."[79] Activists and scholars might challenge Putnam's empirical evidence,[80] but nobody disputes his larger point.

Both of those strategies may seem predictable, even conventional in an era in which the demands of democracy are increasingly driven by technology, but the alacrity with which environmentalists now concentrate on public communications and grassroots mobilization reflects the realities of the moment. In part, it is a consequence of the maturation of a policy domain characterized by an immense body of long-standing laws, regulations, and court precedent at all levels of government. Thirty-five years after passage of the National Environmental Policy Act, environmental concerns seem interwoven into the everyday fabric of American life. Just getting an issue atop an already crowded—or consciously constricted—agenda takes extraordinary effort, as Greenpeace knew when it sent its activists to that ship off Miami.

The widespread commitment to strategies designed to set agendas and mobilize supporters also reflects the opportunity structure of the moment. If "the environment" is woven into the fabric of everyday life, *who* defines its meaning is an open question. Given conservatives' success in reshaping the ideological center of U.S. politics since the environmental era began, it stands to reason that their definition of "common sense" environmental policy is positioned to dominate debates over issues ranging from ANWR to climate change for years to come. Despite their resources and their hard-won legitimacy, environmentalists know that they must offer a compelling and practical alternative if they are to win the discursive battle for the hearts and minds of the American people. The reelection of George W. Bush puts an exclamation point on that reality.

Notes

1. The White House, "President Announces Wetlands Initiative on Earth Day," press release, April 22, 2004, www.whitehouse.gov/news/releases/2004/04/print/20040422-4.html.

2. The White House, "President Bush Presents Environmental Youth Awards," press release, April 22, 2004, www.whitehouse.gov/news/releases/2004/04/20040422-7.html.

3. Elisabeth Busmiller, "Bush Promotes Wetlands Plan to Counter Kerry's Attack," *New York Times,* April 24, 2004, A13.

4. Zachary Coile, "Kerry Blasts Bush's Record on Protecting Environment," *San Francisco Chronicle,* April 21, 2004, A4.

5. Robert Perks, *Rewriting the Rules: The Bush Administration's Assault on the Environment,* 3rd ed. (Washington, D.C.: Natural Resources Defense Council, 2004), iv.

6. Sierra Club, "Sierra Club Leader Carl Pope's New Book Finds Bush Administration Guilty of 'Strategic Ignorance' on the Environment," press release, April 22, 2004, www.sierraclub.org/pressroom/releases/pr2004-04-22.asp.

7. League of Conservation Voters, *2003 Presidential Report Card: The Bush Environmental Record—Putting Corporate Interests over America's Interests* (Washington, D.C.: League of Conservation Voters, 2003).

8. League of Conservation Voters, "LCV Sends over 'Tuna on White—Hold the Mercury'," press release, April 22, 2004, www.lcv.org/news/news.cfm?id=2612&c=26.

9. Charles Seabrook, "Bush Reputation on Environment Mixed," *Los Angeles Times,* January 29, 2004, 8A.

10. Juliet Eilperin, "Endangered Species Act's Protections Are Trimmed," *Washington Post,* July 4, 2004, A01.

11. Eric Pianin, "Panel Backs Faster Environment Review," *Washington Post,* September 25, 2003, A31.

12. Eric Pianin, "Bush Moves to Defuse Environmental Criticism," *Washington Post,* February 2, 2004, A05.

13. National Wildlife Federation, "President Bush's Wetlands Initiative Doesn't Hold Water: NWF's Statement on the President's Earth Day Announcement," press release, April 22, 2004, www.nwf.org/news/.

14. Katherine Q. Seelye and Jennifer 8. Lee, "Court Blocks U.S. Effort to Relax Pollution Rule," *New York Times,* December 25, 2003, A1.

15. "Bush Environmental Policies Endanger Homeland Security, Report Says; Bush Campaign Photo Ops Attempt to Disguise President's Dirty Record," U.S. Newswire, June 28, 2004, http://releases.usnewswire.com/GetRelease.asp?id=110-06282004.

16. Riley E. Dunlap and Lydia Saad, "Only One in Four Americans Are Anxious About the Environment," *The Gallup Poll Monthly,* No. 127 (April 2001): 6–16.

17. "Disturbing Numbers for Mr. Bush," *New York Times,* June 21, 2001, A24; "The House Rebukes the President," *New York Times,* June 23, 2001, 12.

18. The number saying Bush was doing a good job "improving the nation's energy supply" declined by 24 percentage points between March 2001 and March 2004, and the number saying he was "keeping America prosperous" declined by 25 percentage points. Riley E. Dunlap, "Bush and the Environment: Potential for Trouble?" Gallup Poll News Service, April 5, 2004, www.gallup.com/content/print.aspx?ci=11179.

19. "Politics and Pollution," *New York Times,* August 28, 2003, 30.

20. Steven R. Brechin and Daniel A. Freeman, "Public Support for Both the Environment and an Anti-Environmental President: Possible Explanations for the George W. Bush Anomaly," *The Forum* 2 (2004): 1. Edwards et al. note a similar pattern during the presidency of George H. W. Bush. See George C. Edwards III, William Mitchell, and Reed Welch, "Explaining Presidential Approval: The Significance of Issue Salience," *American Journal of Political Science* 39 (1995): 108–134.

21. We define "significant concern" as the combined percentage of respondents who answered "a great deal" (20 percent) or a "fair amount" (26 percent) to the question about acid rain.
22. The 15-percentage-point decline combines the responses "a great deal" and "a fair amount" and compares the years 2001 and 2004.
23. Dunlap, "Bush and the Environment: Potential for Trouble?"
24. In response to the open-ended question "What do you think is the most important problem facing this country today?" 2 percent said the environment or pollution. The Gallup Organization, September 13–15, 2004 [datafile], n = 1,022 adults nationwide, margin of error +/– 3 percentage points.
25. Lydia Saad, "Global Warming on Public's Back Burner," *Gallup Poll Tuesday Briefing,* April 20, 2004; see also Frank Newport and Lydia Saad, "Americans Consider Global Warming Real, but Not Alarming," *The Gallup Poll Monthly,* 127 (April 2001): 2–5.
26. Newport and Saad, "Americans Consider Global Warming Real," 3.
27. The Pew Center for the People and the Press, "Bush's Base Backs Him to the Hilt," April 26, 2001, http://people-press.org/reports/display.php3?ReportID=14.
28. V. O. Key Jr., *Public Opinion and American Democracy* (New York: Knopf, 1961).
29. The Pew Center for the People and the Press, "Democratic Party Image Improvement: Democrats More Confident, Kerry Faring Better in Battleground States," July 21, 2004, http://people-press.org/reports/display.php3?ReportID=220.
30. Neela Banerjeen, "Would More Drilling in America Make a Difference?" *New York Times,* June 20, 2004, 14.
31. Lydia Saad, "Americans Mostly 'Green' in the Energy vs. Environment Debate," *The Gallup Poll Monthly* 126 (2001): 34.
32. Ibid., 35.
33. Dunlap and Saad, "Only One in Four Americans," 13.
34. The Gallup Organization, June 8–10, 2001 [datafile], n = 1,011 adults nationwide, margin of error +/– 3 percentage points.
35. Jack Citrin, Beth Reingold, and Donald P. Green, "American Identity and the Politics of Ethnic Change," *Journal of Politics* 52 (1990): 1126.
36. Luntz Research Companies, *Straight Talk* (Alexandria, Va.: Luntz Research Companies, 2002), 107.
37. Jennifer 8. Lee, "A Call for Softer, Greener Language: G.O.P. Advisor Offers Linguistic Tactics for Environmental Edge," *New York Times,* March 2, 2003, 18.
38. "Environmental Word Games," *New York Times,* March 15, 2003, 16.
39. Alison Mitchell, "Democrats See Gold in Environment," *New York Times,* April 21, 2001, 20; Mike Allen and Eric Pianin, "Democrats See Environment as a Bush Liability: Party Using Issue to Energize Base," *Washington Post,* March 24, 2001, A2.
40. Edward G. Carmines and James A. Stimson, "The Two Faces of Issue Voting," *American Political Science Review* 74 (1980): 78–91; Anthony Downs, "Up and Down with Ecology—The Issue-Attention Cycle," *The Public Interest* 28 (summer 1972): 38–50; Norman Nie, Sidney Verba, and John R. Petrocik, *The Changing American Voter* (Cambridge: Harvard University Press, 1976).
41. Jerry Taylor, "Campaign Trail Littered with Environmental Wrecks," *Plain Dealer,* December 5, 1992, 7b.
42. League of Conservation Voters, "League of Conservation Voters Statement on National Electoral Results," November 4, 2004, www.lcv.org/new/newspring.cfm?id =3430&c=26
43. Deborah Lynn Guber, *The Grassroots of a Green Revolution: Polling America on the Environment* (Cambridge: MIT Press, 2003).
44. The survey was conducted by Princeton Survey Research Associates International and sponsored by Pew Research Center's Forum on Religion and Public Life, August 5–10, 2004 (n = 1,512).
45. The Pew Research Center for the People and the Press, November 5–8, 2004 [datafile], n = 1,209 adults nationwide, margin of error +/– 3 percentage points.

46. Angus Campbell, Philip E. Converse, Warren E. Miller, and Donald E. Stokes, *The American Voter* (Chicago: University of Chicago Press, 1960); Anthony Downs, *An Economic Theory of Democracy* (New York: Harper, 1957).
47. Donald E. Stokes, "Spatial Models of Party Competition," *American Political Science Review* 57 (1963): 368–377.
48. The poll questions cited here were administered by Hart and McInturff Research Companies for NBC News and the *Wall Street Journal.* The first was administered September 17–19, 2004 (n = 1,006), and the second was administered May 1–3, 2004 (n = 1,012). For more on voters' inability to distinguish between candidates' policy positions, see Guber, *The Grassroots of a Green Revolution.*
49. Mark Peffley, Stanley Feldman, and Lee Sigelman, "Economic Conditions and Party Competence: Processes of Belief Revision," *Journal of Politics* 49 (1987): 100–121.
50. Ann McFeatters, "Green Party Candidate Continues to Criticize Bush and, Particularly, Gore," *Pittsburgh Post-Gazette,* November 18, 2000, A8.
51. Robert C. Mitchell, "Public Opinion and the Green Lobby: Poised for the 1990s?" in *Environmental Policy in the 1990s,* ed. Norman J. Vig and Michael E. Kraft (Washington D.C.: CQ Press, 1990); Robert C. Mitchell, Angela A. Mertig, and Riley E. Dunlap, "Twenty Years of Environmental Mobilization: Trends among National Environmental Organizations," in *American Environmentalism: The U.S. Environmental Movement, 1970–1990,* ed. Riley E. Dunlap and Angela G. Mertig (Washington, D.C.: Taylor & Francis, 1992), 11–26.
52. Mark Dowie, *Losing Ground: American Environmentalism at the Close of the Twentieth Century* (Cambridge: MIT Press, 1995), xii.
53. See Christopher J. Bosso, *Environment Inc.: From Grassroots to Beltway* (Lawrence: University Press of Kansas, 2005).
54. Michael E. Kraft, "Environmental Policy in Congress: From Consensus to Gridlock," in *Environmental Policy: New Directions for the Twenty-First Century,* 5th ed., ed. Norman Vig and Michael Kraft (Washington, D.C.: CQ Press, 2003), 127–150.
55. Charles R. Shipan and William R. Lowry, "Environmental Policy and Party Divergence in Congress," *Political Research Quarterly* 54 (June 2000): 245–263.
56. The ASGP split with the more "radical" Green Party of the United States (GPUSA) in 1991.
57. Christopher J. Bosso and Deborah Lynn Guber, "The Boundaries and Contours of American Environmental Activism," in Vig and Kraft, *Environmental Policy: New Directions for the Twenty-First Century,* 5th ed., 79–101.
58. Official election returns provided by the Federal Election Commission indicate that Nader received 97,488 votes in Florida—a state in which George W. Bush's official margin of victory was just 537.
59. Rick Lyman, "Greens Pick a Candidate Not Named Nader," *New York Times,* June 27, 2004, A20.
60. Robert J. Duffy, *The Green Agenda in American Politics: New Strategies for the Twenty-First Century* (Lawrence: University Press of Kansas, 2003).
61. David Vogel, *Fluctuating Fortunes: The Political Power of Business in America* (New York: Basic Books, 1989); Kay Lehman Schlozman and John T. Tierney, *Organized Interests and American Democracy* (New York: Harper and Row, 1983).
62. Charles E. Lindblom, *Politics and Markets* (New York: Basic Books, 1977).
63. Kirkpatrick Sale, "The U.S. Green Movement Today," *The Nation,* July 19, 1993, 94.
64. Jacqueline Vaughn Switzer, *Green Backlash: The History and Politics of Environmental Opposition in the United States* (Boulder: Lynne Reiner, 1997); David Helvarg, *The War Against the West* (San Francisco: Sierra Club Books, 1994); Christopher J. Bosso, "Adaptation and Change in the Environmental Movement," *Interest Group Politics,* 3rd ed., ed. Allan J. Cigler and Burdett A. Loomis (Washington, D.C.: CQ Press, 1991), 151–176.
65. Daniel A. Mazmanian and Michael E. Kraft, "The Three Epochs of the Environmental Movement," in *Toward Sustainable Communities: Transition and Transforma-

tions in Environmental Policy, ed. Daniel A. Mazmanian and Michael E. Kraft (Cambridge: MIT Press, 1999), 3–42.

66. Denise Scheberle, *Federalism and Environmental Policy: Trust and the Politics of Implementation* (Washington, D.C.: Georgetown University Press, 1997).

67. Michael L. Fischer, "Executive Director of the Sierra Club, 1987–1992," an oral history conducted in 1992 and 1993 by Ann Lage, Regional Oral History Office, The Bancroft Library, University of California, Berkeley, 148.

68. Keith Schneider, "Selling Out? Pushed and Pulled, Environment Inc. is on the Defensive," *New York Times,* March 29, 1992, Sect. 4, p. 1; Anne Raver, "Old Environmental Group Seeks Tough New Image," *New York Times,* June 9, 1991, A1, 22.

69. Christopher J. Bosso, *Pesticides and Politics: The Life Cycle of a Public Issue* (Pittsburgh: University of Pittsburgh Press, 1987), 143–177.

70. Kraft, "Environmental Policy in Congress: From Consensus to Gridlock," 139–142.

71. Norman J. Vig, "Presidential Leadership and the Environment," in Vig and Kraft, *Environmental Policy: New Directions for the Twenty-First Century,* 5th ed., 103–126.

72. Elizabeth Shogren, "Hunters, Anglers Gaining Power: President Listens to 'Hook-and-Bullet' Enthusiasts on Environmental Issues," *Los Angeles Times,* January 5, 2004.

73. Rosemary O'Leary, "Environmental Policy in the Courts," in Vig and Kraft, *Environmental Policy: New Directions for the Twenty-First Century,* 5th ed., 151–174; Lettie McSpadden, "The Courts and Environmental Policy," in *Environmental Politics and Policy: Theories and Evidence,* 2nd ed., ed. James P. Lester (Durham, N.C.: Duke University Press, 1994), 242–274.

74. Tom Turner, "The Legal Eagles," in *Crossroads: Environmental Priorities for the Future,* ed. Peter Borreli (Washington, D.C.: Island Press, 1988), 58.

75. Ned Martel and Blan Holden, "Inside the Environmental Groups, 1994," *Outside* (March 1994): 71.

76. Manuel Roig-Franzia, "Judge Dismisses Greenpeace Charges," *Washington Post,* May 20, 2004, A14.

77. Jeffrey M. Berry, *The New Liberalism: The Rising Power of Citizen Groups* (Washington, D.C.: Brookings Institution Press, 1999), 155.

78. Duffy, *The Green Agenda in American Politics,* 4–5.

79. Robert D. Putnam, *Bowling Alone: The Collapse and Revival of American Community* (New York: Simon and Schuster, 2000), 154.

80. Andrew Savage, John Isham, and Christopher McGrory Klyza, "The Greening of Social Capital: An Examination of Land-Based Groups in Two Vermont Counties," *Rural Sociology,* forthcoming.

5

Presidential Leadership and the Environment
Norman J. Vig

*George W. Bush will go down as the worst environmental president
in our nation's history.*

Robert F. Kennedy Jr.[1]

*I earned capital in the campaign, political capital. And now I
intend to spend it. It is my style.*

President George W. Bush,
speaking at a November 4, 2004, press conference[2]

President George W. Bush wasted little time in causing a furor over environmental policy. Within two months of taking office in 2001, he
announced that he would reverse a campaign pledge to impose controls on
carbon dioxide emissions from power plants and that the United States
would withdraw from the Kyoto Protocol on climate change. He argued that
the Kyoto treaty, which President Bill Clinton had signed but the Senate had
not ratified, was "fatally flawed" because it would place unfair burdens on the
U.S. economy without requiring developing countries to control their emissions. Despite pleas from world leaders and much of the scientific community, Bush refused to change his mind.

Bush's rejection of the Kyoto treaty was only the most dramatic shift in
environmental policy during his first term. His administration rescinded or
modified many of the rules and regulations issued by the Clinton administration and adopted more industry-friendly approaches in most areas. It proposed a national energy plan calling for large increases in domestic energy
production, including oil and gas development in the Arctic National
Wildlife Refuge (ANWR) and on other sensitive public lands. It also
blocked a Clinton executive order that would have protected nearly 60 million acres of roadless forests from logging. For these and other reasons, most
environmental organizations opposed the president's reelection in 2004 (see
chapter 4). Although environmental issues played little role in a campaign
dominated by terrorism, the Iraq war, and the economy, the administration
quickly claimed a mandate to proceed with an ambitious environmental
reform agenda in its second term.[3]

Later in this chapter I examine Bush's actions and proposals in some detail. But first, it is important to realize that, although all recent presidents have played an active role in shaping national environmental policy, they operate within a system of constitutional and political constraints that limit their power. Many other actors also influence policy development, and presidents often fail to get their way. Whatever the final verdict on Bush's tenure, then, it is important to examine the powers of the presidency to effect environmental change.

Presidential Powers and Constraints

The formal roles of the president have been summarized as commander in chief of the armed forces, chief diplomat, chief executive, legislative leader, and opinion/party leader.[4] If we look only at environmental policy, the president's role as chief executive has probably been most important.[5] The president's powers to make cabinet and subcabinet appointments, to propose agency and program budgets, to issue executive orders, and to oversee the regulatory process are especially important prerogatives as chief executive. Some presidents have also played a leading role in enacting environmental legislation and in rallying public opinion behind new environmental policies. The role of chief diplomat has also become more important as many environmental problems have required international solutions. The president's power to sign or reject treaties such as the Kyoto Protocol is obviously of paramount importance. Military activities also have major impacts on the environment.

Presidential powers can also be analyzed from a policy cycle perspective such as that introduced in chapter 1. First, presidents have a major role in *agenda setting*. They can bring issues to the public's attention, define the terms of public debate, and rally public opinion and constituency support through speeches, press conferences, and other media events. Second, they can take the lead in *policy formulation* by devoting presidential staff and other resources to particular issues, by mobilizing expertise inside and outside government, and by consulting interest groups and members of Congress in designing and proposing legislation. Third, they can *legitimate policy* by supporting legislation in Congress and brokering compromises. Conversely, they can block unwanted legislation through the use of the veto power. Fourth, presidents use their powers to oversee the bureaucracy in myriad ways to influence *policy implementation*. Finally, they constantly *assess and evaluate* existing policies and propose reforms.

Despite these enormous powers, presidents cannot govern alone; they are only part of a government of "separated powers."[6] They must rely on Congress to enact legislation and provide the funding to carry out all activities of the federal government. When Congress and the presidency are controlled by different parties, the president may have little control over the policy agenda. But even when the president's own party has a majority in one or both houses, majority coalitions on particular issues may be difficult if not impossible to build. Powerful interest groups wage public policy campaigns against legislation that they oppose and can often "veto" policy initiatives. Nearly all major rules and regulations are also challenged in the courts by affected parties, often tying up administrative actions in litigation that goes on for years (see chapter 7). Finally, of course, events beyond the president's control such as the terrorist attacks of September 11, 2001, can profoundly alter the president's agenda and prospects for success.

Presidential success thus rests in large part on circumstances, and some moments in history are more conducive to radical policy change than others.[7] There have been two periods in recent times when the mood of the public has demanded strong presidential leadership on the environment. The first was 1970–1972 when the modern environmental movement that gathered force in the 1960s reached a crescendo. President Nixon understood the strength of this movement and decided to lead rather than follow its momentum. He declared the 1970s "the environmental decade"; signed the National Environmental Policy Act, the Clean Air Act, the Endangered Species Act, and other landmark legislation; and created the U.S. Environmental Protection Agency (EPA) by executive order.[8] With the exception of Theodore Roosevelt at the beginning of the twentieth century, no other president presided over a greater expansion of federal environmental policy. The second recent wave of proenvironmental opinion gathered force in the 1980s during the presidency of Ronald Reagan and peaked during 1988–1990. After serving as Reagan's vice president and then being elected president in 1988, George H. W. Bush declared himself "the environmental president" and supported passage of a major Clean Air Act in 1990, much as Nixon had in 1970. However, public support for new environmental initiatives waned thereafter, and Bill Clinton, like Jimmy Carter in the 1970s, found it more difficult to build support for environmental initiatives.

Classifying Environmental Presidencies

A president's influence on environmental policy can be evaluated by examining a few basic indicators: (1) the president's environmental *agenda* as expressed in campaign statements, policy documents, and major speeches such as inaugural and state of the union addresses, (2) presidential *appointments* to key positions in government departments and agencies and to the White House staff, (3) the relative priority given to environmental programs in the president's proposed *budgets*, (4) presidential *legislative initiatives* or vetoes, (5) *executive orders* issued by the president, (6) White House *oversight* of environmental regulation, and (7) presidential support for or opposition to *international environmental agreements*. By these criteria some presidents can be seen as much more proenvironmental than others.

Measuring actual performance outcomes is more difficult. For example, President Clinton achieved few of the policy changes he espoused during his 1992 campaign yet ended his presidency with a strong contribution to public lands conservation. Incumbents should be judged in terms of not only how much of their initial agenda they achieve but also how successful they are relative to the circumstances and constraints they face. Ultimately, of course, the success of policy changes should be gauged in terms of their effects on the environment. Do they, for example, result in more or less pollution? But given the multitude of factors that affect the environment and the difficulties of monitoring and measuring environmental quality, it is rarely possible to make definitive statements about specific policy outcomes (see chapter 1).

We can, however, classify presidents generally in terms of their attitudes toward the seriousness of environmental problems, the relative priority they give to environmental protection compared with other policy problems, and whether they attempt to strengthen or weaken existing environmental policies. In this broad perspective, recent presidents seem to fall into three main categories: opportunistic leaders, frustrated underachievers, and rollback advocates.[9]

Opportunistic Leaders

Two presidents, Richard Nixon and the elder Bush, held office at the peak of public opinion surges demanding action to strengthen environmental protection. Although both had served as vice president in conservative Republican administrations and neither had a strong record on environmental policy, both adopted the conservationist mantel of Theodore Roosevelt and supported major advances in national environmental protection early in their presidencies. As opposition to further policy changes mounted from traditional Republican constituencies, however, both reverted to more conservative policies later in their terms. Nixon, for example, vetoed the Federal Water Pollution Control Act Amendments of 1972 (which passed over his veto), and Bush declared a moratorium on all new environmental regulation and refused to endorse binding international agreements to deal with climate change and biodiversity at the 1992 Earth Summit in Rio de Janeiro, Brazil.

Frustrated Underachievers

Two Democratic presidents, Jimmy Carter and Bill Clinton, came to office with large environmental agendas and strong support from environmental constituencies but accomplished less than expected. Carter had little success in dealing with the energy crisis of the late 1970s, whereas Clinton had only minor legislative achievements in the field of environmental policy. Both presidents were forced by competing priorities and lack of public and congressional support to compromise their environmental agendas. Yet both achieved belated success in protecting public lands and tightening environmental regulations before leaving office. Carter preserved millions of acres of Alaskan wilderness and helped pass the Superfund bill to clean up toxic waste sites after losing the 1980 election, and Clinton issued executive orders creating or enlarging twenty-two national monuments and protecting millions of acres of forest lands during his waning days in office.

Rollback Advocates

Two presidents have entered office with negative environmental agendas: Ronald Reagan and George W. Bush. Both represented antiregulatory forces in the Republican Party and sought to roll back or weaken existing environmental legislation. Reagan launched a crusade against what he considered unnecessary social regulation that he believed impeded economic growth. His stance on the environment aroused enormous controversy, and he was forced to moderate his policies by 1984. Bush also stressed the importance of economic growth over environmental protection. He launched a wide range of initiatives to soften environmental regulation during his first term but was in a stronger position to pursue his agenda in his second term.

In the following sections I first review the presidencies of Ronald Reagan, George H. W. Bush, and Bill Clinton as examples of these three categories. In each case I examine their use of presidential powers and evaluate their presidencies using the criteria mentioned in this introduction. I then offer a preliminary assessment of George W. Bush's record.

The Reagan Revolution:
Challenge to Environmentalism

The "environmental decade" of the 1970s came to an abrupt halt with Reagan's victory in 1980. Although the environment was not a major issue in the election, Reagan was the first president to come to office with an avowedly antienvironmental agenda. Reflecting the Sagebrush Rebellion—an attempt by several western states to claim ownership of federal lands—as well as long years of public relations work for corporate and conservative causes, Reagan viewed environmental conservation as fundamentally at odds with economic growth and prosperity. He saw environmental regulation as a barrier to "supply side" economics and sought to reverse or weaken many of the policies of the previous decade.[10] Although only partially successful, Reagan's radical agenda laid the groundwork for a renewed attack on environmental policy a decade later.

After a period of economic decline, Reagan's landslide victory appeared to reflect a strong mandate for policy change. And with a new Republican majority in the Senate, he was able to gain congressional support for the Economic Recovery Act of 1981, which embodied much of his program. The law reduced income taxes by nearly 25 percent and deeply cut spending for environmental and social programs. Despite this initial victory, however, Reagan faced a Congress that was divided on most issues and did not support his broader environmental goals. On the contrary, the bipartisan majority that had enacted most of the environmental legislation of the 1970s remained largely intact.

Faced with this situation, Reagan turned to what has been termed an "administrative presidency."[11] Essentially this involved an attempt to change federal policies by maximizing control of policy implementation within the executive branch. That is, rather than trying to rewrite legislation, Reagan used his powers as chief executive to alter the direction of policy.

The administrative strategy initially had four major components: (1) careful screening of all appointees to environmental and other agencies to ensure compliance with Reagan's ideological goals, (2) tight policy coordination through cabinet councils and White House staff, (3) deep cuts in the budgets of environmental agencies and programs, and (4) an enhanced form of regulatory oversight to eliminate or revise regulations considered burdensome by industry.

Reagan's appointment of officials who were overtly hostile to the mission of their agencies aroused strong opposition from the environmental community. In particular, his selection of Anne Gorsuch (later Burford) to head the EPA and James Watt as secretary of the interior provoked controversy from the beginning because both were attorneys who had spent long years litigating against environmental regulation. Both made it clear that they intended to rewrite the rules and procedures of their agencies to accommodate industries such as mining, logging, and oil and gas.

In the White House, Reagan lost no time in changing the policy machinery to accomplish the same goal. He attempted to abolish the Council on Environmental Quality (CEQ), and when that effort failed because it would require congressional legislation, he drastically cut its staff and ignored its members' advice. In its place he appointed Vice President George Bush to head a new Task Force on Regulatory Relief to review and propose revisions or rescissions of regulations in response to complaints from business. All regulations were analyzed by a staff agency, the Office of Information and Regulatory Affairs (OIRA) in the Office of Management and Budget. OIRA held up, reviewed, and revised hundreds of EPA and other regulations to reduce their effect on industry. Although regulatory oversight is an accepted and necessary function of the modern presidency, the Reagan White House's effort to shape and control all regulatory activity in the interests of political clients raised serious questions of improper administrative procedure and violation of statutory intent.[12]

Finally, Reagan's budget cuts had major effects on the capacity of environmental agencies to implement their growing policy mandates. The EPA lost approximately one-third of its operating budget and one-fifth of its personnel in the early 1980s. The CEQ lost most of its staff and barely continued to function. In the Interior Department and elsewhere, funds were shifted from environmental to development programs.[13]

Not surprisingly, Congress responded by investigating OIRA procedures and other activities of Reagan appointees, especially Burford and Watt. Burford came under heavy attack for confidential dealings with business and political interests that allegedly led to sweetheart deals on matters such as Superfund cleanups. After refusing to disclose documents, she was found in contempt of Congress and forced to resign (along with twenty other high-level EPA officials) in March 1983. Watt was pilloried in Congress for his efforts to open virtually all public lands (including wilderness areas) and off-shore coastal areas to mining and oil and gas development. He resigned later in 1983 after making some thoughtless remarks about the ethnic composition of a commission appointed to investigate his coal-leasing policies. By that time he had alienated almost everyone in Congress.[14]

Because of these embarrassments and widespread public and congressional opposition to weakening environmental protection, Reagan's deregulatory campaign was largely spent by the end of his first term. Recognizing that his policies had backfired, the president took few new initiatives during his second term. His appointees to the EPA and Interior after 1983 diffused some of the political conflict generated by Watt and Burford. EPA administrators (William Ruckelshaus and Lee Thomas) were able to restore some funding and credibility to their agency, though the EPA was permanently weakened by the drastic budget and personnel cuts of the early 1980s that made it difficult to cope with new legislative mandates.

Reagan clearly lost the battle of public opinion on the environment. His policies had the unintended effect of revitalizing environmental organizations. Membership in such groups increased dramatically, and polls indicated a steady growth in the public's concern for the environment that peaked in the late 1980s (see chapter 4). It is not surprising that Bush decided to distance himself from Reagan's environmental record in the 1988 election.

The Bush Transition

The elder Bush's presidency returned to a more moderate tradition of Republican leadership, particularly in the first two years. While promising to "stay the course" on Reagan's economic policies, Bush also pledged a "kinder and gentler" America. Although his domestic policy agenda was the most limited of any recent president, it included action on the environment. Indeed, during the campaign Bush declared himself a "conservationist" in the tradition of Teddy Roosevelt and promised to be an "environmental president."[15]

If Bush surprised almost everyone by seizing the initiative on what most assumed was a strong issue for the Democrats, he impressed environmentalists even more by soliciting their advice and by appointing a number of environmental leaders to his administration. William Reilly, the highly respected president of the World Wildlife Fund and the Conservation Foundation, became EPA administrator; and Michael Deland, formerly New England director of the EPA, became chairman of the CEQ. Bush promised to restore the CEQ to an influential role and made it clear that he intended to work closely with the Democratic Congress to pass a new Clean Air Act early in his administration.

Yet Bush's nominees to head the public lands and natural resource agencies were not much different from those of the Reagan administration. In particular, his choice of Manuel Lujan Jr., a ten-term retired congressman

(R-N.M.), to serve as secretary of the interior indicated that no major departures would be made in western land policies. The president's top White House advisers were also much more conservative on environmental matters than were Reilly and Deland. This was especially true of his chief of staff, John Sununu.

Bush pursued a bipartisan strategy in passing the Clean Air Act Amendments of 1990, arguably the single most important legislative achievement of his presidency. His draft bill, sent to Congress on July 21, 1989, had three major goals: to control acid rain by reducing sulfur dioxide emissions from coal-burning power plants by nearly half by 2000, to reduce air pollution in eighty urban areas that still had not met 1977 air quality standards, and to lower emissions of nearly 200 airborne toxic chemicals by 75 to 90 percent by 2000. To reach the acid precipitation goals—to which the White House devoted most of its attention—Bush proposed an innovative approach advocated by environmental economists that relies on marketable pollution allowances rather than command-and-control regulation to achieve emissions reductions more efficiently (see chapter 9).

During the last eighteen months of the administration, Vice President Dan Quayle entered the spotlight as head of the Council on Competitiveness, an obscure White House body that Bush had appointed in 1989. The "Quayle Council" assumed a role similar to that of Bush's own Task Force on Regulatory Relief in the early Reagan administration. Its function was to invite and respond to industry complaints of excessive regulation, to analyze the costs and benefits of regulation, and to question any new regulations that were considered unnecessarily burdensome. It operated in secrecy, frequently pressuring the EPA and other agencies to ease regulations. During 1991 the council began to intervene in regulatory processes to rewrite environmental rules and regulations, raising many of the same procedural issues as during the Reagan administration.[16]

But it was probably Bush's role as chief diplomat that most defined his environmental image. The president threatened to boycott the UN Conference on Environment and Development (the Earth Summit) in June 1992 until he had ensured that the climate change convention to be signed would contain no binding targets for carbon dioxide reduction. He further alienated much of the world as well as the U.S. environmental community by refusing to sign the Convention on Biological Diversity despite efforts by his delegation chief, William Reilly, to seek a last-minute compromise.[17] Thus, despite Bush's other accomplishments in foreign policy, the United States was isolated and embarrassed in international environmental diplomacy.

In summary, what began as a productive environmental administration deteriorated into defensive disarray in its final year. Many environmentalists who had supported Bush were dismayed by the antiregulatory tenor of his reelection campaign, which sounded increasingly like that of Ronald Reagan in 1980. In retrospect, Bush's retreat was an indication of changes to come in the Republican Party.

The Clinton Presidency

Environmental issues were clearly overshadowed by the economy and other controversies during the 1992 election. According to one exit poll, only 6 percent of voters considered the environment one of the most important issues, ranking it ninth in importance. However, "green" voters reported that they voted for Clinton over Bush by more than a 5–1 margin.[18] Clinton and vice presidential candidate Al Gore also received endorsements from the Sierra Club, the League of Conservation Voters, and other environmental organizations.

Clinton's campaign promises included many environmental pledges: to raise the corporate average fuel economy (CAFE) standard for automobiles, encourage mass transit programs, support renewable energy research and development, limit U.S. carbon dioxide emissions to 1990 levels by 2000, create a new solid waste reduction program and provide other incentives for recycling, pass a new Clean Water Act with standards for nonpoint sources, reform the Superfund program and tighten enforcement of toxic waste laws, protect ancient forests and wetlands, preserve ANWR, sign the biodiversity convention, and restore funding to UN population programs.[19]

Beyond this impressive list of commitments, Clinton and Gore departed from traditional rhetoric about the relationship between environmental protection and economic growth. They argued that the jobs-versus-environment debate presented a false choice because environmental cleanup creates jobs and the future competitiveness of the U.S. economy will depend on developing environmentally clean, energy-efficient technologies. They proposed a variety of investment incentives and infrastructure projects to promote such green technologies. All of these promises created high expectations among environmentalists.

Clinton's early actions indicated that he intended to deliver on his environmental agenda. The environmental community largely applauded his appointments to key environmental positions. Perhaps most important, Gore was given the lead responsibility for formulating and coordinating environmental policy. His influence was quickly seen in the reorganization of the White House and in Clinton's budget proposals, which contained elements of the new thinking that he and Gore had espoused during the campaign.

One of the administration's first acts was to abolish the Council on Competitiveness. Plans were announced for a new Office of Environmental Policy (OEP). The new office was to coordinate departmental policies on environmental issues and to ensure integration of environmental considerations into the work of all departments.[20] The OEP director, Kathleen McGinty, and EPA administrator Carol Browner were both former Senate environmental aides of Gore. There was also a considerable strengthening of the president's staff for international environmental affairs. Former senator Timothy Wirth was appointed undersecretary for global affairs at the State Department, and Eileen Claussen, formerly head of atmospheric programs at the EPA, became special assistant to the president for global environmental affairs at the National Security Council. Also, a new President's Council on Sustainable Development was appointed in June 1993.

Other appointments to the cabinet and executive office staffs were largely proenvironmental, though they tended to be competent pragmatists rather than radicals. The most notable environmental leader was Bruce Babbitt, a former Arizona governor and president of the League of Conservation Voters, who became secretary of the interior. In contrast to his predecessors in the Reagan and Bush administrations, Babbitt came to office with a strong reform agenda for western public lands management.[21] Several environmental activists from organizations such as the Wilderness Society and the Audubon Society were appointed to influential policy positions in his department. Overall, it was probably the strongest "green team" in history.

Although Clinton entered office with an expansive agenda and great talent and enthusiasm for policymaking, his environmental agenda quickly got bogged down in Congress. Two events early in the term gave the administration an appearance of environmental policy failure. Babbitt promptly launched a campaign to "revolutionize" western land use policies, including a proposal in Clinton's first budget to raise grazing fees on public lands closer to private market levels (something natural resource economists had advocated for many years). The predictable result was a furious outcry from cattle ranchers and their representatives in Congress. After meeting with several western Democratic senators, Clinton backed down and removed the proposal from the bill. Babbitt was left to fight a humiliating losing battle on the issue without presidential support.[22] Much the same thing happened on the so-called BTU tax. This was a proposal to levy a broad-based tax on the energy content of fuels as a means of promoting energy conservation and raising revenue. Originally included in the president's budget package at Gore's request, it was eventually dropped in favor of a much smaller gasoline tax (4.3 cents per gallon) in the face of fierce opposition from members of both parties in Congress.

Clinton failed to satisfy environmentalists on other issues as well. Many opposed his support for the North American Free Trade Agreement (NAFTA) and the World Trade Organization (see Chapter 16). And although Clinton signed the biodiversity convention rejected by President Bush and announced his intention to stabilize carbon dioxide emissions by 2000, his administration failed to implement either policy. The biodiversity treaty was not submitted for ratification by the Senate, and the administration's climate change action plan announced in October 1993 called only for weak voluntary measures that were inadequate by the administration's own admission.[23]

The 1994 elections gave Republicans control of both houses of Congress and thirty-one governorships. Claiming a mandate for the Contract with America that some three hundred GOP candidates for the House had pledged to support, the new House Speaker, Newt Gingrich, R-Ga., vowed "to begin decisively changing the shape of the government."[24] With the help of industry lobbyists, the new congressional leaders unleashed a massive effort to rewrite the environmental legislation of the past quarter-century.[25]

Clinton saw an opportunity to regain public support by taking a tough stance against the extremism of the new Republican environmental agenda. He campaigned throughout the country against the Republican proposals and appeared to have been successful by early fall 1995 in rallying public opinion against any significant weakening of environmental protection.[26] After a number of defeats in both houses, the GOP leadership switched to a strategy of burying provisions in riders to appropriation bills and in the budget reconciliation bill (see chapter 6). Clinton was largely successful in removing these provisions by threatening to veto budget bills and managed to restore most of the funding for environmental programs.

Like Reagan, Clinton was forced by congressional opposition to rely primarily on his powers as chief executive to pursue his environmental agenda. But, unlike Reagan, he used his powers of appointment, budgeting, reorganization, and regulatory oversight to reform and strengthen environmental protection. A "reinventing environmental regulation" program launched in 1995 produced more than forty new programs. EPA administrator Browner also strengthened existing regulations and enforcement. For example, in 1997 she issued tighter ambient air quality standards for ozone and small particulate matter to protect children, asthmatics, and other vulnerable population groups against lung disease. In the final year of the Clinton administration, the EPA proposed a series of new regulations tightening standards on other forms of pollution, including diesel emissions from trucks and buses and arsenic in drinking water.

In addition to strengthening the EPA, the Clinton administration took numerous measures to protect public lands and endangered species. For example, it helped to broker agreements to protect the Florida Everglades, Yellowstone National Park, and ancient redwood groves in California. The White House actively promoted voluntary agreements to establish habitat conservation plans to protect endangered species and other wildlife throughout the country.[27] More dramatically, Clinton used his executive authority under the Antiquities Act of 1906 to issue proclamations establishing nineteen new national monuments and enlarging three others, the total covering 6.1 million acres.[28] Finally, in January 2001, just prior to leaving office, Clinton issued a long-awaited executive order protecting nearly 60 million acres of roadless areas in national forests from future road construction and hence from logging and development.[29] He could thus claim to have protected more public land in the contiguous U.S. than any president since Theodore Roosevelt.[30]

Even so, the Clinton administration largely failed to develop an effective response to perhaps the greatest challenge of the new century, climate change. Although the administration agreed to support an international protocol setting binding targets and timetables for greenhouse gas reductions, it refused to commit the United States to meaningful reductions prior to the Kyoto treaty negotiations in December 1997. By then the president was severely constrained by congressional opposition to any agreement limiting U.S. emissions.[31] Ultimately Clinton authorized Vice President Gore to break the deadlock at Kyoto with an offer to reduce U.S. greenhouse gas emissions to 7 percent below 1990 levels by 2008–2012, and the United States signed the treaty in 1998. However, Congress made it clear that it would not ratify the agreement and prohibited all efforts to implement it. The administration subsequently proposed a variety of alternative mechanisms for implementing the protocol at the November 2000 conference at The Hague, but these proposals were so divisive that the conference delegates failed to reach agreement (see chapter 13).

President George W. Bush: Back to the Future?

Like Ronald Reagan, George W. Bush has used the administrative powers of the presidency to advance an antiregulatory, probusiness agenda. He has exercised the powers of appointment, budget, regulatory oversight, and rulemaking to alter the direction of existing environmental policies. He has also proposed major new energy and environmental legislation. And like Reagan, he has supported large tax cuts and has balanced environmental protection against other goals such as promoting economic growth, increasing energy production, and deferring to state and local interests.[32] Space constraints do not allow analysis of all of the president's environmental policies here, but they are also discussed in the other chapters (including chapter 17).

An Electoral Mandate?

George W. Bush took office in 2001 with a weak mandate to govern. He had lost the popular vote to Al Gore and had been declared the electoral college winner only after several weeks of legal dispute over contested Florida ballots, culminating with intervention by the Supreme Court. The Republicans also barely controlled the House of Representatives and lost control of the Senate when Sen. James Jeffords, R-Vt., declared himself an independent in May 2001. Not until the mid-term elections of 2002 did Bush secure a majority in both houses of Congress. By then he also had an entirely new leadership mandate as a result of the September 11, 2001, terrorist attacks on New York City and Washington, D.C. As the self-declared "war president," Bush was able to dominate the domestic as well as international scene as few American presidents have done. In addition to launching wars in Afghanistan and Iraq, he presided over passage of a series of large tax cuts, creation of a new Department of Homeland Security, and major education and health care reforms. His reelection in 2004 appeared to confirm support for a conservative agenda in his second term.

However, one could argue that President Bush had no mandate for major changes in environmental policy. Polls indicate that most people are relatively satisfied with present levels of environmental protection and do not want to see environmental laws weakened (see chapter 4). In fact, environmental issues received little attention in either the 2000 or 2004 presidential campaigns. In 2000 Gore attacked Bush's environmental record as governor of Texas and promised to continue Clinton's reforms. Bush argued that more regulatory authority should be devolved to the states and that voluntary pollution controls would be more effective than traditional command-and-control regulation. Although Bush made it clear that he did not support the Kyoto Protocol, he promised that his administration would establish controls over carbon dioxide and mercury emissions from power plants and also reduce other forms of air pollution. He also vowed to protect wetlands and to increase funding for the national parks. At the same time, however, he called for increased energy production in the United States and supported oil and gas drilling in ANWR.

Not surprisingly, environmentalists supported Gore by a wide margin. They viewed Bush as beholden to the oil industry and corporate polluters, especially after he picked Dick Cheney as his running mate. Many environmentalists cast their votes for the Green Party candidate, Ralph Nader (who won 97,000 votes in Florida alone, probably costing Gore the election). In 2004, virtually all environmental organizations supported John Kerry over Bush. Kerry had a strong environmental record in the Senate and proposed stricter controls over pollution and an array of incentives for alternative energy development and conservation.[33] But he did not make environmental issues a prominent theme in his campaign, and they were barely mentioned in the three presidential debates. Nevertheless, following the election Michael O. Leavitt, administrator of the Environmental Protection Agency, proclaimed that "the election is a validation of our philosophy and agenda."[34]

Appointments

Bush's first administration was characterized by some observers as a political restoration because many of his cabinet and agency appointees had served in his father's administration and, indeed, in the Reagan, Ford, and Nixon presidencies. The cabinet included White House veterans such as Donald Rumsfeld and Colin Powell, and several old Bush family friends were chosen for key staff positions (including the chief of staff, Andrew H. Card Jr.). But what stood out most were the intimate corporate connections of most of the appointees. Some commentators viewed Bush's appointees as even more conservative than Reagan's.[35]

Christine Todd Whitman, the former governor of New Jersey who was appointed administrator of the EPA, was considered a moderate and was generally well-received by environmentalists. But she resigned in June 2003 after numerous rebuffs by the White House and was replaced by Michael Leavitt, the conservative governor of Utah.[36] Gale Norton, the secretary of the interior, had served under James Watt in the Reagan administration and was an outspoken proponent of opening ANWR to oil development.[37] The energy secretary, former GOP Michigan senator Spencer Abraham, was a longtime opponent of higher fuel-efficiency standards. Appointees to other cabinet departments and staff positions were suspect because of their close industry ties. In the White House, chief of staff Card had served as chief lobbyist for General Motors, and James Connaughton, the new chair of the CEQ, had represented General Electric and other companies in fights with the EPA over toxic waste cleanups. Vice President Cheney had headed Halliburton, one of the world's largest oil exploration services companies.

Bush's appointments to subcabinet positions with environmental responsibilities were almost all "pro-business advocates who [had] worked on behalf of various industries in battles with the federal government, largely during the Clinton years," while virtually no environmentalists were appointed.[38] Moreover, Bush was slower than any previous president in nominating a White House science adviser, and few other scientists were appointed to senior policy positions.[39] Finally, Bush's choice to head the Office of Information and Regulatory Affairs (the so-called regulations czar) was Harvard professor John D. Graham, who had long questioned the benefits of many environmental regulations.[40]

The president put his own stamp on the cabinet during his second term, replacing nine of the fifteen members. In many cases, loyal staff members were promoted to fill the vacancies. Michael Leavitt was moved from the EPA to secretary of health and human services, and Samuel Bodman, who served as deputy secretary of both commerce and the treasury in the first term, was elevated to secretary of energy.[41] Gail Norton stayed on at interior, and Stephen L. Johnson, a career scientist at the EPA, replaced Leavitt as administrator of that agency.[42]

Budget Priorities

President Bush's first budget proposal, for fiscal year 2002, called for a modest 4 percent increase in overall domestic discretionary spending but an 8 percent reduction in funding for natural resource and environmental programs (the largest cut for any sector). The EPA's budget was to be slashed by nearly $500 million, or 6.4 percent, and the Interior Department budget was slated for a 3.5 percent cut.[43] Congress, however, did not approve these budget cuts; in fact, the EPA's budget was *increased* to $7.9 billion, $600 million more than the president had requested. This pattern continued in subsequent years, with the result that environmental spending grew substantially during 2000–2004 (see appendix 2). Nevertheless, Bush continued to push for cuts in each of his budget messages. For example, his budgets for fiscal years 2005 and 2006 called for cuts in EPA funding of 7.2 percent and 5.6 percent, respectively.[44] The huge deficits caused by Bush's tax cuts and other spending increases will likely constrain environmental programs in the future.

Regulatory Review and Oversight

Even before Bush was inaugurated, he let it be known that he would review and possibly rescind many of Clinton's environmental regulations and executive orders.[45] On his first day in office he placed a sixty-day moratorium (later extended) on Clinton administration rules that had not yet taken effect. He also reiterated that in his administration, state governments would be given more discretion in implementing and enforcing federal environmental regulations (see chapter 2).[46]

Many of Bush's early regulatory decisions aroused public controversy. For example, the EPA announced that it would suspend a proposed regulation that would lower the allowable level of arsenic in drinking water from 50 ppb (parts per billion) to 10 ppb (the World Health Organization standard) in order to reconsider its scientific basis. After Congress voted to impose the new standard and a National Academy of Sciences study suggested that an even lower standard could be justified, the EPA eventually confirmed that it would implement the Clinton standard (see chapters 8 and 10).[47] The administration also suspended implementation of Clinton regulations that would have banned road construction in nearly 60 million acres of national forests,[48] tightened controls over agricultural runoff and other forms of nonpoint water pollution,[49] and restricted use of snowmobiles in Yellowstone National Park.[50] Other rules changes relaxed controls on mountain-top removal in Appalachian coal mining and allowed dumping of mining wastes in rivers and streams.[51] On the other hand, the administration eventually adopted some of the regulatory changes initiated by the Clinton administration, including new pollution control standards for diesel engines and for off-road vehicles and construction equipment, and higher energy efficiency standards for air conditioners.[52] The administration also raised the fuel-efficiency standards for light trucks and sport utility vehicles by 1.5 miles per gallon beginning with the 2007 model year.

Bush has restored tight oversight of the regulatory process similar to that of the Reagan administration. OIRA head John Graham has required strict cost-benefit analyses and risk assessments for all proposed regulations and has not hesitated to intervene in agency decision making to influence rules while they are being developed.[53] OIRA's guidance stresses the need to monetize costs and benefits and to demonstrate the "net benefits" of environmental, health, and safety regulations. Graham has also used the Data Quality Act (an obscure rider in a 2000 appropriations bill) to allow outside organizations (mainly business and industry) to challenge scientific data and analysis that might support regulations.[54] Graham has added scientific staff to OIRA and appointed his own scientific advisory committee, but he has also tried to influence the composition of other peer review committees; some critics have charged that scientists who disagree with the Bush administration's agenda have been excluded from peer reviews.[55] The White House and OIRA have edited government scientific reports and other documents to eliminate references to problems such as global warming and to minimize the importance of findings that might justify regulation.[56] As a result of these and other actions, Graham and the Bush administration have been charged with politicizing science for ideological ends (see chapters 8 and 10). Nevertheless, Graham has boasted, "The Bush administration has cut the growth of costly business regulations by 75 percent, compared to the two previous administrations."[57]

Major Policy Initiatives

Beyond the rollback and revision of many detailed rules and regulations through administrative processes—most of which are not visible to the public—President Bush has launched several highly publicized efforts to alter the direction of national environmental and energy policies. In some cases he has proposed legislation to enact these policies (for example, a national energy bill), but in other cases he has attempted to alter existing laws through reinterpretation and major rules changes. Among his most important policy proposals in the first term were the national energy plan, the Clear Skies initiative, the Climate Change initiative, and the Healthy Forests initiative. Critics were quick to point out that the benign-sounding names of these programs had an Orwellian aura to them because they all concealed threats to environmental protection and natural resource conservation.

The national energy plan, entitled *Reliable, Affordable, and Environmentally Sound Energy for America's Future*, was drafted in secrecy during the spring of 2001 by a task force appointed by Vice President Cheney.[58] By all accounts, virtually all of the outside experts consulted were from energy producers and related industries, and many of the report's 106 recommendations directly reflected these interests.[59] The plan called for major increases in future energy supplies, including domestic oil, gas, nuclear, and "clean coal" development, and for streamlining environmental regulations to accelerate new energy production and to improve the national electricity grid. Although it also proposed $10 billion to be spent over ten years for research and tax incentives for renewable energy development, this amount was less than the Clinton administration had projected. In any case, these ideas were overshadowed by controversial recommendations for easing restrictions on oil, gas, coal, and nuclear power production and opening ANWR to energy development. Approximately 75 percent of the plan's recommendations were administrative in nature and are being carried out without new legislation. A bill incorporating other aspects of the Bush-Cheney plan, together with additional tax breaks for the energy industries (some $32 billion in all), quickly passed the House of Representatives in 2001 but later stalled in the Senate when authorization to drill in ANWR was defeated.[60] Subsequent efforts to revive the bill in the 108th Congress (2003–2005) also failed despite Republican control of both houses (see chapter 6). However, many public lands have been opened for oil and gas exploration, and numerous environmental restrictions on energy production have been relaxed.[61]

President Bush announced his Clear Skies initiative on February 14, 2002, after rejecting a stronger measure drafted by the EPA.[62] Clear Skies called for cuts of about 70 percent in sulfur dioxide, nitrogen oxides, and mercury emissions from power plants between 2008 and 2018. These reductions would be achieved through a new cap-and-trade system modeled after the successful emissions-trading program for sulfur dioxide created by the Clean Air Act Amendments of 1990 (see chapter 9). However, environmentalists were quick to point out that the Clear Skies proposal would actually reduce emissions of sulfur dioxide and nitrogen oxides much *less* than strict enforcement of the existing Clean Air Act would, and argued that mercury emissions could be cut much faster if regulated under the "hazardous emissions" section of the Clean Air Act.[63] The administration was accused of downplaying scientific evidence on the dangers of mercury poisoning under pressure from energy lobbyists (see chapter 8).[64] Nevertheless, Bush submitted to Congress legislation incorporating these and other measures.

Although the Clear Skies bill quickly stalled, the administration began to implement many of its provisions by executive order. For example, in August 2003 it adopted a rule that effectively repealed the new source review section of the Clean Air Act, as amended in 1977. This provision required older coal-fired power plants, oil refineries, and other industrial facilities to install modern pollution control equipment if they were modified to increase production or extend their life. The Clinton administration had sued over fifty of the dirtiest power plants for failing to clean up their emissions under this authority, in some cases resulting in multimillion-dollar settlement agreements. The Bush administration dropped many of these lawsuits and instead adopted rules relaxing the new source review requirements for as many as 17,000 sources, allowing them to *increase* their pollution emissions as they expand.[65] Although the administration argued that this would actually encourage companies to modernize older facilities more quickly while meeting increased energy needs, the Circuit Court of Appeals for the District of Columbia suspended the rules after fourteen states filed suits charging that they violated the Clean Air Act.[66]

When the Clear Skies bill again failed to clear the Senate Environment and Public Works Committee in March 2005, the EPA proceeded to issue separate rules to control sulfur and nitrogen oxides in 28 eastern states and to reduce mercury emissions (see chapter 6). Whether these rules will withstand legal challenges remains to be seen.[67]

None of Bush's proposals required control of carbon dioxide emissions, the most important greenhouse gas. Instead, Bush announced a new Climate Change initiative at the same time that the Clear Skies initiative was launched.[68] The plan called for slowing the growth of global warming emissions so as to cut "greenhouse gas intensity" (the ratio of greenhouse gases to economic output) by 18 percent over the next 10 years. This would be accomplished by encouraging companies to voluntarily report and reduce their emissions and by an expanded climate science research program and incentives to develop new technologies.[69] Critics pointed out that Bush's plan would only continue historic rates of declining carbon intensity while allowing total greenhouse emissions to *increase* over the ten-year period, given the economy's projected growth.[70] Moreover, when the administration's ten-year climate science plan was released by the Commerce and

Energy Departments in July 2003, many scientists criticized it for ignoring existing research and reopening many questions about human impacts on climate change that they regarded as settled.[71] References to climate change were deleted from the 2003 EPA state-of-the-environment report on the grounds that there was insufficient consensus on the science involved.[72] A subsequent report issued by Commerce and Energy in August 2004 appeared to indicate a shift in this position as it affirmed scientific evidence on the human causes of climate change.[73] However, President Bush reiterated that he would not consider any regulation of greenhouse emissions in his second term.[74]

President Bush announced his Healthy Forests initiative in August 2002 at the height of one of the worst wildfire seasons ever experienced in the western states. The plan called for new processes to expedite thinning of forests and "fuel reduction," especially to protect communities and property threatened by catastrophic fires. Congress subsequently passed the Healthy Forests Restoration Act of 2003, which incorporated most of the president's proposal.[75] Among other things, the legislation limited public participation and opportunities for appeal of forest project decisions and "reduced the complexity of environmental analysis" required to support forest planning.[76] Environmental groups were also quick to charge that the new policy amounted to a smoke screen for authorizing increased logging on federal lands, even of mature, healthy trees far from threatened communities. This was viewed as only one of many efforts of the Bush administration to open public lands to increased logging, mining, and energy development (see chapter 14 for a full discussion).[77]

Finally, President Bush declined to perform the role of environmental diplomat. His administration made few efforts to strengthen international environmental cooperation, though actions were announced during the first term to launch a new agreement with Canada to clean up the Great Lakes and to work with other nations to protect the oceans. The administration also supports ratification of the Law of the Sea, a treaty negotiated in 1982.[78] On the other hand, it has sought exemptions from implementation of the atmospheric ozone treaty and cut off funding for UN family planning programs. And despite renewed pressure from European allies, President Bush continued to oppose the Kyoto treaty, which entered into force in February 2005 following its ratification by Russia in late 2004.[79]

Conclusion

The record of recent presidents demonstrates that the White House has had a significant but hardly singular or consistent role in shaping national environmental policy. Presidents Nixon, Carter, and Bush the elder had their greatest successes in supporting successful environmental legislation. Facing more hostile Congresses, Presidents Reagan and Clinton had most influence (for better or worse) as chief executives who used administrative powers to the full in shaping the implementation of environmental policies. George W.

Bush faces fewer checks on his use of presidential powers to redefine America's environmental commitments than any of these previous chief executives. With majorities in both houses of Congress and a public distracted by other issues, Bush may be able to change the direction of environmental and energy policy more decisively than any president since Richard Nixon proclaimed the first environmental decade in 1970.

The context of presidential leadership has changed considerably over the decades since then. The rise of new conservative movements, first under Ronald Reagan and again in the 1990s, has increased the level of ideological partisanship and divided the country over environmentalism as well as over other basic values. At the same time, truly global problems such as climate change, loss of biodiversity, ocean degradation, hazardous and toxic waste pollution, the spread of human and animal diseases, and nuclear proliferation require international collaboration. The United States cannot ultimately lead a world with which it refuses to cooperate in environmental diplomacy. The president thus has a vital role to play in future environmental policymaking on the global as well as the domestic stage.[80]

Suggested Web Sites

BushGreenwatch (www.bushgreenwatch.org) Offers liberal critiques of Bush policies.

Cato Institute (www.cato.org/research/nat-studies/index.html) Promotes conservative analysis and advocacy.

Council on Environmental Quality (www.whitehouse.gov/ceq) Provides analysis of environmental conditions and links to other useful sources throughout the federal government.

Natural Resources Defense Council (www.nrdc.org/bushrecord) Provides analysis and criticism by a leading environmental organization.

OMB Watch (www.ombwatch.org) Follows budgets and regulatory policies.

Pew Center on Global Climate Change (www.pewclimate.org) Provides information from the leading think tank on climate change issues.

President's official Web site (www.whitehouse.gov/infocus/environment)

REP America (www.repamerica.org) Represents moderate Republicans for environmental protection.

Sierra Club (www.sierraclub.org/wwatch) Offers critical analysis of Bush actions.

Notes

1. Robert F. Kennedy Jr., *Crimes against Nature: How George W. Bush and His Corporate Pals Are Plundering the Country and Hijacking Our Democracy* (New York: HarperCollins, 2004), 3.
2. "Transcript of Bush's First News Conference after Winning Second Term," *New York Times,* November 5, 2004, A16.

3. Felicity Barringer and Michael Janofsky, "GOP Plans to Give Environment Rules a Free-Market Tilt," *New York Times*, November 8, 2004; Elizabeth Shogren and Kenneth R. Weiss, "Environment Officials See a Chance to Shape Regulations," *Los Angeles Times*, November 10, 2004.
4. Dennis L. Soden, ed., *The Environmental Presidency* (Albany: State University of New York Press, 1999), 3.
5. Ibid., 346.
6. Charles O. Jones, *The Presidency in a Separated System* (Washington, D.C.: Brookings Institution Press, 1994); *Separate but Equal Branches: Congress and the Presidency* (Chatham, N.J.: Chatham House, 1995).
7. See Frank R. Baumgartner and Bryan D. Jones, *Agendas and Instability in American Politics* (Chicago: University of Chicago Press, 1993).
8. On Nixon's environmental legacy, see John C. Whitaker, *Striking a Balance: Environment and Natural Resources Policy in the Nixon-Ford Years* (Washington, D.C.: American Enterprise Institute, 1976); Charles O. Jones, *Clean Air* (Pittsburgh: University of Pittsburgh Press, 1975); Jonathan Aitken, *Nixon: A Life* (Washington, D.C.: Regnery, 1993).
9. The presidency of Gerald R. Ford is not considered here because he essentially continued Richard Nixon's policies and did not leave a distinctive environmental legacy.
10. For a more detailed analysis of Reagan's environmental record, see Michael E. Kraft and Norman J. Vig, "Environmental Policy in the Reagan Presidency," *Political Science Quarterly* 99 (fall 1984): 414–439; Vig and Kraft, eds., *Environmental Policy in the 1980s: Reagan's New Agenda* (Washington, D.C.: CQ Press, 1984).
11. Richard P. Nathan, *The Administrative Presidency* (New York: Wiley, 1983).
12. See Barry D. Freedman, *Regulation in the Reagan-Bush Era: The Eruption of Presidential Influence* (Pittsburgh: University of Pittsburgh Press, 1995); V. Kerry Smith, *Environmental Policy under Reagan's Executive Order: The Role of Cost-Benefit Analysis* (Chapel Hill: University of North Carolina Press, 1984).
13. On the impact of the Reagan budget cuts, see especially Robert V. Bartlett, "The Budgetary Process and Environmental Policy," and J. Clarence Davies, "Environmental Institutions and the Reagan Administration," in *Environmental Policy in the 1980s*, ed. Vig and Kraft.
14. For a more detailed summary of Watt's policies, see Paul J. Culhane, "Sagebrush Rebels in Office: Jim Watt's Land and Water Policies," in *Environmental Policy in the 1980s*, ed. Vig and Kraft, 293–318; C. Brant Short, *Ronald Reagan and the Public Lands: America's Conservation Debate* (College Station: Texas A&M University Press, 1989). Burford tells her side of the story in Anne M. Burford (with John Greenya), *Are You Tough Enough?* (New York: McGraw-Hill, 1986).
15. John Holusha, "Bush Pledges Aid for Environment," *New York Times*, September 1, 1988; Bill Peterson, "Bush Vows to Fight Pollution, Install 'Conservation Ethic,'" *Washington Post*, September 1, 1988.
16. The most detailed analysis of the Quayle Council is in Charles Tiefer, *The Semi-Sovereign Presidency* (Boulder: Westview Press, 1994), chap. 4.
17. Keith Schneider, "White House Snubs U.S. Envoy's Plea to Sign Rio Treaty," *New York Times*, June 5, 1992.
18. *Newsweek*, special election issue, November–December 1992, 10.
19. Bill Clinton and Al Gore, *Putting People First* (New York: Times Books, 1992), 89–99.
20. Ann Devroy, "Clinton Announces Plan to Replace Environmental Council," *Washington Post*, February 9, 1993. At the end of 1994 the OEP was folded into the CEQ, which continued to play an active role in the White House.
21. Timothy Egan, "Sweeping Reversal of U.S. Land Policy Sought by Clinton," *New York Times*, February 24, 1993.
22. Margaret Kriz, "Turf Wars," *National Journal*, May 22, 1993, 1232–1235; Richard L. Berke, "Clinton Backs Off from Policy Shift on Federal Lands," *New York Times*,

March 31, 1993; James Conaway, "Babbitt in the Woods: The Clinton Environmental Revolution That Wasn't," *Harpers,* December 1993, 52–60.

23. William K. Stevens, "With Energy Tug of War, U.S. Is Missing Its Goals," *New York Times,* November 28, 1995.
24. "Taking Speaker's Mantle, Gingrich Vows 'Profound Transformation,' " *Congressional Quarterly Weekly Report,* December 10, 1994, 3522.
25. For a summary of the Republican agenda and responses to it, see "GOP Sets the 104th Congress on New Regulatory Course," *Congressional Quarterly Weekly Report,* June 17, 1995, 1693–1701.
26. "It's Not Just Owls Anymore," *Newsweek,* September 4, 1995, 23.
27. As an alternative way of implementing the Endangered Species Act, the Clinton administration supported completion of more than 250 habitat conservation plans protecting some 170 endangered plant and animal species while allowing controlled development on 20 million acres of private land. William Booth, "A Slow Start Built to an Environmental End-run," *Washington Post,* January 13, 2001.
28. For a description of these monuments, see Reed McManus, "Six Million Sweet Acres," *Sierra,* September–October 2001, 40–53.
29. Douglas Jehl, "Road Ban Set for One-Third of U.S. Forests," *New York Times,* January 5, 2001; Eric Pianin, "Ban Protects 58.5 Million Forest Acres," *Washington Post,* January 5, 2001.
30. Bill Clinton, *My Life* (New York: Knopf, 2004), 948.
31. In particular, the Byrd-Hagel resolution (passed 95–0 on June 12, 1997) opposed any agreement that would harm the U.S. economy or that did not require control of greenhouse gas emissions by developing countries.
32. Douglas Jehl, "On Rules for Environment, Bush Sees a Balance, Critics a Threat," *New York Times,* February 23, 2003; Jonathan Weisman, "In 2003, It's Reagan Revolution Redux," *Washington Post,* February 4, 2003; Bill Keller, "Reagan's Son," *New York Times Magazine,* January 26, 2003.
33. "The Kerry-Edwards Vision for a Cleaner Environment, a Stronger Economy & Healthier Communities," www.johnkerry.com/pdf/vision.pdf.
34. Barringer and Janofsky, "GOP Plans to Give Environment Rules a Free-Market Tilt."
35. Alison Mitchell, "News Analysis: A Cabinet Conservative at the Core," *New York Times,* January 3, 2001; Dana Milbank and Ellen Nakashima, "Bush Team Has 'Right' Credentials: Conservative Picks Seen Eclipsing Even Reagan's," *Washington Post,* March 25, 2001.
36. David Stout, "E.P.A. Chief Whitman Resigns," *New York Times,* May 21, 2003; John Heilprin, "EPA Administrator Christine Todd Whitman Resigns," *Washington Post,* May 21, 2003; Jennifer 8. Lee, "After Long Delay, Senate Confirms Utah Governor as Head of E.P.A.," *New York Times,* October 29, 2003. Whitman discusses her frustrations in *It's My Party Too* (New York: Penguin, 2005).
37. Douglas Jehl, "Norton Record Often at Odds with Laws She Would Enforce," *New York Times,* January 13, 2001; Eric Pianin, "Norton Argues for Arctic Drilling," *Washington Post,* January 20, 2001.
38. Katherine Q. Seelye, "Bush Picks Insiders to Fill Environmental Posts," *New York Times,* May 12, 2001; "No Greens Need Apply" (editorial), *New York Times,* August 19, 2001.
39. James Glanz, "Balancing the Equation of Science and Politics," *New York Times,* July 3, 2001. Bush appointed Dr. John H. Marburger III, former director of the Brookhaven National Laboratory, as director of the White House Office of Science and Technology Policy (OSTP) in July 2001, but, in contrast to previous science advisers, Bush did not give him the title of assistant to the president and abolished the position of associate director of OSTP for the environment. See William J. Broad, "Government Reviving Ties to Scientists," *New York Times,* November 20, 2001. Marburger's low-key role is discussed in Glanz, "At the Center of the Storm over Bush and Science," *New York Times,* March 30, 2004.

40. See John D. Graham and Jonathan B. Wiener, eds. *Risk vs. Risk: Tradeoffs in Protecting Health and the Environment* (Cambridge: Harvard University Press, 1997).

41. Robert Pear, "Bush Selects E.P.A. Head To Be Secretary of Health," *New York Times*, December 14, 2004; David E. Sanger, "Bush Names New Energy Chief to His Second-Term Cabinet," *New York Times*, December 10, 2004. Although Bodman was a former professor of chemical engineering, he had spent most of his career as CEO of an investment firm and a chemical company.

42. Felicity Barringer, "E.P.A. Scientist Is Bush's Pick As New Chief," *New York Times*, March 5, 2005. It should be noted that Johnson is the first scientist to head the EPA.

43. Glenn Kessler and Amy Goldstein, "First Bush Budget Makes Modest Cuts," *Washington Post*, April 10, 2001; "Bush's Budget: The Losers," *Washington Post*, April 10, 2001; "Who Gets What Slice of the President's First Federal Budget Pie," *New York Times*, April 10, 2001.

44. Diana Jean Schemo and Lynette Clemetson, "Domestic Gains for Education but Not Much Else," *New York Times*, February 3, 2004; David Stout, "Bush Seeks Sweeping Budget Cuts to Rein in Federal Deficit," *New York Times*, February 8, 2005.

45. Robert Pear, "Bush Aides Pledge to Give Clinton's Final Blizzard of Regulations a Hard, Close Look," *New York Times*, December 23, 2000; Douglas Jehl, "G.O.P. to Press for Unraveling of Clinton Acts," *New York Times*, January 6, 2001.

46. Robert Pear, "Shifting of Power from Washington Is Seen under Bush," *New York Times*, January 7, 2001; Douglas Jehl, "Whitman Promises Latitude to States on Pollution Rules," *New York Times*, January 18, 2001.

47. Douglas Jehl, "E.P.A. Delays Its Decision on Arsenic," *New York Times*, April 19, 2001; Katharine Q. Seelye, "E.P.A. to Adopt Clinton Arsenic Standard," *New York Times*, November 1, 2001. See also Whitman, *It's My Party Too*, 157–161.

48. Eric Pianin, "White House Seeks to Scuttle Clinton Ban on Logging Roads," *Washington Post*, April 26, 2001; Douglas Jehl, "White House Considering Plan to Void Clinton Rule on Forests," *New York Times*, May 1, 2001; Felicity Barringer, "Bush Seeks Shift in Logging Rules," *New York Times*, July 13, 2004; Barringer, "Administration Overhauls Rules for U.S. Forests," *New York Times*, December 23, 2004.

49. Douglas Jehl, "E.P.A. Delays Further Rules of Clinton Era," *New York Times*, July 17, 2001; Eric Pianin, "EPA Seeks Clean Water Rule Delay, *Washington Post*, July 17, 2001.

50. Katharine Q. Seelye, "Bush May Lift Park's Snowmobile Ban," *New York Times*, June 24, 2001; Michael Janofsky, "U.S. Would Allow 720 Snowmobiles Daily at Yellowstone," *New York Times*, August 20, 2004.

51. Katharine Q. Seelye, "Bush White House Reverses Clinton Decision on Mining," *New York Times*, October 26, 2001; Michael Shnayerson, "Sale of the Wild," *Vanity Fair*, September 2003, 328–353; James Dao, "Rule Change May Alter Strip-Mine Fight," *New York Times*, January 26, 2004.

52. Jennifer 8. Lee and Andrew C. Revkin, "E.P.A. Backs Stricter Guidelines," *New York Times*, April 16, 2003; Michael Janofsky, "Tough Emission Rules Set for Big Diesel Vehicles," *New York Times*, May 11, 2004; Matthew L. Wald, "Accord Set of Efficiency for Cooling," *New York Times*, November 12, 2004.

53. See "New Regulatory Czar Takes Charge," *Science*, October 5, 2001, 32–33; "Harvard Professor Shakes Up Regulatory Policy," *Science*, December 14, 2001, 2277–2278; Rebecca Adams, "Regulating the Rule-Makers: John Graham at OIRA," *CQ Weekly*, February 23, 2002, 520–526.

54. Rick Weiss, " 'Data Quality' Law Is Nemesis of Regulation," *Washington Post*, August 16, 2004. See also chapter 10 in this volume.

55. Sheryl Gay Stolberg, "Bush's Science Advisers Drawing Criticism," *New York Times*, October 10, 2002; Joel Brinkley, "Out of Spotlight, Bush Overhauls U.S. Regulations," *New York Times*, August 16, 2004; Bruce Barcott, "Changing All the Rules," *New York Times Magazine*, April 4, 2004.

56. Andrew C. Revkin, "With White House Approval, E.P.A. Pollution Report Omits Global Warming Section," *New York Times*, September 15, 2002; Revkin and

Katharine Q. Seelye, "Report by the E.P.A. Leaves Out Data on Climate Change," *New York Times,* June 19, 2003; Bette Hileman, "EPA's State of the Environment," *Chemical & Engineering News,* 81 (June 30, 2003); Jennifer 8. Lee, "U.S. Proposes Easing Rules on Emissions of Mercury," *New York Times,* December 3, 2003; Andrew C. Revkin, "Bush vs. the Laureates: How Science Became a Partisan Issue," *New York Times,* Science Times Section, October 19, 2004.

57. Brinkley, "Out of Spotlight."

58. National Energy Policy Development Group, *Reliable, Affordable, and Environmentally Sound Energy for America's Future,* May 17, 2001, available at www.whitehouse .gov/energy. See also David E. Sanger and Joseph Kahn, "Bush, Pushing Energy Plan, Offers Scores of Proposals to Find New Power Sources," *New York Times,* May 18, 2001; "Energy Report Highlights," *Washington Post,* May 18, 2001; Joseph Kahn, "Cheney Promotes Increasing Supply as Energy Policy," *New York Times,* May 1, 2001.

59. Katharine Q. Seelye, "Bush Task Force on Energy Worked in Mysterious Ways," *New York Times,* May 16, 2001; Joseph Kahn, "Bush Advisers on Energy Report Ties to Industry," *New York Times,* June 3, 2001; Kahn, "Cheney Refuses to Release Energy Task Force Records," *New York Times,* August 4, 2001; Dan Van Natta Jr. and Neela Banerjee, "Documents Show Energy Official Met Only with Industry Leaders," *New York Times,* March 26, 2002.

60. Eric Pianin and Glenn Kessler, "In the End, Energy Bill Fulfilled Most Industry Wishes," *Washington Post,* August 3, 2001.

61. See, for example, Joby Warrick and Juliet Eilperin, "Oil and Gas Hold the Reins in the Wild West: Land-Use Decisions Largely Favor Energy Industry," *Washington Post,* September 25, 2004; Craig Welch, "For Good or Ill, Bush Clears Path for Energy Development," *Seattle Times,* September 26, 2004. A revised energy bill passed the House of Representatives on April 21, 2005, but its fate in the Senate remained doubtful. Carl Hulse, "House Votes to Approve Broad Energy Legislation," *New York Times,* April 22, 2005.

62. White House, "Fact Sheet: President Bush Announces Clear Skies & Global Climate Change Initiatives," February 14, 2002. See also Katharine Q. Seelye, "White House Rejected a Stricter Alternative to Clear Skies Plan," *New York Times,* April 28, 2002.

63. Jennifer 8. Lee, "New Policy on Mercury Pollution Was Rejected by Clinton E.P.A.," *New York Times,* December 16, 2003. The Clinton administration had proposed to regulate mercury as a "hazardous" air emission, which would have allowed more stringent and rapid regulation; see chapter 8 in this volume.

64. Jennifer 8. Lee, "White House Minimized the Risks of Mercury in Proposed Rules, Scientists Say," *New York Times,* April 7, 2004; Felicity Barringer, "E.P.A. Accused of a Predetermined Finding on Mercury," *New York Times,* February 4, 2005.

65. Katharine Q. Seelye, "Administration Adopts Rule on Antipollution Exemption," *New York Times,* August 28, 2003. The new EPA regulations announced in August 2003 would allow plants to modify their facilities up to 20 percent of their total value without meeting new pollution control requirements. Christopher Drew and Richard A. Oppel Jr., "How Industry Won the Battle of Pollution Control at E.P.A.," *New York Times,* March 6, 2004.

66. David Kocieniewski, "States to Fight Relaxation of Power-Plant Pollution Standards," *New York Times,* August 29, 2003; "Bush Plans Pollution Rules by March, Disappointing Utilities," Bloomberg.com, January 21, 2005.

67. Michael Janofsky, "Bush-Backed Emissions Bill Fails to Reach Senate Floor," *New York Times,* March 10, 2005; Janofsky, "E.P.A. Sets Rules to Cut Pollution," *New York Times,* March 11, 2005; Matthew L. Wald, "New Rules Set for Emission of Mercury," *New York Times,* March 16, 2005. Both the Clean Air Interstate Rule and the Clean Air Mercury Rule would establish cap-and-trade systems to reduce emissions by 70 percent when fully implemented.

68. See note 62.

69. The best official summary is perhaps Spencer Abraham, "The Bush Administration's Approach to Climate Change," *Science,* July 30, 2004, 616–617.

70. Andrew C. Revkin, "Climate Plan Is Criticized as a Risky Bet," *New York Times,* February 22, 2002; Revkin, "Climate Plan Is Criticized as Optimistic," *New York Times,* February 26, 2003; Pew Center on Global Climate Change, "Analysis of President Bush's Climate Change Plan," www.pewclimate.org/policy_center/analyses/response_bushpolicy.cfm.

71. Guy Gugliotta, "Taking on Global Climate Change: Planned Study is Decried as Stalling," *Washington Post,* July 24, 2003; Andrew C. Revkin, "Experts Fault Bush's Proposal to Examine Climate Change," *New York Times,* February 26, 2003. The Bush administration claims to be spending $4.5 billion annually on climate-related research and development. One of the more dramatic elements is the hydrogen fuels initiative announced by the president in his 2003 state-of-the-union address. Its goal is to promote the development and commercialization of hydrogen fuel-cell powered cars and trucks by about 2020.

72. Weiss, " 'Data Quality' Law Is Nemesis of Regulation."

73. Andrew C. Revkin, "U.S. Report, in Shift, Turns Focus to Greenhouse Gases," *New York Times,* August 26, 2004. It is noteworthy that the Energy and Commerce Departments manage the climate science program, not the EPA.

74. John Heilprin, "Bush Stands by Rejection of Limits on Gases Blamed for Global Warming," Associated Press, November 8, 2004.

75. See White House, "Healthy Forests: An Initiative for Wildfire Prevention and Stronger Communities," www.whitehouse.gov/infocus/healthyforests.

76. See, for example, Sierra Club, "Debunking the 'Healthy Forests Initiative,' " www.sierraclub.org/forests/fires/healthyforests_initiative.asp. It was pointed out that site-specific "hazardous fuels reduction projects" were categorically excluded from environmental analysis, public participation, and legal appeals.

77. For a long list of such charges, see Natural Resources Defense Council, "The Bush Record," www.nrdc.org/bushrecord.

78. Michael Janofsky, "Officials Lay Groundwork for Cleanup of Great Lakes," *New York Times,* December 4, 2004; Cornelia Dean, "Bush Forms Panel to Coordinate Ocean Policy," *New York Times,* December 18, 2004.

79. Larry Rohter, "U.S. Waters Down Global Commitment to Curb Greenhouse Gases," *New York Times,* December 19, 2004.

80. Alan Cowell, "Blair Calls on United States to Cooperate with Rest of the World," *New York Times,* January 27, 2005.

6

Environmental Policy in Congress

Michael E. Kraft

We must strive to build upon the success of the Clean Air Act, not gut it. . . . This bill allows giant corporate utilities to avoid compliance and stops the enforcement of our existing clean air laws. The big utilities are essentially given ten extra years to pollute. In addition, the measure exempts thousands of sources from the requirements to control hazardous air pollutants that cause cancer and birth defects.

Senator James M. Jeffords, I-Vt., ranking minority
member, Senate Environment and Public Works Committee,
March 9, 2005

[The bill was] killed by the environmental extremists who care more about continuing the litigation-friendly status quo and making a political statement on CO_2 than they do about reducing air pollution.

Senator James M. Inhofe, R-Okla., chair, Senate
Environment and Public Works Committee, March 9, 2005[1]

In March 2005, two striking developments illustrated well the challenges that Congress faces with contemporary environmental and energy issues. One of these challenges is reflected in the statements above by Senators Jeffords and Inhofe. On March 9 the Senate Environment and Public Works Committee deadlocked in a 9–9 vote on President Bush's Clear Skies initiative, a top White House environmental priority since its introduction in 2002. The seven Democrats on the committee were joined by Senator Jeffords, an independent from Vermont and ranking minority member, and Sen. Lincoln Chaffee, a moderate Republican from Rhode Island. Unable to break a long-standing stalemate on the bill despite extended negotiations, the committee vote meant that the measure would not advance to the full Senate and was likely dead for the year. Shortly after the vote the administration announced that it was issuing a fall-back set of administrative rules that it hoped would achieve some of the same goals. Yet the rules are more vulnerable to legal challenge, and they cannot achieve what the legislation promised to do.[2]

At about the same time, the Senate once again was considering proposals to permit drilling for oil in the Arctic National Wildlife Refuge (ANWR) in a reprise of repeated attempts over the previous four years that failed to secure legislative approval. The ANWR dispute had long been one of the most contentious in Congress, reflecting a broad and persistent partisan division on environmental and natural resource issues. It had also become a powerful symbol of divergent party philosophies and policy priorities. Even after many of the largest oil companies signaled their declining interest in ANWR on economic grounds, the congressional battles raged on.[3]

Knowing they stood little chance of success through a direct vote on the measure, Republicans announced a new strategy to avert the threat of yet another Democratic filibuster. The Democrats have routinely used filibusters to block legislative proposals and judicial nominations they opposed (as have Republican senators). So the Republicans decided they would attach a refuge drilling proposal to a must-pass Senate budget resolution; it would take only fifty-one votes to enact rather than the sixty needed to end a filibuster. The 2004 elections gave the party fifty-five seats in the Senate, or four more than when they lost a Senate vote on ANWR in 2003, but they were still short of the votes needed to stop a certain filibuster by drilling opponents. Moreover, the ANWR vote has not split purely along party lines. In 2003 eight Republicans voted against drilling.[4]

As expected, environmental groups mounted a vigorous challenge to the proposed budget strategy. The Sierra Club, the Natural Resources Defense Council (NRDC), and other groups ran radio, television, and print advertisements to bring public pressure on key senators. They also launched a grassroots lobbying campaign that flooded the Senate with postcards urging members to defeat the budget bill maneuver. Former president Jimmy Carter, who in 1980 signed the law that created the Alaskan wildlife refuge, also was enlisted to telephone Democratic senators who leaned toward permitting oil development in ANWR.[5] These efforts proved to be insufficient. On March 16, 2005, by a 51–49 vote, the Senate left the ANWR drilling language in the budget bill.

Environmental Challenges and Political Constraints

The defeat of the president's Clear Skies initiative and the fight over ANWR tell us much about the contemporary role of Congress in environmental and energy policy. They also are fitting examples of the difficulty of resolving policy conflicts in what some analysts call an "era of partisan warfare" on Capitol Hill. Increasingly each party appeals to its core constituency through a continuous political campaign that emphasizes an ideological "message politics." In this context, policy compromise between the parties is never easy, as each often seeks to deny the other any semblance of victory even at the cost of stalemate in dealing with pressing national problems such as energy use.[6]

It was not always so. For nearly three decades, from the late 1960s to the mid-1990s, Congress enacted—and over time strengthened—an extraordinary range of environmental policies (see chapter 1 and appendix 1). In doing so, members within both political parties recognized and responded to rising public concern about environmental degradation. For the same reasons, they stoutly defended and even expanded those policies during the 1980s when they were assailed by Ronald Reagan's White House.[7]

This pattern changed with the election of the 104th Congress in 1994, as the new Republican majority brought to the Hill a very different position on the environment. It was far more critical of regulatory bureaucracies, such as the U.S. Environmental Protection Agency (EPA), and the policies they are charged with implementing.[8] On energy and natural resource issues, such as drilling for oil in ANWR, Republicans have tended to lean heavily toward increasing resource use and economic development rather than conservation. As party leaders pursued these goals from 1995 to 2005, they invariably faced intense opposition from Democrats who were just as determined to block what they characterized as ill-advised attempts to roll back years of progress in protecting public health and the environment.[9]

The 2004 election gave President George W. Bush and the Republican Party the best opportunity to reform environmental policy since the watershed election of 1994. The Republicans increased their margins in both the Senate and the House and seemed likely to maintain their lead for the foreseeable future.[10] Republican leaders signaled their intent to capitalize on their political good fortune by seeking major changes in environmental and natural resource policies they viewed as long overdue. Among them were the Clean Air Act, the Clean Water Act, the Endangered Species Act, the National Environmental Policy Act, and the president's proposals for a national energy policy, of which drilling for oil in ANWR was a central element.[11] Yet the prospects were not as promising as many in the party had hoped.

The short-term effect of political conflict over Clear Skies and ANWR—and many other environmental proposals since 1995—has been partisan polarization and policy stalemate, a state of affairs that seems likely to persist. For the most part, building consensus on the issues has proved to be difficult, and Congress has been unable to approve either the sweeping changes sought by Republicans or the moderate reforms preferred by most Democrats. Thus existing policies—with their many acknowledged flaws—have largely continued in force.[12] The longer-term impacts are less clear. They depend on the outcome of future congressional elections, the effect that environmental and corporate interest groups have on public opinion and political support in Congress, and especially the willingness of members to cooperate in the search for a new generation of environmental policy.

There should be no doubt, however, that ultimately only Congress can redesign environmental policy for the twenty-first century. Thus it is important to understand how Congress makes decisions on environmental issues and why members adopt the positions and take the actions they do. In the sections below I examine efforts at policy change on Capitol Hill and compare them with the way Congress dealt with environmental issues previously. This assessment highlights the many distinctive roles that Congress plays in the policymaking process. I give special attention to the phenomenon of policy stalemate or gridlock, which at times has been a defining characteristic of congressional involvement with environmental policy.

Congressional Authority and Environmental Policy

Under the Constitution, Congress shares authority with the president for federal policymaking on the environment. Every year members of Congress make critical decisions on hundreds of measures, from funding the operations of the EPA and other agencies to supporting highways, mass transit, forestry, farming, oil and gas exploration, energy research and development, and international population and development assistance. All of these decisions can have significant impacts on environmental protection and sustainable development in the United States and around the world. Most of these actions are rarely front page news, and the public may hear little about them, which does not, however, diminish their importance.[13]

As discussed in chapter 1, we can distinguish congressional actions in several different stages of the policy process: agenda setting, formulation and adoption of policies, and implementation of them in executive agencies. Presidents have greater opportunities than does Congress to set the political agenda, that is, to call attention to specific problems and define the terms of debate. Still, members of Congress can have a major impact on the agenda through legislative and oversight hearings as well as through the abundant opportunities they have for introducing legislation, requesting and publicizing studies and reports, making speeches, taking positions, and voting. All of these actions can assist them in framing issues in a way that can promote their preferred solutions.

Because of their extensive executive powers, presidents also can dominate the process of policy implementation in the agencies (see chapter 5). Here too, however, Congress can substantially affect agency actions through its budgetary decisions. These powers translate into an influential and continuing role of overseeing, and often criticizing, actions in executive agencies such as the EPA, the Department of Energy, the Fish and Wildlife Service, and the Forest Service.

Moreover, through its constitutional power to advise and consent on presidential nominations to the agencies and the courts, the Senate has a role in choosing who is selected to fill critical positions. A case in point is President Bush's nomination of William G. Myers III for the Ninth Circuit Court of Appeals. Myers, who was once a lobbyist for the mining and grazing industries, was strongly opposed by the Senate's Democrats in both 2004 and 2005, in part because of his stance on environmental policies.[14]

Even if it cannot compete on an equal footing with the president in some of these policymaking activities, historically, Congress has been more influential than the White House in the formulation and adoption of environmental policies. For much of the modern environmental era, as noted earlier, it also has operated with broad bipartisan agreement on the issues.[15] Yet the way in which Congress exercises its formidable policymaking powers is shaped by several key variables, such as whether the president's party also controls Congress—and by what margins—and its willingness to defer to the president's recommendations.

Congress's actions on the environment also reflect its dualistic nature as a political institution. In addition to serving as a national lawmaking body, it is an assembly of elected officials who represent politically disparate districts and states. Thus members' decisions tend to reflect local and regional concerns and interests. Indeed, powerful electoral incentives continually induce members of Congress to think as much about local and regional impacts of environmental policies as they do about the larger national interest.[16] Such political pressures led members in the early 2000s to drive up the cost of the president's energy proposals with what one journalist called an "abundance of pet projects, subsidies and tax breaks" to specific industries.[17]

Another distinctive institutional characteristic is the system of House and Senate standing committees, where most significant policy decisions take place. Dozens of committees and subcommittees have jurisdiction over environmental policy (see Table 1-1 in chapter 1), and the outcomes of specific legislative battles often turn on which members sit on those committees. The 2005 deadlock in the Senate Environment and Public Works Committee over the president's Clear Skies proposal illustrates the committees' importance.

Taken together, these characteristics have important implications for environmental policy. First, building policy consensus in Congress is rarely easy. Second, policy compromises invariably reflect members' preoccupation with local and regional impacts of environmental decisions. Third, the White House matters a great deal in how the issues are defined and whether policy decisions can be made acceptable to all concerned, but the president's influence is nevertheless limited by independent political calculations on Capitol Hill.

Given these constraints, Congress frequently finds itself unable to make critical decisions on environmental policy. The U.S. public may see a "do-nothing Congress," yet the fundamental reality is that all too often members can find no way to reconcile the conflicting views of multiple interests and constituencies.

There are, however, some striking exceptions to this common pattern of deadlock. In 1990 Congress approved a far-reaching extension of the Clean Air Act, the nation's most demanding environmental statute.[18] In 1996 it ended a long stalemate on pesticide policy through adoption of the Food Quality Protection Act, and in the same year it approved a major revision of the Safe Drinking Water Act. An intriguing question is how Congress can achieve a remarkable consensus on some environmental policies while remaining mired in gridlock on others. A brief examination of the way

Congress has dealt with environmental issues since the early 1970s helps to explain this seeming anomaly. Such a review also provides a useful context in which to examine and assess the actions of recent Congresses, and the outlook for environmental policymaking for the early twenty-first century.

Causes and Consequences of Environmental Gridlock

Policy gridlock refers to an inability to resolve conflicts in a policy-making body such as Congress, which results in government inaction in the face of important public problems. There is no consensus on *what* to do and therefore no movement in any direction. Present policies, or slight revisions of them, continue until agreement is reached on the direction and magnitude of change. Sometimes environmental or other programs officially expire but continue to be funded by Congress through a waiver of the rules governing the annual appropriations process. The failure to renew the programs, however, contributes to administrative drift, ineffectual congressional oversight, and a propensity, as discussed later in the chapter, for members to use the appropriations process to achieve what cannot be gained through statutory change.[19]

Why Does Policy Gridlock Occur?

Political pundits and public officials bemoan policy gridlock in Congress. They are less likely to ask why it occurs or what might be done to overcome the prevailing tendency toward institutional stalemate.[20] There are no simple answers to those questions, but six reasons for gridlock are commonly suggested: the divergent policy views of Democrats and Republicans, a constitutionally mandated separation of powers, the complexity of environmental problems, lack of public consensus on the issues, the influence of organized interest groups, and ineffectual political leadership. It is helpful to understand how these forces affect the way Congress deals with environmental challenges, and thus what might push Congress toward actions more consonant with public needs in the early twenty-first century.

Divergent Policy Views. Despite belief by some observers that little difference exists between the two major parties, there is a wide gulf between them on almost all major environmental protection and natural resource issues. Based on rankings by the League of Conservation Voters (LCV), the two major parties show increasing divergence from the early 1970s through the early 2000s. On average they have differed by nearly 25 points on a 100-point scale, and the differences grew wider during the 1980s and 1990s.[21] LCV scores for 2004 were typical of recent years. Senate Democrats averaged 85-percent support for the positions endorsed by the league and the environmental community. Senate Republicans averaged 8 percent. In the House, Democrats averaged 86 percent and Republicans 10 percent.[22] Each party has members who differ from the norm. Senators John McCain, R-Ariz. (56 percent) and Lincoln Chaffee, R-R.I. (50 percent) come to mind among the Republicans. Yet these exceptions do not diminish the importance of the general polarization between the parties, which extends to many other issues beyond the environment and is now as great as at any time in decades.[23]

Separated Powers and Bicameralism. Overlapping authority for policy-making in the U.S. political system, originally intended to limit the power of government, is a major cause of policy stalemate. The U.S. Constitution divides legislative authority between the president and Congress, and between the House and Senate. Moreover, each institution reflects a somewhat different constituency and set of political incentives, setting the stage for conflict over environmental policy. Political conflicts are more likely under divided government, where the parties split control of Congress and the White House.

Complexity of Environmental Problems. Environmental issues are often conveyed in the mass media as rather simple choices over clean air and water, elimination of toxic chemicals, protection of endangered species, and the like. Yet most environmental problems are in fact multidimensional and highly complex in ways the public barely recognizes. Global climate change is a good example (see chapter 13). Often considerable scientific uncertainty exists over the magnitude of the problems and how best to deal with them. Yet members of Congress are reluctant to accept costly actions until there is compelling scientific evidence of the risks. Such evidence simply may not be available.

Lack of Public Consensus. The more the public agrees on basic policy directions, the easier it is for Congress to act. That relationship should be good news for environmental policy because polls have long indicated widespread public concern over environmental problems and support for policy action. Yet surveys also indicate that environmental issues are rarely among the most salient (see chapter 4). Absent a clear and forceful public voice, members of Congress cannot easily respond to their constituents' generalized concern for the environment. This may help to explain the results of a recent study showing that members of Congress do tend to vote in a way that is consistent with their campaign promises on environmental issues, but that Republicans are "far more likely to break their campaign promises," and that proenvironmental campaign promises are more likely to be broken than are others.[24]

Influence of Organized Groups. Interest groups willingly enter the political vacuum created by an inattentive and disengaged public, and often sharply conflict with one another. Most groups have markedly increased their presence in the nation's capital since the early 1970s, and business groups have become especially well represented.[25] In recent years business and environmental groups have proven highly adept at blocking each other's initiatives in Congress, despite pronouncements in some circles of the "death of environmentalism."[26] Increasingly, however, environmental groups act as an outside force on Congress. Since the Republican takeover of Congress in 1995, the number of times they have testified before congressional committees has plummeted.[27]

Ineffectual Political Leadership. A final explanation for policy gridlock is ineffectual political leadership. The fragmented U.S. political system often requires presidential leadership to get much done. Similarly, strong leadership within Congress either at the committee level or among party leaders may help to forge the majorities needed for enacting legislation, as was evident in the 104th Congress, where House Speaker Newt Gingrich proved adept at forging coalitions for policy change.[28] Without such leadership in the White House or on Capitol Hill, building consensus among disparate interests can be enormously difficult.

Gridlock's Effects

Just as policy stalemate in Congress has a number of causes, there are differing appraisals of its impact on environmental policy. Generally the term *gridlock* has a negative connotation in the press and among the U.S. public. It is seen as something to be ended quickly or avoided in the first place. Environmentalists might argue, for example, that when government cannot act on a pressing problem, human health or the environment will suffer needlessly. Climate change and loss of biodiversity are two examples. Similarly, business interests assert that congressional inability to reform environmental policies such as the Clean Air Act translates into unnecessary costs and burdens that companies (and society) must bear. Along with many policy analysts, they see political stalemate as a lost opportunity to improve the effectiveness and efficiency of those policies.[29]

Yet under some conditions gridlock may also be viewed positively. For example, if political conflict allows the continuation of policies (for example, the Endangered Species Act) that would otherwise be weakened by a legislative body, then environmentalists may welcome the outcome; the policies they prefer are left in place. Similarly, by blocking proposals for oil development in ANWR, environmental groups are maintaining current restrictive policies that apply to the Alaskan wildlife refuge.

Policymaking on the environment from the 1970s through early 2005 indicates two very different outcomes. In some cases Congress overcame the institutional and political obstacles discussed earlier and produced strong and sometimes innovative environmental policy. In other cases legislative stalemate prevailed. The differences between the two results merit brief examination here to provide a context for the last section of the chapter, in which I assess contemporary legislative action in Congress.

From Consensus in the Environmental Decade to Deadlock in the 1990s

As chapter 1 makes clear, the 1970s offer examples of both successful and unsuccessful environmental policymaking. The record for this so-called environmental decade is nevertheless remarkable, particularly in comparison with actions taken during most of the 1980s and 1990s. The National

Environmental Policy Act, Clean Air Act, Clean Water Act, Endangered Species Act, and Resource Conservation and Recovery Act, among others, were all signed into law in the 1970s, mostly between 1970 and 1976. We can debate the merits of these early statutes with the clarity of hindsight and in light of contemporary criticism of them. Nonetheless their enactment demonstrates vividly that the U.S. political system is capable of developing major environmental policies in fairly short order under the right conditions. Consensus on environmental policy could prevail in the 1970s because the issues were new and politically popular, and attention was focused on broadly supported program goals, such as cleaning up the nation's air and water, rather than on the means used to achieve them (command-and-control regulation) or the costs of doing so.

Environmental Gridlock Emerges

The pattern of the 1970s did not last. Congress's enthusiasm for environmental policy gradually gave way to apprehension about its impacts on the economy, and policy stalemate became the norm in the early 1980s. Ronald Reagan's election as president in 1980 also altered the political climate, and threw Congress into a defensive posture. It was forced to react to the Reagan administration's aggressive policy actions. Rather than proposing new programs or expanding old ones, Congress focused its resources on oversight and criticism of the administration's policies, and bipartisan agreement became more difficult. Members were increasingly cross-pressured by environmental and industry groups, partisanship on these issues increased, and Congress and President Reagan battled repeatedly over budget and program priorities.[30] The cumulative effect of these developments in the early 1980s was that Congress was unable to agree on new environmental policy directions.

Gridlock Eases: 1984–1990

The legislative logjam began breaking up in late 1983, as the U.S. public and Congress repudiated Reagan's antienvironmental agenda (see chapter 5). The new pattern was evident by 1984 when, after several years of deliberation, Congress approved major amendments to the 1976 Resource Conservation and Recovery Act that strengthened the program and set tight new deadlines for EPA rulemaking on control of hazardous chemical wastes.

Although the Republicans still controlled the Senate, the 99th Congress (1985–1987) compiled a record dramatically at odds with the deferral politics of the 97th and 98th Congresses (1981–1985). In 1986 the Safe Drinking Water Act was strengthened and expanded, and Congress approved the Superfund Amendments and Reauthorization Act, adding a separate Title III, the Emergency Planning and Community Right-to-Know Act (EPCRA). EPCRA was an entirely new program mandating nationwide reporting for toxic and hazardous chemicals produced, used, or stored in communities (resulting in the now well-known Toxics Release Inventory), as well as state and local emergency planning for accidental chemical releases. Democrats regained control of the Senate following the 1986 election, and Congress reauthorized the Clean Water Act over a presidential veto.

Still, Congress was unable to renew the Clean Air Act and the Federal Insecticide, Fungicide, and Rodenticide Act—the nation's key pesticide control act—as well as new legislation to control acid rain. The disappointment in this limited progress was captured in one analyst's assessment: "Congress stayed largely stalemated on a range of old environmental and energy problems in 1988, even while a generation of new ones clamored for attention."[31] Much the same could be said for the 101st and 102nd Congresses (1989–1993) during George H. W. Bush's administration.

Yet with the election of the elder Bush in 1988, Congress and the White House were able to agree on enactment of the innovative and stringent Clean Air Act Amendments of 1990 and the Energy Policy Act of 1992. The latter was an important if modest advancement in promoting energy conservation and a restructuring of the electric utility industry to promote greater competition and efficiency. Success on the Clean Air Act was particularly important because for years it was a stark symbol of Congress's inability to reauthorize controversial environmental programs. Passage was possible in 1990 because of improved scientific research that clarified the risks of dirty air, reports of worsening ozone in urban areas, and a realization that the U.S. public would tolerate no further delays in acting. President Bush had vowed to "break the gridlock" and support renewal of the Clean Air Act, and Sen. George Mitchell, D-Maine, newly elected as Senate majority leader, was equally determined to enact a bill.[32]

Policy Stalemate Returns

Unfortunately, approval of the 1990 Clean Air Act Amendments was no signal that a new era of cooperative and bipartisan policymaking on the environment was about to begin. Nor was the election of Bill Clinton and Al Gore in 1992, even as Democrats regained control of both houses of Congress. Most of the major environmental laws were once again up for renewal. Yet despite an emerging consensus on many of the laws, in the end the 103rd Congress (1993–1995) remained far too divided to act. Coalitions of environmental groups and business interests clashed regularly on all of these initiatives, and congressional leaders and the Clinton White House were unsuccessful in resolving the disputes.

The search for consensus on environmental policy became more difficult as the 1994 election neared. Republicans increasingly believed they would do well in November, and partisan politics helped to scuttle whatever hopes remained for action in 1994. Like the environmentalists, the Republicans, their conservative Democratic allies in these battles, and business leaders thought they could strike a more favorable compromise in the next Congress.

The 104th Congress:
Revolutionary Fervor Meets Political Reality

Few analysts had predicted the astonishing outcomes of the 1994 midterm elections, even after one of the most expensive, negative, and anti-Washington campaigns in modern times. Republicans captured both houses of Congress, picking up an additional fifty-two seats in the House and eight in the Senate. They also did well in other elections throughout the country, contributing to their belief that voters had endorsed the Contract with America, which symbolized the new Republican agenda.[33]

The contract had promised a rolling back of government regulations and a shrinking of the federal government's role. There was no specific mention of environmental policy, however, and the document's language was carefully constructed for broad appeal to a disgruntled electorate. The contract drew heavily from the work of conservative and probusiness think tanks that for years had waged a multifaceted campaign to discredit environmentalist thinking and policies. Those efforts merged with a carefully developed GOP plan to gain control of Congress to further a conservative political agenda.[34]

The preponderance of evidence suggests that the Republican victory in November conveyed no public mandate to roll back environmental protection.[35] Yet the political result was clear enough. It put Republicans in charge of the House for the first time in four decades and set the stage for an extraordinary period of legislative action on environmental policy characterized by bitter relations between the two parties.

The resulting environmental policy deadlock should have come as no surprise. With several notable exceptions, consensus on the issues simply could not be built, and the revolution failed for the most part. The lesson seemed to be that a direct attack on popular environmental programs could not work because it would provoke a political backlash. Those who supported a new policy agenda turned instead to a strategy of evolutionary or incremental environmental policy change through a more subtle and less visible exercise of Congress's appropriations and oversight powers. Here they were more successful.[36]

Environmental Policy Actions in Recent Congresses

As discussed earlier, Congress influences nearly every environmental and resource policy though exercise of its powers to legislate, oversee executive agencies, advise and consent on nominations, and appropriate funds. Sometimes these activities take place largely within the specialized committees and subcommittees and sometimes they reach the floor of the House and Senate, where they may attract greater media attention. Some of the decisions are made routinely and are relatively free of controversy (e.g., appropriations for the national parks) whereas others stimulate more political conflict, as was the case with George W. Bush's Clear Skies bill and the

ANWR dispute. In this section I briefly review some of the most notable congressional actions from 1995 to 2005 within three broad categories: regulatory reform initiatives (directed at the way agencies make decisions), appropriations (funding levels and use of budgetary riders), and proposals for changing the substance of environmental policy. For those who wish to follow ongoing debate over how Congress acts on environmental policy issues, a number of key Web sites are listed at the end of the chapter.

Regulatory Reform: Changing Agency Procedures

Regulatory reform has long been a central theme in U.S. environmental policy (see chapters 1 and 5). There is no real dispute about the need to reform agency rulemaking that has been widely faulted for being too inflexible, intrusive, cumbersome, and adversarial and sometimes based on insufficient consideration of science and economics.[37] However, considerable disagreement exists over precisely what elements of the regulatory process need to be reformed and how best to do so to ensure the changes are both fair and effective.

Beginning in 1995 and continuing for several Congresses, the Republican Party and conservative Democrats favored omnibus regulatory reform legislation that would affect all environmental policies by imposing broad and stringent mandates on bureaucratic agencies. Those mandates were directed particularly at the use of cost-benefit analysis and risk assessment in proposing new regulations (see chapters 8 and 9). Proponents of such legislation also sought to open agency technical studies and rulemaking to additional legal challenges to help protect the business community against what they viewed as unjustifiable regulatory action.

Opponents of both kinds of measures argued that such impositions and opportunities for lawsuits would wreak havoc within agencies, such as the EPA, that already faced daunting procedural hurdles and frequent legal disputes as they developed regulations. Thus they preferred more limited changes that would be considered as each environmental statute came up for renewal. They also sought to give agency professionals more discretion in considering how to weigh pertinent evidence and set program priorities.

Debate over regulatory reform measures in Congress has provided ample opportunity for the kind of message politics described earlier. Members have recounted colorful anecdotes of alleged regulatory abuses and pleas for relief for the business community. Opponents just as often challenged these arguments as only weakly linked to scientific or economic reality.[38] In the end, the House favored broad regulatory reform bills during the mid-1990s as part of the Contract with America, but the Senate failed to go along. GOP leaders were more successful, however, in gaining approval of several less ambitious, but nonetheless important, reform measures.

One of these bills was the Unfunded Mandates Reform Act, which Congress approved and the president signed in early 1995. The act erected new procedural barriers to keep Congress from approving statutes likely to impose federal requirements on state and local governments without providing funding to cover the costs. Another was the Small Business Regulatory Enforcement Fairness Act of 1996, which was attached to an unrelated but "must-pass" bill raising the public debt limit. It required agencies to assist small business in complying with regulations and forced agencies to submit proposed rules to Congress for review and possible rejection. A third was the Data Quality Act of 2000, enacted as a budgetary rider (see below) and designed to ensure the accuracy of data on which agencies base their regulations. Its effect on the role of science in agency rulemaking is discussed in chapter 10.

With the election of George W. Bush in 2000, the regulatory reform agenda shifted from imposing these kinds of congressional mandates on Clinton administration agencies to direct intervention by the White House. Bush appointed conservative and probusiness officials to nearly all environmental and natural resource agencies, and rulemaking shifted decisively toward the interests of the business community (see chapters 5, 8, 10, and 14).[39] Equally important was the president's appointment of John Graham to head the Office of Information and Regulatory Affairs, a White House clearance body for all major agency regulations (discussed in chapters 5 and 10).

Appropriations Politics: Budgets and Riders

The implementation of environmental policies depends heavily on the funds that Congress appropriates each year. Thus if certain policy goals cannot be achieved through changing the governing statutes, or altering the rulemaking process, attention may turn instead to appropriations. This was the case during the Reagan administration in the 1980s, which severely cut environmental budgets, and it has been a major element of the Republican strategy since 1995. One of the most avid revolutionaries in the GOP freshman class of 1995, Rep. David McIntosh, of Indiana, explained the logic of this approach: "The laws would remain on the books, but there would be no money to carry them out. It's a signal to the agencies to stop wasting time on these regulations."[40]

The appropriations process has been used in two distinct ways to achieve policy change. One is through riders. These are legislative stipulations attached to appropriations bills to achieve policy goals such as restricting, remaking, or even eliminating federal programs. The other is through changes in the level of funding, typically involving a cut in spending for programs that are not favored.

Appropriations Riders. Use of appropriations riders became a common strategy following the 1994 election. In the 104th Congress, for example, more than fifty antienvironmental riders were included in seven different budget bills, largely with the purpose of slowing or halting enforcement of laws by the EPA, the Interior Department, and other agencies until Congress could revise them. In one of the most controversial cases, seventeen riders were appended to the EPA appropriations bill in 1995 in an attempt to prohibit the agency from enforcing certain drinking-water and water quality standards and to keep it from regulating toxic air emissions from oil and gas refineries, among many other provisions. The EPA was told flatly that it could not spend any money on these activities.[41] President Clinton vetoed the bill.

The use of riders has continued in subsequent years, as has opposition to the strategy by environmental groups. A rider on a transportation appropriations bill in 2000 (as in previous years) barred the Department of Transportation from even considering an increase in auto fuel-efficiency standards. Another in 2000, if approved, would have prohibited the EPA from collecting fees from pesticide manufacturers to fund safety reviews that are mandatory under 1996 legislation.[42]

In late 2004, as Congress rolled a number of budget measures together in an omnibus package in a final effort to complete work on the fiscal year 2005 budget, a number of environmental riders were attached to the measure. These included exclusion of grazing permit renewals from environmental review and limitations on judicial review and public participation in logging projects in the Tongass National Forest. Some other riders were defeated, including several that would have weakened protection under the Endangered Species Act.

Why use these kinds of riders to achieve policy change? Such a strategy is attractive to its proponents because appropriations bills, unlike authorizing legislation, typically move quickly and Congress must enact them each year to keep the government operating. Many Republicans and business lobbyists also argue that use of riders is one of the few ways they have to rope in a bureaucracy that they believe needs additional constraints. They feel they are unable to address their concerns through changing the authorizing statutes themselves, a far more controversial and uncertain path to follow.[43]

Yet relying on riders is widely considered to be an inappropriate way to institute policy changes. The process provides little opportunity to debate the issues openly, and there are no public hearings or public votes. For example, provisions of the Data Quality Act of 2000, noted earlier, were written largely by an industry lobbyist and were enacted quietly as twenty-seven lines of text buried in a massive budget bill that President Clinton had to sign.[44] In a retrospective review in 2001, NRDC counted hundreds of antienvironmental riders attached to appropriations bills since 1995. Clinton blocked more than seventy-five of them, but many became law, including the Data Quality Act.[45]

Cutting Environmental Budgets. The history of congressional funding for environmental programs was discussed in chapter 1, and it is set out in appendix 2 for selected agencies and in appendix 4 for overall federal spending on natural resources and the environment. Despite a general increase in federal spending between 1980 and 2004, these budgets are the focus of continuing conflict within Congress. For example, in the 104th Congress, GOP leaders enacted deep cuts in environmental spending only to face President Clinton's veto of the budget bill. Those conflicts led eventually to a temporary shutdown of the federal government, with the Republicans receiving the brunt of the public's wrath for the budget wars. Most of the environmental cuts were reversed. Disagreements over program priorities continued throughout the 1990s, yet in 1998 the Clinton administration managed to gain full funding for its $1.7 billion Clean Water Action Plan (a five-year initiative to deal with polluted runoff from cities and farms), a 23-percent boost for programs to protect rare and endangered species, and a big jump in spending on global climate change research.[46]

George W. Bush had fewer budgetary conflicts with Congress in his first year of office than did Clinton. But once Democrats regained control of the Senate, Bush was forced to compromise on environmental funding. For instance, his fiscal year 2002 budget proposed $2.3 billion in cuts for a range of environmental programs, and EPA spending was to decline by $498 million.[47] Democrats in both houses opposed cuts in the EPA's enforcement budget, and they won the support of some of their Republican colleagues. Congress went on to approve an EPA budget that was nearly $600 million more than Bush had requested.[48]

For subsequent years Bush again sought cuts in the EPA's budget, but Congress generally resisted. However, as concern over federal budget deficits rose, Bush was more successful. The fiscal year 2004 budget gave the EPA a budget of about $8.4 billion, an increase over the president's proposal. Yet for the fiscal year 2005 budget, Congress was finally persuaded to go along with some of the cuts recommended by the Bush White House, reducing the EPA's budget to $8 billion. The president's fiscal year 2006 budget proposals call for another 5.6-percent cut in the EPA's budget, much of it targeted at the agency's clean water state loan program, and a total cut for all environmental programs of over 10 percent. The long-term projections in the White House budget documents incorporate further substantial reductions in environmental spending, though it remains to be seen whether Congress will go along.[49]

Legislating Policy Change

As discussed earlier, in any given year Congress makes decisions on hundreds of environmental or resource programs. In this section I highlight selective actions in recent Congresses, with particular attention to energy policy and clean air programs. Given the emphasis throughout the chapter on constraints that often keep Congress from reaching across party lines to find common ground, several cases of bipartisan agreement on policy changes merit brief mention first.

Successful Enactment of Policy Change. Among the most notable achievements of the otherwise antienvironmental 104th and 105th Congresses are three conspicuous success stories involving control of pesticides and other agricultural chemicals, drinking water, and transportation. Especially for the first two of these actions, years of legislative gridlock were overcome as Republicans and Democrats uncharacteristically reached agreement on new policy directions. Two more recent cases of successful legislation are discussed as well.

The Food Quality Protection Act of 1996 was a major revision of the nation's pesticide law, which for decades had been a poster child for policy gridlock as environmentalists battled with the agricultural chemical and food industries. The act required the EPA to use a new, uniform, reasonable-risk approach to regulating pesticides used on food, fiber, and other crops, and it required that special attention be given to the diverse ways in which both children and adults are exposed to such chemicals. The act sped through Congress in record time without a single dissenting vote because the food industry was desperate to get the new law enacted after court rulings that would have adversely affected it without the legislation. In addition, after the bruising battles of 1995, GOP lawmakers were eager to adopt an election-year environmental measure.[50]

The 1996 rewrite and reauthorization of the Safe Drinking Water Act sought to address many long-standing problems with the nation's drinking water program. It dealt more realistically with regulating contaminants based on their risk to public health and authorized $7 billion for state-administered loan and grant funds to help localities with compliance costs. It also created a new right-to-know provision that requires large water systems to provide their customers with annual reports on the safety of local water supplies. Bipartisan cooperation on the bill was made easier because it aided financially pressed state and local governments and, like the pesticide bill, allowed Republicans to score some election-year points with environmentalists.[51]

Another important legislative enactment took place in the 105th Congress. After prolonged debate over renewal of the nation's major highway act, in 1998 the House and Senate overwhelmingly approved the Transportation Equity Act for the 21st Century. It was a sweeping six-year, $218 billion measure that provided a 40-percent increase in spending to improve the nation's aging highways and included $5.4 billion for mass transit systems.[52] Members of Congress find it easier to reach agreement when federal dollars are distributed among the states and congressional districts.

In 2001 President Bush gained congressional approval of important legislation to reclaim so-called urban brownfields. The measure represented an unusual compromise between House Republicans who sought to reduce liability for small businesses under Superfund and Democrats who wanted to see contaminated and abandoned industrial sites in urban areas cleaned up.[53] The final bill authorized $250 million a year for five years to help states clean up and redevelop contaminated industrial sites. The compromise ended a long-standing dispute over liability provisions of the Superfund law that left abandoned more than 450,000 brownfield sites around the nation.

In a somewhat similar action, the 108th Congress in 2003 approved one of the Bush administration's environmental priorities, the Healthy Forests initiative. The measure was designed to permit increased logging in national forests to reduce the risk of wildfires. It reduced the number of environmental reviews that would be required for such logging projects and sped up judicial reviews of legal challenges to these projects. Environmental groups opposed the legislation, but bipartisan concern over communities at risk from wildfires was sufficient for enactment. Wildfires struck Southern California only days before the Senate voted 80–14 to approve the bill.[54]

These five cases are dissimilar in many respects, but they indicate that, under certain conditions, members can work across party lines. Still, Congress finds it difficult to agree on many other measures where the political rewards are less evident or policy disagreements between the parties and their constituencies are too great to overcome.

Partisan Conflict and Stalemate. Several examples illustrate the continuing political conflict. Among the most long standing of these are renewal of the Superfund program and the Endangered Species Act. Newer disputes that have proved to be equally contentious are revision of the Clean Air Act and national energy policy, especially given its linkage to ANWR and to climate change.

The Superfund program has not been reauthorized for over two decades, and except for the brownfields measure discussed earlier, congressional agreement has not been forthcoming. In 1995 Congress let the special industry tax that funds the program expire, and it has yet to be renewed. The inaction has shifted the program from one for which "polluters pay" to one for which general tax revenues must be used instead. The result is that the program's cleanup fund is no longer adequate for cleanup of contaminated sites across the nation. Congressional reaction to Bush administration proposals on the program late in 2004 suggests that agreement will remain hard to come by.[55]

The Endangered Species Act presents a similar level of conflict and lack of resolution. In 2001, then–House Resources Committee chair James Hansen, R-Utah, captured the dilemma well: "We haven't reauthorized it because no one could agree on how to reform and modernize the law. Everyone agrees there are problems with the Act, but no one can agree on how to fix them."[56] By late 2004, most Republican-backed proposals sought to require greater consideration of the rights of property owners and to force the Fish and Wildlife Service to rely more on peer-reviewed science in its species decisions. Opponents have argued that such bills would gut the act to appease small landowners and corporate developers, and that requirements for such "sound science" are mere ploys to prevent the service from acting.[57]

The Bush administration's Clear Skies initiative, proposed in 2002, was to make the first major changes to the Clean Air Act since the amendments of 1990. It was offered initially as an improvement to the act that would incorporate market incentives and create greater certainty over requirements on industry. Supporters of the Bush bill said it would significantly cut emissions at some 1,300 power plants across the country and help to bring most of the nation into compliance with federal clean air standards.

Opponents asserted that the legislation was far too weak and did not cut emissions as fast as would be required under the existing Clean Air Act.

They also objected to the bill's omission of any regulation of carbon dioxide even as nearly all other industrialized nations sought to rein in the greenhouse gas.[58] In response to that omission, Senators John McCain, R-Ariz., and Joseph Lieberman, D-Conn., cosponsored the Climate Stewardship Act of 2003. It was designed to cap greenhouse gas emissions by power plants, refineries, and other industries and would use tradable allowances to do so. The bill gained forty-three votes in the Senate in 2003, but ultimately was blocked, in McCain's words by "the power and influence of the special interest lobby, especially public utilities and automobile manufacturers."[59] The bill was reintroduced in both houses in 2005. As noted earlier, the Clean Skies bill itself was defeated in the Senate in March 2005, and the Bush administration chose to pursue its goals through administrative rules instead.

The last measure, Bush's 2001 proposal for a national energy policy, is perhaps the most important environmental initiative of recent years and yet also the most frustrating. As stated in the chapter opening, controversy over ANWR would prove to be a main sticking point. Yet it was by no means the only one.

The Bush energy plan was formulated in 2001 under closely guarded conditions by a task force headed by Vice President Dick Cheney in the aftermath of a short-term energy crisis in California and rising gasoline prices. The president's recommendations to Congress called for an increase in the production and use of fossil fuels and nuclear energy, gave modest attention to the role of energy conservation, and sparked intense debate on Capitol Hill with its emphasis on oil and gas drilling in ANWR. The Republican House quickly approved the measure in 2001, after what the press called "aggressive lobbying by the Bush administration, labor unions and the oil, gas and coal industries."[60] The vote largely followed party lines. The bill provided generous tax and research benefits to the oil, natural gas, coal, and nuclear power industries; and it rejected provisions that would have forced the auto industry to improve fuel efficiency for sport utility vehicles.

The Senate was far more skeptical about the legislation and remained so over the next four years. To no one's surprise, ANWR became symbolic of the party split on energy issues: "I don't see any way around ANWR," said former senator J. Bennett Johnston, D-La., now an energy lobbyist. "It's a theological issue."[61]

Competing energy bills were debated on the Hill through mid-2005 without resolution. Senate Democrats favored measures that balanced energy production and environmental concerns, including increases in auto and truck fuel-efficiency standards; they drew strong support from environmentalists and denunciation by industry and Republicans. Neither side was prepared to compromise as lobbying by car manufacturers, labor unions, the oil and gas industry, and environmentalists continued. Regional splits over whether to approve a liability waiver for the gasoline additive and groundwater contaminant MTBE also undercut consensus-building efforts. As one writer put it in 2002, the "debate between energy and the environment is important to core constituencies of both parties, the kind of loyal followers vital in a congressional election year."[62] Ironically the two sides were in agreement on most of the issues, such as tax incentives for energy production and conservation and new energy research programs.[63] A corporate tax cut bill enacted in 2004 incorporated some of those elements, such as oil and gas drilling tax breaks, renewable energy tax credits, and accelerated depreciation for an Alaskan natural gas pipeline. In April 2005 the House voted to approve President Bush's energy bill, but Senate action remained uncertain.[64]

Conclusions

From many perspectives, U.S. environmental policies are at a critical crossroads. They have achieved much since the late 1960s, but future gains cannot be assured by relying solely on conventional regulatory approaches governed by the existing statutes. A serious search for new policy strategies has been under way since at least the early 1990s as appraisals of existing programs have made clear their deficiencies. Innovative policy designs and experiments in the use of market-based approaches, selective devolution to state and local governments, information disclosure, public-private partnerships, collaborative decision-making, and much more suggest the promise of new directions.[65] Such policy change can succeed at the federal level, however, only with the active assistance of Congress.

The political struggles on Capitol Hill summarized in this chapter reveal sharply contrasting visions for environmental policy. Consensus may exist on broad principles of reform, but few signs point to an early resolution of conflict over the all-important details. The revolutionary rhetoric of the 104th Congress had dissipated by 2005, and Congress has been able to revise several major statutes in an uncommon display of bipartisan cooperation. Nonetheless, for most other environmental programs, policy gridlock continued to frustrate all participants, and partisan differences prevented emerging issues such as climate change from being seriously addressed.

The constitutional divisions between the House and Senate guarantee that newly emergent political forces such as those represented in the House in the 1990s cannot easily push their legislative agendas. The same applies to George W. Bush's ascent to the presidency. His administration shares many of the same concerns voiced by conservatives on Capitol Hill (see chapter 5). In the U.S. political system, however, effective policymaking will always require cooperation between the two branches and leadership within both to advance sensible policies and secure public approval for them. The public clearly has a role to play in these deliberations as well, and the availability of information about Congress and the legislative process could facilitate a level of public involvement that might alter the outcome.

Suggested Web Sites

Library of Congress Thomas search engine (http://thomas.loc.gov) This search engine for locating key congressional documents is one of the most comprehensive public sites available for legislative searches. See also www.house.gov and www.senate.gov for portals to the House and Senate, and the committee and individual member Web sites.

Environmental Protection Agency (www.epa.gov/epahome/rules .html) The EPA site for laws, rules, and regulations includes the full text of the dozen key laws administered by the EPA. It also has a link to current legislation before Congress.

Sierra Club (www.sierraclub.org) The Sierra Club is one of the leading national environmental groups that tracks congressional legislative battles.

League of Conservation Voters (www.lcv.org) The LCV compiles environmental voting records for all members of Congress.

Natural Resources Defense Council (www.nrdc.org) Perhaps the most active and influential of national environmental groups that lobby Congress, NRDC also provides detailed news coverage of congressional legislative developments.

National Association of Manufacturers (www.nam.org) This leading business organization offers policy news, studies, and position statements on environmental issues as well as extensive resources for public action on the issues.

National Federation of Independent Businesses (www.nfib.com) NFIB is the nation's largest advocacy group for small business and has been especially active on regulatory reform issues.

Heritage Foundation (www.heritage.org) This leading conservative research institute offers news and studies on a range of environmental and energy issues.

Competitive Enterprise Institute (www.cei.org) This conservative, probusiness group has been active on regulatory reform and many environmental issues. The site offers analyses and positions on a range of topics.

Notes

1. Jeffords's statement is taken from the Senate Environment and Public Works Committee Web site, as a minority press release, http://epw.senate.gov. Inhofe's statement is drawn from Michael Janofsky, "Bush-Backed Emissions Bill Fails to Reach Senate Floor," *New York Times*, March 10, 2005, A21.
2. Michael Janofsky, "E.P.A. Sets Rules to Cut Pollution," *New York Times*, March 11, 2005, 1, A14. Within a week the EPA also announced new rules to control mercury emissions, though they were sharply criticized by environmental and public health groups.
3. See Jeff Gerth, "Big Oil Steps Aside in Battle over Arctic," *New York Times*, February 21, 2005, A12. As Gerth reports, one Bush administration adviser, speaking anonymously, went so far as to say, "No oil company really cares about ANWR."
4. Sheryl Gay Stolberg, "Senate Gearing Up for Fight over Oil Drilling in Alaska," *New York Times*, March 9, 2005, A13.
5. Ibid.
6. See Eric Schickler and Kathryn Pearson, "The House Leadership in an Era of Partisan Warfare," in *Congress Reconsidered*, 8th ed., ed. Lawrence C. Dodd and Bruce I. Oppenheimer (Washington, D.C.: CQ Press, 2005). For a similar perspective on the contemporary Senate, including the pattern of "message politics," where position

taking displaces legislative deliberation, and the rising frequency of filibusters, see C. Lawrence Evans and Daniel Lipinski, "Obstruction and Leadership in the U.S. Senate," in the same volume.

7. See chapter 1 in this volume; and Michael E. Kraft, "Congress and Environmental Policy," in *Environmental Politics and Policy: Theories and Evidence*, 2nd ed., ed. James P. Lester (Durham, N.C.: Duke University Press, 1995).

8. Ed Gillespie and Bob Schellhas, eds., *Contract with America* (New York: Times Books/ Random House, 1994); Bob Benenson, "GOP Sets the 104th Congress on New Regulatory Course," *Congressional Quarterly Weekly Report*, June 17, 1995, 1693–1705.

9. For a general review of this period, see Lawrence C. Dodd and Bruce I. Oppenheimer, "A Decade of Republican Control: The House of Representatives, 1995–2005," in *Congress Reconsidered*, 8th ed., ed. Dodd and Oppenheimer.

10. Lawrence C. Dodd and Bruce I. Oppenheimer, "Prologue: Perspectives on the 2004 Congressional Elections," in *Congress Reconsidered*, 8th ed., ed. Dodd and Oppenheimer.

11. Margaret Kriz, "Out of the Loop," *National Journal*, February 5, 2005, 344–349; Mary Clare Jalonick, "After November Election, Change Could Be in the Air—and Water," *CQ Weekly*, October 23, 2004, 2520–2522; and Jalonick, "Energy and Environment: GOP Plans to Kick-Start Business-Friendly Legislation That Stalled in Previous Session," *CQ Weekly*, January 3, 2005, 16–17. To underscore the legitimacy of its policy agenda, then–EPA administrator Michael Leavitt asserted that "the election is a validation of our philosophy and agenda." The quote is from Felicity Barringer and Michael Janofsky, "G.O.P. Plans to Give Environment Rules a Free-Market Tilt," *New York Times*, November 8, 2004, A14.

12. See Daniel A. Mazmanian and Michael E. Kraft, eds., *Toward Sustainable Communities: Transition and Transformations in Environmental Policy* (Cambridge: MIT Press, 1999); and Robert F. Durant, Daniel J. Fiorino, and Rosemary O'Leary, eds., *Environmental Governance Reconsidered: Challenges, Choices, and Opportunities* (Cambridge: MIT Press, 2004).

13. For a general analysis of roles that Congress plays in the U.S. political system, see Roger H. Davidson and Walter J. Oleszek, *Congress and Its Members*, 9th ed. (Washington, D.C.: CQ Press, 2002).

14. Neil A. Lewis, "Democrats on Senate Panel Pummel Judicial Nominee," *New York Times*, March 2, 2005, A18.

15. Kraft, "Congress and Environmental Policy."

16. Davidson and Oleszek, *Congress and Its Members*. See also Gary C. Jacobson, *The Politics of Congressional Elections*, 6th ed. (New York: Pearson Longman, 2004).

17. Carl Hulse, "Consensus on Energy Bill Arose One Project at a Time," *New York Times*, November 19, 2003, A14.

18. Richard E. Cohen, *Washington at Work: Back Rooms and Clean Air*, 2nd ed. (New York: Macmillan, 1995); Gary C. Bryner, *Blue Skies, Green Politics: The Clean Air Act of 1990*, 2nd ed. (Washington, D.C.: CQ Press, 1996).

19. For a general discussion of the effects of programs that continue without formal reauthorization, see David Baumann, "Government on Autopilot," *National Journal*, March 13, 1999, 688–692.

20. For example, see Alex Wayne and Bill Swindell, "Capitol Hill Gridlock Leaves Programs in Limbo," *CQ Weekly*, December 4, 2004, 2834–2860. The phenomenon, of course, affects many other policy areas, not just the environment. One of the few scholarly analyses of the subject is Sarah A. Binder, *Stalemate: Causes and Consequences of Legislative Gridlock* (Washington, D.C.: Brookings Institution Press, 2003).

21. See Charles R. Shipan and William R. Lowry, "Environmental Policy and Party Divergence in Congress," *Political Research Quarterly* 54 (June 2001): 245–263.

22. League of Conservation Voters (LCV), "National Environmental Scorecard" (Washington, D.C.: LCV, November 2004). The scores are available at the league's Web site (www.lcv.org).

23. See, for example, Robin Toner, "Good-Will Reserves Run Low for Social Security Talks," *New York Times,* December 19, 2004, which includes general data on the ideological divide between the parties. Morris Fiorina argues that this polarization does not extend to the general electorate. That is, American society is not polarized even if party activists and members of Congress are. See Fiorina (with Samuel J. Abrams and Jeremy C. Pope), *Culture War? The Myth of a Polarized America* (New York: Longman, 2005).

24. See Evan J. Ringquist and Carl Dasse, "Lies, Damned Lies, and Campaign Promises? Environmental Legislation in the 105th Congress," *Social Science Quarterly* 85 (June 2004): 400–419. The quotation is from p. 417.

25. Jeffrey M. Berry, *The Interest Group Society,* 3rd ed. (New York: Longman, 1997), chap. 2. On the general influence of business groups on the environment, see Sheldon Kamieniecki, *Corporate America and Environmental Policy: How Much Does Business Get Its Way?* (Palo Alto, Calif.: Stanford University Press, 2005); and Michael E. Kraft and Sheldon Kamieniecki, eds., *Business and Environmental Policy* (Cambridge: MIT Press, forthcoming).

26. Kriz, "Out of the Loop." On the lobbying activities of environmental groups, see Robert J. Duffy, *The Green Agenda in American Politics: New Strategies for the Twenty-First Century* (Lawrence: University Press of Kansas, 2003).

27. Christopher J. Bosso, *Environment, Inc.: From Grassroots to Beltway* (Lawrence: University Press of Kansas, 2005), 134.

28. Schickler and Pearson, "The House Leadership in an Era of Partisan Warfare."

29. See National Academy of Public Administration (NAPA), *Environment.gov: Transforming Environmental Protection for the 21st Century* (Washington, D.C.: NAPA, 2000); Mazmanian and Kraft, *Toward Sustainable Communities*; and Durant, Fiorino, and O'Leary, *Environmental Governance Reconsidered.*

30. Mary Etta Cook and Roger H. Davidson, "Deferral Politics: Congressional Decision Making on Environmental Issues in the 1980s," in *Public Policy and the Natural Environment,* ed. Helen M. Ingram and R. Kenneth Godwin (Greenwich, Conn.: JAI, 1985). See also Norman J. Vig and Michael E. Kraft, eds., *Environmental Policy in the 1980s: Reagan's New Agenda* (Washington, D.C.: CQ Press, 1984).

31. Joseph A. Davis, "Environment/Energy," *1988 Congressional Quarterly Almanac* (Washington, D.C.: Congressional Quarterly, 1989), 137.

32. For a fuller discussion of the gridlock over clean air legislation, see Bryner, *Blue Skies, Green Politics.*

33. Rhodes Cook, "Rare Combination of Forces May Make History of '94," *Congressional Quarterly Weekly Report,* April 15, 1995, 1076–1081.

34. Katharine Q. Seelye, "Files Show How Gingrich Laid a Grand G.O.P. Plan," *New York Times,* December 3, 1995, 1, 16. See also John B. Bader, "The Contract with America: Origins and Assessments," in *Congress Reconsidered,* 6th ed., ed. Lawrence C. Dodd and Bruce I. Oppenheimer (Washington, D.C.: CQ Press, 1997).

35. Everett Carll Ladd, "The 1994 Congressional Elections: The Postindustrial Realignment Continues," *Political Science Quarterly* 110 (spring 1995): 1–23; Alfred J. Tuchfarber et al., "The Republican Tidal Wave of 1994: Testing Hypotheses about Realignment, Restructuring, and Rebellion," *PS: Political Science and Politics* 28 (December 1995): 689–696.

36. Allan Freedman, "GOP's Secret Weapon against Regulations: Finesse," *CQ Weekly,* September 5, 1998, 2314–2320; Charles Pope, "Environmental Bills Hitch a Ride through the Legislative Gantlet," *CQ Weekly,* April 4, 1998, 872–875.

37. See J. Clarence Davies and Jan Mazurek, *Pollution Control in the United States: Evaluating the System* (Washington, D.C.: Resources for the Future, 1998); and Durant, Fiorino, and O'Leary, *Environmental Governance Reconsidered.*

38. John H. Cushman Jr., "House Passes Bill That Would Limit Many Regulations," *New York Times,* March 4, 1995, 1, 8; Tom Kenworthy, "Letting the Truth Fall Where It May," *Washington Post National Weekly Edition,* March 27–April 2, 1995, 31.

39. The trend has been documented exhaustively by both environmental groups and journalists. See, for example, the Natural Resources Defense Council's "Rewriting the Rules (2005 Special Edition): The Bush Administration's First Term Environmental Record, January 2005, www.nrdc.org/legislation/rollbacks/rollbacksinx.asp; Bruce Barcott, "Changing All the Rules," *New York Times Magazine*, April 4, 2004, 39–44, 66, 73, 76–77; and Felicity Barringer, "Bush Record: New Priorities in Environment," *New York Times*, September 14, 2004, 1, A18.

40. Quoted in Bob Herbert, "Health and Safety Wars," *New York Times*, July 10, 1995, A11.

41. John H. Cushman Jr., "G.O.P.'s Plan for Environment Is Facing a Big Test in Congress," *New York Times*, July 17, 1995, 1, A9.

42. White House press release, "Defending the Environment and Public Health against the Latest Wave of Republican Riders" (Washington, D.C.: White House, June 9, 2000).

43. Pope, "Environmental Bills Hitch a Ride."

44. Andrew Revkin, "Law Revises Standards for Scientific Study," *New York Times*, March 21, 2002, A24.

45. Susan Zakin, "Riders from Hell," *Amicus Journal* (spring 2001): 20–22.

46. Carroll J. Doherty and the staff of *CQ Weekly*, "Congress Compiles a Modest Record in a Session Sidetracked by Scandal: Appropriations," *CQ Weekly*, November 14, 1998, 3086–3087 and 3090–3091.

47. Special report on the Bush budget, *CQ Weekly*, April 14, 2001, 840–841.

48. Adriel Bettelheim, "VA-HUD Spending Bill Clears after Deal on Drinking Water, Drug-Related Crimes," *CQ Weekly*, November 10, 2001, 2678–2680.

49. Details of the budgetary battles can be followed through coverage by *CQ Weekly*. The president's budget proposals can be found at the Web site for the Office of Management and Budget (www.omb.gov), and commentary on it by environmental groups can be seen in reports by the NRDC, among others. See NRDC's special report of its "Legislative Watch" on legislative and budgetary actions of the 108th Congress issued in December 2004, and available at www.nrdc.org.

50. David Hosansky, "Rewrite of Laws on Pesticides on Way to President's Desk," *Congressional Quarterly Weekly Report*, July 27, 1996, 2101–2103; Hosansky, "Provisions: Pesticide, Food Safety Law," *Congressional Quarterly Weekly Report*, September 7, 1996, 2546–2550.

51. David Hosansky, "Drinking Water Bill Clears; Clinton Expected to Sign," *Congressional Quarterly Weekly Report*, August 3, 1996, 2179–2180; Allan Freedman, "Provisions: Safe Drinking Water Act Amendments," *Congressional Quarterly Weekly Report*, September 14, 1996, 2622–2627.

52. Alan K. Ota, "What the Highway Bill Does," *CQ Weekly*, July 11, 1998, 1892–1898.

53. Rebecca Adams, "Pressure from White House and Hastert Pries Brownfields Bill from Committee," *CQ Weekly*, September 8, 2001, 2065–2066.

54. Mary Clare Jalonick, "Healthy Forests Initiative Provisions," *CQ Weekly*, January 24, 2004, 246–247.

55. Michael Janofsky, "Changes May Be Needed in Superfund, Chief Says," *New York Times*, December 5, 2004, A24. On the drop in program revenues, see Jennifer 8. Lee, "Drop in Budget Slows Superfund Program," *New York Times*, March 9, 2004, A23.

56. Cited in *Science and Environmental Policy Update*, the Ecological Society of America on-line newsletter, April 20, 2001.

57. Mary Clare Jalonick, "Environmental Panels' Chairmen Chip Away at Endangered Species Act, Refocusing Resources and Definitions," *CQ Weekly*, March 27, 2004, 756; Jalonick, "House Panel OKs Softening of Species Act," *CQ Weekly*, July 24, 2004, 1811.

58. Michael Janofsky, "Climate Debate Threatens Republican Clean-Air Bill," *New York Times*, January 27, 2005; Janofsky, "Vote Nearing, Clean Air Bill Prompts Rush of Lobbying," *New York Times*, February 15, 2005, A14.

59. Cited in Juliet Eilperin, "Standoff in Congress Blocks Action on Environmental Bills," *Washington Post,* October 18, 2004, A02.
60. Chuck McCutcheon, "House Passage of Bush Energy Plan Sets Up Clash with Senate," *CQ Weekly,* August 4, 2001, 1915–1917.
61. Rebecca Adams, "Politics Stokes Energy Debate," *CQ Weekly,* January 12, 2002, 109.
62. Ibid., 108.
63. For example, see Mary Clare Jalonick, "Encouraged by GOP Election Sweep, Energy Industry Likes Odds in 109th," *CQ Weekly,* November 13, 2004, 2696–2697.
64. Carl Hulse, "House Votes to Approve Broad Energy Legislation," *New York Times,* April 22, 2005.
65. Mazmanian and Kraft, *Toward Sustainable Communities*; Durant, Fiorino, and O'Leary, *Environmental Governance Reconsidered*; and NAPA, *Environment.gov.*

7

Environmental Policy in the Courts

Rosemary O'Leary

In 1966, on one of her frequent trips to a family cabin in rural upstate New York, Carol Yannacone was shocked to find hundreds of dead fish floating on the surface of Yaphank Lake, where she had spent her summers as a child. After discovering that the county had sprayed the foliage surrounding the lake with DDT to kill mosquitoes immediately prior to the fish kill, Yannacone persuaded her lawyer husband to file suit on her behalf against the county mosquito control commission. The suit requested an injunction to halt the spraying of pesticides containing DDT around the lake.

Although the Yannacones initially were able to win only a one-year injunction, they set into motion a chain of events that would permanently change environmental policy in the courts. It was through this lawsuit that a group of environmentalists and scientists formed the Environmental Defense Fund (EDF), a nonprofit group dedicated to promoting change in environmental policy through legal action. After eight years of protracted litigation, EDF won a court battle against the U.S. Environmental Protection Agency (EPA) that Judge David Bazelon heralded as the beginning of "a new era in the . . . long and fruitful collaboration of administrative agencies and reviewing courts."[1] That judicial decision triggered a permanent suspension of the registration of pesticides containing DDT in the United States.

Fast forward to 2004. By the end of his first term as president, George W. Bush was fully immersed in the concept of environmental policymaking in the courts. Environmental advocates were waging an all-out attack in the courts in an effort to challenge the president's attempted change of environmental policies.

The Southern Utah Wilderness Alliance, for example, had filed suit against the Bush administration alleging that the Bureau of Land Management was not properly managing off-road vehicles on federal lands designated as wilderness study areas. The Bush administration countered that federal courts have no authority to review the Interior Department's management of public lands. By the time the case reached the Supreme Court in 2004, eight former chairs of the President's Council on Environmental Quality, dating back to the Nixon administration, had filed a friend-of-the-court brief backing the environmental groups and arguing that the president's policy was wrong-headed.[2]

At the same time, in response to an EPA rule promulgated by the Bush administration that would exempt hundreds of power plants from upgrading pollution controls when they expand and modernize, New York and several other states filed suit.[3] The rule, the states argued, was illegal because it created a loophole that would allow industrial facilities to circumvent the new source review standards of the Clean Air Act. The U.S. Court of Appeals for the District of Columbia Circuit issued an injunction ordering the EPA not to implement the most significant rollback in rules after finding it might lead to irreversible harm to the environment. The Bush administration defended itself by saying that the new source review standards were designed only for new plants, not for expanded or modernized plants, and that this interpretation of the Clean Air Act was consistent with congressional intent.

These are just two current examples of the role of courts in environmental policymaking. In chapter 1, Michael Kraft and Norman Vig described and analyzed the policymaking process. The courts are often an integral part of this process.

One important aspect of environmental conflicts, however, is that multiple forums exist for decision making. Litigation is by no means the only way to resolve environmental disputes. Most environmental conflicts never reach a court, and an estimated 50 to 90 percent of those that do are settled out of court. Discussion and debate are informal ways of resolving environmental conflict. Enacting legislation is another way to deal with such conflict. Environmental conflict resolution approaches, ranging from collaborative problem solving to mediation, are becoming more common in environmental policy.

The focus of this chapter, however, is environmental policy in the courts. First, a profile of the U.S. court system and a primer on judicial review of agency actions are offered. Next, the focus changes to how courts shape environmental policy, with several in-depth case analyses provided. The chapter concludes with a view to the future.

The Organization and Operation of the U.S. Court System

To understand environmental policy in the courts, a brief profile of the U.S. court system is essential. The United States has a dual court system, with different cases starting both in federal courts and in state or county courts. Keeping in mind that most legal disputes never go to court (they are resolved through one of the informal methods mentioned in the introduction to this chapter), this section describes the organization of the U.S. court system (Figure 7-1).

When legal disputes do go to court, most are resolved in state courts. Many of these disputes are criminal or domestic controversies. They usually start in trial courts and are heard by a judge and sometimes a jury. If the case is lost at the trial court level, appeal to an intermediate court of appeals is possible. At this level, the appeals court usually reviews only questions of law, not fact. If a party to a case is not satisfied with the outcome at the intermediate level, then the party may appeal to the state supreme court. In cases involving federal questions, final appeal to the U.S. Supreme Court is possible, but the Court has wide discretion as to which cases it will review.

Figure 7-1   The Dual Court System

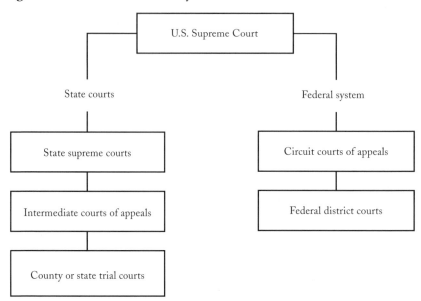

Most of the environmental cases discussed in this chapter began in the federal court system because they concerned interpretations of federal statutes or the Constitution. Cases that begin in the federal court system usually begin in the federal district courts. There are eighty-nine federal district courts staffed by 649 judges. (There are also so-called specialty courts such as the U.S. bankruptcy courts, the U.S. court of appeals for the armed forces, and the U.S. court of federal claims.)

Some statutes, however, provide for appeal of decisions of federal regulatory agencies directly to the federal courts of appeals, rather than through district courts. These cases, coupled with appeals from federal district courts make for a full docket for the federal courts of appeals. There are thirteen federal circuit courts of appeals with 179 judges in total. Here, judges sit in groups of three when deciding cases. When there are conflicting opinions among the lower federal district courts within a circuit, all the judges of the circuit will sit together and hear a case. An unsatisfactory outcome in a circuit court can be appealed to the U.S. Supreme Court. Less than 10 percent of the requests for Supreme Court review usually are granted.

Sources of Law

The decisions of appellate courts are considered precedent. Precedent is judge-made law that guides and informs subsequent court decisions involving similar or analogous situations. But precedent is only one of several sources of environmental law. The major sources of environmental law are as follows:

- Constitutions (federal and state)
- Statutes (federal, state, and local)
- Administrative regulations (promulgated by administrative agencies)
- Treaties (signed by the president and ratified by the Senate)
- Executive orders (proclamations issued by presidents or governors)
- Appellate court decisions

Judicial Review of Agency Actions

One of the pivotal issues in environmental law today is the scope of judicial review of an agency's action. The purpose of judicial review of administrative decision making generally is to assure at least minimum levels of fairness. It has been said that the scope of review for a specific administrative decision may range from 0 to 100 percent, meaning that depending on the issue in question, a reviewing court may have broad or narrow powers to decide a case—or somewhere in between.

When an agency makes a decision, it usually does three things. First, it interprets the law in question. Second, it collects facts concerning a particular situation. Third, it uses its discretionary power to apply the law to the facts. The review by a court of an agency's actions in each of these three steps is very different. (At the same time, it must be acknowledged that separating an agency's actions into three categories can be difficult, as in instances when there are mixed questions of law and fact.)

An agency's *interpretation of the law* usually demands a strong look by a reviewing court. When constitutional issues are of concern, judges will rarely defer to administrative interpretations. However, when an agency's interpretation of its own regulation is at issue, it is said that deference is "even more clearly in order."[4] The general practice is that a court will give less deference to an agency's legal conclusions than to its factual or discretionary decisions.

At the same time, courts have shown deference to administrative interpretations of the law. The premier case that illustrates this point is *Chevron v. NRDC [Natural Resources Defense Council]*,[5] which concerned the EPA's "bubble concept" pursuant to the Clean Air Act. Under the bubble concept, the EPA allows states to adopt a plant-wide definition of the term *stationary source.* Under this definition, an existing plant that contained several pollution-emitting devices could install or modify one piece of equipment without meeting the permit conditions, if the alteration did not increase the total emissions from the plant. This allowed a state to treat all of the pollution-emitting sources within the same industrial group as if they were encased in a single bubble.

Environmentalists sued the EPA, asserting that this definition of stationary source violated the Clean Air Act. In a unanimous decision, the Supreme Court held that the EPA's plant-wide definition was permissible.

The Supreme Court's opinion is now referred to as the *Chevron* doctrine. It holds that when Congress has spoken clearly to the precise question at issue the rule of law demands agency adherence to its intent. However, if Congress has not addressed the matter precisely, then an agency may adopt any reasonable interpretation—regardless of whether a reviewing court may consider some other interpretation more reasonable or sensible. As such, the *Chevron* doctrine is often thought of as making it more difficult for courts to overrule agency interpretations.

An agency's *fact finding* usually demands less scrutiny by reviewing courts than do legal issues. Although an agency's decision may be reversed if it is unwarranted by the facts, courts generally acknowledge that agencies are in a better position to ascertain facts than is a reviewing court.

Judicial review of an agency's *discretionary powers* is usually deferential to a point, while maintaining an important oversight role for the courts. A court usually will make sure the agency has done a careful job of collecting and analyzing information, taking a hard look at the important issues and facts.

Even if a reviewing court decides that the agency correctly understood the law involved and concludes that the agency's view of the facts was reasonable, it may still negate the decision if the agency's activity is found to be "arbitrary, capricious, an abuse of discretion, or otherwise not in accordance with the law."[6] This can involve legal, factual, or discretionary issues. This type of review has been called several things: a rational basis review, an arbitrariness review, and an abuse of discretion review.

How Courts Shape Environmental Policy

As they decide environmental cases to assure minimum levels of fairness, courts shape environmental policy in many ways. First, the courts determine who does or does not have standing, or the right, to sue. Although many environmental statutes give citizens, broadly defined, the right to sue polluters or regulators,[7] procedural hurdles must still be jumped in order to gain access to the courts. Plaintiffs usually must demonstrate injury in fact, which is often not clear-cut and is subject to interpretation by judges. By controlling who may sue, courts affect the environmental policy agenda.

Second, and related to the first power, courts shape environmental policy by deciding which cases are ripe, or ready for review. For a case to be justiciable, an actual controversy must exist. The alleged wrong must be more than merely anticipated. Deciding which cases are ripe and which are not makes the courts powerful gatekeepers.

A third way in which courts shape environmental policy is by their choice of standard of review. Will the court, for example, take a hard look at the actions of public environmental officials in this particular case, or will it defer to the administrative expertise of the agency? Under what conditions will government environmental experts be deemed to have exceeded their legislative or constitutional authority? To what standards will polluters be held?

A fourth way in which courts shape environmental policy is by interpreting environmental laws. Courts interpret statutes, administrative rules and regulations, executive orders, treaties, constitutions, and prior court decisions. Often these laws are ambiguous and vague. Situations may arise that the laws' drafters did not anticipate. Hence, judicial interpretation becomes of paramount importance. And given the precedent-setting nature of court orders, a judicial interpretation made today may determine not only current environmental policy but also that of the future.

A final major way in which courts shape environmental policy is through the remedies they choose. Will the court, for example, order a punitive fine for polluters, or probation? Judges generally have great discretion in their choice of remedy, thus affecting environmental policy.

The Supreme Court, the final arbiter of many precedent-setting environmental cases, shapes environmental policy primarily through the selection of cases it chooses to hear, the limits it places on other branches of government, and the limits it places on the states.[8] Justices' values, ideological backgrounds, and policy preferences at times influence the outcome of environmental court decisions.

A study examining the impact of over two thousand federal court decisions on the EPA's policies and administration found that from an agency-wide perspective, compliance with court orders has become one of the EPA's top priorities, at times overtaking congressional mandates.[9] The courts have dictated which issues get attention at the EPA. In an atmosphere of limited resources, coupled with unrealistic and numerous statutory mandates, the EPA has been forced to make decisions among competing priorities. With few exceptions, court orders have been the winners in this competition. Thus the implications of courts shaping environmental policy are formidable. The cases discussed in the sections that follow paint a vivid portrait of environmental policymaking in the courts.

Standing and Citizen Suits: The Case of Water Pollution

As alluded to earlier in this chapter, to have standing to sue, the Supreme Court consistently has ruled that a party must demonstrate injury in fact, "a concrete and particularized, actual or imminent invasion of a legally protected interest."[10] In federal cases this requirement arises out of the U.S. Constitution's "case or controversy" requirement.[11] The case of *Friends of the Earth, Inc. v. Laidlaw Environmental Services* is a good illustration of both of these requirements.[12]

In 1986 Laidlaw Environmental Services (Laidlaw) bought a hazardous waste incinerator facility in Roebuck, South Carolina, that included a wastewater treatment plant. Soon thereafter the South Carolina Department of Health and Environmental Control (DHEC) granted Laidlaw a National Pollution Discharge Elimination System (NPDES) permit authorizing the company to discharge treated water into the North Tyger River. With the permit came limits on Laidlaw's discharge of several pollutants, including mercury.

Laidlaw repeatedly violated the conditions of its permit, discharging pollutants numerous times into the river. In particular, Laidlaw consistently failed to meet the permit standard for daily average limit on mercury discharges. In response to Laidlaw's illegal activity, on April 10, 1992, a consortium of environmental groups, including Friends of the Earth, Citizens Local Environmental Action Network, and the Sierra Club, sent a letter to Laidlaw notifying the company of its intention to sue. The Clean Water Act allows citizen suits against polluters after a mandatory sixty-day notice period. If the plaintiff is victorious in court, possible remedies include an injunction to halt the polluting activity and payment of actual damages, punitive damages, and attorneys' fees.

In an effort to block the lawsuit by the environmentalists, and figuring that it could negotiate a better deal with the government, Laidlaw's lawyer responded by asking DHEC to file a lawsuit against the company. DHEC agreed to file the lawsuit. Laidlaw's lawyer then wrote the complaint for DHEC and paid the fee for filing the lawsuit in court.

On June 9, 1992, the last day before the environmentalists' sixty-day notice period expired, DHEC and Laidlaw announced a settlement of the lawsuit, which required Laidlaw to pay $100,000 in civil penalties and to make "every effort" to comply with its permit obligations. The environmentalists were livid and continued to pursue their own lawsuit.

On June 12 the environmental consortium filed its citizen suit against Laidlaw, alleging noncompliance with the requirements of the NPDES permit and seeking an injunction to halt the pollution as well as civil penalties. Laidlaw immediately countered, arguing that there was no injury in fact to the environmentalists and that there was no case or controversy as is required by Article III of the U.S. Constitution. Therefore, Laidlaw maintained, the environmentalists lacked standing to sue.

Nearly five years later, on January 22, 1997, a federal district court issued a judgment in favor of the environmentalists and against Laidlaw. Although it found that Laidlaw had enjoyed a total economic benefit of $1,092,581 by violating its NPDES permit, the court concluded that a lesser civil penalty of $405,800 was appropriate, taking into account the judgment's "total deterrent effect." The environmental consortium appealed the decision to the court of appeals, arguing that the penalty was inadequate. In its lawsuit the environmental group cited new evidence that Laidlaw's violation of pollution standards had continued even after its deal with DHEC. Laidlaw also appealed the decision, arguing again that the environmentalists lacked standing to sue.

On July 16, 1998, the U.S. Court of Appeals for the Fourth Circuit issued its judgment, reversing the lower court and finding on behalf of Laidlaw. The case had become moot when Laidlaw came into compliance with its NPDES permit, the court reasoned, and so the environmentalists did not have standing to sue. The court remanded the case to the lower court with instructions to dismiss the action and not to grant the environmentalists' requests for attorneys' fees.

Undaunted, the environmental group appealed to the U.S. Supreme Court. In a 7-2 decision, the Supreme Court found in favor of the environmentalists and against Laidlaw, reversing the court of appeals. The Court reasoned, first, that the environmentalists had standing, given that they had demonstrated that individual members of their groups lived by the plant and the river and were affected by the pollution. Further, the environmental consortium had demonstrated that the civil penalties it sought carried with them a deterrent effect that would most likely address its members' injuries and prevent future injuries.

Second, the Court reasoned that the matter was not moot. There were very real disputed factual matters for the lower courts to grapple with: whether Laidlaw now was truly in compliance with its NPDES permit, whether it was absolutely clear that Laidlaw's permit violations could not reasonably be expected to recur, and the prospect of future Laidlaw violations.

This landmark case illustrates how courts shape environmental policy by determining who has standing pursuant to citizen suit provisions of environmental laws. Without the citizen suit provision of the Clean Water Act, the environmentalists most likely would not have sued Laidlaw and the violations of the statute most likely would have continued. Without a finding by the Supreme Court that the environmentalists had standing, they would not have had the legal authority to sue. This combined citizen suit–standing decision delivered a one-two punch that strengthened the role of citizens and environmentalists in environmental policy.

Ripeness and Standard of Review: The Case of Timber Cutting

The U.S. national forest system is vast. It includes 155 national forests, 20 national grasslands, 8 land utilization projects, and other lands that together occupy nearly 300,000 square miles of land located in forty-four states, Puerto Rico, and the Virgin Islands. To manage those lands the National Forest Service, housed in the U.S. Department of Agriculture, develops land and resource management plans, as mandated by the National Forest Management Act of 1976. In developing the plans the Forest Service must take into account both environmental and commercial goals.

In the late 1980s the Forest Service developed a plan for the Wayne National Forest located in southern Ohio. When the plan was proposed, several environmental groups, including the Sierra Club and the Citizens Council on Conservation and Environmental Control, protested in administrative hearings that the plan was unlawful in part because it allowed below-cost timber sales and so encouraged clear-cutting. Opposing the environmental groups was the Ohio Forestry Association.

When the plan was not changed, the Sierra Club brought suit in federal court against the Forest Service and the secretary of agriculture. Among its requests to the district court, the Sierra Club asked for a declaration that the plan was unlawful because it authorized below-cost timber cutting. The Sierra Club also asked for an injunction to halt below-cost timber harvesting.

In a case full of twists and turns[13] the Supreme Court eventually ruled in favor of the Ohio Forestry Association in the 1998 case *Ohio Forestry Association, Inc. v. Sierra Club*.[14] Among the many arguments cited in its rationale, the Court said that the case was not ripe for review because it concerned abstract disagreements over administrative policies. Immediate judicial intervention would require the Court to second-guess thousands of technical decisions made by scientists and other forestry experts and might hinder the Forest Service's efforts to refine its policies, the Court said. Further, delayed judicial review would not cause significant hardship for the parties.

This case is a good example of how courts shape environmental policy by applying the concepts of standard of review and ripeness. Notable is the Court's reluctance to second-guess the judgments of government scientists and other technical analysts. In a case in which there is no showing of arbitrary or capricious government action, the Court will give great deference to experts in its review. Also notable is the Court's reluctance to review a plan that had not yet been implemented. Because no clear-cutting or timber sales had occurred, there was not yet a case or controversy, and so the case was not ripe for review. Regrettably, however, this means that concrete damage to the environment is needed before the court will act. Though wise from a legal perspective, this approach may be short-sighted from an environmental perspective when applied to future environmental challenges (for example, climate change) for which proactive policy actions are needed now.

Standard of Review: The Case of Air Quality

The Clean Air Act mandates that the EPA administrator promulgate National Ambient Air Quality Standards for each air pollutant for which air quality criteria have been issued. Once a standard has been promulgated, the administrator must review the standard, and the criteria on which it is based, every five years and revise the standard if necessary. On July 18, 1997, the EPA administrator revised the standards for particulate matter and ozone. Because ozone and particulate matter are both nonthreshold pollutants—that is, any amount harms the public health—the EPA set stringent standards that would cost hundreds of millions of dollars to implement nationwide.

The American Trucking Association, as well as other business groups and the states of Michigan, Ohio, and West Virginia, challenged the new standards in the U.S. Court of Appeals for the District of Columbia Circuit and then in the U.S. Supreme Court. Among other things, the plaintiffs argued that the statute that delegated the authority to the EPA to set the standards was unconstitutionally vague. They also argued that the EPA should perform a cost-benefit analysis when setting national air quality standards in order to keep costs in check.

In a unanimous decision, in the case of *Whitman v. American Trucking Association*, the Supreme Court mostly upheld the EPA and its new regulations.[15] The statute, while ambiguous, was not overly vague, wrote the Court, reversing the court of appeals. Furthermore, no cost-benefit analysis was needed. The EPA, based on the information about health effects contained in the technical documents it compiled, is to identify the maximum airborne concentration of a pollutant that the public health can tolerate, decrease the concentration to provide an adequate margin of safety, and set the standard at that level. Nowhere are the costs of achieving such a standard made part of that initial calculation, according to the Court.

Concerning the appropriate standard of review, the Court invoked the rule that if a statute is silent or ambiguous with respect to an issue, then a court must defer to a reasonable interpretation made by the agency administrator. The key words for understanding the concept of standard of review are *ambiguous, reasonable,* and *defer.* The statute must be silent or ambiguous, the agency's actions must be judged by the court to be reasonable, and then the court will defer to the agency.

The key word for understanding the essence of this specific case is *reasonable,* for in one ambiguous instance in this case the Court found the EPA's actions reasonable, whereas in another ambiguous instance in the same case the Court found the EPA's actions unreasonable. Specifically the EPA's actions concerning cost-benefit analysis were found to be reasonable. Contrasted to this, the EPA's interpretation concerning the implementation of the act in another ambiguous section was found to be unreasonable. In the second instance, the EPA read the statute in a way that completely nullified text meant to limit the agency's discretion. This, the Court said, was unlawful.

Once again we have a case that is a clear example of how courts shape environmental policy—here by choosing and applying a standard of review. What is an appropriate standard of review can, and should, change from case to case. In addition, reasonable judges can differ as to their view of what constitutes an appropriate standard of review. Further, once a standard of review is selected, the application of that standard becomes important. Crucial in this case were judgments concerning whether the EPA administrator acted reasonably. Hence, when judges are selected, an examination of their judicial philosophies and predispositions becomes important.

Interpretation of Environmental Laws

Judges shape environmental policy in how they interpret laws. Environmental laws are often broad and vague. Circumstances arise that the drafters of the laws did not foresee. Different stakeholders interpret mandates contrarily. The cases analyzed in this section exemplify how courts shape environmental policy through judicial interpretation of laws.

Interpreting Statutes: The Case of the Endangered Species Act

The Endangered Species Act (ESA) of 1973 contains a variety of protections designed to save from extinction species that the secretary of the interior designates as endangered or threatened.[16] Section 9 of the act makes it unlawful for any person to "take" any endangered or threatened species. *Take* is defined by the law as "harassing, harming, pursuing, hunting, shooting, wounding, killing, trapping, capturing or collecting any of the protected wildlife."[17] In the early 1990s the secretary promulgated a regulation that defined the statute's prohibition on takings to include "significant habitat modification or degradation where it actually kills or injures wildlife."[18]

A group calling itself Sweet Home Chapter of Communities for a Great Oregon filed suit alleging that the secretary of the interior exceeded his authority under the ESA by promulgating that regulation. The plaintiff group comprised small landowners, logging companies, and families dependent on the forest products industries of the Pacific Northwest. They argued that the legislative history of the ESA demonstrated that Congress considered, and rejected, such a broad definition. Further, they argued that the regulation as applied to the habitat of the northern spotted owl and the red-cockaded woodpecker had injured them economically, because there were now vast areas of land that could not be logged. If the secretary wanted to protect the habitat of these endangered species, they maintained, the secretary would have to buy their land.

The district court entered summary judgment for the secretary of the interior, finding that the regulation was a reasonable interpretation of congressional intent.[19] In the U.S. Court of Appeals for the District of Columbia, a divided panel first affirmed the judgment of the lower court. After granting a rehearing, however, the panel reversed the lower court. The confusion, and final decision, centered on how to interpret the word *harm* in the ESA, looking at the totality of the act.

The secretary of the interior appealed to the U.S. Supreme Court. In a 6-3 decision, in the case of *Babbitt v. Sweet Home Chapter of Communities for a Great Oregon,* the Supreme Court reversed the court of appeals and upheld the Department of the Interior's regulation.[20] Examining the legislative history of the ESA, and applying rules of statutory construction, the majority of the Court concluded that the secretary's definition of *harm* was reasonable. Further, the Court concluded that the writing of this technical and science-based regulation involved a complex policy choice. Congress entrusted the secretary with broad discretion in these matters, and the Court expressed a reluctance to substitute its views of wise policy for those of the secretary.

This path-breaking endangered species case demonstrates how courts shape environmental policy by the way they interpret statutes. Different judges at different stages of review in this case interpreted the statutory word *harm* differently. The protection of endangered species hinged on these interpretations. Tied in with this is the important notion of which rules of statutory construction courts choose to apply and how they apply them. Further, this case is another example of how courts are hesitant to substitute their view for the views of experts in scientific and technical matters, absent a showing of arbitrary or capricious action, or obvious error. The final

Supreme Court decision set a precedent that strengthened endangered species policy throughout the United States.

Interpreting Statutes and the Constitution: The Case of Wetlands and Waste Disposal

The Solid Waste Agency of Northern Cook County (SWANCC) is a consortium of twenty-three suburban Chicago cities and counties in Cook County, Illinois, representing 700,000 residents. SWANCC needed a new landfill for nonhazardous solid waste. The Chicago Gravel Company informed SWANCC of the availability of a 533-acre parcel that had been the site of a sand and gravel pit mining operation until 1960. SWANCC purchased the land, which contained several small ponds and gravel pits left over from mining operations.

During the period in which SWANCC was seeking various permits to open the new landfill, the U.S. Army Corps of Engineers initially said it had no jurisdiction over the site. The Corps changed its mind, however, after being informed by the Illinois Nature Preserves Commission that migratory birds were observed on the site. A total of 121 species of birds, including several migratory species, were counted at the proposed project. The parcel also provided breeding habitat for more than fifty species, including a few bird species listed as endangered or threatened under Illinois law.

SWANCC filed for a permit pursuant to Section 404 of the Clean Water Act. The Corps denied the permit in July 1994. SWANCC filed suit. The district court held for the Corps,[21] and the court of appeals affirmed. SWANCC appealed to the U.S. Supreme Court.

In *Solid Waste Agency v. U.S. Army Corps of Engineers,* a 5–4 opinion split along ideological lines, the Supreme Court overruled the lower courts and found in favor of SWANCC. The statutory meaning of the *navigable waters* that the Corps is to protect pursuant to the Clean Water Act cannot be stretched to include rain-filled gravel pits, the Court majority said. Moreover, the regulation of land use is traditionally performed by local governments. To allow an encroachment on such traditional state powers, a clear indication of congressional intent is required. No such intent is manifested either in the statute or in the legislative history of the act, posing grave constitutional concerns, the five justices wrote.

The controversial issue in this case was whether to expand the regulatory powers of the Corps, something that Republican-appointed justices traditionally have been reluctant to do. Without an obvious showing of congressional intent, the conservative majority of the Court (Justices Rehnquist, O'Connor, Scalia, Kennedy, and Thomas) was hesitant to take such action. Acknowledging past cases in which the Court deferred to the interpretation of a statute by a federal agency, the Court said that this case was different because it affected the federal-state balance. "This requirement stems from our prudential desire not to needlessly reach constitutional issues and our assumption that Congress does not casually authorize administrative agencies to interpret a statute to push the limit of congressional authority," they wrote.[22]

The dissent (Justices Stevens, Souter, Ginsburg, and Breyer), drawing on the original intent of the Clean Water Act, countered that a broad statutory interpretation posed no serious constitutional question because the Corps was regulating an intrastate activity (the filling of a pond with landfill waste) that substantially affects interstate commerce. Reasonable people could disagree on the interpretation of the Clean Water Act in this case as well as the application of the Constitution, they said. Neither the statute nor the precedent was clear. If reasonable people could disagree, then deference should be paid to the expert interpretation of the federal agency and the broad intent of the act, which was to protect the environment.

This complex case is in part an example of how justices' values and policy preferences affect environmental policy through court decisions. It demonstrates the importance of Supreme Court appointments and why the stakes are so high. It also helps us understand why so many people are waiting to see if any justices retire soon, and with whom President Bush will replace them.

As of the writing of this chapter, several states (e.g., Wisconsin, South Carolina, Minnesota, California) had passed stricter regulatory standards tightening their wetlands laws in response to the SWANCC case. Contrasted to this, the Bush administration issued a wetlands directive in 2003, also in response to the SWANCC case, that environmental advocates charged has left wetlands even more vulnerable.[23] In addition, a handful of bills seeking to clear up uncertainties created by the court decision have been introduced in Congress.

Interpreting Statutes and the Constitution: Two Cases of Regulatory Takings and Land Use

In 1986, David H. Lucas purchased two vacant oceanfront lots on the Isle of Palms in Charleston County, South Carolina, for $975,000. He intended to build single-family residences on the lots, but in 1988 the South Carolina Legislature enacted the Beachfront Management Act (BMA).[24] In Lucas's case this act prohibited him from constructing any permanent structure (including a dwelling) except for a small deck or walkway on the property. Lucas filed suit in the court of common pleas, asserting that the restrictions on the use of his lots amounted to government taking his property without justly compensating him, a so-called *regulatory taking*. The lower court agreed with Lucas, maintaining that the BMA rendered the land valueless, and awarded him over $1.2 million for the regulatory taking. Upon appeal the Supreme Court of South Carolina reversed the lower court's decision. The judges maintained that the regulation under attack prevented a use seriously harming the public. Consequently, they argued, no regulatory taking occurred.[25]

On June 29, 1992, however, the U.S. Supreme Court, in a 6-3 decision, reversed the holding of the highest court in South Carolina and remanded the case to it for further action.[26] In its decision, the Court articulated several pivotal principles that constitute a test for regulatory takings. First, the justices emphasized that regulations denying a property owner all "economically viable use of his land" require compensation, regardless of the public interest advanced in support of the restraint. As such, even when a regulation addresses or prevents a "harmful or noxious use," government must compensate owners when their property is rendered economically useless to them.

At the same time, however, the Court threw back to the South Carolina courts the issue of whether a taking occurred in Lucas's case. The lower courts had to examine the context of the state's power over the "bundle of rights" Lucas acquired when he took title to his property. Put differently, the pivotal question for all state regulators today is this: Do state environmental regulations merely make explicit what already was implicit in any property title (that is, the right to regulate its use), or are they decisions that come after a person acquires title that were not originally implied? In the latter case, they are takings that governments must compensate.

Equally important in *Lucas* was what the Court did *not* discuss in its narrowly worded opinion. First, the Court did not say that Lucas was entitled to compensation. Rather, it implied that the South Carolina Supreme Court was hasty in concluding that Lucas was not entitled to recompense. Second, the Court did not address the issue of property that is merely diminished in value—a far more common occurrence. Instead, it addressed only the issue of property that was rendered totally valueless. Finally, in pushing the regulatory takings issue back onto the state, the Court did not say that state laws may never change. Indeed, the majority held that "changed circumstances or new knowledge may make what was previously permissible no longer so." Hence, the Court left the door open for some regulation of newly discovered environmental harms after title to a property changes hands. Still, Lucas did prevail. Upon remand the South Carolina Supreme Court reversed its earlier decision and awarded Lucas over $1.5 million.

A few years later, the Supreme Court continued to develop the area of regulatory takings in a local government planning and zoning case that also is having profound effects on environmental policy. In *Dolan v. Tigard* (1994), the owner of a plumbing and electrical supply store applied to the city of Tigard, Oregon, for a permit to redevelop a site.[27] The plaintiff wanted to expand the size of her store and to pave the parking lot.

The city, pursuant to a state-required land use program, had adopted a comprehensive plan, a plan for pedestrian-and-bicycle pathways, and a master drainage plan. As such, the city's planning commission conditioned Dolan's permit on her doing two things. First, she had to dedicate (that is, convey title) to the city the portion of her property lying within a 100-year floodplain so that the city could improve a storm drainage system for the area. Second, she had to dedicate an additional fifteen-foot strip of land adjacent to the floodplain as a pedestrian-and-bicycle pathway. The planning commission argued that its conditions regarding the floodplain were "reasonably related" to the owner's request to intensify use of the site, given its impervious surface. Likewise, the commission claimed that creating the pedestrian-and-bicycle pathway system could lessen or offset the increased traffic congestion that the permit would cause.

In a previous case, *Nollan v. California Coastal Commission* (1987), the Court had ruled that an agency must be prepared to prove in court that a "legitimate state interest" is "substantially advanced" by any regulation affecting property rights.[28] Doing so required agencies to show that an "essential nexus" exists between the "end advanced" (that is, the enunciated purpose of the regulation) and the "condition imposed" by applying the regulation. However, the Court was silent about how judges should interpret these terms.

After reviewing various doctrines that state courts had used to guide such analyses, the Court in *Dolan* enunciated its own test of "rough proportionality." It stated that "[n]o precise mathematical calculation is required, but the city must make some sort of individualized determination that the required dedication is related both in nature and extent to the impact of the proposed development." If there is rough proportionality, then there is no taking. In this instance, the Court decided that the city had not made any such determination and concluded that the city's findings did not show a relationship between the floodplain easement and the owner's proposed new building. Furthermore, the city had failed to quantify precisely how much the pedestrian-and-bicycle pathway would proportionately offset some of the demand generated.

The implications of the Court's doctrine in this case are profound. The facts are hardly unique and represent the types of zoning decisions that local governments make daily. What is more, its logic potentially extends to all local government regulatory activities. Finally, the decision means that the courts can become even more involved than they are already in reviewing and judging the adequacy—the dissent in *Dolan* said the "micromanaging"—of local regulatory decisions.

These and other cases together indicate that with the burden of proof in takings cases now falling on the government, considerable litigation is inevitable. As such, local governments will have to do more individualized analysis of the expected impacts of land use changes and the conditions they impose on them. Not only will this be more costly but it will likely have a chilling effect on regulatory activity at that level. Finally, because no clear guidance exists concerning how to operationalize concepts such as *rough proportionality*, local regulators should expect continuing litigation in different regulatory contexts. Lower and appellate courts will have to begin clarifying this test for them, a decidedly time-, labor-, and uncertainty-intensive exercise.

Consider, for example, what has happened to date in this regard. At any one time, more than two hundred takings cases have been pending in the

U.S. court of federal claims. The majority of these cases on any given day are likely to concern environmental and natural resource regulations. Statutes most affected to date are the Clean Water Act, the Endangered Species Act, and the Wilderness Act. Nor are the stakes miniscule. Environmental advocates charge that if takings suits are successful, the trend will destroy years of hard-fought incremental progress in protecting the environment. Government regulators agree, adding that the trend could devastate already ailing government budgets. This will be true especially if proposed federal legislation is enacted that would take compensation payments from the coffers of the agency that issued such regulations.

In December 2003, for example, the U.S. court of federal claims ordered the federal government to pay California irrigators $26 million for water diverted to protect fish listed under the Endangered Species Act. The case, *Tulare Lake Basin Water Storage District v. United States*,[29] was the first time the government had been ordered to pay a monetary award for a takings claim filed under the Act. Thus regulatory takings cases are being watched closely by all stakeholders. Indeed, several new cases have already been appealed to the Supreme Court. These are excellent examples of how courts help shape environmental policy.

Choice of Remedy

A final way in which courts affect environmental policy is through their choice of remedies. When a recalcitrant polluter is taken to court, the two most common actions ordered by a court are mandatory compliance with environmental law and punitive monetary penalties to deter future violations. In the Clean Water Act case discussed earlier in this chapter, *Friends of the Earth, Inc. v. Laidlaw Environmental Services*, for example, the settlement decree ordered Laidlaw to comply with the Clean Water Act, and the district court assessed punitive monetary penalties.[30] In a case involving criminal violations of environmental law, the penalty might involve jail time or probation. In each of these scenarios, considerable judicial discretion is involved.

The Clean Air Act, the Clean Water Act, the Resource Conservation and Recovery Act, and the Emergency Planning and Community Right-to-Know-Act also allow those who win citizen suits to seek monetary penalties, which go to the U.S. Treasury rather than to the plaintiff. In these circumstances, again, a judge has immense discretion. Most often the only curbs on judges in these circumstances are statutorily set maximum amounts as well as lists of factors that judges must weigh.

A relatively new remedy being used more often in both judicial decrees and administrative orders is a supplemental environmental project (SEP). SEPs are alternative payments in the form of projects or activities. Examples include environmental restoration, environmental education, and the establishment of green space such as parks. The Clean Air Act, for example, contains the following language concerning SEPs:

The court in any action under this subsection. . .shall have discretion to order that such civil penalties, in lieu of being deposited in the [U.S. Treasury Fund], be used in beneficial mitigation projects which are consistent with this chapter and enhance the public health or the environment.[31]

To award SEPs, judges must have the statutory authority to do so or at least be assured that the statute does not forbid them to do so. The vague language of the Clean Water Act, for example, has prompted some judges to be hesitant about awarding SEPs under that statute. Still, judges retain considerable discretion in setting up SEPs.

Although the EPA has included SEPs in its orders in various forms and under various names since the late 1970s, they became more widely accepted in the 1990s. In February 1994, President Clinton issued Executive Order 12898, which directed federal agencies to integrate environmental justice issues into agency policy (see chapter 11). The EPA seized this opportunity by incorporating into many consent decrees SEPs that address environmental challenges in minority and low-income neighborhoods. The EPA's policy on SEPs was finalized in 1998.

An example SEP is the case in which the EPA's Region 1 received an anonymous tip to check out properties of the Massachusetts Highway Department (MHD). There they found nearly 200 barrels of illegally stored hazardous wastes in 149 MHD facilities. The resulting settlement, negotiated in less than a year and approved by a court, included over $20 million in cleanup costs and $5 million in SEPs.[32] A relatively small penalty of $100,000 also was ordered to be paid to federal government coffers. The SEPs undertaken by the MHD made a concrete difference in a way that traditional penalties often do not. They ranged from the development of an environmental education program for MHD personnel and for the public to the cleanup of environmentally contaminated minority neighborhoods throughout Massachusetts.

Recent SEPs have branched into other areas. In 2004, for example, Mobil Exploration and Producing U.S., Inc., paid a $515,000 penalty for illegally releasing produced water and oil into a creek, failing to develop an oil spill prevention plan, and failing to develop a spill response plan. Also part of their agreement with the U.S. Department of Justice was a SEP to extend a water line to provide drinking water to local residents in the vicinity of McElmo Creek, Utah.[33] Also in 2004, but on the state level, Marathon Oil Company not only paid $149,340 to the state of Texas for violating Texas air permit regulations but also implemented a SEP that included the donation of 445 acres of land to the TransPecos Foundation for a nature trail along the Pecos River in Crockett County, Texas.[34] Other entities prosecuted for violating environmental laws that recently have implemented SEPs (in addition to paying fines) are as diverse as Wal-Mart (for violating storm water rules),[35] the city of Monroe, Louisiana (for illegal wastewater discharge),[36] and the Bibb County Board of Commissioners in Georgia (for underground storage tank violations).[37]

These are just a few examples from the hundreds of SEPs ordered annually. Although mandatory compliance with environmental laws and monetary penalties remain the most often court-ordered remedies, the use of SEPs is growing. The EPA now has a special Web site on SEPs[38] and maintains a list of ideas for potential SEPs. The choice of remedy is yet another way in which courts shape environmental policy.

Conclusion: A View to the Future

Judge Bazelon was right: Since 1971, administrative agencies and reviewing courts have collaborated fruitfully, especially in the area of environmental policy. The courts in the United States have become permanent players in environmental policymaking. Supporting this conclusion are dozens of Web sites concerning environmental policy in the courts. The most useful of these sites are listed at the end of this chapter. Although the extent of judicial involvement in environmental cases will ebb and flow over the years, the courts will always be involved in environmental policy to some degree.

As this chapter has demonstrated, courts have a major influence in how environmental laws work in practice. Courts shape environmental policy in many ways. The most significant ways are by determining who has standing to sue, by deciding which cases are ripe for review, by the court's choice of standard of review, by interpreting statutes and the Constitution, by the remedies judges choose, and simply by resolving environmental conflicts.

Environmental court decisions are influenced by the state of the law, such as precedent and rules for interpreting statutes. They are also influenced by the courts' environment, such as mass public opinion, litigants and interest groups, congressional expansion or perhaps narrowing of jurisdiction, and presidential appointments. Environmental court decisions are influenced as well by justices' values: liberal, moderate, conservative, or somewhere in between. In addition, environmental court decisions are affected by group interaction on the bench, with individual justices at times influencing others.

Making predictions concerning environmental policy in the courts during the next decade is risky business, but three trends seem to be emerging. First, some studies indicate a trend of partisan voting tendencies on environmental issues by judges. One study, for example, concluded that conservative judges are part of a trend of antienvironmental judicial activism.[39] The report, written by the Alliance for Justice, Community Rights Counsel, and NRDC, examined federal rulings from 1990 to 2000 and found that a group of highly ideological conservative judges are increasingly striking down environmental protections. A more recent study by the Judicial Accountability Project of the Defenders of Wildlife accused the Bush administration of consistently making arguments in court that were hostile to the National Environmental Policy Act. The study also accuses Republican-appointed judges of being nearly twice as likely as Democrat-appointed judges to accept these hostile arguments. "Despite the existence of several outstanding Republican-appointed jurists," the report concluded, "the reality is that partisanship and ideology now increasingly influence the judicial review of executive branch actions to an unprecedented extent."[40] President Bush is likely to have a major impact on environmental policy in his second term through appointment of more conservative judges to the federal courts, including the Supreme Court.

A second trend concerns less aggressive enforcement of environmental laws by the EPA and the Department of Justice. A report issued in October 2004 by the nonpartisan Environmental Integrity Project,[41] compared the enforcement track record of the first three years of the Bush EPA to the last three years of the Clinton-era EPA. Among the reported conclusions are the following:

- *Decrease in air pollution enforcement.* Nine Clean Air Act lawsuits were filed by the EPA from January 19, 2001, through January 18, 2004, compared with sixty-one in the three years prior to January 19, 2001.
- *Decrease in water pollution enforcement.* Clean Water Act lawsuits declined from fifty-six between 1998 and mid-January 2001 to twenty-two between 2001 and mid-January 2004.
- *Decrease in hazardous waste cases.* Lawsuits for violation of the Resource Conservation and Recovery Act dropped from nineteen to five over the comparable three-year time periods.
- *Decrease in lawsuits against largest energy companies.* Although the Department of Justice has continued to litigate the cases it inherited from the previous administration, it has filed new lawsuits against only three energy companies between January 19, 2001, and January 18, 2004. That represents an approximately 90-percent decline when compared with the twenty-eight lawsuits filed against power companies, oil companies, and pipelines in the three years leading up to January 19, 2001.

In defense of these figures, the Bush administration argued that its focus has been on voluntary compliance and outcome measures—such as the amount of pollution reduced—rather than output measures—such as the number of lawsuits filed or the amount of fines assessed.

A third possible future trend concerns the increased use of environmental conflict resolution (ECR). ECR is effectively group problem solving. Advocates of ECR produce two primary criticisms of litigation as a dispute resolution process for environmental conflicts. First, litigation does not allow for adequate public participation in important environmental decisions. The costs of litigation are often prohibitive to interest groups, especially groups that are small or that represent local interests. The process of litigation is also extremely time consuming, often taking months for cases to come to trial. After accounting for appeals time, the entire litigation process can take years. These time delays inherent in litigation are costly to all of the parties involved. Second, litigation is ineffective for resolving the issues at stake in environmental disputes, ECR advocates charge. Court decisions frequently fail to resolve the basic issues in dispute between the parties. This is because the courts are often limited in their ability to address the substantive dimensions of environmental conflicts and thus render decisions only on procedural grounds.[42] Many of the underlying controversies remain unresolved; hence, more lawsuits often emerge in the future.

Despite these criticisms, the environmental policies that are developed, expanded, narrowed, and clarified in our courts will continue to affect the air we breathe, the water we drink, and the food we eat. The United States is the most litigious country in the world. Clearly environmental policy in the courts—at least in the United States—is here to stay.

Suggested Web Sites

Natural Resources Defense Council (www.nrdc.org) Provides expert analyses of issues and reports that are relevant to ongoing legal decisions.

Environmental Law Institute (www.eli.org) Provides objective, nonpartisan analysis of current environmental law issues.

U.S. Environmental Protection Agency (www.epa.gov/epahome/lawregs.htm) Links to laws, regulations, the U.S. Code, and pending legislation in Congress concerning the EPA.

U.S. Department of Interior (www.doi.gov/non-profit/lawx) Lists laws and regulations for the major agencies within Interior.

U.S. Forest Service (www.fs.fed.us/publications) Useful for laws, regulations, and publications concerning federal forests.

Council for Environmental Quality (www.whitehouse.gov/ceq) Links to important environmental and natural resource agencies, as well as to reports. Especially helpful is the CEQ National Environmental Policy Act (NEPA) link (http://ceq.eh.doe.gov/nepa/nepanet.htm).

Lexis and Westlaw (www.lexis.com; www.westlaw.com) Excellent commercial Web sites for basic materials concerning domestic environmental law.

Notes

1. *Environmental Defense Fund v. Ruckelshaus*, 439 F.2d 584 (1971).
2. *Norton v. Southern Utah Wilderness Alliance*, 124 S.Ct. 2373 (2004).
3. *New York v. EPA*, 2003 U.S. App LEXIS 26520 (December 24, 2003).
4. *Udall v. Tallman*, 308 U.S. 1 (1965).
5. *Chevron v. NRDC*, 467 U.S. 837 (1984).
6. Administrative Procedure Act, Section 706[2][A].
7. Six of the EPA's seven major environmental statutes have citizen suit provisions.
8. See, for example, Lettie Wenner, *The Environmental Decade in Court* (Bloomington: Indiana University Press, 1982).
9. Rosemary O'Leary, *Environmental Change: Federal Courts and the EPA* (Philadelphia: Temple University Press, 1993).
10. For a good discussion of this requirement, see *Lujan, Secretary of the Interior v. Defenders of Wildlife et al.* 504 U.S. 555 (1992).

11. See U.S. Constitution, Article III, Section 2.
12. *Friends of the Earth, Inc. v. Laidlaw Environmental Services,* 890 F.Supp. 470 (1995); 956 F.Supp. 588 (1997); 149 F.3d 303 (1998); 120 S.Ct. 693 (2000).
13. *Sierra Club v. Thomas,* 105 F.3d 248 (1997).
14. *Ohio Forestry Association, Inc. v. Sierra Club,* 523 U.S. 726 (1998).
15. *Whitman v. American Trucking Association,* 531 U.S. 457 (2001).
16. 87 Stat. 884, 16 U.S.C. Section 1531 (1988 ed. and Supp.V).
17. 16 U.S.C. Section 1538 (a)(1).
18. 50 C.F.R. Section 17.3 (1994).
19. *Sweet Home Chapter of Communities for a Great Oregon v. Lujan,* 806 F.Supp. 279 (1992); 1 F.3d 1 (1993);17 F.3d 1463 (1994).
20. *Babbitt v. Sweet Home Chapter of Communities for a Great Oregon,* 515 U.S. 687 (1995).
21. *Solid Waste Agency of Northern Cook County v. United States Army Corps of Engineers,* 998 F.Supp. 946 (1998); 191 F.3d 845 (1999); 536 U.S. 159 (2001).
22. Ibid., at 173.
23. Earthjustice, NRDC, NWF, Sierra Club, *Reckless Abandon,* August 12, 2004, www.earthjustice.org/news/documents/8-04/CWA_Jurisdiction_8-12-04.pdf, March 5, 2005.
24. S.C. Code Ann. (1989) Sections 48-39-10 et seq.
25. *Lucas v. South Carolina Coastal Council,* 304 S.C. 376 (1991).
26. *Lucas v. South Carolina Coastal Council,* 505 U.S. 1003 (1992).
27. *Dolan v. Tigard,* 512 U.S. 374 (1994).
28. *Nollan v. California Coastal Commission,* 483 U.S. 825 (1987).
29. Fed Cl. No. 98-101 (2003).
30. *Friends of the Earth, Inc. v. Laidlaw Environmental Services,* 120 S.Ct. 693 (2000).
31. Clean Air Act, Section 113.
32. *In the Matter of: The Commonwealth of Massachusetts, Massachusetts Highway Department,* EPA Docket No. RCRA-I-94-1071, Consent Agreement and Order, October 3, 1994.
33. *United States v. Mobil Exploration and Producing U.S. Inc.,* D. Utah, No. 2:98-CV-220 (August 3, 2004).
34. *State of Texas v. Marathon Oil Co.* (August 26, 2004).
35. *United States v. Wal-Mart Stores, Inc.,* D.Del., No. 04-301 (May 12, 2004).
36. *United States v. Monroe,* W.D. La., No. 040944 (April 27, 2004).
37. *United States v. Bibb County Board of Commissioners* (July 9, 2004).
38. U.S. Environmental Protection Agency, "Supplemental Environmental Projects," February 10, 2004, www.epa.gov/compliance/civil/programs/seps, June 1, 2005.
39. Environmental Media Services, "Senators, Environmental Groups Respond to Report Finding Pattern of Conservative Judicial Activism," July 18, 2001. Full report available at www.ems.org; press releases available via Ascribe newswire via LEXIS and PR Newswire Assoc. Inc. (www.prnewswire.com).
40. William Snape III and John M. Carter II, "Weakening the National Environmental Policy Act: How the Bush Administration Uses the Judicial System to Weaken Environmental Protections," 2003, www.defenders.org/publications/nepareport.pdf, June 1, 2005.
41. Eric Schaeffer, *Report: EPA Taking 75% Fewer Polluters to Court, Major Polluter Cases Down 90%,* October 12, 2004, www.environmentalintegrity.org/pubs/101204_eip_news_release_final3.doc, June 1, 2005.
42. See Rosemary O'Leary and Lisa Bingham, eds., *The Promise and Performance of Environmental Conflict Resolution* (Washington D.C.: Resources for the Future, 2003).

8

Improving Environmental Regulation at the EPA: The Challenge in Balancing Politics, Policy, and Science

Walter A. Rosenbaum

We will use strong science. Scientific analysis should drive policy. Neither policy nor politics should drive scientific results.

EPA administrator Christine Todd Whitman, statement to Senate Committee on Environment and Public Works, January 17, 2001

Oh, the President is who was elected to run the country. I am a part of, or was a part of his administration. So the President sets overall environmental policy.

EPA administrator Christine Todd Whitman, "Clearing the Air: Christine Todd Whitman on Life in and Outside the EPA," interview on the PBS program *NOW with Bill Moyers,* September 19, 2003

In the cornucopia of the top presidential job appointments there are plums and prunes. One of Washington's most trusted guidebooks for political insiders awards the Environmental Protection Agency (EPA) administrator a prune. "One of the toughest jobs in Washington," it warns.[1] One former EPA administrator compared his job to racing a train to an intersection. Another EPA chief, considered the EPA's most successful and popular leader, complained that the EPA was "Congress' designated whipping boy." If political trouble is the administrator's daily bread, what did Christine Todd Whitman, George W. Bush's newly appointed EPA administrator, think about her job? "I love it," she said emphatically in 2001. "The more time I spend in this job, the more I realize that the issues are so important that it is worth the hassles."[2] She spoke too soon. By June 2003, despite formidable political skills and experience, Whitman was out of a job. She had vastly underestimated the complexity of the EPA's mission and the punishing cross-pressures on her that resulted. The troubles that Whitman encountered at the EPA continued under her successor, former Utah governor Mike Leavitt, who left the EPA less than two years later to become Secretary of Health and Human Services. The Administrator's revolving door suggests that the job rating at George W. Bush's EPA is unlikely to improve.

A Collision of Responsibilities: Presidential Leadership, Congressional Accountability, and "Sound Science"

One matter that hastened Whitman's departure was a conflict over "sound science" at the EPA, a controversy that has become a defining issue in the EPA's turbulent relationship with George W. Bush's administration. Troubles with "sound science" vexed Whitman's tenure from the start. Among the most publicized matters were two controversies inherited from the Clinton administration: what should the regulatory standards be for arsenic in drinking water and for mercury air emissions from electric power plants?

These issues created a collision between several of the many tasks inherited by the EPA and its leadership. As part of the executive branch of the federal government, the EPA and its administrator are expected to be responsive to the president's policy initiatives and to White House political leadership—and the White House had very definite and outspoken opinions about what both standards should be. At the same time, Congress also expects the EPA, as an environmental regulatory agency, to enforce a multitude of scientifically complex environmental laws whose implementation often requires the EPA's staff to use sound scientific information and judgment as a basis for policymaking—for example, when setting the arsenic and mercury standards. Unfortunately for Whitman, environmental and science advocacy groups vigorously opposed Bush's preferred standards as scientifically dubious. Like other EPA administrators, Whitman quickly inherited the tribulations involved in trying to satisfy both White House and congressional expectations concerning what constituted "sound science" in policy implementation. These conflicting expectations accelerated Whitman's exit from Washington. Still, her departure could not banish the discordant "sound science" debate settling about the EPA.

The controversies stirred by the arsenic and mercury standards unfolded differently yet grew from common ground. They originated in the EPA's fundamental regulatory responsibility to integrate science into policymaking and explain especially well the nature of current contention over "sound science" in the EPA's relationship with the Bush White House. However, in a larger and more important perspective, the disputes are embedded in deeper conflicts of expectations and responsibilities inherent in all aspects of the EPA's mission and in the administrator's job. An understanding of these inherent, often dissonant aspects of the EPA's mission is essential to understanding all facets of the EPA's activities and explaining its behavior. Thus interpreting almost any aspect of EPA policymaking necessarily begins with its basic organization and mandated activities.

An Essential and Arduous Mission

Measured by the size of its budget and workforce, the EPA is the federal government's largest regulatory agency. Created by presidential order in 1970, the EPA at the beginning of George W. Bush's second term employed about 18,000 staff with an annual budget in fiscal year 2005 of approximately $8 billion. By any measure, the scope of its responsibilities and the resulting workload are enormous.

A Very Mixed Performance

As demonstrated in chapter 1, the nation's environmental quality has undoubtedly improved, in some cases dramatically, as a consequence of the EPA's regulatory programs. The quality of this achievement is often obscured by impatience with the pace of environmental improvement, or by dissatisfaction with the regulatory costs involved, or by lack of appreciation for the scientific and technical difficulties regulation may entail. Still, the luster dims when the agency's entire regulatory performance is considered. Few EPA programs dependably produce attractive headlines, and bad news is only an official report away. In 2001, for instance, the Government Accountability Office (formerly the General Accounting Office, or GAO) reported the following:

- Water quality information was not available about the condition of more than 90 percent of the nation's ocean shorelines, 80 percent of its river and stream miles and 60 percent of its lake acreage.[3]
- Essential data about human exposure to potentially harmful chemicals, which EPA was required to obtain, were available for only 2 percent of 476 priority chemicals affected by the Toxic Substances Control Act and for only 13 percent of the 243 pesticides of most concern to EPA agricultural chemical regulators.
- Only about 8 percent of the 3,700 solid waste treatment and storage facilities requiring cleanup by the EPA had completed the work by 1999.[4]

Additionally, the EPA's programs are increasingly expensive. Many factors account for the sharply rising regulatory costs, and many programs are not grossly over budget. But the EPA's program costs *seem* to rise relentlessly, and, in politics, appearance often matters as much as reality.

The EPA's Mission: A Dozen Different Directions

Almost every environmental problem seems to end in some manner at the EPA's doorstep. The EPA is wholly or largely responsible for the implementation of thirteen major environmental statutes and portions of several dozen more (Table 8-1). The major laws embrace an extraordinarily large and technically complex set of programs across the

Table 8-1   Major Environmental Laws Administered by the EPA

Statute	Provisions
Toxic Substances Control Act	Requires that EPA be notified of any new chemical prior to its manufacture and authorizes EPA to regulate production, use, or disposal of a chemical.
Federal Insecticide, Fungicide, and Rodenticide Act	Authorizes EPA to register all pesticides and specify the terms and conditions of their use, and to remove unreasonably hazardous pesticides from the marketplace.
Federal Food, Drug, and Cosmetic Act	Authorizes EPA in cooperation with FDA to establish tolerance levels for pesticide residues on food and food products.
Resource Conservation and Recovery Act	Authorizes EPA to identify hazardous wastes and regulate their generation, transportation, treatment, storage, and disposal.
Superfund (Comprehensive Environmental Response, Compensation, and Liability Act)	Requires EPA to designate hazardous substances that can present substantial danger and authorizes the cleanup of sites contaminated with such substances.
Clean Air Act	Authorizes EPA to set emission standards to limit the release of hazardous air pollutants.
Clean Water Act	Requires EPA to establish a list of toxic water pollutants and set standards.
Safe Drinking Water Act	Requires EPA to set drinking water standards to protect public health from hazardous substances.
Marine Protection, Research, and Sanctuaries Act	Regulates ocean dumping of toxic contaminants.
Asbestos School Hazard Act	Authorizes EPA to provide loans and grants to schools with financial need for abatement of severe asbestos hazards.
Asbestos Hazard Emergency Response Act	Requires EPA to establish a comprehensive regulatory framework for controlling asbestos hazards in schools.
Emergency Planning and Community Right-to-Know Act	Requires states to develop programs for responding to hazardous chemical releases and requires industries to report on the presence and release of certain hazardous substances.
Food Quality Protection Act	Creates health-based safety standards for pesticide residues in food and adds special safety standard for children and infants. Requires EPA to create program for endocrine testing of new chemicals. Requires consumer right-to-know information about pesticide residues on food.

Source: Environmental Protection Agency, *Environmental Progress and Challenges: EPA Update* (Washington, D.C.: Environmental Protection Agency, 1988), 113; and author.

whole domain of environmental management. This staggering range of responsibility is one major reason the EPA has been chronically over-worked and repeatedly targeted for sweeping organizational reform for more than twenty years.

Over the years since the EPA's creation, Congress has continued to load the agency with an enlarging agenda of ambitious regulatory programs without much guidance about how to establish priorities among major programs or within them when they compete for scarce resources or administrative attention. The result is an incoherent regulatory agenda, comprising a massive pile of legislative mandates for different regulatory actions, many armed with unachievable deadlines, and leaving the agency without any firm and consistent sense of direction.[5] After a searching study of the EPA's organization and performance in the mid-1990s, the National Academy of Public Administration (NAPA) put the blame largely on Congress:

> The EPA lacks focus, in part, because Congress has passed more than a dozen environmental statutes that drive the agency in a dozen directions, discouraging rational priority-setting or a coherent approach to environmental management. The EPA is sometimes ineffective because, in part, Congress has set impossible deadlines and unrealistic expectations, given the Agency's budget.[6]

In the absence of an orderly mission statement, the EPA must create priorities according to whatever programs have the largest budgets, have the most demanding deadlines, attract the most politically potent constituencies, or excite the greatest congressional attention. A case in point is the Food Quality Protection Act (FQPA), passed by Congress in 1996. One significant portion of the FQPA was a hasty legislative reaction to a surge of national publicity concerning the possible existence of chemicals called 'endocrine disruptors.' Some scientists and environmental organizations asserted that these chemicals, widely distributed in pesticide residues and food products, could be potent human carcinogens or might dangerously damage human and animal reproductive systems. Little is known about these substances, but Congress felt compelled to act. The FQPA ordered the EPA—while continuing its other regulatory responsibilities—to review immediately the relevant scientific literature, identify the chemical compounds that should be examined, create the appropriate testing protocols, and report the results to Congress in two years. Because these tasks required a review of scientific literature involving more than 600,000 chemicals and chemical compounds even before the testing protocols could be developed, the EPA's two-year mandate was a predestined failure.[7] Equally unachievable EPA mandates can be found in most other major environmental measures passed by Congress. The continual appearance of imperious deadlines and other kinds of disruptive micromanagement in legislation entrusted to the EPA exemplifies a chronic tension between Congress and the EPA that severely complicates the agency's mission.

Figure 8-1   EPA Organizational Structure

Administrator
Deputy Administrator

Assistant Administrator for Administration and Resources Management	Assistant Administrator for Air and Radiation	Assistant Administrator for Enforcement and Compliance Assurance
Office of the Chief Financial Officer	Office of General Counsel	Office of Inspector General
Assistant Administrator for International Affairs	Assistant Administrator for Environmental Information	Assistant Administrator for Prevention, Pesticides, and Toxic Substances
Assistant Administrator for Research and Development	Assistant Administrator for Solid Waste and Emergency Response	Assistant Administrator for Water

Region 1 Boston	Region 2 New York	Region 3 Philadelphia	Region 4 Atlanta	Region 5 Chicago
Region 6 Dallas	Region 7 Kansas City	Region 8 Denver	Region 9 San Francisco	Region 10 Seattle

Source: Environmental Protection Agency, "EPA Organizational Structure," www.epa.gov/epahome /organization.htm, February 10, 2005.

A Media-Based Organization

From its beginning, the most important organizational units in the EPA have been its program offices—usually called media offices. These offices are committed to controlling pollution in a specific medium such as air or water, or to dealing with a specific form of pollution such as pesticides or toxics (Figure 8-1). Each office lives with its own statutory support system: legislatively mandated programs, deadlines, criteria for decisions, and, usually, a steel grip on large portions of its office budget, to which it is entitled by the laws it enforces. Thus the Office of Toxic Substances administers the massive Superfund program, follows the mandated statutory procedures and deadlines in the law, and, in fiscal year 2005, claimed $1.3 billion of the EPA budget earmarked for toxic waste site cleanup.

Each of the offices is populated by a variety of professionals: engineers, scientists, statisticians, economists, professional planners, managers, lawyers, and mathematicians. "Along with this expertise," observes Thomas McGarity, "comes an entire professional [worldview] that incorporates attitudes and biases ranging far beyond specialized knowledge and particular facts"—viewpoints shaped by the specific mission of the program office and focused on that mission's tasks.[8] This tenacious media-based design appeals to Congress, environmentalists, pollution control professionals, and many other influential interests, albeit for different reasons. Each media office, in effect, has its own political and professional constituency. Most important, any proposal to change the EPA's organizational design will incite apprehension about the possible damage to existing programs and raises the specter of a bitter political battle over the alternatives.

Creating Regulations: Interpreting the Law

Most of the statutes for which the EPA is responsible require the agency to create regulations—administrative rules having the force of law, as if written by Congress—that define details or procedures for implementing pollution control laws. This delegated authority is the grounding of all the regulation writing through which the EPA translates federal environmental laws into specific and detailed statements defining how the laws will be interpreted and applied to control specific pollutants or polluting activities. Most often, this means creating environmental standards for various hazardous or toxic pollutants and prescribing what technologies or procedures must be used to control or eliminate them.[9]

For example, the Clean Air Act (1970), the foundation of national air quality standards, directs the EPA to set permissible levels of air quality for numerous hazardous and toxic substances—major pollutants such as nitrogen oxides, sulfur oxides, and carbon monoxide—at levels that protect public health and create "an adequate margin of safety for the most sensitive populations" such as infants, the elderly, or those with asthma.[10]

The EPA's professional staff is expected to determine the specific ambient air quality standard for each of these pollutants, to set the permissible emissions levels for these pollutants from each source, and design an enforcement procedure to assure compliance with these standards from each source emitting a regulated pollutant. Congress routinely grants the EPA this delegated authority with each major environmental law assigned to the agency because Congress itself lacks the scientific expertise and resources required to make these complex technical decisions. In the case of the Clean Air Act, for instance, the EPA was largely responsible not only for setting air quality standards for each regulated pollutant but also for identifying which populations should be considered "most sensitive" to specific air pollutants and what "an adequate margin of safety" should be in setting standards.

Writing regulations to implement any environmental legislation is likely to be arduous, prolonged, and often contentious. This is particularly true for environmental regulations based on scientific information and judgment. As we shall observe in the case of the arsenic and mercury emissions standards, needed scientific data may be insufficient, contradictory, or subject to different interpretation.[11] Interests affected by the regulations, such as environmental groups, scientists, corporations, local governments, states, and even other federal agencies, may battle over what scientific evidence is valid or where environmental standards should be set and how they should be enforced. Congress and the White House almost certainly will get involved. All this makes regulatory writing difficult enough without the additional problems created because crucial portions of the laws the EPA is expected to administer may be vague, contradictory, or silent on important matters of interpretation. Thus the EPA's staff may have to navigate the complexities of legislative language with meager interpretive guidance, sure only of certain contention among stakeholders who stand to gain or lose from the agency's eventual interpretation.

An Edgy Congressional Partnership

Congress must necessarily delegate authority to the EPA, but it still treats the agency with almost schizophrenic inconsistency. Congress firmly advocates aggressive environmental protection in all its guises and expects the EPA to enforce vigorously the legislation it creates for that purpose. Legislators have been quick to protect the agency's basic structure and programs from emasculation but unwilling to provide realistic and dependable budget support for the programs they protect. Congressional frustration with the frequent delay in enforcing environmental laws leads to the habitual reliance on extravagant, extraordinarily detailed, and inflexible language in environmental law; to the constant mandating of precise deadlines for completing various programs; and to prescribing in exquisite detail how administrators are to carry out program activities. Impatience with the EPA's often laggard regulatory pace is further exacerbated when, as observed in chapter 6, congressional factions—usually Democrats—suspect that the EPA is deliberately weakening the enforcement of environmental regulations when Republicans control the presidency.

In another perspective, the EPA often seems to Congress to be an unending source of unwelcome political controversy. With the possible exception of the Internal Revenue Service, few other federal agencies have a more legislatively troublesome regulatory mission. Thus, from its inception, the EPA's work has been a matter of intense, unrelenting legislative scrutiny, concern, and criticism. And there are plenty of congressional committees available for the work. The EPA's programs currently fall within the jurisdiction of thirteen congressional committees and thirty-one subcommittees. Probably no other federal agency is exposed to so much congressional oversight. So regularly is the EPA a subject of congressional investigations that until recently Congress's own watchdog agency, the GAO, maintained a large, permanent branch at EPA headquarters. In short, Congress may be admirably supportive of the EPA, but in many respects Congress is the most disruptive presence in the EPA's work life. It has been difficult for the agency to function with predictable effectiveness in such a volatile political climate agitated by tensions inherent in a system of divided governmental institutions and by the highly divisive partisan differences over environmental policy within Congress since 1980.[12]

Data Deficiencies and Ambiguities

The nature of environmental science guarantees technical and political controversy over some of the EPA's scientific determinations. In particular, when the agency is compelled to make a regulatory decision, the relevant scientific data may be fragmentary, inconclusive, or at least contentious.[13] For example, data on the extent of human exposure to more than 1,400 chemicals considered to pose a threat to human health—and thus potentially subject to EPA regulation—is available for less than 8 percent of the chemicals.[14] State water quality reports are commonly haphazard; consequently, only about one-third of all U.S. surface waters have been surveyed for environmental quality.[15] Sometimes the data are conflicting, as often happens with estimates of the cancer risk from indoor exposure to numerous chemicals.

Moreover, a continually rising tide of ecological research often produces new data indicating that prior policy decisions may have been based on inadequate information and must be revised. For instance, twenty-five years after the EPA set its original air pollution standards for airborne particulates, a recognized health problem, the agency had to revise the standard, making it more stringent and compliance much more expensive because ongoing scientific research demonstrated that the earlier standards were based on insufficient data, though they were the best available at the time.

Another abundant source of scientific difficulty is that the effects of many suspected health hazards may not become clearly apparent until decades after their risks are first suspected and frequently long after the EPA may be compelled to make decisions about how they should be regulated. For instance, more than 25 percent of workers with significant workplace exposure to asbestos have died of lung cancer, but the effects of exposure often did not appear for twenty years or more. The human health risk from many newer industrial or commercial substances also may be latent and slow to appear, yet the EPA may have to decide whether they require regulation long before these consequences are manifest. Given these realities, scientific experts themselves can reach conflicting interpretations about the accuracy and policy implications of scientific data involved in regulatory decisions. "Very high quality, peer reviewed, scientific research articles and reports by highly respected research teams can, and often do, reach differing conclusions and results on substantially the same research," observes Bruce Alberts, president of the National Research Council. "This is not a weakness of science, of the scientists performing the research. . . . It is simply characteristic of the initial difficulties often encountered in charting the unknown."[16]

Regulatory Federalism

Chapter 2 illustrated that the essential partnership between the EPA and the state governments, while generally cooperative, is also contentious. States are quick to complain that the EPA is often an intrusive "federal nanny," interfering excessively and inappropriately when states attempt to adjust federal regulations in response to uniquely local conditions. At the same time, states sometimes complain that the EPA is not aggressive enough in enforcing federal environmental regulations when the states are adversely affected by pollution. Most of these complaints are generic, inevitable in an environmental regulatory system grounded on federalism yet continually requiring attention and remediation from the EPA and Congress.

There has also been a fundamental transformation in the competence of the states as environmental regulators over the past several decades—a political sea-change to which both the EPA and Congress have been slow to adjust. As state regulatory experience and competence grows, state pressure has increased on Congress and the EPA to promote more collaboration and less command-and-control in working with the states, to demonstrate greater confidence in state regulatory skill, and, in general, to give the states a more assertive voice in the EPA's management.

A Tale of Two Standards:
The Battle over Arsenic and Mercury Emissions

The EPA's experience with setting environmental standards for mercury air emissions and waterborne arsenic illustrate especially well how contending political forces, differing and complex legislative mandates, competing data interpretations, and delegated authority converge during EPA's routine responsibilities—in this case, using scientific data to formulate and implement essential toxic substance regulations. Moreover, the narrative raises an important question often involved in this regulatory work: When is White House involvement in the EPA's scientific decision making appropriate?

Regulating with "Sound Science"

To regulate arsenic, mercury emissions, or other substances, the EPA is customarily expected to use a complex array of scientific strategies.[17] It must create the relevant database; identify when and where human exposures to the potentially hazardous pollutant may occur; and then determine the appropriate environmental standards, control procedures, and enforcement measures to be adopted.

The EPA has evolved over considerable time a comprehensive organizational structure to promote sound scientific research and its appropriate integration into regulatory policymaking. This structure includes (1) a high-level Science Advisory Board composed of respected, independent scientific experts drawn from the professions, science, and industry who set standards, periodically review scientific research, and advise the EPA administrative leaders on science issues, (2) a Science Policy Council composed of high-level EPA scientific staff who directly advise the administrator, (3) a carefully developed "peer review policy" to ensure that all outside scientific evaluators of research used in the EPA's regulatory work (commonly called peer reviewers) are competent and independent in their judgments, and (4) staff specifically trained to monitor and report on the scientific quality of detailed program research in all of the EPA's program offices such as those regulating air pollution, water pollution, and toxics. In addition to these internal quality controls, the EPA continually receives oversight of its scientific fact finding from numerous committees in both congressional chambers and scrutiny from a multitude of scientific and technical organizations concerned with the professional quality of its work. In reality, most of the EPA's scientific decision making customarily provokes little public scientific or political controversy—no small matter considering that the agency in a typical year may produce more than eight hundred scientific documents reviewed, or scheduled for review, by external and internal experts.

Like other presidents, George W. Bush arrived at the White House with a policy agenda including changes in environmental regulations for which the EPA is responsible. At the time—and, again, like other presidents—Bush also assured the nation after his inauguration that his administration was "strongly supporting science and applying the highest scientific standards in decision-making," at the EPA and elsewhere in the federal government. However, the arsenic issue arrived in the headlines almost as soon as Bush entered the White House and quickly fixed the idea of "sound science" in the firmament of controversies likely to surround Bush and the EPA throughout his White House tenure.

Should the Arsenic Standard Be Changed?

Arsenic is a widespread environmental element, the twelfth most common in the human body. Created by weathering of rocks, fossil fuel combustion, ore smelting, and fabrication and transported mainly by water, long-term exposure to high arsenic levels is associated with increased skin, lung, liver, and bladder cancer risk. Several national surveys of public drinking water systems have found arsenic in 3 to 39 percent of the samples taken, with an average concentration of less than 10 parts per billion (ppb). Arsenic concentrations are generally highest in groundwater but may also reach levels of health concern in surface water. Most people, however, are exposed to arsenic by consumption of seafood.[18]

New EPA administrator Whitman was outspokenly supportive of the president's environmental policy agenda and, within a month of her appointment, announced a plan initiated by the White House to withdraw and restudy a regulatory rule, made during the Clinton administration, that updated a sixty-year-old federal standard limiting arsenic in community drinking water systems from 50 ppb to 10 ppb. The Clinton-era proposal, based on the EPA's delegated authority to revise federal drinking water standards when justified by new scientific evidence, originally would have set the standard at a very stringent 5 ppb but subsequently adopted the higher limit as more reasonable. Environmentalists, many public health authorities, and scientists had long pressured the EPA to revise the historic standard (environmentalists strongly favored the 5 ppb figure), which they considered dangerously high in light of considerable current research. In particular, the newly proposed standard of 10 ppb had been adopted by the World Health Organization, which based its decision partially on recommendations by the National Academy of Sciences, the federal government's most prestigious scientific authority. "Certainly the standard should be less than 50 ppb," Whitman noted in announcing the restudy, "but scientific indicators are unclear as to whether the standard needs to go as low as 10 ppb. . . . I want to be sure that the conclusions about arsenic in the rule are supported by the best available science."[19]

The Political Setting. The arsenic issue was firmly caught in a vortex of colliding political forces. The Clinton administration had declared the 10 ppb standard on January 18, 2001, just days before President Bush assumed office and despite a congressional decision to extend the deadline for the new standard until June 2001. This last-minute decision angered many congressional Republicans, especially those who had long opposed the Clinton standard as too strict and who believed that Clinton and his EPA administrator, Carol Browner, had blatantly maneuvered to deny the incoming Republican administration an opportunity to evaluate the issue itself. Thus congressional Republicans and their allies cheered Whitman's proposal to review the standard, arguing that President Bush, not the Clinton EPA, had followed congressional intentions by insisting that the standard be delayed until the new administration had assumed office and had the chance to review all the relevant scientific evidence.

Congressional Democrats, joined by most environmental spokespersons, public health advocates, and allied scientific interests, were angered by what they suspected would be a rollback in the Clinton standard for which they had long campaigned. The Natural Resources Defense Council (NRDC), an important environmental organization, threatened to draw the federal courts into the fray by suing the EPA to reverse Whitman's decision, which it called "a craven capitulation to the mining industry and other corporate interests at the expense of the health of millions of Americans."[20] (NRDC had already used the courts to compel the Clinton administration to hasten its revised standard.) Critics argued that the Bush administration was catering to the mining industry, which had long criticized the 10 ppb standard, because the industry had contributed more than $5.6 million to the Republican Party during the 2000 presidential campaign. The American Waterworks Association, representing most of the nation's 54,000 municipal water systems, had reluctantly accepted the 10 ppb standard but also pressured Congress to provide financial assistance to offset part of the estimated $1 billion annual cost to upgrade existing water systems.

Mining interests were among the most politically potent of the many organized interests dissatisfied with the Clinton proposal and eager to have it reconsidered. Western mining corporations, whose arsenic wastes would be heavily regulated under the Clinton proposal, were represented by the influential National Mining Association, which charged that the Clinton standard was "a political decision . . . not supported by science." Western miners had long contended that that they did not create significant arsenic wastes and that most arsenic in western ground and surface water originated naturally. Mining companies had earlier been joined in a lawsuit opposing the Clinton standard by the states of Nebraska and New Mexico (whose officials resisted imposition of standards from Washington), by many smaller community water systems (whose managers believed their costs of compliance with the new regulation would be excessive), and by some conservative think tank analysts who rejected the EPA's scientific justification for the strict standard.

Scientific Data and Regulatory Dollars. Critics also assailed the scientific justification for the Clinton proposal, noting especially that the EPA's own Science Advisory Board had been unable to specify a precise safe arsenic threshold, leaving a much wider range of scientifically defensible options than the 10 ppb standard advocated. The Clinton standard was also criticized as "prohibitively expensive," especially for more than three thousand smaller municipal water systems that would have to undertake the most extensive facility upgrading.[21] Opponents of the Clinton standard, citing data from several well-respected Washington think tanks, also asserted that the EPA's calculations had underestimated the real cost of the proposed regulation by more than $20 million and that the same health objectives could be achieved in cheaper ways.[22]

A Science Referee Supports the EPA. The rapidly escalating public controversy resulting from the Bush administration's proposal to reconsider the arsenic standard seemed to surprise the White House and to disconcert the EPA's new leadership. The media attention surrounding the issue threatened to produce a prolonged, and possibly distracting, controversy for the administration when its more important policy priorities lay elsewhere. Moreover, the controversy could thrust the EPA's new administrator into a lengthy, and perhaps politically damaging, conflict with the scientific community at the outset of her tenure while simultaneously creating an internally divisive issue at the EPA. Not least important, the extensive scientific research related to the arsenic standard reviewed by the EPA during the Clinton administration appeared to leave the agency with a range of defensible arsenic standards from which to select. The data did not point conclusively to any single figure; thus the EPA appeared to be well within the limits of its delegated authority in selecting the 10 ppb standard. In short, neither the White House nor the EPA's critics could achieve a strategic advantage by claiming to have *the* single, scientifically defensible number.

Given these circumstances, in March 2001, only weeks after Whitman had announced the EPA's review of the arsenic standard and after consultation with the White House, the controversy took a new turn. The EPA asked the National Research Council (NRC), the federal government's most important scientific research organization, to review the most recent scientific data to ascertain the best current estimate of risks involved with drinking water with arsenic concentrations between 3 and 20 ppb. Although the NRC review committee was not asked to recommend a new standard to the EPA, the committee report seemed to justify a range of possible standards, including the 10 ppb proposed by the Clinton EPA. Moreover, the committee also reported that a link could be established between bladder and lung cancer and exposure to arsenic in drinking water and that the association was stronger than was revealed by available data only two years earlier. The report was widely perceived to validate the Clinton EPA's arsenic standard.[23] Shortly after the NRC report was released, the White House and EPA administrator Whitman announced that the EPA would adopt the standard as it was originally proposed under Clinton.

What Standard for Mercury Emissions?

The arsenic controversy was the opening chapter in a narrative of increasingly acrimonious debate between the Bush administration, environmentalists, and the scientific community over the administration's involvement in scientific decisions related to policymaking throughout the federal government. Despite Whitman's departure in 2003, the EPA remained a main stage for these disputes, as the subsequent conflict over mercury air emissions demonstrates.

The Mercury Emissions Problem. Small amounts of mercury are created naturally in the environment, but most hazardous exposures come from anthropogenic sources, that is, from human activities. The federal government now regulates mercury emissions from medical and municipal waste incinerators, leaving electric power plants, chlorine chemical manufacturing, and iron and steel plants recycling automobile parts as the remaining sources of human exposure to mercury. The major unregulated source is the nation's 1,100 coal-fired electric-generating facilities, which discharge 40 percent of the mercury air emissions in the United States—approximately forty-eight tons yearly. Deposited on the ground, often with rain, mercury commonly migrates to water bodies. It has contaminated an estimated 12 million acres of lakes, estuaries, and wetlands, as well as 437,000 miles of streams, rivers, and coastlines, where it may also cause death or developmental disorders in fish and other wildlife. Forty-four states have issued warnings about consumption of mercury-contaminated fish.[24]

All sides of the mercury issue agree on little more than the imperative to regulate mercury air emissions. Mercury is a potent neurotoxin that is especially dangerous to fetuses and growing children, in whom it can create severe developmental and neurological problems. Americans are exposed to high concentrations of mercury by consuming fish, particularly in the tissue of large predators including shark, swordfish, and tuna, where it appears as methyl mercury.[25]

Conflicting Proposals. In December 2003, EPA administrator Michael Leavitt, who had replaced Whitman, released for the first time publicly the EPA's proposal for the first federal regulations controlling mercury emissions from electric power plants. The proposed new standard represented another Bush administration initiative and departed substantially from an earlier Clinton administration plan, which had never been formally proposed. Like the earlier arsenic controversy, the Bush initiative provoked a critical backlash among environmentalists and their allies, who argued again that the new EPA standard was based on a flawed interpretation of the relevant scientific data, which many critics asserted was deliberate.

Until the late 1990s the EPA considered mercury emissions from electric power plants to be adequately controlled as a "health hazard" under Section 112 of the Clean Air Act. However, in early 2004 the environmental advocacy group Earthjustice initiated a lawsuit compelling the EPA to reclassify mercury as a neurotoxin and, thus, a "hazardous air pollutant" to be regulated by a different provision of the Clean Air Act, Section 111. The EPA imposed more stringent, and much costlier, controls on mercury emissions from electric power plants than would have been required if the emissions had still been classified as a health hazard. In early 2000 the Clinton administration had considered new regulations that the EPA estimated could reduce power plant mercury emissions by as much as 90 percent if, as it hoped, the best available (but most expensive) technological controls were used.[26] These controls could cost the electric power industry between $2 billion and $6 billion annually.[27] With Bush's presidential victory in 2000, however, this initiative was abandoned.

A critical EPA decision following Bush's inauguration was to cite scientific data that, it asserted, demonstrated airborne mercury was *not* a "hazardous air pollutant," thereby significantly weakening and delaying the Clinton administration's earlier regulatory plan. By treating mercury again as a health hazard under the Clean Air Act, the Bush proposal relieved power plants from the requirement to achieve maximum possible mercury control by 2008, which would have been required if the emissions were considered a hazardous air pollutant. Instead, by treating the emissions as simply a health hazard, the Bush plan would not fully implement mercury controls until 2050 and would achieve only an estimated 29-percent reduction in mercury emissions by 2010, although it planned to achieve a 70-percent reduction by 2018. The reclassification also enabled electric power plants to trade mercury emissions rights for several decades (much like sulfur dioxide emissions were already traded to control acid rain under the Clean Air Act) and, in other ways, slowed the implementation of stringent mercury emissions controls throughout the electric power industry.[28]

Spokespersons for the Bush administration asserted their proposal would enable electric utilities to implement mercury emissions controls less expensively and more cost-effectively than the Clinton plan while reducing the total air pollution emissions from all coal-burning electric utilities. Additionally, they cited more than a decade's experience with acid rain emission trading to demonstrate that utilities would have strong incentives to exceed the minimum pollution control standards required for mercury regulation.[29]

The Conflict Evolves. By December 2003 the EPA's proposal was a major public controversy. The agency had already logged more than 540,000 public comments during its review of mercury emission controls, and 60,000 more would arrive the next year—the greatest volume of public response to an air pollution regulation ever recorded. The contention involved a multitude of inherently complex matters—economic, engineering, and technological issues as well as partisan political disputes, regional economic rivalries, and interstate conflicts—all of which drew into the fray associated advocacy groups of national and international importance, as well as partisans of both major political parties. No issue, however, provoked more contention than the reliability of the scientific data cited by the EPA to justify its decision to rewrite the Clinton administration proposals.

A Campaign to Suppress Science? Environmentalists asserted that the White House had flagrantly subverted the EPA's scientific research by creating a scientific justification for the EPA proposal that misstated and misrepresented the relevant scientific information. To support these indictments, critics cited newspaper articles reporting that "EPA veterans say they cannot recall another instance where the agency's technical experts were cut out of developing a major regulatory proposal."[30] The mercury regulations, claimed the critics, confirmed the Bush administration's pervasive intervention in scientific research throughout the federal government. "Mercury is just a particularly vivid example of what's going on in environmental protection and public policy in general," claimed a *New York Times* editorial.[31]

Copied Memos and Flyspecking. Evidence of the Bush administration's influence in shaping the scientific justification for the EPA's proposal was abundant. Several paragraphs of the proposed regulations were nearly identical to those in a memorandum to the White House from a Washington law firm where several former EPA air pollution officials were employed. Additionally, environmental spokespersons pointed to numerous instances in which White House advisors and agencies had "flyspecked" the EPA's scientific report—that is, meticulously edited numerous important and often subtle details—so that the toxic risks associated with mercury exposure appeared less certain. For example:

- An Office of Management and Budget economist apparently altered all references to the confirmed health risks of mercury by eliminating the word *confirmed.*
- The EPA's original statement that "recent published studies have shown an association between methyl mercury exposure and an increased risk of heart attacks and coronary disease in adult men" had been changed to read "It has been hypothesized that there is an asso-

ciation between methyl-mercury exposure and an increased risk of coronary disease; however, this warrants further study as the new studies currently available present conflicting results."
- A staff member of the president's Council on Environmental Quality deleted EPA statements that children born to women with elevated mercury levels were at increased risk of "adverse health effects."[32]

A Matter of Interpretation? Undoubtedly, White House editing of the EPA's original scientific analysis created a much greater element of uncertainty to conclusions about the health effects of mercury exposure. EPA administrator Leavitt and his EPA spokespersons were unapologetic. The scientific data relevant to the mercury exposure, they argued, was subject to differing interpretations even among scientific experts, and the Bush EPA had chosen an interpretation with different policy implications that would ultimately produce more economically efficient and timely pollution control than the Clinton EPA's approach. In short, the science allowed for different regulatory options and the EPA was exercising its inherent authority to interpret the data and to recommend a policy response.

Moreover, although scientific critics of the Bush administration's mercury regulations attracted most of the media attention, other scientists found the EPA's interpretation of the mercury data appropriate: Six of ten members on the National Academy of Sciences panel that prepared the report from which the EPA's own data were taken asserted that the EPA's changes "did not introduce inaccuracies" and that "many of the revisions sharpened scientific points being made and that justification could be made for or against other changes."[33] At the same time, many panel members expressed concern because the White House consistently minimized health risks when there would be disagreement. "What they're saying is not scientifically invalid on its face," observed one panel member. "Partially, they edited for clarity and relevance from a scientific viewpoint. But there appears to be an emphasis on wordsmithing that is not necessarily dictated by the science."[34] In brief, for many experts the controversy appeared to involve different *shadings* and *emphasis* in the way scientific information was translated into policy proposals rather than sharply conflicting sets of data.

From the perspective of most environmentalists and many scientific spokespersons, however, the EPA had failed to protect its scientific decision making from "political interference." These criticisms were reinforced a few months later, when the respected science advocacy group, Union of Concerned Scientists (UCS), issued a widely publicized report, signed by sixty well-know scientists, including twenty Nobel laureates and a former EPA administrator, severely indicting the Bush administration for undermining the integrity of scientific research throughout federal agencies. "There is significant evidence that the scope and scale of the manipulation, suppression and misrepresentation of science by the Bush administration is unprecedented," concluded the UCS.[35]

An Ongoing Controversy. The EPA's proposal for the mercury emissions standard was issued March 15, 2005, but the decision, regardless of its substance, is unlikely to put the conflict over the standard or the argument over interference with EPA science to rest. Regardless of which side prevails in the EPA's eventual mercury emission proposal, the opposition is almost certain to bring the federal courts back into the fray by contesting the EPA's decision for many reasons, predictably including an assertion that the EPA had misinterpreted or misrepresented the scientific data related to the mercury emission standard. In the most significant perspective, however, the mercury emission issue, like the arsenic dispute, involves enduring problems in reconciling good science with the political pressures inherent in the EPA's mission as an environmental regulator.

Different Conclusions, One Continuing Challenge

The arsenic and mercury emissions controversies illustrate clearly the challenge confronting EPA administrators in implementing their legally mandated environmental responsibilities and in making regulatory decisions with scientific competence while navigating conflicting political currents, all of which is necessary if their decisions are to be scientifically grounded *and* practically achievable. The two controversies, however, present contrasting consequences in this effort to manage the volatile interplay of science and politics in the EPA's work.

In the case of the arsenic standard for drinking water, "sound science" appears to have prevailed when the EPA's interpretation of the relevant scientific data and its resulting choice of a regulatory standard were accepted by independent scientific experts, (reluctantly) by the Bush administration and EPA administrator Whitman. However, the EPA staff seemed less able to isolate or to protect its interpretation of the scientific data related to mercury emissions from a politically nuanced restatement created by the White House and more congenial to the president and his newly appointed EPA administrator.

One certain conclusion from these otherwise different episodes, however, is that the EPA will never be able to isolate completely its scientific data or its science decision making from political pressures or political influence. The challenge is to achieve a high standard of "good science" within the constraints imposed by the political realities of environmental regulation.

The Pluralistic Politics of Regulation

Disputes over the EPA's science can easily divert awareness that the EPA's mission is ultimately political. Despite its extensive dependence on science, the EPA is not primarily a scientific research institution or an environmental consultant to the White House but rather a governmental agency responsible for inherently political regulatory decisions heavily dependent on science. Even if the accuracy of the EPA's scientific information itself was seldom contested, the data would still provoke political contention and intervention by a multitude of political interests who will advance competing claims concerning whether the data justify a specific regulatory proposal in which they have a stake.

Thus the EPA's most routine regulatory decisions will always be saturated with political interest, and the agency's regulatory course will always cross unsettled political seas.[36] The EPA implements congressionally mandated policies. Thus its mission, the specific laws it enforces, and its priorities are framed by officials politically accountable for the manner in which they guide the agency and oversee its activities. The EPA's administrative procedures essential to its legislative mandates are constantly scrutinized by hundreds of advocacy groups of all persuasions with a vested interest in its regulatory policies. And, as we noted earlier, the EPA's administrators are vested by law and custom with delegated authority. Where freedom of choice exists in environmental regulation, the play of competing political forces is inevitable.

Other federal bureaucracies as well as state and local governments, all with their own policy agendas, are equally interested parties to EPA's regulatory decision making. For example, immediately following the Bush administration's proposed mercury regulations, the attorneys general of ten states publicly declared the proposals inadequate and requested the substitution of much stricter controls.

Washington's political culture nourishes all sorts of folkways that promote the politicizing of the EPA's regulatory decisions, as well. EPA staff unhappy with the agency's regulatory decision making, regardless of the issue or the presidency, can frequently feed a public controversy by leaking information (as they did in the mercury emission controversy) about conflicting scientific evidence or expert disagreements to a sympathetic outside public official, media reporter, or interested advocacy group. Often the Washington media need no assistance in launching a scientific controversy but create their own through investigative journalism.

An Inevitable Presidential Presence

The president, however, exercises a uniquely intimate and powerful political influence on the EPA because the agency's mission is an expression of executive authority. The EPA is part of the executive branch of government and, thus, is primarily responsible to the president. This relationship involves both the EPA's legal accountability to the president acting in his role of constitutional chief executive and—within broad limits—the agency's responsiveness to the White House policy agenda when the president acts as the head of government. It doesn't matter that the EPA is consequently thrust into frequently fierce controversy over the limits of its legal and political responsibilities to the White House. Nor does it matter that these dual obligations sometimes conflict. That is life at the EPA. That is why administrators rate a prune, not a plum, in some Washington quarters.

Because the White House, regardless of the occupant, will be deeply concerned with what happens at the EPA, it is predictable that the president and his White House staff will be involved with regulatory issues such as the arsenic and mercury standards (see chapter 5). Because the EPA is embedded in the executive branch, presidents also possess many effective constitutional and political means of exerting their influence on the EPA's decision making.[37] These resources include the ability to appoint the EPA's administrator and a multitude of upper- and middle-level managers; to review and modify the agency's proposed budget; to direct the White House Office of Management and Budget, the most important executive management agency; to review the EPA's regulatory and policy initiatives; and much more (see chapter 5).

Inevitably, then, the EPA's administrator and staff continually struggle with balancing conflicting political, scientific, and institutional pressures embedded in the nature of their job. Although the EPA is more often criticized than commended for its work, it is no small accomplishment that it has been able to carry out its regulatory responsibilities with reasonable competence and consistency, often in the most turbulent, unpredictable political settings. Still, the EPA always walks a political tightrope, on which balance is essential and never predictable.

Meeting the Challenge

In light of the insistent political pressures inseparable from its mission, and despite the high-profile disputes described previously, EPA professional staff have been able to maintain a credible level of integrity in their acquisition and interpretation of scientific information. Indeed, the arsenic and mercury issues illustrate that important controversies relating to the integrity of the EPA's science frequently involve how the EPA's political leadership chooses to interpret the data, or how it revises scientific documents prepared by the professional staff, rather than about the quality of the EPA's fundamental science gathering and analysis itself.

Competent scientific decision making depends, however, on continuing the circumstances that sustain it and creating tripwires warning when the integrity of the process may be threatened. These circumstances include the following:

- Ongoing improvement in the EPA's existing organizational structure for acquisition, review, and critical interpretation of scientific data, including, especially, adequate funding.
- Opportunities for the EPA's professional staff to provide publicly available interpretations of scientific findings associated with regulatory proposals free of editing by White House officials or appointees at the EPA.
- Aggressive, independent monitoring of scientific activities by advocacy groups and regulatory stakeholders.

- Oversight by respected scientific societies and research institutions.
- Transparency of scientific procedures to the public and appropriate media.

These are not conclusions for those who like their politics neat, the issues cleanly resolved, and the ambiguities banished. Politics and science have a troublesome and durable affinity in government policymaking. This attraction can never been eliminated, but at best it can be constrained so that political values taint scientific determinations as little as possible. After George W. Bush departs the White House, another president, regardless of party, will undoubtedly be tempted to intervene in EPA regulatory science as well and for reasons that may seem to the White House quite defensible. And there is always a point at which scientific evidence alone cannot resolve regulatory decisions and political determinations have to be made. Thus the EPA's scientific mission will always be arduous and controversial, grounded in an edgy relationship with the White House and other political interests, including Congress. And the EPA's critics themselves may not agree about the correct boundary between science and politics in EPA policymaking or know precisely when the agency's overall performance is balanced properly.

Postscript

In May 2005, Stephen L. Johnson replaced Michael Leavitt as EPA administrator. Johnson, an EPA staff member for twenty-four years, is the first professional scientist and career employee to hold that position. While his appointment was greeted with widespread approval among EPA's diverse political constituency, it remains to be seen whether Johnson will be able to still environmentalist criticism of EPA science policy.

Suggested Web Sites

U.S. Environmental Protection Agency (www.epa.gov) Numerous links exist from this site to all major activities and issues of concern to the EPA, including a very useful document library. Best place to start: "Site Map."

National Academy of Sciences (www.nas.edu) Links to many environmental topics where detailed reports and publications of the Academy are available. Especially useful links are to the "Environment" and "Policy" sections.

Union of Concerned Scientists (www.ucsusa.org) A nationally important, highly respected policy analysis and advocacy organization representing numerous scientific disciplines. A major source for nonpartisan, science-based analysis.

Office of Management and Budget (www.whitehouse.gov/omb) The OMB is the most important White House agency providing administrative staff and management for the president and is a major actor on environmental policy issues. An important source of information and analysis of presidential policy initiatives.

Natural Resources Defense Council (www.nrdc.org) Among the oldest and most influential national environmental advocacy organizations, the NRDC offers valuable analysis of national environmental policy issues from an environmentalist perspective.

Notes

1. John H. Trattner, *The 2000 Prune Book* (Washington, D.C.: Brookings Institution Press, 2000), 250.
2. Raymond Hernandez, "Hitting the Ground Limping," *New York Times,* May 6, 2001, 14NJ.
3. U.S. Government Accountability Office (GAO), *Major Performance and Accountability Changes: Environmental Protection Agency,* Document No. GAO-01-257 (January 2001), 16. See also Environmental Working Group, *Clean Water Report Card* (Washington, D.C.: Friends of the Earth, March 2000).
4. Ibid., 4.
5. Among the literature on the EPA's organizational problems, see, especially, National Academy of Public Administration (NAPA), *Resolving the Paradox of Environmental Protection* (Washington, D.C.: NAPA, 1998); National Commission on the Environment, *Choosing A Sustainable Future* (Washington, D.C.: Island Press, 1993); Marc K. Landy, Marc J. Roberts, and Stephen R. Thomas, *The Environmental Protection Agency: Asking the Wrong Questions from Nixon to Clinton* (New York: Oxford University Press, 1998); and Walter A. Rosenbaum, "The EPA at Risk: Conflicts over Institutional Reform," in *Environmental Policy,* 4th ed., ed. Norman J. Vig and Michael E. Kraft (Washington, D.C.: CQ Press, 1997), 143–167.
6. NAPA, *Setting Priorities, Getting Results: A New Direction for the Environmental Protection Agency* (Washington, D.C.: NAPA, 1995), 8.
7. On endocrine disruptors, see Center for Bioenvironmental Research, Tulane and Xavier Universities, *Environmental Estrogens: What Does the Evidence Mean?* (New Orleans: Center for Bioenvironmental Research, 1996); Center for the Study of Environmental Endocrine Disruptors, *Significant Government Policy Developments* (Washington, D.C.: Center for the Study of Environmental Endocrine Disruptors, 1996); Center for the Study of Environmental Endocrine Disruptors, *Effects: State of Science Paper* (Washington, D.C.: Center for the Study of Environmental Endocrine Disruptors, 1995); and EPA, *Endocrine Disruptor Screening Program Overview,* February 6, 2004, www.epa.gov/scipoly/oscpendo/edspoverview, February 10, 2005.
8. Thomas O. McGarity, "The Internal Structure of EPA Rulemaking," *Law and Contemporary Problems* 54 (autumn 1991): 59.
9. This process, most often in the form of risk analysis, is informatively described in National Research Council, Commission on Life Sciences, Committee on the Institutional Means for Assessment of Risks to Public Health, *Risk Assessment in the Federal Government: Managing the Process* (Washington, D.C.: National Academies Press, 1983), chap. 1.
10. A useful summary of the Clean Air Act and its important subsequent amendments is found in Gary C. Bryner, *Blue Skies, Green Politics: The Clean Air Act of 1990 and Its Implementation,* 2nd ed. (Washington, D.C.: CQ Press, 1995).
11. On problems associated with data interpretation, see National Research Council, *Risk Assessment in the Federal Government,* esp. chap. 1; Walter A. Rosenbaum, "Regulation at Risk: The Controversial Politics and Science of Comparative Risk Assessment," in *Flashpoints in Environmental Policymaking: Controversies in Achieving Sustainability,*

ed. Sheldon Kamieniecki, George A. Gonzalez, and Robert O. Vos (Albany: State University of New York Press, 1997), 31–62.

12. The turbulent history of congressional oversight of the EPA since the mid-1980s is discussed in Richard J. Lazarus, "The Tragedy of Distrust in the Implementation of Federal Environmental Law," *Law and Contemporary Problems* 311 (1991): 315–317; Richard A. Harris and Sidney M. Milkis, *The Politics of Regulatory Change* (New York: Oxford University Press, 1989); Mark J. Landy, Marc J. Roberts, and Stephen R. Thomas, *The Environmental Protection Agency,* chap. 8; Walter A. Rosenbaum, "The EPA at Risk"; Gary Bryner, "Congressional Decisions about Regulatory Reform: The 104th and 105th Congresses," in *Better Environmental Decisions,* ed. Ken Sexton, Alfred A. Marcus, K. William Easter, and Timothy D. Burkhardt (Washington, D.C.: Island Press, 1999), 91–112; Rogelio Garcia, "Federal Regulatory Reform Overview," CRS Issue Brief for Congress, No. IB95035 (May 22, 2001).

13. On problems of data deficiencies and discretionary judgment involved in the EPA's regulatory responsibilities, see National Research Council, *Risk Assessment in the Federal Government,* chap. 1; Walter A. Rosenbaum, "Regulation at Risk," 31–62.

14. GAO, "EPA: Major Challenges and Program Risks," Report No. GAO/OGC 99-17 (January 1999).

15. GAO, "Water Quality: Identification and Remediation of Polluted Waters Impeded by Data Gaps," Report No. GAO/T-RCED 00-88 (February 2000), 5.

16. Letter of Bruce Alberts to the Executive Office of the President on OMB's Proposed Bulletin on Peer Review and Information Quality, www.whitehouse.gov/omb/inforeg/2003iq/115.pdf, December 4, 2004.

17. A useful review of scientific decision making at the EPA is found in Mark P. Powell, *Science at EPA: Information in the Regulatory Process* (Washington, D.C.: Resources for the Future, 1999).

18. For a usefully updated technical and medical analysis of environmental arsenic, see Medical News Today, "New Arsenic Drinking Water Standard May Still Be Toxic," September 26, 2004, www.medicalnewstoday.com/medicalnews.php?newsid=14032, February 10, 2005. Basic environmental and toxicological aspects of arsenic are discussed in National Research Council, Division of Earth and Life Sciences, Board of Environmental Studies and Toxicology, Committee on Toxicology, Subcommittee to Update the 1999 Arsenic in Drinking Water Report, "Summary," in *Arsenic in Drinking Water: 2001 Update* (Washington, D.C.: National Academies Press, 2001).

19. A history of the arsenic in drinking water rule can be found at EPA, "Arsenic in Drinking Water," February 1, 2005, www.epa.gov/safewater/arsenic.html, February 10, 2005.

20. Natural Resources Defense Council, "NRDC Denounces Bush Administration Suspension of Arsenic-in-Drinking-Water Protections," May 22, 2001, www.nrdc.org/media/pressreleases/010522a.asp, December 3, 2004; see also Rachel Massey, "Bush Mandates Arsenic in Your Tap Water," *Rachel's Environment & Health News,* 722 (April 12, 2001), 1.

21. U.S. Water News Online, "EPA Proposes Arsenic Water Limits" June 2000, www.uswaternews.com/archives/arcpolicy/tepapro6.html, December 3, 2004.

22. See, for example, AEI-Brookings Joint Center for Regulatory Study, *Drinking Water Standard for Arsenic* (Washington, D.C.: AEI-Brookings Joint Center for Regulatory Analysis, 2001); see also Jason K. Burnett and Robert W. Hahn, *EPA's Arsenic Rule: The Benefits of the Standard Do Not Justify the Costs* (Washington, D.C.: AEI-Brookings Joint Center for Regulatory Studies); Robert Raucher, "Arsenic Drinking Water Standards," Report No. RSP 2000-18, September 19, 2000, www.mercatus.org/regulatorystudies/article.php?id=762&, February 10, 2005.

23. National Research Council, "Summary."

24. For a comprehensive review of scientific and technical issues associated with mercury emissions, see EPA, "Controlling Power Plant Emissions: Overview,"

www.epa.gov/mercury/control_emissions/, December 4, 2004; see also Mark Clayton, "Mercury Rising," *Christian Science Monitor,* April 29, 2004, 1.

25. Michael Shore, *Out of Control: Close and Close to Home: Mercury Pollution from Power Plants* (Washington, D.C.: Environmental Defense, 2003).

26. For the complete Clinton proposal and its related documents, see EPA, "Electric Utility Steam Generating Units Section 112 Rule Making," June 14, 2004, www.epa.gov/ttn/atw/combust/utiltox/utoxpg.html, December 4, 2004.

27. U.S. Department of Energy, Office of Fossil Energy, "Mercury Emission Control R&D," www.fossil.energy.gov/programs/powersystems/pollutioncontrols/overview_mercurycontrols.html, September 19, 2004; Thomas Brown, William O'Dowd, Robert Reuther, and Dennis Smith, *Control of Mercury Emissions from Coal-Fired Power Plants: A Preliminary Cost Assessment* (Washington, D.C.: U.S. Department of Energy, Federal Technology Center, undated), www.netl.doe.gov/publications/proceedings/98/98ps/ps3b-6.pdf.

28. For a comprehensive analysis of the Bush proposal, see EPA, "National Emission Standards for Hazardous Air Pollutants for Industrial/Commercial/Industrial Boilers and Process Heaters," *Federal Register* 68 (January 13, 2003): 1659–1763; U.S. Energy Information, "Executive Summary," in *Reducing Emission of Sulfur Dioxide, Nitrogen Oxides and Mercury from Electric Power Plants,* October 17, 2001, www.eia.doe .gov/oiaf/servicerpt/mepp/, December 5, 2004.

29. Rachael L. Swarns, "Bush Defends New Environmental Rules," *New York Times,* September 16, 2003, A22; see also Union of Concerned Scientists, "Executive Summary," in *Scientific Integrity in Policymaking: An Investigation into the Bush Administration's Misuse of Science* (Union of Concerned Scientists, 2004).

30. Tom Hamburger and Alan C. Miller, "EPA Let Industry Dictate Policy on Mercury, Some Staffers Say," *Los Angeles Times,* March 3, 2004, 1.

31. Paul Krugman, "Editorial Desk: The Mercury Scandal," *New York Times,* April 6, 2004, A23.

32. Lisa Heinzerling and Rena Steinzor, "Political Intervention: The White House Doctors Mercury Conclusions," April 16, 2004, www.americanprogress.org/site/pp.asp?c=biJRJ8OVF&b=45899, September 16, 2004.

33. Jennifer 8. Lee, "White House Minimized the Risks of Mercury in Proposed Rules, Scientists Say, *New York Times,* April 7, 2004, A16.

34. Ibid.

35. Union of Concerned Scientists, *Scientific Integrity in Policymaking,* 2.

36. For a discussion of the political and economic issues implicit in the EPA's mission, see J. Clarence Davies and Jan Mazurek, *Regulating Pollution: Does the U.S. System Work?* (Washington, D.C.: Resources for the Future, 1997); Paul Portney and Robert N. Stavins, eds., *Public Policies for Environmental Protection,* 2nd ed. (Washington, D.C.: Resources for the Future, 2000); Harris and Milkis, *The Politics of Regulatory Change;* NAPA, *Setting Priorities, Getting Results.*

37. For a useful political and historical review of the president's role in environmental policy making, see Dennis L. Soden, ed., *The Environmental Presidency* (Albany: State University of New York Press, 1999). Discussions of particularly significant environmental presidencies include Barry D. Freedman, *Regulation in the Reagan-Bush Era* (Pittsburgh: University of Pittsburgh Press, 1995); John C. Whitaker, *Striking a Balance: Environmental and Natural Resources Policy in the Nixon-Ford Years* (Washington, D.C.: American Enterprise Institute, 1976); and Norman J. Vig, "Presidential Leadership and the Environment," in *Environmental Policy: New Directions for the Twenty-First Century,* ed. Norman J. Vig and Michael E. Kraft (Washington, D.C.: CQ Press, 2003), 103–125.

9

Economics, Incentives, and Environmental Policy

A. Myrick Freeman III

The environment can be viewed as a resource system that contributes to human welfare in a variety of ways. It provides the basic means of support for all life forms—clean air, clean water, a hospitable climate, and so forth. It is the source of minerals and other raw materials used in the production of food and the goods and services that support modern society's standard of living. The environment can be used for a variety of recreational activities such as hiking, fishing, and observing wildlife. It is also the source of amenities and esthetic pleasure, providing scenic beauty and inspiring our awe at the wonder of nature. Finally, the environment is the place where we deposit the wastes from the economic activities of production and consumption. This latter use and the conversion of natural environments to more intensively managed agricultural ecosystems and to residential and commercial development give rise to today's environmental problems.

The environment is a scarce resource. It cannot provide all the desired quantities of all its services at the same time. Greater use of one type of environmental service usually means that less of some other type of service is available. Thus the use of the environment involves trade-offs. Increasing the life-sustaining or amenity-yielding services it provides may require reducing the use of the environment's waste-receiving capacities or cutting back on development, and vice versa. Economics is about how to manage the activities of people and the ways we use the environment to meet our material needs and wants in the face of scarcity. Environmental protection and pollution control are costly activities. We wish to protect the environment and reduce pollution presumably because the value we place on the environment's life-sustaining and life-enhancing services is greater than the value we place on what we must give up to achieve environmental improvement.

Devoting more of our scarce resources of labor, capital, and so forth to controlling pollution necessarily means that fewer of these resources are available to do other things that we value. Similarly, the protection of a particular environmental resource to preserve amenities or wildlife habitat typically requires reductions in other uses of that resource, such as mining and timber and paper production. The costs of environmental protection are the values of these alternative uses that are forgone and the labor, capital, materials, and energy used up in controlling the flow of wastes to the environment.

Because pollution control and environmental protection are costly, it is in our best interest to be economical in our decisions about environmental protection and improvement. This idea is true in two senses. First, we need to be economical about our objectives for environmental protection. If we are to make the most of our endowment of scarce resources, we should compare what we receive from devoting resources to pollution control and environmental protection with what we give up by taking resources from other uses. We should set higher targets for pollution control only if the results are worth more to us than what we give up by diverting resources from other uses such as producing food, shelter, and comfort. This approach is basically what benefit-cost analysis is about.

Second, whatever pollution control targets are chosen, the means of achieving these targets should minimize the costs of meeting them. It is wasteful to use more resources than is absolutely necessary to achieve pollution control objectives. Yet many environmental protection and pollution control policies are wasteful in just this sense. One of the major contributions of economic analysis to environmental policy is that it can reveal when and how these policies can be made more cost-effective.

In the first section of this chapter I describe how benefit-cost analysis can be used to decide how far to go in the direction of environmental protection. I also discuss recent applications of benefit-cost analysis to environmental policy decisions and contributions that this approach to environmental policymaking might make in the future.

In the second section I describe briefly the basic approach to achieving pollution control objectives that is embodied in the major federal statutes—the Clean Air Act of 1970 and the Clean Water Act of 1972. The third section is devoted to the concept of cost-effectiveness. In the remaining sections I describe and evaluate a variety of economics-based incentive devices (such as pollution taxes, deposit-refund systems, and tradable pollution discharge permits) that encourage pollution control activities by firms and individuals and reduce the overall costs of achieving environmental protection targets. I also discuss possible additional uses of economic incentives in environmental policy.

Benefit-Cost Analysis and Environmental Policy

The basic premise underlying benefit-cost analysis is that the purpose of economic activity is to increase the well-being of the individuals who make up society. If we are to make the most of our scarce resources, we should compare what we receive in the form of increased well-being from pollution control and environmental protection activities with what we give up by taking resources from other uses that also contribute to well-being. We should measure the values of what we gain (the benefits) and what we lose (the costs) in terms of the preferences of those who experience these gains and losses. We should undertake environmental protection and pollution control only if the results are worth more, in terms of individuals' values, than what is given up by diverting resources from other uses. This is the under-lying principle of the economic approach to environmental policy. Benefit-cost analysis is a set of analytical tools designed to measure the net contribution of any public policy to the economic well-being of the members of society.

Although in some respects benefit-cost analysis is nothing more than organized common sense, the term is typically used to describe a more nar-rowly defined, technical economic calculation that attempts to reduce all benefits and costs to a common monetary measure (that is, dollars). It seeks to determine if the aggregate of the gains that accrue to those made better off is greater than the aggregate of losses to those made worse off by the policy choice. The gains and losses are measured in dollars and are defined as the sums of each individual's willingness to pay to receive the gain or to prevent the policy-imposed losses. If the gains exceed the losses, then the policy should be accepted, according to the logic of benefit-cost analysis. Policies under which the aggregate gains outweigh the aggregate costs can be justified on ethical grounds because the gainers could fully compensate the losers with monetary payments and still be better off with the policy. Thus if the compensation were actually made, there would be no losers, only gainers. Whether losers should be compensated is considered to be an ethical ques-tion. In practice, losers are rarely compensated. For most environmental poli-cies, costs are typically widely distributed across the population in the form of higher prices for products.[1]

Setting Environmental Standards

The setting of environmental quality standards illustrates some of the issues involved in using benefit-cost analysis for environmental policy-making. An environmental quality standard is a legally established minimum level of cleanliness or maximum level of pollution in some part of the envi-ronment. Once established, a standard can form the basis for enforcement actions against polluters whose discharges cause the standard to be violated. Benefit-cost analysis provides a basis for determining what the standard should be. In general, economic principles require that each good be pro-vided at the level for which the marginal willingness to pay for it (the max-imum amount that an individual would be willing to give up to get one more unit of the good) is just equal to the additional cost of providing one more unit of the good (its marginal cost).[2]

Consider an environment that is badly polluted by industrial activity. Suppose that successive one-step improvements are made in some measure of environmental quality. For the first step, individuals' marginal willing-nesses to pay for a small improvement are likely to be high. The cost of the first step is likely to be low. The difference between them is the net benefit of the first step. Further increases in cleanliness bring further net benefits as long as the aggregate marginal willingness to pay is greater than the mar-ginal cost. But as the environment gets cleaner, the willingness to pay for additional units of cleanliness typically decreases, at least beyond some point, whereas the marginal cost of further cleanliness rises. At that point where marginal willingness to pay equals marginal cost, the net benefit of an increase in cleanliness is zero, and the total benefits of environmental improvement are at a maximum. This is the point at which the environmental quality standard should be set, if economic reasoning is followed.

The logic of benefit-cost analysis does not require that those who benefit pay for those benefits or that those who ultimately bear the cost of meeting a standard be compensated for those costs. Whether compensation should be paid is considered to be a question of equity or distributive fairness. Benefit-cost analysis is concerned exclusively with economic efficiency as represented by the aggregate of benefits and costs. If standards are set to maximize the net benefits, then the gainers could fully compensate the losers and still come out ahead. But when beneficiaries do not compensate losers, political asymmetry occurs. Those who benefit call for ever-stricter standards and more cleanup because they obtain the benefits and bear none of the costs, whereas those who must bear the costs of controlling pollution call for less strict standards. This conflict between the interests of those who benefit from environmental cleanup and those who bear its costs must be resolved through some kind of political process.

An environmental quality standard set according to the benefit-cost rule will almost never call for complete elimination of pollution. Contrast this economic approach to setting standards with what the Clean Air Act says about establishing air quality standards for conventional air pollutants such as fine particles and ozone. Section 109 requires that these standards be set so as to "protect human health" with "an adequate margin of safety." If even the smallest amount of pollution increases the risk of disease or death at least for some sensitive individuals (as is apparently the case for ozone and fine particles), a literal reading of the Clean Air Act would require the complete cleanup of these pollutants. But this may result in marginal costs that are substantially greater than society's willingness to pay for additional cleanup.

Uses of Benefit-Cost Analysis

Benefit-cost analysis is often used to evaluate proposed regulations and new environmental policies to determine whether they are likely to increase economic welfare.[3] The use of benefit-cost analysis is presently authorized by the Toxic Substances Control Act of 1976; the Federal Insecticide, Fungicide, and Rodenticide Act (FIFRA) of 1972; and the 1996 amendments to the Safe Drinking Water Act. But its use is effectively precluded for setting standards under the Clean Air Act and the Clean Water Act. Since the mid-1970s the U.S. Environmental Protection Agency (EPA) has been conducting benefit-cost analyses of major regulations even though in many cases it could not base decisions on the results. These analyses are major components of the regulatory impact assessments required under a series of executive orders issued by recent presidents from Jimmy Carter to George W. Bush.

In a comprehensive study of the economic analyses of proposed federal regulations, Robert Hahn found that over half of the 106 rules promulgated between 1981 and mid-1996 had estimated costs that exceeded estimated benefits. This was true even for rules promulgated under the three acts allowing balancing of benefits and costs.[4] This finding suggests that the criterion of economic efficiency for environmental policy has not been a predominant concern under either Republican or Democratic administrations.

Among the winners in terms of net economic benefits are the removal of lead from gasoline, the control of particulate matter air pollution, the reduction of the amount of lead in drinking water, and the setting of standards for some volatile organic compounds in drinking water. These winners all involve threats to human health, especially mortality, and widespread exposures of people. The environmental rules that appear to be losers in terms of net economic benefits include mobile source air pollution control; much of the control of discharges into the nation's waterways, with the exception of some lakes and rivers that were especially polluted; and many of the regulations, standards, and cleanup decisions taken under FIFRA, the Toxic Substances Control Act, the Safe Drinking Water Act, and Superfund.[5]

Congress in 2000 required that the Office of Information and Regulatory Affairs (OIRA), the branch of the Office of Management and Budget charged with overseeing regulatory decisions of federal agencies, report annually its estimates of the benefits and costs of federal regulations. The most recent report (2003) showed total annual benefits of regulations issued by EPA of $120–190 billion, whereas total annual costs were in the range of $23–27 billion. This result was dominated by the very high benefits relative to costs of rules regulating air emissions and ambient concentrations of fine particle air pollution. Regulations affecting water pollution had costs that were on average greater than benefits by about three to one.[6]

Benefit-cost analysis can also be used after the fact to evaluate existing policies by estimating the benefits realized and comparing them with the costs of the policies. In 1990 Congress directed the EPA to carry out a retrospective benefit-cost assessment of the Clean Air Act. The analysis revealed benefits that exceed costs by as much as perhaps a factor of forty. Almost all of the benefits came from the control of particles and airborne lead.[7] However, a similar analysis of the benefits of the Clean Water Act found benefits that were a fraction of the best available estimates of the costs of the act.[8] When these kinds of analyses show that costs have exceeded benefits, it may be possible to reduce the costs through more cost-effective policies (more on this below). But excessive costs may also indicate that the targets or environmental standards need to be reconsidered.

Benefit-Cost Analysis: An Assessment

A major question is whether the state of the art of measurement is sufficiently well developed to provide reliable estimates of benefits and costs. The physical and biological mechanisms by which environmental changes affect people are often not well understood. And the economic values people place on environmental changes can seldom be measured with precision. As a consequence, the results of a benefit-cost analysis are usually (or at least should be) expressed as most likely values with ranges of uncertainty. But even with wide ranges of uncertainty, information on the ranges of benefits and costs should be useful for decision makers who are concerned with how proposed policies would affect people's welfare.

Another question concerns the political context in which analyses of benefits and costs are carried out and used.[9] The typical textbook discussions of the use of benefit-cost analysis implicitly assume a disinterested decision maker who has access to all the relevant information on the positive and negative effects of a policy and who makes choices based on this information so as to maximize social welfare. The real world, however, seldom corresponds to the textbook model. First, decision makers seldom have perfect information on benefits and costs. But more important, environmental policy decisions are usually made in a highly politicized setting in which the potential gainers and losers attempt to influence the decision.

Some observers contend that the benefits of environmental regulation are difficult to quantify and value compared with the costs. They point out that in such a setting the businesses that would bear the costs will be better organized to represent their views. If this is correct, then relying on benefit-cost analysis as the basis for setting environmental standards would appear to justify less environmental protection and pollution control than is really desirable. There are three responses to this argument.

First, this is not so much an argument for rejecting benefit-cost analysis of choices as it is for electing and appointing decision makers who are more capable and for trying to achieve greater objectivity and balance of conflicting views. Second, the argument is based on, at best, an oversimplified view of the process. To be sure, proindustry groups will present information that minimizes estimates of benefits and maximizes estimates of costs. However, policy analysts within government seldom accept industry estimates at face value and, for major regulations, usually prepare their own estimates of benefits and costs or have them prepared by consultants. At the EPA, the benefit-cost analyses of all significant rules are now subject to rigorous peer review by panels of outside experts. (However, see chapters 8 and 10 for discussions of the Bush administration's efforts to introduce political factors into the process of obtaining scientific advice relating to policy questions.)

Finally, it is not true that benefit-cost analysis is always biased against environmental protection. For many years, funding decisions regarding federal water resource development projects were based nominally on benefit-cost analyses. But these analyses used techniques that systematically overstated the benefits of development, understated the economic costs, and ignored the environmental costs of building dams, diverting water for irrigation, and so forth. As a consequence, a number of economically wasteful and environmentally damaging projects were undertaken. Competent and objective benefit-cost analyses clearly demonstrated that many of these projects were uneconomical even without taking into account their environmental costs. More recently several major rules governing the emissions of air and water pollutants have been adopted after economic analyses showed that their benefits exceeded their costs.[10]

The Future of Benefit-Cost Analysis

The United States has made substantial progress in controlling some forms of pollution since the 1970s. Examples include emissions of soot and dust from coal-burning power plants and municipal trash incinerators and the discharge of sewage and other organic wastes into rivers. Such progress was made partly because these problems were highly visible and the costs of cleaning them up were relatively low. But dealing with the pollution problems of the present and future is likely to be much more costly. Thus it will be important to try to estimate the benefits of cleanup.

The twin questions of whether to conduct benefit-cost analyses of environmental policies and how decision makers should use the results were brought to center stage after the Republicans gained control of Congress in 1995. The Republicans pushed for several bills that would have required that all new and existing major regulations be subjected to a benefit-cost analysis and that only those regulations that passed a benefit-cost test could be approved or retained. Although most economists lauded the principles expressed in these proposals,[11] many had serious reservations about some of their specific features. None of these bills was enacted.

In 2001 George W. Bush signaled his intent to give a more prominent role to benefit-cost analysis in regulatory decision making by appointing John Graham to head OIRA. Graham is a well-known advocate of the use of benefit-cost analysis in policymaking. Graham has increased the role of OIRA in reviewing and approving the economic analyses prepared by regulatory agencies such as the EPA. But he has also begun the practice of writing so-called prompt letters to agencies suggesting that they consider promulgating regulations when it appears that benefits substantially exceed costs (see chapter 10).[12]

For some kinds of problems—for example, how far to go in controlling greenhouse gas emissions—analysis of the benefits and costs is made difficult by the scientific uncertainties concerning the physical and ecological consequences of certain policies. Nevertheless, some effort to describe and quantify benefits and costs may provide useful information to decision makers as they consider alternative policies. Estimating the benefits and costs of different proposals for controlling greenhouse gas emissions is made difficult by the problems of projecting the following variables for up to one to two centuries into the future: global population; the rate of technological improvement in energy conversion, conservation, and emissions control; and how future populations will adapt to changing climate. In a comprehensive integrated assessment of alternative policies, William Nordhaus and Joseph Boyer estimated the global benefits and costs for several alternative proposals. They found that a "modest" program of emissions reductions is justified on economic grounds but that more aggressive proposals to meet specific emissions reductions targets (for example, those of the Kyoto Protocol), to stabilize emissions at some rate, or to stabilize global average temperatures at 1.5 or 2.5 degrees Celsius above preindustrial levels would have costs substantially in excess of benefits.[13] However, as the authors acknowledged, these estimates contain substantial uncertainties, and the possibility of catastrophic changes and nonlinear climate responses cannot be ruled out. Further, the authors did not consider that controlling carbon dioxide emissions from coal-burning power plants (a major source) will yield substantial benefits in the near term from reduced emissions of particulate matter and other conventional pollutants.

Direct Regulation in Federal Environmental Policy

The major provisions of the federal laws controlling air and water pollution embody what is often termed a direct regulation (or command-and-control) approach to achieving the established targets. This direct regulation approach involves placing limits on the allowable discharges of polluting substances from each source, coupled with an administrative and legal system to monitor compliance with these limits and to impose sanctions or penalties for violations.

In this approach the pollution control authority must carry out a series of four steps:

1. Determine the rules and regulations for each source that will achieve the given pollution control targets. The regulations typically establish maximum allowable discharges of polluting substances from each source. They also could require the installation of certain types of pollution control equipment, restrict certain activities, or limit such things as the sulfur content of fuels.
2. Establish penalties or sanctions for noncompliance.
3. Monitor sources so that incidents of noncompliance can be detected. Alternatively the authorities might establish a system of self-reporting with periodic checks and audits of performance.
4. Punish violations. If violations of the regulations are detected, the authorities must use the administrative and legal mechanisms spelled out in the relevant laws to impose penalties or to require changes in the behavior of the sources.[14]

Economists have criticized the direct regulation approach on two grounds. First, the regulations require a pattern of pollution control activities that tends to be excessively costly—in other words, not cost-effective. Second, the incentive structure created for firms and individuals is inappropriate. Because compliance is so costly, there is no positive incentive to control pollution, although there is the negative incentive to avoid penalties. Not only is there no incentive to do better than the regulations require, but also the incentives to comply with the regulations themselves may be too weak to overcome the disincentive of bearing the costs of compliance, resulting in a high rate of noncompliance with the rules.

Efficiency and Cost-Effectiveness

Even if one objects to basing environmental policy on benefit-cost analysis for either philosophical or pragmatic reasons, it still makes good sense to favor cost-effective environmental policies. Cost-effectiveness means the stated environmental quality standards are achieved at the lowest possible total cost. The importance of achieving cost-effective pollution control policies should be self-evident: Cost savings free resources that can be used to produce other goods and services of value to people.

When several sources of pollution exist in the same area, a pollution control policy must include some mechanism for dividing the responsibility for cleanup among the several sources. The direct regulation form of policy typically does this by requiring all sources to clean up by the same percentage. But such a policy will rarely be cost-effective. A pollution control policy is cost-effective only if it allocates the responsibility for cleanup among sources so that the incremental or marginal cost of achieving a one-unit improvement in environmental quality at any location is the same for all sources of pollution. Differences in the marginal costs of improving environmental quality can arise from differences in the marginal cost of treatment or waste reduction across sources; also, discharges from sources at different locations can have different effects on environmental quality.

Suppose that targets for air pollution control have been established by setting an ambient air quality standard for sulfur dioxide. To illustrate the importance of differences in marginal costs of control, suppose that two adjacent factories are emitting sulfur dioxide. A one-ton decrease in emissions gives the same incremental benefit to air quality whether it is achieved by factory A or factory B. Now suppose that to achieve the ambient air quality standard, emissions must be reduced by fifty tons per day. One way to achieve the target is to require each factory to clean up twenty-five tons per day. But suppose that with this allocation of cleanup responsibility, factory A's marginal cost of cleanup is $10 per ton per day, whereas at factory B the marginal cost is only $5 per ton per day. Allowing factory A to reduce its cleanup by one ton per day saves it $10. If factory B is required to clean up an extra ton, total cleanup is the same and the air quality standard is met. And the total cost of pollution control is reduced by $5 per day. Additional savings are possible by continuing to shift cleanup responsibility to B (raising B's marginal cost) and away from A (reducing A's marginal cost). This shifting should continue until B's rising marginal cost of control is made equal to A's now lower marginal cost.

Nothing in the logic or the procedures for setting pollution control requirements for sources ensures that the conditions for cost-minimization will be satisfied. In setting discharge limits, federal and state agencies usually do not consider the marginal cost of control, at least in part because of the difficulties they would have in getting the data. Thus discharge limits are not likely to result in equal marginal costs of reducing discharges across different sources of the same pollutant. One analysis of the marginal cost of removing oxygen-demanding organic material under existing federal water pollution standards found a thirtyfold range of marginal costs within the six industries examined.[15]

Another way to look at the question of cost-effectiveness is to ask how to get the greatest environmental improvement for a given total expenditure on pollution control. The answer is to spend that money on pollution control activities with the highest level of pollution control benefit per dollar spent. For example, if society decides for whatever reason to spend $1 million to control organic forms of water pollution, it should require that the money be spent on industries with the highest pollutant removal per dollar, which is to say, the lowest cost per pound of removal. The study cited in the preceding paragraph shows that spending an extra dollar for controlling organic pollution in a low-cost industry will buy thirty times more pollution removal than spending the same dollar in an industry with high marginal costs.

A number of environmental protection and public health policies are cost-ineffective because of large differences across activities in the marginal costs of control, or in the benefit per dollar spent. For example, a study of the costs of regulating toxic chemicals in the environment and the workplace found that the costs of each life-year-saved varied widely, both across chemicals and for different regulations on the same chemical. The costs of meeting an exposure standard for benzene varied from $76,000 per life-year-saved in rubber and tire factories to $3 million per life-year-saved in coke and coal chemical factories. And the costs of controlling arsenic emissions varied from $74,000 per life-year-saved at copper smelters to $51 million at glass manufacturing plants.[16] These examples show that it would be possible both to lower the compliance cost burden for industry and to increase the number of life-years-saved by somewhat reducing the requirements imposed on the highest-cost factories and placing stricter requirements on those sources with the lowest cost of compliance.

Probably the greatest opportunities for more cost-effective pollution control are in the realm of the conventional pollutants of air and water. The problem of cost-effectiveness has stimulated many empirical studies comparing the costs of direct regulation policies (under provisions of the Clean Air Act and the Federal Water Pollution Control Act) with cost-effective alternatives based on equalizing the marginal costs of meeting environmental quality standards across all sources of pollution. In his review of these studies, Tom Tietenberg found that least-cost pollution control planning could generate cost savings of 30 to 40 percent, and in some cases more than 90 percent.[17] This means that in some instances pollution control costs are ten times higher than they need to be.

How can cost savings of this magnitude be realized? Can pollution control policies be made more cost-effective without causing further environmental degradation? The answer lies in changing the incentives that face polluters.

Incentives versus Direct Regulation

In an unregulated market economy, pollution arises because of the way individuals and firms respond to market forces and incentives. Firms find that safe and nonpolluting methods of disposing of wastes are usually more costly than dumping them into the environment, even though such disposal harms others. Because polluters are generally not required to compensate those who are harmed, they have no incentive to alter their waste disposal practices.

Incentives under Direct Regulation

In deciding how to respond to a system of regulations and enforcement, polluters will compare the costs of compliance with the likely costs and penalties associated with noncompliance. The costs of compliance may be substantial, but the costs of noncompliance are likely to be uncertain. Incidents of noncompliance might not be detected. Minor violations, even if detected, might be ignored by the authorities. Rather than commit itself to the uncertain legal processes involved in imposing significant fees and penalties, the overburdened enforcement arm of the pollution control agency might negotiate an agreement with the polluter to obtain compliance at some future date. And even if cases are brought to court, the process is time consuming and the court might be more lenient than the pollution control agency would wish. These problems of monitoring and enforcement of regulations add up to a weak incentive for polluters to comply with the regulations.

Among the consequences of these weak incentives have been high rates of violations of existing standards. In one early study, the U.S. General Accounting Office (since renamed the Government Accountability Office) compared the actual discharges of a sample of water polluters with the permissible discharges under the terms of their discharge permits. Eighty-two percent of the sources studied had at least one month of noncompliance during the study period. Twenty-four percent of the sample was in "significant noncompliance," with at least four consecutive months during which discharges exceeded permitted levels by at least 50 percent.[18] More recently the GAO found that in 1994 about one in six of the major industrial and municipal sources that were inspected were in significant violation of their discharge permits.[19] Finally, in 1998 the EPA's own inspector general reported finding serious enforcement problems for both air and water pollution control at the state level, where most of the responsibility for enforcement resides.[20]

Improving the Incentives

Economists have long argued for an alternative approach to pollution control policy based on the creation of strong positive incentives for firms to control pollution. One form that the incentive could take is a charge or tax on each unit of pollution discharged. The tax would be equal to the monetary value of the damage that pollution caused to others. Each discharger wishing to minimize its total cost (cleanup cost plus tax bill) would compare the tax cost of discharging a unit of pollution with the cost of controlling or preventing the discharge. As long as the cost of control was lower than the tax or charge, the firm would want to prevent the discharge. In fact, it would reduce pollution to the point at which its marginal cost of control was just equal to the tax and, indirectly, equal to the marginal damage caused by the pollution. The properly set tax would cause the firm to undertake on its own accord the optimum amount of pollution control.

The pollution tax (or charge) strategy has long appealed to economists because it provides a sure and graduated incentive to firms by making pollution itself a cost of production. And it provides an incentive for innovation and technological change in pollution control. Also, because the polluters are not likely to reduce their discharges to zero, the government would collect revenues that could be used to finance government programs, reduce the deficit, or make possible cuts in taxes.

A system of marketable or tradable discharge permits (TDPs) has essentially the same incentive effects as a tax on pollution. After establishing a maximum allowable level of emissions (a cap), the government would issue a limited number of pollution permits, or "tickets." Each ticket would entitle its owner to discharge one unit of pollution during a specific time period. The government could either distribute the tickets free of charge to polluters on some basis or auction them off to the highest bidders. Dischargers could also buy and sell permits among themselves. This has come to be known as a cap-and-trade system. The cost of purchasing a ticket or of forgoing the revenue from selling the ticket to someone else has the same incentive effects as a tax on pollution of the same amount.

Polluters can respond to the higher cost of pollution imposed by a tax or a TDP system in a variety of ways. They could install some form of conventional treatment system if the cost of treatment were less than the tax or permit price. Alternatively, polluters can consider changing to processes that are inherently less polluting. They can recover and recycle materials that otherwise would remain in the waste stream. They can change to inputs that produce less pollution. For example, a paper mill's response to a tax on dioxin in its effluent might be to stop using chlorine as a bleaching agent. Finally, because the firm would have to pay for whatever pollution it did not bring under control, this cost would result in higher prices for its products and fewer units of its products being purchased by consumers. The effects of higher prices and lower quantities demanded would be to reduce the production level of the firm and, other things being equal, to further reduce the amount of pollution being generated.

A system of pollution taxes or TDPs can make a major contribution to achieving cost-effectiveness. If several sources are discharging into the environment, they will be induced to minimize the total cost of achieving any given reduction in pollution. This is because each discharger will control discharges up to the point at which its marginal or incremental cost of control is equated to the tax or permit price. If all dischargers face the same tax or price, their marginal costs of pollution control will be equal. This is the condition for cost-effectiveness. Low-cost sources will control relatively more, thus leading to a cost-effective allocation of cleanup responsibilities. There is no reallocation of responsibilities for reducing discharges that will achieve the same total reduction at a lower total cost.

One difficulty with implementing a pollution-charge system is in knowing what the charge should be. In some cases enough is already known about the costs of control for average polluters so that the appropriate charge can be calculated. The charge can be adjusted, too, if experience reveals that it was initially set too high or too low. One advantage of the TDP system is that the pollution control agency does not have to determine the level of the tax. Once the agency determines the number of permits, the market determines the permit price. Another advantage of a TDP system in comparison with effluent charges is that it represents a less radical departure from the existing system. Because all sources are presently required to obtain permits specifying the maximum allowable discharges, it would be relatively easy to rewrite permits in a divisible format and to allow sources to buy or sell them. A source with low marginal costs of control should be willing to clean up more and to sell the unused permits as long as the price of a permit were greater than the marginal cost of control. A source with high pollution control costs would find it cheaper to buy permits than to clean up itself.

Incentives in Practice

Since 1992, the EPA has published a series of reports describing and assessing the use of a variety of incentive-based strategies by federal, state, and local governments. These reports are available on the Internet.[21]

During the 1980s the EPA found two ways to use economic incentives in more limited ways to introduce greater flexibility into the existing legal framework and to foster cost-effectiveness in meeting existing targets: the creation of so-called bubbles, and pollution control offsets. Many industrial facilities often have several separate activities or processes discharging the same substances. Regulators can apply pollution control requirements to the aggregate of emissions leaving the plant rather than to each stack or source. This approach allows plant managers to adjust the levels of control at different activities if they can lower total control costs while holding total emissions of the substance constant.

The offset policy was meant to resolve a potential conflict between meeting federal air quality standards and allowing economic growth in a region. The Clean Air Act prohibits the licensing of new air pollution sources if they would interfere with the attainment of federal air quality standards. The EPA allows new sources to be licensed in areas not meeting air quality standards provided they can show there would be offsetting reductions in emissions from existing sources of pollution in the area beyond what has already been required. New sources can do this either by installing additional controls on these sources or by shutting them down. The offset rules provide an incentive for new sources to reduce emissions from existing sources in the region and to seek offsets from other firms. The policy also encourages technological innovation to find means of creating offsets and probably encourages older, dirty facilities to shut down sooner than they otherwise would in order to sell offsets.

The Clean Air Act Amendments of 1990 established a marketable permit program as a key component of the federal effort to reduce acid deposition resulting from emissions of sulfur dioxide. The act called for a reduction of sulfur dioxide emissions of 10 million tons per year (to about 50 percent of 1980 levels) by the year 2000. Since 1995, major sources of these emissions (primarily coal-burning electric power plants) have been receiving tradable permits for emissions (called allowances) equal to a percentage of their historical emissions levels. The number of permits has been reduced to the target level. The cost savings relative to direct regulation have been estimated to be of the order of 50 percent or several billion dollars per year.[22]

The Air Quality Management District in Los Angeles set up a TDP system for oxides of nitrogen and sulfur in 1994 as part of its plan to achieve compliance with ambient air quality standards. Each year for the next ten years, the number of permits was reduced. Each source has the choice of reducing emissions in step with the reduced number of permits it receives, reducing emissions by more than the required amount and selling the extra permits, or keeping emissions constant and purchasing additional permits, depending on whether the marginal costs of reducing emissions are less than or greater than the market price of a permit. Although the market worked well for the first six years or so, the price of permits skyrocketed in 2000 and 2001, largely as a consequence of the California electricity crisis and the botched deregulation of electricity rates. The TDP system for nitrogen oxides was suspended and has not yet been reinstated.[23] The use of taxes on emissions has not been a major feature of U.S. environmental policy, although it has become relatively common in several European countries. There are significant taxes on emissions of sulfur in Sweden, Norway, and Denmark; on nitrogen oxides emissions in Sweden; and on carbon dioxide emissions in Sweden and Norway. Poland, France, and Spain have emissions taxes on sulfur and nitrogen oxides, but these taxes are set at levels that do not provide significant incentives to reduce emissions. The Netherlands has effective charges for discharges to water bodies. Sweden also has a tax on energy production to provide an incentive for energy conservation.[24]

Many state and local governments have also been experimenting with forms of pollution fees and cap-and-trade systems in other contexts. Examples include the regional cap-and-trade program for nitrogen oxides in the northeastern United States, tying the annual fee paid for licenses to operate industrial facilities to the expected quantities of emissions of air and water pollutants, charging households and others by the bag for trash collection and disposal, and taxing purchases of automobile tires and motor oil and using the revenues for safe disposal of these products.[25]

Incentives and Environmental Policy in the Twenty-First Century

In this section I briefly discuss several possible applications of economic incentive strategies. They include President Bush's Clear Skies proposal, using taxes or tradable permits to reduce carbon dioxide emissions, using deposit-refund systems to prevent improper disposal of hazardous wastes, and "getting the prices right" to prevent excessive use of scarce resources.

The Clear Skies Cap-and-Trade Proposal

In July 2002 President Bush submitted legislation to Congress that would set new, more stringent limits (caps) on emissions of sulfur dioxide, nitrogen oxides, and mercury and establish a national permit trading program for each pollutant.[26] The caps would result in emissions reductions of almost 70 percent for each pollutant. Trading would achieve these goals at the lowest possible cost. Environmental advocates criticized the proposal on several grounds:

1. The proposal would slow progress toward cleaner air, because compliance with the final cap limits would not be required until 2018.
2. The cap-and-trade programs would replace other provisions of the Clean Air Act that, if pursued vigorously, would achieve larger reductions more quickly. These other provisions are the strict-interpretation new-source-review requirements for coal-burning power plants that are modified or updated and the imposition of maximum attainable control requirements on major sources of mercury emissions as required under the hazardous air pollutant program. The Clinton administration had pushed for stricter enforcement of new source review and had won substantial reductions in emissions of small particles as well as substantial fines. But the Bush administration has backed off strict enforcement of new source review.
3. Trading of permits, especially for mercury, could lead to increased concentrations of emissions at some locations, resulting in so-called pollution hot spots.

On the last issue, it should be noted that the trading of sulfur allowances has not resulted in significant concentrations of emissions or hot spots. In any event, relatively minor modifications of the trading rules could prevent the emergence of hot spots without seriously impairing the cost-effectiveness of the trading program.

At this writing, one Republican senator has joined with the Democratic minority on the Senate Environment and Public Works Committee to stall this legislation in Congress. In the meantime, the EPA has promulgated two new regulations. One is called the Clean Air Interstate Rule (CAIR), which creates a cap-and-trade program for sulfur dioxide and nitrogen oxides in twenty-eight eastern states. CAIR has the support of at least some environmental groups,[27] and benefit-cost analyses show that the rule has benefits, in the form of improved health, that are well in excess of its costs. The second rule creates a national cap-and-trade program for mercury. However, some controversy exists about whether the EPA has the legal authority to establish such a rule under the terms of the Clean Air Act. The benefits and costs of the mercury program are highly uncertain, and consensus is lacking on whether the rule would pass a benefit-cost test.

Carbon Dioxide Emissions

If present trends in emissions and atmospheric concentrations of carbon dioxide continue, average temperatures worldwide could increase by 1.4 to 5.8 degrees Celsius by the year 2100.[28] If this global warming is to be avoided, or at least substantially retarded, global emissions of carbon dioxide must be reduced. This issue was addressed by 160 nations meeting in Kyoto, Japan, in December 1997. The result was the Kyoto Protocol, which commits the industrialized nations of the world to reducing carbon dioxide emissions by an average of about 5 percent below 1990 levels by sometime between 2008 and 2012. The Clinton administration signed the Protocol and committed the United States to a 7-percent reduction in emissions. But the Bush administration reversed the U.S. position and withdrew from further negotiations about implementation of the protocol. (For further discussion, see chapter 13.)

Two major policy questions are facing nations engaged in any cooperative effort to control greenhouse gas emissions. The first question is, What policy instruments should each nation choose to meet its own commitment? One possibility is to implement an economic incentive system such as a tax or a TDP program. A strong case can be made for using an incentive-based system over direct regulation such as mandatory controls on power plant emissions. In terms of incentives, enforcement, cost-effectiveness, and administrative ease, both the tax and the TDP system come out ahead of direct regulation. One important consideration in choosing between a tax and a TDP system is the different ways in which the consequences of uncertainty are felt. With a tax, there is uncertainty about the magnitude of the reduction in emissions that will be achieved for any given tax rate. With a TDP system, there is no uncertainty because the reduction in emissions is determined by the number of permits the government chooses to issue. But uncertainty remains about the price of permits and the costs incurred in achieving the required emissions reduction. Thus, given a specific commitment to stabilize greenhouse gas emissions, the certainty about the size of the emissions reductions makes a TDP system more attractive than a tax on carbon dioxide emissions. Along this line, Senators McCain, R-Ariz., and Lieberman, D-Conn., proposed a cap-and-trade program for emissions of carbon dioxide and other greenhouse gases in 2003. The bill was defeated on a 43–55 vote.[29]

If no such commitment has been made, however, a stronger case could be made for taxing carbon dioxide emissions. This is because little is known about the economic costs of controlling these emissions, leaving a TDP system at a disadvantage. A compromise position would be to start off with a relatively modest tax on carbon dioxide emissions. The response to the tax would then provide information on the relationship between the marginal cost of controlling emissions and the size of the emissions reduction. Various tax rate proposals have been made, with most falling in the range of $10 to $100 per ton of carbon content of the fuel. To put these numbers in perspective, a tax of $75 per ton of carbon is equivalent to an increase in the gasoline tax of about fifty cents per gallon.

The second question facing those nations ratifying the Kyoto Protocol is, What should be the role of emissions rights trading between countries? Economists argue that the total costs of controlling carbon dioxide emissions could be reduced substantially if nations were allowed to trade carbon dioxide emissions permits with other nations. The Kyoto Protocol allows for the development of a trading system for emissions rights among industrialized nations. The United States has been clear that trading among nations must be part of any framework to which it would agree. In fact, the European Union has established an emissions credit trading system that started in 2005.[30]

A variation on this strategy is to allow the industrialized nations, or firms in those nations, to pay for reductions in emissions in the developing nations and then to take credit for these reductions in meeting their own commitments for emissions reductions. Most observers believe that there are many options for low-cost emissions reductions in developing countries through improvements in energy efficiency and reductions in conventional pollutants. However, for such a system to work, there must be agreement on how to establish the baseline emissions levels against which reductions are measured.

Hazardous Waste Disposal

Federal policy on hazardous wastes focuses on regulating disposal practices. The effectiveness of this policy is highly dependent on the government's ability to monitor and enforce these disposal regulations and to detect and penalize illegal practices. Both industry and government have recognized that the problem of safe disposal can be made more manageable by reducing the quantities of hazardous wastes being generated. The high cost of complying with disposal regulations is itself an incentive for industry to engage in source reduction, but it is also an incentive to violate the regulations on safe disposal, the so-called midnight-dumping problem.

For some types of wastes, a deposit-refund system could provide better incentives to reduce hazardous wastes at their source as well as to dispose of them safely. The system would resemble the deposits on returnable soda and beer cans and bottles established in some states. For example, the manufacturer of a solvent that becomes a hazardous waste after it is used could be required to pay the EPA a deposit of so many dollars per gallon of solvent produced. The amount of the deposit would have to be at least as high as the cost of recycling the solvent or disposing of it safely. Because paying the deposit becomes, in effect, part of the cost of producing the solvent, the manufacturer would have to raise its price. This would discourage the use of the solvent and encourage source reduction. The deposit would be refunded to whoever returned one gallon of the solvent to a certified safe disposal facility or recycler. Thus the user of the solvent would find it more profitable to return the solvent than to dispose of it illegally. In this way, private incentives and the search for profit are harnessed to the task of environmental protection.[31] A deposit-refund system has potential applications for a variety of products for which improper disposal is environmentally damaging but difficult to prevent. Examples include motor oil, car tires, and mercury and lead-acid batteries.

Getting the Prices Right

A surprising number of environmental problems are caused, at least in part, by inappropriate prices for some of the goods and services that people buy and by barriers to the effective functioning of markets. A basic economic principle is that if the price of a good is increased, the quantity purchased decreases while the quantity that producers are willing to sell increases. Many environmental problems are linked to government policies that keep the prices of some things artificially low. For example, the federal government sells water to farmers in the West at prices that are far below the government's cost of supplying the water. And most states in the arid West either prohibit or place substantial restrictions on the ability of private owners of water rights to sell their water to others who might be able to make better use of it. As a consequence, vast quantities of water are wasted in inefficient irrigation practices while some urban areas face water shortages. This system increases the political pressure to build more dams and to divert larger quantities of water from rivers already under ecological stress from inadequate water flows.

The U.S. Forest Service often sells rights to harvest its timber at prices that do not cover the government's own cost of supervising the harvest and constructing access roads. Not only do taxpayers bear the direct financial cost (estimated at over $2 billion between 1992 and 1997), but also there is an indirect cost in that too much forest land is subject to cutting with the attendant loss of wildlife habitat and recreation opportunities.[32] Rather than discontinue the practice of below-cost timber sales, the Forest Service has stopped calculating the costs of these sales so that it is no longer possible to determine the magnitude of the economic losses to taxpayers.[33]

Free access to public facilities is a special case of a low price. In many urban areas, access to the public highway system is free. Even where tolls are charged, these tolls do not always cover the cost of constructing and maintaining the highways. More important, the tolls do not reflect the costs that each driver imposes on others when he or she enters an already congested highway, slows traffic even further, and increases the emissions of air pollution. If each driver were charged a toll that reflected his or her marginal contribution to congestion, drivers would have less incentive to use the highway during peak traffic hours. Average speeds would be higher with more efficient use of fuel and less air pollution. This would diminish the pressure to build more roads with their impacts on land use, and so forth.[34]

In some cases, prices are too high. In the past the government has supported the prices of some agricultural products at artificially high levels. Thus farmers had incentives to plant more of these crops on less productive lands and to apply excessive quantities of pesticides and fertilizers. The result was excess soil erosion and pollution of streams and rivers in rural areas as runoff carried sediments, pesticides, and nutrients into adjacent waters. Congress attempted to phase out these price supports and subsidies in the Freedom to Farm Act of 1996. But declining prices of farm crops and the resulting low incomes of farmers have renewed pressure to restore the subsidies and to continue environmentally damaging agricultural practices. In the summer of 2001 the Bush administration proposed replacing the current system of price supports and subsidies to farmers with a more widely distributed set of payments based on the adoption of improved cultivation practices for conservation and environmental protection. But the proposal met with strong opposition in Congress. And in 2002 Congress passed and President Bush signed legislation that reinstituted price supports and subsidies for farmers.

Conclusion

Economic analysis is likely to be increasingly useful in grappling with the environmental problems of the twenty-first century for at least four reasons. First, as policymakers address the more complex and deeply rooted national and global environmental problems, they are finding that solutions are more and more costly. Thus it is increasingly important for the public to get its money's worth from these policies. This means looking at benefits and comparing them with costs. Therefore, some form of benefit-cost analysis will likely play a growing role in policy debates and decisions in the future.

Second, the slow progress since 1970 in dealing with conventional air and water pollution problems shows the need to use private initiative more effectively through altering the incentive structure. This means placing greater reliance on pollution charges, tradable discharge permits, and deposit-refund systems. I have suggested several possible applications of incentive-based mechanisms to emerging problems, but the list of potential applications is much longer. The institution of tradable permit programs at the federal level and in Southern California demonstrates the political feasibility of this type of instrument. However, the current political climate appears to be quite hostile to any form of tax increase, even taxes on "bads" such as pollution.

Third, the high aggregate cost of controlling various pollutants and environmental threats makes it imperative to design cost-effective policies. Incentive-based mechanisms can play an important role in achieving pollution control targets at something approaching the minimum possible social cost.

Finally, economic analysis can help us to identify cases in which government policies result in prices that send the wrong signals to consumers and producers and fail to provide the right incentives to make wise use of scarce resources and the environment.

Suggested Web Sites

Resources for the Future Inc. (www.rff.org) A nonprofit research organization devoted to environmental and resource management issues.

EPA's National Center for Environmental Economics (http://yosemite1.epa.gov/ee/epa/eed.nsf/pages/homepage) The NCEE Web site has research reports, regulatory impact analyses, and other EPA publications.

OMB's Office of Information and Regulatory Affairs (www.whitehouse.gov/omb/inforeg/regpol.html) OIRA's Web site provides a variety of information on its regulatory oversight mission, including pending regulations, the status of regulatory reviews, and prompt letters that encourage federal agencies to consider regulations that appear to have benefits greater than costs.

Notes

1. For more discussion of the principles of benefit-cost analysis and applications in the realm of environmental policy, see one of the textbooks on environmental economics. Examples include Tom Tietenberg, *Environmental and Natural Resource Economics*, 6th ed. (Reading, Mass.: Addison Wesley Longman, 2003) and Barry C. Field, *Environmental Economics: An Introduction*, 3rd ed. (New York: McGraw-Hill, 2002).
2. *Marginal* is an economic concept that refers to the effects of small changes. For example, if the total cost of production of a good increased from $10,000 to $10,010 when production increased from a rate of 500 to 501, then the marginal cost of the 501st unit is $10.
3. For discussions of the role of economic analysis in federal environmental policies, see Richard D. Morgenstern, ed., *Economic Analysis at EPA: Assessing Regulatory Impact*, (Washington, D.C.: Resources for the Future, 1997); Paul R. Portney and Robert N. Stavins, eds., *Public Policies for Environmental Protection*, 2nd ed. (Washington, D.C.: Resources for the Future, 2000); and Randall Lutter and Jason F. Shogren, eds., *Painting the White House Green: Rationalizing Environmental Policy Inside the Executive Office of the President*, (Washington, D.C.: Resources for the Future, 2004).
4. Robert N. Hahn, *Reviving Regulatory Reform: A Global Perspective* (Washington, D.C.: AEI–Brookings Joint Center for Regulatory Studies, 2000). Regulatory analyses done for EPA regulations can be examined at EPA, National Center for Environmental Economics, "Regulatory Economic Analyses," http://yosemite1.epa.gov/ee/epa/eed.nsf/webpages/regulatoryimpactanalyses.html.

5. For a review of the available information on the benefits and costs of U.S. environ-mental policy, see A. Myrick Freeman III, "Environmental Policy since Earth Day I: What Have We Gained?" *Journal of Economic Perspectives* 16 (winter 2002): 125–146.

6. U.S. Office of Management and Budget, Office of Information and Regulatory Affairs (OIRA), *Informing Regulatory Decisions: 2003 Report to Congress on the Costs and Ben-efits of Federal Regulations and Unfunded Mandates on State, Local and Tribal Entities,* 2003, www.whitehouse.gov/omb/inforeg/2003_cost-ben_final_rpt.pdf.

7. U.S. Environmental Protection Agency (EPA), *The Benefits and Costs of the Clean Air Act: 1970 to 1990* (Washington, D.C.: EPA, 1997). For an indication of some of the controversy stimulated by this report, see Randall Lutter and Richard Belzer, "EPA Pats Itself on the Back," *Regulation* 23 (2000): 23–28, and the letter response from Freeman et al., *Regulation* 24 (2001): 4–5.

8. Tayler H. Bingham et al., *A Benefits Assessment of Water Pollution Control Programs since 1972* (Research Triangle Institute, 2000), http://yosemite1.epa.gov/ee/epa/eerm.nsf/vwrepnumlookup/ee-0429?opendocument; Freeman, "Environmental Policy since Earth Day I," p. 138.

9. For a critique of the use of benefit-cost analysis in environmental policy and a response by a well-known economist, see Frank Ackerman, Lisa Heiserling, and V. Kerry Smith, "Choice Cuts: Cost-Benefit Analysis Is Often Used to Support Industry Wish Lists. Should We Blame the Method or the Masters?" *American Prospect,* May 12, 2004, www.prospect.org/web/view-web.ww?id=7696. Ackerman and Heiserling are the authors of *Priceless: On Knowing the Price of Everything and the Value of Nothing,* (New York: The New Press, 2004).

10. Examples include new effluent limitations for consolidated animal feeding operations and emissions standards for several types of sources of fine particles.

11. See, for example, Kenneth J. Arrow et al., "Is There a Role for Benefit-Cost Analysis in Environmental, Health, and Safety Regulation?" *Science,* April 12, 1996, 221–222.

12. See the OIRA Web site (www.whitehouse.gov/omb/inforeg/regpol.html) for infor-mation on OIRA activities and examples of prompt letters.

13. William D. Nordhaus and Joseph Boyer, *Warming the World: Economic Models of Global Warming* (Cambridge: MIT Press, 2000).

14. For more detailed discussions of the major provisions of federal air and water pollu-tion laws, see Paul R. Portney, "Air Pollution Policy," and A. Myrick Freeman III, "Water Pollution Policy," in Portney and Stavins, *Public Policies for Environmental Pro-tection,* 2nd ed.

15. Wesley A. Magat, Alan J. Krupnick, and Winston Harrington, *Rules in the Making: A Statistical Analysis of Regulatory Agency Behavior* (Washington, D.C.: Resources for the Future, 1986), table 6–1.

16. Tammy O. Tengs et al., "Five-Hundred Life-Saving Interventions and Their Cost-Effectiveness," *Risk Analysis* 15 (1995): 369–390.

17. T. H. Tietenberg, *Emissions Trading: An Exercise in Reforming Pollution Policy* (Wash-ington, D.C.: Resources for the Future, 1985), 38–47.

18. U.S. General Accounting Office (GAO), *Waste Water Dischargers Are Not Complying with EPA Pollution Control Permits* (Washington, D.C.: GAO, 1983).

19. GAO, *Water Pollution: Many Violations Have Not Received Appropriate Enforcement Attention* (Washington, D.C.: GAO, 1996).

20. See John H. Cushman Jr., "EPA and States Found to Be Lax on Pollution Control," *New York Times,* June 7, 1998, 1.

21. See EPA, National Center for Environmental Economics, *The United States Experi-ence with Economic Incentives for Pollution Control,* January 2001, http://yosemite1.epa.gov/ee/epa/eed.nsf/webpages/usexperiencewitheconomicincentives.html.

22. For reviews of the sulfur allowance trading program, see Dallas Burtraw, "Trading Emissions to Clean the Air: Exchanges Few but Savings Many," *Resources* 122 (winter 1996): 3–6; Richard Schmalensee et al., "An Interim Evaluation of Sulfur Dioxide Emissions Trading," *Journal of Economic Perspectives* 12 (1998) 53–68; Robert N.

Stavins, "What Can We Learn from the Grand Policy Experiment? Lessons from SO_2 Allowance Trading," *Journal of Economic Perspectives* 12 (1998) 69–88; and A. Danny Ellerman, Paul Joskow, and David Harrison Jr., *Emissions Trading in the U.S.: Experience, Lessons, and Considerations for Greenhouse Gasses,* Pew Center on Global Climate Change, 2003, www.pewclimate.org/global-warming-in-depth/all_reports/emissions_trading/index.cfm.

23. See Ellerman et al., *Emissions Trading in the U.S.*

24. For more details, see Thomas Sterner, *Policy Instruments for Environmental and Natural Resource Management* (Washington, D.C.: Resources for the Future, 2003) and Winston Harrington and Richard D. Morgenstern, eds., *Choosing Environmental Policy: Comparing Instruments and Outcomes in the United States and Europe* (Washington, D.C.: Resources for the Future, 2004). A comprehensive database on the use of economic instruments in environmental policy in developed nations is available at www.oecd.org/env/tax-database.

25. See Robert N. Stavins, "Market-Based Environmental Policies," in Portney and Stavins, *Public Policies for Environmental Protection,* 2nd ed.

26. For details, see EPA, "Clear Skies," www.epa.gov/clearskies.

27. For example, see Environmental Defense, "Big Win for Clean Air! EPA Unveils Rule to Slash Power Plant Pollution," March 9, 2005, www.environmentaldefense.org/article.cfm?ContentID=4358.

28. J. T. Houghton et al., eds., *Climate Change 2001: The Science of Climate Change* (New York: Cambridge University Press, 2001).

29. See Pew Center on Global Climate Change, "Summary of the McCain-Lieberman Climate Stewardship Act," www.pewclimate.org/policy_center/analyses/s_139_summary.cfm.

30. For information on current developments in the system, see International Emissions Trading Association, www.ieta.org/ieta/www/pages/index.php?idsitepage=523.

31. See Clifford S. Russell, "Economic Incentives in the Management of Hazardous Waste," *Columbia Journal of Environmental Law* 13 (1988): 1101–1119; and Molly K. Macauley, Michael D. Bowes, and Karen L. Palmer, *Using Economic Incentives to Regulate Toxic Substances* (Washington, D.C.: Resources for the Future, 1992).

32. Taxpayers for Common Sense, *Forest Service Terminates Timber Subsidy Report,* October 19, 2001, http://www.taxpayer.net/TCS/PressReleases/10-19-01gaoforest.htm.

33. GAO, *Financial Management: Annual Costs of Forest Service's Timber Sales Program Are Not Determinable,* Publication No. GAO-01–1101R (Washington, D.C.: GAO, September 21, 2001).

34. Kenneth A. Small, Clifford Winston, and Carol A. Evans, *Road Work: A New Highway Pricing and Investment Strategy* (Washington, D.C.: Brookings Institution Press, 1989); James J. MacKenzie, Roger C. Dower, and Donald D. T. Chen, *The Going Rate: What It Really Costs to Drive* (Washington, D.C.: World Resources Institute, 1992).

10

Risk-Based Decision Making:
Policy, Science, and Politics

Richard N. L. Andrews

Environmental regulation today is pervaded by the language of risk, and environmental policy analysis by the concepts and methods of quantitative risk assessment. Three of the first major environmental controversies of George W. Bush's presidency focused on risk issues: the human health risks of arsenic in drinking water, the ecological risks of oil drilling in the Arctic National Wildlife Refuge, and the economic and ecological risks of global warming. In 1984 the administrator of the U.S. Environmental Protection Agency (EPA), William Ruckelshaus, first officially endorsed "risk assessment and risk management" as the primary framework for EPA decision making.[1] In 1987 a major agency report stated flatly that "the fundamental mission of the Environmental Protection Agency is to reduce risks." Another influential report, issued in 1990, recommended that the EPA "target its environmental protection efforts on the basis of opportunities for the greatest risk reduction."[2] Risk-based decision making is now the dominant language for discussing environmental policy in the EPA and in many other environmental and health regulatory agencies.[3]

The adoption of this risk-based framework has important implications for U.S. environmental policy. Risk assessment was developed as a technical procedure for evaluating the human health risks of toxic chemicals, but the risk-based approach has since been promoted for comparing environmental and other issues, setting priorities, justifying regulations, setting limits on cleanup requirements and expenditures, and rationalizing other environmental policy decisions. It also has become the focus of intensive political debate over trade-offs between environmental concerns and regulatory burdens more generally.

Risk assessment remains controversial, however, both among scientists and policymakers and in general political debate. Even many of its advocates are sometimes uneasy that it is often oversold or abused. Risk-based decision making may also be too narrow and too negative to deal adequately with many of the most important environmental policy issues of the present and future. To appraise its significance, one must first understand what it is, how it has come to be used so widely, why it is controversial, and how it is now being applied.

The Regulatory Legacy

U.S. environmental policy before 1970 included more than seven decades of experience in managing the environment as a natural resource base—lands and forests, minerals, water, fish and wildlife—but pollution control had been left almost exclusively to state and local governments. Beginning in 1970, however, U.S. policy shifted dramatically from managing the environment to regulating it, and from state and local to national primacy. The EPA was created by reorganizing most of the few existing regulatory programs into one agency. Within a decade Congress enacted more than a dozen major new regulatory statutes for federal pollution control, each requiring many individual standards and permits for particular technologies, practices, and substances (see chapter 8).

Initially these laws emphasized the use of known technologies to reduce the most obvious problems: urban sewage, automotive air pollution, and the major industrial pollutants of air and water. The Clean Air Act of 1970, for instance, directed the EPA to set national minimum ambient air quality standards for six major pollutants, based on health criteria, and to set technology-based standards for new pollution sources and so-called technology-forcing statutory timetables for reducing emissions from motor vehicles. The Federal Water Pollution Control Act Amendments of 1972 required federal permits for all new water pollution sources, again using technology-based standards—that is, best-practicable and best-available technologies—to force improved control of wastewater discharges from each industrial process.

As these measures took effect, however, environmental politics became increasingly linked with public fears that pesticides and other manufactured chemicals might cause cancer.[4] The environmental control agenda was broadened and redirected, therefore, to address the far larger domain of chemical hazards: toxic air and water pollutants, pesticides, drinking-water contaminants, hazardous wastes, and toxic substances in commerce generally. This domain included thousands of compounds, far too many to address explicitly in statutes. Many of these compounds had not even been well studied, and many were not just wastes but also had important economic uses.[5]

These substance-by-substance decisions raised serious new problems for environmental protection policy. Asbestos, for instance, clearly caused cancer in shipyard workers who were continuously exposed to it at high concentrations as they installed it in ships during World War II. But did this mean that asbestos in floor and ceiling tiles was a serious threat to children? Was the threat serious enough to require that every school and day care center spend large sums to remove it rather than to improve their educational programs? Similar questions about risk and cost could be raised about many other chemicals: industrial chemicals such as PCBs (polychlorinated biphenyls); pesticides such as DDT; trace contaminants such as radon in drinking water; and consumer products such as lead in gasoline, PCP (pentachlorophenol, a wood preservative in outdoor paint), and others. Which of these thousands of chemicals should the EPA regulate, and how should it decide? Should it ban them outright, and lose their valuable uses as well as their hazards—and risk substitution of other products with their own unstudied hazards? Should it regulate them to eliminate all risk (if that were even possible)? Or to reduce the risk to some minimum level (one in a million, for instance)? Or to some level comparable to other risks people routinely accept voluntarily (driving a car or crossing the street, for instance)? Or to a level justified by economic estimates of the costs and benefits of control? Finally, how much proof of these risks should the agency be required to present before regulating?

To control toxic chemicals, Congress enacted risk-based and risk-balancing statutes. These laws required the EPA to assess the risks of each substance it proposed to regulate and then either to protect the public with "adequate margins of safety" against "unreasonable risks" or to make choices that would balance those risks against economic benefits. In turn, the EPA had to develop methods for *setting risk priorities* among many possible candidates for regulation; for *justifying particular regulatory decisions,* balancing risks against benefits; and for *approving site decisions,* based on an "acceptable risk" for certifying a cleaned-up hazardous waste site or permitting construction of a new facility.[6] A U.S. Supreme Court decision in 1980, the so-called *Benzene* decision, added a legal precedent that the agencies must demonstrate a factual basis, not merely well-reasoned professional judgment, to justify regulatory proposals; and in 1981 President Reagan issued an executive order directing the agencies to propose regulations only when they could document benefits greater than costs.[7]

Risk Assessment and Risk Management

Quantitative risk assessment has been defined as "the process of obtaining quantitative measures of risk levels, where risk refers to the possibility of uncertain, adverse consequences."[8] To the EPA, *risk* usually means "the probability of injury, disease, or death under specific circumstances," and *risk assessment* means "the characterization of the potential adverse health effects of human exposure to environmental hazards."[9] These definitions combine two concepts: hazard (adverse consequence) and probability (quantitative measure of likelihood or uncertainty). This mixing of two concepts is one cause of the confusion and controversy that surrounds risk assessment.

One fundamental doctrine of this approach is that risk assessment should be clearly distinguished from risk management. Risk assessment, in this view, is a purely scientific activity based on expert analysis of facts. Risk management is the subsequent decision process in which the scientific conclusions are considered along with other elements such as statutory requirements, costs, public values, and politics. A National Research Council report endorsed this view in 1983, and it was adopted as the agency's policy by Ruckelshaus, then EPA administrator. It remains a basic tenet in the literature on risk assessment, though Ruckelshaus himself later acknowledged the difficulty of maintaining such a clear distinction in practice.[10]

Risk Assessment

Quantitative health risk assessment has become a detailed analytical procedure that includes four elements:

1. *Hazard identification,* in which the analyst gathers information on whether a substance may be a health hazard
2. *Dose-response assessment,* in which the analyst attempts to describe quantitatively the relationship between the amount of exposure to the substance and the degree of toxic effect
3. *Exposure assessment,* in which the analyst estimates how many people may be exposed to the substance and under what conditions (that is, how much of it, how often, for how long, and from what sources)
4. *Risk characterization,* in which the analyst combines information from the previous steps into an assessment of overall health risk, for example, an added risk that one person in a thousand (or a hundred, or a million) will develop cancer after exposure at the expected levels over a lifetime

Suppose, for instance, that the EPA decides to assess the health risks of an organic solvent used to degrease metal parts: a liquid, moderately volatile, that is somewhat soluble in water and degrades slowly in it.[11] The hazard identification step uncovers several experimental animal studies between 1940 and 1960, all showing lethal toxicity to the liver at high doses but no toxic effects below an identifiable threshold dose; cancer was not studied. A more recent study, however, appears to show that lifetime exposure to much lower doses causes significant increases in liver cancers in both mice and rats. The only human data are on exposed workers, too few to draw statistically valid conclusions (two cases of cancer diagnosed in fewer than 200 workers, when one case might have been expected). From these data the EPA decides that the solvent is a "possible" (as opposed to "probable" or "definite") human carcinogen.

In dose-response assessment, the analyst then uses a mathematical model to predict a plausible upper-bound estimate of human cancer risk by extrapolating from the animal studies: from high to low doses, and from laboratory species (such as rats and mice) to humans. Applying these models to the measured animal data, the EPA estimates a unit cancer risk (the risk for an average lifetime exposure to 1 milligram per kilogram [mg/kg] of body weight per day) of about 2 in 100 for lung cancer from inhalation, based on studies of male rats, and about 5 in 100 for liver cancer from ingestion, based on studies of male mice.

In exposure assessment, the analyst then uses monitoring data and dispersion models to calculate that approximately 80 neighbors may be exposed to about 0.0008 mg/kg of body weight per day, and 150 workers to about 0.001 mg/kg per day; and through gradual groundwater contamination, about 50,000 people may be exposed to 0.001 to 0.002 mg/kg per day in their drinking water after about twenty years.

Finally, the risk characterization combines these calculations into numerical upper-bound estimates of excess lifetime human cancer risk. In this hypothetical case, the result might be 8 in 100,000 of the general population, 1 in 1,000 nearby residents, and 3 in 1,000 workers. Note from the previous paragraph that the actual numbers of neighbors and workers are far smaller, but risk assessments are usually expressed in numbers per thousand for consistency's sake. The EPA's risk managers—the officials responsible for the agency's regulatory decisions—then use these estimates to decide what risks should have the highest priority for regulation and what regulatory action (if any) is justified.

Risk Management

In the context of the EPA's statutory authorities, risk management primarily means choosing and justifying regulatory decisions. The EPA administers a complex patchwork of statutes, each of which addresses a particular set of problems, establishes its own range of authorized management actions (usually regulations), and specifies its own criteria for making decisions. Some laws direct that health risks be minimized regardless of costs; others that the risks be balanced against costs; and still others that the best-available technology be used to minimize risks, allowing some judgment about what technologies are economically available, or that new technologies be developed to meet a standard.[12]

In practice the EPA and other regulatory agencies appear to apply their own rules of thumb, based on risk and cost, to manage health risks. In one study that examined 132 federal regulatory decisions on environmental carcinogens from 1976 through 1985, two clear patterns emerged. Every chemical with an individual cancer risk greater than four in a thousand was regulated, and, with only one exception, no action was taken to regulate any chemical with an individual risk less than one in a million. In the risk range between these two levels, cost-effectiveness was the primary criterion. That is to say, risks were regulated if the cost per life saved was less than $2 million, but not if the cost was higher.[13]

Science and Values

Quantitative risk assessment is now used to varying degrees by all federal environmental and health regulatory agencies. It also has been institutionalized in a professional society (the Society for Risk Analysis); several journals; and a large professional community of practitioners in government agencies, chemical and other industries, consulting firms, universities and research institutes, and advocacy organizations.

Despite its widespread use, however, serious dispute remains regarding how much of risk assessment is really scientific and how much is merely a recasting of value judgments into scientific jargon. The language of risk assessment is less accessible to the general public. Does it nonetheless provide a more scientifically objective basis for public policy decisions?

Risk Assessment Policy

Risk assessment in practice is permeated by judgments that cannot be reduced to science. One such judgment governs the selection of substances for risk assessment in the first place. These judgments are based not only on preliminary evidence of risk but also on publicity, lawsuits, and other political pressures. Another judgment concerns what effects, or endpoints, are considered. Most assessments focus on cancer, with less attention and usually far less data for other health hazards, species, ecosystems, and environmental consequences.

In conducting each risk assessment, the analysts' own value judgments come into play whenever they must make assumptions or draw inferences in the absence of objective facts. Such judgments are identified collectively as risk assessment policy. Hazard identification, for example, relies on evidence from epidemiological studies of human effects, from animal bioassays, from short-term laboratory tests, or simply from comparison of the compound's molecular structure with other known hazards. These data are sometimes few and fragmentary, often collected for different purposes, and of varied quality; the analyst must make judgments about their applicability.

For both dose-response and exposure assessments, analysts must routinely use mathematical models to generate risk estimates. Even the best dose-response models, however, are based on simplified biology and fragmentary data. Scientists must interpolate the dose-response relationship from a small number of observations, extrapolate the relationship to lower doses (often far beyond the observed range), and adjust for the many possible differences between species and conditions of exposure.

Similarly, in exposure assessment, analysts must make many assumptions about variability in natural dispersion patterns and population movements, about other sources of exposure, and about the susceptibility of those exposed (for instance, healthy adults compared with children or chemically sensitive persons).

Finally, analysts must synthesize a characterization of overall risk out of the diverse, uncertain, and sometimes conflicting estimates derived from the previous three steps. Such choices include weighing the quality, persuasiveness, and applicability of differing bodies of evidence; deciding how to estimate and adjust for statistical uncertainties; and even choosing which estimates to present (best estimate or upper bound, for instance, or a range defined by degree of probability).

Given these many unavoidable judgments, the conclusions of health risk assessments often are shaped as much by their assumptions as by facts. The EPA and other agencies therefore developed guidance documents called inference guidelines, which specify the assumptions and rules of thumb to be used in calculating risks and in presenting risk assessments. Such guidelines are policy directives, not scientific documents themselves, based on a mixture of scientists' judgments and political choices about the appropriate level of prudence.[14]

A Precautionary Bias?

There has been intense and continuing debate, both scientific and political, over whether the regulatory agencies' decisions—and even their risk estimates—are systematically biased in favor of excessive caution. If each assumption includes a "safety factor" favoring health protection, for instance, and especially if those factors are then multiplied (as they often must be), the overall safety factor might be far greater than any of them individually and sometimes far costlier to achieve. Regulated industries and other critics have argued that these practices make the agencies' risk assessments excessively cautious, and that they should instead calculate only "best estimates" of risk rather than large margins of safety.[15] Some of these critics could be viewed as merely self-serving industrial interests or antiregulatory publicists,[16] but others include respected academic scientists and commentators. British epidemiologists Richard Doll and Richard Peto argued that no clear epidemiological evidence demonstrated increases in most cancers from general public exposure to industrial chemicals. Biochemist Bruce Ames, inventor of the Ames toxicity test, argued that people routinely ingest natural carcinogens far more potent than most exposures to manufactured chemicals, without evident ill effects. The late Philip Abelson, former editor of *Science,* repeatedly questioned the assumptions and extrapolations used in the EPA's risk assessments, arguing that they raised needless public fears and wasted money on costly and unnecessary protective measures.[17]

Other risk experts have argued, however, that some of these assumptions might not be excessively cautious at all: Both human susceptibility and exposure levels can be underestimated as well as overestimated, as can the toxicity of a substance itself and its interaction with other risk factors. One respected research team, for instance, identified plausible biological reasons showing that existing risk assessment methods—despite all their safety factors—might still underestimate some risks of low-level exposure. Given scientific uncertainty, moreover, best-estimate methods could not themselves avoid value judgments, errors, and biases. They might simply substitute different ones, favoring less prudence regarding health protection.[18] Many risk experts therefore argued against using any single point estimate of risk as a basis for decisions, and for substituting a range defined by degrees of probability or uncertainty.[19] Others identified additional risks that had not yet been carefully studied, such as hormonal hazards posed by dioxin owing to its estrogen-mimicking properties. A major review by the National Academy of Sciences also reaffirmed the EPA's risk assessment methods and assumptions.[20]

Despite these counterarguments, however, skeptics have gained increasing influence in challenging the EPA's use of scientific risk claims to justify its regulatory decisions.

Multiple Risks and Risk Management

Quantitative health risk assessment was developed to estimate health risks associated with specific chemicals and exposures and thus to permit comparisons among the magnitudes of health hazards they posed. It was not originally designed for setting priorities among more diverse kinds of environmental problems, such as a chemical threatening health versus a development project threatening a wetland—or even for analyzing situations in which complex combinations of risks to many different sorts of endpoints are present. A broader problem for risk assessment as a decision tool, therefore, is that many of the risk management decisions that the EPA and other agencies must make involve far more complex choices, and more complex judgments even about the risks involved in them, than the single-substance cases discussed above. Such decisions often involve combinations of hazards causing multiple kinds of risks to different populations.

Imagine, for instance, a relatively common type of decision: the EPA must establish requirements for toxic air and water releases and hazardous waste storage permits at a new facility for chemical reprocessing and incineration. Many risks must be considered: cancer, respiratory illness, fish mortality, stream eutrophication, crop damage, diminished visibility, and economic hardship to the surrounding community, to list just a few. There may be beneficial effects as well: reduced damage to health and ecosystems because of improved waste disposal practices, economic benefits to the community, and others.

In principle, risk assessment can estimate the probability of each of these effects individually. It does not, however, specify which should be considered, nor make them commensurable, nor provide weights specifying their relative importance; and it may not even estimate their interactions well. In practice, risk assessment has often dealt with these issues by simplifying them, focusing on just a few primary human health effects. This simplification may obscure or bias rather than illuminate the many considerations that must be balanced in many decisions.

Comparative Risk Analysis:
Unfinished Business and *Reducing Risk*

Beginning in the mid-1980s, nonetheless, EPA administrators undertook a more ambitious initiative: to use the language of risk as an agency-wide framework for setting priorities among all its programs and mandates.

A pioneering study by the EPA in 1987, entitled *Unfinished Business*, compared the relative risks of thirty-one environmental problems spanning the full range of the agency's responsibilities in relation to four different kinds of risk: cancer, noncancer health risks, ecological effects, and other effects on human welfare. This study was *not* a formal quantitative risk assessment, because both data and methodology were lacking for most noncancer risks. Rather, it was based on a consensus of judgments by some seventy-five EPA senior managers and on comparisons of those judgments with opinion-poll data on perceptions held by the general public.

The *Unfinished Business* study found that the agency's actual risk management priorities were more consistent with public opinion than with the problems EPA managers thought most serious. For example, the agency was devoting far more resources to the problem of chemical waste disposal than to indoor air pollution and radon, which appeared to have much greater health risks. The study also found that in most of its programs, the EPA had been far more concerned with public health than with protecting the natural environment itself; but that even for public health effects, localized hazards caused much higher risks than overall risk estimates revealed.[21] Finally, it noted that the information available to assess risks for virtually any of these problems was surprisingly poor.

A follow-up study by the EPA's Science Advisory Board in 1990, entitled *Reducing Risk,* encouraged the EPA to go further with this approach and made substantive recommendations for addressing several high-priority environmental threats. It recommended increased emphasis, for instance, on reducing human destruction of natural habitats and species and on slowing stratospheric ozone depletion and global climate change—and correspondingly less emphasis on more localized concerns such as oil spills and groundwater contamination. Finally, it urged the EPA to use a wider and more flexible range of market-oriented incentives to promote cost-effective reduction of environmental risks—pollution charges, tradable emissions permits, emissions disclosure requirements, and liability principles, for instance—in place of the more rigid prescriptive regulatory requirements that had been its primary policy tools so far.[22] EPA administrator William Reilly publicly endorsed the report and made its implementation a personal priority. EPA offices and regions were to use comparative risk studies to justify their annual budget requests, and enforcement priorities were to be based on relative-risk estimates.[23]

In practice, however, the EPA's programs and priorities continued to be directed by its statutes and annual appropriations, which authorized specific and separate regulatory solutions for particular environmental problems and left others—agricultural runoff and global warming, for instance—without specific regulatory authority. The result was that without statutory changes, the EPA administrator had little authority to implement risk-based priorities and incentive-based instruments except on an experimental basis.[24]

Risk Assessment and Environmental Decisions

By the end of the 1980s, risk assessment had become established as the EPA's primary language of analysis and management. The agency's statutes did not contain this consistency of discourse, but most EPA administrative decisions were now couched in terms of how much risk they would reduce. Why?

The most fundamental reason was a major shift in the standards by which the courts reviewed the agencies' regulatory decisions. Before 1980 the courts had generally deferred to the agencies' expertise and responsibility to write rules applying the regulatory statutes to particular environmental hazards. As late as 1976, for instance, the courts upheld the EPA's decision to ban lead in gasoline—one of its greatest public health successes—even though at the time the scientific evidence supporting this action was still quite limited.[25] In 1980, however, the Supreme Court set a new and far more restrictive requirement, demanding that the agencies must demonstrate factually that a risk is "significant" before regulating it.[26] In 1991 the Fifth Circuit Court of Appeals took an even tougher position, overturning the EPA's rule banning five uses of asbestos—even after ten years of rulemaking, thousands of scientific studies, and over 100,000 pages of documentation—because the agency had not proven a significant risk of exposure in all of these uses (asbestos cement sewer pipes, for instance).[27]

In effect, the courts greatly increased the burden of proof on the regulatory agencies, severely limiting their discretion to regulate on a precautionary basis—to prevent harm before it happened—based on a consensus of expert judgments. The agencies therefore adopted quantitative risk assessment as a method for satisfying the courts, and shifted their regulatory priorities toward risks for which they could present a more detailed scientific record.

From the perspective of Ruckelshaus and other EPA administrators, risk assessment also was a useful management tool. It provided a scientific procedure and a common denominator—human health risk—by which the administrator could rationalize and defend the agency's regulatory decisions, both among individual chemicals and across the agency's many mandates. Assistant administrator Milton Russell argued, for instance, that risk balancing was the only alternative to a much cruder and more fragmented approach, in which priorities were set mainly by historical accident and political influence, and uncoordinated actions might create new risks as great as those they were correcting (for instance, simply moving pollutants from water to land or land to air).[28]

Finally, risk assessment strengthened the EPA's position externally against compliance-cost arguments. During the early 1980s the Reagan administration had greatly expanded the authority of the Office of Management and Budget (OMB) to impose cost-benefit requirements—regulatory impact assessments—on environmental regulatory proposals. Whatever its imperfections, risk assessment focused the regulatory process on environmental and health consequences, and cast the issues in primarily scientific terms. The agency's expertise carried more weight in this area than in the broader domain of economics, where the OMB and the regulated industries themselves had greater influence.[29]

Although risk assessment strengthened the EPA's hand in dealing with the OMB, it increased conflict between the agency and the public over the question of how much proof the agency should have to document before regulating. Environmental advocacy groups generally argued that, if in doubt, the government should regulate to protect health, whereas businesses argued that, if in doubt, it should not regulate until it showed clear proof of harm. Quantitative risk assessment seemed to tip such controversies in favor of business, demanding proof rather than prudence and imposing heavy new analytical burdens before regulatory action could be taken.[30] Yet why, environmental groups asked, were technical estimates of hypothetical cancer risks any more real or legitimate than public concerns about exposures to imperfectly understood chemicals; about unanticipated leaks, spills, or plant malfunctions; or about harm to their community because of industrial waste disposal?[31]

Risk assessment thus remained a controversial procedure, even as it increasingly became the dominant language for justifying regulatory decisions. Like cost-benefit analysis, it became an important tool, though it remained controversial as a decision rule, for environmental policymaking.[32]

The Political Debate over Environmental Risks

By the 1990s risk-based decision making became the focal point for a far broader political battle about trade-offs between environmental protection and public health on the one hand and the burdens, costs, and effectiveness of regulation on the other. In essence, three competing approaches to environmental policy were being promoted: risk based, technology based, and incentive based.

Advocates of the risk-based approach argued for more universal and consistent use of risk analysis as a basis both for setting regulatory priorities and for justifying individual regulations. They included many scientists and economists whose ideal was to base regulatory decisions on "good science" and "rational choice" rather than public apprehensions, and conservative judges who demanded proof rather than merely prudence as justification for government decisions. They also included business interests who saw risk assessment as a weapon for blocking unwanted regulations, by diverting the agencies' efforts into elaborate analytical requirements and endless legal battles over scientific and economic proof. In the early 1990s, for instance, Sen. Patrick Moynihan, D-N.Y., proposed legislation to make risk assessment an explicit basis for setting EPA priorities. Others proposed to prescribe changes in risk assessment methodology by statute, and still others proposed to add industry representatives to scientific peer reviews and to open EPA risk assessments to additional litigation and judicial review.

Advocates of the technology-based approach, meanwhile, argued that the risk-based approach was ineffective in practice even if logical in principle, precisely because it could so easily be manipulated to paralyze the regulatory process with excessive demands for proof ("paralysis by analysis"). They argued instead for specific technology-based mandates, because even if they were rigid—perhaps even *because* they were clear and rigid—they got effective results. Advocates of this approach included many environmental lawyers, engineers, and advocacy groups who saw clear, enforceable require-ments as the most effective way to assure environmental results from unwilling businesses. They also included some businesses preferring the sim-plicity of one-time technological compliance ("just tell me what to do") and manufacturers of pollution-control equipment.

In the 1990 Clean Air Act, for instance, Congress concluded that risk-based regulation of hazardous air pollutants had failed and instead directed the EPA to issue technology-based standards (requiring maximum achiev-able control technology [MACT]), with risk-based regulation as a back-up option if MACT did not sufficiently reduce the risk.

Finally, incentives advocates argued that market-based incentives—pollution taxes, tradable emissions permits, information disclosure require-ments, strict liability, and others—would be more efficient and more effective than either risk- or technology-based regulations. The regulatory process itself was too inflexible and inefficient, they argued, and technology-based regulations merely "locked in" a one-time improvement with no incen-tive to improve further. Incentives advocates included economists and some businesses seeking greater flexibility. They also included some environmental advocates who saw regulation as gridlocked and sought new leverage for improvements, though many also were fearful of replacing enforceable requirements with "flexible" incentives.

In the 1990 Clean Air Act Amendments, for example, incentives advo-cates created a cap-and-trade system for sulfur emissions from electric power plants, capping (at a significantly reduced level) total emissions nationwide but allowing the utilities to trade permits and to use a wide range of methods—low-sulfur western coal, for instance, rather than end-of-pipe scrubbers—to stay within this limit. The results included significant reduc-tions of sulfur emissions, though far more of them due to fuel switching—and perhaps to merely "banking" these emissions credits for future use—than to actual market trading of permits.[33]

A series of expert reports during the 1990s called for statutory reforms incorporating more systematic use of risk assessment and market incen-tives.[34] In 1997 the Presidential/Congressional Commission on Risk Assess-ment and Risk Management recommended that risk management be redefined away from the fragmented and increasingly cumbersome proce-dures for analyzing individual substances toward a more comprehensive framework for considering the multiple contaminants and sources of expo-sure, and the multiple value perspectives, that are characteristic of most real risk management decisions.[35] In practice, however, congressional policy-making from 1994 on was stalemated between a Republican majority com-mitted to reducing environmental regulation and defenders of the existing regulations who could still summon enough public and judicial support to block major rollbacks.

The main exceptions to this legislative impasse were two risk-based statutes passed during the 1996 election campaign, the Food Quality Pro-tection Act and amendments to the Safe Drinking Water Act. Significantly, both were initially developed not by the Congress but through multi-stakeholder negotiations, and then brought to Congress for ratification. Both also were followed by protracted political struggles over their implementation.

Pesticide Residues in Foods

The Food Quality Protection Act replaced the 1958 Delaney clause of the Food, Drug, and Cosmetic Act—which flatly prohibited the addition of any potential human carcinogen to food products—with new criteria based on risks, particularly to children. Passage of the act achieved a long-standing goal of agribusiness and other opponents of environmental regulation, many of whom believed that such an absolute ban was unwarranted and impractical. But it also achieved major reforms desired by environmentalists, by requiring documentation of all risks of pesticide residues rather than just cancer risks, particularly risks to children rather than just to the general adult population. In addition, it required the EPA to look at the cumulative risks of exposure to multiple pesticide residues in food, rather than just one chemical at a time, and it required consideration of all sources of exposure, such as from household pesticides and drinking-water contaminants as well as from food. Finally, it required food stores to post information about chemical residues on their products—a right-to-know provision—which environmental advocates hoped would substitute consumer pressures for the difficulties of achieving effective government regulation.

As the EPA began to propose rules for implementing the law, however, agribusiness lobbyists mounted a fierce campaign to weaken them. Under the law, the EPA was given ten years to review nearly 10,000 tolerance limits for pesticide residues in food. Beginning in 1998 the EPA reviewed the first ninety of these and proposed extra margins of safety to protect children in nine cases; and it began moving toward a review of two of the most potent and widely used classes of pesticides, organophosphates and carbamates. In response, an industry coalition mounted an intensive lobbying initiative claiming that the EPA was not using "sound science" and was moving too aggressively to take pesticides off the market. By the end of 2000 only two additional pesticides had been regulated.[36]

Drinking-Water Contaminants: The Arsenic Controversy

The 1996 amendments to the Safe Drinking Water Act, meanwhile, directed the EPA to focus on the most hazardous drinking-water contaminants, thus requiring more risk-based priorities and easing the burdens on the EPA and local water utilities, but it also required the utilities to disclose contaminant levels to their customers—another right-to-know policy. The EPA issued disclosure rules in 1998, and by spring 2000, four years after the law was passed, the agency finally proposed tighter regulations for one serious drinking-water contaminant: arsenic.

Arsenic causes cancer and is found at harmful levels in at least one out of ten community drinking-water supplies, often due to natural sources of contamination. A National Research Council study in 1999 concluded that in some communities as many as 1 person in 100 might be at risk, a risk level far higher than most EPA regulations allow. After some fifteen years of scientific study, and consultation with both environmentalists and water utilities—and in the face of a lawsuit by the Natural Resources Defense Council—the EPA finally proposed new rules in May 2000, reducing permitted arsenic levels from 50 to 5 parts per billion (ppb). Environmental groups argued that even these restrictions were too lax, still allowing a cancer risk of 1 in every 10,000 people; but water utilities argued for a standard of 10 ppb, the same as that used by the European Union and the World Health Organization. They contended that compliance costs were already too great, especially for many small water systems that would be affected, and that the estimated health benefits were not worth the additional costs.[37] During President Clinton's last week in office, the EPA administrator signed regulations adopting the 10-ppb standard.

Bush's EPA administrator Christine Todd Whitman initially suspended the arsenic rule and commissioned detailed restudies of its scientific justification by a new National Research Council panel and of its cost estimates by an EPA advisory panel. Environmental groups and the press attacked her decision as confirmation of the Bush administration's lack of commitment to environmental protection: Arsenic had already been well studied, the proposed standard had already been adopted by Europe and the World Health Organization, and it had even been supported by many water utilities themselves the previous year. The House and Senate each passed legislation directing the EPA to implement stricter standards immediately, and when the restudies also confirmed that the Clinton administration's estimates were justified, Whitman adopted the 10-ppb standard. Although the ultimate outcome was unchanged, the suspension and additional months of restudy increased public cynicism about the potential for political use of demands for greater scientific proof of risks before regulating.[38] (See chapter 8 for further discussion of the arsenic standard.)

Executive Oversight: Good Science or Political Agenda?

More broadly, the Bush administration beginning in 2001 sought to impose far more active executive oversight over all the federal regulatory agencies, both by the White House itself and through the OMB. The OMB's Office of Information and Regulatory Affairs (OIRA) had been authorized by President Reagan to impose greater scrutiny and accountability on the regulatory agencies for the costs and information burdens their decisions imposed on those who were regulated. Its legal authority to overrule agency decisions was limited—it had no role in the agencies' regulatory statutes—but under presidential executive orders and several procedural laws, it exercised growing authority to oversee the agencies' paperwork requirements, the methods they used in performing risk assessments and cost-benefit analyses, and after 2000 even the data disseminated by government agencies and used in regulatory decisions. In short, it gained increasing power to either encourage or block the development of environmental and other regulations by influencing the agencies' risk assessment procedures and risk management decisions.

As head of OIRA, President Bush appointed John Graham, former director of the Harvard Center for Risk Analysis and an outspoken advocate of limiting government regulation to those proposals that could pass stringent quantitative risk assessment and cost-benefit analyses. Under Graham's direction, OIRA promoted what he labeled "smart regulation": "to accelerate the adoption of good rules, modify existing rules to make them more effective and less costly, and rescind outmoded rules whose benefits do not justify their costs."[39] In his first six months, Graham sent back twenty regulatory proposals to the agencies for restudy, signaling more skeptical review of their risk assessment methods and justifications. He added scientists and engineers to OIRA's staff of mostly economists, signaling that the scientific as well as the economic justifications for regulatory proposals would be scrutinized more closely. He approved and even encouraged several high-cost regulatory proposals, such as emissions standards for off-road diesel engines and labeling requirements for trans-fatty acids in food products, when he believed them justified by strong scientific evidence of risk and high benefit-cost ratios. At the same time, he also claimed credit for sharply reducing the flow of high-cost regulations that he believed did not meet these tests.[40]

Graham also sought to impose more centralized analytical and procedural requirements on the regulatory agencies, including procedures for risk assessments, cost-benefit analyses, and peer review and for external challenges to the quality of data used in regulatory decisions or disseminated by the agencies. OIRA's drafts of these guidelines provoked strong objections, however, even from many experts. The analytical guidelines, for instance, directed the agencies to quantify the "value of a statistical life" and to estimate people's willingness to pay for saving such a life as a standard for assessing regulatory proposals, implicitly ignoring inequities in such judgments based on highly unequal incomes and wealth (as well as serious practical problems in measuring them).[41] They also required discounting future costs and benefits, implicitly devaluing impacts on future generations, and proposed to use age-adjusted risk estimates, implying that the lives of the elderly were worth less than those of younger victims (a "senior death discount"); the latter proposal was reversed after a political outcry.[42] The peer review proposal would have imposed a cumbersome centralized process on top of the agencies' own procedures, including increased participation by scientists associated with regulated industries and increased skepticism toward academic scientists funded by federal agencies—in effect, a prescription for increased influence by regulated industries—and this too was moderated after strong opposition from the scientific community.[43]

Finally, two new procedural laws gave OIRA, as well as interested parties outside the government, far greater power to challenge not just regulatory proposals but also the scientific studies and risk assessments used to justify them. First, a 1998 rider to an appropriations bill, the Shelby amendment or Data Access Act, directed the OMB to declare as public records all data produced under federally funded research grants—university research grants, for instance—subject to information requests under the Freedom of Information Act.[44] This decision greatly broadened the definition of public records and opened the potential for harassment of academic scientists by industries seeking to discredit or block research critical of their impacts (significantly, the disclosure requirement applied only to government-funded studies, not to industry-funded studies that might also be used to influence public policy decisions).[45] Second, an appropriations bill rider in 2000, the Data Quality Act—drafted by an industry lobbyist and former OMB official[46]—directed the OMB to issue policy and procedural guidance for "ensuring and maximizing the quality, objectivity, utility, and integrity of information . . . disseminated by Federal agencies," and to establish administrative mechanisms by which "affected persons" can "seek and obtain correction of information . . . that does not comply with the guidelines."[47]

In effect these provisions opened the door for additional challenges to the agencies, both by the OMB and by industries and other parties affected by their decisions. Rather than make decisions based on professional judgments about the "preponderance of the evidence," the agencies must now be prepared to defend themselves on every data point before regulating. The paint industry, for instance, argued that because of alleged errors in one document of a large public record supporting a model rule for regulating volatile organic compounds, all state air-pollution-control plans based on the model rule should be invalidated.[48] The data-quality mandate could of course be used by environmental advocates as well as by regulated industries: Early challenges came both from industries challenging data on the harmful effects of pesticides, rocket fuel, overfishing, and global climate change, and from environmental groups challenging data used to support Forest Service timber contracts, Bureau of Land Management decisions allowing more grazing, and Army Corps of Engineers river projects.[49]

In both cases, the effect was to use demands for "good science" to require a higher and higher standard of proof before government action. Many past regulations that have saved numerous lives might not have been approved under such a rigorous standard of proof, for example, removing lead from gasoline and reducing vinyl-chloride exposure in the workplace.[50] Dr. John Snow, father of modern epidemiology, stopped a cholera epidemic in 1852 by insisting that the handle be removed from a public well in London, decades before the "good science" of Pasteur and others identified the waterborne pathogen responsible for it. Should government regulate hazards only after proof and cost-benefit analysis, or should it have authority to prevent them? Yet if government agencies exercise such authority, how can they be held accountable for political abuses of it?

Graham's stated goal—using executive oversight to hold the agencies accountable for improving the level of rational and consistent analysis applied to regulatory decisions—was also undercut by widespread political interventions, by Bush's political appointees and by the White House itself, both in risk-based decisions and even in the risk assessments and scientific reports underlying them. Examples included studies on the impacts of mercury emissions from power plants (see chapter 8), of global warming (see chapter 13), of tuna fishing on dolphins (see chapter 16), and of mountaintop coal mining, as well as many endangered-species studies, among others. In 2004 a large group of scientists signed two reports charging the Bush administration with more "systematic distortion" of scientific findings in the pursuit of political goals than any previous presidency; signers included 20 Nobel laureates and even some Republican advisors to previous presidents.[51] Whatever Graham's personal commitment to "good science" and rational analysis, OIRA appeared far less willing or able to challenge the political intrusions into science and risk assessment that occurred throughout the Bush administration. Without such a commitment, and a principled willingness to resign over it if necessary, OIRA's oversight process was vulnerable to the perceptions of skeptics that it served as much to advance the administration's antiregulatory business agenda as to improve regulation.

Environmental Risks: The Twenty-First Century

For all the rhetoric advocating "good science" and risk assessment as a basis for regulation, the science is rarely certain, and government decisions inevitably represent judgments balancing the likelihoods and consequences of different outcomes. In this context, arguments favoring higher or lower standards of scientific proof are often advanced for political rather than scientific reasons, by those opposing or advocating regulation. Over the past several decades, risk-based regulation has arguably been less effective in reducing environmental risks than either technology- or incentive-based approaches, precisely because it is vulnerable to endless arguments over scientific proof prior to mandating action.[52] In the process, it also has diverted significant amounts of scientific effort into studies to justify regulations and win court battles.

The EPA's statutes, meanwhile, remain a fragmented patchwork of separate mandates, with little discretion either for risk-based priorities or for more effective incentives to motivate solutions. Some pollutants that appear to pose only remote risks continue to be regulated, whereas other important environmental risks remain ineffectively managed, for example, nonpoint sources of water pollution, urban smog, losses of natural habitat, and global climate change.

The Precautionary Principle and "Risk-Risk" Trade-offs

Is there a better way to prevent damage to human health and the environment? During the same period, from the 1970s through the 1990s, European governments developed and adopted the "precautionary principle" as a basis for such decisions. Contrary to some public assumptions, this principle is not an alternative to risk assessment and cost-benefit analysis. Indeed, it specifically requires the consideration of available scientific technical data and of the costs and benefits of either action or inaction, and it also requires that actions be proportional to the level of protection intended (a "balancing" criterion). It differs from the U.S. risk-cost-benefit balancing approach, however, in specifically stating that the decision criterion should be based on a high level of health and environmental protection, and that preventive action is legitimate even when the science is still uncertain—in contrast to the increased demand for proof in U.S. regulatory proposals since the *Benzene* decision. In the 1992 United Nations Rio Declaration, the principle was further stated as "Where there are threats of serious or irreversible damage, lack of full scientific certainty shall not be used as a reason for postponing cost-effective measures to prevent environmental degradation." The decision maker's responsibility, in short, is to determine as a political judgment what level of risk is acceptable to the public and how all the public concerns affected by it—including long-term and noneconomic concerns such as health and other impacts, in addition to economic costs and benefits—should be balanced to reach an appropriately protective outcome.[53]

In practice, some U.S. environmental laws are more precautionary than their European counterparts, whereas European laws are more precautionary toward other risks.[54] The practical effect of the precautionary principle, however, is to establish a more explicit presumption on the side of environment and health protection, and to allow greater administrative discretion to regulate risks to those outcomes in the absence of scientific certainty, and to place more of the burden of proof on businesses to prove safety rather than on the regulator to prove harm. Before becoming EPA administrator, New Jersey governor Christine Todd Whitman argued publicly that "policymakers need to take a precautionary approach to environmental protection. . . . We must acknowledge that uncertainty is inherent in managing natural resources, recognize it is usually easier to prevent environmental damage than to repair it later, and shift the burden of proof away from those advocating protection toward those proposing an action that may be harmful."[55] However, the Bush administration strongly opposed moving U.S. risk-based decision making in this direction.

An essential issue for either approach is how to assure explicit consideration and appropriate balancing of "risk-risk comparisons," that is, of the hazards that might result from regulating a risk along with those resulting from not doing so. Banning one chemical may lead to increased use of another with different or even greater hazards, for instance, and restricting some pesticides may allow the increased spread of disease organisms or food-crop damage.[56] Such judgments are both legitimate and necessary, but the precautionary principle should not be used so one-sidedly that the possible consequences are ignored.

Policy Integration

Reducing many important environmental risks will require changes not just in the EPA's policies but also across many economic sectors, and across all the agencies whose policies create important incentives for these sectors. A prominent example is the risk of accelerated global warming, to which human emissions from fossil fuels are believed to be significant contributors. The global warming issue represents by far the largest-scale combination of environmental risks and economic trade-offs identified to date, and although the Kyoto Protocol was not a perfect solution, it represented an extraordinary investment of effort by scientists as well as diplomats to craft first steps to reduce its risks (see chapter 13 for fuller discussion). Even in the face of widespread scientific agreement, however, the Bush administration chose to defer any serious U.S. actions to address it: to create systematic incentives to reduce greenhouse gas emissions from power plants, industries, and motor vehicles. So far, the United States at the national level has no effective institutional mechanism—nor the political will—to orchestrate such government-wide risk-reduction initiatives.

From Risk Reduction to Sustainable Development

Many issues framed as environmental risk decisions are not so much about environmental risks themselves as about conflicting views of their significance and conflicting public preferences. The proposal to open the Arctic National Wildlife Refuge to oil drilling is often presented as an issue about the ecological risks to the caribou herds that live there, but it is really about conflicting preferences between advocates for oil extraction and opponents who intensely value the idea of permanently protected natural wilderness areas.

Even more important, the most serious environmental challenges for the future include international and global issues for which a national risk-regulation approach by itself is inadequate. Examples include the depletion of ocean fisheries, stratospheric ozone damage, global climate change, genetic manipulation of other species for foods and drugs, nanotechnology, and unsustainable pressures of population and economic development on natural processes worldwide.

Are these problems amenable to quantitative risk assessment? In principle, perhaps. But in practice these decisions are about far more complex choices than risk alone. They are also about other environmental values—sustainability of natural resources and ecosystems, and aesthetics and the appreciation of nature, for instance—and about legitimate non-environmental values as well, such as self-determination, fairness, human needs and wants, and other considerations. The vocabulary of risk-based decision making is a valuable step forward from the patchwork of conflicting laws that still defines much of U.S. environmental regulation. But it is ultimately too narrowly focused on justifying the regulation of adverse outcomes to provide an adequate framework for the more complex and creative tasks of environmental management. These questions require a broader understanding of the interactions between human societies and their environments and a more systematic and positive vision of their future.

The United Nations World Commission on Environment and Development (WCED) proposed in 1987 the concept of "sustainable development" as a broader framework for environmental decision making. Sustainable development sets as a principle the goal of meeting the needs of the present in ways that do not compromise the ability of future generations to meet their own needs. In doing so, it integrates environmental and social as well as economic needs. The WCED report reaffirmed the importance of economic development, especially for the millions of people who still live in economic poverty and degraded environments, but it argued that the *pattern* of economic development for the future must incorporate ecological sustainability and social equity as well. These ideas were further developed by the United Nations Conference on Environment and Development (the Earth Summit) in Brazil in 1992, in its Agenda 21. Perhaps the highest priority tasks for environmental policy in the twenty-first century are to move from risk reduction to sustainable development as its core language and goal, to develop agreement on its details and priorities, and to achieve its implementation.[57]

Suggested Web Sites

Society for Risk Analysis (www.sra.org/resources_government.php) This Web page offers dozens of risk-related government links.

Regulations.gov (www.regulations.gov) This Web site enables users to find and comment on current regulatory proposals.

U.S. Environmental Protection Agency (www.epa.gov) At the EPA Web site, users can find information on specific topics and programs.

U.S. Office of Management and Budget, Office of Information and Regulatory Affairs (www.whitehouse.gov/omb/inforeg) This Web site provides documentation on OMB regulatory review policies and actions for risk assessment and cost-benefit analysis by federal agencies.

Harvard Center for Risk Analysis (www.hcra.harvard.edu) The Harvard Center for Risk Analysis is one of the leading academic organizations promoting and conducting quantitative risk analyses of environmental and health regulations.

Center for Progressive Reform (www.progressivereform.org, formerly the Center for Progressive Regulation) The Center for Progressive Reform's Web site provides analyses by a network of legal and other scholars who are strongly critical of many of the current methods and uses of risk and cost-benefit analysis.

The Center for Regulatory Effectiveness (www.thecre.com) The Center for Regulatory Effectiveness's Web site provides information and analyses on a wide range of regulatory issues, particularly from the perspective of the regulated businesses.

OMB Watch (www.ombwatch.org) OMB Watch provides information on risk assessment and other regulatory issues involving OMB oversight from the perspective of a nonprofit citizen watchdog group.

Union of Concerned Scientists (www.ucsusa.org) The Union of Concerned Scientists' Web site provides critical analyses of uses and abuses of science in governmental decisions from the perspective of a nonprofit organization of scientists and citizens.

Notes

1. William D. Ruckelshaus, "Science, Risk, and Public Policy," *Science* 221 (1983): 1027–1028.
2. U.S. Environmental Protection Agency (EPA), *Risk Assessment and Risk Management: Framework for Decisionmaking* (Washington, D.C.: EPA, 1984); EPA, *Unfinished Business: A Comparative Assessment of Environmental Problems* (Washington, D.C.: EPA, 1987), 1; EPA, *Reducing Risk: Setting Priorities and Strategies for Environmental Protection* (Washington, D.C.: EPA, 1990), 16.
3. Curtis C. Travis et al., "Cancer Risk Management: A Review of 132 Federal Regulatory Decisions," *Environmental Science and Technology* 21 (1987): 415–420.
4. Mark E. Rushefsky, *Making Cancer Policy* (Albany: State University of New York Press, 1986), 74–80.
5. Ibid., 59–84.
6. Milton Russell and Michael Gruber, "Risk Assessment in Environmental Policy-Making," *Science* 236 (1987): 286–290.
7. *Industrial Union Department, AFL-CIO v. American Petroleum Institute*, 448 U.S. 607 (1980), "the *Benzene* decision"; Executive Order No. 12291, February 17, 1981. As a legal matter, the extent to which quantitative risk assessment is required depends on the language of the specific statute involved. Although the *Benzene* decision involved a proposed standard by the Occupational Safety and Health Administration, it influenced all the regulatory agencies to put increased emphasis on quantitative risk assessment, as did Reagan's executive order.
8. Vincent Covello and Joshua Menkes, *Risk Assessment and Risk Assessment Methods: The State of the Art* (Washington, D.C.: Division of Policy Research and Analysis, National Science Foundation, 1985), xxiii.
9. ENVIRON Corp., *Elements of Toxicology and Chemical Risk Assessment*, rev. ed. (Washington, D.C.: ENVIRON, July 1988), 9; National Research Council, *Risk Assessment in the Federal Government: Managing the Process* (Washington, D.C.: National Academies Press, 1983), 18.
10. National Research Council, *Risk Assessment in the Federal Government*; Ruckelshaus, "Science, Risk, and Public Policy"; Ruckelshaus, "Risk in a Free Society," *Risk Analysis* 4 (1984): 157–162.
11. Example adapted from the EPA, "Workshop on Risk and Decision Making" (materials prepared for the EPA by Temple, Barker, and Sloane Inc. and ENVIRON Corp., 1986).
12. For a list of examples of each of these types of laws, see Rushefsky, *Making Cancer Policy*, 68–70.
13. Travis et al., "Cancer Risk Management."

14. EPA, "Health Risk and Economic Impact Assessments of Suspected Carcinogens: Interim Procedures and Guidelines," *Federal Register* 41, May 25, 1976, 21402–21405; *Federal Register* 51, September 24, 1986, 33992–34054; *Federal Register* 53, June 30, 1988, 24836–24869; Rushefsky, *Making Cancer Policy*, chaps. 3–6.

15. See, for example, Philip H. Abelson, "Risk Assessments of Low-Level Exposures," *Science* 265 (1994): 1507.

16. The American Industrial Health Council, for instance, was formed in the 1980s to develop industry-wide positions on environmental health risks and risk assessment methods. See, for example, "Special Edition: Need for Re-Examination of Risk," *AIHC Science Commentary* 5 (1994): 1–26. Popular-literature critiques included Edith Efron, *The Apocalyptics: Cancer and the Big Lie* (New York: Simon and Schuster, 1984); and Elizabeth Whelan, *Toxic Terror* (Ottawa, Ill.: Jameson Books, 1985).

17. Richard Doll and Richard Peto, "The Causes of Cancer: Quantitative Estimates of Avoidable Risks of Cancer in the United States Today," *Journal of the National Cancer Institute* 66 (1981): 1191–1285; Bruce Ames, Renae Magaw, and Lois Swirsky Gold, "Ranking Possible Carcinogenic Hazards," *Science* 236 (1987): 271–280; Abelson, "Risk Assessments of Low-Level Exposures," 1507.

18. See, for instance, Adam M. Finkel, "Has Risk Assessment Become Too 'Conservative'?" *Resources* (summer 1989): 11–13; John C. Bailar III, Edmund A. C. Crouch, Rashid Shaikh, and Donna Speigelman, "One-Hit Models of Carcinogenesis: Conservative or Not?" *Risk Analysis* 8 (1988): 485–497. See also Adam M. Finkel and Dominic Golding, eds., *Worst Things First? The Debate over Risk-Based National Environmental Priorities* (Baltimore: Johns Hopkins University Press, 1995).

19. National Academy of Public Administration (NAPA), *Setting Priorities, Getting Results: A New Direction for EPA* (Washington, D.C.: NAPA, 1995), 41–43.

20. Theodora Colborn, Frederick von Saal, and Ana M. Soto, "Developmental Effects of Endocrine-Disrupting Chemicals in Wildlife and Humans," *Environmental Health Perspectives* 101 (1993): 378–384; National Academy of Sciences–National Research Council, *Science and Judgment in Risk Assessment* (Washington, D.C.: National Academies Press, 1994). See also Adam Finkel, "A Second Opinion on an Environmental Misdiagnosis: The Risky Prescriptions of Breaking the Vicious Circle," *NYU Environmental Law Journal* 3 (1994): 295–381.

21. EPA, *Unfinished Business*.

22. EPA, *Reducing Risk*.

23. William Reilly, "Aiming Before We Shoot: The Quiet Revolution in Environmental Policy," *Northern Kentucky Law Review* 18 (1991): 159–174.

24. During the George H. W. Bush and Clinton administrations, EPA administrators tried to implement some of these proposals by administrative initiatives, such as risk-based enforcement priorities, sector-wide negotiation of environmental performance improvement in high-pollution industrial sectors (the Common Sense Initiative), and economic incentives for improvements beyond regulated levels by high-performing businesses (Project XL, for "eXcellence and Leadership"). Most of these initiatives fell far short of their champions' hopes for them, however, due in part to the continued requirements of statutory mandates and precedents and the associated risk of litigation.

25. *Ethyl Corp v. EPA*, 541 F.2d 1 (D.C. Circuit) (en banc), *cert.* denied 426 U.S. 941 (1976). The evidence supporting this decision was confirmed only several years later, by public health scientists who documented significant reductions in blood lead levels in inner-city children after the lead phase-down had occurred.

26. *Industrial Union Dept., AFL-CIO v. American Petroleum Institute*, 448 U.S. 607 (1980). For fuller discussion of the changing expectations of the courts, see Gail Charnley and E. Donald Elliott, "Risk versus Precaution: Environmental Law and Public Health Protection," *Environmental Law Reporter* 32 (March 2002): 10363–10366.

27. *Corrosion Proof Fittings v. EPA*, 947 F.2d 1201 (Fifth Circuit).

28. Russell and Gruber, "Risk Assessment," 286–290.

29. Terry F. Yosie, "Science and Sociology: The Transition to a Post-Conservative Risk Assessment Era" (plenary address to the annual meeting of the Society for Risk Analysis, Houston, Texas, November 2, 1987). Yosie was then director of the EPA's Science Advisory Board.

30. Rushefsky, *Making Cancer Policy*, 92–94; see also, for example, American Industrial Health Council (AIHC), *AIHC Recommended Alternatives to OSHA's Generic Carcinogen Proposal* (Scarsdale, N.Y.: AIHC, 1978).

31. Sheldon Krimsky and Alonzo Plough, *Environmental Hazards: Communicating Risks as a Social Process* (Dover, Mass.: Auburn House, 1989). See also K. S. Shrader-Frechette, *Risk and Rationality: Philosophical Foundations for Populist Reforms* (Berkeley and Los Angeles: University of California Press, 1991).

32. The tool-versus-rule issue has also been discussed in relation to cost-benefit analysis of regulatory proposals: see Richard N. L. Andrews, "Cost-Benefit Analysis as Regulatory Reform," in *Cost-Benefit Analysis and Environmental Regulations: Politics, Ethics, and Methods*, ed. Daniel Swartzman, Richard A. Liroff, and Kevin G. Croke (Washington, D.C.: Conservation Foundation, 1982).

33. Donald Munton, "Dispelling the Myths of the Acid Rain Story," *Environment* 40 (July–August 1998): 4–7, 27–34.

34. See, for example, EPA, *Reducing Risk*; NAPA, *Setting Priorities*; NAPA, *Resolving the Paradox of Environmental Protection* (Washington, D.C.: NAPA, 1997); NAPA, *Environment.gov* (Washington, D.C.: NAPA, 2000).

35. Presidential/Congressional Commission on Risk Assessment and Risk Management, *Risk Assessment and Risk Management in Regulatory Decisionmaking*, Final Report, Vol. 2, 1997, www.epa.gov/ncea/pres_com/riskcom2/v2epaa.htm.

36. Cindy Skrzycki, "In Which the EPA Observes Chemical Reactions," *Washington Post*, May 8, 1998, D1; Tom Kenworthy, "A Pesticide Balancing Act: EPA Caught between Farmers, Food Safety Fears," *Washington Post*, August 2, 1999, A1; Kenworthy, "EPA Limits Use of 2 Pesticides," *Washington Post*, August 3, 1999, A2.

37. John H. Cushman Jr., "E.P.A. Proposes New Rules to Lower Arsenic in Tap Water," *New York Times*, May 25, 2000, A20.

38. Anita Huslin, "Debate Swells over Arsenic in Water Supply," *Washington Post*, July 5, 2000, B1; Elizabeth Shogren, "Senate Orders Tougher Arsenic Limit for Water," *Los Angeles Times*, August 2, 2001, A22; Shogren, "EPA Study Undercuts Arsenic Step," *Los Angeles Times*, August 24, 2001, A20.

39. John D. Graham, "Reining in the Regulatory State: The Smart-Regulation Agenda," Cato Institute Hill Briefing, October 3, 2003, www.whitehouse.gov/omb/inforeg/speeches/031003graham.pdf.

40. Ibid.

41. OMB Circular A-4, September 17, 2003, www.whitehouse.gov/omb/circulars/a004/a-4.pdf

42. Ibid.; see also Lisa Heinzerling and Frank Ackerman, *Pricing the Priceless: Cost-Benefit Analysis of Environmental Protection*, (Washington, D.C.: Georgetown University Law Center, 2002), www.law.georgetown.edu/gelpi/papers/pricefnl.pdf.

43. OMB, "OMB Proposes Draft Peer Review Standards for Regulatory Science," press release, August 29, 2003, www.whitehouse.gov/omb/pubpress/2003-34.pdf; critical comments by Bruce Alberts, president of the National Academy of Sciences, at www.whitehouse.gov/omb/inforeg/2003iq/115.pdf.

44. P.L. No. 105-277, 112 *Stat.* 2681 (1998).

45. Donald T. Hornstein, "Accounting for Science: The Independence of Public Research in the New, Subterranean Administrative Law," *Law & Contemporary Problems* 66 (autumn 2003): 230–232; Wendy E. Wagner, "The 'Bad Science' Fiction: Reclaiming the Debate over the Role of Science in Public Health and Environmental Regulation," *Law & Contemporary Problems* 66 (autumn 2003): 63 ff.

46. Chris Mooney, "Paralysis by Analysis: Jim Tozzi's Regulation to End All Regulation," *Washington Monthly*, May 2004.

47. Ibid.; §515, 114 *Stat.* 2763A-153-154.

48. Letter from the Center for Progressive Regulation to Michael Leavitt and John Graham, August 3, 2004, www.progressivereform.org/articles/paint_dqa_0804.pdf.

49. OMB/OIRA, *Information Quality: A Report to the Congress, Fiscal Year 2003,* www.whitehouse.gov/omb/inforeg/infopoltech.html#iq.

50. Frank Ackerman, Lisa Heinzerling, and Rachel Massey, "Applying Cost-Benefit Analysis to Past Decisions: Was Protecting the Environment *Ever* a Good Idea?" (white paper), Center for Progressive Regulation, July 2004, www.progressivereform .org/articles/cb_wrong.pdf.

51. Union of Concerned Scientists, *Scientific Integrity in Policymaking: An Investigation of the Bush Administration's Misuse of Science,* February 2004, and *Scientific Integrity in Policymaking: Further Investigation of the Bush Administration's Misuse of Science,* July 2004, www.ucsusa.org, July 31, 2004.

52. See, for instance, Oliver Houck, "Tales from a Troubled Marriage: Science and Law in Environmental Policy," *Science* 302 (2003): 1926–1929.

53. Commission of the European Communities, *Communication from the Commission on the Precautionary Principle,* February 2, 2000, http://europa.eu.int/comm/dgs/ health_consumer/library/pub/pub07_en.pdf. See also Theofanis Christoforou, "The Precautionary Principle, Risk Assessment, and the Comparative Role of Science in the European Community and the US Legal Systems," and Jonathan Wiener, "Convergence, Divergence, and Complexity in US and European Risk Regulation," chaps. 1 and 3 in *Green Giants? Environmental Policies in the United States and the European Union,* ed. Norman J. Vig and Michael G. Faure (Cambridge: MIT Press, 2004).

54. Wiener, "Convergence, Divergence, and Complexity." The United States, for example, is more precautionary with respect to risks of fine particulates (diesel emissions), hazardous waste disposal, "right to know" mandates, and rights to sue for compensation for environmental or health damage (tort claims), whereas Europe is more precautionary with respect to hormones in beef and milk, genetically modified foods, toxic chemicals, and global climate change.

55. Christine Todd Whitman, quoted in *Scientific American,* 284 (January 1, 2001): 18.

56. Wiener, "Convergence, Divergence, and Complexity."

57. World Commission on Environment and Development, *Our Common Future* (New York: Oxford University Press, 1987); Ismail Serageldin and Andrew Steer, eds., *Making Development Sustainable: From Concepts to Action* (Washington, D.C.: World Bank, 1994). See also chapter 15 in this volume.

11

Environmental Justice: Normative Concerns, Empirical Evidence, and Government Action

Evan J. Ringquist

Chester, Pennsylvania, is a town of almost 40,000 residents located near Philadelphia. For over half a century the town was a center of industry, but the deindustrialization of the rust belt and a decline in defense procurement caused many of Chester's factories to close their doors. Even so, the city has one of the highest concentrations of industrial facilities in the state. Chester and the adjoining township also contain a remarkably large number of hazardous waste facilities, including a municipal waste incinerator; a medical waste treatment plant; and eight commercial treatment, storage, and disposal facilities (TSDFs) capable of handling over two million tons of hazardous waste each year. Two-thirds of Chester residents also happen to be black. By contrast, the remainder of Delaware County is only 6 percent black and contains only three commercial TSDFs. In 1996 the Pennsylvania Department of Environmental Protection (PA DEP) issued a permit for yet another commercial TSDF in Chester. In response, citizens filed a lawsuit against the agency, claiming that they were the victims of environmental racism.[1]

The Chester case is not an isolated example. As early as 1971, federal regulators recognized that exposure to environmental pollutants was not distributed equally: minority communities experienced disproportionately high levels of environmental risk.[2] These inequities were largely ignored until the late 1980s, when a number of studies concluded that minority neighborhoods generally experienced worse air quality, worse water quality, more landfills, more sources of toxic pollution, more hazardous waste sites, and weaker enforcement of environmental regulations than did wealthier neighborhoods with smaller minority populations. Concerns over racial and class biases in environmental protection have mobilized hundreds of grassroots groups into what is generally referred to as the environmental justice movement. This movement has the potential to broaden the base of support for traditional environmentalism, and it may reinvigorate and refocus the forces of progressive politics behind environmental concerns.[3] In short, it has the potential to change the face of environmental politics and policy. In this chapter I chronicle the development and demands of the environmental justice movement, examine the empirical evidence that supports (and sometimes refutes) the claims of environmental justice advocates, consider five potential causes of environmental inequities, and summarize actions taken by government officials to remedy environmental inequities. Finally, I evaluate the prospects for continued progress in addressing perceived racial and class biases in environmental protection.

The Environmental Justice Movement

Despite examples like Chester, the initial prospects for a coalition between the environmental movement and advocates for civil rights and social justice looked bleak. Early in their history, environmental groups sought to keep the environmental movement separate from general social justice concerns because they feared that an alliance might dilute their effectiveness and detract from their ability to attract members. In addition, mainstream environmental groups often emphasize wilderness preservation and the protection of endangered species over reducing pollution in inner cities, and the membership lists and leadership positions of these groups are hardly crowded with racial minorities.[4]

Partially in response to criticism from environmental justice advocates, partially in recognition that social justice and the environment are intimately linked, and partially because poor and minority citizens provide an opportunity to increase their membership base, most mainstream environmental groups have become involved in the environmental justice movement. In 1989 the ten largest environmental groups embarked on an outreach campaign to increase minority membership and the number of minorities in leadership positions. Some of these groups, particularly Greenpeace and the National Wildlife Federation, now actively seek partnerships with local grassroots groups to combat environmental injustice. Today the common interests of environmentalists and social justice advocates are advanced through a multifaceted nationwide network of organizations generally referred to as the environmental justice movement.

Origins of the Environmental Justice Movement

Nearly all observers agree that the environmental justice movement began in 1982 outside a small town in North Carolina. A hazardous waste management firm, in conjunction with the U.S. Environmental Protection Agency (EPA) and the state of North Carolina, proposed construction of a large hazardous waste landfill in Warren County. The residents of Warren County initially received little information about the proposed landfill. When they were finally alerted to the nature of the facility, large demonstrations ensued, during which more than five thousand arrests were made. The local residents were not the only ones protesting the landfill. Representatives from the United Church of Christ, the Southern Christian Leadership Conference, and the Congressional Black Caucus also took part in the demonstrations. Because Warren County was the poorest county in the state, with a population that was 65 percent African American (more than three times the state average), many of the protesters believed this landfill was as much a violation of the residents' civil rights as it was a threat to public health and environmental quality. By linking environmental and civil rights concerns, opponents of the Warren County landfill served as the prototype for the modern environmental justice movement.[5]

From Warren County to Washington, D.C., and Beyond

After the Warren County episode, local civil rights and social justice groups throughout the United States began to protest the location of polluting facilities. Soon these temporary groups that had mobilized around a single facility began to maintain a permanent presence in local politics in order to advance the cause of environmental justice. As the number of these groups increased and their activities expanded, local activists inevitably came into contact with each other. Through these contacts, environmental justice advocates throughout the United States realized that they shared similar values, used similar tactics, and faced similar obstacles in pressing for environmental justice. Although local groups initially surmounted these obstacles with the help of national environmental organizations, increasingly these groups banded together into large, regional assistance networks.[6]

In 1990, representatives from several environmental justice groups organized the nation's first conference on race and the incidence of environmental hazards. The final report from this conference was forwarded to the EPA, and several of the coalition's suggestions served as the basis for agency efforts to promote environmental equity. In 1991, environmental justice groups from throughout the United States participated in the first People of Color Leadership Summit on the Environment, held in Washington, D.C. The summit drew more than six hundred participants from all fifty states and several foreign countries and also attracted the participation of the leaders of most of the nation's mainstream environmental groups. The major product of the summit was a statement of the principles of environmental justice. These principles serve as criteria for developing and evaluating policies aimed at attaining social and environmental justice.[7] To accomplish these goals the statement calls for full representation of minority groups and the poor in the policymaking process through membership in traditional environmental groups and through government provision of the legal and technical advice required for effective participation, for increased emphasis on pollution prevention, and for resident participation in corporate decisions affecting the well-being of their communities.[8] Currently, local groups and regional networks are at the center of a thriving environmental justice community on the Internet (see list at the end of this chapter). Many environmental justice groups are also engaged in partnerships with university-based environmental justice programs such as the Ecojustice Network at Harvard University, the Environmental Justice Resource Center at Clark Atlanta University, and the Center for Environmental Equity and Justice at Florida A & M University.

Environmental Injustice: A Look at the Evidence

The city of Chester has the lowest birth rate, the highest infant mortality rate, and among the highest cancer death rates in Pennsylvania. Not surprisingly, in Chester and elsewhere the most serious concern of environmental justice advocates is that inequities in exposure to environmental risks will result in higher rates of disease and death among minorities and the poor. It is extraordinarily difficult to test this concern directly. First, many diseases caused by environmental pollution have other causes as well. Thus, even if we find that poor and minority populations have higher rates of these ailments, we can't be sure that these diseases are caused by exposure to pollution. Second, the United States is the only advanced industrial nation that does not gather disease data by income and education, and environmental health data are not routinely collected by race and income.[9]

As a substitute for these data, we can evaluate the evidence we do have regarding the complex chain of causal relationships that lead to adverse environmental health effects among poor and minority populations. In the sections that follow I evaluate this evidence. First, I examine the charge that polluting facilities are located closer to these communities. Second, I assess the evidence that racial minorities and the poor are exposed to higher levels of pollution. Third, I examine evidence that residents of poor and minority communities are exposed to larger environmental health risks. If proximity to facilities leads to higher levels of pollutant exposure, if increased exposure leads to increased health risk, if increased risk leads to increased disease, and if poor and minority populations experience disproportionately high levels of proximity, exposure, risk, and disease, then we might logically conclude that at least some of this disease is caused by their greater exposure to environmental threats.

The Location of Polluting Facilities

Solid Waste Landfills and Incinerators. The earliest research into environmental racism in facility siting examined the location of solid waste landfills and incinerators. One study found that all the landfills constructed in King and Queen County, Virginia, between 1969 and 1990 were located in communities in which a majority of the residents were African American. In another study, sociologist Robert Bullard found that although only 28 percent of Houston's population was African American, 82 percent of Houston's waste facilities were located in majority black neighborhoods. Bullard claimed that the results from the Houston and Virginia studies are not uncommon and that minority communities throughout the United States receive more than their fair share of landfills and incinerators.[10] A more systematic study by the U.S. Government Accountability Office (GAO, formerly the General Accounting Office), however, reached a different conclusion. After examining the characteristics of populations surrounding nearly three hundred nonhazardous waste facilities, the GAO found no evidence that poor or minority residents were overrepresented near these landfills.[11]

Hazardous Waste Treatment, Storage, and Disposal Facilities. Most of the research examining the location of polluting facilities has focused on hazardous waste TSDFs, and the degree to which these facilities are located disproportionately in poor or minority communities is the subject of some debate. In 1983 the GAO examined the location of the four commercial hazardous waste landfills in the EPA's Region 4 (the Southeast). The average minority population of this region was 20 percent, but these landfills were located in communities where racial minorities made up, respectively, 38 percent, 52 percent, 66 percent, and 90 percent of the local populations. Moreover, poverty rates in these communities were significantly higher than for the region as a whole. The GAO concluded that there was enough evidence to be concerned about inequities in the siting of these facilities.[12] Studies of TSDF locations in several cities have also produced evidence that these facilities are located in neighborhoods with disproportionately large concentrations of poverty and people of color.[13]

The first nationwide study of the location of TSDFs was undertaken in 1987 by the United Church of Christ's Commission for Racial Justice (CRJ). The CRJ's statistical analysis demonstrated that as the percentage of poor and minority residents of a neighborhood increased, so did the likelihood that the neighborhood had a TSDF. This relationship held even when controlling for region, urbanization, and land value. An update to the CRJ report found these same relationships in the 1990s.[14] At least one group of researchers, however, disputed the conclusion that hazardous waste facilities are located in poor and minority communities. Douglas Anderton and his colleagues at the University of Massachusetts concluded that the positive association between race and facility location is an artifact of data aggregation. Indeed, when these scholars compared the demographics of census tracts (areas smaller than zip codes) that had commercial TSDFs with nearby census tracts with no facilities, they found no relationship between race, poverty, and the location of TSDFs.[15] Other scholars have also found little evidence of inequities in TSDF location when using census tracts as the unit of analysis, though these studies have focused on individual states and municipalities.[16] Vicki Been, however, demonstrated that the results reached by Anderton and his colleagues are themselves artifacts of a peculiar and questionable research design. While finding that the relationship between race, class, and facility location is more pronounced at the zip code level, Been also found that census tracts with commercial TSDFs have significantly higher percentages of Latino and African American residents.[17]

A potential limitation of these studies is that they only examine the location of commercial TSDFs (that is, facilities that accept hazardous wastes generated elsewhere). Fewer than one in ten hazardous waste facilities are commercial facilities, however, and commercial facilities handle less than 5 percent of all hazardous wastes generated in the United States. In an examination of all TSDFs nationwide, I found that race is an important

244 Evan J. Ringquist

Table 11-1 Population Living in Air Pollutant Nonattainment Areas (in percent)

Pollutant	White	Black	Latino
Particulates	14.7%	16.5%	34.0%
Carbon monoxide	33.6	46.0	57.1
Ozone	52.5	62.2	71.2
Sulfur dioxide	7.0	12.1	5.7
Lead	6.0	9.2	18.5

Source: Ken Sexton et al., "Air Pollution Health Risks: Do Class and Race Matter?" *Toxicology and Industrial Health 9*, no. 5 (1993): 843–878.

predictor of facility location, but that poverty is not, when controlling for other factors.[18] In a recent examination of noncommercial TSDF location at the census tract level, however, researchers at the University of Massachusetts found no such relationship.[19]

Exposure to Environmental Pollutants

Simply because a person lives close to a polluting facility does not mean he or she is exposed to higher levels of pollution. If regulated facilities are operating properly, if the pollution control equipment on these facilities is working correctly, and if environmental regulations are enforced diligently, then the level of exposure near these facilities should be minimal. We must look at the pollution data themselves to determine if pollutant exposure is distributed inequitably.

Air Pollutants. Early research into the distribution of air quality within cities found that air pollution was more severe in neighborhoods with high concentrations of poor and minority residents, and subsequent studies have continued to find significant inequities in the distribution of air pollution.[20] Table 11-1 illustrates the general conclusion that African American and Latino residents are much more likely than white residents to live in areas with unhealthy levels of air pollutants.

Toxics Release Inventory Pollutants. The 1986 Superfund Amendments and Reauthorization Act requires thousands of factories throughout the United States to report their releases of toxic chemicals. Together, this information makes up the Toxics Release Inventory (TRI). Researchers have demonstrated that TRI pollutants are concentrated in poor and minority communities in Florida, South Carolina, Ohio, and Los Angeles but not in Pittsburgh or Cleveland.[21] Two nationwide studies have also concluded that TRI pollutants tend to be concentrated in minority communities.[22] Table 11-2 presents a simple illustration of this relationship. The table shows clear inequities in the distribution of TRI pollutants in 2001, as the production of these pollutants increases with the percentage of blacks, Latinos, minorities, and the poor in residential zip codes. Finally, all previous analyses of TRI data studied the release of these pollutants under normal operating conditions at firms. Accidental releases of these pollutants, however, are typically more dangerous to surrounding residents. Two recent nationwide studies have shown that these accidental releases of toxic chemicals are also concentrated in poor and minority communities.[23]

Other Harmful Pollutants. John Hird and Michael Reese examined the distribution of several different environmental pollutants and concluded that, by most measures, pollution is significantly worse in counties with large concentrations of African American and Latino residents.[24] Moreover, certain subpopulations of the United States are exposed to exceptionally high levels of some pollutants. For example, agricultural workers, especially migrant farm laborers, are exposed to far more pesticides than are other citizens, and roughly 90 percent of all migrant farm laborers are African American or Latino.[25] Similarly, African American residents in Detroit, and Native Americans throughout the United States, are exposed to significantly higher levels of PCB (polychlorinated biphenyl) and mercury contamination because these subpopulations eat four to five times the amount of fish assumed by EPA models when setting safe levels of these pollutants. One study in Wisconsin concluded that the number-one environmental threat faced by Native Americans was the contamination of their food supply, particularly fish, by toxic pollutants.[26]

Exposure to Environmental Health Risks

Early environmental justice research provided ample evidence that both noxious facilities and the pollution emanating from them were concentrated in lower income neighborhoods and communities of color. Until recently, however, we did not know whether this greater exposure to facilities and pollution actually posed greater environmental health risks to these affected populations. In what may be the first environmental equity analysis to examine environmental health risks, James Hamilton and Kip Viscusi

Table 11-2 Toxic Pollutant Production in Poor and Minority Zip Code Areas (in pounds)

Percentage of the Population	African American	Latino	Minority	Poor
5%	2,522,616	2,886,732	2,033,501	1,972,796
5–25	3,345,747	3,039,788	3,543,274	3,277,288
>25	4,793,625	3,733,397	4,133,507	3,424,568

Source: Compiled from the EPA Toxics Release Inventory 2001 and U.S. Bureau of the Census 2000 STF 3B.

concluded that the risks posed by Superfund sites are concentrated dispro-portionately among residents of poor and minority communities.[27] More recently, researchers have begun to make use of two risk modeling tools developed by the EPA. The Cumulative Exposure Project (CEP) estimates human exposure to outdoor hazardous air pollutants, links these exposure data to toxicity data, and calculates human health cancer risks aggregated to the census tract level. The Risk Screening Environmental Indicators (RSEI) model is similar to the CEP in that it focuses on the health risks posed by toxic air pollutants. However, the RSEI model includes far more of these pollutants and incorporates more refined dispersion and toxicity models than does the CEP. Consequently the RSEI allows researchers to link pollution exposure to toxicity information and calculate an environmental health risk score for each square kilometer region in the United States.

Using the CEP data, Rachel Morello-Frosh, Manuel Pastor, and James Sadd found that minority residents in Southern California were exposed to significantly larger environmental cancer risks than were white residents, even after controlling for other economic, land use, and population factors.[28] In addition, using RSEI risk estimates for 1996, Marc Shapiro found that environmental health risks were greater in areas with large minority popula-tions but that these risks did not vary systematically with respect to the income of area residents. In addition, Shapiro's analysis concluded that envi-ronmental health risks worsened for African Americans between 1988 and 1996 but that these risks were reduced for Latinos and Asian Americans. Risk reductions between 1988 and 1996 were also greater in higher income areas.[29] Most important for our purposes, analyses using data from Super-fund sites, the CEP, and the RSEI all illustrate that the environmental inequities associated with the location of noxious facilities and the concen-tration of environmental pollutants generally translate into inequities with respect to environmental health risks.

Overall Evaluations of Environmental Inequities

Several scholars have attempted to complete comprehensive reviews of primary research regarding the distribution of environmental risk. Most of these reviews have concluded that environmental inequities are significant and generalizable,[30] although at least two have dissented from this conclu-sion.[31] A superior approach to overall assessments of environmental inequities is to conduct a meta-analysis of all extant environmental equity studies. Meta-analysis is a tool for quantitatively extracting the most gener-alizable conclusions from a large body of sometimes contradictory research. In the only meta-analysis of environmental inequity to date, I found that both polluting facilities and pollution emissions are concentrated in minority communities but that there is little evidence that these environmental risks are located in areas of hardcore poverty. Rather, these risks tend to be located in working-class neighborhoods.[32]

Environmental Inequities and Environmental Health

As we have seen, strong evidence indicates that poor citizens and members of minority groups live closer to polluting facilities and are exposed to higher levels of pollution. We have also seen that these factors create situations in which these same poor and minority citizens are exposed to greater environmental health risks. Literally dozens of studies show that adverse health effects stem from exposure to environmental pollutants or elevated levels of environmental risk.[33] Finally, we know that minorities and the poor experience more illnesses and have shorter life expectancies. Although all of this research provides a mountain of circumstantial evidence, the data limitations described in the introduction to this section prevent us from stating absolutely that environmental pollution disproportionately harms the health of minorities and the poor. Indeed, after surveying much of the same evidence presented here, the EPA concluded that "although there are clear differences between ethnic groups for disease and death rates, there are virtually no data to document the environmental contribution to these differences."[34] Moreover, after reviewing the available evidence, the Institute of Medicine concluded that "adequate data are not available in most instances to examine the relationships among the environmental, racial, ethnic, and other socioeconomic determinants of adverse health outcomes. More research is needed to clarify these relationships."[35] The National Environmental Health Association concurred with the Institute of Medicine and the EPA, and all three institutions have called for detailed, high-quality studies to investigate connections between environmental risk and public health in low-income and minority communities.[36]

Causes of Environmental Inequity

The evidence is clear that minorities and the poor face disproportionately high levels of environmental risk, even if the health consequences of this exposure remain unclear. Simply describing this situation, however, is not enough. Social scientists, policymakers, and the citizens who live in these polluted communities are all interested in causation: How and why did this situation arise? Five explanations are generally given for the distribution of polluting facilities and thus for the distribution of environmental risk: scientific rationality, market rationality, neighborhood transition, political power, and explicit discrimination. The appropriate role for government in ensuring environmental equity depends on which causes of environmental injustice are most important.

Scientific Rationality

Engineers, EPA officials, and others are extremely skeptical of the claims of environmental justice advocates. According to these experts, the siting of polluting facilities, especially landfills and hazardous waste TSDFs, is driven by technical criteria. When looking to site a hazardous waste land-fill, for example, companies will regard the area's demographics as irrelevant. What matters, they would argue, are the geological characteristics of the site. (For example, does the site sit on top of an important drinking-water aquifer?) If the scientific rationality explanation is correct, then these facilities should be randomly distributed in all types of communities. The reality that polluting facilities are concentrated in poor and minority areas strongly suggests that technical criteria alone do not explain the distribution of these facilities.

Market Rationality

According to proponents of the market rationality explanation, economic factors drive decisions regarding the location of hazardous waste facilities. For companies, the most important economic factors in deciding where to site facilities are cheap land, available labor, access to transportation infrastructure, and access to raw materials. Ignoring these factors in order to target poor and minority communities for polluting facilities would be economically irrational. Although certain economic forces may lead a company to locate a facility in a poor community, economics rather than discrimination drive this decision. The evidence supports the notion that economic considerations are important in siting polluting facilities. In Chester, one reason given for the concentration of hazardous waste TSDFs was the integrated system of railroads, highways, and port facilities, and the abundance of raw materials (that is, industrial wastes). Moreover, the CRJ study discussed earlier in this chapter found that commercial hazardous waste facilities were located in areas with low property values, and the sociologists at the University of Massachusetts concluded that these same facilities were located in areas with large numbers of skilled manufacturing employees. My own research demonstrated that hazardous waste TSDFs are more likely to be located where land is cheap and where raw materials (in this instance, hazardous wastes) are abundant. Much of this same research, however, concluded that the racial and class characteristics of the surrounding area are important even after controlling for these economic factors. In other words, economic rationality alone is unlikely to explain the distribution of these facilities.[37]

Neighborhood Transition

The Chester example is unusual in that all but one of the commercial hazardous waste TSDFs opened after 1987. In most communities, any attempt to evaluate the degree of discrimination in siting polluting facilities faces one very large problem: Which came first, the facility or the people in the surrounding neighborhood? The neighborhood transition explanation paints the following scenario: Many polluting facilities originally located in urban, working-class areas for many of the reasons cited by the market rationality explanation. Over time, those residents with the resources to move away did so. Because these facilities had reduced the value of the surrounding property, the departing residents were replaced by people who were poor or members of minority groups. Thus, although the present-day risks from these facilities may be distributed inequitably, the process of siting these facilities was not discriminatory.

Considered carefully, the neighborhood transition thesis poses two propositions. First, neighborhoods receiving hazardous waste facilities were no different from those that did not receive them at the time the facilities opened. Second, the proportion of poor or minority residents has increased more rapidly in neighborhoods that host hazardous waste facilities than in those that do not. Social scientists have been able to test these propositions only recently. With respect to the first proposition, the group at the University of Massachusetts found that commercial hazardous waste facilities built during the 1970s and 1980s were not placed in neighborhoods with larger than average concentrations of poor and minority residents.[38] Vicki Been found the same to be true for landfills in Houston, Texas. In other analyses, however, Been found that hazardous waste facilities in EPA Region 4 were originally located in areas with disproportionately large poor and minority populations.[39] Moreover, Been found once again that the null results of researchers at the University of Massachusetts were a function of a peculiar research design. Her own research found that commercial hazardous waste facilities built in the 1970s were more likely to be located in African American and Latino areas, whereas those built in the 1980s were more likely to be located in Latino areas. Been found the strongest relationship between race and facility location for firms that opened for business prior to 1970.[40] There is more consensus with respect to the second proposition. No study has found that building hazardous waste facilities causes white flight or unusual increases in the concentrations of poor and minority residents in the surrounding area.[41]

Political Power

Although the right to vote is distributed equally, political power is not. Political power is a function of wealth, education, group organizational skills, frequent participation in the political process, and so forth. Certain citizens, particularly members of minority groups and the poor, have fewer of these resources. Because the rational political actor will attempt to site polluting facilities where they will face the least amount of political resistance, political rationality, rather than outright discrimination, may best explain the location of polluting facilities.

A report commissioned by the state of California explicitly recommended that the state target areas that "lack social power" when trying to site incinerators. Moreover, when investigating which hazardous waste facilities seek to expand their capacity, James Hamilton of Duke University found that neither race nor class matters much. Instead, facilities are least likely to expand when they are located in neighborhoods where the residents are politically active. Hamilton and Viscusi also found that the designation and remediation of hazardous waste sites are significantly affected by the political power of area residents.[42] Finally, my own research showed that one of the best predictors of whether a permit to operate a hazardous waste TSDF will be approved or denied is not the demographic characteristics of the surrounding neighborhood but rather characteristics usually associated with political efficacy.[43] To sum up, nearly all of the available evidence suggests that when it comes to siting hazardous waste facilities, neighborhood political power matters.

Intentional Discrimination

Assessing the intentional discrimination hypothesis requires the adoption of a new unit of analysis—the individual decisions of public and private actors—rather than the more traditional and spatially defined "community" or "neighborhood." Intentional discrimination can occur in at least four dimensions. For example, intentional discrimination can motivate the behavior of public or private actors, and these behaviors can affect the location of noxious facilities or the environmental management decisions of existing facilities. We have at least some evidence regarding the presence of intentional discrimination in individual decisions across all four dimensions.

The location of polluting facilities is determined jointly by private and public officials. Private actors choose the sites for these facilities (usually in consultation with municipal officials), and government officials accept or reject these choices by approving or denying the required permits. Many observers, including prominent members of the environmental justice movement such as Robert Bullard, claim that minority and poor neighborhoods are explicitly targeted to receive polluting facilities during this process. Not surprisingly, both corporate and governmental officials reject these claims. These objections not withstanding, an intensive case study of the history of waste management in Chicago concluded that the process of facility siting discriminated against poor and minority residents.[44] We can also observe indirect evidence of intentional discrimination in our Chester example; recall that in Chester, officials chose to approve the permit for an additional TSDF even though an EPA study had concluded that "Chester residents probably run a higher than average chance of developing cancer and non-cancer health effects due to environmental risk factors."[45]

Once noxious facilities are sited, private actors must decide how to manage the pollution produced by these facilities, and government actors are responsible for enforcing pollution control regulations on these facilities. Intentional discrimination can influence both types of decisions. In general, there is little evidence that intentional discrimination influences the environmental management decisions of firms. Wayne Gray and Ronald Shadbegian found that facilities in poorer areas produce more air and water pollution but facilities in minority communities actually release fewer of these pollutants.[46] More comprehensive analyses showed that the decisions to recycle, reuse, or release toxic pollutants are unrelated to the characteristics of communities surrounding polluting facilities,[47] that pollution control expenditures are higher for firms in poorer (and wealthier) communities and unaffected by the minority status of these communities,[48] and that compliance with environmental regulations is not lower for facilities in poor and minority neighborhoods.[49] Possible intentional discrimination is only somewhat more evident in the environmental management decisions of government officials. For example, Gray and Shadbegian found that regulatory enforcement actions are less frequent in poor communities but more frequent for facilities in minority communities.[50] Moreover, a 1992 study by reporters at the *National Law Journal* found that average civil penalties for violating environmental laws are higher in white, wealthy neighborhoods than in poor or minority neighborhoods.[51] These conclusions do not hold up under statistical scrutiny, however. In fact, penalties for violating environmental laws are neither larger nor smaller in areas with large numbers of poor and minority residents.[52] On the other hand, my own research indicates that EPA officials are significantly more likely to approve permits for hazardous waste facilities in neighborhoods with large numbers of minority residents.[53]

In many ways the intentional discrimination theory is the most difficult to test. Although suggestive, the evidence presented here does not prove discriminatory intent. As the other explanations for environmental inequities make plain, discriminatory intent is not necessary to produce discriminatory outcomes. Nevertheless, even though intentional discrimination may not be the most plausible explanation for environmental inequities, we would do well to remember that "harm perpetuated by benign inadvertence is as injurious as harm by purposeful intent."[54]

Complexity and Caution When Assessing Environmental Inequity

In 1990, Federated Technologies, Inc., offered to purchase a long unused ranch in Noxubee County, Mississippi, on which the company proposed to construct three hazardous waste landfills and a hazardous waste incinerator. The racial and economic characteristics of Noxubee County made it unusual, even in Mississippi. African Americans constituted 69 percent of county residents (the state average was 36 percent), 41 percent of county residents had income below the official poverty line (more than twice the state average), and roughly 50 percent of adult county residents did not have a high school diploma (this figure was an astounding 86 percent among African American adults). Finally, the median income for African American households in Noxubee County was $14,205, well below the state median of $20,136 (the figure for white households in the county was $23,198).

On the surface, the Federated Technologies plan for Noxubee County looks to be a good example of an environmental inequity. Looks can be deceiving, however. One of the reasons Federated Technologies selected the

Noxubee site was that it enabled the company to buy a very large tract of land, with access to highway and rail infrastructure, for a comparably low price. In short, market rationality played a large part in selecting the location for this facility. In addition, the Noxubee County site was one of four state-approved areas for a hazardous waste facility, largely because the site sat on top of nearly 700 feet of impermeable chalk. The geological suitability of the site, coupled with the fact that the tract of land was large enough to place a substantial buffer zone between the facility and area residents, clearly illustrates that scientific rationality played a significant role in site selection as well. Finally, although the Federated Technologies plan generated significant public opposition, especially from out-of-state groups, more notable was the local support for the project. Both African American members of the county board of supervisors supported the Federated plan, as did all of the African American elected municipal officials in the county. Even the local chapter of the NAACP supported the construction of the hazardous waste facility in Noxubee County—which placed it at odds with the state chapter of the organization. In fact, one African American municipal alderman explicitly "rejected the. . .charge of environmental racism, countering that the racism was in not allowing African-Americans in Noxubee County to make their own decisions and to try to improve their own welfare." [55] The lesson of Noxubee County, then, is that it is sometimes difficult to establish the existence of environmental inequities in the first place, let alone identify their causes.

Remedying Environmental Injustice

In response to pressure from environmental justice advocates and the evidence reviewed in this chapter, private and government actors are undertaking a variety of activities to remedy environmental inequities.

Policy Changes at the National Level

Presidential Actions. In February 1994 President Clinton issued Executive Order (EO) 12898, which requires that "each federal agency . . . make achieving environmental justice part of its mission by identifying and addressing, as appropriate, disproportionately high and adverse human health or environmental effects of its programs, policies, and activities on minority populations and low-income populations in the United States and its territories and possessions." Accompanying EO 12898, Clinton released a Memorandum on Environmental Justice that requires all federal agencies to (1) ensure that all programs or activities receiving federal financial assistance that affect human health or the environment do not discriminate on the basis of race, color, or national origin, (2) analyze the environmental and health effects on poor and minority communities whenever an Environmental Impact Statement is required under the National Environmental Policy Act, and (3) ensure that poor and minority communities have adequate access to public information relating to human health, environmental planning, and environmental regulation. One might have expected George W. Bush to take very different positions on environmental justice issues than his predecessor. Bush, however, has thus far taken no actions to either advance or roll back previous presidential initiatives regarding environmental justice. Rather surprisingly, he has allowed EO 12898 and the accompanying presidential memorandum to remain in force and has done nothing to dismantle the environmental justice infrastructure within the EPA. Moreover, Bush's first EPA administrator, Christine Todd Whitman, went on record supporting environmental justice as a top agency priority.[56] Similar support has not yet been articulated by Bush's second (though short-lived) EPA administrator, Michael Leavitt, nor current EPA head Stephen Johnson.

Congressional Actions. In 1992 Congress enacted the Residential Lead-Based Paint Reduction Act. This legislation authorized $375 million for inspection and lead abatement actions in low-income housing, required the EPA to set up training and certification programs for lead abatement contractors, and provided grants to the states to develop their own lead abatement and training programs.[57] Other than this, Congress has taken no meaningful action to address environmental justice. Indeed, the most significant recent actions by Congress in this area have impeded addressing environmental inequities. Since 2000, EPA's appropriations bills have contained language preventing the agency from spending any money to implement or administer environmental justice programs under Title VI of the Civil Rights Act—the agency's highest profile environmental justice initiative. Thus it is extraordinarily unlikely that policy leadership in this area will come from Congress in the near future.

Administrative Actions. The EPA has undertaken three types of efforts aimed at producing environmental justice: agency reorganization, research and education, and litigation. After the issuance of EO 12898, the EPA created an Office of Environmental Justice, currently located within the Office of Enforcement and Compliance Assurance. In addition, the EPA now houses (1) an environmental justice steering committee, made up of senior managers from all EPA offices and regions, with responsibility for strategic planning, (2) an environmental justice policy working group, made up of high-level policy staff and responsible for the design of cross-media environmental justice policies, (3) an Office of Civil Rights, located within the office of the administrator, and (4) environmental justice coordinators within each headquarters office and each region, responsible for implementing environmental justice policies.

In several areas the EPA is going beyond the requirements of EO 12898, embarking on additional research and education activities with respect to environmental justice. For example, in 1992 the EPA created the Minority Academic Institutions Task Force to enhance the interaction between the agency and historically minority academic institutions. Responding to the recommendations of this task force, the EPA created the Cooperative Progression Program, with which the EPA recruits promising minority students to pursue careers in the environmental field and eventually work at the agency. More recently the EPA has focused on developing a geographic information system-based protocol for identifying environmental justice problem areas and has embarked on an ambitious program to devise measures of cumulative risk from exposure to multiple environmental hazards.[58] These initiatives will significantly improve the scientific and technical apparatus on which sound environmental justice policy should be based.

Finally, one way to reduce inequitable exposures to environmental risk is to sue the actors responsible for producing that risk, and it is in this area that the EPA has moved most aggressively to promote environmental justice. Title VI of the 1964 Civil Rights Act prohibits the use of federal funds in programs having discriminatory effects. Because the EPA provides federal grant money to all state environmental agencies and many nongovernment actors, legal experts saw Title VI as a potential weapon to use against the siting of noxious facilities in poor and minority neighborhoods. In 1993 the EPA's Office of Civil Rights began an investigation into the process by which permits were granted to operate polluting facilities in Louisiana's so-called cancer alley. This investigation bore fruit in 1994, when the EPA sued Borden Chemicals and Plastics for illegally storing and disposing of large quantities of hazardous chemicals that eventually contaminated the groundwater in nearby poor and minority communities. The Borden case is the first in which the EPA raised the issue of environmental racism.[59]

The most carefully watched court case regarding the environmental justice implications of facility siting arose out of our continuing Chester example. In 1996 a local grassroots environmental justice group, Chester Residents Concerned for Quality Living (CRCQL), filed suit against the PA DEP, claiming racial discrimination and disproportionate impact under Title VI of the Civil Rights Act. The case was dismissed by a district court judge, but the U.S. Court of Appeals for the Third Circuit overturned the district court decision, finding that (1) Title VI does not require discriminatory intent, only discriminatory impact, and (2) that there was an implied private right of action under Title VI. Pennsylvania appealed this decision. *Seif v. CRCQL* was placed on the U.S. Supreme Court's docket in 1998, but before the high court could rule on the case, the state agency revoked the permit for the commercial TSDF in accordance with the wishes of the facility owner.

In 1998 the EPA moved to formalize its civil rights policy by issuing interim guidelines for investigating complaints and for challenging permits under Title VI, and in 2000 the agency published draft guidance documents further formalizing its policy in this area. These efforts to craft a formal policy regarding the use of Title VI to remedy environmental inequities, however, may be for naught. In *Alexander v. Sandoval,* the Supreme Court significantly compromised the ability of litigants to prosecute disparate impacts under Title VI, which in turn will limit, if not eliminate, Title VI as a vehicle for pursuing environmental equity.[60]

Policy Changes at the State and Local Levels

Many state and local governments have struck out on their own to address the issues raised by environmental justice advocates. A comprehensive survey of state efforts was recently completed by the American Bar Association and Hastings College of Law, which focused on environmental justice actions in three areas: generating information relevant for assessing the extent of environmental inequity in the state, reorganizing the state environmental protection bureaucracy to address environmental justice concerns, and changing state environmental policy to remedy or prevent environmental inequities. Fifteen states have taken no environmental justice actions in any area, whereas eight states have taken at least one action in all three areas. Not surprisingly, California has addressed environmental inequity most aggressively, followed by New York and Massachusetts. Pennsylvania, home of our continuing Chester example, has also taken action in all three areas. With respect to information provision, Pennsylvania created the Environmental Justice Work Group to review and identify any environmental inequity concerns in the state's environmental programs. In addition, the state has reformed its environmental protection bureaucracy (PA DEP) by creating a permanent Environmental Justice Advisory Board and an Office of Environmental Advocate to facilitate community involvement in PA DEP decision making. Finally, in 2002, Pennsylvania incorporated environmental justice into policy actions by placing equity concerns at the center of the state's Performance Partnership Agreement with the EPA.[61]

Several municipalities also have taken steps to promote environmental justice. The contemporary model for local efforts to ensure environmental justice is New York City's fair share policy. In 1989 New York adopted a new city charter with two unique provisions ensuring that each borough and neighborhood bears its fair share of locally undesirable land use burdens (for example, prisons, waste facilities, and homeless shelters). The city has developed explicit criteria for determining each borough's fair share. Each year the mayor produces a list of undesirable facilities that must be built, expanded, or closed. The list specifies the exact location of these facilities in accordance with the fair share criteria and also takes into account the extent to which the character of the neighborhood will be changed by the concentration of these facilities. Borough presidents and community residents then have at least two years to comment on these plans.[62]

Although we can find several examples of states and localities being generally responsive to the concerns of environmental justice activists, this support has not been without reservation. Most notable is the cool reception received by the EPA's Title VI guidance documents at the state and local levels. In fact, after studying these documents, the U.S. Conference of Mayors and the Environmental Council of the States (made up of the heads of all state environmental agencies) opposed the plan.[63] To the extent that federal environmental justice policy emphasizes challenging facility permits under Title VI, state and local governments will be far less willing partners in the future than they have been in the past.

Obstacles to Remedying Environmental Injustice

The environmental justice movement has been quite successful at getting its concerns onto the environmental policy agenda. The movement has also instigated a large amount of research assessing the presence and causes of inequities in the distribution of environmental risk and in some instances has prompted policy solutions that seek to remedy these inequities. However, continued progress will require significant changes in the national political climate, the science underlying claims of environmental inequity, and the environmental justice movement itself.

This assessment is shared by Christopher Foreman, author of one of the best evaluations of the environmental justice movement to date.[64] Foreman identified five difficulties faced by activists seeking to pursue social justice through environmental policy. First, the evidence supporting inequities in the distribution of environmental risks is inconclusive. Second, the current national political climate is generally unreceptive to new initiatives in the area of environmental protection—especially those dealing with the redistribution of environmental risk or compensatory actions—and the leading role of state and local governments in environmental protection leaves the movement's focus on the federal level misplaced. Third, environmental justice activists are motivated by more than a concern over environmental quality; they are driven by aspirations for political empowerment, social justice, improved public health, and other goals that are difficult to address through environmental means. Fourth, aggressive pursuit of environmental justice concerns by the EPA may exacerbate well-known problems with its traditional environmental regulations (for example, difficulty in setting priorities and inefficient use of resources with respect to risk). Finally, efforts to remedy perceived environmental inequities may divert attention away from more serious threats to the health and well-being of minority communities (for example, lifestyle choices) and thus be counterproductive.

The strength of some of these conclusions is open to debate. For example, the evidence for significant inequities in the distribution of environmental risk is much stronger than Foreman admits. Moreover, criticizing environmental justice efforts for diverting attention and resources away from other factors contributing to the low quality of life in poor and minority neighborhoods is like criticizing crime policy for diverting attention and resources away from education. We know that the latter may have a larger effect on addressing certain social ills than the former, but public policy decisions that take these cross-issue substitution effects into account are extraordinarily rare. Nevertheless, Foreman has identified the most important factors limiting the political effectiveness of the environmental justice movement today. Specifically, his last three points are emblematic of what he characterizes as a "chronic inability to define and pursue a coherent policy agenda." In calling for social empowerment, pollution prevention, direct access to environmental decision making, attention to community preferences in environmental priorities, and the redistribution of economic power, the environmental justice movement is "almost boundary-less, covering all races and classes, and all manners of perceived environmental slights."[65]

A National Normative Consensus Regarding Environmental Justice

What *should* government do about observed environmental inequities? According to Foreman, the environmental justice community's response to this question is "everything," which in a world of limited political and economic resources is the same as nothing. The difficulties faced in answering this question, however, go beyond those identified by Foreman. To answer this question, we must forge a national consensus first on what constitutes discrimination in environmental protection and second on what we mean by equity.

Defining Discrimination. Does every decision-making process that produces discriminatory outcomes deserve the government's attention, or are such decisions legally actionable only when there is discriminatory intent? This is a difficult question, and even our laws apply different definitions of discrimination. For example, violating the Fourth Amendment's equal protection clause requires discriminatory intent, whereas violating Title VI of the 1964 Civil Rights Act requires only that an action produce a discriminatory outcome. If we adopt the discriminatory intent definition when examining the five causes of environmental inequity presented earlier in this chapter, only the fifth cause is clearly an example of discrimination. If we adopt the discriminatory outcome definition, however, then any of the causes of environmental inequities presented earlier require government remedy.

Defining Equity in the Distribution of Polluting Facilities. We routinely use the term *equity* as if there were one, universally accepted definition. There are, however, many different definitions. For example, an economist might characterize as equitable a system that requires those who benefit from the production of pollution to also pay its costs. Because wealthy individuals consume more and thus produce more pollution, equity requires that these individuals either live with higher numbers of polluting facilities or pay others to accept them. A geographic conception of equity, in contrast, might require that all states, cities, or communities have equal numbers of polluting facilities. Still other conceptions might require that polluting facilities be divided proportionately among income classes, racial groups, or even individuals.

One problem with these definitions of equity is that a distribution that is equitable at one level often produces inequities at another level. For example, even if polluting facilities were distributed equally between rich and poor, and white and minority neighborhoods, not every neighborhood would receive a facility. Moreover, each of these facilities would not be equally risky.

Thus, some poor, rich, African American, Latino, or white residents will be exposed to higher levels of environmental risk than will others. In short, an equitable distribution of facilities according to group status may produce an inequitable distribution of environmental risk among individuals. Finally, some experts argue that when it comes to disposing of hazardous and radioactive wastes, we should either lock them away from the environment for hundreds of years (for example, in sealed landfills) or ship them to other countries for disposal. But eventually all landfills leak, which only transfers the environmental risk across generations, and shipping the wastes to other nations for disposal simply produces environmental inequities on an international scale.

What Definitions of Discrimination and Equity Mean for Public Policy. Defining *discrimination* and *equity* is of more than academic interest. How we define these two terms determines the dividing line between acceptable and unacceptable government responses to the concerns of environmental justice advocates. If discrimination includes only those actions with clear discriminatory intent, and equity is defined as communities paying the full costs of the pollution they produce, then government efforts to ensure environmental equity are relatively simple: Narrowly enforce antidiscrimination laws, prevent the illegal disposal of wastes, and have rich communities pay poor communities for accepting polluting facilities. In short, government would do few things differently. However, if we define discrimination as any action that produces a discriminatory outcome and equity in very broad terms (for example, equalizing exposure to all environmental risks for all individuals and generations), ensuring environmental equity would require the government to intervene in developers' decisions to build houses and factories; to redistribute income and political power; and to guarantee equal access to medical care, the political process, and so forth. Regardless of the definitions one selects, until we have clearly defined criteria for what constitutes discrimination and equity, it is difficult to develop practical policies to address the problem of environmental inequity.[66]

Conclusion

We can draw several conclusions from the material presented in this chapter. First, solid evidence indicates that minority groups and the poor experience higher levels of exposure to environmental risk, though the evidence on just what causes these inequities is less certain. Moreover, there is a strong likelihood that members of these same groups experience higher levels of environmentally generated disease and death as a result of this elevated risk. Second, national, state, and local governments (and mainstream environmental groups) have all responded to the concerns of environmental justice advocates. Few of these policy responses, however, have produced long-lasting changes in the process of allocating environmental risk. Third, the resources and strategies necessary for mobilizing a constituency and moving an issue on to the public agenda are very different from those necessary for articulating a coherent policy agenda and for forging consensus regarding policy change. Although the environmental justice movement has experienced significant success at the former, the latter hampers realization of the movement's full potential. Fourth, we will have no standards with which to judge either the adequacy or the effectiveness of government efforts to ensure environmental equity until we can arrive at some common social understanding of what *discrimination* and *equity* mean in the context of environmental protection. Finally, for the foreseeable future, environmental justice concerns will continue to occupy a place next to risk assessment, federal mandates to the states, property rights, and economic incentives as the major forces reshaping the context of environmental policymaking in the twenty-first century.

Suggested Web Sites

West Harlem Environmental Action (www.weact.org)
Concerned Citizens of South Central Los Angeles (www.ccscla.org)
Southwest Network for Environmental and Economic Justice (www.sneej.org)
Action PA (www.actionpa.org)
Ecojustice Network (Harvard University) (www.ecojustice.net)
Environmental Justice Resource Center (Clark Atlanta University) (www.ejrc.cau.edu)
Center for Environmental Equity and Justice (Florida A & M University) (www.famu.edu/acad/colleges/esi/CEEJ/welceej.html)
EPA Office of Environmental Justice (www.epa.gov/compliance/environmentaljustice)

Notes

1. Barry Hill, "Chester, Pennsylvania—Was It a Classic Example of Environmental Injustice?" *Vermont Law Review* 23 (1999): 479–528.
2. U.S. Council on Environmental Quality, *Environmental Quality 1971* (Washington, D.C.: U.S. Government Printing Office, 1971).
3. See Robert Bullard, ed., *Confronting Environmental Racism: Views from the Grassroots* (Boston: South End Press, 1993); Robert Paehlke, *Environmentalism and the Future of Progressive Politics* (New Haven: Yale University Press, 1989).
4. Philip Shabecoff, "Environmental Groups Told They Are Racist in Hiring," *New York Times,* February 1, 1990, Sec. A.
5. Robert Bullard, "Environmental Justice for All," and Ken Geiser and Gerry Waneck, "PCBs and Warren County," in *Unequal Protection: Environmental Justice and Communities of Color,* ed. Robert Bullard (San Francisco: Sierra Club, 1994).
6. Andrew Szasz, *Ecopopulism: Toxic Waste and the Movement for Environmental Justice* (Minneapolis: University of Minnesota Press, 1994).
7. Environmental Justice Resource Center, "Principles of Environmental Justice," October 27, 1991, www.ejrc.cau.edu/princej.html, February 17, 2005.
8. Szasz, *Ecopopulism*; Benjamin Chavis, "Foreword," Karl Grossman, "The People of Color Environmental Summit," and Regina Austin and Michael Schill, "Black, Brown, Red, and Poisoned," in Bullard, *Unequal Protection.*

9. U.S. Environmental Protection Agency (EPA), *Environmental Equity: Reducing Risk for All Communities*, Vol. 1 (Washington, D.C.: EPA, 1992).

10. Robert Bullard, *Dumping in Dixie: Race, Class, and Environmental Quality* (Boulder: Westview Press, 1990). See also Bullard, *Confronting Environmental Racism.*

11. U.S. Government Accountability Office (GAO), *Hazardous and Nonhazardous Waste: Demographics of People Living Near Waste Facilities* (Washington, D.C.: U.S. Government Printing Office, 1995).

12. GAO, *Siting of Hazardous Waste Landfills and Their Correlation with Racial and Economic Status of Surrounding Communities* (Washington, D.C.: U.S. Government Printing Office, 1983).

13. Bullard, *Confronting Environmental Racism*; Paul Mohai and Bunyan Bryant, "Environmental Racism: Reviewing the Evidence," in Bryant and Mohai, ed., *Race and the Incidence of Environmental Hazards* (Boulder: Westview Press, 1992).

14. Commission for Racial Justice, *Toxic Wastes and Race in the United States* (New York: United Church of Christ and Public Data Access, Inc., 1987); Benjamin Goldman and Laura Fitton, *Toxic Wastes and Race Revisited* (Washington, D.C.: Center for Policy Alternatives, 1994).

15. Douglas Anderton, Andy Anderson, John Michael Oakes, and Michael Fraser, "Environmental Equity: The Demographics of Dumping," *Demography* 31 (1994): 229–248.

16. Susan Cutter, D. Holm, and L. Clark, "The Role of Geographic Scale in Monitoring Environmental Justice," *Risk Analysis* 16 (1996): 517–526.

17. Vicki Been, "Analyzing Evidence of Environmental Justice," *Journal of Land Use and Environmental Law* 11 (1995): 1–36.

18. Evan Ringquist, "Race, Class, and the Politics of Environmental Risk" (unpublished manuscript, 1998).

19. Pamela Davidson and Douglas Anderton, "Demographics of Dumping II: A National Environmental Equity Survey and the Distribution of Hazardous Materials Handlers," *Demography* 37 (2000): 461–466.

20. Peter Asch and Joseph Seneca, "Some Evidence on the Distribution of Air Quality," *Land Economics* 54 (1978): 278–297; Julian McCaull, "Discriminatory Air Pollution: If Poor, Don't Breathe," *Environment* 18 (1976): 26–31; American Lung Association, "Urban Air Pollution and Health Inequities: A Workshop Report," *Environmental Health Perspectives* 109 (June 2001): 357–374.

21. Lauretta Burke, "Race and Environmental Equity: A Geographic Analysis in Los Angeles," *Geo Info Systems* (October 1994): 44–50; Susan Cutter, "The Burdens of Toxic Risks: Are They Fair?" *Business and Economic Review* 40 (1994): 101–113; Philip Pollock III and M. Elliot Vittas, "Who Bears the Burdens of Environmental Pollution? Race, Ethnicity, and Environmental Equity in Florida," *Social Science Quarterly* 76 (1995): 294–310; T. S. Glickman and R. Hersh, "Evaluating Environmental Equity: The Impacts of Industrial Hazards on Selected Social Groups in Allegheny County, Pennsylvania," Discussion Paper 95-13 (Washington, D.C.: Resources for the Future, 1995); William Bowen, M. J. Salling, K. Haynes, and E. Cyran, "Toward Environmental Justice: Spatial Equity in Ohio and Cleveland," *Annals of the Association of American Geographers* 85 (1995): 641–663.

22. Evan J. Ringquist, "Equity and the Distribution of Environmental Risk," *Social Science Quarterly* 78 (1997): 811–829; Susan Perlin, R. Woodrow Setzer, John Creason, and Ken Sexton, "Distribution of Industrial Air Emissions by Income and Race in the United States," *Environmental Science and Technology* 29 (1995): 69–80.

23. Daniel Dresinski, Michael Lay, and Paul Stretesky, "Chemical Accidents in the United States, 1990–1996," *Social Science Quarterly* 84(1) (2003): 122–143; M. R. Elliot, Y. Wang, R. A. Lowe, and P. R Kleindorfer, "Environmental Justice: Frequency and Severity of U.S. Chemical Industry Accidents and the Socioeconomic Status of Surrounding Communities," *Journal of Epidemiology and Community Health* 58 (2004): 24–30.

24. John Hird and Michael Reese, "The Distribution of Environmental Quality," *Social Science Quarterly* 79 (1998): 693–716.

25. EPA, *Environmental Equity*, Vol. 1; Ivette Perfecto and Baldemar Velasquez, "Farm Workers: Among the Least Protected," *EPA Journal* 18 (1992): 13–14.

26. EPA, *Environmental Equity: Reducing Risk for All Communities*, Vol. 2 (Washington, D.C.: EPA, 1992); Patrick West, "Health Concerns for Fish-Eating Tribes," *EPA Journal* 18(1) (1992): 15–16. See also "Invitation to Poison? Detroit Minorities and Toxic Fish Consumption from the Detroit River," in Bryant and Mohai, *Race and the Incidence of Environmental Hazards.*

27. James Hamilton and W. Kip Viscusi, *Calculating Risks: The Spatial and Political Dimensions of Hazardous Waste Policy* (Cambridge: MIT Press, 1999).

28. Rachel Morello-Frosh, Manuel Pastor, and James Sadd, "Environmental Justice and Southern California's 'Riskscape'," *Urban Affairs Review* 36 (2001): 551–578.

29. Marc Shapiro, "Information Regulation, Environmental Justice, and Risk," *Journal of Policy Analysis and Management* 24(2) (2005): 373–398.

30. Mohai and Bryant, "Environmental Racism"; Benjamin Goldman, *Not Just Prosperity: Achieving Sustainability with Environmental Justice* (Washington, D.C.: National Wildlife Federation, 1993); David Allen, James Lester, and Kelly Hill, "Prejudice, Profits, and Power: Assessing the Eco-Racism Thesis at the County Level" (paper presented at the annual meeting of the Western Political Science Association, Portland, Oregon, 1995).

31. GAO, *Hazardous and Nonhazardous Waste*; William Bowen, *Environmental Justice Through Research Based Decision Making* (New York: Garland, 2001).

32. Evan J. Ringquist, "Assessing Evidence of Environmental Inequities: A Meta-Analysis," *Journal of Policy Analysis and Management* 24(2) (2005): 223–248.

33. A few examples include S. W. Lagatos, B. J. Wessen, and M. Zelen, "An Analysis of Contaminated Well Water and Health Effects in Woburn, Massachusetts," *Journal of the American Statistical Association* 81 (1986): 583–596; J. Griffith et al., "Cancer Mortality in United States Counties with Hazardous Waste Sites and Groundwater Pollution," *Archives of Environmental Health* 44 (1989): 69–74; Lisa Croen et al., "Maternal Residential Proximity to Hazardous Waste Sites and Risk for Selected Congenital Malformations," *Epidemiology* 8 (1997): 347–359; Sandra Geschwind, "Risk of Congenital Malformations Associated with Proximity to Hazardous Waste Sites," *American Journal of Epidemiology* 135 (1993): 1197–1207; Dennis Peck, ed., *Psychosocial Effects of Hazardous Toxic Waste Disposal on Communities* (Springfield, Ill.: Charles C. Thomas, 1989); National Research Council, *Environmental Epidemiology: Public Health and Hazardous Wastes* (Washington, D.C.: National Academies Press, 1991); American Lung Association, "Urban Air Pollution and Health Inequities: A Workshop Report," *Environmental Health Perspectives* 109 (June 2001): 357–374.

34. EPA, *Environmental Equity*, Vol. 1, 3.

35. Institute of Medicine, *Toward Environmental Justice* (Washington, D.C.: National Academies Press, 1999).

36. National Environmental Health Association, "NEHA's Position on Environmental Justice," *Journal of Environmental Health* 59 (1996): 40–42.

37. Commission for Racial Justice, *Toxic Wastes and Race*; Anderton et al., "Environmental Equity"; Ringquist, "Race, Class, and the Politics of Environmental Risk."

38. John Oakes, Douglas Anderton, and Andy Anderson, "A Longitudinal Analysis of Environmental Equity in Communities with Hazardous Waste Facilities," *Social Science Research* 25 (1996): 125–148.

39. Vicki Been, "Locally Undesirable Land Uses in Minority Neighborhoods: Disproportionate Siting or Market Dynamics?" *Yale Law Journal* 103 (1994): 1383–1422.

40. Vicki Been, with Francis Gupta, "Coming to the Nuisance or Going to the Barrios? A Longitudinal Analysis of Environmental Justice Claims," *Ecology Law Quarterly* 24 (1997): 1–56.

41. Ibid.; Oakes et al., "A Longitudinal Analysis of Environmental Equity Claims"; Manuel Pastor, James Sadd, and James Hipp, "Which Came First? Toxic Facilities, Minority Move-In, and Environmental Justice," *Journal of Urban Affairs* 23 (2001): 1–21.

42. Hamilton and Viscusi, *Calculating Risks.*

43. Cerrell and Associates Inc., *Political Difficulties Facing Waste-to-Energy Conversion Plant Siting: Report for the California Waste Management Board* (Los Angeles: Cerrell & Associates, 1984); James Hamilton, "Politics and Social Costs: Estimating the Impact of Collective Action on Hazardous Waste Facilities," *Rand Journal of Economics* 24 (1993): 101–125; Hamilton, "Testing for Environmental Racism: Prejudice, Profits, Political Power?" *Journal of Policy Analysis and Management* 95 (1995): 107–132; Ringquist, "Race, Class, and the Politics of Environmental Risk."

44. David Pellow, *Garbage Wars: The Struggle for Environmental Justice in Chicago* (Cambridge: MIT Press, 2002).

45. EPA, *Chester Environmental Risk Study: Findings and Recommendations* (Washington, D.C.: EPA, 1994).

46. Wayne Gray and Ronald Shadbegian, "Optimal Pollution Abatement: Whose Benefits Matter, and How Much?" *Journal of Environmental Economics and Management* 47 (2004): 510–534.

47. Evan J. Ringquist and Michael Martin, "Environmental Equity and Management at the Firm Level" (paper presented at the annual meetings of the Midwest Political Science Association, 2004).

48. Randy Becker, "Pollution Abatement Expenditure by U.S. Manufacturing Plants: Do Community Characteristics Matter?" (Center for Economic Studies, U.S. Bureau of the Census, 2003).

49. Matthew Potoski and Aseem Prakash, "Green Clubs and Voluntary Governance: ISO 14001 and Firms' Regulatory Compliance" *American Journal of Political Science* 49(2) (2005): 235–248.

50. Gray and Shadbegian, "Optimal Pollution Abatement."

51. Marianne Lavelle and Marcia Coyle, "Unequal Protection: The Racial Divide on Environmental Law," *National Law Journal* (September 21, 1992): S1.

52. Evan J. Ringquist, "A Question of Justice: Equity in Environmental Litigation, 1974–91," *Journal of Politics* 60 (1998): 1148–1165.

53. Ringquist, "Race, Class, and the Politics of Environmental Risk."

54. Deeohn Ferris, "A Challenge to EPA," *EPA Journal* 18 (1992): 28–29.

55. Eduardo Rhodes, *Environmental Justice in American: A New Paradigm* (Bloomington: Indiana University Press, 2003), 176.

56. Christine Todd Whitman, "EPA's Commitment to Environmental Justice" (internal agency memorandum), August 9, 2001, www.epa.gov, October 1, 2001.

57. Michael E. Kraft and Denise Scheberle, "Environmental Justice and the Allocation of Risk: The Case of Lead and Public Health" *Policy Studies Journal* 23 (spring 1995): 113–122.

58. EPA, *1997–98 Waste Programs Environmental Justice Accomplishments Report* (Washington, D.C.: Office of Solid Waste and Emergency Response).

59. "Clinton Actions on Race and the Environment," *National Law Journal,* December 6, 1993, 1; "Agency Watch," *National Law Journal,* December 5, 1994, A16.

60. Evan J. Ringquist, "Environmental Justice," in Robert Durant, Daniel Fiorino, and Rosemary O'Leary, eds., *Environmental Governance Reconsidered* (Cambridge: MIT Press, 2004).

61. Steven Bonorris, ed., *Environmental Justice for All: A Fifty-State Survey of Legislation, Policies, and Initiatives* (Washington, D.C.: American Bar Association and Hastings College of Law, 2004).

62. Vicki Been, "What's Fairness Got to Do with It? Environmental Justice and the Siting of Locally Undesirable Land Use," *Cornell Law Review* 78 (1993): 1001–1009.

63. John Cushman, "Pollution Policy Is Unfair Burden, States Tell EPA," *New York Times,* May 10, 1998; Janet Ward, "Mayor's Environmental Racism Policy Wrong Headed," *American City and County* 113 (August 1998): 4.

64. Christopher Foreman, *The Promise and Peril of Environmental Justice* (Washington, D.C.: Brookings Institution Press, 1998).

65. Ibid., 12.

66. Been, "What's Fairness Got to Do with It?"

12

The Greening of Industry: Combining Government Regulation and Voluntary Strategies

Daniel Press and Daniel A. Mazmanian

The greening of industry has emerged as an important topic among business, environmental, and government leaders only since the mid-1980s. At this early stage in what will require a profound transformation by the time it is complete, debate exists over which business and industry practices are most in need of change and how to bring such change about: Is policy intervention best applied at the stage of waste management, air and water pollution control, or energy usage? Can the most change be realized in production methods, product design, or the end products themselves? Will the strongest drive for change come at the stage of consumption and usage of products?

Equally unclear is the best position for society to adopt in order to promote the most comprehensive yet cost-effective transformation.[1] Four broad approaches to this question illustrate the differences of opinion about how best to achieve industrial greening. The first approach involves government imposing on all business and industry prescribed environmental protection technologies and methods of emissions reduction. A second, more flexible approach, would allow businesses to select their own most cost-effective strategies for reducing emissions, under the watchful eye of government. A third way is to use market-based incentives that provide bottom-line rewards for environmentally friendly business behavior, leaving change to the natural workings of the marketplace. The fourth approach is to rely largely on volunteerism, wherein businesses commit to environmental goals that match or exceed those required in exchange for relief from the prescribed technology and command-and-control regulations that would otherwise be imposed.

Since the mid-1990s, the amount of research on these approaches has expanded rapidly and heated debate has ensued about which approach or which mix of approaches to use. (These exchanges have been especially noticeable since the publication of the fifth edition of this book.) Some reformers focus their attention mainly on the shortcomings of the nation's long-standing environmental policies—variously referred to as "command-and-control," "top-down," "deterrence-based" policies for air, water, land-use, noise, and endangered species protection—and the need to roll back these policies. Other reformers focus mainly on the growing importance of the corporate responsibility and quality management movements within and across industries—domestically and internationally—and how this shift is moving many businesses toward a greener path. All reformers want to know how best to accelerate this trend through various flexible governmental and voluntary policies, particularly in light of the unrelenting challenges to the environment posed by modern technological society and a growing global population.

In assessing the contending positions and approaches, it is reasonable to assume that all else being equal, business and industry owners, managers, and workers would prefer to live and work in a cleaner, more environmentally sustainable world. Yet seldom is all else equal. The market economy in which businesses operate has a long history of freely using natural resources and nature's goods, such as clean air, water, and soil as well as food and fodder, and shielding both producers and consumers from the environmental pollution and resource degradation associated with the extraction of these goods, their use in production, and their consumption. This is the very same market economy, after all, that nurtures consumer tastes and expectations, ultimately their demands, for ever more goods and services, resulting in the extraordinary material consumption of today's modern lifestyle.[2]

Consequently, the greening of industry is neither a private business matter nor a minor marketplace imperfection so much as a serious "public" problem, in need of a public policy solution. Because real costs are associated with the transformation into a green business, we do not expect businesses to automatically or enthusiastically assume these costs. Indeed, it is typically in a firm's best interest to minimize if not avoid the additional costs of transformation to the extent that doing so does not demonstrably improve its near-term market position. This is precisely why the first generation of environmental laws, starting in the 1970s in the United States, was compulsory for all business, creating the "command-and-control" regulatory regime of the first environmental epoch. As this chapter shows, a good deal of progress resulted but at great expense; arguably many unnecessary costs were incurred by business and government, costs that might be avoided under a different approach.

The Dilemma of Collective Action for Environmental Protection

How to bring about significant changes that are in the best interest of all sectors can be understood as one of a category of problems known as "collective action problems" or "collective action dilemmas."[3] These occur when individuals would be better off if they cooperate in pursuit of a common goal, but for one reason or another each chooses a less optimal course of action—one that typically satisfies some other highly important goal. The challenge to policymakers when facing collective action problems is to devise an approach that anticipates and counteracts the normal (in the language of game theory, the "rational") tendency of actors to forego the better *joint* gain for a nearer-term assured and secure, but lesser, *individual* gain.

Figure 12-1 Green Industry as a Collective Action Dilemma

Firm's choice

	Evasion	Self-policing
Flexible regulation	**Cell A** Government as potential "sucker"	**Cell B** Win-win: superior outcomes for government and industry
Deterrence (through command-and-control)	**Cell C** Suboptimal for both government and business but a typical outcome	**Cell D** Green industry initiatives of the 1980s to today, with industry as potential "sucker"

Government's choice

Source: Based on Matthew Potoski and Aseem Prakash, "The Regulation Dilemma: Cooperation and Conflict in Environmental Governance," *Public Administration Review* 64 (March/April 2004): 137–148.

The collective action dilemma in the case of the greening of industry has been portrayed by Matthew Potoski and Aseem Prakash as a two-dimensional game-theoretic problem, which we have adapted in Figure 12-1. The vertical and horizontal labels show the options available to each player, and the four cells represent the payoff (or benefits) and risk (or costs) to each of the actors based on the combinations of each option. For example, should they decide to cooperate to maximize the gains to each (cell B)? Or should they not cooperate in order to avoid the possibility of being taken advantage of by the other or incurring some other cost (cell C), such as the loss of public confidence and trust on the part of government and market share and profitability on the part of business?

Although simplified, the game situation approximates closely the real world of the relations between business and government. Consequently, if left to its own devices, business would choose to have little or no governmental requirement placed on it to protect the environment. This would be only reasonable (rational) for a business trying to maximize its profits in a market economy. This option is represented by the "evasion" position on the horizontal dimension, on the "Firm's choice" axis. However, if compelled by law to provide environmental protection and safeguards, and possibly go even further to transform itself into a green company, business would prefer an approach that allowed for self-policing and regulatory flexibility. It would find this superior to being heavily regulated by a command-and-control government bureaucracy.

Government, in turn, has the choice of opting for a policy of "deterrence," which experience has shown to be workable based on the command-

and-control regulatory approach taken to environmental protection since 1970. The downside, as experience has also shown, is that this approach has required the growth and support of a large government bureaucracy to carry out the oversight and regulation of businesses, the suppression of the creative energy on the part of firms that could be used to develop their own green business strategies, and ultimately the less than promised and far less than imaginable transformation of industry than could have occurred. Conversely, government could choose to be more flexible and lenient on industry, relying instead on a modest amount of monitoring combined with market forces, consumer demands, and new technology to ensure greater protection of the environment. There is risk in this approach for the government. It embraces the promise of an eventually large payoff, but as market forces and modest oversight combine to bring about the desired green transformation of business in the short term, some, if not most, businesses will not change their behavior or will do so insufficiently or slowly, absent stringent regulation.

And this is the dilemma: As the logic of game theory suggests and a fair amount of experience affirms, under flexible regulatory systems that rely on market forces to bring about changed behavior, the market forces are insufficient and many businesses do not change or do so only minimally. When firms know that they are unlikely to be detected or penalized even when caught, they too often opt for evasion over committing the capital required to transform themselves. The result is that government (and thus the public) ends up being betrayed, realizing even less movement toward the green transformation than under a command-and-control approach: Government finds itself in the position of the "sucker," which is the worst possible outcome in a collective action game.

Armed with the insights of game theory, we find it logical that, left to its own resources and absent compulsion, business will choose evasion over greening. Government, in turn, will choose command-and-control over flexibility, not because it is optimal but to avoid the risk of ending up the sucker. Thus game theory tells us that most of the activity surrounding environmental protection can be expected to take place in the lower-left cell of Figure 12-1, cell C, the zone in which government regulates with a heavy hand to prevent business from evading environmental protection laws and regulations. This is precisely where the action took place throughout the first environmental epoch, which began in the 1970s.[4]

A second epoch began in the 1980s and continues today, characterized by recognition of the collective action dilemma and efforts to extricate government and business from its grasp. The challenge is how to combine flexible regulatory strategies with market forces to move the central theater of action out of the lower-left cell C to the upper-right cell B.

A number of pilot and experimental programs by government and business have been initiated and are reviewed below. The experience underscores how difficult it has been to dislodge the players from their long-standing positions. This should come as no surprise in light of the dilemma they face and the amount of time they have spent living and working under the command-and-control approach. The crux of the matter remains that, by and large, government is loath to relinquish its reliance on deterrence and business can be expected to evade when circumstances allow.

Yet the need for society to find a win-win solution—a more optimal mix of flexibility and self-policing—continues and has motivated the continuing search for the needed policy breakthrough. A growing body of research on strategies that appear to work is guiding these efforts, at least on an experimental basis among self-motivated businesses. Thus devising a new hybrid public policy approach seems feasible, at least in principle, within a game-theoretic framework. Of course, the direction of public policy is set by the politics of policymaking, not simply the logic of policy analysis, so this too will be considered in our final assessment.

What follows is an overview of the efforts made since 1970 to address the problems of environmental pollution and the degradation of our natural resources base by greening the practices of business and industry. This overview moves through the strict command-and-control environmental policy epoch, located schematically in cell C, and then turns to the market-oriented and flexible regulatory strategies that reflected a significant change in the understanding of the problem. In actuality, the debate and center of activity has moved only part way, with the innovative action taking place "under the shadow of regulation" (in cell D).

We examine several impressive examples of corporate self-regulation and voluntary green approaches of individual firms, often in conjunction with government, as illustrative of how change has occurred and can occur. These accomplishments need to be juxtaposed with the efforts by George W. Bush's administration to slow down, if not derail, the greening of industry movement. The chapter ends with an assessment of how we can best accomplish the much-needed green transformation of America's business and industry.

The Accomplishments of
Command-and-Control since 1970

Although the needed green transformation of business is actively being researched and dominates the policy debate today, command-and-control regulation is the most widespread regulatory approach in practice. In a number of important respects, the approach has worked and continues to work to clean up the environment, in some instances quite admirably.[5] Moreover, evidence indicates that the nation's strict environmental regulations have spurred innovation in businesses, which ultimately provides them a source of competitive advantage in the market economy.[6] Also, one can point to the creation of jobs in the pollution control technology sector as a source of economic growth and employment that has resulted from the traditional form of environmental regulation.[7]

Since the 1970s, government rules and regulations have spurred reductions throughout the nation in air, water, and soil contamination; these reductions are noted at numerous points throughout this book (see especially chapter 1). Nationwide air emissions trends from all industrial sources (including electricity-generating power plants) show that air emissions reached a peak in the early to mid-1970s, declined, and then plateaued from the mid-1980s onward.

Between 1990 and 2001, sulfur oxides emissions declined consistently (perhaps by as much as one-third), very likely as a consequence of the 1990 Clean Air Act's Acid Rain program. Lead and volatile organic compounds also declined, by 3.5 percent and 20 percent, respectively. Other air pollutants exhibited more worrisome trends. Carbon monoxide from industrial processes fluctuated throughout the 1990s, probably as a function of economic conditions, but overall industry emitted 29 percent more carbon monoxide in 1999 than in 1990. Nitrogen oxides also increased, by 5.6 percent from 1990 to 1999.[8] Official records for all environmental data are often unavailable for the same years (here we present ranges for the closest years); however, all of these figures should be viewed as rough approximations. Although the U.S. Environmental Protection Agency (EPA) officially reports impressive emissions reductions in its annual inventories, the agency admits, when pressed, that "estimates for the non-utility manufacturing sector are some of the most unreliable data we have in the national emission inventory."[9]

Water quality is even harder to assess reliably but has also improved somewhat, thanks largely to the thousands of municipal wastewater treatment plants built with financing from the federal government since 1970 (see chapter 1).[10] Today, almost every American can expect drinkable water as a matter of course, with regular monitoring for quality and reasonably rapid responses to contamination threats. It is less clear, however, how industry's overall contribution to water quality protection has changed over the years, because such data are not routinely collected or centrally distributed.

Energy consumption presents an equally mixed picture. Manufacturing firms slowly reduced their annual energy consumption between the 1970s and early 1990s, going from 23.97 quads (quadrillion British thermal units, or BTUs) in 1970 to 20.26 quads in 1991 (a savings sufficient to power about 30 million American homes for a year).[11] However, energy use gradually rose during the 1990s, up to 21.66 quads in 1994 and 23.80 quads in 1998.[12]

This roughly 20-percent overall (or total) increase in energy consumption from 1991 to 1998 occurred while manufacturing output increased nearly 37 percent during the same time period.[13] At the same time, manufacturing industries reduced their energy intensity (the amount of energy it takes to manufacture a product) by 26.7 percent (usually measured in BTUs per dollar value of shipments and receipts) between 1980 and 1988.[14] Those reductions continued during the 1990s as the consumption per dollar value of shipments for those industries decreased 16 percent, from 5,500 BTUs in 1991 to 4,600 BTUs in 1998.[15]

A great deal of money has been spent to accomplish these results, in terms of total dollars and as a percentage of the gross national product, and with them the costs borne by industry. This is reflected in the increasing level of expenditures by industry. In 1973, U.S. industries spent about $4.8 billion on pollution abatement, split almost equally between capital and operating costs. They spent a total of about $28.6 billion on pollution abatement in 1994: $7.9 billion on capital costs and $20.7 billion on operating costs.[16] Chemical and petroleum companies spent almost half of this total, $12.8 billion.

After a hiatus of five years, the Department of Commerce updated national pollution abatement expenditures by American industries; however, because it used different estimation methods, the 1999 figures are not perfectly comparable with earlier periods. Nonetheless, industry spent about $27 billion on pollution abatement, prevention, recycling, and remediation. The 1999 figure represents a decrease of 5.6 percent (over 1994 expenditures) in total pollution spending by manufacturing, which also reflects less spending per dollar of product value than in the early 1990s. Thus, until the mid-1990s, manufacturing industries were consistently spending more on pollution abatement for every dollar of value their products made; and overall, some gains in environmental quality were achieved. That is, the levels of some air pollutants decreased and overall toxic releases seem to have declined. However, far more energy was used and the levels of some air pollutants (carbon monoxide, nitrogen oxides) increased substantially. One clear conclusion is that industry's pollution abatement spending today achieves less per dollar than it did in the 1970s. This is to be expected: Prior to 1970, uncontrolled pollutant releases were common; therefore, early pollution abatement expenditures achieved dramatic improvements over no treatment, which had been the norm.

Is the news about industrial pollution good, bad, or uncertain? Undeniably, the country's air would have been far worse if industry had not been installing abatement equipment since 1970. Moreover, it is remarkable that, thus far, air pollution seems to rise at a smaller rate than economic growth. The bad news is that, overall, industry is consuming more energy and raw materials, which in turn creates serious pollution and resource degradation, and is burdening the nation's air, land, and water with larger pollutant loads each year. Thus, even if the rate of increase is small, the overall burden grows, which is not the right direction for protecting public and environmental health.

Regulatory Experiments in Industrial Greening

Command-and-control approaches have clearly resulted in better environmental practices in business and industry and a significant curbing of traditional patterns of environmental pollution, but they ultimately fall short of the fundamental transformation needed in business and industry. The best end-of-pipe pollution management has not sufficiently reduced the overall pollution load generated by an economy that is ever expanding to satisfy the needs of a global population projected to grow by 50 percent over the next fifty years.

Therefore, attention has begun to shift from pollution reduction to pollution prevention, and to do so by devising incentive-based, self-regulatory and voluntary policy approaches (see chapter 9). Building on the successes and limitations of command-and-control regulation, U.S. industry and government moved on a limited basis toward an industrial greening approach (see Figure 12-1, cell D). Characterized by industry self-policing and government deterrence, this approach has achieved some successes but is clearly suboptimal—from economic and environmental perspectives—to the relationship that could exist if the situation in cell B were the case (across-the-board cooperation by both business and industry).

A first phase in the movement toward greening has used market incentives, self-reporting, and environmental management systems to improve corporate environmental performance. More recently, bolder experiments in self-regulation have advanced industry closer to the cooperative zone.

Phase I: Market Incentives, Self-Reporting, and Environmental Management Systems

As indicated in chapter 9, incentive-based approaches to environmental policy—such as emissions taxes, tradable permit systems, and deposit-refund programs—can be both effective at preventing pollution and more economically efficient. The EPA and many states have experimented with a wide range of market incentives, mostly since the 1980s, many of which have demonstrated promising results.[17] Experimentation with these "efficiency-based regulatory reforms" characterizes the second epoch of the environmental movement.[18]

Two of the most well-known experiments with market incentives include the Acid Rain program of the 1990 Clean Air Act and the tradable permits program in the Los Angeles basin. By most accounts, the Acid Rain program made good on economists' predictions: Emissions decreased, and industry spent less money overall. As discussed in chapter 9, the Los Angeles program has worked less well, at least in keeping down pollution control costs.

In the case of the Acid Rain program, the Clean Air Act allowed sulfur dioxide emissions trading throughout the Midwest (where power plants burn a great deal of acid-rain-producing coal). Prior to the Acid Rain program, new plants were required to "scrub"—remove at the smokestack—70 to 90 percent of their sulfur dioxide emissions. They thus were motivated only to reduce costs to meet the standard, not to increase the effectiveness of their scrubbers or find less costly methods. After the program began, however, and as was predicted, desulfurization rates increased substantially, because now power plants could reap the economic benefits of scrubber technology innovations.[19] Overall, the EPA estimates that the Acid Rain program is responsible for reducing sulfur dioxide emissions by 35 percent over 1990 levels at a cost of only one-quarter what was expected under the old command-and-control regulation.[20]

Another significant second-epoch regulatory experiment consisted of self-reporting, auditing, and disclosure requirements, beginning in 1986 with the Superfund Amendments and Reauthorization Act. This legislation created the Toxics Release Inventory (TRI), the first major federal environmental program that moved away from the traditional command-and-control approach (characterized by heavy fines, specified emissions levels, and mandatory pollution abatement technologies) toward a "softer, gentler" self-reporting and cooperative framework. The TRI requires companies that have ten or more employees, and that use significant amounts of any one of the hundreds of listed chemicals, to report their annual releases and transfers of these chemicals to the EPA, which then makes these data available to the public through an annual report, the TRI *Public Data Release.*

Originally only about 300 chemicals (referred to as core chemicals) were listed under the TRI reporting requirements, but the list has grown to include more than 650. The reporting requirements are extensive, including the maximum amount of chemicals on site; the number of pounds released either on or off site to different media (air, land, water); and information on whether discharges are treated, recovered for energy, or recycled.

The TRI requires companies to report their activities but does not require that they change their behavior. To view such policies as "all study and no action," however, would be to miss their contribution to what David Morell calls "regulation by embarrassment."[21] Indeed, environmental groups such as Citizens for a Better Environment, INFORM, and Greenpeace have seized on TRI data to publicize particularly heavy polluters. Some organizations make TRI data easily available over the Internet, allowing communities to view local toxic releases in map form.[22] Moreover, many state environmental agencies are basing their rulemaking on the TRI reports for industries in their states. Some industries have called for ending the TRI reporting process because of these new regulatory uses.

In 2002, U.S. industry generated over 13 million tons of toxic waste—or just under 100 pounds per American—about a fifth of which was released to air, land, and water untreated.[23] Making year-to-year comparisons in toxic releases is difficult, because the EPA has expanded the kinds of facilities required to report releases as well as added to the list of chemicals to report. But if we limit ourselves to the three hundred or so core chemicals from the original reporting industries, total on- and off-site releases decreased 45 percent from 1989 to 2002.[24] If we expand reporting to include all the common chemicals reported since 1995 (roughly six hundred chemicals) by the original industries, total on- and off-site releases increased a whopping 77 percent between 1995 and 2002.[25] This was much higher than the increase in industrial output for the same period, which grew by about 12 percent.[26]

Thus the overall record is mixed. First, total production-related waste (TPRW)—the amount of toxics produced before any treatment, recycling, or release occurs—is down by about 10 percent from the early 1990s to 2002. Industry is producing less total toxics but is releasing more to air, land, and water. And 10 percent over a decade constitutes relatively little fundamental reduction. Second, not all sectors are responding equally well to the challenge of toxics reduction. Although the original industries required to report to the TRI have decreased their chemical releases, they have not changed the amount of chemicals they generate as waste, which must then be recycled, used as a source of energy, treated, or released. The only way to accomplish significant lasting decreases in TPRW is through reducing the use of toxics in the production process. The data for total releases suggest that the transition from waste management to such fundamental reduction is not occurring as rapidly as needed.

Of TPRW generated in 1995, roughly 8 percent was recycled, 2 percent was recovered as energy, 1 percent was treated, and 10 percent was released. Those percentages worsened by 2002—with about the same recycled (7.6 percent), recovered for energy (3 percent), or treated (1 percent), but more released to air, land, and water (about 14 percent).[27] If facilities were moving up the waste management hierarchy, then not only would TPRW be decreasing, but the percentage of recycled materials would be increasing, and the percentage of treated or released materials would be decreasing.

While the EPA and industry applaud declines in toxic releases with every new TRI report, critics of the program have raised serious doubts about the validity of TRI data. For example, the Environmental Integrity Project (EIP) challenged the TRI results in a 2004 report entitled "Who's Counting? The Systematic Underreporting of Toxic Air Emissions." The EIP compared TRI reports for refineries and chemical facilities in Texas with actual smokestack emissions, in some cases using infrared scanners aboard aerial surveys. The EIP and the Texas Commission on Environmental Quality found that, for ten of the most common hydrocarbons, the EPA's reports underestimated actual emissions by 25 percent to 440 percent, raising serious concerns about outdated or inaccurate estimation methods that never actually measure releases themselves.[28]

The TRI is the most widely known and used database of self-reported information, but it is not unique. Thousands of companies around the world implement corporate environmental reports (CERs) every year and submit annual documents similar to their financial reports. These include "management policies and systems; input/output inventor[ies] of environmental impacts; financial implications of environmental actions; relationships with stakeholders; and the [company's] sustainable development agenda."[29]

Despite the appealing logic of self-reporting and auditing, it is exceedingly difficult to tell what such information achieves. Firms may be reluctant to accurately disclose potential problems with their facilities, fearing that regulators or third-party organizations (such as environmental litigants) may seize on the data to impose fines, facility changes in equipment and operation, or both.[30] The relatively small amount of research done on self-reporting suggests that, at best, CER systems improve company data collection and internal management, while possibly rendering environmental issues more transparent to government and the public.[31] More critical research shows that self-audits overwhelmingly reveal inventory and reporting violations (for example, of hazardous materials) rather than the much more serious unlawful emissions releases that the EPA discovers during its standard enforcement procedures.[32]

The third innovation of industrial greening actually modifies company management philosophies and practices. To implement green strategies, firms have adopted Environmental Management Systems (EMSs) that include corporate environmental pledges, internal training programs, environmental education programs, and use of cradle-to-grave systems of management control such as full-cost accounting, total quality management (TQM), and other environmental management systems.[33]

Given their interest in avoiding environmental protection costs, why do firms adopt EMSs? After all, they are costly—in terms of both money and staff time—and they open private firms to external scrutiny that may not be welcome. Potoski and Prakash reported that annual third-party audits for ISO 14001 certification (an international EMS discussed later in this chapter) can cost a small firm from $25,000 to $100,000 and much, much more for larger firms.[34]

In their survey of over two hundred U.S. manufacturing plants, Richard Florida and Derek Davison found that the three most important reasons for adopting EMSs included management "commitment to environmental improvement. . .corporate goals and objectives . . . , and business performance." Compliance with state and federal regulations, as well as improved community relations, were other frequently cited reasons.[35]

Firms that go green can also be rewarded by the financial markets. Some investment brokers have begun to respond to the greening movement with socially responsible environmental investment portfolios, although they are only a small part of the investments market. By the mid-1990s about forty mutual funds were managing $3 billion of green investments.[36] In 2003 the Social Investment Forum reported that socially responsible investment portfolios—those that select companies through a wide range of social screens, include shareholder advocacy, or invest in communities—had reached $2.16 trillion in assets, or a little over 11 percent of the total investment assets under U.S. management.[37]

Managers of green mutual funds are constantly updating their social ratings of industries worthy of investment. Indeed, a number of studies now suggest a strong correlation between profitability and greening, although researchers are quick to point out that just how a company's profits are tied to its investments in pollution prevention or abatement is not clear.[38]

Do EMSs make a difference? Because of the difficulty linking management changes to verifiable, objective environmental outcomes, the jury is still out on that question. Some researchers conclude that EMSs are effective when they have strong support from top management, who in turn rely on EMSs to greatly improve company environmental awareness and to better track the flow of raw materials, energy, labor, quality, and costs throughout the firm's operations.[39] And "EMS adopters" report that they recycle more, release fewer air, water, and waste emissions, and use less electricity than do non-EMS firms, but such findings are not based on third-party audits.[40]

Phase II: Self-Regulation

More recently, greening includes voluntary self-regulation efforts by firms around the world; some of these efforts are "invited" by regulators, whereas others are initiated and implemented by corporate leaders themselves. The primary attraction of voluntary, self-regulation is cost. Regulators simply cannot keep up with the cost of regulating many thousands of large firms. Industries should adopt environmental programs if, by doing so, they can lower their operating costs. Critics raise several objections to self-regulation. First, self-regulation may be nothing more than "greenwashing" by firms wishing to improve their public image without fundamentally changing their production practices, although some companies escape such charges by subjecting their environmental practices to third-party audits and then reporting the results using widely accepted indicators.[41] Second, by its very nature—adopting changes internal to a firm—the exact effect of self-regulation may be exceedingly difficult to assess; regulators and the public, in effect, must trust that firms are honest when reporting on their voluntary activities. Third, cleaner manufacturing often requires management, labor, equipment, or process changes, usually up front, before potential savings can be realized. As a result, these initial costs of self-regulation can seriously discourage participation. Finally, voluntary environmental management can lead to lower productivity if new practices are cleaner but less efficient than old ones.[42]

Since the mid-1980s the EPA has launched about two dozen voluntary programs. These programs are managed by the agency's Office of Policy, Economics, and Innovation (formerly the Office of Reinvention) and its Partnership Programs Coordinating Committee. One of the earliest and most successful is the 33/50 toxics reduction program. The favorable responses it received inside and outside the EPA helped usher in the other initiatives, most of which began between 1991 and 1995.

In 1989 the EPA had sufficient TRI data to rank the largest polluters and the chemicals they release. Just nine chemical and petroleum manufacturers were responsible for vast releases of toxics. Rather than call for further regulation of these companies, EPA administrator William Reilly convened meetings with their senior management, environmental organizations, and agency staff. He emerged with a pledge to lead the way in industrywide voluntary reductions.

In 1991 the EPA launched the 33/50 program, named for its goal of reducing releases of seventeen high-priority chemicals by 33 percent by 1992 and 50 percent by 1995. The seventeen chemicals were selected from the TRI list based on "their relative toxicity, volumes of use, and the potential for pollution prevention opportunities."[43] Significant decreases in the release levels for these chemicals were not the program's only objective. The EPA also wanted to promote flexibility by challenging corporations to reduce toxic emissions by whatever means they felt most appropriate. Participants were encouraged to adopt source reduction rather than end-of-pipe control methods. More than 8,000 companies were identified as potential program participants and invited to enroll in the program. According to the *1995 TRI Public Data Release*, roughly 1,300 companies signed up more than 6,000 facilities for the 33/50 program.

The EPA reported that the cumulative reduction achieved by participants during the program's first five years (1988–1993) totaled 46 percent.[44] The 1996 TRI report indicated a 60-percent overall reduction in the releases and transfers of the seventeen chemicals between 1988 and 1996.[45]

In many ways, the 33/50 program is a success story. Not only were the reduction goals achieved, but also an EPA-sponsored study revealed that source reduction accounted for 58 percent of the decrease in releases and transfers for the 33/50 chemicals.[46] In 1997 the program was recognized by the Innovations in American Government Award program as one of the twenty-five best government innovations in the country. At the same time, caution is warranted. The Government Accountability Office (GAO, formerly the General Accounting Office) has pointed out that so-called paper reductions accounted for 400 million pounds—or 27 percent—of the reductions achieved between 1988 and 1991. In addition, many of the reductions in 33/50 program chemicals cannot be attributed directly to the program because 26 percent of the 1988–1991 reductions were reported by nonparticipants, and 40 percent of the reductions occurred before the program was established.[47]

Ultimately the EPA's pollution prevention programs are still relatively new and must be evaluated cautiously. Benefits have been forthcoming. However, Walter Rosenbaum points out that these programs are also part "fanfare and guesswork." For example, the problems with the self-reported industry data—on energy and material inputs and waste streams—make it very difficult to assess what is truly happening in a firm. Moreover, EPA evaluators have not performed life-cycle assessments to determine if greening is truly occurring, as opposed to problems being displaced to other media.[48]

The EPA is not alone in its efforts to promote green management, however. In 1996 the International Organization for Standardization (ISO) released its ISO 14001 environmental management standards. A company registering for ISO 14001 certification must (1) develop an environmental management system, (2) demonstrate compliance with all local environmental laws, and (3) demonstrate a commitment to continuous improvement.[49] By December 2002 over 49,000 firms had been ISO 14001–certified worldwide, but the United States—with about 2,600 certified firms—lagged behind most other developed countries in the proportion of its companies that sought and obtained this voluntary certification.[50] Increasingly, large manufacturers require that their suppliers become ISO 14001 certified as well. Ford Motor Company led the way in the mid-1990s but was soon followed by all the major automakers.[51]

Potoski and Prakash analyzed ISO 14001–certified firms in the United States, asking whether their air emissions were significantly lower than those of noncertified firms, and indeed they were. Their explanation is that, on the spectrum of voluntary measures, ISO 14001 represents a "weak sword," because it requires only third-party audits. A "strong sword" system, like the EPA's Performance Track program, requires third-party monitoring, public disclosure of audit information, and sanctions by program sponsors.[52] It remains to be seen just how much more environmental performance strong sword environmental management systems can spur over weak sword programs.

Industry trade associations also lead voluntary self-regulation efforts by their member companies; the chemical industry provides one notable example. In response to extensive and highly negative media coverage, the Synthetic Organic Chemical Manufacturers Association (SOCMA) adopted its Responsible Care program in 1988. This sectorwide code of conduct is now required of all CMA members and has been adopted in some form by chemical manufacturers in forty-six countries.[53] It consists of ten guiding principles and six management practice codes. The guiding principles emphasize responding to community concerns; ensuring safety in all phases of production, transportation, use, and disposal; developing safe chemicals and supporting research on health, safety, and environmental effects of products, processes, and wastes; and helping to create responsible laws and regulations. The management codes are designed to improve each facility's emergency response capabilities; pollution prevention efforts; and safety in production, sales, distribution, and final disposal. The CMA has been adopting quantitative benchmarks to measure its members' progress on each of these codes.[54]

The Responsible Care program has also spawned an extensive mutual assistance network within the chemical industry, a network that includes very senior management. Companies that are far along in their implementation of the codes are asked to help those companies having difficulty complying. Through its Partnership Program, the CMA actively pushes the envelope of Responsible Care beyond the chemical industry. Partners are industries and associations that are not CMA members but that make, use, formulate, distribute, transport, treat, or dispose of chemicals.[55]

Early assessments of the Responsible Care program revealed disappointing progress. In one study of sixteen medium- to large-sized firms, about half took the Responsible Care codes seriously—mostly by adopting environmental management systems and integrating environmental principles throughout the firm.[56] A study comparing the environmental performance of firms adopting Responsible Care with those that had not revealed essentially no difference, a discouraging result suggesting that management changes may not be resulting in measurable environmental improvements.[57]

Box 12-1   DuPont Chemical: A Leading Company Strives to Change Its Image and Practices

The DuPont Corporation, one of the country's oldest, largest, and most profitable companies, has for years been leading the chemical industry's efforts to improve its environmental management and reputation with the public at large. Has the company succeeded? As is so often the case with industrial greening, the results have been mixed.

On the positive side, DuPont leads industry efforts to protect the ozone layer and to mitigate climate change. Before the Montreal Protocol was signed in 1988, DuPont was responsible for a quarter of the world market for chlorofluorocarbons (CFCs)—and in 1989 announced it would phase them out well ahead of the schedule expected by treaty negotiators. In 1999, DuPont's executive vice president and chief operating officer Dennis H. Reilly announced a three-point goal for addressing climate change by 2010, including cutting its greenhouse gas emissions by 65 percent over 1990 levels; holding total energy use constant, again using 1990 as the base year; and using renewable resources for 10 percent of its global energy needs. More recently, DuPont won a 2003 Green Chemistry Award from the EPA for a microbial process that produces 1,3-propanediol (PDO) from glucose, the first time an engineered microorganism will be used to convert a renewable resource into a high-volume chemical. PDO is used to make polyester.

(Continues)

Other critics point to a large gap between improvements to which CMA members have committed themselves and what companies have actually achieved. Part of the problem is that some of the management codes lack clear performance indicators and company statistics are not yet independently validated by third-party observers.[58]

All critiques aside, the U.S. chemical industry certainly pollutes less for each gallon of product than it did in prior decades. Toxic releases, energy consumption, and air emissions data all show that the industry's total production has grown faster than its pollution levels. (See Box 12-1 for a discussion of one chemical company's environmental performance.)

Building on Pilot Programs and Policy Experiments

Overall, the national effort to reduce the air pollution emitted by business and industry, particularly in major urban areas across the nation, under the Clean Air Act, has been reasonably successful. Significantly helping this

---

Box 12-1   *(Continued)*

Tempering these successes, critics point out that DuPont's CFC patents were set to expire, so it was going to lose money in that business anyway (and DuPont is heavily involved in global production of HFC, the major CFC replacement, including production in China, the largest growing market). Regarding climate change, DuPont would likely reap several hundred million dollars in profit by selling emissions reduction credits in some future global emissions trading market. Thanks to its sheer size, DuPont still released more chemicals than many of its competitors in 2002; DuPont has four facilities in the top ten chemical company releasers nationally. Finally, DuPont has fielded major litigation throughout the years over pollutant releases, the most recent involving allegations that the company contaminated groundwater with perfluoroctanoic acid (also known as PFOA or C-8, which DuPont uses to make Teflon and other products) and exposed workers to illegal doses of the chemical.

Source: William R. Moomaw, "Expanding the Concept of EMSs to Meet Multiple Goals," in Cary Coglianese and Jennifer Nash, eds., *Regulating from the Inside: Can Environmental Management Systems Achieve Policy Goals?* (Washington D.C.: Resources for the Future, 2001); Andrew Wood, "DuPont, Süd-Chemie, AgraQuest among EPA Green Chemistry Award Winners," *Chemical Week,* July 2/9, 2003, 14; "DuPont Finalizes China HFCs Venture," *Chemical Week,* March 24, 2004, 14; U.S. EPA, *2002 Toxics Release Inventory Public Data Release,* www.epa.gov/triexplorer; and Robert Westervelt, "DuPont Charged with TSCA Violations over C-8 Disclosure," *Chemical Week,* July 14, 2004, 14.

---

effort has been a dramatic reduction since 1970 of emissions per automobile on the road today. Many of our most polluted waterways have been cleaned up over this time period as well.

Balanced against this record, there is little evidence that the emissions reduction and cleanup was accomplished in the most cost-effective manner. Possibly more important in looking forward, more than three decades of experience did not result in any visible commitment by the majority of businesses in the United States to a comprehensive, green transition.

As a result, we cannot be sure to continue abating large-scale pollution, nor that the aggregate of emissions from American industry will remain below previous levels. That is, businesses have made little commitment to moving beyond the long-standing command-and-control regulatory approach to a life-cycle environmental analysis of their products. We are even less likely to see widespread closed-system toxics management in manufacturing or product use, or sustained attention to more global and growing problems such as greenhouse gases emissions, destruction of natural habitats, or depletion of ocean resources. Equally important, no national policy goals or mandated regulations exist in the United States to move industry in this direction.

An instructive lesson from the voluntary programs established since 1991 is that when businesses form an alliance within their sector, either voluntarily or under the pressure of government policy, significant reductions can be realized, as illustrated by the chemical industry. Yet this very example suggests that chemicals may be the proverbial exception to the rule since the change in that industry was due to the extraordinary public pressure brought to bear in the early 1990s as a result of the few colossal environmental disasters experienced in the United States and abroad and the fact that the industry is fairly well concentrated. Thus cooperation was brought about among a relatively few number of actors. In effect, the conditions for moving into a win-win game position for both government and the chemical industry existed, in that flexible regulation and volunteerism could be achieved, and the action moved into cell B of Figure 12-1. Today, few other such examples can be found within major business and industrial sectors.

How might this situation be changed? After a thorough review of the pilots and experiments in flexible regulation, self-regulation, and voluntary approaches since the mid-1990s, Marc Eisner has woven together the best components from each into a promising synthesis.[59] His approach is designed to overcome the natural (that is, rational) reticence of business and industry, and move the greening agenda beyond cell D, into cell B. He focuses on bridging the gap between business and government, on "harnessing the market and industrial associations to achieve superior results by creating a system of government-supervised self-regulation." [60]

The central propositions of his policy synthesis are as follows:

- Market rewards should be the primary motivator (placing emphasis on the "carrot") while retaining in reserve the traditional regulatory "stick."
- Reliance should be placed on trade and business associations; these sectoral and quasigovernmental organizations can serve as the central implementers of greening policy (they are "quasi" in that they are nonprofit organizations, although they would be imbued with governing authority).
- Emphasis should be placed on disclosure and "sunshine" provisions over government-prescribed techniques of emissions reduction and on-site government inspection.
- Sectoral associations would serve as intermediary entities, both to implement policy and to assure the government that policy would be carried out as intended.

The proposal does not require significant new public laws or the creation of new government bureaucracy because they can be woven together from existing programs and authority.

The critical virtue of this approach is that, if adopted as the overall framework for greening, it would mitigate the government's fear of becoming a "sucker," as well as business' fear of an overbearing regulatory regime, on the one hand, and of other businesses evading their responsibilities to go green, on the other. In short, we have in Eisner's proposal a game-theoretic and pragmatically attractive approach to moving government and business into cell B. As we mentioned at the outset, policy is set by the politics of policymaking and not simply by the logic of policy analysis, as attractive as it may be, and to which we now turn.

Mixed Signals from Industry and Washington

Despite the good image nurtured by corporate public relations officers, many industry lobbyists still work assiduously at blocking or rolling back environmental mandates.[61] Industry political action committees are keeping up a steady stream of campaign contributions to antienvironmentalist legislators, just as they have done for years.[62] Indeed, the chemical industry's strong political lobbying to weaken existing environmental protection legislation and to prevent new legislation undermines the credibility of its own Responsible Care program. The American Chemistry Council became concerned enough with its industry's poor reputation that it adopted third-party auditing as part of a newly reinvigorated Responsible Care initiative.[63]

For its part, George W. Bush's administration did little to move industry and the government toward win-win outcomes depicted in cell B; rather, the administration's general retreat from regulatory enforcement moved the country further into cell A (in which the federal government can end up being a "sucker").

From the start of the Bush administration, proenforcement advocates took a back seat while the EPA was instructed to drop air pollution lawsuits that were close to successful settlement, relax standards for mercury in air emissions and for arsenic in drinking water, and advance energy production goals over conservation and habitat protection.[64] The most significant retreat from command-and-control regulation came when the administration yielded to industry pressure on the subject of new source review. In place for decades, new source review required new, better pollution controls when industries upgraded or expanded their facilities. Led by electric power utilities burning coal in old plants, lobbyists argued that new source review would impose hundreds of millions of dollars in new, unnecessary costs—and could prevent much-needed expansion of the country's electric-power-generating capacity.[65] In the end, the revised regulations "said utilities would not have to add new pollution-control devices if upgrades and construction projects did not cost more than 20 percent of the plant's value—a loophole all sides said was huge."[66] The inevitable conclusion is that not even conventional deterrence, much less win-win strategies, will be pursued without a change of administrations or a much more aggressively environmental Congress.

Reaching beyond Win-Win

We assume that devising ways to improve protection of the environment will need to build on the several generations of existing law and public policy, and any thought of disregarding these and starting anew is unrealistic. For this reason, the synthetic approach conceived by Eisner, designed to harness the core self-interested impulses of business and government on behalf of protection of the natural environment, is appealing. To be successful, these policies require business to improve the production of material goods and services while reducing to a minimum the adverse impacts on the natural environment. Indeed, this is not only the win-win of game theory but also the "double bottom-line" aspiration of industrial ecology today. As a blueprint for a politically realistic, near-term policy goal, we believe Eisner provides an ambitious though realizable approach to environmental protection and the greening of industry.

Not even the best policy ideas succeed in the real world, of course. With this in mind, should the Eisner approach fail and it becomes necessary to look for more ambitious though over-the-horizon approaches, they do exist. We can suggest two options in particular to underscore the point. These are the "theory of economic dynamics of environmental law" articulated recently by David Driesen,[67] and steady-state, or "true cost economics," long advocated by Herman Daly.[68] In a recent treatise on law and the environment, Driesen argues that dramatic greening is unlikely until the priority given to efficiency and benefit-cost thinking in neoclassic microeconomic behavior is replaced by the goal of encouraging "dynamic technology change" and adaptation, in a world of growing natural resources scarcity.

A second and similarly ambitious and transformative approach consists of efforts to refocus attention at the macroeconomic level away from the exclusive attention on production of material goods and human services to balancing production with the costs to natural assets and the environment, a movement led by Daly and a small but growing number of "ecological economists" around the world.

Ultimately, however, the presidential election results of 2004 bode poorly for industrial greening. The Bush administration's focus on reduced enforcement pulls the rug out from under agency officials' feet, making it likely that voluntary programs will be much less effective. U.S. industry makes strides in environmental protection when credible regulatory enforcement is paired with flexibility and innovation. None of these approaches will be forthcoming in Bush's second term, and so we can expect advances in greening—if there are to be any—to arise from different quarters. The challenge will be for environmental groups, consumers, forward-thinking industries, and pro-greening legislators to work around this administration's shortsightedness.

Suggested Web Sites

Independent Analysis of Corporate Environmental and Social Performance

Innovest Strategic Advisors Group (www.innovestgroup.com) A research and advisory firm specializing in analyzing companies' performance on environmental, social, and strategic governance issues.

Corporate Social Responsibility Network (www.csrnetwork.com) A third-party "benchmarking" consulting group that offers corporate social and environmental responsibility auditing.

Six Sigma (www.isixsigma.com) Promoting in business the adoption, advancement, and integration of Six Sigma, a management and auditing methodology to identify errors or defects in manufacturing and service.

The Global Reporting Initiative (www.globalreporting.org) An independent nongovernmental organization charged with developing and disseminating globally applicable sustainability reporting guidelines.

Business Sustainability Councils

World Business Council for Sustainable Development (www.wbcsd .ch) A global green industry clearinghouse.

World Resources Institute (http://povertyprofit.wri.org) Global environmental clearinghouse with programs tying industry to development.

Leading Business and Environment Journals

Business Strategy and the Environment (www3.interscience.wiley.com/ cgi-bin/jhome/5329) Publishes scholarship on business responses to improving environmental performance.

The Green Business Letter (www.greenbizletter.com) A monthly newsletter providing information for businesses and universities wishing to integrate environmental thinking throughout their organizations in profitable ways.

Environmental Quality Management (www3.interscience.wiley.com/ cgi-bin/jhome/60500185) An applied and practice-oriented journal demonstrating how to improve environmental performance and exceed new voluntary standards such as ISO 14000.

Corporate Social Responsibility and Environmental Management (www3.interscience.wiley.com/cgi-bin/jhome/90513547) A journal specializing in research relating to the development of tools and techniques for improving corporate performance and accountability on social and environmental dimensions.

U.S. Environmental Protection Agency Sites

Energy Star (www.energystar.gov) A good site for learning about energy efficiency programs and efficient equipment, lighting, and buildings.

Toxics Release Inventory (www.epa.gov/triexplorer) The nation's list of toxic chemical releases from manufacturing, power generation, and mining facilities.

Partners for the Environment (www.epa.gov/epahome/hi-voluntary .htm) A clearinghouse for the EPA's voluntary pollution prevention and management programs.

National Environmental Performance Track (www.epa.gov/ performancetrack) An EPA program inviting companies to join as members that receive recognition for achieving leading-edge environmental performance.

Notes

1. Robert B. Gibson, ed., *Voluntary Initiatives: The New Politics of Corporate Greening* (Peterborough, Ontario: Broadview Press, 1999).
2. Thomas Princen, Michael Maniates, and Ken Conca, eds. *Confronting Consumption* (Cambridge: MIT Press, 2002).
3. Huib Pellikaan and Robert J. van der Veen, *Environmental Dilemmas and Policy Design* (New York: Cambridge University Press, 2002); Nives Dolak and Elinor Ostrom, eds., *The Commons in the New Millennium: Challenges and Adaptation* (Cambridge: MIT Press, 2003).
4. Daniel A. Mazmanian and Michael E. Kraft, "The Three Epochs of the Environmental Movement," in *Toward Sustainable Communities: Transition and Transformations in Environmental Policy,* ed. Daniel A. Mazmanian and Michael E. Kraft (Cambridge: MIT Press, 1999).
5. U.S. Environmental Protection Agency (EPA), *EPA FY 1999 President's Budget* (Washington, D.C.: EPA, spring 1998).
6. Michael E. Porter and Claas van der Linde, "Green and Competitive: Ending the Stalemate," *Harvard Business Review* 73 (September–October 1995): 120–134.
7. Doris Fuchs and Daniel A. Mazmanian, "The Greening of Industry: Needs of the Field," *Business Strategy and Environment* 7 (1998): 193–203.
8. EPA, Technology Transfer Network, Clearinghouse for Inventories & Emissions Factors, *National Air Pollutant Emissions Inventory, 1970–2002,* www.epa.gov/ttn/chief/ net/2002inventory.html, March 5, 2005.
9. Roy Huntley, Environmental Engineer, Emission Factor and Inventory Group, EPA, personal communication, August 26, 2004.
10. Cary Coglianese and Jennifer Nash, eds., *Regulating from the Inside: Can Environmental Management Systems Achieve Policy Goals?* (Washington D.C.: Resources for the Future, 2001).
11. U.S. Department of Energy (DOE), Energy Information Administration, *Annual Energy Review* (Washington, D.C.: DOE, 1980, 1985, 1991, 1997).
12. DOE, Energy Information Administration, *1998 Energy Consumption by Manufacturers,* August 14, 2001, www.eia.doe.gov/emeu/mecs/mecs98/datatables/contents .html, March 1, 2005.
13. EPA, *1999 Toxics Release Inventory Public Data Release,* EPA 260-R-01–001 (Washington, D.C.: EPA, April 2001).
14. DOE, Energy Information Administration, *Annual Energy Review* (Washington, D.C.: DOE, 1991, 1997).

15. DOE, Energy Information Administration, data from 1998, 1994, and 1991 *Energy Consumption by Manufacturers* reports, www.eia.doe.gov/emeu/mecs/, March 1, 2005.
16. U.S. Department of Commerce, *Pollution Abatement Costs and Expenditures*, MA-200(80)-1 (Washington, D.C.: U.S. Department of Commerce, Bureau of the Census, 1980, 1985, 1993, 1994).
17. Walter A. Rosenbaum, *Environmental Politics and Policy*, 6th ed. (Washington, D.C.: CQ Press, 2005), 163.
18. Mazmanian and Kraft, "The Three Epochs of the Environmental Movement."
19. David Popp, "Pollution Control Innovations and the Clean Air Act of 1990," *Journal of Policy Analysis and Management*, 22 (2003): 641–660.
20. EPA, *The EPA Acid Rain Program 2002 Progress Report* EPA-430-R-03-011, November 21, 2003, www.epa.gov/airmarkets/cmprpt/arp02/index.html, March 1, 2005.
21. David Morell, STC Environmental, personal communication, 1995.
22. For an example, see the Right-to-Know Network (www.rtknet.org) or Environmental Defense's Web site (www.scorecard.org).
23. EPA, *2002 Toxics Release Inventory Public Data Release*, August 2, 2004, www.epa.gov/triexplorer, March 1, 2005.
24. Ibid.
25. Ibid.
26. U.S. Department of Commerce, Economics and Statistics Administration, Census Bureau, *Manufacturers' Shipments, Inventories and Orders, 1992–2002*, August 2003, www.census.gov/prod/2003pubs/m3-02.pdf, March 1, 2005.
27. EPA, *2002 Toxics Release Inventory Public Data Release.*
28. Environmental Integrity Project, "Who's Counting? The Systematic Underreporting of Toxic Air Emissions," June 22, 2004, www.environmentalintegrity.org/pub205.cfm, March 1, 2005.
29. David Annandale, Angus Morrison-Saunders, and George Bouma, "The Impact of Voluntary Environmental Protection Instruments on Company Environmental Performance," *Business Strategy and the Environment* 13 (2004): 1–12.
30. Alexander Pfaff and Chris William Sanchirico, "Big Field, Small Potatoes: An Empirical Assessment of EPA's Self-Audit Policy," *Journal of Policy Analysis and Management* 23 (summer 2004): 415–432.
31. Annandale et al., "The Impact of Voluntary Environmental Protection Instruments."
32. Pfaff and Sanchirico, "Big Field, Small Potatoes."
33. John T. Willig, ed., *Environmental TQM*, 2nd ed. (New York: McGraw-Hill Executive Enterprises Publications, 1994); Coglianese and Nash, *Regulating from the Inside*; Marc Allen Eisner, "Corporate Environmentalism, Regulatory Reform, and Industry Self-Regulation: Toward Genuine Regulatory Reinvention in the United States," *Governance: An International Journal of Policy, Administration, and Institutions,* 17 (April 2004): 145–167.
34. Matthew Potoski and Aseem Prakash, "Covenants with Weak Swords: ISO 14001 and Firms' Environmental Performance," paper delivered at the annual meeting of the American Political Science Association, Chicago (September 2–5, 2004).
35. Richard Florida and Derek Davison, "Why Do Firms Adopt Advanced Environmental Practices (and Do They Make a Difference)?," in Coglianese and Nash, *Regulating from the Inside.*
36. Ricardo Sandoval, "How Green Are the Green Funds?" *Amicus Journal* 17 (spring 1995): 29–33. One widely respected eco-rating of Fortune 500 companies is provided by the Investor Responsibility Research Center in Washington, D.C., www.irrc.org.
37. Social Investment Forum, *2003 Report on Socially Responsible Investing Trends in the United States,* December 2003, www.socialinvest.org/areas/research, March 1, 2005.

38. David Austin, "The Green and the Gold: How a Firm's Clean Quotient Affects Its Value," *Resources* 132 (summer 1998): 15–17.
39. Annandale et al., "The Impact of Voluntary Environmental Protection Instruments;" Bruce Smart, ed., *Beyond Compliance: A New Industry View of the Environment* (Washington, D.C.: World Resources Institute, 1992).
40. Florida and Davison, "Why Do Firms Adopt Advanced Environmental Practices?"
41. Eisner, "Corporate Environmentalism."
42. Natalie Stoeckl, "The Private Costs and Benefits of Environmental Self-Regulation: Which Firms Have Most to Gain?" *Business Strategy and the Environment* 13 (2004): 135–155.
43. EPA, *1995 Toxics Release Inventory Public Data Release,* EPA 745-R-97–005 (Washington, D.C.: EPA, April 1997).
44. EPA, *1993 Toxics Release Inventory Public Data Release,* EPA 745-R-95–010 (Washington, D.C.: EPA, 1995).
45. EPA, *1996 Toxics Release Inventory Public Data Release,* EPA 745-R-98-005 (Washington, D.C.: EPA, 1996).
46. EPA, *1995 Toxics Release Inventory Public Data Release.*
47. U.S. Government Accountability Office (GAO), *Toxic Substances: Status of EPA's Efforts to Reduce Toxic Releases* (Washington, D.C.: GAO, 1994).
48. Walter A. Rosenbaum, "Why Institutions Matter in Program Evaluation: The Case of EPA's Pollution Prevention Program," in *Environmental Program Evaluation: A Primer,* ed. Gerrit J. Knaap and Tschangho John Kim (Urbana: University of Illinois Press, 1998); Douglas J. Lober, "Pollution Prevention as Corporate Entrepreneurship," *Journal of Organizational Change Management* 11 (1998): 26–37.
49. Information on ISO 14001 is available at www.ecology.or.jp/isoworld/english/english.htm.
50. International Organization for Standardization (ISO), *Twelfth cycle: The ISO Survey of ISO 9000 and ISO 14001 Certificates,* www.iso.ch/iso/en/iso9000-14000/pdf/survey12thcycle.pdf.
51. Eisner, "Corporate Environmentalism," 150.
52. Potoski and Prakash, "Covenants with Weak Swords."
53. Synthetic Organic Chemical Association (SOCMA), "Overview of Responsible Care," 2004, www.socma.com/responsiblecare/index.htm.
54. Lois R. Ember, "Responsible Care: Chemical Makers Still Counting on It to Improve Image," *Chemical and Engineering News,* May 29, 1995, 12.
55. Ibid., 11.
56. J. Howard, J. Nash, and J. Ehrenfeld, "Standard or Smokescreen? Implementation of a Voluntary Environmental Code," *California Management Review* 42 (2000): 63–82.
57. A. King and M. Lenox, "Prospects for Industry Self-Regulation without Sanctions: A Study of Responsible Care in the Chemical Industry," *The Academy of Management Journal* 43 (2000): 698–716.
58. Ember, "Responsible Care," 13.
59. Eisner, "Corporate Environmentalism."
60. Ibid., 145.
61. Marc S. Reisch, "Twenty Years after Bhopal: Smokescreen or True Reform? Has the Chemical Industry Changed Enough to Make Another Massive Accident Unlikely?" *Chemical and Engineering News,* June 7, 2004, 19–23.
62. Larry Makinson and Joshua Goldstein, *The Cash Constituents of Congress* (Washington, D.C.: Center for Responsive Politics, 1994).
63. Marc S. Reisch, "Track Us, Trust Us: American Chemistry Council Says Will Supply the Facts to Earn the Public's Trust," *Chemical and Engineering News,* June 7, 2004, 24–25.
64. Christopher Drew and Richard A. Oppel Jr., "How Industry Won the Battle of Pollution Control at E.P.A.," *New York Times,* March 6, 2004; Rosenbaum, *Environ-*

mental Politics and Policy; Maurie J. Cohen, "George W. Bush and the Environmental Protection Agency: A Midterm Appraisal," *Society and Natural Resources* 17 (2004): 1–21.

65. Bruce Barcott, "Changing All the Rules," *New York Times*, April 4, 2004.

66. Drew and Oppel, "How Industry Won the Battle of Pollution Control."

67. David M. Driesen, *The Economic Dynamics of Environmental Law* (Cambridge: The MIT Press, 2003).

68. Herman Daly, *Beyond Growth: The Economics of Sustainable Development* (Boston: Beacon Press, 1996). For a discussion of true cost economics, see Brendan Themes, "True Cost Economics: The Current Economic Model Has Failed Us," *Utne Reader*, August 26, 2004, www.utne.com/webwatch/2004_163/news/11366-1.html.

13

Climate Policy on the Installment Plan
Lamont C. Hempel

Climate change may be the most significant and enduring environmental problem of the twenty-first century, especially if it exacerbates the twentieth century's most pervasive and insidious ecological problem: loss of biodiversity. Human alterations of climate epitomize what are sometimes called third-generation environmental issues—global in scale; long term in scope; plagued by scientific uncertainty; and seemingly unmanageable within the boundaries of conventional policy, practices, and institutions. Prior generations of issues featured local and regional concerns about air and water quality, land use, and nonrenewable resource depletion. They centered on health-based, point-source regulation of pollution, along with compartmentalized approaches to natural resource management. Today they are giving way to a new generation of environmental concerns and a new direction in environmental policy, one shaped principally by the worldwide implications of enhanced greenhouse warming.

This new direction calls for more "glocal"—that is, transboundary and multilevel—approaches to environmental problem solving, while at the same time requiring more flexible, contingent, and collaborative forms of policy design and implementation. The policy approaches and jurisdictional responsibilities that functioned reasonably well to limit resource use and pollution in the past—at least when faithfully executed and enforced—are proving inadequate for the emerging task of managing the Earth's climate system.

The United States emits nearly a quarter of all anthropogenic greenhouse gases. While unquestionably a world leader in many aspects of environmental protection, the United States is increasingly viewed as the world's leading laggard when it comes to global warming issues. The energy and climate initiatives announced by President George W. Bush in 2001 added to this perception, as did Bush's reelection in 2004. In the aftermath of September 11 and the resulting war on terrorism, it became easy for the Bush administration to defer action on the climate front, despite growing evidence that rapid responses might be warranted. Climate issues were seldom mentioned during the 2004 presidential campaign. But that did not mean they were absent from the policy agenda. Perhaps in anticipation of campaign pressure from Democratic nominee Senator John Kerry, key members of the Bush administration endorsed a report released at the time of the Republican National Convention acknowledging significant risks from changes in climate caused in part by human activities.[1] Whether their endorsements marked the beginning of a new era or merely the posturing necessary to sustain a policy of inaction remains to be seen.

This chapter examines U.S. climate policy within the larger context of the international climate change debate. The role of U.S. science and politics is unquestionably central to this debate, though developments in other countries have also played an influential and sometimes decisive role. The focus here is on policy evolution and on the political and economic dilemmas that have shaped international climate negotiations.[2] Evolving climate policy is then examined within the domestic framework of U.S. energy policy—all part of a continuing struggle to convert contestable science into prudent policy and to transform promising technology into economically affordable action.

"Political" Science

The conversion of science into policy is seldom a smooth process, particularly if scientific consensus is tentative—and therefore fragile—and the economic implications of that fledgling consensus are inimical to the interests of powerful stakeholders. The climate change debate exemplifies this tension better perhaps than any other issue of our time. Uncertain, potentially catastrophic, complex beyond human comprehension, and susceptible to costly overreaction and underreaction by partisan policymakers, climate issues offer a revealing glimpse of what happens when probabilistic science meets the crystallized objectives of interest group politics.

Science has been a powerful force in environmental policymaking for many decades, but emerging climate concerns have elevated science higher than ever before, although seemingly without an accompanying rise of influence on policy. Before climate change became an issue, science-based environmental policymaking was largely a matter of quantifying and managing potential harm to the health of people and ecosystems. Today, however, environmental scientists are confronted with the inherently unmanageable and chaotic behavior of climate systems. They may never be able to predict adequately the changes in climate caused by human activity.

This growing realization has not been lost on political leaders, many of whom are probably relieved that science remains too uncertain to drive policy, directly, hence preserving their political options for dealing with what could be enormously costly, high-stakes issues of climate change. Those who yearn for a rigorous science that provides indisputable authority for policy action may have to settle for the vagaries of "acceptable risk."

Risk Assessment

Because it goes to the heart of policy decisions about energy, transportation, natural resource management, and many other issues, the climate debate can be characterized as a high-stakes political contest between so-called risk takers and risk avoiders. Risk takers oppose action unless there is solid proof that the benefits of proactive policy outweigh the potential costs of adaptation to climate change. Risk avoiders adhere to the so-called precautionary principle, which calls for proactive policy in the absence of scientific proof, especially when large-scale threats with potentially irreversible outcomes are involved (see chapter 10).

Framing the issue in terms of risk behavior presumes that participants in the climate debate agree on the probability and severity of climate threats. They do not. Nor do they agree on what constitutes risky behavior. For example, opponents of climate protection initiatives claim to be responsibly risk averse, arguing that it is the environmentalists who are the true risk takers, foolishly promoting costly prevention measures that will disrupt our way of life and our free-market economy without compelling evidence that such measures are necessary, now. Environmentalists counter that such rationales merely shift the risk exposure to future generations. Inaction, in their view, poses the highest risk of all for our descendants and for millions of other species.

Many scientists believe that enhanced greenhouse warming may have severe effects on human settlement patterns, food and freshwater supplies, energy production, and the health and integrity of natural ecosystems. Potential impacts include loss of wetlands and other wildlife habitat; increased frequency and severity of storms and droughts; reduced forest productivity; changes in species composition; ocean flooding; increased saltwater intrusion in estuaries; and myriad other problems resulting from interactive shifts in temperature, precipitation, wind patterns, sea level, ocean currents, and cloud behavior.

But it is also possible that climate change will occur slowly enough to permit incremental adaptation without severely straining the capacities of natural systems or human ingenuity. Some scientists believe the central challenge of climate policy will be "adapting to the inevitable."[3] Whereas some regions may benefit from changes in climate, those that are less fortunate may have plenty of time to prepare for a less favorable climate. In the long run, advances in science and technology may prove adequate to the challenges of climate adaptation and environmental protection, without having to alter human lifestyles and economic priorities. The key question in the face of potentially large and irreversible climate risks is whether it is prudent to assume that such advances will occur in a timely fashion. Moreover, even if human beings possess sufficient technoscientific capacity to cope with climate change, many other living species remain vulnerable to change. Their migration and adaptation rates may not be fast enough to keep pace with human alterations of climate.

Regardless of how the problem is framed, the debate over climate policy involves two key questions that inevitably bring together science and politics. The first question addresses the need for action on potential climate threats; the second addresses our ability to influence outcomes through public policy, market forces, lifestyle changes, and new technologies.[4] The usual response to the "need for action" question begins with a scientific risk assessment and ends with a political judgment about what constitutes an *acceptable* risk. The response to the "ability to influence" question begins with an assessment of institutional and financial capacity and culminates in a judgment about political and technical feasibility, administrative competence, and the efficacy of markets to implement decisions and policies.

Policy responses to climate threats are inevitably a product of such reasoning, whether consciously and systematically or by some haphazard process of trial and error. Policies are constructed not only from tentative agreements about what the facts are but also from even more tentative agreements about what the facts *mean*. Positions on climate policy reflect political needs assessments that influence the funding and interpretation of scientific needs assessments. They also reflect beliefs about the desirability of government, market, technological, and lifestyle solutions—that is, the ability to influence outcomes—that draw heavily on the claims-making activities of scientists and political leaders. Following this logic, some observers acknowledge a need for action in climate protection while rejecting proactive public policies on grounds that government may be less capable of positively influencing outcomes than is, say, the market.[5]

Claims of Scientists

Life as we know it depends on the greenhouse effect, whereby incoming ultraviolet radiation from the sun is partially absorbed at the Earth's surface, redistributed through the oceans and atmosphere, and then radiated back to space in infrared "heat" wavelengths. Because of infrared trapping by natural greenhouse gases—mostly water vapor, along with carbon dioxide (CO_2) from cellular respiration—the Earth's surface temperature is about 33°C (59°F) warmer than it would otherwise be. Before the industrial era, outgoing heat radiation was roughly in balance with incoming solar radiation, thanks to relatively stable concentrations of these natural greenhouse gases. In the past 150 years, however, human activities have measurably enhanced the greenhouse effect by increasing the concentrations of key trace gases—principally CO_2, chlorofluorocarbons, methane, nitrous oxides, and tropospheric ozone (in the form of urban smog).

Atmospheric concentrations of CO_2, arguably the most important of these gases, are projected to double by the middle of the twenty-first century from preindustrial levels of about 270 parts per million by volume (ppmv), due primarily to fossil fuel combustion, deforestation, and other large-scale transformations wrought by industrial and agricultural development.[6] Unfortunately there is no reason to assume that concentrations will stop increasing at that point.

The consequences of increased greenhouse warming are much harder to predict than is the warming itself. Although virtually all scientists agree that the chemistry of our atmosphere is changing and that the average surface temperature of the Earth is rising, there is much less consensus about the rate, magnitude, and duration of any resulting climate disturbances that can be attributed to emissions from human activities. Scientists recognize that other factors—some natural, some anthropogenic—may play a significant role in the observed warming. Most agree that a combination of greenhouse gases, aerosols (for example, sulfates, fine particles of dust, volcanic emissions), deforestation, and changes in our sun (for example, sunspot activity) may be forcing perceptible changes in climate.

The overall global climate trend can be summarized as warmer and wetter, with rising sea levels; however, regional variations and microclimatic conditions make prediction hazardous. Modeling the interaction of feedback mechanisms for climate systems is exceedingly complex. Further complicating efforts at prediction are recent marine geochemistry studies suggesting that incremental global warming may trigger abrupt cooling by shutting down major ocean currents. Of particular concern is the enormous current that carries heat to the North Atlantic. Researchers studying this ocean "conveyor belt" and its interactions with other climate systems have warned that global warming may cause sudden shifts in ocean circulation, plunging much of Europe and Asia into a steep cooling trend.[7] Some researchers conclude that such a shift could occur within a single decade, producing catastrophic consequences for agriculture and jeopardizing the integrity of major ecosystems.

Issue Evolution

The evolution of climate issues and policies can be divided roughly into five developmental stages: Stage I. scientific assessment (1950s–1988); Stage II. agenda setting (1988–1992); Stage III. policy frameworks (1992–1997); Stage IV. national targets and timetables (1997–2012); and Stage V. contingent implementation (early to mid–twenty-first century). Obviously these stages overlap and often repeat. For example, today's climate negotiators anticipate that a new set of targets and timetables will be needed before 2012. The temporal demarcations represent approximate shifts in emphasis and in the preoccupations of policymakers. They distinguish the relative importance of different preoccupations in shaping the development of climate policy issues.

Scientific assessment has occurred and will continue to occur throughout each stage. But this does not mean that the visibility and influence of science remain constant over time. The focus of policy debate has already shifted from scientific risk assessment to the economic implications of recently adopted targets and timetables for greenhouse gas reduction. In the future the focus will presumably shift more toward political matters of implementation and compliance. And, if implementation follows its usual pattern, the focus will continue shifting as setbacks in compliance or advances in science and technology result in the reformulation of policy responses.

Like Anthony Downs's famous issue attention cycle,[8] the five eras suggested here can be thought of as common stages in the development of many environmental policies. The cycle is almost certain to repeat itself as new questions and issues arise in the scientific and political realms. Hence it is likely that over periods of months and years climate issues will move on and off the policy agenda as successive advances in science alarm or calm the attentive public, and as displacement by other emerging issues occurs. It is equally likely that changes in economics, politics, and technology will provide an impetus for new policy frameworks and revised targets and timetables. These changes will affect the scale and speed of efforts at implementing climate protection measures, not to mention the content of what is being implemented.

The five stages or evolutionary phases that have helped to frame the climate debate can be described historically in terms of key issues, actors, and focusing events (summarized in Box 13-1), beginning with the scientific production of climate research findings.

Stage I. Scientific Assessment

Although calculations of the greenhouse effect of CO_2 were made in the 1890s, not until the 1950s did scientists begin testing the theory of global warming, using the Mauna Loa Observatory in Hawaii to measure a possible atmospheric buildup of CO_2.[9] By the late 1960s, warnings by scientists about human-induced climate change began to appear in the popular literature. As evidence of rising CO_2 levels and possible warming effects accumulated in the 1970s, the climate debate became sharper and more closely tied to questions of energy and environmental policy. Prominent scientists began to call for serious and sustained attention to the climate implications of energy consumption. For example, Wallace Broeker, a leading expert on greenhouse geochemistry, argued in 1977 that the warming effects of fossil fuel combustion "could become the single most important environmental issue of the next 30 years."[10] Twenty years later he amplified his claim, warning that greenhouse effects on ocean currents could spur catastrophic cooling in Eurasia.[11]

Stage II. Agenda Setting

Before the summer of 1988 the debate over global warming was confined largely to a few thousand scientists. It was only in the midst of that summer's intense heat spells and droughts that widespread media attention was drawn to the issue and public interest was piqued. The political focusing event came in the form of much publicized testimony before the Senate Committee on Energy and Natural Resources by Dr. James Hansen, director of NASA's Institute for Space Studies. At the invitation of Sen. Tim Wirth, D-Colo., Hansen testified that the "signal" of climate change had been detected with a high level of confidence and, furthermore, that human activities were almost certainly the major cause.

Within a week following Hansen's testimony, an international group of scientists and policymakers meeting in Toronto called for a 20-percent

Box 13-1 Important Events in Climate Policy Evolution

1979   World Meteorological Organization and UN Environment Program establish World Climate Program and sponsor first World Climate Conference.

1988   Summer weather disasters are linked by news media to global warming; NASA scientist James Hansen testifies about climate threats before U.S. Senate; United Nations establishes Intergovernmental Panel on Climate Change (IPCC).

1989   G-7 Summit endorses proposal for an international climate protection treaty.

1990   IPCC First Assessment released, projecting mean global temperature increases of 3.5–8° C by the year 2050; Second World Climate Conference convened; United Nations establishes International Negotiating Committee to draft Framework Convention on Climate Change.

1992   Framework Convention on Climate Change signed by more than 150 nations meeting at the Earth Summit meeting in Rio de Janeiro.

1993   President Bill Clinton's proposed energy consumption tax rejected by Congress; Clinton pledges to stabilize U.S. greenhouse gas emissions at 1990 levels by 2010; U.S. Climate Change Action Program announced, based on voluntary actions.

1995   First Conference of the Parties (COP-1) is held in Berlin, resulting in the Berlin Mandate, which temporarily exempts developing countries from future limits on emissions.

1996   Parties attending COP-2 in Geneva endorse second IPCC Assessment, which includes a statement that "discernible human influence" on climate systems is now evident. The United States, in a reversal of position, endorses mandatory emissions reduction targets.

1997   Clinton, in address to the United Nations, calls for "realistic and binding limits" on emissions. Senate resolution passed 95–0 instructing the Clinton administration to refrain from signing any forthcoming climate protocol that does not include measures to be undertaken by developing countries. Clinton announces U.S. commitment to reducing emissions to 1990 levels by 2012. COP-3 is held in Kyoto, Japan (December),

(Continues)

Box 13-1 *(Continued)*

leading to agreements in concept on a protocol for binding emissions targets and timetables.

1998   The Kyoto Protocol is signed by the United States at COP-4 in Buenos Aires, Argentina. Parties develop a plan of action to develop rules for achieving legally binding emissions reductions, averaging 6–8 percent below 1990 levels, during the period 2008–2012.

1999   COP-5 held in Bonn, Germany. Parties consider technical and political mechanisms needed to implement the Kyoto Protocol.

2000   Talks collapse at COP-6 in The Hague, Netherlands, because of disagreements between the United States and the European Union over "flexibility mechanisms."

2001   George W. Bush rejects Kyoto Protocol but pledges unspecified support for climate research and policy development. U.S. National Research Council releases report indicating climate change impacts may become severe by the end of the century. COP-6.5 talks resume in Bonn, with most parties agreeing to proceed without U.S. support. The IPCC's Third Assessment is released, providing new and stronger evidence of climate risks. COP-7 in Marrakech, Morocco, ends with late-hour agreement on rules to implement Kyoto Protocol.

2002   Bush administration announces voluntary global warming plan to achieve modest improvements in U.S. emissions intensity (ratio of greenhouse gas emissions to total gross domestic product). COP-8 takes place in New Delhi, India.

2003   Senators McCain, R-Ariz., and Lieberman, D-Conn., introduce Climate Stewardship Act, which fails by vote of 43–55. COP-9 held in Milan, Italy. Defines role of forests in carbon emissions reduction strategies.

2004   McCain-Lieberman climate initiative placed on hold in Congress. Kerry and Bush campaigns downplay climate issues. Arctic Climate Impact Assessment released, showing rapid melting of ice pack. Russia ratifies Kyoto Protocol. Over six thousand delegates from 194 nations gather in Buenos Aires, Argentina, for COP-10. Plans for post-Kyoto climate negotiations are dismissed by United States as "premature."

2005   Kyoto Protocol enters into force (February 16).

reduction in global carbon emissions by 2005. Convinced that conclusive evidence of atmospheric destruction would arrive too late for preventive measures to be effective, they implored world leaders to act on the basis of incomplete information. Greenhouse skeptics in science and industry, fearing that a small group of overzealous scientists were prematurely setting the policy agenda, began a lobbying campaign of their own to emphasize the uncertainty in the research data and the extent of counterevidence.[12] They did not have to dig deeply to uncover disagreement.

The resulting battle of the experts led to the creation of the Intergovernmental Panel on Climate Change (IPCC), an international scientific review body that serves informally as a climate "science court" of last resort. This high-level group of scientists and related experts advises world leaders on the technical aspects of climate change, its impact on human and other life forms, and possible policy responses. The UN General Assembly's establishment of the IPCC in December 1988 brought together the activities of scientific assessment and agenda setting in a highly visible manner. Almost from its inception the panel's assessment activities strongly influenced the scope and pace of policy debate on climate issues. In fact, virtually all national and international climate initiatives to date have been crafted in light of the IPCC's science assessments. By enlisting hundreds of the world's leading climate scientists and thousands of noted technical advisors and reviewers, the IPCC has become the principal source of authoritative information about the science of climate change and its societal implications. Readers are encouraged to visit the IPCC Web site (www.ipcc.ch) for copies of their latest assessments.

Scientists, more than any other group, shaped the policy debate before 1992, but once they succeeded in moving climate issues high on the institutional agendas of governments, the political and economic determinants of policy became dominant once again. For some policymakers, this meant that scientific advice could be safely judged on the basis of its political and economic acceptability, rather than on its technical merits.

Stage III. Policy Frameworks

The political mobilization following the weather disasters of the late 1980s, the IPCC assessments, and orchestrated warnings by prominent scientists succeeded in placing climate issues at the center of international environmental policy discussions, but these discussions did not produce a ready consensus about *which* climate protection measures to adopt and how fast to introduce them. For that purpose a general guide for climate action—a framework convention—was needed, one that could secure general commitments from many different nations without threatening to jeopardize their economic development with specific mandates. Recognizing this need, the United Nations established the International Negotiating Committee in 1990 to draft a climate policy framework. The committee's work culminated in the Framework Convention on Climate Change, which was signed in

1992 by more than 150 governments at the Earth Summit in Rio de Janeiro. Today, 188 countries are parties to the convention.

Although international in scope, the framework convention bore the unmistakable imprint of U.S. negotiators, who succeeded in keeping emissions targets and timetables for greenhouse gas abatement out of the initial agreement. This was in keeping with the steadfast position of George H. W. Bush's administration that abatement measures were too costly and that existing scientific evidence did not justify economic sacrifices. Instead of mandates, the United States and other industrialized democracies publicly embraced the nonbinding goal of reducing their own carbon and other greenhouse gas emissions to 1990 levels by the year 2000. Few, however, adopted effective strategies or policies for accomplishing this goal. They agreed merely to prepare inventories of their emissions and to adopt unspecified national policies for future abatement and mitigation.

While hailed as a major first step, the climate treaty signed in Rio de Janeiro permitted a great deal of political posturing. Whether naively or strategically, it combined very demanding objectives and very weak instruments for achieving them. The principal objective of the convention was, as stated in Article 2,

> stabilization of greenhouse gas concentrations in the atmosphere at a level that would prevent dangerous anthropogenic interference with the climate system. Such a level should be achieved within a time frame sufficient to allow ecosystems to adapt naturally to climate change, to ensure that food production is not threatened and to enable economic development to proceed in a sustainable manner.

Given the enormous emissions reductions needed to stabilize greenhouse gas concentrations, the nonbinding measures agreed to in the convention were widely viewed as palliatives. All parties agreed to develop emissions inventories and action plans, cooperate in research, and share relevant information and technology. But from the very start a division between North and South threatened to impede more meaningful action. Developing countries, by downplaying their role in future emissions and pointing to the heavy responsibility of the United States and other industrialized countries for past emissions, argued successfully for a two-track approach that confined the need for action initially to the North.

Separating the duties of rich and poor countries under the framework convention was essential for achieving international consensus, but it threatened to further undermine U.S. support. Countries that were already developed or in transition—listed in the convention as Annex I parties—were assigned most of the burden for climate protection. This seemed acceptable at the time because these countries were annually producing two-thirds of global emissions. Today, however, annual emissions from non–Annex I countries, which include most of the developing world, are expected to surpass Annex I countries as early as 2015. In anticipation of increasing emissions from the South, opponents of the convention have complained that it sacrifices equity and science for the sake of political expediency.

On closer inspection the focus on annual emissions rates is itself highly political. Annual accounting methods attribute greater responsibility to developing countries than is warranted, because their cumulative emissions remain small in comparison with those of their industrial counterparts, and the cumulative emissions determine the atmospheric concentrations of CO_2 and other gases. Given the long residence time of some greenhouse gases in the atmosphere, it may take until the end of the twenty-first century before developing countries surpass the industrialized world in cumulative emissions. Eventually, however, this unwitting emissions race is one the developing countries are likely to win. No matter how one calculates future greenhouse gas emissions, the expected CO_2 contributions of non–Annex I countries, especially China, loom increasingly large on the horizon. Hence the complaints of critics from the United States, although premature, may ultimately be justified.

Opponents of aggressive climate protection policies were effective from the start in framing climate issues as trade-offs between economic vitality and environmental risk. Led by the fossil fuel industry's Global Climate Coalition and by business-funded public relations consortia, such as the Global Climate Information Project, they pressed for inexpensive and, at most, incremental responses to the problem of greenhouse gas emissions. Their lobbying campaigns severely limited efforts by President Bill Clinton's administration to achieve a domestic consensus on climate policy. As a consequence, the administration's Climate Change Action Plan, which was called for by the framework convention and released in October 1993, relied almost exclusively on voluntary actions and gradual shifts in energy consumption and investment. These measures quickly proved inadequate for achieving the national goal of reducing projected greenhouse gas emissions by roughly 100 million tons by the year 2000.

Stage IV. National Targets and Timetables

Following the agreement on a framework convention, a series of international meetings to refine and extend climate protection policy were held in Berlin, Geneva, Kyoto, Buenos Aires, Bonn, The Hague, Marrakech, New Delhi, and Milan. Known officially as conferences of the parties (COPs), these meetings were prescribed in the framework convention to provide a deliberative process out of which might emerge realistic targets and timetables for emissions reduction beyond the year 2000.

From the outset, controversy developed over the differential treatment of greenhouse gas emissions from developed and developing countries. The First Conference of the Parties (COP-1, Berlin, 1995) called for "quantified limitation and reduction objectives within specified time frames," but delegates also agreed that developing countries would not have to meet these objectives for the time being. From a developing country perspective, the immediate goal was to reduce the "luxury" emissions of the North without impinging on the "survival" emissions of the South. This approach had both ethical and strategic merit. However, by excluding developing countries from any new and additional commitments, COP-1 created one of the most contentious issues for opponents of climate action to exploit during subsequent negotiations.

U.S. acceptance of differential treatment was easier when voluntary action was the official position. But by the end of COP-2 (Geneva, 1996), the U.S. position had shifted in support of international emissions trading with a "realistic, verifiable and binding medium-term emissions target."[13] Reactions in Congress were strong. In July 1997 the Senate voted 95–0 in favor of the Byrd-Hagel Resolution instructing the president to refrain from signing any prospective climate protocols that did not include developing countries in the prescribed actions. Although merely advisory, the unanimous support for the resolution signaled a major escalation in the climate treaty controversy.

Against this backdrop, delegates arrived in Kyoto in December 1997 for COP-3, many expressing strong doubts about the prospects for a meaningful outcome. After eleven days of grueling negotiations, the nearly exhausted delegates came to agreement in an all-night session on the final day of the meeting. As part of the agreement, they established country-by-country emissions targets using 1990 emissions levels as the baseline. The proposed Kyoto Protocol was to become legally binding ninety days after being ratified. The protocol called for thirty-nine industrialized nations (Annex B parties) to achieve emissions reductions averaging about 5 percent below 1990 levels by 2012. The United States agreed to a 7-percent cut, though it should be noted that this translated into a 30- to 35-percent reduction from projected "business-as-usual" levels for 2012.[14] Members of the European Union pledged to cut emissions collectively by 8 percent (though cuts by individual members would vary), and Japan committed to a 6-percent reduction.

The protocol was comprehensive in that it applied to all major greenhouse gases not already controlled under the Montreal Protocol for Ozone Protection. It also established a number of mechanisms to promote flexibility in national policy responses. Most important were provisions for emissions trading among Annex B parties (Article 17); joint implementation—a project-based crediting system for offsetting carbon emissions within developed countries (Article 6); and a major new program called the Clean Development Mechanism (Article 12), which encourages developed countries to provide financial and technical assistance programs to developing countries for the purpose of achieving certified emissions reductions.

In other respects the agreement left many issues unresolved, including one of great importance to U.S. negotiators: the form and extent of emissions trading to be permitted among developed countries. Also unclear was the degree to which compliance with the protocol could be made verifiable and enforceable. As in so many other policy domains, flexibility in climate policy came at the cost of increased complexity.

The Clinton White House used the occasion of COP-4 (Buenos Aires, 1998) to become the sixtieth signatory to the Kyoto Protocol. Rebuke by U.S. senators was immediate and strong, suggesting a difficult road ahead for ratification.[15] Critics were quick to point out that Kyoto was the most complex environmental treaty ever conceived. In addition to concerns about the Kyoto mechanisms, binding consequences for noncompliance, credits for carbon sequestration, and assistance to developing countries, they complained that even if faithfully implemented the protocol would have little effect on climate risks.

On many of the crucial issues, the United States and so-called Umbrella Group Parties (Australia, Canada, Japan, and Russia) found themselves at odds with the European Union and with the Group of 77 and China. The rift between the United States and the European Union was particularly troublesome: The United States accused the Europeans of being inflexible, and the Europeans criticized the United States for pursuing trading and sequestration schemes that would introduce numerous loopholes and measurement difficulties. Ironically, the European Union later adopted a carbon emissions trading system that raised the prospect of a joint U.S.–E.U. carbon trading scheme.[16]

Within two months of taking office, President Bush renounced the Kyoto Protocol (March 2001), insisting that its implementation would weaken the U.S. economy while exempting 80 percent of the world's people from compliance. The Bush administration reaffirmed U.S. support for the framework convention and for additional scientific research but insisted that the United States would not be bound by the protocol or any of its implementation measures.

The timing of the U.S. withdrawal from Kyoto corresponded with the preparation of the administration's ambitious new energy plan—a plan notable for its heavy reliance on fossil fuel development and nuclear energy. Reactions in Europe and many other regions were predictably negative. The Bush administration's decision appeared to undermine the only process available for international climate protection. It also made it easier for other parties to exploit the political vacuum left by the U.S. departure. Before the Kyoto Protocol could take effect, 55 percent of the parties, *representing 55 percent of the developed countries' emissions,* must ratify it. This threshold could be met without U.S. participation if all the other major parties—including Russia, Japan, and all members of the European Union—ratified the protocol. In terms of bargaining power, however, this demanding arrangement yielded new political leverage for nations seeking to loosen the protocol's rules and penalties as a condition of their governments' support.

Against this background and the specter of terrorist threats against the United States, it is hardly surprising that subsequent meetings of the parties focused on "package deals" for achieving ratification without U.S. commitments. Delegates had to confront the trade-off between a protocol with teeth and a toothless imitation designed to assure political acceptance by the Russian Federation and others. With strong leadership from the European

Union and the support of most developing countries, delegates to COP-7 in Marrakech, COP-8 in New Delhi, and COP-9 in Milan managed to craft compromise agreements that retained significant requirements and penalties for Annex B parties while rejecting for the time being any binding commitments for developing countries. As a result, the United States continued to criticize the protocol as unworkable. In late 2004, however, the prospects for Kyoto changed abruptly. The Russian Federation, after withholding its ratification for several years, surprised the world by accepting the treaty and thereby permitting it to become legally binding on its more than 140 parties.

Stage V. Contingent Implementation

The Kyoto Protocol entered into force February 16, 2005. Implementation by each party will presumably be contingent on the efforts made by other parties to the agreement, as well as on advances in science and technology, economic development, and perceived fairness. In the special case of the United States, implementation is all about alternatives to Kyoto and may be more contingent on political and military developments related to the war on terrorism.[17] The U.S. withdrawal from Kyoto had left many parties waiting anxiously to see what climate measures the Bush administration would offer in its place. A cabinet-level review of U.S. climate options was promised but had to be shelved in the aftermath of the September 11 terrorist attacks. Finally, in February 2002, President Bush announced a voluntary climate plan designed to reduce greenhouse gas emissions per unit of gross domestic product by 18 percent in the year 2012. Critics noted that overall emissions would still be 30 percent above 1990 levels, given the president's assumptions about growth in gross domestic product. Furthermore, they argued that the voluntary nature of U.S. climate actions would introduce great uncertainty for implementation planning by the other 186 members of the framework convention.

Despite uncertainty about U.S. contributions, the broad outlines of a generic implementation strategy have been discernible for more than a decade: Make the cheapest cuts first, tie performance levels to the progress of other parties, and promote "no regrets" measures to limit and reduce emissions. Such measures (for example, energy-efficiency improvements) serve collaterally to improve domestic economies, even if climate threats turn out to be false alarms. This strategy, which is popular in many countries, represents a compromise between bold international mandates based on precise abatement targets and timetables, and voluntary, incremental domestic adjustments based on the need for economic flexibility in policy responses. Before the Bush administration's energy plan was unveiled in May 2001, this was widely presumed to be the long-term strategy of the U.S. government.

The Bush administration's retreat from binding targets and timetables reflected a deeper problem in implementation strategy: a lack of correspondence between the relatively ambitious emissions targets developed by international negotiators and the rather anemic reduction measures promoted by domestic implementers. As with so many other international breakthroughs in environmental protection, negotiators have tended to evaluate the success of the climate convention and protocol in terms of multilateral cooperation. Domestic implementers tend to focus on incentive structures and compliance mechanisms that benefit subnational interests and regions. Sadly the ability of climate negotiators to secure cooperation among themselves is often greater than the ability of the governments they represent to secure cooperation from their own citizens, in the form of reduced energy consumption, stronger protection of forests, and so forth. Within the United States, gaining the cooperation of other branches of the government may prove even more difficult than gaining general public support. In 1999, leaders of Congress declared the Kyoto Protocol "dead on arrival" (for ratification) unless China, India, and other major developing countries were prepared to join the Annex I parties in abatement efforts. But in 2001, following political shifts in the White House and U.S. Senate, the policy preferences were reversed. Senate leaders defended the protocol against what they viewed as the rash actions of an "oil man" in the White House.

The contests between executive and legislative leaders, and between international and domestic politics, are not the only sources of tension that block effective implementation of climate policy. Throughout the negotiating process the climate debate has been embedded in a much older and more familiar debate about theoretically elegant policies versus workable programs. Solutions that looked good on paper have too often failed in practice, especially when the roles of policy designers and implementers have been functionally and temporally separated.

In the case of greenhouse gas abatement the practicality debate has revolved around the use of market-based policy instruments—principally emissions trading—to meet agreed-on targets and timetables. The idea of trading is to allow those for whom emissions reduction is expensive to buy abatement services or emissions allowances from those for whom it is relatively cheap. Advocates of trading seek to harness the power of markets to ensure that climate protection measures are accomplished at the least cost and with incentives that encourage participants to achieve more than the minimum reductions required.

The United States has steadfastly maintained that the best way to inject flexibility and efficiency into climate policy responses is to rely on trading schemes. In fact, 75 percent of the costs of planned reductions in U.S. emissions under President Clinton were premised on trading approaches.[18] Critics contend that market solutions have been oversold, that they appear much more promising in academic circles than in real policy environments. Even some leading academic economists have questioned the feasibility of international trading to achieve binding targets and timetables. They point to the difficulty of finding allocation rules for emissions credits that would be acceptable to all the major emitters of greenhouse gases.[19] Noting the powerful tendency of parties to international treaties to behave as free riders, some critics argue that the only workable climate policy is to tax fossil energy consumption or emissions.[20]

Tax opponents argue that emissions taxes are politically unwise and that their supporters are "out of touch with reality."[21] The feasibility of emissions trading, they argue, has already been demonstrated with the U.S. experiment in sulfur trading begun in 1990.[22] The only remaining obstacles to an effective trading system for greenhouse gases, in their estimation, arise from standard disputes over the allocation of credits, monitoring and enforcement measures, and questions about banking of credits. This last item has become particularly troublesome in the case of Russia, which seeks to bank all carbon emissions reductions that have resulted from its continuing economic crisis as "paper tons" that can be credited toward meeting future targets. In essence, Russia wants to treat a severe economic problem as a greenhouse gas solution, a view that critics regard as trading in hot air.

Implementation of climate stabilization programs and policies, whether of the market-based, technology-based, or command-and-control (regulatory) variety, will require extensive cooperation among China, North America, the European Union, and the newly industrializing countries of Asia and Latin America. Eventually development and population pressures in developing countries will necessitate truly global levels of cooperation.[23] Because of large differences in the capacities and capabilities of these nations to curb their emissions, joint action will almost surely be guided by the principle of common but differentiated responsibilities, whereby the richest nations are expected to undertake the most costly climate stabilization programs. The Bush administration's position on Kyoto could be seen as a rejection of this principle, but the position will be hard to sustain in the face of growing evidence that only rich countries have the resources required to make timely transformations of energy, transportation, and other systems responsible for soaring greenhouse gas emissions. By far the most important of these changes center on energy consumption.

The Role of U.S. Energy Policy in Climate Protection

Mapping the constraints that impede action on climate issues leads inexorably to matters of energy policy. Fossil energy combustion alone accounts for nearly 90 percent of U.S. greenhouse gas emissions, most of it in the form of CO_2. Whereas other emissions sources, such as landfills, chlorofluorocarbon-based refrigerants, and nitrogen fertilizers, emit greenhouse gases that are much more potent than CO_2, molecule for molecule, their aggregate and cumulative contribution to potential global warming remains far below that of carbon-based fuels. Further complicating the picture is the fact that coal, oil, and gas vary significantly in their carbon emissions per unit of energy produced, with coal being the highest (worst) and natural gas the lowest. Hence the most critical factors in controlling greenhouse gas emissions may be the choice of fuel type and the efficiency with which it is used. Given the enormous quantities of coal, oil, and natural gas consumed in global trade and development, it is not surprising that efforts to reduce carbon emissions through energy conservation and alternative energy technologies have become the centerpiece of climate stabilization strategies.

The energy policy community believes that it holds the key to climate stabilization. But it remains to be seen whether energy policy can prove as effective as market forces in determining future carbon emissions. For example, the sharp rise in gasoline prices during 2004 probably slowed emissions (reduced rate of gasoline consumption and sport-utility vehicle sales) more than any climate policies. At the same time, a boom in coal production and associated plans for new coal-fired power plants in 2004 promised long-term growth in worldwide coal consumption.

The Bush administration's energy plan unveiled in 2001 appeared to move U.S. energy policy in the opposite direction of international climate accords. Citing what turned out to be a contrived California electricity crisis as evidence of energy shortages that threatened the U.S. economy, the plan's authors called for increased reliance on energy industry initiatives and technological know-how. Although disparaging comments about conservation and renewable energy were muted in the final plan, the administration's energy policy remained, unabashedly, to increase production of fossil fuels and to expand the nation's energy supply infrastructure. Included in measures to expand supply were subsidies for coal, drilling for oil in the Arctic National Wildlife Refuge (ANWR), and calls for the relaxation of clean air regulations thought to impinge excessively on fossil fuel development.

Most elements of the Bush administration's energy plan remain stalled in Congress, many of them mired in disputes over drilling in ANWR or over efforts of House Republicans to shield manufacturers of MTBE, a controversial fuel additive, from environmental lawsuits. Efforts by the Bush political team to transform a close election into a mandate for change may alter this picture with renewed and stronger efforts to pass major energy legislation. The implications for U.S. carbon emissions are potentially alarming.

Perhaps the lone source of hope for congressional climate initiatives remains the McCain-Lieberman bill, a modest effort to cap U.S. greenhouse gas emissions. The bill was first voted on in 2003 and attracted support from 43 senators, a strong showing that signaled Senate interest in moving beyond the White House position. Subsequent efforts to pass the bill in 2004 also failed, but the bill's success in garnering limited bipartisan support was heartening to many critics of the president's climate policy.

Timely reductions in carbon probably require close cooperation between the White House and the leadership of Congress. Specifically they require progress in at least three distinct areas of energy policy: (1) promotion of energy-efficiency improvement and use of energy-saving devices, (2) desubsidization of fossil energy extraction and use, and (3) development of alternative energy technologies such as hydrogen vehicles, wind turbines, photovoltaics, fuel cells, and gas turbines. The success of each of these measures depends largely on the interaction of market and political forces in setting energy prices. Although this is obvious in the case of desubsidization strategies, getting energy prices "right" (that is, internalizing externalities) is also fundamental for making alternative energy sources and efficiency improvements more attractive.

Energy conservation is by many accounts the key to emissions avoidance and reduction. Most experts agree that major efficiency improvements are both possible and desirable, but sharp differences of opinion exist over which improvements are cost-effective, in which combinations, and under what circumstances. Even if climate concerns were to evaporate, many energy conservationists claim that investments in energy efficiency will produce large net savings by avoiding the costs of constructing new power plants and by reducing energy consumption of households, manufacturers, and the transportation sector.[24] Skeptics argue that massive investments in energy efficiency, especially if induced by carbon taxes or draconian efficiency standards, will mean a lower standard of living for most of the world.[25] Record high oil prices in 2004 served only to strengthen objections to the notion that fossil energy prices should be increased now, as a matter of prudent policy, in order to internalize potential social costs of carbon that cannot be authoritatively estimated.

Many energy reformers argue that energy prices are grossly distorted. Opponents of subsidies claim that efforts to perpetuate them, ostensibly to maintain economic stability, are more often than not the self-serving strategies of special interests that benefit directly from these redistributive policies. Direct government subsidies for fossil energy sources and technologies worldwide are estimated at $200 billion annually. U.S. government support for fossil energy sources and technologies—particularly gasoline-powered vehicles—is well over $100 billion annually.[26] Reducing these subsidies inevitably pits environmental and energy conservation enthusiasts against powerful stakeholders in the energy, manufacturing, and transportation sectors. Not surprisingly, desubsidization has shown less progress than the other two major approaches to energy reform.

The hoped-for silver bullet of climate protection is often said to lie in the third approach: alternative energy technology. Although oversold in some instances, technological solutions show genuine promise for reducing carbon emissions sharply by the middle of the twenty-first century, if not before.[27] Among the exciting innovations already emerging are hybrid electric vehicles made of super-lightweight materials; fuel cells and solar-powered hydrogen production systems; and a new generation of wind turbines, which have been growing in generating capacity by 25 percent per year. Advanced nuclear power systems, while controversial, may also play a significant role in future climate protection, although remaining problems with waste management, safety, and security are likely to perpetuate perceived risks within the U.S. investment community.

Whereas most of these technologies provide carbon-free energy services, low-carbon technologies such as gas-fired absorption heat pumps and advanced repowering systems for fossil-fuel-fired plants are likely to contribute more to emissions reduction goals in the short term than are technologies based on renewable energy. Even so-called clean-coal programs are showing some progress in reducing carbon emissions or capturing them before they get into the atmosphere. Most promising in the near term are advanced technologies for energy conservation, such as super-efficient windows, lights, appliances, and electric motors, all of which provide alternatives that increase end-use efficiency and thereby reduce emissions, regardless of the carbon content of the energy input. The major impediments to widespread use of these technologies appear to be consumer ignorance about, or indifference to, life-cycle cost and the associated tendency of consumers to apply very high discount rates to energy-efficiency investments (that is, expecting a payback of between three and thirty-six months for any new energy-saving device).[28]

If the most promising alternative energy sources and efficiency improvements were combined and swiftly introduced, it might be possible to keep atmospheric CO_2 concentrations below about 500 ppmv, a level many scientists believe would produce only modest shifts in climate, thereby allowing humans and many other species to adapt without significant stress. Few energy analysts, however, believe that action of this magnitude is achievable without the use of steep carbon taxes or other drastic measures to wean consumers from heavy reliance on fossil fuels. In view of President Bush's rejection of the Kyoto Protocol, even fewer believe that the United States is politically ready to accept the taxes or regulations such a transformation may require.

Lack of presidential commitment is only part of the problem. Consider President Clinton's unsuccessful attempt in 1993 to establish a broad-based tax on the heat content of fuels—the so-called BTU tax—which would have added about $3.47 to the price of a barrel of oil (nearly 60 cents per million BTUs, or 8.3 cents per gallon of gasoline). Coal, natural gas, and nuclear energy would have been taxed at about twenty-six cents per million BTUs. Although energy conservation and carbon emissions reductions were cited as benefits of the BTU tax, most of the public debate centered on the tax implications for deficit reduction and economic competitiveness. Critics argued that the tax would unfairly hamper U.S. firms competing in the global market. Congress, bowing to pressure from the fossil fuel lobby and energy-intensive industries, not only discarded the broad-based tax proposal in favor of a much narrower gasoline tax but also reduced the tax rate by about 50 percent (to 4.3 cents per gallon).

Framing the energy tax proposal as a large, new, and additional burden on the economy—an economy designed to run on cheap energy—ensured congressional opponents an easy victory in terms of public opinion. Carbon taxes and similar alternatives to the BTU tax have not fared any better in U.S. politics, although some have succeeded in Europe. Polling results show that climate issues continue to have low salience for most Americans, and few are willing to support significant taxes on carbon fuels or emissions (see chapter 4).[29]

Interestingly, when energy tax proposals are presented to the public in the form of revenue-neutral tax shifts, public opinion is far more positive. A poll conducted in the summer of 1998 revealed that over 70 percent of respondents favored a proposed tax shift from income and payroll to fossil fuel consumption.[30]

On a global level, tax shifting could have profound effects on greenhouse gas emissions of all kinds. When combined with government desubsidization strategies, carbon taxes could quickly dampen demand for fossil fuels, depending on how gradually they were phased in. A tax-shift strategy developed at the Worldwatch Institute would arguably lead to massive emissions savings within a few decades. The global strategy calls for sharp reductions in government subsidies for environmentally destructive activities—estimated at $650 billion per year—plus a gradual shift of an additional $1 trillion per year in taxes on income, savings, and investment to consumption taxes that "make prices tell the ecological truth" and, in the process, provide a net tax cut of approximately $500 for each American.[31] Although such a massive tax shift and desubsidization effort appears politically inconceivable today, the long-term outlook for such measures may improve with developments in climate science, international trade, and public awareness of climate threats. Ultimately the political climate for tax shifts may depend on whether those who pay the taxes personally experience shifts in the physical climate that adversely affect their surrounding temperature, precipitation, and sea level—and by extension their food, water, and material production systems.

Conclusion

Climate policy directions for the twenty-first century are likely to be shaped by how governments respond to three cross-cutting dilemmas: (1) the treatment of risks and rewards in measuring present costs and future benefits of climate action, (2) the choice between prescriptive precision and adaptive flexibility in climate policy design, and (3) the challenge of integrating international and domestic climate politics.

The temporal separation of costs and benefits creates perverse incentives to defer needed policy responses. If climate threats are real, leaders who resist taking action today will probably be safely out of office by the time unambiguous climate impacts are felt by the general public. By the same token, leaders who push for precautionary abatement measures may incur high political costs, while finding no tangible climate benefits in the short term to serve as justification. Inaction may turn out to be the most costly policy option of all, but because the costs are borne predominantly by future generations, the political system remains biased in favor of inaction. To overcome this bias, more attention will have to be devoted to the goals of sustainability and intergenerational equity.

Tensions between the goals of comprehensive policy and adaptive management continue to confound climate protection efforts. In the future, both policy and management will have to be more adaptive and flexible, using abatement targets and tools that can be rapidly adjusted in step with advancing scientific knowledge and economic opportunities, much like the "flip-flop" pattern of past climate change itself. Although emissions trading and other market approaches look promising in this regard, practical barriers remain.

Good policy design will reflect the creative tensions between international and domestic politics as well as the tensions between theory and practice in the choice of policy instruments and implementation plans. Eventually policymakers may have to move beyond the conventional two-level test of international and domestic political acceptability toward a more "glocal" perspective on climate issues.[32] In the United States, state and local climate initiatives may surpass those of the federal government for years to come.[33] In the meantime, however, increasing efforts to distinguish survival emissions from luxury emissions will ensure that tensions within and between nations remain high.

Because of what scientists call atmospheric commitment, there is little margin for error in today's policy responses to climate threats. Today's emissions are producing effects on climate that may not show up for fifty years or more. Even the modest abatement targets and timetables agreed to in Kyoto will not prevent massive new commitments. That is why many observers argue that the Kyoto Protocol is but the first step in a long journey.

It remains to be seen whether the U.S. withdrawal from Kyoto is tantamount to a derailment or merely a bump on the chosen track of international climate negotiations. Any future attempts to harmonize U.S. energy policy and the aims of climate protection may prove inadequate in the long run unless China, India, Brazil, and other developing countries participate in meaningful emissions reductions. It appears likely that major new and additional measures for prevention, abatement, and adaptation will be needed in the next few decades. Reducing atmospheric commitment will require environmental commitment on the part of policymakers. At the intersection of such commitments will emerge the next installment in what is likely to be a long line of policy responses to climate change.

Notes

1. In late August 2004, the secretaries of Energy and Commerce and the president's chief science advisor endorsed a report, "Our Changing Planet: The U.S. Climate Change Science Program for Fiscal Years 2004 and 2005," which appeared to signal a shift in the Bush administration's position on climate change. See, also, Spencer Abraham, "The Bush Administration's Approach to Climate Change," *Science,* July 30, 2004, 616–617. Critics dismissed the apparent shift as a campaign ploy.
2. For a detailed analysis of climate negotiations, see the *Earth Negotiations Bulletin,* published by the International Institute for Sustainable Development, www.iisd.ca/climate. See also the Pew Center on Global Climate Change, www.pewclimate.org.
3. Martin Parry et al., "Adapting to the Inevitable," *Nature,* October 22, 1998, 741.

4. A systematic treatment of these questions is provided by Susan Walter and Pat Choate, *Thinking Strategically: A Primer for Public Leaders* (Washington, D.C.: Council of State Planning Agencies, 1984).

5. Designing markets to faithfully capture the true costs and benefits of climate actions may require significant government intervention.

6. Since preindustrial times (circa 1750), atmospheric concentrations of CO_2, methane, and nitrous oxides have increased by approximately 30 percent, 145 percent, and 15 percent, respectively. The Intergovernmental Panel on Climate Change projects increases in concentrations of CO_2 the most important of the long-lived trace gases, from today's level of about 380 ppmv to between 500 and 980 ppmv by the end of the twenty-first century, depending on the emissions scenario selected.

7. Richard Kerr, "Warming's Unpleasant Surprise: Shivering in the Greenhouse?" *Science,* July 10, 1998, 156–158.

8. Anthony Downs, "Up and Down with Ecology: The Issue Attention Cycle," *Public Interest* (summer 1972): 38–50.

9. Svante Arrhenius, "On the Influence of Carbonic Acid in the Air upon the Temperature of the Ground," *The London, Edinburgh, and Dublin Philosophical Magazine and Journal of Science* 41 (April 1896): 237–276.

10. Quoted in "Is Energy Use Overheating World?" *U.S. News and World Report,* July 25, 1977.

11. Described in Kerr, "Warming's Unpleasant Surprise," 156.

12. Among the most influential of these critics were members of the Marshall Institute, a small group of scientists whose opinions were repeatedly used by George H. W. Bush's chief of staff, John Sununu, to oppose climate protection initiatives.

13. Address by Timothy Wirth to the Second Conference of the Parties, Framework Convention on Climate Change, Geneva, Switzerland, July 17, 1996.

14. Because of changes in accounting methods for carbon sequestration and changes in the baseline years—from 1990 to 1995—for three synthetic greenhouse gases, the overall 7-percent cut agreed to by U.S. negotiators at Kyoto represented no more than a 3-percent real reduction from President Clinton's pre-Kyoto proposal.

15. For example, U.S. senator Chuck Hagel, R-Neb., coauthor of the 1997 resolution opposing unilateral climate action by the United States and its allies, declared tersely, "In signing the Kyoto Protocol, the President blatantly contradicts the will of the U.S. Senate," press release, November 14, 1998.

16. Stuart Eizenstat and David Sandalow, "The Years after Tomorrow," *New York Times,* July 6, 2004, A15.

17. For a lively discussion of future scenarios for U.S. policy, see David Victor, *Climate Change: Debating America's Policy Options* (Washington, D.C.: Council on Foreign Relations, 2004).

18. President's Council of Economic Advisors, *The Kyoto Protocol and the President's Policies to Address Climate Change* (Report to Congress, July 31, 1998).

19. See, for example, Richard Cooper, "Toward a Real Global Warming Treaty," *Foreign Affairs* 77 (March–April 1997): 66–79.

20. The free-rider problem posits that "the wide distribution of expected but distant benefits in response to collective action provides an incentive for every country to encourage all to act but then to shirk itself." Ibid., 69.

21. Stuart Eizenstat, "Stick with Kyoto" (Response to Richard Cooper), *Foreign Affairs* 77 (May–June 1997): 119.

22. The permits traded for sulfur dioxide emissions reduced emissions in 2000 by approximately 50 percent from 1980 levels while providing savings of at least $2 billion to participating utilities when compared with conventional regulatory approaches.

23. See, for example, Frederick Myerson, "Population, Carbon Emissions, and Global Warming: The Forgotten Relationship at Kyoto," *Population and Development Review* 24 (March 1998): 115–130.

24. See, for example, Howard Geller et al., "The Role of Federal Research and Development in Advancing Energy Efficiency: A \$50 Billion Contribution to the U.S. Economy," *Annual Review of Energy* (1987).

25. See, for example, Ronald Cooper, "Energy Conservation and Renewable Energy Supplies: A Survey," *Journal of Energy and Development* 21 (1997): 259–281. Cooper complains that "many energy conservation enthusiasts have forgotten that the improvement in living standards among industrial nations has come about through technological development, exploitations of natural resources, and large increases in energy consumption, particularly electricity" (p. 269).

26. Christopher Flavin and Seth Dunn, "Rising Sun, Gathering Winds: Policies to Stabilize the Climate and Strengthen Economies," *Worldwatch Paper* 138 (November 1997).

27. Despite such advances, both U.S. and UN energy models indicate that large regions of the world are likely to remain dependent on fossil fuels for many decades to come—perhaps until late in the twenty-first century—even if major breakthroughs in alternatives can be commercialized rapidly in industrial countries.

28. Cooper, "Energy Conservation and Renewable Energy Supplies," 263.

29. Robert O'Connor and Richard Bord, "Implications of Public Opinion for Environmental Policy: Risk Perceptions, Policy Preferences, and Management Options for Climate Change" (paper presented at the annual meeting of the American Political Science Association, Boston, September 3–6, 1998). For more recent polling results, see the University of Maryland's Program on International Policy Attitudes, www.pipa.org.

30. International Communications Research, poll conducted for Friends of the Earth, June 1998.

31. David Roodman, *The Natural Wealth of Nations* (Washington, D.C.: Worldwatch Institute, 1998).

32. For a discussion of the two-level approach, see Robert D. Putnam, "Diplomacy and Domestic Politics: The Logic of Two-Level Games," *International Organization* 42 (summer 1988): 427–460. For a discussion of "glocal" perspectives, see Lamont C. Hempel, *Environmental Governance: The Global Challenge* (Washington, D.C.: Island Press, 1996).

33. California's 2004 initiative to reduce automotive emissions of CO_2 is a prime example. See, also, Barry Rabe, *Statehouse and Greenhouse: The Emerging Politics of American Climate Change Policy* (Washington, D.C.: Brookings Institution Press, 2004).

14

A Return to Traditional Priorities in Natural Resource Policies

William R. Lowry

Changes in natural resource policies under the George W. Bush administration are noticeable in ecosystems all over the country. Consider, for instance, the national forests of the Sierra Nevada in California. After years of deliberation, including nearly two hundred public hearings, and collaboration among different stakeholder groups, the Sierra Nevada Framework produced a sophisticated plan for logging, fire management, and habitat protection on 11 million acres of national forests in the state. The plan was finalized during the last year of Bill Clinton's presidency. Upon taking office, members of the incoming Bush administration, including the new head of forestry policy, Mark Rey, lauded the plan for its balanced approach.

Today, the Sierra Nevada Framework has been replaced by a plan that will more than double the amount of timber to be removed from the forests each year and will end restrictions on cutting of millions of acres of old-growth forests. The Bush administration's spokespersons claim the plan will better protect the forests from fire, but critics argue that specific provisions such as allowing the cutting of large, fire-resistant trees suggest instead that it was motivated by timber interests, not fire protection. Indeed, the new plan was produced not after public consultation but rather from a handful of invitation-only discussions, a process that has raised questions even from the state administration of Republican governor Arnold Schwarzenegger.[1]

The situation in California's forests is not atypical. Natural resource policies have been evolving toward collaborative efforts at balanced approaches to ecosystems management. The Bush administration has slowed, if not stopped, this evolution in favor of an emphasis on traditional priorities of resource use and extraction. In this chapter I argue that the impact of the Bush administration must be understood within the broader context of the evolution of natural resource policies. The first stage of this evolution, running from colonial times through much of the nineteenth century, involved little government control and a view of resources as perpetually abundant. In the second stage, natural resource policies in the twentieth century were developed within the public sector, allowing government a prominent policymaking role. Public agencies pursued policies that were often criticized as controversial, ineffective, and inefficient in their emphasis on assisting the subsidized use of resources. Dissatisfaction with these conventional public sector mechanisms for resolution of disputes over land, water, and species stimulated a variety of proposals that could constitute a third stage. Recent programs, such as the Sierra Nevada Framework, emphasized coordination between economic and environmental goals to pursue sustainability, innovative techniques for area management, scientific input into planning, and cooperation between people who have traditionally disagreed over the handling of natural resources. Momentum toward this third stage has slowed since 2000, however, as the Bush administration has de-emphasized science-based, collaborative resolutions in order to reinstate use and extraction as priorities for natural resource policies.

In the first half of this chapter I review the evolution of natural resource policies, including some examples of efforts that could herald the third stage. In the second half I discuss the impact of the Bush administration on this evolution.

The Evolution of Natural Resource Policies

The first stage of natural resource policies was characterized by a lack of understanding about environmental destruction, a public sense of perpetual abundance, and the omnipresent opportunity to move farther west. Well into the nineteenth century, settlers and entrepreneurs cleared whole forests, destroyed rangeland through overgrazing, and eliminated entire species through overhunting, overfishing, and other activities. Evidence that the lack of systematic management of natural resources caused significant environmental damage as well as unsustainable economic use led to a new, second stage in policies regarding public lands and waters.

The Growth of Federal Management

Starting in the nineteenth century, the federal government assumed a greater role in management of natural resources. That role grew until the 1980s, when serious questions were raised about the efficacy and efficiency of federal practices. By then the federal government owned nearly one-third of the total U.S. land area, and its policies affected natural resources even on lands that were not publicly owned. Federal management of natural resources produced varying degrees of success. In many cases, practices that caused damage to land and water were halted. In other instances, however, the delegation of responsibility to a public agency led to detrimental policy-making arrangements: subgovernments—so-called iron triangles composed of local economic interests, congressional representatives, and public sector employees—emerged, each element assisting the others in exploiting the resource under agency management. Policymakers organized the institutional framework for federal management around the different types of resources discussed below.

Waterways. The earliest federal policies regarding management of natural resources concerned rivers and harbors, largely because they provided such an important means of transportation. The federal government explicitly assumed responsibility for these resources in 1802 with the creation of the U.S. Army Corps of Engineers. Congress charged the Corps with making and keeping inland waterways navigable. As its name suggests, the Corps early on displayed a fondness for "engineering" waterways, an approach that translated into the use of structural modifications such as dams, dredging, and levees that could divert and seemingly control wetlands and waterways. When Congress established the Bureau of Reclamation (BuRec) to pursue water projects in the arid West a century later, this agency too adopted a structural approach.

This approach to waterways was instituted within a subgovernment of water users. Members of Congress, by supplying the fiscal resources, could claim credit for dams and other water projects. Public agencies overseeing these projects were rewarded with larger budgets. And local economic interests gained federal dollars and the jobs and revenue that come with new programs. Both BuRec and the Corps thrived in this supportive environment and developed an ability to expand in response to shifting demands. Their statutory responsibilities grew to include flood control, hydroelectric power generation, and, eventually, environmental protection. The Corps in particular benefited, enabling it to command significant political resources.[2]

Forests. National policies regarding forest resources in the United States have long centered on the goal of multiple use. These policies first appeared at the end of the nineteenth century amid growing recognition of the damages resulting from unsustainable logging. Created in 1905, the U.S. Forest Service quickly adopted the philosophy that forests should provide the greatest good for the greatest number of people. All potential uses of national forests, ranging from timber harvesting to watershed protection to grazing to recreation, were to be balanced. The Multiple Use-Sustained Yield Act of 1960 served to sanction this already ingrained agency ethos.

In practice, however, the multiple use policy often translated into "tree farming" of vast areas of national forests. Timber was the one forest output that could be easily measured and used to quantify incentives for local forest managers. The amount of board feet of timber produced from the national forests increased each year until the 1970s. Although that total has declined since then, the devastating result of Forest Service-sanctioned tree farming is apparent in that today less than 15 percent of the original, old-growth forests remain.[3]

Parklands. The national park system contains what are often called the purest or most precious of America's natural resources. Beginning with the establishment of Yellowstone in 1872, Congress and the president have since set aside more than 380 parks, monuments, battlefields, and other areas containing almost 80 million acres of land. Congress created the National Park Service (NPS) in 1916 to manage this system for the enjoyment of current visitors but also to preserve these sites in "unimpaired" condition for future generations.

Since 1916 the NPS has faced the difficult task of balancing these often conflicting policy goals of use and preservation. The agency has been criticized, with some justification, for everything from "locking up" precious lands to catering too much to concessionaires and developers. In fact, the NPS is one of the most micromanaged agencies in the federal government. The specific policies pursued and the lands designated for protection are as likely to be determined by congressional overseers as by agency personnel.[4]

Rangelands. Public rangelands are supervised by the federal government's largest landlord, the Bureau of Land Management (BLM). The BLM evolved in 1946 out of an executive branch reorganization of largely ineffectual public land agencies. Its creation stemmed in large part from the demands of cattle ranchers and their congressional representatives who recognized that, without greater institutional control, public grazing lands were doomed to "dust bowl" futures from overuse and severe erosion.

Because the new agency did not receive authorizing legislation from Congress until 1976, it developed its own policy emphasis, one consistent with the needs of its closest constituents—ranchers and miners. This service focus has been sustained through a classic subgovernment involving agency personnel, grazing and mining interests, and cooperative western state representatives and senators.[5] Reformers have attempted numerous changes since 1976, with some success, but the basic policies preferred by the subgovernment remain largely in place.[6]

Wildlife Refuges and Endangered Species. Policies toward species and wildlife refuges are largely the jurisdiction of the U.S. Fish and Wildlife Service. Like the BLM, the Fish and Wildlife Service was created by an executive reorganization of weak existing agencies. Ultimately it gained responsibility for over 90 million acres of wetlands, hatcheries, and wildlife refuges.

A relatively vague policy mission of protecting the nation's fish and wildlife resources was made much more prominent with passage of the Endangered Species Act in 1973. Congress mandated that the Fish and Wildlife Service list and provide for the protection of threatened and endangered species. Specific sections of the act called for designation of critical habitat areas for species recovery and for federal actions to be cleared through the Fish and Wildlife Service when those actions might affect endangered species.[7] As discussed later in this chapter, the Endangered Species Act has been one of the most controversial of resource policies.

Other Land and Water Designations. The lands described in the preceding sections constitute the majority of federal land designations in the United States, but they do not exhaust the targets of natural resource policies in this country. The 1964 Wilderness Act called for the designation of undeveloped federal lands as wilderness areas to be kept in their natural state. These lands have been designated in national parks, forests, and refuges and are managed by the agency responsible for the relevant geographic location.[8] Public agencies are also responsible for maintaining the pristine nature of the wild and scenic rivers that traverse their jurisdictions. Since 1968, Congress has designated portions of over two hundred rivers, covering roughly 10,000 miles of waterways.[9] Finally, state and local governments have their own policies concerning natural resource protection. For instance, every state has its own system of parks.

Minerals and Energy Sources. Federal natural resource policies also control the use of minerals and energy sources existing on public lands or in public waters. The United States is responsible for nearly one-fourth of the world's energy consumption. The vast majority of its energy supplies comes from fossil fuel sources such as coal, oil, and natural gas. Although imports play a major role in meeting our petroleum needs, domestic production of energy sources on public lands is also significant. Over the years, federal policies targeted at mineral and energy source protection have included regulation of the price of natural gas and other commodities as well as subsidization of exploration for fossil fuels and nuclear development. However, the United States has never had a comprehensive energy policy and today continues its precarious reliance on fossil fuels.[10]

Summary. Natural resource policies have evolved as a series of separate and fairly ambiguous mandates. The failure of Congress to specify any overarching vision of natural resource policies is consistent with its tendency to delegate difficult tasks rather than make explicit decisions. The resulting segmentation and lack of prioritization has led to chronic disagreement and numerous controversies.

Policy Controversies

Since the early 1800s, federal government approaches to natural resource management evolved in response to perceptions of abuse and neglect in the absence of adequate government supervision of resources. Recently, controversies over federal policies have fostered arguments in favor of new approaches.

Lack of Consensus. Consensus over the ultimate disposition of natural resources has never existed. In recent decades, however, the intensity of disputes between different advocacy groups escalated dramatically.

The growth of the environmental movement since the late 1960s spawned a variety of groups focused on natural resource issues (see chapter 4). Some of the more recent groups, such as Friends of the Earth and Earth First!, were formed precisely to pursue a less compromising, more confrontational approach than their more traditional counterparts. Opponents of environmental groups also became more visible and outspoken. The Sagebrush Rebels of the 1970s, a group focused on diminution of federal authority, gave way to the Wise Use and County Supremacy movements in the 1980s and 1990s. The Wise Use movement specifically proposes more development of public lands as well as increased construction of visitor accommodations in places such as national parks.[11] The County Supremacy movement calls for a drastic reduction in the role of the federal government in management of natural resources.[12]

The heightened intensity of debate between interest groups over natural resource policies has often been matched by confrontations between the two major political parties. Differences between the parties intensified during the 1980s as the Reagan administration pursued a deregulatory agenda that included selling off large parcels of public lands and opening up other areas for oil, gas, and mineral development. Reagan's first secretary of the interior, James Watt, openly advocated privatizing and developing public lands. Unresolved issues such as proposed oil drilling in the Arctic National Wildlife Refuge, discussed later in this chapter, festered through the 1990s.[13]

When the Republicans gained the majority position in Congress in 1995 and began considering major changes in environmental laws, party differences were again magnified. An early indication of the Republican agenda was given when the new majority party changed the name of one major House committee from Natural Resources to just Resources. Party differences became increasingly apparent in specific debates, notably the one over reauthorization of the Endangered Species Act. Eventually, Speaker of the House Newt Gingrich encouraged his party to find less confrontational approaches to the act and other environmental issues.[14] Gingrich managed to tone down his party's rhetoric, but his efforts produced little change in their environmental agenda. Analyses of League of Conservation Voters scores for members of Congress show, as discussed in chapter 6, that the two parties have diverged substantially over time.[15]

Many of these debates are now being fought in the courts. Property rights advocates have gained considerable attention in recent years as a result of "takings" litigation. These cases involve claims that government actions may affect the use of private property to the point of unlawful violation of the Fifth Amendment (see chapter 7). In many ways these cases and the land rights groups pursuing them have shifted the debate from controversy over use of public lands to reconsideration of just how public these lands really are.[16]

Lack of Efficacy. The second stage of natural resource policies produced many positive results such as the recovery of some endangered species and an enviable system of national parks. For all the positives, however, policy shortcomings in many other issue areas have received considerable attention in recent years.

Some of these critiques are directed at areas of apparent success. Good news concerning revitalization of specific species such as the bald eagle and California condor is tempered by the fact that hundreds of species await listing or specific plans for recovery. Prominent scientists decry the lack of systematic protection for species and warn that "humanity has initiated the sixth great extinction spasm," eliminating a large number of species within a single generation.[17] Even the most revered of natural resources, the national parks, have often been characterized as overcrowded, underfunded, and excessively commercial.[18]

Other complaints focus on how resources are used. Major floods during the 1990s elicited compelling questions regarding the structural policy approach toward waterways. According to critics, the subgovernment that traditionally dominates water policy decisions produced modifications to rivers resulting in a loss of floodplains, thus contributing to flooding during periods of high precipitation and severe property damage.[19] These criticisms renewed debates over the historical tendency of the Corps and BuRec to support structural modifications and their ability to justify such changes using questionable cost-benefit analyses.[20] Analyses of Forest Service behavior have been critical as well. Critics suggest that catering to timber interests with the use of clear-cuts and other land abuses has left the national forests on the verge of losing their regenerative abilities.[21]

Lack of Efficiency. Natural resource policies are also criticized for inefficiency. For example, not only do the structural policies of the Corps contribute to flooding, but also they cost significant amounts of taxpayer money both in capital contributions up front and in disaster relief afterward. Taxpayers pay more than $200 million annually for flood claims, many of them in areas that flood on a regular basis. Many of these arguments assign blame to bureaucrats who, at least theoretically, have few incentives to pursue efficient behavior.[22]

Critics condemn the fiscal behavior of the Forest Service and the BLM. The Forest Service annually brings in less revenue than it spends. This deficit is largely the result of subsidies to loggers who pay below-market rates for timber and to recreationists who often pay no fees to use forest lands. The price to U.S. taxpayers is hundreds of millions of dollars each year.[23] The BLM has been chastised for years for its subsidization of grazing and mining. The BLM traditionally spends two to three times as much on administering an acre of rangeland as it receives in grazing fees.[24]

The easiest target for the inefficiency criticism involves mining fees and royalties paid on use of public lands. These prices are still determined by the 1872 Mining Law. Basically, mining companies can patent claims to public land at 1872 prices (generally $5 per acre) and then, if they spend a minimum of $100 per year on improvements, can treat the land like private property. Unlike the 8- to 12-percent royalty payments from mining of coal, oil, or natural gas, mining of hard-rock minerals involves no payment of royalties at all. By simply imposing an 8-percent royalty on hard-rock minerals, the government could generate millions of dollars of revenue every year. Instead, mining companies enjoy incredibly sweet deals. In 1995, for example, ASARCO Inc. patented 347 acres of national forest containing an estimated $2.9 billion worth of minerals for just $1,735.[25] Attempts to change such gross underpricing of public lands have consistently been unsuccessful in the face of stiff opposition from western lawmakers sympathetic to mining interests.[26]

Summary. Criticisms regarding lack of efficacy and inefficient use of natural resources are summarized in Table 14-1. These problems have fueled demands for change in natural resource policies. When criticisms reinforce one another, they are particularly powerful arguments for reform. In numerous instances (for example, hard-rock mining and clear-cutting), conventional policies have been both economically inefficient and environmen-

Table 14-1   Criticisms of Existing Resource Policies

Resource	Efficacy	Efficiency
Waterways	Destroyed floodplains; destroyed wetlands	Dollar losses from flooding; unjustified capital expenses
Forests	Excessive clear-cutting; damaged habitat/topsoil	Subsidized logging; subsidized recreation
Parklands	Inadequate protection; excessive commercialization	Subsidized concessions; subsidized recreation
Species	Inadequate protection; insufficient habitat	High expenditures on some species; impacts on jobs and property values
Minerals	Use of fragile areas; failure to reclamate	Subsidized development; artificially low fees

tally destructive. This creates the potential for development of powerful coalitions between fiscal conservatives and environmentalists.[27]

Recent Policy Proposals

Demands for systematic reconsideration of natural resource policies have become increasingly prominent since the early 1980s. While broad proposals such as privatization and devolution have been suggested, more momentum developed for collaborative efforts at sustainable development. Such innovative efforts could constitute a third major stage in the evolution of natural resource policies.

Privatization. One set of proposals to overhaul natural resource policies centers on demands to privatize the public sector. Privatization proposals are motivated by the recognition that scarce natural resource commodities can theoretically be used in ways that maximize the value of net output. Advocates criticize public bureaucracies as centralized and inefficient and claim that without direct incentives, agency employees will not manage natural resources to achieve the greatest benefits for society. Privatizing resource policies, particularly through establishment of private property rights, could enable the use of market-determined prices to provide measures of true social preference.[28]

Privatization proposals are compelling for several reasons, not the least of which are persuasive analyses of past public sector failures. They are not, however, immune to criticism. First, most such proposals are based on assumptions of an idealized market economy in which perfect knowledge and proper incentives always exist. Such conditions are, as one critic notes, "elegant, alluring, and hopeless."[29] Second, although markets are well suited to reveal individual preferences, they are less adept at assessing collective values for qualities such as clean air and water.[30] Third, the emphasis on efficiency may neglect crucial questions of equity, questions that may be resolved only through distinctions between different types of land and resources.[31] Fourth, critics argue that people benefit just by knowing that certain resources, such as preserved lands, are there for perpetuity. Privatization advocates counter that if there is a demand, then private ownership will retain wilderness conditions.[32] However, the long-term effects of privatization are anything but certain. Economists recognize that markets do not easily assess demand from future generations. As Nobel laureate Robert Solow says, "The future is not adequately represented in the market, at least not the far future."[33]

Privatization proposals received considerable attention in the 1980s and again with George W. Bush's administration. Such proposals are most compelling when applied to commodity extraction policies such as those guiding timber harvesting.[34] Some versions of increased use of market forces in resource policies, often referred to as New Resource Economics, call for the appropriate pricing of uses ranging from production to recreation.[35] Other privatization proposals have been less successful at valuing wilderness and land preservation efforts.

Devolution. Devolution proposals call for decentralization of natural resource policies to the state, local, or county level (see chapter 2). Inspired by severe distrust of the federal government, advocates of these proposals argue that state and local governments are more attuned to the needs of their constituents and more capable of addressing specific circumstances affecting natural resources within their jurisdictions. Thus transfers of power would arguably facilitate wiser decision making and be more consistent with the spirit of local democratic processes.[36]

If devolution were adopted, how would it affect natural resource policies? Scholars have offered predictions that cover a wide range of possible outcomes, from intensive development as state legislatures cater to and compete for business and industry to increased environmental regulation as local citizens worry more about their own spaces.[37] Other scholars suggest that devolution may enhance greater collaboration between diverse interests in management of ecosystems at local levels.[38] From my own research on state approaches to pollution control and park management, I would expect three outcomes. First, empowered states would display considerable variance in emphases. Second, many policies would be altered significantly. Comparisons of national and state parks, for instance, reveal a greater emphasis on financial self-sufficiency, more development, and greater commercialization of parks at subnational levels. Third, conflict over resource usage would not be reduced; it would simply resume at more local levels of government.[39]

Support for devolution remains inconsistent. The Sagebrush Rebellion received considerable attention in some state legislatures in the late 1970s. Sporadic support since then, even in western states where so much federal land is located, has slowed the momentum of devolution proposals. Nevertheless, some specific policy proposals, such as the issue regarding roadless rules discussed below, contain considerable emphasis on decentralization of decision making. However, advocates of devolution continue to find little systematic support through either popular referenda or judicial rulings.[40] Wholesale devolution of federal power in natural resource policies thus remains unlikely.

Collaborative Ecosystem Management. Perhaps the most promising third-stage proposals for resource policies are those that attempt collaborative, science-based resolutions to achieve innovative management of natural ecosystems. Such efforts bring together public and private sectors and involve different levels of government in participatory, voluntary attempts at resolving contentious situations.[41] As one study of these programs concludes, "For all its faults, collaborative planning is worth the effort if it succeeds in reconciling otherwise intractable environmental and development issues."[42]

To oversimplify somewhat, the desirable end-state under which these proposals often unite is the pursuit of sustainable development. The term *sustainable development* dates to the 1987 UN Commission on Environment and Development, which called for development that meets the needs of present generations without compromising those of future generations. This concept has received significant international attention as well as domestic support.[43] The broad goal is to maximize both environmental and economic benefits in resource policy. Specific targets include participatory planning, greater incorporation of scientific data, facilitation of both commodity usage and resource protection, realistic pricing of various forms of resource use, and concern for long-term as well as short-term outcomes. Several different versions of these efforts are evident.

Ecosystem management proposes to protect biodiversity in areas large enough to sustain evolutionary processes and genetic potential through dynamic use of scientific techniques, such as geographic information systems, over long periods of time.[44] Proponents of collaborative approaches have been critical of existing efforts to protect natural resources as mere landscape maintenance that does not really afford holistic protection of areas or species.[45] Thus even high profile areas such as the Greater Yellowstone Ecosystem are affected by an uncoordinated set of federal and state agencies as well as by private landowners.

One recent case may provide a blueprint for ecosystem management efforts. Stimulated by controversial court cases involving protection of the northern spotted owl in the Pacific Northwest, the Clinton administration encouraged development of a wide-ranging project to protect old-growth forest ecosystems. Planning involved as many as four different federal agencies and hundreds of scientists. The plan includes a system of forest and aquatic reserves, strong emphasis on scientific input, and dynamism through the inclusion of adaptive areas for experimentation. Ambitious in scope, the ultimate success of the plan will not be known for some time.[46]

In a review of over one hundred ecosystem management projects in the United States, one group of analysts expressed overall optimism but admitted that obstacles have been challenging. Specific obstacles include high information needs, hesitant collaboration between diverse interests, limited time and resources available to essential partners, and mistrust of government intrusion on what are seen as private property rights. Thus implementation remains preliminary.[47] Members of some agencies have also expressed at least rhetorical support for biodiversity goals, although real acceptance of ecosystem goals among personnel remains uncertain.[48]

Collaborative planning has been quite evident in the use of habitat conservation plans. These plans are motivated by provisions in the Endangered Species Act allowing developers to seek "incidental taking" permits if their proposed actions might affect, harm, or harass an endangered species. To receive the permit, a plan must be offered that specifies steps taken to minimize impact on threatened species, why alternatives to the taking were not pursued, how funding will be supplied for the plan, and other issues. The planning process usually involves a steering committee made up of representatives from all relevant interests, a technical committee of experts (often biologists), and the use of outside consultants to prepare the plan.

One prominent example involves the San Diego Multiple Species Conservation Plan. Initiated in 1997, the project is centered around a fifty-year plan to reconcile natural preservation and development interests in the areas surrounding this fast-growing city. The plan calls for economic interests to give up the rights to develop thousands of acres of remaining natural habitat in return for freedom from any future obligations to protect imperiled species on already developed lands. In other words, existing property owners are guaranteed a "no surprises" policy in the future. If completed, the 900-square-mile region would include 172,000 acres of protected habitat. Proponents, including then-secretary of the Interior Bruce Babbitt and the Republican mayor of San Diego, promised that this arrangement would assist an entire ecosystem, one that is home to nearly two hundred imperiled species, without impairing economic growth. The plan required six years of collaborative negotiations among developers, preservationists, scientists, and politicians at both state and federal levels.[49] Though some environmental groups have criticized habitat conservation plans as giving too much to developers, the Clinton administration embraced the concept, approving hundreds of them. One review of these plans calls them a "badly needed pressure-release valve" for otherwise intense confrontations.[50]

Another innovative approach to sensitive, controversial ecosystem protection efforts is adaptive management. Adaptive management uses experimentation to provide a scientific basis for policy change by an explicit, voluntary, authoritative body. Specifically, policymakers try different ways to modify management of an ecosystem, closely monitor the results of the controlled experiment, and then adjust decision making accordingly. Adaptive management has been touted as a process that can incorporate scientific data with attempts to build consensus among the numerous, often conflicting, perspectives about how best to manage an ecosystem.[51] Adaptive management is now being used to manage a number of ecosystems in North America, including parts of the Colorado River. On the Colorado, a decision-making body of twenty-seven representatives of agencies and interest groups has initiated and monitored several experiments, including the simulated "flood" of

1996, involving management of the Glen Canyon Dam upstream of the Grand Canyon.[52] Though most of these programs are relatively new, analysts already cite variable success and recognize that adaptive management faces significant barriers, not the least being the ability to overcome fundamental value conflicts over land use. Still, those analysts also admire the potential created through the emphasis on science and the incorporation of different viewpoints.[53]

Numerous other policy innovations are consistent with a new stage's emphasis on scientifically based collaborative resolutions. The Federal Energy Regulatory Commission has developed, since 1994, an alternative licensing process for dam renewals. In brief, the alternative licensing process frontloads dam relicensing by bringing together different stakeholders early in the renewal process to develop scientific analyses of the impacts of dam operations and to facilitate negotiations over possible modifications. This approach provides a substantial change from traditional procedures of issuing the license and then letting the different stakeholders fight it out in court.[54] Another innovation involves forest conservation easements. Organizations like the Trust for Public Land and the Nature Conservancy have developed legal agreements with private forest owners in which the owner restricts the type and amount of development in the forest in return for compensation for the lost activities. Such arrangements can potentially increase the size of semiprotected habitat for ecosystems.[55] Still other innovative resolutions are continually being developed in grassroots restoration efforts. These efforts are not guided by federal agencies or national organizations, but they are focused on sustainable biodiversity, receptive to scientific analyses, and cognizant of economic as well as ecological concerns. These efforts include self-governing agreements to protect common-pool resources, such as lobster fisheries, from potential destruction.[56]

The Bush Administration and Natural Resource Issues

The Bush administration made its priorities in natural resource policies apparent soon after taking office. Appointments to important positions involving these policies were drawn from resource industries and their associated law firms, most notably Gail Norton as secretary of the interior. Once in place, the Bush team suspended numerous Clinton administration programs and, as discussed below, pursued its own goals on public lands and waters. Administration policymakers also displayed a willingness to deride as "junk science" any independent scientific analyses that did not support their policy goals, a willingness that has inspired criticism from objective journals such as *Science* and from organizations such as the Union of Concerned Scientists (UCS). In a scathing report, the UCS concluded, "A growing number of scientists, policymakers, and technical specialists both inside and outside the government allege that the current Bush administration has suppressed or distorted the scientific analyses of federal agencies to bring these results in line with administration policy."[57]

Table 14-2   Natural Resource Controversies

Controversy	Pre-Bush Emphasis	Bush Administration Emphasis
Arctic National Wildlife Refuge	Prohibit oil drilling	Open to oil drilling
Roadless areas in national forests	Prohibit roads and logging	Increase timber production
Endangered species	Habitat conservation plans	Reduce listing of species
Yellowstone snowmobiles	Phase out and eliminate	Allow up to maximum levels

As a result of the administration's actions, the evolution in natural resource policies toward participatory, collaborative, science-based approaches was replaced with a reinstatement of traditional goals of use and extraction. President Reagan's secretary of the interior Watt summed it up well early in George W. Bush's term when he stated, "Everything Cheney's saying, everything the president's saying—they're saying exactly what we were saying twenty years ago, precisely."[58] The revised forest plan described at the start of the chapter was perhaps typical but also less visible than several other prominent cases illustrating this shift. Table 14-2 summarizes the shifting emphases in the prominent controversies discussed below.

Energy Policies and the Arctic National Wildlife Refuge

The administration's energy policies display renewed emphasis on traditional priorities and diminished emphasis on public involvement in policymaking. The policies were a product of Vice President Dick Cheney's energy task force deliberations in 2001. The administration, citing executive privilege, has refused to divulge details on who the task force met with and how often. Organizations such as the liberal Sierra Club and the conservative Judicial Watch as well as the U.S. Government Accountability Office (GAO) persisted in attempts to gain this information until 2004, when the Supreme Court ruled that the records could remain secret.

If such secrecy recalled policy deliberations before the increased public participation of recent decades, the task force's recommendations also reestablished traditional energy priorities. The administration called for increased support of fossil fuels and intensified development of domestic sources of energy. Those recommendations have been backed up with more than two-thirds of the energy-related subsidies and tax incentives in the administration's energy budgets going to fossil fuel and nuclear power industries. The most prominent issue involves the Arctic National Wildlife Refuge (ANWR; also discussed in chapter 6). This 19-million acre refuge on the northeast slope of Alaska is incredibly controversial, containing perhaps the largest unexplored oil field in North America but also the last intact Arctic habitat for thousands of mammals and birds. The debate in Congress over the proposed energy bill, and especially the ANWR provision, has been intense.[59] In the meantime, the administration continued to intensify drilling in other parts of Alaska and elsewhere. Indeed, throughout 2003 and 2004, the administration opened up hundreds of thousands of acres of BLM and Forest Service land to oil and gas development. Efforts to drill in ANWR gained considerable momentum in 2005 when Republican leaders inserted a drilling provision into a budget bill. This maneuver is important in that budget legislation is not subject to filibuster. After a heated debate on March 16, the Senate rejected an effort to remove this provision by a 51–49 vote (seven Republicans voted against drilling, three Democrats voted for). If the House and Senate budget bills are reconciled to include the provision and signed by President Bush, then ANWR will be open for oil exploration.

Forest Policies and the Roadless Areas

The story at the beginning of this chapter hints at another major area of controversy involving natural resource policies. In 1999 the Clinton administration proposed a ban on road-building in 58 million acres of national forests. In an extensive notice-and-comment period, the proposal received over two million comments, more than 90 percent of which were in favor of the ban. Just prior to leaving office in early 2001, the outgoing administration published the final rule, immediately prompting legal challenges in court. After taking office, the Bush administration announced it would allow revisions to the ban on a case-by-case basis, again prompting legal challenges. In 2003 the Ninth Circuit Court of Appeals upheld the roadless ban. Nevertheless, in December 2003 the Bush administration exempted nine million acres of the Tongass National Forest from the rule. Today, a wide range of groups, from environmentalists to companies making outdoor gear and shoes such as Nike, is urging the administration to reinstate the roadless rule.

The administration has argued, as part of its Healthy Forests Initiative, that it needs to allow thinning of forests, including current roadless areas, without extensive public review, in order to reduce fire danger. Proponents criticized environmental groups for causing too many legal delays in forest management plans. Environmental groups counter that many of the worst fires in recent years occurred on logged areas where the extra space allows more oxygen for fuel. Further, the GAO found very little evidence (less than 1 percent of fuel reduction projects had been appealed, none litigated) of obstruction by environmental groups.[60] Nevertheless, the Bush administration stuck to its proposal, a position consistent with the theme of moving away from public participation and stakeholder collaboration and toward traditional uses of natural resources. During the summer of 2004, President Bush's Agriculture secretary, Ann Veneman, publicly rejected the Clinton roadless rule, calling instead for devolution of decision responsibilities over roadless areas to state governors.[61] This policy change received little attention from the media, largely because, typical of so many of the Bush administration's actions, it was achieved through administrative fiat rather than legislation. The potential consequences, however, are enormous. The initial proposal allowed governors to petition the federal government to open roadless areas in their states. The proposal later evolved to the point that governors now have to petition the federal government to allow them to retain roadless areas. Even then, the Forest Service has the power to reject those petitions. Indeed, under the rules adopted in May 2005, forest managers have much greater discretion to quickly approve, with significantly reduced environmental oversight, plans for any forest use.

Land Use Policies and Endangered Species

Since passage in 1973, the Endangered Species Act has been one of the most controversial environmental statutes. One reason is that the act protects individual species rather than ecosystems that support species. This is part of the impetus behind the shift to a focus on ecosystems described earlier. Another reason is that the legislation has real teeth, including provisions that severely restrict economic activities that might impact endangered or threatened species. Thus, as described earlier, policymakers developed habitat conservation plans in efforts to allow economic growth even while protecting plant and animal species.

Rather than emphasizing either of these approaches, both of which rely on scientific analyses and collaboration, the Bush administration has attempted other changes to the Endangered Species Act. One change would restrict additions to the list of threatened and endangered species by removing from the act a provision allowing citizen groups to sue the Interior Department to get species listed. As of March 2005, 1,264 plant and animal species were listed, with hundreds more waiting for the necessary studies.[62] The administration has refused to list many proposed species—wolverines, for example—even though scientific analyses support listing. Instead, the administration has displayed an eagerness to delist species, even when the science does not support it. A classic example involves wild salmon in the Pacific Northwest. As long as salmon species are listed, timber companies can't cut trees along relevant rivers. If salmon counts increase substantially, then the species can be delisted and the trees cut. The administration, acting through the National Marine Fisheries Service and to the dismay of fish biologists, has proposed counting hatchery salmon along with wild salmon, a sure way to increase salmon counts even though these are very different creatures. Another proposal calls for stopping the designation of "critical habitat" for species recovery. Currently, about half the listed species have approved recovery plans. Finally, in numerous cases, such as the battle over water in the Klamath River, the administration has sided with resource users even when scientific analyses showed that such actions would harm threatened and endangered species. On the Klamath, despite the fact that the National Marine Fisheries Service determined that freshwater releases were essential to salmon survival in the river, farmers demanded and received diversions of water for irrigation. The result was a fish kill of 33,000 salmon. Government biologist Michael Kelley said of the administration's attempt to get the National Marine Fisheries Service to revise its study, "We are under pressure to get the right results. . . . This administration is putting species at risk for political gains."[63]

National Park Policies and the Yellowstone Snowmobiles

While campaigning for the presidency, candidate George W. Bush made numerous promises about protecting and improving the national parks. Early in his term, his administration's rhetoric, including the National Parks Legacy Project, was so positive that the National Parks Conservation Association was considerably more supportive of the new president than was nearly any other established environmental group. Disappointment with administration actions, however, eroded that support to the point that the association gave the Bush administration an overall midterm grade of D–. Those actions included altering the Clean Air Act in ways that would increase air pollution in parks, efforts to outsource 70 percent of NPS staff, allowing more road-building in protected areas, and a failure to increase funding to promised levels. Even Interior Secretary Norton admitted, in the summer of 2004, that the administration had not achieved the funding levels for parks it had promised. Not surprisingly, then, a 2003 survey of 1,300 NPS employees by the Campaign to Protect America's Lands found that two-thirds of the respondents believed that current policies were in the "wrong direction."[64] The most visible parks issue, and the one most illustrative of the theme of deemphasizing public participation while reemphasizing resource use, is that of the Yellowstone snowmobiles.

The controversy surrounding the snowmobile issue increased along with their usage. Whereas some parks have banned snowmobiles for decades, Yellowstone has allowed them since 1971. Since the mid-1990s, the number of snowmobiles entering Yellowstone and Grand Teton Parks during winter months has increased to an average of over 800 daily and as many as 1,650 per day on holiday weekends. Critics contend that snowmobiles cause significant problems with noise and air pollution as well as altering the natural behavior of park wildlife. Following years of study, the Clinton administration conducted an Environmental Impact Statement analysis of the potential reduction of snowmobiles entering Yellowstone. Over three years of debate, the issue received more than 45,000 public comments. In the final comment period, 83 percent favored elimination of snowmobiles from Yellowstone.[65] The Clinton administration thus put into place a three-year phase-out of snowmobiles with a complete ban by the winter of 2003–2004. Winter visitors would instead be carried into the park by less-intrusive snow coaches. The plan prompted legal challenges from the state of Wyoming and the International Snowmobile Manufacturers Association.

Upon taking office, the Bush administration stated that it would revisit the issue. Over a one-year period, the administration received 350,000 comments, more than on any single park issue. Those comments again supported the ban at a four-to-one rate. The administration also conducted its own scientific study of the impact of snowmobiles, only to have the study conclude that the park's environment and winter employees would be best protected by banning the snowmobiles and that the economic impacts on surrounding communities would be "negligible to minor."[66] Nevertheless, the administration stopped the Clinton phase-out, instead proposing to allow snowmobiles up to a limit of 1,100 vehicles in the two parks each day. The Greater Yellowstone Coalition and other groups immediately challenged the Bush proposal in federal court. The courts have not clarified the issue. One federal judge, Emmet Sullivan, aborted the new Bush-supported plan in December 2003, calling it "completely politically driven."[67] The U.S. Court of Appeals for the D.C. Circuit upheld Judge Sullivan's order to implement the Clinton-era plan in early 2004. The debate on the issue continues, however. In June 2004, an amendment calling for ending snowmobile use in Yellowstone failed in the U.S. House of Representatives by a 198–222 vote. In October 2004, another federal judge, Clarence Brimmer, responded to a suit by snowmobile manufacturers by rejecting the ban.

Conclusion

The third stage of the evolution of natural resource policies, emphasizing participatory, collaborative, science-based management of diverse ecosystems, offers great potential toward achieving sustainable use of lands and waters in the United States and elsewhere. However, as discussed above, this evolution is currently stalled for many ecosystems and in many natural resource policies. A highly charged, contentious political atmosphere and a presidential administration determined to reestablish historical patterns of use of resources has renewed traditional priorities and processes in natural resource policymaking. With reelection in 2004 and stronger Republican majorities in both houses of Congress, the Bush administration can be expected to pursue these policies even more vigorously in a second term. Specific policy outcomes will likely include oil drilling in ANWR, intensified logging on national forest lands, substantial revisions to the Endangered Species Act, and more snowmobiles in Yellowstone.

Suggested Web Sites

American Petroleum Institute (http://api-ec.api.org) The major trade association of the oil and natural gas industries.

American Rivers (www.amrivers.org) A nonprofit conservation organization focused on U.S. waterways.

Greater Yellowstone Coalition (www.greateryellowstone.org) A conservation organization dedicated to lands in and around Yellowstone.

National Parks Conservation Association (www.npca.org) The environmental group focused on protecting America's national parks.

Property and Environment Research Center (www.perc.org) An institute dedicated to using market principles on environmental issues.

Sierra Club (www.sierraclub.org) One of America's oldest and largest environmental groups.

Union of Concerned Scientists (www.ucsusa.org) A nonprofit alliance of citizens and scientists concerned with environmental issues.

U.S. Department of Energy (www.energy.gov) The federal agency responsible for U.S. energy policies.

U.S. Fish and Wildlife Service (www.fws.gov) The federal agency largely responsible for endangered species and wildlife refuges.

U.S. Forest Service (www.fs.fed.us) The federal agency responsible for America's national forests.

U.S. Geological Survey (www.usgs.gov) A federal agency responsible for scientific information on the environment.

U.S. National Park Service (www.nps.gov) The federal agency responsible for America's national parks.

Notes

1. Cosmo Garvin, "Old-Growth Trees to Fall in the Sierra," *High Country News,* March 1, 2004, 4.
2. For more on the Corps, see Jeanne Nienaber Clarke and Daniel C. McCool, *Staking Out the Terrain,* 2nd ed. (Albany: State University Press of New York, 1996), 17–49, 129–156; Daniel A. Mazmanian and Jeanne Nienaber, *Can Organizations Change?* (Washington, D.C.: Brookings Institution Press, 1979).
3. Clarke and McCool, *Staking Out the Terrain,* 49–66; Roger C. Dower et al., eds., *Frontiers of Sustainability* (Washington, D.C.: Island Press, 1997), 191–280; George Hoberg, "From Localism to Legalism," in *Western Public Lands and Environmental Politics,* ed. Charles Davis (Boulder: Westview Press, 1997), 47–73; Herbert Kaufman, *The Forest Ranger* (Baltimore: Johns Hopkins University Press, 1960).
4. Ronald A. Foresta, *America's National Parks and Their Keepers* (Washington, D.C.: Resources for the Future, 1984); John Freemuth, *Islands under Siege* (Lawrence: University Press of Kansas, 1991); Michael Frome, *Regreening the National Parks* (Tucson: University of Arizona Press, 1992); William Lowry, *The Capacity for Wonder* (Washington, D.C.: Brookings Institution Press, 1994).
5. Clarke and McCool, *Staking Out the Terrain,* 157–175; Charles Davis, "Politics and Public Rangeland Policy," in *Western Public Lands and Environmental Politics,* ed. Davis, 74–94; Robert F. Durant, *The Administrative Presidency Revisited* (Albany: State University of New York Press, 1992); Philip O. Foss, *Politics and Grass* (Seattle: University of Washington Press, 1960).
6. Davis, "Politics and Public Rangeland Policy."
7. Clarke and McCool, *Staking Out the Terrain,* 107–125; Winston Harrington and Anthony C. Fisher, "Endangered Species," in *Natural Resource Policy,* ed. Paul R. Portney (Washington, D.C.: Resources for the Future, 1982), 117–148.

8. Craig W. Allin, "Wilderness Policy," in *Western Public Lands and Environmental Politics*, ed. Davis, 172–189; Walter A. Rosenbaum, *Environmental Politics and Policy*, 3rd ed. (Washington, D.C.: CQ Press, 1995), 297–328.

9. Tim Palmer, *Endangered Rivers and the Conservation Movement* (Berkeley: University of California Press, 1986).

10. David H. Davis, *Energy Politics*, 4th ed. (New York: St. Martin's Press, 1993); Christopher M. Klyza, "Reform at a Geological Pace," in *Western Public Lands and Environmental Politics*, ed. Davis, 95–121.

11. Alan Gottlieb, *The Wise Use Agenda* (Bellevue, Wash.: Free Enterprise Press, 1989), xvii.

12. Ron Arnold, "Overcoming Ideology," and John Freemuth, "Wise Use Movement and the National Parks," in *A Wolf in the Garden*, ed. Philip D. Brick and R. McGreggor Cawley (Lanham, Md.: Rowman and Littlefield, 1996), 15–26, 207–213; William L. Graf, *Wilderness Preservation and the Sagebrush Rebels* (Savage, Md.: Rowman and Littlefield, 1990); S. L. Witt and L. R. Alm, "County Government and the Public Lands," in *Public Lands Management in the West*, ed. Brent S. Steel (Westport, Conn.: Praeger, 1997), 95–110.

13. Paul J. Culhane, "Sagebrush Rebels in Office," in *Environmental Policy in the 1980s*, ed. Norman J. Vig and Michael E. Kraft (Washington, D.C.: CQ Press, 1984), 293–317.

14. Margaret Kriz, "Aiming for the Green," *National Journal*, October 4, 1997, 1958–1960.

15. Charles Shipan and William Lowry, "Environmental Policy and Party Divergence in Congress," *Political Research Quarterly* 54 (June 2001): 245–263.

16. Philip D. Brick and R. McGreggor Cawley, "Knowing the Wolf, Tending the Garden," and Glenn P. Sugameli, "Environmentalism: The Real Movement to Protect Property Rights," in *A Wolf in the Garden*, ed. Brick and Cawley, 1–12, 59–72.

17. Edward O. Wilson, *The Diversity of Life* (New York: Norton, 1992), 32; see also Rosenbaum, *Environmental Politics and Policy*, 333–340.

18. Frome, *Regreening the National Parks*; Lowry, *The Capacity for Wonder*.

19. Karl Hess Jr., "John Wesley Powell and the Unmaking of the West," in *The Next West*, ed. John A. Baden and Donald Snow (Washington, D.C.: Island Press, 1997), 151–180; Todd Shallat, *Structures in the Stream* (Austin: University of Texas Press, 1994).

20. Mazmanian and Nienaber, *Can Organizations Change?*, 22–23.

21. Rocky Barker, "New Forestry in the Next West," in *The Next West*, ed. Baden and Snow, 29; Nels Johnson and Daryl Ditz, "Challenges to Sustainability in the U.S. Forest Sector," in *Frontiers of Sustainability*, ed. Dower et al., 191–280.

22. Terry L. Anderson and Pamela Snyder, *Water Markets* (Washington, D.C.: Cato Institute, 1997).

23. Norman Myers and Jennifer Kent, *Perverse Subsidies: How Misused Tax Dollars Harm the Environment and the Economy* (Washington, D.C.: Island Press, 2001), 170; Robert H. Nelson, "The Future of Federal Forest Management," in *Federal Lands Policy*, ed. Philip O. Foss (New York: Greenwood, 1987), 159–176; Randal O'Toole, *Reforming the Forest Service* (Washington, D.C.: Island Press, 1988).

24. John Baden and Dean Lueck, "Bringing Private Management to the Public Lands," in *Controversies in Environmental Policy*, ed. Sheldon Kamieniecki, Robert O'Brien, and Michael Clarke (Albany: State University of New York Press, 1986), 54; John G. Francis, "Public Lands Institutions and Their Discontents," in *Federal Lands Policy*, ed. Foss, 61–76; and Gary D. Libecap, *Locking Up the Range* (Cambridge, Mass.: Ballinger, 1981).

25. "Merry Christmas, Mining Companies," editorial, *St. Louis Post-Dispatch*, December 11, 1995, 6B.

26. Charles Davis, "Gold or Green? Efforts to Reform the Mining Law of 1872," *Natural Resources and Environmental Administration* 19 (February 1998): 2–4.

27. Nelson, "The Future of Federal Forest Management," 161; Donald Snow, "Introduction," in *The Next West*, ed. Baden and Snow, 1–9.

28. B. Delwourth Gardner, "The Case for Divestiture," in *Rethinking the Federal Lands,* ed. Sterling Brubaker (Washington, D.C.: Resources for the Future, 1984), 169; see also Terry L. Anderson and Peter J. Hill, "Introduction," in *The Political Economy of the American West,* ed. Terry L. Anderson and Peter J. Hill (Lanham, Md.: Rowman and Littlefield, 1994), x; Nelson, "The Future of Federal Forest Management," 170–171.

29. R. W. Behan, "The Polemics and Politics of Federal Land Management," in *Federal Lands Policy,* ed. Foss, 180.

30. Joseph Sax, "The Claim for Retention of the Public Lands," in *Rethinking the Federal Lands,* ed. Brubaker, 139.

31. Christopher K. Leman, "How the Privatization Revolution Failed," in *Western Public Lands,* ed. John G. Francis and Richard Ganzel (Towota, N.J.: Rowman and Allanheld, 1984), 115.

32. Gardner, "The Case for Divestiture," 174.

33. Robert M. Solow, "Sustainability," in *Economics of the Environment,* 3rd ed., ed. Robert Dorfman and Nancy S. Dorfman (New York: Norton, 1993), 182.

34. Some of the most interesting analyses come from the Property and Environment Research Center (www.perc.org).

35. John Baden and Andrew Dana, "Toward an Ideological Synthesis in Public Land Policy," in *Federal Lands Policy,* ed. Foss 1–20; Mark Sagoff, "Saving the Marketplace from the Market," in *The Next West,* ed. Baden and Snow 131–149.

36. John G. Francis and Richard Ganzel, "Introduction," in *Western Public Lands,* ed. Francis and Ganzel, 1–22; Hess, "John Wesley Powell," 177.

37. Francis and Ganzel, "Introduction"; Howard E. McCurdy, "Environmental Protection and the New Federalism," in *Controversies in Environmental Policy,* ed. Kamieniecki, O'Brien, and Clarke, 85–107.

38. Edward P. Weber, *Pluralism by the Rules* (Washington, D.C.: Georgetown University Press, 1998).

39. William Lowry, "State Parks Found to Be Source of Innovation," *Public Administration Times* 19(10) (1996): 1, 12–13; see also Francis, "Public Lands Institutions," 74.

40. Christopher A. Simon, "The County Supremacy Movement and Public Lands in Oregon," in *Public Lands Management in the West,* ed. Steel, 111–127; Witt and Alm, "County Government and the Public Lands."

41. David A. Salvesen and Douglas R. Porter, "Introduction," in *Collaborative Planning for Wetlands and Wildlife,* ed. Douglas Porter and David A. Salvesen (Washington, D.C.: Island Press, 1995), 1–6. See also Rosemary O'Leary and Lisa Bingham, *The Promise and Performance of Environmental Conflict Resolution* (Washington D.C.: Resources for the Future, 2003).

42. Douglas R. Porter and David A. Salvesen, "Conclusion," in *Collaborative Planning for Wetlands and Wildlife,* ed. Porter and Salvesen, 275; Timothy Beatley, "Preserving Biodiversity through the Use of Habitat Conservation Plans," in *Collaborative Planning for Wetlands and Wildlife,* ed. Porter and Salvesen, 57–68; Julia M. Wondolleck and Steven L. Yaffee, *Making Collaboration Work* (Washington D.C.: Island Press, 2000).

43. Herman E. Daly, *Beyond Growth* (Boston: Beacon Press, 1996); Dower et al., eds., *Frontiers of Sustainability,* 3; National Commission on the Environment, *Choosing a Sustainable Future* (Washington, D.C.: Island Press, 1993); Daniel Sitarz, ed., *Sustainable America* (Carbondale, Ill.: EarthPress, 1998).

44. Jerry F. Franklin, "Ecosystem Management: An Overview," in *Ecosystem Management,* ed. Mark S. Boyce and Alan Haney (New Haven: Yale University Press, 1997), 21–53; Reed F. Noss and Allen Y. Cooperrider, *Saving Nature's Legacy* (Washington, D.C.: Island Press, 1994); Steven L. Yaffee, Ali F. Phillips, Irene C. Frentz, Paul W. Hardy, Sussanne M. Maleki, and Barbara E. Thorpe, *Ecosystem Management in the United States* (Washington, D.C.: Island Press, 1996).

45. Alan Haney and Mark S. Boyce, "Introduction," in *Ecosystem Management,* ed. Boyce and Haney, 9. See also Reed F. Noss and J. Michael Scott, "Ecosystem Protection and Restoration," in *Ecosystem Management,* ed. Boyce and Haney, 239–264.

46. Franklin, "Ecosystem Management," 47–48; see also the April 1994 issue of *Journal of Forestry.*

47. Yaffee et al., *Ecosystem Management in the United States,* 39.

48. Noss and Cooperrider, *Saving Nature's Legacy,* 87, 329; Jack Ward Thomas, "Foreword," in *Ecosystem Management,* ed. Boyce and Haney, x–xi; Yaffee et al., *Ecosystem Management in the United States,* 33–34; Hanna J. Cortner and Margaret A. Moote, *The Politics of Ecosystem Management* (Washington, D.C.: Island Press, 1999); William R. Lowry, *Dam Politics* (Washington D.C.: Georgetown University Press, 2003); Todd Wilkinson, *Science Under Siege* (Boulder: Johnson Books, 1998).

49. B. Drummond Ayres Jr., "San Diego Council Approves 'Model' Nature Habitat Plan," *New York Times,* March 20, 1997, A14; Judith A. Layzer, *The Environmental Case* (Washington, D.C.: CQ Press, 2002); William K. Stevens, "Disputed Conservation Plan Could Be Model for Nation," *New York Times,* February 16, 1997, A8.

50. Timothy Beatley, "Preserving Biodiversity through the Use of Habitat Conservation Plans," in *Collaborative Planning for Wetlands and Wildlife,* ed. Porter and Salvesen, 57, 35–74; Scott Sonner, "Clinton Administration Has 'Junked the Law,' Critics Charge," *St. Louis Post-Dispatch,* May 9, 1997, 3A.

51. Lance H. Gunderson, C. S. Holling, and Stephen S. Light, "Barriers Broken and Bridges Built: A Synthesis," in *Barriers and Bridges to the Renewal of Ecosystems and Institutions,* ed. Gunderson et al. (Washington D.C.: Island Press, 1995), 489–532; Kai N. Lee, *Compass and Gyroscope* (Washington D.C.: Island Press, 1993).

52. Lowry, *Dam Politics,* chap. 5; National Research Council, *Downstream: Adaptive Management of Glen Canyon Dam and the Colorado River Ecosystem* (Washington, D.C.: National Academies Press, 1999), 140.

53. Carl Walters, "Challenges in Adaptive Management of Riparian and Coastal Ecosystems," *Conservation Ecology* 1(2) (1997): 1–22.

54. Lowry, *Dam Politics,* chap. 6.

55. Mark Mathews, "Out of the Woods," *Land & People* (spring 2004): 33–43. See also the Web site for Trust for Public Land (www.tpl.org).

56. Elinor Ostrom, "Reformulating the Commons," in *Protecting the Commons,* ed. Joanna Burger (Washington, D.C.: Island Press, 2001); William K. Stevens, *Miracle under the Oaks* (New York: Pocket Books, 1995).

57. For the complete report, see Union of Concerned Scientists, "Scientific Integrity in Policy Making," July 2004, www.ucsusa.org.

58. Todd Wilkinson, "The Undoing of Our Wildlands?" *Defenders* 76 (summer 2001): 19. See also Margaret Kriz, "Working the Land," *National Journal,* February 23, 2002, 532–539.

59. Useful Web sites include those favoring drilling (for example, Department of Energy at www.energy.gov), those opposed (for example, www.savearcticrefuge.org), and those providing scientific assessments (for example, U.S. Geological Survey at www.usgs.gov).

60. The U.S. Government Accountability Office (GAO, formerly the General Accounting Office), *Forest Service: Appeals and Litigation of Fuel Reduction Projects* (Washington, D.C.: GAO, August 31, 2001). For additional information on forest management plans, see the U.S. Forest Service Web site (www.fs.fed.us).

61. Felicity Barringer, "Bush Seeks Shift in Logging Rules," and Greg Hanscom, "Outsourced," *New York Times,* July 13, 2004, 1.

62. For a current listing of endangered and threatened species in the United States and the world, see the U.S. Fish and Wildlife Service's Threatened and Endangered Species System "Summary of Listed Species," ecos.fws.gov/tess_public/TESSBoxscore.

63. Carl Pope and Paul Rauber, "Strategic Ignorance," *Sierra* (May/June 2004): 43.

64. The study is available at www.protectamericaslands.org.

65. Benjamin Long, "Desperately Seeking Silence," *National Parks* (November/December 2001): 28–32.
66. Tom Kenworthy, "Study Supported Ban on Snowmobiles," *USA Today*, January 30, 2003. See also the Web sites for the Greater Yellowstone Coalition (www.greateryellowstone.org) and for the National Parks Conservation Association (www.npca.org).
67. Scott McMillion, "Yellowstone Snowmobilers Suffer Whiplash," *High Country News*, January 19, 2004, 3.

15

Environment, Population, and the Developing World
Richard J. Tobin

Environmental problems occasionally make life in the United States unpleasant, but most Americans tolerate this situation in exchange for the comforts associated with a developed economy. Most Europeans, Japanese, and Australians share similar lifestyles, so it is not surprising that they too typically take modern amenities for granted.

When lifestyles are viewed from a broader perspective, however, much changes. Consider, for example, what life is like in much of the world. The U.S. gross national product (GNP) per capita was about $35,000 per year, or almost $675 per week, in 2002, but millions of people live in countries where weekly incomes are less than 5 percent of this amount, even when adjusted for differences in prices and purchasing power. In Sierra Leone, the world's most impoverished country, real per-capita incomes are about one-seventieth of those in the United States. Among all developing countries, a majority of people live on less than two dollars per day, including more than three-quarters of the population in South Asia and sub-Saharan Africa.[1]

Low incomes are not the only problem facing many of the world's inhabitants. In some developing countries, women, often illiterate and with no formal education, will marry as young as age thirteen. In several African countries, 45 percent or more of all females are married before their twentieth birthday. In parts of Africa, girls commonly marry at age seven or eight. In one Indian state, a survey in the early 1990s found that nearly one in five women had married before they were age ten. Marriage at early ages typically leads to motherhood at young ages.[2] During their childbearing years, women in many developing countries will deliver as many as six or seven babies, most without trained medical personnel at hand. This absence is not without consequences. The chance of a woman dying due to complications associated with pregnancy, childbirth, or an unsafe abortion is hundreds of times higher in many poor countries than it is in the United States.

Many of the world's children are also at risk. Only eight out of one thousand American children die before the age of five; in some Asian and African countries as many as 25 to 30 percent do. *Every day* more than 30,000 children under age five die in developing countries from diseases that rarely kill Americans. Most of the deaths are caused by tetanus, measles, malaria, diarrhea, whooping cough, or acute respiratory infections, most of which could be easily and cheaply cured or prevented.[3]

Of the children from these poor countries that do survive their earliest years, millions will suffer brain damage because their pregnant mothers had no iodine in their diets; others will lose their sight and die because they lack vitamin A. Many will face a life of poverty, never to taste clean water, learn to read or write, visit a doctor, have access to even the cheapest medicines, or eat nutritious food regularly. To the extent that shelter is available, it is rudimentary, rarely with electricity or proper sanitary facilities. Because their surroundings have been abused or poorly managed, millions in the developing world will also become victims of floods, famine, desertification, water-borne diseases, infestation of pests and rodents, and noxious levels of air pollution. Most sewage in developing countries is discharged without any treatment, and pesticides and human wastes often contaminate well water. In China, according to one estimate, animal or human waste contaminates the water supplies of about half the population.[4]

As children in developing countries grow older, many will find that their governments do not have or cannot provide the resources to ensure them a reasonable standard of living. Yet all around them are countries with living standards well beyond their comprehension. The average American uses about fifteen to twenty times more energy and consumes about 50 percent more calories per day—far in excess of minimum daily requirements—than does the typical Indian. An Indian mother might wonder why Americans consume a disproportionate share of the world's resources when she has malnourished children she cannot clothe or educate.

In short, life in much of Asia, Africa, and Latin America provides an array of problems different from those encountered in developed nations. Residents of poor countries must cope with widespread poverty and a lack of economic development. Yet both developed and developing nations often undergo environmental degradation. Those without property, for example, may be tempted to denude tropical forests for land to farm. Alternatively, pressures for development often force people to overexploit their base of environmental resources.

These issues lead to the key question addressed in this chapter: Can the poorest countries, with the overwhelming majority of the world's population, improve their lot through sustainable development? According to the World Commission on Environment and Development, sustainable development meets the essential needs of the present generation for food, clothing, shelter, jobs, and health without "compromising the ability of future generations to meet their own needs."[5] Achieving this goal will require increased economic development without irreparable damage to the environment.

Whose responsibility is it to achieve sustainable development? One view is that richer nations have a moral obligation to assist less fortunate ones. If the former do not meet this obligation, not only will hundreds of millions of people in developing countries suffer but the consequences will be felt in the developed countries as well. Others argue that poorer nations must accept responsibility for their own fate because outside efforts to help them only worsen the problem and lead to an unhealthy dependence. Advocates of this position insist that it is wrong to provide food to famine-stricken nations because they have exceeded their environment's carrying capacity.[6]

The richer nations, whichever position they take, cannot avoid affecting what happens in the developing world. It is thus useful to consider how U.S. actions influence the quest for sustainable development. At least two related factors affect this quest. The first is a country's population; the second is a country's capacity to support its population.

Population Growth: Cure or Culprit?

Population growth is one of the more contentious elements in the journey toward sustainable development. Depending on one's perspective, the world is either vastly overpopulated or capable of supporting as many as thirty times its current population (about 6.4 billion in mid-2004 and increasing at an annual rate of about 76 million per year).[7] Many of the developing nations are growing faster than the industrial nations (Table 15-1), and more than 80 percent of the world's population lives outside the developed regions. If current growth rates continue, the proportion of those in developing countries will increase even more. Between 2000 and 2050 about 98 percent of the world's population increase will occur in the latter

Table 15-1   Estimated Populations and Projected Growth Rates

Region or Country	Estimated Population (millions)			Rate of Annual Natural Increase	Number of Years to Double Population
	2004	2025	2050		
World total	6,396	7,934	9,276	1.3	53
More developed countries	1,206	1,257	1,257	0.1	690
United States[a]	294	349	420	0.6	115
Japan	128	121	101	0.1	690
Canada	32	36	37	0.3	230
Less developed regions	5,190	6,677	8,019	1.5	46
China	1,300	1,476	1,437	0.6	115
India	1,087	1,363	1,628	1.7	41
Sub-Saharan Africa	733	1,120	1,701	2.5	28
Brazil	179	211	221	1.3	53
Philippines	84	118	147	2.0	35
Nigeria	137	206	307	2.9	24
Mexico	106	132	150	2.1	33
Uganda	26	48	83	3.0	23
Yemen	20	40	71	3.3	21

Source: Population Reference Bureau, *2004 World Population Data Sheet* (Washington, D.C.: Population Reference Bureau, 2004), www.prb.org.

[a] Although rates of natural increase in the United States are modest, immigration accounts for much of the projected increase in the U.S. population.

regions, exactly where the people and the environment can least afford such a surge.

Africa is particularly prone to high rates of population growth, with some countries facing increases of 3 percent or more per year. This may not seem to be much until we realize that such rates will double the countries' populations in about twenty-three years. Fertility rates measure the number of children an average woman has during her lifetime. Seventeen of the nineteen countries with fertility rates at six or above are in Africa. By comparison, the birth rate in the United States was fourteen per thousand in 2004, and its fertility rate was two.

Although many countries have altered their attitudes about population growth, many have also realized the immensity of the task. The prevailing theory of demographic transition suggests that societies go through three stages. In the first stage, in premodern societies, birth and death rates are high; therefore, populations remain stable or increase at low rates. In the second stage, death rates decline and populations grow more rapidly because of vaccines, better health care, and more nutritious foods. As countries begin to reap the benefits of economic development, they enter the third stage. Infant mortality declines but so does the desire or need to have large families. Population growth slows considerably.

This model explains events in many developed countries. As standards of living increased, birth rates declined. The model's weakness is that it assumes economic development; in the absence of such development, many nations are caught in a "demographic trap."[8] They get stuck in the second stage. This is the predicament of many countries today. In some African countries the situation is even worse. Their populations are growing faster than their economies, and living standards are declining. These declines create a cruel paradox. Larger populations produce increased demands for health and educational services; stagnant economies make it impossible to provide them.

The opportunity to lower death rates can also make it difficult to slow population growth. In almost thirty-five Asian and African countries the average life expectancy at birth is less than fifty years (and less than forty years in a few African countries), compared with seventy-seven in the United States and eighty-two in Japan, as of 2004. If these Asians and Africans had access to the medicines, vitamins, and nutritious foods readily available in the developed nations, then death rates would drop substantially. Life expectancies in these countries could be extended by twenty years or more.

There is some reason to expect death rates to decline. Despite the devastating impact of HIV/AIDS, especially in sub-Saharan Africa, development agencies have attempted to reduce infant mortality by immunizing children against potentially fatal illnesses and by providing inexpensive cures for diarrhea and other illnesses. These programs have met with enormous success, and more progress is anticipated. Reduced mortality rates among children should also reduce fertility rates. Nonetheless, the change will be gradual, and millions of children will be born in the meantime. Most of the first-time mothers of the next twenty years have already been born.

The best-known and most controversial population programs are in India and China. India's family planning program started in the early 1950s as a low-key educational effort that achieved only modest success. The program changed from being voluntary to compulsory in the mid-1970s. The minimum age for marriage was increased, and India's states were encouraged to select their own methods to reduce growth.

Several states chose coercion. Parents with two or more children were expected to have themselves sterilized. To ensure compliance, states threatened to withhold salaries or to dismiss government workers from their jobs if they did not get sterilized. Public officials were likewise threatened with sanctions if they did not provide enough candidates for sterilization. One result was a massive program of forced sterilization that caused considerable political turmoil.[9] Although the program was eventually relaxed, India has been able to cut its fertility rate significantly. This is remarkable progress, but cultural resistance may stifle further gains. India currently adds about 18 million inhabitants each year. If such growth continues, India could become the world's most populous country by 2035.

Whether India becomes the world's most populous nation depends on what happens in China. To reduce the country's population growth rate, the Chinese government discourages early marriages. It also adopted a one-child-per-family policy in 1979, and the policy is applied in most urban areas. The government gives one-child families monthly subsidies, educational benefits for their child, preferences for housing and health care, and higher pensions at retirement. Families that had previously agreed to have only one child but then had another are deprived of these benefits and penalized financially.

The most controversial elements of the program involve the government's monitoring of women's menstrual cycles; instances of forced sterilizations and abortions, some occurring in the last trimester; and even female infanticide in rural areas. Chinese officials admit that abortions have been forced on some unwilling women. These officials quickly add, however, that such practices represent aberrations, not accepted guidelines, and that they violate the government's policies.

China's initial efforts lowered annual rates of population growth considerably. Total fertility rates declined from 5.8 in 1970 to 1.7 in 2004. Perhaps because of this success, the program began to encounter extensive resistance and, in some areas, outright disregard. Consequently the government relaxed its restrictions and exempted certain families, particularly in rural areas, from the one-child policy. Rather than mandating limits on the number of children a couple can have, China has gradually adopted approaches to population control that encourage women to have fewer children. These policy changes led to a 20-percent increase in the birth rate between 1985 and 1987, and China soon announced that it had abandoned its goal of a population of 1.2 billion by 2000, which the country exceeded in 1997.[10]

For many years the U.S. government viewed rapidly growing populations as a threat to economic development. The United States backed its rhetoric with money; it was the single largest donor to international population programs. The official U.S. position changed dramatically during the Reagan administration. Due to its opposition to abortion, the administration said the United States would no longer contribute to the UN Population Fund because it subsidized some of China's population programs. None of the fund's resources are used to provide abortions, but the U.S. ban on contributions nonetheless continued during George H. W. Bush's administration.

Within a day of taking office, President Bill Clinton announced his intention to alter these policies, to provide financial support to the fund, and to finance international population programs that rely on abortions. The Clinton administration also dramatically increased financial support for family planning in developing countries even in the face of cuts in the overall U.S. budget for foreign assistance. With the Republicans gaining control of the Congress in 1995, however, much of this momentum was soon reversed. In the federal budget for fiscal year 1996, for example, Congress cut by 35 percent U.S. foreign assistance for population and family planning programs in developing countries.

Just as Clinton had acted quickly, so too did George W. Bush. Within two days of becoming president in 2001, he reinstated President Reagan's policy banning the use of federal funds by international organizations to support abortions or to advocate abortions overseas.

Concerns about abortion are not the only reason many people have qualms about efforts to affect population increases. Their view is that large populations are a problem only when they are not used productively to enhance development. The solution to the lack of such development is not government intervention, they argue, but rather individual initiatives and the spread of capitalist, free-market economies. Advocates of this position also believe that larger populations can be advantageous because they enhance political power, contribute to economic development, encourage technological innovation, and stimulate agricultural production.[11] Other critics of population control programs also ask if it is appropriate for developed countries to impose their preferences on others.

Another much-debated issue involves the increased access to abortions, and who chooses to have them. The consequences of efforts to limit population growth are not always gender neutral. In parts of Asia, male children are highly prized as sources of future financial security, whereas females are viewed as liabilities. In years past, the sex of newborns was known only at birth, and in most countries newborn males slightly outnumber newborn females. With the advent of ultrasound, however, the sex of a fetus is easily ascertained months before a child is due. This knowledge is often the basis of a decision to abort female fetuses, notably in parts of India.[12] Other practices also seem to disadvantage females. In China, for example, the infant mortality rate for females is more than 30 percent higher than it is for males.

In sum, the appropriateness of different population sizes is debatable. There is no clear answer to whether growth by itself is good or bad. The important issue is a country's carrying capacity. Can it ensure its population a reasonable standard of living?

Providing Food and Fuel for Growing Populations

Sustainable development requires that environmental resources not be overtaxed so that they are available for future generations. As Lester Brown points out, however, when populations exceed sustainable yields of their forests, aquifers, and croplands, "they begin directly or indirectly to consume the resource base itself," gradually destroying it.[13] The eventual result is an irreversible collapse of biological and environmental support systems. Is there any evidence that these systems are now being strained or will be in the near future?

The first place to look is in the area of food production. Nations can grow their own food, import it, or, as most nations do, rely on both options. The Earth is richly endowed with agricultural potential and production. Millions of acres of arable land remain to be cultivated, and farmers now produce enough food to satisfy the daily caloric and protein needs of a world population exceeding 12 billion, far more than are already alive.[14] These data suggest the ready availability of food as well as a potential for even higher levels of production. This good news must be balanced with the realization that hundreds of millions of people today barely have enough food to survive.

As with economic development, the amount of food available in a country must increase at least as fast as the rate of population growth; otherwise, per-capita consumption will decline. If existing levels of caloric intake are already inadequate, then food production (and imports) must increase faster than population growth in order to meet minimum caloric needs. Assisted by the expanded use of irrigation, pesticides, and fertilizers, many developing countries, particularly in Asia, dramatically increased their food production in the 1970s and 1980s. Asia's three largest countries— China, India, and Indonesia—are no longer heavily dependent on imports.

Despite these and a few other notable successes, much of the developing world is in the midst of an agricultural crisis. Thirty-two African countries produced less food per capita in 2003 than they did in 1990. In many developing countries the average daily caloric consumption, already below subsistence levels in the early 1980s, declined still further by the late 1990s as agricultural productivity per capita plunged in many places (Table 15-2). These nations consequently face severe problems with food security.

It is possible to increase agricultural outputs, but in many countries there is not enough land suitable for cultivation to support existing populations. Some developing countries have already reached or exceeded the sustainable limits of production. Their populations are already overexploiting

Table 15-2   Changes in Agricultural Production and Daily Caloric
Intake

Country	Index of Food Production per Capita (1989–1991 = 100) Year 2001	Daily Caloric Supply per Capita Years			Proportion of Population Undernourished (%) Years
	2001	1979–1981	1989–1991	1999–2001	1999–2001
United States	108	3,190	3,480	3,770	—
Canada	109	2,900	3,010	3,180	—
Bangladesh	109	1,980	2,070	2,160	32
China	167	2,330	2,680	2,970	11
Cuba	58	2,880	2,880	2,610	11
India	108	2,080	2,370	2,490	21
Kenya	80	2,180	1,960	2,040	37
Madagascar	80	2,370	2,110	2,070	36
Malawi	156	2,270	1,940	2,170	33
Sierra Leone	69	2,110	1,990	2,170	50
Zambia	83	2,260	2,000	1,900	50

Source: Food and Agriculture Organization (FAO), *Compendium of Food and Agriculture Indicators: 2003,* (Rome: FAO, 2003); FAO, *The State of Food and Agriculture 2003–04* (Rome: FAO, 2004).

Note: "—" signifies not available.

the environment's carrying capacity. These people are thus using their land beyond its capacity to sustain agricultural production. One estimate suggests that farmers in India, Pakistan, Bangladesh, and West Africa are already farming virtually all the land suitable for agriculture. Unless changes are made soon, production will eventually decline. Millions of acres of barren land will be added to the millions that are already beyond redemption.

Many developing nations rely on fish as their major source of protein. Unfortunately the state of many of the world's fisheries is perilous. Nearly 30 percent of the most important marine fish stocks are depleted, overharvested, or recovering from overharvesting. Almost half are being exploited at their biological limit.[15] So desperate are some subsistence fishers that they rely on cyanide or dynamite to catch the few fish that remain. Although production from aquaculture is increasing, many poor people cannot afford to purchase what they could formerly acquire without the need for cash.

It is important to appreciate as well that the nature of diets changes as nations urbanize. Irrespective of differences in prices and incomes, according to the International Food Policy Research Institute, "urban dwellers consume more wheat and less rice and demand more meat, milk products, and fish than their rural counterparts." This preference leads to increased requirements for grain to feed animals, the need for more space for forage, greater demands for water, and increased pollution from animal waste. Changes in the composition of diets can be anticipated in many countries. In fact, in virtually every low-income country, urbanization is increasing faster than overall population growth (in many instances, three to four times faster).

China provides an illustration of this phenomenon. One recent estimate from the United Nations suggests that the percentage of Chinese living in urban areas doubled, to 40 percent, in just over 25 years. Between 1982 and 2002, the per-capita consumption of meat more than tripled in China (compared with an 18-percent increase in the United States over the same time period).[16]

Increased demand for meat has several environmental consequences. More grain must be produced to feed the livestock and poultry. In a typical year, as much as 35 to 40 percent of the world's grain production is used for animal feed, but the conversion from feed to meat is not a neat one. As many as ten pounds of grain are required to produce one pound of beef. Ruminant livestock need grazing land, which is already in short supply in many areas. Throughout the world, about twice as much land is devoted to animal grazing as is used for crops. If a land's carrying capacity is breached due to excessive exploitation, then the alternative is to use feedlot production, which requires even higher levels of grain and concentrates waste products in smaller areas.

Imports offer a possible solution to deficiencies in domestic production, but here, too, many developing countries encounter problems. To finance imports, countries need foreign exchange, usually acquired through their own exports or from loans. Few developing countries have industrial products or professional services to export, so they must rely on minerals, natural resources (such as timber or petroleum), or cash crops (such as tea, sugar, coffee, cocoa, and rubber).

Economic recessions and declining demand in the developed world cause prices for many of these commodities to fluctuate widely. To cope with declining prices for export crops, farmers are forced to intensify production, which implies increased reliance on fertilizers and pesticides, or to expand the area under cultivation in order to increase production. Unfortunately these seemingly rational reactions are likely to depress prices even further as supply outpaces demand. As the area used for export crops expands, less attention is given to production for domestic consumption.

Opportunities exist to increase exports, but economic policies in the developed world can discourage expanded activity in developing countries. Every year farmers in Japan, Europe, and the United States receive billions of dollars in subsidies and other price-related supports from their governments. In the estimation of the Organization for Economic Cooperation and Development, government aid to farmers in a few developed countries, including Japan, the United States, and the European Union, reached $257 billion in 2003. The U.S. share of this total was almost $39 billion. Subsidies, which represent a portion of this total, reached an historic high in 2000 and provided nearly half of net farm income to U.S. farmers.[17]

Not to be outdone, the European Union spent over $121 billion in 2003 on agricultural supports. Almost half of the European Union's annual budget is devoted to farm subsidies. So large are these supports, noted the president of the World Bank in 2003, that the average European cow received a subsidy of about $2.50 per day, or more than the average daily income of about three billion people.[18] Japanese cows are even more fortunate. They receive a daily subsidy of about $7.50, or more than 1,800 times as much foreign assistance as Japan provides to sub-Saharan Africa each day.

Subsidies often lead to overproduction and surpluses, which discourage imports from developing countries, remove incentives to expand production, encourage the use of environmentally fragile land, and can increase prices to consumers in countries that provide the subsidies. Rice, sugar, cotton, wheat, and peanuts are easily and less expensively grown in many developing countries, but the U.S. government subsidizes U.S. farmers heavily to grow these crops or imposes tariffs on their importation.

Farmers in many European countries typically produce far more milk than can be consumed in these countries, so they often look for opportunities to export the surplus, even at a loss. In Jamaica, this situation has devastated much of the local dairy industry, which cannot compete with the subsidized dairy products, including powdered milk, imported from Europe.

Developing countries are increasingly irritated with trade and agricultural policies that they consider to be discriminatory. In response to a complaint from Brazil, the World Trade Organization (WTO) agreed in 2004 that European subsidies for sugar exports violate international trade rules. This decision followed another WTO decision in which it ruled that U.S. price supports for cotton result in excess production and exports as well as low international prices, thus causing "serious prejudice" to Brazil. African producers of cotton have also called for an end to government support for the production of cotton in developed countries, especially the United States, the world's largest exporter of cotton. Without access to export markets, developing countries are denied their best opportunity for development, which, historically, has provided the best cure for poverty and rapid population growth.

Developing countries could once depend on loans from private banks or foreign governments to help finance imports. Now, however, many developing countries are burdened with massive debts, which reached almost $2.5 trillion in 2002. This debt often cannot be repaid because of faltering economies, as governments in Indonesia, Korea, Russia, and Thailand learned in the late 1990s. Failures to make interest payments are common, and banks are understandably hesitant to lend more money to countries with poor records of repayment.

A common measure of a nation's indebtedness is its debt service, which represents the total payments for interest and principal as a percentage of the country's exports of goods and services. These exports produce the foreign currencies that allow countries to repay their debts and to import foreign products, including food, medicines, petroleum, and machinery. When debt service increases, nations find that more of their export earnings are required to repay loans, and less money is available for development. Many developing nations have encountered this problem, especially in Africa and Latin America. Several of the countries have agreed to write off the debt of some developing countries, but this may have few positive consequences because these countries were not repaying the debt—they cannot afford to do so.

The Destruction of Tropical Forests

Shortages of fuelwood point to a much larger and potentially catastrophic problem: the destruction of tropical forests. The rain forests of Africa, South America, and Southeast Asia are treasure chests of incomparable biological diversity. These forests provide irreplaceable habitats for as much as 80 percent of the world's species of plants and animals, most of which remain to be discovered and described scientifically. More than one-quarter of the prescription drugs used in the United States have their origins in tropical plants. Viable forests also stabilize soils, reduce the impact and incidence of floods, and regulate local climates, watersheds, and river systems.[19] In addition, increasing concern about the effect of excessive levels of carbon dioxide in the atmosphere (the greenhouse effect) underscores the global importance of tropical forests. Through photosynthesis, trees and other plants remove carbon dioxide from the atmosphere and convert it into oxygen.

At the beginning of the twentieth century, tropical forests covered approximately 10 percent of the Earth's surface, or about 5.8 million square miles. The deforestation of recent decades has diminished this area by about one-third. If current rates of deforestation continue unabated, only a few areas of forest will remain untouched. Humans will have destroyed a natural palliative for the greenhouse effect and condemned half of all species to extinction.

Causes and Solutions

Solutions to the problem of tropical deforestation depend on the root cause.[20] One view blames poverty and the pressures associated with growing populations and shifting cultivators. Landless peasants, so the argument goes, invade tropical forests and denude them for fuelwood, for grazing, or to grow crops with which to survive. Frequent clearing of new areas is necessary because tropical soils are typically thin, relatively infertile, and lacking in sufficient nutrients. Such areas are ill suited for sustained agricultural production.

Another explanation for deforestation places primary blame on commercial logging intended to satisfy demands for tropical hardwoods in developed countries. Whether strapped for foreign exchange, required to repay

loans, or subjected to domestic pressure to develop their economies, governments in the developing world frequently regard tropical forests as sources of
ready income. Exports of wood now produce billions of dollars in annual revenues for developing countries, and some countries impose few limits in
their rush to the bank. In Latin America, as an illustration, exports of
unprocessed logs increased by at least 70 percent in the 1990s.

Recognizing the causes and consequences of deforestation is not
enough to bring about a solution. Commercial logging is profitable to those
who own the logging concessions, and few governments in developing countries are equipped to manage their forests properly. These governments often
let logging companies harvest trees in designated areas under certain conditions. All too frequently, however, the conditions are inadequate or not well
enforced.

An Alternative View of the Problem

As the pace of tropical deforestation has quickened, so have international pressures on developing countries to halt or mitigate it. In response,
leaders of developing countries quickly emphasize how ironic it is that developed countries, whose increasing consumption creates the demand for tropical woods, are simultaneously calling for a reduction of logging and shifting
cultivation in developing countries.

In addition, the developing countries correctly note Europe's destruction of its forests during the industrial revolution and the widespread cutting
in the United States in the nineteenth century. Why then should developing
countries be held to a different standard than the developed ones? Just as
Europeans and Americans decided how and when to extract their resources,
developing countries insist that they too should be allowed to determine
their own patterns of consumption.

International collaboration between wood-producing and wood-
consuming nations offers one hope in the battle against deforestation. To
date, however, such collaboration has only a modest record. The International Tropical Timber Organization (ITTO), created in 1983, was on the
brink of collapse just a few years later.[21] Several importing nations had
refused to pay their full dues, Japanese importers boycotted ITTO meetings,
and the organization could claim few accomplishments other than its ten-
uous survival. The ITTO issued best-practice guidelines for the management of tropical forests in 1990; it asked all countries to adhere to these
guidelines by 2000 and to ensure that all exports of tropical timber after that
year be from sustainably managed forests. Less than a year later the ITTO
weakened its objective and asked that its member countries merely progress
toward achieving sustainable management of tropical forests by 2000. No
producing country achieved the original goal by that year.

A review of progress in late 2000 concluded that it is nearly impossible
to estimate how many tropical forests are managed sustainably, although
some estimates are as low as 1 percent.[22] In addition, the review noted that,

although many timber-producing nations have developed new policies for their forests and forestry, little evidence indicates that the policies are being implemented.

Will tropical forests survive? Solutions abound. What is lacking, however, is a consensus about which of these solutions will best meet the essential needs of the poor, the reasonable objectives of timber-exporting and timber-importing nations, and the inflexible imperatives of ecological stability.

Fortunately there is a growing realization that much can be done to stem the loss of tropical forests. For example, many countries have developed national forest programs that describe the status of their forests as well as strategies to preserve them for future generations. Unfortunately, implementation of these plans does not always parallel the good intentions associated with them. Likewise, rather than seeing forests solely as a source of wood or additional agricultural land, many countries are now examining the export potential of forest products other than wood. The expectation is that the sale of these products—such as cork, rattan, oils, resins, and medicinal plants—will provide economic incentives to maintain rather than destroy forests.

Other proposed options to maintain tropical forests include programs to certify that timber exports are from sustainably managed forests. Importers and potential consumers would presumably avoid timber products without such certification. For such programs to be successful, however, exporters would have to accept the certification process and there would have to be widespread agreement about what sustainable management means. That agreement is still absent. In addition, no country would want to subject itself to the process only to be told that its timber exports do not meet the requirements for certification or to learn that less-expensive timber is available from a country that does not participate in the certification program.

Another approach would impose taxes on timber exports (or imports). The highest taxes would be imposed on logging that causes the greatest ecological costs; timber from sustainable operations would face the lowest taxes. Yet another option would increase reliance on community-based management of forest resources. Rather than allowing logging companies with no long-term interest in a forest to harvest trees, community-based management would place responsibility for decisions about logging (and other uses) with the people who live in or adjacent to forests. These people have the strongest incentives to manage forest resources wisely, particularly if they reap the long-term benefits of their management strategies.

Conflicting Signals from the Industrial Nations

Improvements in the policies of many developing countries are surely necessary if sustainable development is to be achieved. As already noted, however, industrial countries sometimes cause or contribute to environmental problems there.

Patterns of consumption provide an example. Although the United States and other industrial nations can boast about their own low rates of population growth, developing nations reply that patterns of consumption, not population increases, are the real culprits. This view suggests that negative impacts on the environment are a function of population growth plus consumption and technology.

Applying this formula places major responsibility for environmental problems on rich nations, despite their relatively small numbers of global inhabitants. The inhabitants of these nations consume far more of the Earth's resources than their numbers justify. Consider that the richest one-quarter of the world's nations control about 75 percent of the world's income (and, according to the UN Development Programme, the richest 10 percent of Americans have a combined income greater than two billion of the world's poorest people). In addition, these nations consume a disproportionate share of all meat and fish and most of the world's energy, paper, chemicals, iron, and steel. These few nations similarly generate more than 90 percent of all hazardous and industrial wastes. The United States leads the world in per-capita production of trash and has one of the lowest rates of recycling among industrialized countries. Consider as well that these rich nations, most able to afford pollution control and conservation, produce at least two-thirds of all greenhouse gases.[23]

In contrast, consumption patterns among the 20 percent of the world's population living in the lowest income countries account for less than 1.5 percent of the world's private consumption and only about 5 percent of the world's consumption of meat and fish. According to the UN Development Programme, consumption declined in seventy countries between the early 1970s and the mid-1990s.[24]

Comparing such a decline with the situation in the United States is instructive. Americans represent less than 5 percent of the Earth's inhabitants, yet they consume almost one-quarter of the world's commercial energy. Much of this energy is used to fuel Americans' love for the automobile. Whereas Americans increased their numbers by about 20 percent in the 1970s and 1980s, the total number of automobiles in use in the United States grew by more than 50 percent. There are now more vehicles than licensed drivers in the United States, and the average horsepower of the typical American vehicle doubled between 1980 and 2004.[25] American drivers also encounter some of the world's lowest prices for gasoline and consume more than five times as much of it per year as the typical European. Despite many Americans' belief that gasoline prices are outrageously high, the price of gasoline in much of western Europe is about than two and one-half times higher than in the United States.

Although the United States made sizable gains in fuel efficiency in the 1970s and 1980s, many of these gains are being eroded as Americans drive faster and farther, and as they increasingly rely on sport utility vehicles rather than cars. In 1980, small cars represented about 43 percent of all new vehicles purchased; by 2004 this percentage was less than 25. As a result, the fuel economy of 2003 model year vehicles sold in the United States was lower than in 1982. An average increase of just a few miles per gallon would decrease annual emissions of carbon dioxide by more than 100 million metric tons per year.[26] Since 1999, transportation has been the largest single source of carbon dioxide emissions in the United States.

Americans' profligacy with fossil fuels provides part of the explanation for U.S. production of more than one-fifth of the emissions that contribute to global warming. With the exception of a few ministates, no country produces as many metric tons of carbon dioxide per capita as does the United States, which produced 20 metric tons versus 6.8 and 9.4 metric tons per capita in France and the United Kingdom, respectively, in 2002.[27]

Americans' patterns of food consumption are also of interest. As noted in Table 15-2, an average American consumes over 3,700 calories per day, one of the highest levels in the world. About one-sixth of these calories come from sugars. Not surprisingly, almost two-thirds of American adults are either obese or overweight. One study, released in early 2004, noted that American teenagers had higher rates of obesity than did teenagers in each of the other fourteen countries included in the study. Weight-related illnesses are responsible for the deaths of more Americans each year than are motor vehicle accidents. The United States (along with Denmark and New Zealand) leads the world in annual per-capita meat consumption. Few nations waste as much food as does the United States. The U.S. Department of Agriculture once estimated that Americans waste about 96 billion pounds of edible food each year—about one-quarter of all the food available to them and about a pound a day for each American.[28]

As environmental scholar Paul Harrison notes, because of such inequalities in consumption, continued population growth in rich countries is a greater threat to the global environment than is such growth in the developing world. He adds that if relative consumption and levels of waste output remain unchanged, the 57 million extra inhabitants born in rich countries in the 1990s will pollute the globe more than the extra 900 million born elsewhere. Other experts suggest that if Americans want to maintain their present standard of living and levels of energy consumption, then their ideal population is between 40 and 100 million, far less than the mid-2004 U.S. population of about 294 million.[29]

Causes for Optimism?

Although there is cause for concern about the prospects for sustainable development among developing countries, the situation is neither entirely bleak nor beyond hope. Millions of people throughout the world have been the beneficiaries of considerable social and economic development. The number of chronically malnourished people in developing countries declined by more than 150 million between 1970 and 1990, and by another 40 million by 1996–1998. The number of families in developing countries with access to sanitary facilities and clean water surged in the 1990s. Smallpox, a killer of millions of people every year in the 1950s, has been eradicated (except in laboratories). Polio may soon be the next scourge to be eliminated. Between 1970 and 2002, infant mortality rates declined in nearly all developing countries—in many by significant amounts.

Further recognition of the global challenges associated with development came in 2000, when all members of the United Nations adopted eight Millennium Development Goals and agreed to achieve them by 2015. These goals seek to eradicate extreme poverty and hunger; achieve universal primary education; promote gender equity; reduce child mortality; improve maternal health; combat HIV/AIDs, malaria, and other diseases; ensure environmental sustainability; and develop a global partnership for development. Progress has already been made in many of the areas, and the World Bank was able to report that the economies of all developing regions were growing faster in the early 2000s than their average growth rates of the 1980s and 1990s. Far more important, the Bank was optimistic that such growth, even if it moderated slightly, could halve the incidence of poverty in many developing countries by 2015.[30]

In another positive sign, in response to pressure from developing countries and through the auspices of the WTO, the United States and the European Union agreed, in 2004, to substantial reductions in agricultural supports for their farmers. The Europeans agreed to the eventual elimination of all export subsidies, and the United States said it would reduce export credits for cotton and reduce subsidies for corn, rice, wheat, and soybeans.

The international community is also demonstrating recognition of the Earth's ecological interconnectedness. The World Commission on Environment and Development was established in 1983 and charged with formulating long-term environmental strategies for achieving sustainable development. In its report, *Our Common Future,* the commission forcefully emphasized that although environmental degradation is an issue of survival for developing nations, failure to address the degradation satisfactorily will guarantee unparalleled and undesirable global consequences from which no nation will escape.[31] The report's release in 1987 prompted increased international attention to environmental issues.

This attention manifested itself most noticeably in the UN Conference on Environment and Development in Rio de Janeiro, Brazil, in 1992 and a World Summit on Sustainable Development in Johannesburg, South Africa, in 2002. The 1992 conference led to the creation of the UN Commission on Sustainable Development, which meets annually to review nations' efforts to implement international environmental agreements and their progress in achieving sustainable development.[32]

Delegates at the Rio conference also approved Agenda 21, a plan for enhancing global environmental quality. The price tag for the recommended actions is huge. Rich nations could provide the amount needed to meet the goals of Agenda 21 if they donated as little as 0.70 percent (*not* 7 percent, but seven-tenths of 1 percent) of their gross national income to the developing world each year. Only Denmark, Luxembourg, the Netherlands,

Norway, and Sweden exceeded this target in 2003. Belgium, Finland, and Ireland pledged to move toward the recommended target, but U.S. foreign aid was less than 0.15 percent of its gross national income in 2003. U.S. foreign aid was thus well below the target level and the lowest among twenty-two advanced industrial countries, leading one observer to label the United States as the "global Scrooge."

Of the U.S. aid that is provided, much is given to further U.S. foreign policy objectives rather than to help the poorest countries and those most in need. Egypt and Israel are annually among the largest recipients of U.S. aid. Much U.S. foreign aid never leaves the United States because American firms are hired to implement aid programs, and "Buy American" provisions often require recipients to purchase U.S. products. Moreover, according to several opinion surveys, most Americans believe that the U.S. government provides far more assistance than it actually does to poor countries.[33] This belief may explain why a large number of Americans also think that U.S. foreign assistance should be reduced.

In contrast to Americans' seeming reluctance to share their wealth, other nations have demonstrated an increased willingness to address globally shared environmental problems. The international community now operates a Global Environment Facility, a multibillion-dollar effort to finance environmental projects in developing countries. It distributes funds to address global warming, loss of biological diversity, pollution of international waters, and depletion of the ozone layer.

In addition, more than 165 countries have ratified the Convention on Biological Diversity (although not the United States, the only major industrialized country not to have done so).[34] Participating nations meet regularly to discuss accomplishments and next steps. Many of these nations approved a Convention to Combat Desertification in late 1996. The next year, representatives from more than 160 countries met in Kyoto, Japan, to discuss implementation of the 1992 UN Framework Convention on Climate Change, which 188 countries have ratified. In an historic agreement, the Kyoto Protocol, industrialized nations agreed to reduce emissions that contribute to global warming by an average of about 5 percent below 1990 levels in the five-year period from 2008 to 2012. The United States agreed to reduce these emissions by 7 percent and the European Union by 8 percent.

According to many scientists, the protocol was more than timely. An international panel of scientists endorsed a report predicting a future of catastrophic floods, droughts, and violent storms because of global warming.[35] Even so, and despite a campaign pledge to impose stringent limits on emissions of the greenhouse gas carbon dioxide, President Bush reversed himself soon after taking office in 2001. Asserting that he would not do anything to harm the U.S. economy, Bush declared that the United States would not comply with the provisions of the Kyoto Protocol (see chapter 13). With Russia's ratification of the protocol in November 2004, however, the protocol had enough signatories for its requirements to take effect in February 2005.

As a result, thirty industrialized countries are now legally bound to reduce or limit their greenhouse emissions.

Many developing nations recognize their obligations to protect their environments as well as the global commons. At the same time, however, these nations argue that success requires technical and financial assistance from their wealthy colleagues. However desirable the protection of tropical forests and biological diversity and the prevention of global warming and a depleted ozone layer, the poor nations cannot afford to address these problems in the absence of cooperation from richer nations. The prospects for achieving such cooperation are uncertain. Developing nations such as China and India want to provide refrigerators to as many of their inhabitants as possible. These hundreds of millions of refrigerators will require extraordinary amounts of chlorofluorocarbons (CFCs) unless companies in developed nations are willing to share the commercial secrets associated with substitutes for the CFCs. These companies are reluctant to do so, arguing that they are in business to make money, not to give away valuable trade secrets.

This reluctance has important consequences. China's economic growth since the mid-1980s boosted its share of the world's CFC emissions from 3 percent in 1986 to nearly 13 percent in 1999. From 1990 to 1997 alone, China's emissions of carbon into the atmosphere increased by more than 35 percent, and its consumption of petroleum nearly doubled between 1992 and 2002. This pattern of growth continues. Between 1999 and 2003, China accounted for about 40 percent of the total increase in world demand for petroleum, and the U.S. Energy Information Administration estimates that Chinese demand for petroleum will more than double between 2003 and 2025.

China's emissions of gases that contribute to global warming will also increase rapidly as the country continues to industrialize. If recent projections are accurate, China will provide the world's largest absolute increases in carbon dioxide emissions between 2000 and 2020. China has vast reserves of coal, which are used to produce as much as 80 percent of the country's electricity, often without the pollution control devices typically installed on power plants elsewhere. The consumption of electricity in China is expected to triple between 1995 and 2015. Unfortunately the Chinese are among the least efficient users of energy in the world. They consume about three times as much energy per dollar of GDP as the world average and twice the average for all developing countries.[36]

The economic, population, and environmental problems of the developing world dwarf those of the industrial nations and are not amenable to quick resolution. Nonetheless, immediate action is imperative. Millions of people are steadily destroying their biological and environmental support systems at unprecedented rates in order to meet their daily needs for food, fuel, and fiber. Driven by poverty and the need to survive, they have become ravenous leeches on a planet approaching the limits of its tolerance and resilience. Whether this situation will change depends on the ability of residents in the developing countries not only to reap the benefits of sustained development but also to meet the demands of current populations while using their natural resources in a way that accommodates the needs of future generations. Unless the developing nations are able to do so soon, their future will determine ours as well. In the past, we reaped the benefits associated with pollution. Unless we act soon and in collaboration with other nations, Americans may increasingly suffer the consequences of pollution from these countries without the corresponding benefits. In short, it is both naive and unreasonable to assume that the consequences of population growth, environmental degradation, and abysmal poverty in developing countries will remain within their political boundaries.[37] Just as the events of September 11, 2001, demonstrated to us, our lives and our future are not always ours to chart or plan. Similarly, we must appreciate that our ecological future depends on others as much as ourselves.

Notes

1. World Bank, *World Development Report 2004: Making Services Work for Poor People* (New York: Oxford University Press, 2004), 252–253, www.econ.worldbank.org/wdr/wdr2004/text-30023/; and World Bank, *Global Economic Prospects: Overview and Global Outlook* (Washington, D.C.: World Bank, 2005), 22. Due to differences in the costs of goods and services from one country to another, GNP per capita does not provide comparable measures of economic well-being. To address this problem, economists have developed a measure that reflects purchasing-power parity (PPP). Such a measure attempts to equalize the prices of identical goods and services across all countries, with the United States as the base economy. For an explanation and application of the PPP concept, see the "Big Mac Index" of *The Economist,* at www.economist.com, which compares the price of a McDonald's Big Mac hamburger in more than sixty countries.
2. UNICEF, *Early Marriage: Child Spouses* (Florence, Italy: UNICEF, 2001), www.unicef-icdc.org/publications/pdf/digest7e.pdf.
3. UNICEF, *The State of the World's Children 2004* (New York: Oxford University Press, 2004), www.unicef.org/sowc04. UNICEF's annual report on this subject is an excellent source of information about the status of children in developing countries. Other sources of information about the environment and development include the UN Development Programme's annual report on human development, http://hdr.undp.org; the Food and Agriculture Organization, www.fao.org; and the World Bank's annual *World Development Report,* www.econ.worldbank.org/wdr.
4. "A Great Wall of Waste," *The Economist,* August 21, 2004, 56; Elizabeth C. Economy, *The River Runs Black: The Environmental Challenge to China's Future* (Ithaca, N.Y.: Cornell University Press, 2004).
5. World Commission on Environment and Development, *Our Common Future* (London: Oxford University Press, 1987), 8, 43.
6. John N. Wilford, "A Tough-Minded Ecologist Comes to Defense of Malthus," *New York Times,* June 30, 1987, C3.
7. Population Reference Bureau, "2004 World Population Data Sheet" (Washington, D.C.: Population Reference Bureau), www.prb.org/pdf04/04WorldDataSheet_Eng.pdf. See also Paul Ehrlich and Anne Ehrlich, *Extinction* (New York: Random House, 1981), 243. For a discussion of the world's carrying capacity, see Vaclav Smil, "How Many People Can the Earth Feed?" *Population and Development Review* 2 (June 1994): 255–292.
8. Lester R. Brown, "Analyzing the Demographic Trap," in *State of the World 1987,* ed. Lester R. Brown (New York: Norton, 1987), 20.

9. For a discussion of India's family planning programs, see Sharon L. Camp and Shanti R. Conly, *India's Family Planning Challenge: From Rhetoric to Action* (Washington, D.C.: Population Crisis Committee, 1992).

10. UN Population Fund, "Report of the China Independent Assessment Team," (2002) at www.unfpa.org/news/related_docs/usfundingreport03.pdf. See also Elisabeth Rosenthal, "For One-Child Policy, China Rethinks Iron Hand," *New York Times*, November 1, 1998, A1; Hannah Beech, "China's Lifestyle Choice," *Time*, August 6, 2001, 32.

11. For example, see Julian Simon, *The Ultimate Resource* (Princeton: Princeton University Press, 1981).

12. Stephen Klasen and Claudia Wink, "A Turning Point in Gender Bias in Mortality?: An Update on the Number of 'Missing Women'," Department of Economics, University of Munich, Discussion Paper 2001-13, October 2001, http://epub.ub .uni-muenchen.de/archive/00000023; Amartya Sen, "Missing Women—Revisited," *British Medical Journal*, December 6, 2003, 1297–1298, http://bmj.bmjjournals.com /cgi/reprint/327/7427/1297.

13. Brown, *State of the World 1987*, 21.

14. Per Pinstrup-Anderson, former director general of the International Food Policy Research Institute, believes the world can easily feed 12 billion people 100 years from now. See "Will the World Starve?" *The Economist*, June 10, 1995, 39.

15. UN Development Programme, UN Environment Programme, World Bank, and World Resources Institute (WRI), *World Resources, 2000–2001: People and Ecosystems* (Washington, D.C.: WRI, 2000), 48, www.wri.org/wr2000. See also Yumiko Kura, Carmen Revenga, Eriko Hoshino, and Greg Mock, *Fishing for Answers: Making Sense of the Global Fish Crisis* (Washington, D.C.: WRI, 2004), http://pubs.wri.org /pubs_pdf.cfm?PubID=3866.

16. "China's Growth Spreads Inland," *The Economist*, November 20, 2004, 13; FAO, FAOSTAT Database, "Food Supply, Livestock and Fish Primary Equivalent," http://faostat.fao.org/faostat/collections?subset=nutrition.

17. Organization for Economic Cooperation and Development (OECD), *Agricultural Policies in OECD Countries: At a Glance 2004* (OECD: Paris, 2004). U.S. Government Accountability Office (GAO, formerly the General Accounting Office), *Farm Programs: Information on Recipients of Federal Programs*, GAO-01-606 (Washington, D.C.: GAO, 2001), www.gao.gov.

18. David T. Cook, "Excerpts from a Monitor Breakfast on Poverty and Globalization," http://video.csmonitor.com/2003/0613/p25s02-usmb.htm.

19. National Academy of Sciences (NAS), *Population Growth and Economic Development: Policy Questions* (Washington, D.C.: NAS, 1986), 31; FAO, Committee on Food Development in the Tropics, *Tropical Forest Action Plan* (Rome: FAO, 1985), 2, 47.

20. For useful discussions of the causes of deforestation, see Helmut J. Geist and Eric Lambin, "Proximate Causes and Underlying Driving Forces of Tropical Deforestation," *BioScience*, 52 (February 2002): 143–150; and John Roper and Ralph W. Roberts, "Deforestation: Tropical Forests in Decline," (1999), a report by the Canadian International Development Agency, www.rcfa-cfan.org/english/deforestation .htm.

21. Marcus Colchester, "The International Tropical Timber Organization: Kill or Cure for the Rainforest?" *Ecologist* (September–October 1990).

22. Duncan Poore and Thang Hooi Chiew, *Review of Progress towards the Year 2000 Objective* (Yokohama, Japan: International Tropical Timber Council, 2000), www.itto.or .jp/inside/report.html#review.

23. UN Development Programme, *Human Development Report 1998*, 2, http://hdr .undp.org; "Trash as Treasure," *Washington Post*, October 17, 1998, A14; UN Development Programme, *World Resources 2000–2001*, table ERC.5.

24. UN Development Programme, *Human Development Report 1998*, 7.

25. Jonathan Weisman, "No Guzzle, No Glory," *Washington Post,* June 13, 2004, F1; "At $2 a Gallon, Gas Is Still Worth Guzzling," *New York Times,* May 16, 2004, 14.

26. U.S. Environmental Protection Agency (EPA), *Light-Duty Automotive Technology and Fuel Economy Trends: 1975 through 2004,* (Washington, D.C.: EPA, 2004), A-6, http://epa.gov/otaq/fetrends.htm.

27. U.S. Department of Energy, Energy Information Administration, *International Energy Annual 2002,* June 2004, www.eia.doe.gov/pub/international/iealf/tableh1cco2.xls

28. Nancy Hellrich, "Six in 10 in USA Weigh Too Much," *USA Today,* October 9, 2002, A1; "U.S. Teens Fattest in 15-Nation Study," *Washington Post,* January 6, 2004, A6; Linda Scott Kantor, Kathryn Lipton, Alden Manchester, and Victor Oliveira, "Estimating and Addressing America's Food Losses," *Food Review,* 20 (January–April 1997).

29. Paul Harrison, *The Third Revolution: Environment, Population and a Sustainable World* (New York: I. B. Taurus, 1992), 256–257; David Pimentel and Marcia Pimentel, "Land, Energy and Water: The Constraints Governing Ideal U.S. Population Size," *NPG Forum* (January 1990), 5.

30. Information on the Millennium Development Goals and their implementation can be found at www.un.org/millenniumgoals. World Bank, *Global Economic Prospects,* 2.

31. World Commission on Environment and Development, *Our Common Future.*

32. *Linkages—A Multimedia Resource for Environment and Development Policy Makers* (www.iisd.ca/) provides a handy way to remain informed about the formulation and implementation of international environmental agreements.

33. See Chicago Council on Foreign Relations and German Marshall Fund of the United States, "American Public Opinion and Foreign Policy," (2002) www.worldviews .org/detailreports/usreport/index.htm; and Program on International Policy Attitudes, "Americans on Foreign Aid and World Hunger: A Study of U.S. Public Attitudes," February 2, 2001, www.pipa.org/OnlineReports/BFW/introduction.html. For an extended treatment of U.S. foreign assistance, see Paul G. Harris, "International Development Assistance and Burden Sharing," in *Green Giants? Environmental Policies of the United States and the European Union,* ed. Norman J. Vig and Michael G. Faure (Cambridge: MIT Press, 2004). The OECD's Development Assistance Committee tracks information on nations' expenditures for development assistance at www.oecd.org/home.

34. In addition to not ratifying the Kyoto Protocol, the United States also has not ratified international treaties on war crimes, land mines, arms control, the rights of children, the prohibition on the execution of juveniles, and the elimination of discrimination against women.

35. Philip P. Pan, "Scientists Issue Dire Prediction on Warming," *Washington Post,* January 23, 2001, A1.

36. U.S. Energy Information Administration, "The People of China," www.eia.doe.gov /emeu/cabs/china/part1.html.

37. Lester R. Brown and Christopher Flavin, "A New Economy for a New Century," in *State of the World 1999,* ed. Lester R. Brown (New York: Norton, 1999), 3–21.

16

International Trade and Environmental Regulation

David Vogel

Neither environmental nor trade issues figured prominently in the 2004 presidential election campaign. Nevertheless, John Kerry and George W. Bush held different positions with respect to both policy areas. Kerry, along with much of the environmental community, was sharply critical of the president's environmental record. Green groups called Bush the "Toxic Texan," and the League of Conservation Voters stated that "George Bush is well on his way to compiling the worst environmental record in the history of our nation."[1] Kerry made a number of well-received speeches in which he attacked the Bush administration for trying to weaken the nation's environmental laws and regulations. Kerry also criticized the president's support of free trade, arguing that the outsourcing of American jobs threatened the future of the American middle class. He promised, if elected, to review each of the nation's current trade agreements. He suggested furthermore that it was important that these agreements contain labor and environmental provisions to prevent American workers from being disadvantaged by imports from countries whose weaker labor and environmental standards gave them an unfair competitive advantage.

Kerry's policy proposals reflected his outreach to trade unions and environmentalists, both of whom have become critical of trade liberalization, though for different reasons. Yet the differences between the two candidates on the importance of linking trade policy and environmental regulation were more rhetorical than substantive. As this chapter demonstrates, the Bush administration has sought to include environmental provisions in trade agreements negotiated by the United States. The obstacles to doing so are more the result of opposition from developing countries than from American industry.

This chapter begins by explaining why the two policy areas of trade and environment have become more closely linked. It then reviews environmentalists' criticisms of trade liberalization. The next three sections explore the politics surrounding environmental dimensions of the General Agreement on Tariffs and Trade (GATT), the World Trade Organization (WTO), and the North American Free Trade Agreement (NAFTA). It then addresses the contemporary politics of trade and environmental linkages in the United States and their role in the trade agreements both negotiated and being negotiated by United States. The concluding section examines the debate over the impact of trade liberalization on environmental quality.

The Growth of Policy Linkages

The growth of policy linkages between the formerly distinct policy areas of trade and environmental regulation is related to the convergence of two contemporary trends: an increase in the volume of world trade and an increase in the amount and scope of environmental regulation.[2]

Thanks to the GATT and the WTO at the global level, and to other treaties and agreements at a regional level, such as those associated with the European Union (EU), tariff levels have declined steadily since World War II. As a consequence, trade negotiations have begun to pay greater attention to nontariff barriers (NTBs)—government policies that discriminate against imports through means other than tariffs. Examples of NTBs include quotas, procurement policies favoring domestic producers, and subsidies. Another important category of NTBs consists of government regulations and, more specific to the topic of this chapter, environmental standards. Many of these regulations, often inadvertently but sometimes intentionally, restrict trade by imposing greater burdens on foreign producers than on domestic ones.

Accordingly, reducing the role of government regulations as obstacles to trade has become an important priority of both regional and international trade negotiations and agreements. In the second half of the 1980s, for example, the EU's precursor, the European Community (EC), chose to harmonize many environmental and consumer regulations to prevent them from being used to restrict trade among member states. EC law also required its member states to admit any product approved for use in another member state. Likewise, a major result of the Uruguay Round GATT negotiations, which created the World Trade Organization in 1995, was to strengthen the Standards Code, originally established in 1979 to prevent national standards from serving as "technical barriers to trade." NAFTA also includes a number of provisions that seek to restrict its members (Canada, Mexico, and the United States) from using NTBs to undermine regional economic integration.

Economic integration has thus subjected to both regional and international scrutiny an increasing number of public policies that were formally the exclusive purview of national governments. Trade liberalization has made the politics of environmental protection more global: It means that governments, in formulating their environmental policies, must now take into account the impact of these policies not only on national producers but also on their foreign competitors. At the same time—as the trade disputes discussed in this chapter illustrate—trade agreements have provided foreign producers with a legal vehicle for challenging the domestic regulations of their trading partners, if those regulations appear to unfairly discriminate against their exports. Consequently, agreements to expand trade have frequently challenged national regulatory sovereignty.

The second trend fostering increased policy linkages between trade and regulation has been the steady expansion of environmental regulation.

Since around 1970 the number of government regulations that directly or indirectly affect traded goods has increased significantly. These regulations include automobile emissions standards; rules governing the content and disposal of packaging; chemical safety regulations; regulations for the processing, composition, and labeling of food; and rules to protect wildlife and natural resources. The steady growth of protective regulations has forced exporters to cope with an increasingly diverse and complex array of national standards, many of which have made trade more difficult. Because nations generally want to maintain their own standards in spite of—or sometimes because of—the burdens they impose on imports, the continual growth of national environmental regulations represents a growing source of trade conflict.

The geographic scope of environmental policy has also changed. Many environmental issues have taken on a global dimension that requires the coordination of national regulatory policies. These issues include saving endangered species located in foreign lands or international waters, protecting the ozone layer, safeguarding the shipment and disposal of hazardous wastes, and preserving tropical forests in developing countries. The coordination associated with international environmental agreements often involves trade restrictions, either as a means to prevent "free riding" or because the harm itself is trade related.

As a result of the expansion of both trade and regulation, the debate between supporters of environmental regulation and advocates of free trade has become more visible and more contentious. Free trade advocates want to limit the use of regulations as barriers to trade, whereas environmentalists and consumer advocates want to prevent trade agreements from serving as barriers to regulation. The trade community worries about an upsurge of so-called eco-protectionism—the justification of trade barriers on environmental grounds. For their part, consumer and environmental organizations fear that trade liberalization will weaken their own countries' regulatory standards as well as those of their trading partners.

Environmentalists and Free Trade

Many environmental groups have become increasingly critical of treaties and trade agreements that promote liberalization. As one activist put it, "When they call me protectionist, I respond, 'Well, if protecting the earth, if protecting the air, if protecting the water, and indeed human life is protectionist, then I have to admit I am protectionist.' "[3] Although their views are by no means uniform, those within the environmental community share a number of criticisms of free trade.

A primary concern of environmentalists is that growing international competition will weaken national regulatory standards. As tariffs and other trade barriers between developed and developing nations fall, producers in the developed nations are increasingly forced to compete with goods produced in nations with laxer standards. Environmentalists fear that producers in industrial nations will demand the relaxation of their countries' regulatory standards in order to remain competitive; alternatively, they may relocate their production to so-called pollution havens, thus giving developing nations a still greater incentive to keep their standards lax or even to lower them further. Hence, environmentalists are concerned that trade liberalization is likely to result in a regulatory "race to the bottom" as nations compete with one another by weakening their environmental standards.

They also worry that trade liberalization is directly harming environmental quality. Trade liberalization increases the level of global economic activity; indeed, that is among its major purposes. But the Earth's ability to sustain current levels of economic growth could be limited. By increasing the rate at which the Earth's scarce natural resources such as forests, fossil fuels, and fisheries are consumed, free trade is said to undermine sustainable development. Liberal trade policies may also indirectly contribute to the greenhouse effect by stimulating an increase in the use of fossil fuels, thus endangering the welfare of the entire planet. Finally, environmentalists worry that accelerating the rate at which goods and raw materials are transported around the world increases not only energy use but also the likelihood of accidents such as oil or chemical spills in international waters.

The General Agreement on Tariffs and Trade (GATT)

The Tuna-Dolphin Case

Environmentalists have been particularly critical of international trade rules that limit a signatory nation's ability to use trade measures to influence the environmental policies of its trading partners. This was a central issue in the tuna-dolphin case, the most visible and controversial trade-dispute panel decision in the GATT's nearly fifty-year history. Indeed, environmental opposition to the Uruguay Round GATT agreement was largely a reaction to the 1991 decision that declared sections of the Marine Mammal Protection Act to be in violation of U.S. obligations under the GATT.

In the eastern tropical Pacific, where approximately one-quarter of the world's tuna is harvested, dolphins commonly swim above schools of tuna. As a result, the large purse-seine nets used to catch tuna also kill large numbers of dolphins. By the late 1960s, dolphin fatalities had reached roughly 500,000 per year. To protect dolphins, the United States imposed limits on the number of dolphins that could be killed annually by U.S. commercial tuna-fishing vessels.

By the late 1980s, thanks to the tightening of U.S. regulatory standards, along with various improvements in fishing technology, incidental dolphin mortality by U.S.-registered vessels had declined by more than 90 percent. Foreign fishing fleets, however, continued to kill dolphins at a higher rate than did their U.S. counterparts. A major portion of these tuna was then exported to the U.S. market, which accounts for approximately half of global tuna consumption. Following a 1990 federal court decision, the United

States prohibited imports of tuna from Mexico, Venezuela, and the Pacific islands of Vanuatu. This embargo affected approximately $30 million worth of tuna imports annually.

Mexico challenged the U.S. embargo on the grounds that GATT rules prohibit a nation from using trade policies to affect regulatory policies outside its legal jurisdiction. The GATT dispute panel ruled in favor of Mexico. According to the panel, GATT rules permit signatory nations to issue regulations to protect their own citizens or land. Thus a nation can impose whatever restrictions it wishes on products consumed within its borders—provided they do not discriminate between foreign and domestic products—as well as on the production of goods or natural resources within its borders. The panel ruled, however, that a nation cannot regulate how foreign nationals produce goods or raw materials outside its legal jurisdiction. Accordingly, the United States cannot dictate to Mexico how it can harvest tuna: It cannot make access to its domestic market contingent on Mexico adopting dolphin protection practices similar to its own.

This decision outraged U.S. environmentalists. As an article in the magazine of the Sierra Club put it, "Meeting in a closed room in Geneva . . . three unelected trade experts . . . conspired to kill Flipper."[4] An environmental activist predicted: "In the 1990s, free trade and efforts to protect the environment are on a collision course."[5] Lori Wallach, a spokesperson for Congress Watch, a public interest lobbying group founded by Ralph Nader, proclaimed, "This case is the smoking gun. We have seen GATT actually declaring that a U.S. environmental law must go. These [trade] agreements must be modified to allow for legitimate consumer and environmental protections."[6]

Environmentalists specifically argued that the GATT dispute panel ruling rested on an artificial and outdated distinction between domestic and extrajurisdictional environmental regulations. They claimed that because all humanity shares a common biosphere, the U.S. environment *is* adversely affected by the killing of dolphins by Mexican fishing fleets, even if it takes place in international waters. As two environmental lawyers argued, "The panel's domestic limitation is nonsensical because it fails to take into account the fact that domestic environmental harms are now, increasingly, being traced to actions occurring beyond a nation's borders. Limiting the reach of a nation's environmental laws to domestic activities substantially undercuts its ability to protect itself from adverse extraterritorial activities."[7] Moreover, "the GATT's focus on 'products' makes it virtually incapable of capturing the environmental costs of externalities related to methods of production."[8]

In May 1992 the United States, Mexico, and eight other tuna-catching nations signed the first major international accord to protect dolphins. This agreement was endorsed by the Earth Island Institute and other U.S. environmental organizations. In October 1992 Congress approved the International Dolphin Conservation Act, which authorized the United States to pursue an international agreement to establish a global moratorium on the use of purse-seine nets that encircle dolphins and provided for an embargo of up to 40 percent of a nation's fish exports to enforce compliance. David Phillips, executive director of the Save the Dolphins Project at the Earth Island Institute, described the legislation as "a breakthrough proposal for dolphins."[9]

After three years of intensive negotiations, a compromise was reached between the United States and the Latin American nations whose vessels fished in the eastern tropical Pacific. In exchange for allowing their tuna to be sold in the United States, Mexico and ten other countries pledged to cap their annual dolphin kill at five thousand animals per year. This compromise bitterly divided the environmental community. A number of important environmental organizations including Greenpeace and the World Wildlife Fund supported it on the grounds that opening U.S. markets was the best way to encourage more countries to fish in a dolphin-friendly manner. However, eighty-five environmental and animal rights groups strongly opposed the compromise because they viewed it as a trade treaty masquerading as environmental policy. After intensive lobbying by the Mexican government and Bill Clinton's administration, legislation was enacted in the summer of 1997 that ended the seven-year tuna embargo.

The CAFE Dispute

After the Uruguay Round negotiations were concluded, but before the Uruguay Round agreement was voted on by Congress, a GATT dispute panel issued a decision in a second trade dispute involving a challenge to a U.S. environmental regulation. The EU had requested the convening of a dispute panel to determine the GATT consistency of three U.S. automobile regulations and taxes, namely corporate average fuel economy (CAFE) standards, the so-called gas-guzzler tax, and a tax on luxury cars. The former two were environmental/conservation measures, whereas the third was revenue related. The EU claimed that all three measures were discriminatory because their burdens fell disproportionately on European car exports to the United States. Although vehicles manufactured in Europe accounted for only 4 percent of U.S. car sales in 1991, they contributed 88 percent of the revenues collected by these measures.

Of the three regulations and taxes addressed in the EU's complaint, CAFE was the most politically important. Established in 1975 in the midst of the energy crisis, and subsequently tightened in 1980, CAFE standards are designed to promote fuel efficiency. They are based on the miles per gallon achieved by the sales-weighted average of all vehicles sold by each manufacturer. If a manufacturer's vehicles fall below this standard, they are subject to a substantial financial penalty. Although the penalty applies equally to all carmakers doing business in the United States, it has been paid exclusively by European firms. U.S. and Japanese firms have been able to avoid CAFE penalties by averaging their smaller, more fuel-efficient vehicles with their larger, less fuel-efficient ones. However, the European car manufacturers do not have this option because they export only inefficient, luxury vehicles to the United States; they have no smaller cars to bring up the average fuel-efficiency of their fleet.

The *Financial Times* predicted that "should the United States lose this case, it would face as much outcry as the so-called 'tuna-dolphin decision.' "[10] However, in October 1994, the GATT dispute panel ruled in favor of the United States. It concluded that product regulations were GATT consistent as long as they did not explicitly discriminate on the basis of country of origin and were necessary to protect public health or the environment. This GATT panel decision helped diffuse environmental opposition to the Uruguay Round agreement, which was approved by Congress two months later.

The Uruguay Round Agreement

The Uruguay Round agreement, which concluded in 1994 and was ratified by Congress the following year, addressed few of the specific criticisms of environmentalists. But largely as a response to environmentalists' criticisms of the GATT, it explicitly acknowledged one formerly tacit principle. The preamble to the Standards Agreement, now incorporated into the provisions of the newly established WTO, marks the first mention of the word *environment* in the GATT itself. It states that each country "may maintain standards and technical regulations for the protection of human, animal, and plant life and health and of the *environment*" [emphasis added].[11] It also notes that a country should not be prevented from setting technical standards (which include environmental regulations) "at the levels it considers appropriate," a phrase meant to discourage nations from harmonizing standards in a downward direction.[12] In addition, the Agreement on Subsidies and Countervailing Measures permits governments to subsidize up to 20 percent of one-time capital investments to meet new environmental requirements, provided that its subsidies are directly linked and proportional to environmental improvements. This provision makes the granting of environmental subsidies somewhat easier.

The World Trade Organization (WTO)

The Shrimp-Turtle Dispute

After the WTO came into existence, the United States found itself embroiled in another environmentally related trade dispute. In 1989 Congress passed legislation requiring that U.S.-registered shrimp boats be fitted with a device to protect turtles from becoming entrapped in their nets. In 1995 this regulation was applied to foreign fishing vessels. As a result, shrimp and products from shrimp caught by foreign nationals whose countries did not require turtle protection devices could no longer be imported into the United States. India, Malaysia, Pakistan, and Thailand requested the formation of a WTO dispute panel in October 1996. The four countries, whose complaint was supported by a number of other Pacific Rim nations including Australia, argued that WTO rules prohibit a nation from imposing its domestic environmental laws outside its borders. The United States countered that international trade rules permit nations to take measures that are necessary "to protect natural resources" and that most of the turtle species being killed by shrimpers were endangered.

Although Thailand had enacted legislation mandating turtle exclusion devices (TEDs) on the shrimp-crawl nets used by its fisherman, and was therefore exempt from the U.S. ban, it supported the complaint as a "matter of principle." [13] For its part, the U.S. shrimp industry was divided. Although firms that did business with shrimp importers criticized the law as discriminatory, U.S. shrimpers endorsed the ban on the grounds that it created a level playing field. In May 1998 a WTO dispute panel ruled against the United States, basing its decision on principles similar to those the GATT had applied in the tuna-dolphin decision. Although the political heat generated by this decision was less intense than that produced by the tuna-dolphin ruling—in part because no trade agreement was being negotiated or considered by Congress at the time—it reinforced environmentalists' criticisms of the WTO. American environmentalists claimed that the TEDs could save 97 percent of the 150,000 sea turtles killed in shrimp nets each year.

The panel decision was upheld on appeal. But in a significant concession to environmentalists, the WTO's appellate body's decision departed significantly from the language of the tuna-dolphin ruling. It stated that trade restrictions based on production methods *could* be used to protect the environment and to guard natural resources outside a nation's borders. This meant that the United States was permitted to exclude shrimp from vessels that had not installed appropriate turtle protection devices.

The appellate body decision noted that the turtles in question were covered by the Convention on International Trade in Endangered Species of World Flora and Fauna (CITES) and thus could be considered an "exhaustive natural resource," which WTO rules permit national laws to protect, particularly as they migrate between national and international waters. In another major victory for environmentalists, the appellate body stated that dispute settlement bodies could consider legal submissions from nongovernmental organizations.

However, the appellate body found the U.S. embargo inconsistent with WTO rules on two grounds. First, the United States had insisted that its trading partners adopt regulations essentially identical to its own, and it had not applied the same turtle protection standard to each of its trading partners. Second, the appellate body faulted the United States for not having done enough to pursue bilateral or multilateral approaches before applying its own unilateral sanctions. [14]

In January 2000 the United States indicated that it had implemented the panel's decision. It revised and clarified its guidelines for enforcing the U.S. shrimp-turtle law, assuring all countries equal treatment; it launched negotiations for the protection of sea turtles in the Indian Ocean region; and

it offered technical training to shrimp producers. In June 2001 a dispute settlement panel found the revised U.S. implementation of its sea turtle protection law to be fully consistent with WTO rules. By broadening the
conditions under which a nation could restrict imports on environmental
grounds, the final decisions in the shrimp-turtle case represent a significant
change in WTO rules and have been heralded as signaling the belated
"greening" of the WTO.[15]

Biotech Products

In 2003, however, the WTO found itself found confronted with
another environmentally related trade dispute that threatens to be at least as
contentious as the tuna-dolphin and shrimp-turtle disputes. The United
States, joined by Canada and Argentina, requested the formation of a dispute settlement panel to judge the legality of EU policies that had restricted
the approval of genetically modified agricultural products on the grounds
that the restrictions were not based on sufficient scientific evidence that the
products posed a danger to consumers and the environment. The use of
biotech foods and seeds is widespread in the United States but has been
severely limited in the EU and in a number of member states largely because
of popular fears about their health effects, safety, and environmental impacts.
At issue in this dispute is the basis on which governments can, under WTO
rules, legally restrict the import of agricultural products on health, safety, or
environmental grounds.

The economic and political stakes in this trade dispute are substantial.
Not only have American exports of genetically modified agricultural products and seeds to the EU been reduced significantly, but many developing
countries have been reluctant to approve the planting of genetically modified
seeds produced by American firms on the grounds that they will not be able
to export their crops to the EU.[16] This situation has further disadvantaged
American farmers and the American biotech industry. However, the EU
maintains that it should have the right to determine the conditions under
which potentially dangerous agricultural products should be approved for
consumption and cultivation, and that in light of the novelty of biotech agriculture, a more cautious or precautionary approach to assessing the safety
and environmental impact of these products is appropriate.[17] It remains to be
seen whether this approach will be found consistent with the EU's obligations under the WTO agreement.

The American complaint to the WTO rests primarily on two grounds.
First, beginning in October 1998, the EU applied a de facto moratorium on
the approval of any new biotech products. Second, a number of member
states have refused to permit the import or marketing of biotech products
approved by the EU. Since the United States filed its brief with the WTO,
the European Commission has granted regulatory approval for the planting
of seventeen varieties of a strain of corn developed by Monsanto, although it
is unclear whether any of the corn will be planted. In addition, the commis-

sion has approved the import of several genetically altered food products. However, the EU has also adopted strict labeling requirements, under which food products containing more than 0.9 percent genetically modified ingredients must be labeled as such. American exporters are concerned that in light of strong consumer opposition to genetically modified foods in much of Europe, this labeling requirement will discourage companies from marketing these foods. By contrast, the United States does not require such labeling because these foods are considered "substantially equivalent" to food grown from conventional seeds.[18]

The WTO Committee on Trade and the Environment

At the GATT's April 1994 ministerial meeting, during which the Uruguay Round agreement was formally ratified, a resolution was approved committing the soon-to-be-established WTO to undertake a systematic review of "trade policies and those trade-related aspects of environmental policies which may result in significant trade effects for its members."[19] In January 1995 the WTO General Council officially established a Committee on Trade and the Environment (CTE). This committee, which is open to all WTO members, has met four to six times each year. It has debated a number of issues, including WTO rules governing the export of domestically prohibited goods and the growing use of eco-labeling by developed countries.

The EU as well as a number of individual European countries have made widespread use of eco-labels, which certify that a product is environmentally friendly. Many of these countries' trading partners, however, have expressed concern that the criteria used to award labels are biased in favor of domestically produced goods. A similar controversy has arisen over the WTO compatibility of national packaging and recycling requirements because many of these regulations privilege domestic producers.

In 2001, trade ministers and negotiators met in Doha, Qatar, to begin a new round of trade negotiations. They agreed to place on the international trade agenda the relationship between multinational environmental agreements (MEAs) and WTO rules. This issue is important because a number of international environmental agreements contain provisions obligating their signatories to restrict the importation of goods that either are proscribed as environmentally harmful or are produced in harmful ways. For example, CITES restricts or prohibits trade in endangered species, whereas the Montreal Protocol restricts trade in ozone-depleting chemicals as well as in products made using proscribed chemicals. If a nation is a signatory to both an MEA and the WTO, the two obligations complement one another. But a problem can arise if a nation is a member of the WTO but not a signatory to an MEA, because, under current WTO rules, exports from all countries must be treated equally.

The EU, which maintains that "trade measures can be necessary to achieve the environmental objectives of these [environmental] agreements," supports a change in the WTO agreement that would exempt from WTO challenges any trade restrictions sanctioned by MEAs.[20] However, the EU's proposal has been strongly opposed by developing nations, which fear that it could be used to coerce them into adopting the environmental policies and priorities of their greener trading partners. For its part, the United States is not persuaded of the urgency of any change in WTO rules governing MEAs on the grounds that no dispute has come before the WTO regarding the provisions of any MEA. According to the United States, "Increased information exchange between MEAs and the WTO and more predictable observer status could go a long way in ensuring that the two systems of international obligations remain compatible and mutually supportive."

U.S. representatives to the CTE have supported changes in WTO rules that would liberalize trade in environmental goods and services in order to promote the dissemination of state-of-the-art environmental technologies. In addition, the United States has supported proposals to reduce governmental subsidies that undermine sustainable development, such as for fisheries and agriculture.

The CTE has been unable to address any of the critical substantive issues surrounding the impact of WTO rules on environmental regulations. Part of the reason for this standstill is the inability of the EU and the United States to agree on how specifically the WTO should be made greener. For example, the EU favors a more permissive policy toward eco-labels than does the United States because the former makes much more extensive use of them. The EU is also more concerned than is the United States about a possible WTO dispute settlement ruling against the trade provisions of an international environmental agreement, because it is a party to more MEAs than is the United States. In addition, the United States has differed with the EU about the extent to which environmentally harmful subsidies should be restricted under WTO rules.

But a far more important reason for the CTE's lack of progress is the sharp divisions that exist between developed and developing nations. The latter are highly suspicious of any rules changes that would make it easier for environmental standards that restrict trade to pass WTO scrutiny. They fear that any effort to relax WTO rules on NTBs will be used by producers in rich countries not so much to protect the environment as to protect their domestic markets from imports from developing nations. In this context, recall that two of the most controversial trade-environment disputes to come before the GATT/WTO—namely, the tuna-dolphin and shrimp-turtle disputes—pitted less developed countries against a coalition of U.S. environmentalists and domestic producers.

Nonetheless, the CTE has had some accomplishments. It has increased the visibility of environmental issues within the WTO bureaucracy, as revealed, for example, by the steady stream of reports on the impact of trade liberalization on environmental protection that have flowed from the organization's headquarters in Geneva since the mid-1990s.[21] It has also promoted increased coordination between the WTO and the secretariats of international environmental meetings and treaties. Finally, it has helped provide states with more information about each other's domestic regulations that affect trade.[22]

The North American Free Trade Agreement (NAFTA)

Terms of NAFTA

NAFTA, the free trade agreement negotiated among the United States, Mexico, and Canada, addresses a number of environmental issues.[23] The agreement's most innovative feature is its supplemental agreement on the environment, though this is not part of NAFTA itself. The supplemental agreement was negotiated by the Clinton administration with considerable input from U.S. environmental organizations. It established a Commission for Environmental Cooperation (CEC), headed by a secretariat and a council composed of senior environmental officials from each country and advised by representatives of environmental organizations. Addressing some of the criticisms of GATT dispute resolution procedures made by environmental groups following the tuna-dolphin decision, it extends to citizens the right to make submissions to the commission on any environmental issue, requires the secretariat to report its responses to these submissions, and, under certain circumstances, permits its reports to be made public. In fact, these provisions provide more opportunities for nonbusiness participation than does current U.S. law, which permits only aggrieved producers to file complaints with or to sue the International Trade Commission, the body responsible for enforcing U.S. trade laws.

In addition, the CEC was given the authority to consider the environmental implications of production methods or, in its words, the "environmental implications of products throughout their life-cycles." This ruling departed from the position of the GATT tuna-dolphin dispute panel, which had ruled that no nation may regulate how other nations produce goods or raw materials outside its borders.[24] Although the side agreement does not require any of the three signatories to enact new environmental laws, it does authorize the use of fines as well as trade sanctions for the nonenforcement of new or existing laws, though only fines may be applied against Canada. Although the CEC is empowered to address any environmental or natural resource issue, the range of issues subject to dispute settlement panels is limited to the enforcement of those environmental laws related to trade or competition among the parties.

NAFTA seeks to prevent its signatory nations from using environmental regulations to gain a comparative advantage by making such regulations either too strict or too lax. The agreement prohibits any country from lowering its environmental standards to attract investment and permits its signatories to impose more stringent environmental standards on new investments, provided they apply equally to foreign and domestic investors. It also requires all three countries to cooperate on improving the level of environmental protection and encourages, but does not require, the raising of regulatory standards.

As the direct response to environmentalists' concerns over the GATT decision in the tuna-dolphin case, the agreement specifically states that the provisions of several international environmental agreements—including the Montreal Protocol, the Basel Convention on hazardous wastes, and CITES—take precedence over NAFTA. In some cases it also allows each nation to continue to enforce "generally agreed upon international environmental or conservation rules or standards," provided they are "the least trade-restrictive necessary for securing the protection required."[25] At the same time, "while NAFTA in no way attempts to reduce national standards to a lowest common denominator, . . . it does seek to limit the ability of signatories to use such regulations as surreptitious protectionist devices."[26] The Committee on Standards-Related Measures was made responsible for developing common criteria for determining the environmental hazards of products as well as methodologies for risk assessment.

Environmentalists were disappointed that the supplementary agreement did not include any procedure for raising environmental standards or their enforcement to the highest common denominator. Nonetheless, due to the leverage exercised by the environmental community, NAFTA represents the greenest trade agreement ever negotiated by the United States.[27]

The Impact of NAFTA

The CEC, which established its office in Montreal, has received a number of complaints from environmental organizations alleging noncompliance with various national environmental laws. These complaints have included, for example, a petition requesting the CEC secretariat to prepare a factual record explaining the death of 40,000 migratory birds in the Silva Reservoir, located 200 miles northwest of Mexico City and another that alleged the Mexican government had failed to follow its own environmental laws when it authorized the construction of a 500-meter pier and cruise ship terminal that threatened an important coral reef at Cozumel. In the latter case, the Mexican government agreed to scale back the size of the development project and declared the reef to be a protected area. However, to date neither trade sanctions nor fines have been imposed for noncompliance. CEC submissions have functioned primarily to call public attention to environmental problems in the three signatory nations.

The CEC has a number of accomplishments, however. For example, it established a North American environmental research program, developed a North American Pollutant Release and Transfer Registry to monitor the release and transportation of chemicals harmful to air quality, and initiated an ambitious biodiversity conservation program to protect threatened and endangered species. Most important, the three NAFTA signatories have agreed to phase out or reduce the use of a number of dangerous chemicals and pesticides, including DDT. "Taken together, these actions suggest that the CEC may be developing into an institution that could have significant effect on some environmental issues in North America." [28]

NAFTA has had a modest impact on the most pressing environmental issue associated with Mexico-U.S. relations—namely, the reduction of transboundary pollution. Although sixteen transborder projects have been approved with a combined cost of $230 million, progress remains limited on reducing air and water pollution on the Mexican-U.S. border. The impact of NAFTA on domestic Mexican environmental policies and practices has been uneven. A number of Mexican environmental standards have been tightened, and indeed most Mexican standards are now comparable with American ones. More than four hundred firms have signed environmental compliance action plans, and serious environmental violations in the industrial region bordering the United States were reduced by 72 percent shortly after NAFTA was signed. But whereas enforcement was strengthened around the time of NAFTA's approval, it has since declined. Likewise, government spending to assist Mexican firms to comply with the nation's environmental laws has not increased over the past decade, and Mexico spends considerably less on environmental protection than does any other country in the Organization for Economic Cooperation and Development. As a result, Mexican firms, especially smaller ones, typically lack adequate resources to adopt environmental controls.

One NAFTA provision that created little controversy when the agreement was signed has since proved highly contentious. Chapter 11 of NAFTA gives firms the right to sue a government if its regulations "unfairly" penalize foreign investors. Acting under this provision, the Ethyl Corporation forced Canada to reverse its ban on the sale of a gasoline additive, and Metalclad Corporation won a judgment requiring Mexico to pay compensation of $16.7 million on the grounds that environmental laws prohibiting construction of a toxic waste processing plant were the equivalent of expropriation. These Chapter 11 decisions and disputes have been widely denounced by consumer and environmental groups, though these are the only two cases among the ten filed in which firms were awarded damages.

Although environmentalists' fears that Mexico would become a pollution haven have not come to fruition, "for the majority of key environmental indicators, there is no sign of a turnaround regarding environmental degradation in Mexico." [29] The inability of NAFTA to improve Mexican environmental standards has left many U.S. environmentalists disillusioned with trade liberalization. As a specialist on trade policy for the Sierra Club put it a few years ago, "The side agreements really haven't delivered on commitments made by the Clinton administration in 1993." [30] According to Richard Gephardt, the former Democratic House leader from Missouri, NAFTA has proven a failure: Along the Mexican border "each day the environment dies another death." [31] Environmental organizations that supported the passage of NAFTA now insist that the environment become a priority "on the par with other negotiating objectives" in trade talks rather than be included in a side agreement as it was under NAFTA.[32] Not surprisingly, those

organizations that opposed NAFTA also strongly oppose the Bush administration's proposed free trade agreement of the Americas, fearing that it is
likely to further undermine environmental quality in the Americas.

The Domestic Politics of Trade-Environment Linkages

The mass demonstrations at the third ministerial meeting of the WTO
in Seattle in December 1999 both reflected and made more politically visible
domestic political opposition to the role of WTO. Although most of the
demonstrators who chanted "Hey-Hey! Ho-Ho! The WTO has got to go!"
were upset about the impact of trade liberalization on labor standards and
workers, the WTO was also attacked on environmental grounds. A number
of protestors dressed up as turtles to dramatize their opposition to the WTO's
ruling in the shrimp-turtle trade dispute, whereas others demonstrated in
favor of dolphins. The Public Citizen Global Trade Watch, associated with
Ralph Nader, helped organize the Seattle demonstrations and has played a
critical role in mobilizing nongovernmental opposition to the WTO and a
new trade round, especially within the environmental community.[33]

Shortly before he left office, President Clinton signed a new executive
order requiring the United States to undertake formal environmental reviews
of all new trade agreements, and in Seattle he announced his willingness to
include labor and environmental standards in future trade agreements. The
Bush administration renewed this executive order. Further, at the April 2001
Quebec summit, President Bush called for a free trade agreement of the
Americas and expressed the need to combine trade liberalization with "a
strong commitment to protecting our environment and improving labor
standards."[34] However, both the president and then–U.S. trade representative Robert Zoellick subsequently emphasized that such standards should be
not be used as a form of protectionism. They wanted linkages to take the
form of incentives rather than trade sanctions.[35]

Congress has been sharply divided on this issue. Many Democrats in
Congress, reflecting the influence of environmental lobbies and trade unions,
have insisted that any new trade agreement include strong labor and environmental protections—backed up by sanctions. But many congressional
Republicans are strongly opposed to incorporating environmental or labor
standards in future trade agreements, and they are especially opposed to
making such standards enforceable through sanctions. The U.S. business
community is also divided. Although the Business Roundtable and the
Emergency Committee for American Trade—representing the largest multinational corporations—have asked the Bush administration to make labor
and environmental standards part of any future trade talks, the American
Chamber of Commerce opposes any linkages.

Finally, in August 2002, after eight years of debate and delay, Congress
voted to grant the president Trade Protection Authority, thus enabling him
to negotiate further trade agreements. (Under Trade Protection Authority,
formally known as "fast track," Congress agrees to vote on any trade agree-

ment negotiated by the U.S. trade representative either up or down, with no amendments.) This legislation explicitly addressed the relationship between trade and environmental policies. It specifically requested that American trade negotiators seek to include provisions in trade agreements that "strive to ensure that they do not weaken or reduce the protections afforded in domestic environmental laws as an encouragement to trade."

Bilateral and Regional Trade Agreements

Partly because of the delay in reaching agreement on a new multilateral round of trade negotiations, the United States has recently entered into a number of new trade agreements with individual countries. Significantly, three of these agreements, with Jordan (2001), Chile (2003), and Singapore (2003), include environmental clauses. In each case, the U.S. trade representative conducted and published an extensive review of the agreement's environmental impact and identified how trade liberalization could promote sustainable development. Each agreement contains a clause similar to NAFTA: The parties agree to enforce any environmental laws that might affect trade and promise not to weaken or reduce any environmental laws in order to attract trade or investment. A dispute settlement mechanism was established to address any disputes arising from these provisions. However, in contrast to NAFTA, the remedies for violations are fines rather than trade sanctions.

The United States is currently negotiating two regional trade agreements, one for Central America and another that would include all the Americas. Although the United States has sought to include similar "green" clauses in these agreements, there is considerable opposition to doing so by the governments of virtually all Central and Latin American countries, who fear that any environmental clauses will be used by American producers and environmentalists as an excuse to keep out their products. These negotiations have yet to be concluded, and it is unclear whether these agreements, if and when they are reached, will include any environmental provisions.

The Environmental Impact of Trade Liberalization

What has been the overall impact of more liberal trade policies on environmental protection? To a significant extent, any assessment of the environmental impact of trade liberalization depends largely on one's analysis of the relationship between environmental quality and economic development. If the two are viewed as incompatible, then clearly trade liberalization will, by definition, have adverse environmental consequences, especially for developing countries. Alternatively, if economic development is understood to enable an improvement in environmental quality, then trade liberalization can have a positive environmental impact.

For relatively poor countries, increased economic growth and economic interdependence generally result in a deterioration of domestic environmental quality: Pollution levels increase, and natural resources are depleted at an accelerating rate. But environmental quality tends to improve as per-capita income rises because nations have more resources to devote to conservation and pollution control. With the important exception of carbon emissions, economic development generally contributes to improved environmental quality.

Nor is it the case that trade liberalization necessarily results in more environmentally irresponsible economic practices. On the contrary, the experiences of many Latin American countries and the formerly communist nations of eastern and central Europe reveal that the most polluting and energy-inefficient firms are often also economically inefficient. By exposing these firms to global competition, trade liberalization improves local environmental conditions.[36] Further, among the most important sources of environmental degradation in both the developed and developing worlds are government subsidies for mining, agriculture, forestry, energy, and fisheries. To the extent that trade agreements and economic liberalization promote the phasing out of these subsidies, environmental quality is likely to improve. In addition, trade barriers often prevent the importation of pollution control equipment or advanced technologies that are less polluting.[37]

Numerous cross-national empirical studies of environmental performance have failed to find any evidence of a race to the bottom. For example, a study by David Wheeler examined trends in urban air quality in China, Mexico, and Brazil from the mid- to late 1980s through the mid- to late 1990s.[38] During this period, each of these developing countries became increasingly integrated into the global economy as both foreign investment and trade expanded. During this same time period, the levels of particulate pollution declined steadily in urban areas in all four countries. Or consider the United States. Its pollution standards are among the strictest in the world, yet the United States has received more foreign investment than any other country.

There are a number of reasons a race to the bottom has not occurred with respect to environmental standards and conditions. First, for all but a handful of industries, the costs of compliance with environmental standards are too modest to encourage firms to migrate to pollution havens to lower their production costs, even with the removal of barriers to trade.[39] Second, even in many poor countries, community groups have organized to demand that firms reduce their pollution levels. Third, as countries become more affluent, they regulate pollution more strictly. Finally, in part because of increased public scrutiny, many large multinational firms have chosen to adhere to the stricter environmental standards of their home countries in their developing country operations.[40]

In many cases, stricter domestic regulatory standards represent a source of competitive advantage because it is often easier for domestic firms to comply with them. For example, recycling requirements almost invariably work to the advantage of those firms that produce close to their customers, thus providing domestic firms with an important incentive for supporting the requirements. Moreover, the lure of access to green export markets has played a critical role in encouraging firms to support stricter domestic product standards. For example, in the early 1970s, Japan modeled its automobile emissions standards on those of the United States—its major export market. Similarly, an important factor underlying the support of German auto firms for stricter EC emissions standards during the 1980s was the fact that the vehicles they were producing for sale in California were already meeting the world's stricter emissions standards.

Likewise, according to a study conducted by the U.S. Government Accountability Office (formerly the General Accounting Office), countries that export significant quantities of agricultural products to the United States frequently take U.S. standards into account in establishing their domestic pesticide regulations.[41] Moreover, as Michael Porter has argued, stricter regulatory standards can encourage domestic firms to develop improved pollution control technologies, which they can then export as the regulatory standards of their trading partners become stronger.[42] Thus, in a number of cases, increased economic interdependence has led to the strengthening rather than the weakening of environmental standards—a "race to the top" that has been characterized as "the California effect."[43]

Many of the environmental abuses attributable to trade liberalization have more to do with domestic politics than with international economics. Trade liberalization does not dictate the rate at which a nation allows its natural resources to be exploited or the value it accords to hardwood forests, jungles, clean water, or endangered wildlife. These determinations are made by national governments. All developed nations have made considerable progress in protecting their domestic environments; there is nothing in the terms of international trade agreements that prevents developing nations from doing likewise. Moreover, if the developed nations are dissatisfied with the environmental practices of developing nations, they have no shortage of instruments to help improve them. Trade restrictions are rarely the most effective or efficient mechanism.

The tension between trade liberalization and environmental regulation should not be exaggerated. Only three U.S. environmental regulations have been held to be inconsistent with the GATT/WTO agreement, and to date none has been weakened by NAFTA. Both the WTO and NAFTA explicitly protect the right of nations to establish whatever regulatory standards they deem appropriate, provided they can be scientifically justified and are as "least trade-restrictive" as possible. Even more important, neither agreement has prevented a steady increase in the number and scope of regional and international environmental treaties. Nonetheless, tension between both national and international environmental policies and trade liberalization will persist.

Notes

1. "Energy and the Environment," *Economist,* October 9, 2004, 30.
2. See David Vogel, *Trading Up: Consumer and Environmental Regulation in a Global Economy* (Cambridge: Harvard University Press, 1995).
3. Quoted in Stewart Hudson, "Coming to Terms with Trade," *Environmental Action* (summer 1992): 33.
4. Paul Rauber, "Trading Away the Environment," *Sierra* (January–February 1992).
5. James Brooke, "America—Environmental Dictator?" *New York Times,* May 3, 1992, 7.
6. Stuart Auerbach, "Endangering Laws Protecting the Endangered," *Washington Post National Weekly Edition,* October 7–13, 1991, 22.
7. Robert Housman and Durwood Zaelke, "The Collusion of the Environment and Trade: The GATT Tuna-Dolphin Decision," *Environmental Law Reporter* (April 1992): 10271.
8. Matthew Hurlock, "The GATT, U.S. Law, and the Environment: A Proposal to Amend the GATT in Light of the Tuna-Dolphin Decision," *Columbia Law Review* 92 (1992): 2100.
9. "Congress Considers New Bill to Save Dolphins," *Dolphin Alert* (fall 1992): 2.
10. Quoted in "U.S. Auto Fuel-Efficiency Taxes to Be Examined by GATT Panel," *Trade and the Environment: News and Views from the GATT,* June 3, 1993, 4.
11. Richard Steinberg, "The Uruguay Round: A Legal Analysis of the Final Act," *International Quarterly* 6 (April 1994): 35.
12. Ibid.
13. Chana Schoenberger, "Shrimp Dispute Tests U.S. Use of Trade to Protect Environment," *Wall Street Journal,* July 18, 1997, A14.
14. Nancy Perkins, "The World Trade Organization Holds That Trade Barriers May, If Properly Designed and Applied, Be Used to Protect the Global Environment," *Legal Times,* February 8, 1999.
15. See Michael Weinstein and Steve Charnowitz, "The Greening of the WTO," *Foreign Affairs* 80 (November–December 2001): 147–156.
16. See Robert Paarlberg, *The Politics of Precaution: Genetically Modified Crops in Developing Countries* (Baltimore: Johns Hopkins University Press, 2001).
17. For a discussion of the contrast between European and American approaches to risk assessment, see Theofanis Christoforou, "The Precautionary Principle, Risk Assessment, and the Comparative Role of Science in the European Community and the U.S. Legal Systems," in *Green Giants? Environmental Policies of the United States and the European Union,* ed. Norman Vig and Michael Faure (Cambridge: MIT Press, 2004), 17–52.
18. For an extensive discussion of U.S.-E.U. differences on food biotechnology, see Thomas Bernauer, *Genes, Trade, and Regulation* (Princeton: Princeton University Press, 2003).
19. "Decisions Adopted by Ministers in Marrakesh," *Focus: The GATT Newsletter* (May 1994): 9.
20. Quoted in William Lasch III, "Green Showdown at the WTO," *Contemporary Issues Series* 85, Center for the Study of American Business (March 1997): 12.
21. For the annual reports of the CTE as well as the numerous WTO reports and studies on trade and environment, see www.wto.org.
22. For a comprehensive analysis of the impact of the CTE, see Gregory Shaffer, "The World Trade Organization under Challenge: Democracy and the Law and Politics of the WTO's Treatment of Trade and Environment Matters," *Harvard Environmental Law Review* 25 (2000): 74–81.
23. For a detailed discussion of the politics surrounding the approval of NAFTA by the United States, see John Audley, *Green Politics and Global Trade: NAFTA and the Future of Environmental Politics* (Washington, D.C.: Georgetown University Press, 1997).
24. Quoted in James Sheehan, "NAFTA—Free Trade in Name Only," *Wall Street Journal,* September 9, 1993, A21.

25. Michelle Swenarchuk, "NAFTA and the Environment," *Canadian Forum* 71 (January–February 1993): 13.
26. Roberto Salinas-Leon, "Green Herrings," *Regulation* (winter 1993): 31.
27. For criticisms of the environmental provisions of both NAFTA and the side agreement, see Gary Hufbauer and Jeffrey Scott, *NAFTA: An Assessment*, rev. ed. (Washington, D.C.: Institute for International Economics, 1993), 92–97.
28. Richard Steinberg, "Trade-Environment Negotiations in the EU, NAFTA, and WTO: Regional Trajectories of Rule Development," *American Journal of International Law* 91 (1997): 250–251.
29. Kevin Gallagher, "The CEC and Environmental Quality," in *Greening NAFTA: The North American Commission for Environmental Cooperation*, ed. David Markell and John Knox (Palo Alto, Calif.: Stanford University Press, 2003), 119.
30. Anthony DePalma, "NAFTA Environmental Lags May Delay Free Trade Expansion," *New York Times*, May 21, 1997, A4.
31. David Sanger, "Republicans Say the Trade Bill Is in Big Trouble," *New York Times*, October 1, 1997, A14.
32. Nancy Dunne, "Chile's NAFTA Hopes Fade as Trade Pacts Lose U.S. Favor," *Financial Times*, October 2, 1997, 6.
33. See, for example, Lori Wallach and Michelle Sforza, *The WTO: Five Years of Reasons to Resist Corporate Globalization* (New York: Seven Stories Press, 1999) and Lori Wallach and Michelle Sforza, *Whose Trade Organization? Corporate Globalization and the Erosion of Democracy* (Washington D.C.: Public Citizen, 1999).
34. "A Cautious Yes to Pan-American Trade," *Economist*, April 28, 2001.
35. "Calming the Waters: A Talk with the U.S. Trade Rep," *Business Week*, July 23, 2001, 41.
36. See, for example, Nancy Birdsall and David Wheeler, "Trade Policy and Industrial Pollution in Latin America: Where Are the Pollution Havens?" in *International Trade and the Environment*, ed. Patrick Low (Washington, D.C.: World Bank, 1992), 159–168. For a more critical view of the impact of economic globalization on ecological policy, see *Ecological Policy and Politics in Developing Countries*, ed. Uday Desai (Albany: State University of New York Press, 1998).
37. For a comprehensive analysis of the impact of trade liberalization on both economic efficiency and environmental quality, see *The Greening of World Trade Issues*, ed. Kym Anderson and Richard Blackhurst (Ann Arbor: University of Michigan Press, 1992).
38. David Wheeler, "Racing to the Bottom? Foreign Investment and Air Pollution in Developing Countries," *Journal of Environment and Development* 10 (September 2001): 225–245. For an alternative perspective that describes substantial deterioration in environmental conditions in China, see Elizabeth Economy, *The River Runs Black* (Ithaca, N.Y.: Cornell University Press, 2004).
39. An extensive literature is available on the relationships among economic regulation and trade patterns, international competitiveness, and corporate location decisions. See, for example, Richard Stewart, "Environmental Regulation and International Competitiveness," *Yale Law Journal* 102 (June 1993): 2077–2079; Judith Dean, "Trade and the Environment: A Survey of the Literature," in *International Trade and the Environment*, ed. Low, 16–20.
40. See, for example, G. Dowell, S. Hart, and B. Yeung, "Do Global Environmental Standards Create or Destroy Market Value?" *Management Science* 46 (2000): 1059–1074.
41. Quoted in Charles Pearson, "Trade and Environment: The United States Experience" (New York: U.N. Conference on Trade and Development, January 1994), 52.
42. See Michael Porter, *The Competitive Advantage of Nations* (New York: Free Press, 1990), 685–688; and Curtis Moore and Alan Miller, *Green Gold* (Boston: Beacon Press, 1994).
43. See Vogel, *Trading Up*, chap. 8.

17

Toward Sustainable Development?

Norman J. Vig and Michael E. Kraft

What is now plain is that the emission of greenhouse gases, associated with industrialization and strong economic growth from a world population that has increased sixfold in 200 years, is causing global warming at a rate that began as significant, has become alarming and is simply unsustainable in the long-term. And by long-term I do not mean centuries ahead. I mean within the lifetime of my children certainly; and possibly within my own. And by unsustainable, I do not mean a phenomenon causing problems of adjustment. I mean a challenge so far-reaching in its impact and irreversible in its destructive power, that it alters radically human existence.

British Prime Minister Tony Blair,
September 14, 2004

Our alliance is determined to show good stewardship of the Earth, and that requires addressing the serious long-term challenge of global climate change. All of us expressed our views on the Kyoto Protocol, and now we must work together on the way forward.

President George W. Bush,
Brussels, February 21, 2005

The world has changed" was a common response to the terrorist attacks of September 11, 2001. Indeed, we may never again have the sense of national security we enjoyed before these tragic events. But the world is changing in many other ways as well because of the growing population and industrialization of the planet. Global trends such as accelerated climate change; loss of biological diversity; and chemical contamination of air, water, and soils are altering the life support systems on which we all depend. In the early years of the twenty-first century, it is no longer certain that our way of life is sustainable.[1] The softer but more numerous threats to the quality of our environment may become the ubiquitous security issue of the future.

The concept of sustainable development has emerged as the most widely recognized framework for addressing environmental concerns throughout the world. The concept was first defined and popularized in the 1987 UN report *Our Common Future* as "development that meets the needs of the present without compromising the ability of future generations to meet their own needs."[2] It was further elaborated at the 1992 UN Conference on Environment and Development in Rio de Janeiro, Brazil, and incorporated into several international environmental conventions and the treaty of the European Union in the 1990s. It was also the focus of the World Summit on Sustainable Development in Johannesburg, South Africa, in August–September 2002.[3]

As Robert Paehlke indicates in chapter 3, sustainability has broad policy implications because it demands changes in basic patterns of economic, social, and personal life that degrade natural resources and ecosystems over the long term.[4] First-generation environmental problems involved primarily direct regulation of air, water, and soil pollution from major point sources such as factories and power plants. Second-generation issues required broader, more flexible and cost-effective methods to control smaller generators and other sources of widely dispersed contamination. In contrast, third-generation problems (such as climate change) are often global in scope and require more comprehensive and integrated approaches to get at the roots of human behavior that threaten the stability of ecosystems for future generations.[5] Indeed, sustainable development supercedes environmental policy in the sense that all public policy and private activities ultimately must be concerned with environmental sustainability.

In 1993 the National Commission on the Environment, a prestigious group of private individuals including four former heads of the U.S. Environmental Protection Agency (EPA), called for rethinking environmental policies in terms of this concept:

> U.S. leadership should be based on the concept of *sustainable development.* By the close of the twentieth century, economic development and environmental protection must come together in a new synthesis: broad-based economic progress accomplished in a manner that protects and restores the quality of the natural environment, improves the quality of life for individuals, and broadens the prospects for future generations. This merging of economic and environmental goals in the concept of sustainable development can and should constitute a central guiding principle for national environmental and economic policymaking.[6]

President Bill Clinton took up the challenge by appointing a new President's Council on Sustainable Development. The council, consisting of some twenty-five leaders from industry, government, and the environmental community, met over a period of six years and issued several reports.[7] However, after 1994 the Republican-dominated Congress was indifferent or hostile to the idea of sustainability, and the council's work was largely disregarded by other federal agencies. The EPA did introduce some new programs for community-based environmental protection to encourage state and local governments to adopt sustainable development projects, and other departments attempted to define sustainability goals.[8] For the most part, however, sustainable development was regarded as "someone else's problem" and remained outside the vocabulary of U.S. politics, particularly at the national level.[9]

President George W. Bush has not given even rhetorical support to the idea of sustainable development, preferring instead the older concept of environmental "stewardship."[10] His policies appear to assume that scientific and technological advances brought about by global economic growth will allow humans to overcome or adapt to future environmental challenges. As in the Reagan administration, environmental concerns have thus been pushed to the margins of policymaking.

In fact, empirical evidence indicates that the United States does not fare very well on measures of environmental sustainability. One quantitative index, developed at Yale and Columbia Universities, ranks the U.S. only 45th out of 146 countries studied—behind nations such as Japan, Germany, Russia, and even Botswana, Croatia, and Estonia.[11] The fact that the United States has not ratified international environmental treaties such as the Kyoto Protocol (1997), the Convention on Biological Diversity (1992) and its Biosafety Protocol (2000), the Basel Convention on transboundary movement of hazardous wastes (1989), the Stockholm Convention on persistent organic pollutants (2001), and the Convention on the Law of the Sea (1982) also does not speak well of our global environmental stewardship.

Environmental sustainability is important not only for the health and well-being of future generations but also for the peace and security of the world. Strains brought about by population growth, climate change, declining biodiversity, deforestation, desertification, competition for resources such as fresh water, and the spread of human and animal diseases are likely to contribute to future international conflicts. As Prime Minister Blair stated in announcing Britain's commitment to reduce greenhouse gas emissions by 60 percent over the next half-century, "there will be no genuine security if the planet is ravaged by climate change."[12]

In the remainder of this chapter we focus on seven persisting environmental policy issues that the nation must address and discuss a number of alternative policy strategies and tools that might contribute to greater policy effectiveness in the future.

Critical Policy Issues

As noted throughout this book, many important environmental policy issues remain unresolved despite the progress made since 1970. Here we briefly note some of the most important problems likely to confront the nation in the future. It should be emphasized that this list is not exhaustive and that Congress and the public are likely to attach different orders of priority to the issues than that suggested here. In all cases, sustainable development will require major new efforts in the future.

Energy Consumption and Climate Change

Fossil fuel burning is the source of many of our environmental problems, but its greatest potential impact is on global climate change (see chapter 13). Although many uncertainties remain, evidence continues to mount that carbon dioxide and other greenhouse gases generated by human activity are altering the Earth's temperature and climate patterns.[13] The ten warmest years since 1861, when accurate temperature records began to be kept, have occurred since 1990.[14] The Third Report of the Intergovernmental Panel on Climate Change (IPPC), released in January 2001, cited "new and stronger evidence that most of the observed warming of the last 50 years is attributable to human activities" and suggested that continuing greenhouse gas accumulations could lead to average temperature increases in the range of 2.5–10.4 degrees Fahrenheit by the end of this century.[15] This estimate expands the upper bounds of possible temperature increases considerably over the IPPC's report just five years earlier, mainly because of new evidence suggesting a wider range of future climate scenarios.[16] In any case, most climate models suggest a high probability of disastrous impacts such as rising sea levels, an increased volume and intensity of hurricanes and other storms, shifts in rainfall patterns and, consequently, in patterns of droughts and flooding, massive loss of species and habitats, and the spread of pests and infectious diseases to new geographical areas.

President George W. Bush's rejection of the Kyoto Protocol—which entered into effect on February 16, 2005—has isolated the United States from virtually all of the rest of the world on climate change diplomacy. More than 140 other nations have ratified the protocol, including all other industrialized nations except Australia. Moreover, the United States has attempted to block negotiations on targets for further greenhouse gas reductions following the end of the Kyoto period in 2012.[17] President Bush's separate plan for gradually reducing U.S. greenhouse gas "emission intensity" (the volume of emissions per unit of economic output) by inviting companies to voluntarily submit data to a national emissions registry is not likely to have much effect. According to one estimate, under Bush's policy, total U.S. greenhouse gas emissions will *rise* 14 percent over 2000 levels and 30 percent above 1990 levels by 2010.[18] However, his support for new technologies such as vehicles powered by hydrogen fuel cells and zero-emissions coal-fired power plants may help to provide solutions in the decades beyond that.[19]

Several climate change bills have been introduced in the U.S. Congress. The Climate Stewardship Act of 2003, sponsored by Senators Joseph Lieberman, D-Conn., and John McCain, R-Ariz., failed by a 43–55 vote on October 30, 2003. This bipartisan legislation, which is likely to be considered again in the 109th Congress (2005–2007), would cap greenhouse gas emissions from electricity generation, transportation, industrial, and commercial sectors in the United States at 2000 levels in 2010 and at 1990 levels in 2016. These reductions would be achieved through a tradable allowance system and other flexibility mechanisms.[20] The European Union has already created a cap-and-trade program covering about half of its industrial carbon dioxide emissions, beginning in 2005. Because many multinational corporations are subject to these and other national restrictions (for example, in Japan and China), pressure will likely mount for a similar U.S. system that might be linked to an international trading regime in the future.[21] In the meantime, many state and local governments in the United States are taking actions to stem greenhouse gas emissions without waiting for the federal government to act.[22]

Biodiversity and Endangered Species

Loss of biodiversity ranks with climate change as the greatest long-term threat to the global environment. Scientists believe that the current rate of extinction is 1,000 to 10,000 times the normal rate, and amounts to the sixth great extinction in geological history.[23] The World Wildlife Fund reported in 2004 that, on average, populations of land, freshwater, and marine species declined 40 percent between 1970 and 2000.[24] One major international study published in 2004 predicted that 15 to 37 percent of the species it studied will become extinct over the next fifty years due to global warming alone.[25] Natural systems that support the greatest diversity of species—such as rainforests, wetlands, and coastal estuaries—are threatened by human development throughout the world.

We are just beginning to inventory and understand the full richness of biological diversity in the United States.[26] Over 200,000 native species are currently known to exist, more than 10 percent of all documented species on Earth. Of nearly 21,000 species recently assessed, one-third are considered at risk, with 8 percent imperiled, 7 percent critically imperiled, and 1 percent missing or extinct.[27] The Endangered Species Act (ESA) has protected a relatively small share of these species, with 518 animals and 746 plants listed as endangered or threatened as of March 1, 2005.[28] Nevertheless, the ESA has aroused considerable opposition among private landowners who are required to protect the habitat of endangered species on their property. With Congress unable to agree on reauthorization of the act since 1993, the Clinton administration actively supported the negotiation of voluntary "habitat conservation plans" among public and private stakeholders (see chapters 6 and 14). The Bush administration has further weakened administration of the law by refusing to list new endangered species unless ordered to by a court, by exempting military activities from the law, by severely limiting funds for critical habitat restoration, and by refusing to defend the law against property-rights litigation.[29] As noted earlier, the United States has also failed to ratify the Convention on Biological Diversity, the principal international treaty for the protection of biotic resources.

Air and Water Pollution

As noted in chapter 1, considerable progress has been made in improving air quality since the Clean Air Act (CAA) was enacted in 1970, but serious problems remain. More than half of all Americans still live in and around counties that do not meet current air pollution standards, including those for ozone and fine particles.[30] These air pollutants cause thousands of deaths and countless cases of asthma and acute bronchitis each year.[31] The Bush administration has a mixed record on air pollution. To its credit, it has adopted the first regulations for controlling diesel emissions from trucks and off-road equipment. It has also attempted to enact further controls on coal-fired power plants through a proposed interstate rule for sulfur dioxide and nitrogen oxide emissions covering twenty-eight eastern states and through a proposed rule limiting mercury emissions; it pursued both actions administratively when the president's Clear Skies initiative faltered in March 2005 (chapter 5). The EPA claims that its clean diesel program together with the Clear Skies legislation would bring nearly every county in the nation into compliance with ozone and fine particle standards.[32] At the same time, the administration has weakened current controls under the new source review provisions of the CAA and has proposed weaker limits on mercury emissions from power plants than many scientists and environmental groups have suggested (see chapter 8).[33] Moreover, an interim report by the National Academy of Sciences concluded that Bush's Clear Skies proposal is unlikely to control power plant emissions as effectively as would strict compliance with existing CAA requirements.[34] The Clear Skies bill is also likely to remain bogged down in Congress if it fails to address greenhouse gas emissions (see chapter 6).[35] Thus air pollution is certain to remain a contentious issue.

Despite more than thirty years of regulation under the Clean Water Act of 1972, it is questionable whether overall surface water quality has improved in the United States (see chapter 1). Although some lakes and rivers have improved dramatically, others have continued to deteriorate. Overall, some 40 percent of all freshwater bodies and much higher percentages of coastal estuaries and Great Lakes shorelines are regarded as impaired. Most of the continuing problem is due to nonpoint pollution caused by runoff from agricultural and mining operations; construction sites; and urban streets, lawns, and golf courses. Under the 1987 Clean Water Act revisions, states are required to develop plans for control of such indirect sources of water pollution, but these plans are not mandatory. In 1998 President Clinton launched a new Clean Water Action Plan to help state and local governments deal with this problem. Shortly before leaving office, his administration introduced new rules requiring states to draw up detailed plans for bringing 21,000 impaired bodies of water into compliance with national standards. The Bush administration canceled these regulations and eased Clinton-era rules for protecting wetlands.[36] However, on Earth Day 2004, President

Bush announced a series of new initiatives to preserve and restore wetlands over the next five years.[37] Bush also launched a new program to coordinate cleanup efforts in the Great Lakes, and, following two major reports on ocean pollution, to coordinate policies in that area.[38] Whether these policy initiatives will begin to reduce runoff of land-based pollutants remains to be seen.

Hazardous and Nuclear Waste

The storage, treatment, and disposal of hazardous and toxic wastes present another series of intractable problems in our industrial society. Despite growing efforts by manufacturers to reduce the use of hazardous and toxic materials (see chapter 12), the volume of dangerous waste continues to grow. Many solid and hazardous waste facilities have been closed, whereas others, such as incinerators, are meeting increasing public opposition. Nuclear power plants built in the 1960s and 1970s are running out of space for storing spent fuel long before a permanent repository for civilian high-level radioactive wastes will be available. The Department of Energy has spent billions of dollars studying the site feasibility of the proposed national repository at Yucca Mountain, Nevada. In February 2002 President Bush approved the site despite continuing controversy over its long-term safety, and Congress approved it over fierce opposition from Nevada's senators.[39] Whether the site will ever be opened remains to be seen. The cleanup of contaminated nuclear weapons production facilities and the storage and disposal of radioactive military wastes will also present enormous ongoing challenges for the Department of Energy.

Under the Comprehensive Environmental Response, Compensation and Liability ("Superfund") Act of 1980, more than nine hundred of the most contaminated toxic waste dumps in the United States have been cleaned up. The costs of cleanup have been allocated whenever possible to parties responsible for the contamination (the polluter-pays principle), with a federal trust fund (the Superfund) financed by taxes on oil and chemical production used for unrecoverable costs and emergency actions. However, since 1995 Congress has failed to reauthorize the taxes needed to replenish the trust fund, and President Bush has shifted funding to general taxpayer revenues.[40] However, the funds appropriated by Congress (about $1.25 billion in fiscal year 2005) are woefully inadequate for the task. The EPA estimates that as many as 355,000 sites could require cleanup over the next thirty years at a cost of $250 billion.[41] On the more positive side, the president proposed and Congress passed a bipartisan bill in 2002 to help states and cities clean up and redevelop less contaminated areas known as brownfields. Bush requested $210 million in his 2006 budget to support work at some six hundred sites of this kind.

Suburban Sprawl and Sustainable Communities

Environmentalists and policymakers increasingly have argued that sustainable development can best be pursued at local and regional levels—in a manner consistent with the well-established axiom "think globally, act locally." As chapter 3 makes clear, the movement toward sustainable communities, or what the EPA called "community-based environmental protection," spread across the nation during the 1990s and fostered hundreds of local efforts to address interrelated environmental, economic, and social issues. At the local level citizens have come together to identify the major problems affecting a community, such as degradation of local surface water or loss of natural habitats, and to develop appropriate solutions. Winning support for such new ways of thinking is never easy. Yet many of these community-based initiatives have involved formation of innovative partnerships among government, business, and citizen groups to help overcome conflicts that often arise in environmental protection. The EPA experimented with a variety of new community programs during the Clinton administration and continues to support low-profile "smart growth" and "green communities" programs under Bush.[42] For example, in January 2005 the EPA announced a new joint program with the National Oceanic and Atmospheric Administration to help coastal communities to balance natural resource protection with economic development.

It is still too early to tell how successful such intriguing community sustainability efforts will be, but there is little question of their appeal. This is particularly so in areas affected by rapid growth and suburban sprawl, and thus by problems such as highway congestion, air pollution, and loss of open space. In the November 2004 elections, for instance, voters throughout the country endorsed 120 of 161 state and local land conservation measures on the ballot.[43] In addition, many states have approved so-called smart growth policies that encourage communities to develop long-term and integrative land use plans, typically through highly participatory and collaborative processes.[44]

Environmental Justice

Another side of community development on which policy must continue to focus is the distributive effects of activities that negatively affect people and the environment. Substantial evidence indicates that low-income and minority groups are disproportionately exposed to environmental hazards such as lead poisoning, industrial air pollution, and toxic waste sites (see chapter 11). African Americans, Hispanics, Asians, and Native Americans have formed hundreds of new grassroots organizations to fight pollution in their communities, and mainstream environmental groups have become more sensitive to such inequities.

Beginning in George H. W. Bush's administration and accelerating under Clinton, the EPA and other federal agencies have been documenting unequal patterns of pollution exposure and investigating their causes. In February 1994 President Clinton issued Executive Order 12898, which called for all federal agencies to develop strategies for achieving environmental justice. The EPA established an Office of Environmental Justice and a civil rights office in the Office of the Administrator. The agency became more active in the late 1990s in supporting legal actions under Title VI of the 1964 Civil Rights Act, which prohibits racial discrimination by agencies receiving federal funds (see chapter 11). Christine Todd Whitman, the first EPA administrator under George W. Bush, strongly supported these efforts, but they have produced few positive results to date.[45]

International Leadership and Environmental Security

It is increasingly being recognized that most critical environmental problems are global issues that will require much greater international cooperation in the future. These issues include population growth; transboundary pollution; decline of ocean fisheries; international hazardous waste management; export and use of agricultural pesticides and toxic chemicals; the spread of human and animal diseases; and many issues relating to nuclear, biological, and chemical weapons proliferation. The United States cannot deal effectively with problems such as these unless it reengages with the world across a broad spectrum of diplomacy.[46] This means, among other things, that the United States needs to rebuild its ties with the United Nations and with its European allies if the country is to restore its leadership position.

The United States has been a leader in international environmental diplomacy in the past. The U.S. government played an active role in promoting the UN Conference on the Human Environment in Stockholm, Sweden, in 1972 and in supporting UN programs for the environment and population policy in subsequent years. Even during the Reagan administration—which was suspicious of multilateral agreements and imposed restrictions on population programs—the United States took the lead in negotiating the 1987 Montreal Protocol to protect the ozone layer.[47] Since that time, however, the United States has more often than not sought to block new international environmental agreements.[48] The United States has also shown indifference to the needs of developing nations (see chapter 15). Indeed, U.S. official development assistance declined in the aftermath of the Rio summit to less than one-tenth of 1 percent of the gross national product, placing the United States at the very bottom of developed nations in this regard.[49] Although in 2002 President Bush pledged an additional $10 billion to the Millennium Challenge Account, the goal of which is to reduce by half the number of people worldwide who are living in poverty by 2015, little of the additional funding has been forthcoming.[50]

Economic globalization brought about by trade liberalization has led to rapid economic growth in some developing countries, but also to growing threats to the environment.[51] China, for example, is experiencing horrendous air and water pollution, and within a decade most of the greenhouse gases emitted in the world will come from developing countries.[52] Many of these problems will affect the United States directly. Increased international trade under the World Trade Organization (WTO) may also produce conflicts between the rules of trade and existing national and international environmental protections (chapter 16). Although the WTO has created a Committee on Trade and the Environment to discuss these potential conflicts, it has accomplished little to date. The Bush administration, to its credit, has promised to include environmental safeguards in future trade agreements such as the proposed Central American Free Trade Agreement (CAFTA).[53] However, it is unclear whether these provisions will be effective or will be upheld by international courts in the future.

Many environmental problems are also beginning to be perceived as serious threats to national and international security. For example, environmental degradation has been recognized as a source of local and regional conflicts that result in large numbers of international refugees.[54] Global warming is also increasingly viewed as a security issue. A 2003 report commissioned by the U.S. Department of Defense warned that rapid climate change during the next twenty years could lead to catastrophes such as destructive storm surges, massive flooding and droughts, crop failures, famine, rioting throughout the world, and even nuclear conflict.[55] Many military analysts are concerned about our dependence on Middle Eastern oil and have called for far-reaching energy conservation measures.[56] The chief scientific adviser to the British government, Sir David King, has warned of global warming symptoms already affecting Europe and has stated that "climate change is the most severe problem we are facing today—more serious even than the threat of terrorism." [57] Differences over climate change and other environmental issues have become a major source of divergence between the United States and Europe, contributing to the weakening of the transatlantic alliance in recent years.[58] Unless these differences among the wealthiest nations are overcome, the rest of the world is unlikely to be willing or able to halt environmental devastation.

New Strategies and Methods

The 1990s saw major new efforts to "reinvent government" to make it more efficient and effective. The EPA has been a leader in this campaign. Yet in most areas the agency is still charged with writing detailed regulations requiring individual polluters to install specific technologies to mitigate emissions or discharges at "the end of the pipe." Such command-and-control regulation of major pollution sources has had considerable success in improving environmental quality (see chapter 1) and will continue to be needed to protect public health and environmental resources from many immediate threats. However, consensus is growing that new environmental strategies and policy instruments can often achieve better results at less cost. For the first time we have solid empirical evidence that many of these new approaches are effective, at least as a supplement to traditional regulation.[59] At the same time, however, we need to rethink the basic purposes of environmental policies if we are to move in the direction of sustainability. The following sections briefly discuss sustainability principles and alternative policy instruments.

Policy Integration

At a minimum, sustainable development requires much greater integration of environmental considerations into all sectors of governance. It is no longer sufficient to expect an independent agency such as the EPA to "take care of" pollution or for scattered agencies such as the U.S. Forest Service (Department of Agriculture) or the Fish and Wildlife Service (Interior Department) to handle natural resource issues. Departments such as Energy, Interior, Agriculture, Transportation, Commerce, Housing and Urban Development, Health and Human Services, and Defense all have major environmental responsibilities that need to be coordinated. The Clinton administration created a short-lived Office of Environmental Policy to coordinate cabinet policies, but it lacked the stature to intervene in departments and was soon abandoned. The President's Council on Sustainable Development also lacked operational powers. Although the Council on Environmental Quality still exists, it has lost most of its policy functions; and the Office of Management and Budget and its Office of Information and Regulatory Affairs are too narrowly focused on regulatory cost analysis to consider broader issues. Some new institutional authority or intergovernmental mechanism for sustainability policy analysis and planning may thus be necessary (the new Department of Homeland Security and the position of national intelligence director come to mind as examples of what could be done). Federal environmental laws, each of which was written to address a separate problem or medium, also need to be integrated through a comprehensive statute that cuts across regulatory domains and establishes overall sustainability goals and priorities.[60]

Pollution Prevention

The first principle of caregivers is "do no harm." Although it is unrealistic to pursue policies for zero-pollution discharge or absolute preservation of resources, sustainability requires that unnecessary harms be prevented whenever possible. It is better to eliminate pollution at the source than to try to clean it up later. Indeed, the Pollution Prevention Act of 1990 made prevention a priority goal for the nation. Unfortunately most of the other statutes governing environmental protection (see appendix 1) call for end-of-the-pipe controls or after-the-fact cleanup. Because state-of-the-art pollution controls are expensive, companies can often save money and increase profitability by reducing energy and material inputs or by redesigning processes to avoid pollution and waste generation. Hundreds of firms have joined voluntary pollution prevention and energy efficiency programs or have adopted new environmental management systems (see chapter 12). A broader national and international movement toward "green production" calls for more radical approaches to reducing ecological impacts throughout the entire life-cycle of products.[61] Planning for urban restoration and redesign can also eliminate many sources of unnecessary pollution and help to preserve open spaces (see chapter 3).

Precautionary Principle

Scientific risk assessment is an essential tool for setting regulatory standards and priorities. But as chapters 8 and 10 make clear, scientific evidence is often inconclusive and risk assessment methodologies have their limits. This is especially the case when complex, multidimensional issues such as climate change or biodiversity decline are being analyzed. In such cases the "precautionary principle" may be a better guide to action. This principle, found in the 1992 Rio Declaration on Environment and Development and several international environmental treaties, holds that "where there are threats of serious or irreversible damage, lack of full scientific certainty shall not be used as a reason for postponing cost-effective measures to prevent environmental degradation." [62] This approach has been widely adopted in Europe and since 1992 has been formally incorporated into the treaty of the European Union.[63] The precautionary principle is more controversial in the United States because it is often viewed as an excuse for trade barriers or as an invitation to policy based on irrational fears.[64] Yet, several of our basic environmental laws are highly precautionary, including the National Environmental Policy Act (in requiring prospective environmental impact assessments), the Clean Air Act (in setting ambient air quality standards based on health criteria alone), the Endangered Species Act (in requiring protection of species that could go extinct), and the Toxic Substances Control Act (in requiring premarket testing of chemicals). The precautionary approach can supplement "sound science" by providing a margin of safety and extra time for research without foreclosing future options; this is especially important when considering long-term intergenerational consequences such as those from global warming.

Economic Instruments

Economists have long espoused the concept of internalizing environmental costs by taxation or other means of pricing externalities. As A. Myrick Freeman points out in chapter 9, use of devices such as environmental taxes or fees and tradable pollution allowances can often achieve environmental goals more efficiently than command-and-control regulation. In an era of scarce public resources, it makes sense to maximize environmental quality benefits from pollution control expenditures. The idea of using market incentives to encourage behaviors that prevent pollution and conserve resources now has broad support among environmentalists as well as in the business community. Indeed, many observers believe that if environmental damage were fully accounted for (through "full cost pricing"), the level of environmental protection would be much higher than it is at present.

Environmental fees and taxes have been widely used in Europe and in some American states to reduce pollution, save energy, and encourage waste recycling (see chapter 2). For example, gasoline prices are extremely high in Europe compared to the United States in order to discourage driving and conserve energy (as well as raise revenues). It has been much more difficult to impose federal taxes to internalize environmental costs in the United States. The failure of President Clinton's proposed BTU tax on energy in 1993 suggests that tax increases affecting powerful sectors of the economy (such as agriculture and trucking) stand little chance in Congress. At the same time, many polluting and resource-consuming industries have enjoyed large tax breaks and other subsidies. These are unfortunately much greater than the tax incentives that Congress has enacted to encourage positive environmental behavior (such as tax credits for technological innovation). Tax shifts that would reward good behavior and punish bad could offset each other and thus be revenue neutral. For example, Germany's "ecological tax reform" of 1999 raised taxes on energy consumption while lowering social security taxes.[65]

If the United States has resisted green taxes, it has been the leader in creating marketable permit systems. Beginning with "bubble" and "offset" policies to increase flexibility in meeting air quality standards in the late 1970s, the EPA has introduced mechanisms to allow regulated companies to buy and sell pollution rights within overall limits. Cap-and-trade systems lower the costs of compliance by equalizing marginal abatement costs in meeting overall reduction goals (see chapter 9). Such regimes have been successfully used in phasing out leaded gasoline and chlorofluorocarbons (CFCs) and in reducing sulfur dioxide and nitrogen oxide emissions from coal-burning power plants in the United States.[66] Virtually all current proposals for further improving air quality (including Bush's Clear Skies program) and reducing greenhouse gas emissions (including the McCain-Lieberman Climate Stewardship Act) would use similar cap-and-trade systems. The European Union has already created a tradable permit system for carbon dioxide emissions from heavy industry as part of its effort to meet its Kyoto Protocol obligations. In general, cap-and-trade regimes can be highly efficient and effective, but much depends on the level at which caps are set and the timetables for achieving them.

Devolution to States and Communities

States vary greatly in their commitment to environmental protection and in their capacity to implement policies effectively.[67] Nevertheless, as Barry G. Rabe argues in chapter 2, the long-term trend in most states is toward improved regulatory capabilities, and in many cases states are now at the forefront of policy innovation. In this light, policy experts are increasingly arguing that more environmental authority should be delegated to the states.[68] Much of the rationale for the proposed devolution stems from the fact that the states already issue 75 to 80 percent of the permits required by federal environmental statutes.[69] They do so under more or less strict supervision by the EPA, often under excessively detailed and conflicting guidelines. Greater flexibility is needed if states are to take more integrated, cross-media approaches to protecting natural resources and improving community health. Increased trust and cooperation between levels of government is essential for improving policy implementation.[70]

Since the mid-1990s the EPA has experimented with selective devolution to states through its National Environmental Performance Partnership System. It has also experimented with a variety of programs such as Project XL, under which companies or local governments are given greater flexibility in meeting regulatory requirements in return for a commitment to superior environmental performance. Although these programs have proven difficult to implement, they nevertheless hold promise for the future.[71] It is important, however, that national performance standards (for example, for pollution reduction) be maintained as states are given more flexibility in achieving them. One way of ensuring this is through "accountable devolution," in which states with strong performance records would be granted greater flexibility than those with weaker records.[72]

Collaborative Planning

Within the federal-state structure, enormous opportunities exist for improving environmental performance through new collaborative planning and decision-making processes. Collaborative planning involves a search for voluntary, consensual solutions to environmental problems through joint participation by federal, state, and local agencies; business and industry; environmental groups; other interested nongovernmental organizations; and citizens.[73] Such processes can be used to address a wide range of problems such as preservation of endangered species, wetlands, and other natural resources; development of areawide pollution prevention strategies; and siting of facilities to promote social and racial justice. One popular form of collaborative planning is the development of habitat conservation plans that protect endangered species while permitting some development in surrounding areas.[74] Several hundred of these agreements have been completed (see chapter 14). By intervening before an ecosystem becomes so degraded that few options are left, this approach facilitates carefully planned trade-offs between environmental protection and economic growth and thus supports the goal of sustainable development. However, care must be taken to ensure that such agreements are enforced and that they are flexible enough to permit revision if new scientific information demonstrates their inadequacy.[75]

Sustainability Indicators

The concept of sustainable development itself has many meanings and requires much more discussion and research than it has had so far in the United States. Whatever the precise definition, however, concrete indicators are needed by which to measure progress toward sustainability in different sectors. This work requires development not only of better measures of environmental quality per se—that is, the health of ecosystems and the limits to the stresses we can place on them—but also of improved gauges of progress in human activity to reduce society's impacts on natural systems. For example, all nations need to focus on trends in energy consumption, greenhouse gas emissions, land use, waste generation, recycling and reuse of materials, agricultural practices, and driving habits. But broad social and cultural factors such as income inequality, population growth, educational patterns, political representation, and access to information can also be considered important indicators of sustainability. Many governmental and nongovernmental organizations are working on such indicators, including the EPA and other federal agencies as well as state and local bodies.[76]

Traditional measures of economic welfare need to be modified in this light. Standard national accounting indexes that measure gross national product or gross domestic product in monetary terms fail to capture many facets of human and environmental well-being. For example, these indexes count all expenditures for pollution control and cleanup as part of the output of goods and services but do not subtract the economic value of losses caused by environmental degradation and depletion of nonrenewable resources.[77] Increased pollution thus counts positively rather than negatively, whereas depreciation of environmental capital is ignored. A number of scholars and international agencies, including the World Bank, have been developing alternative measures of welfare that more accurately value environmental goods and services and overall quality of life. The United States does considerably less well on some of these scales than on conventional economic indexes.[78] Until we begin to think differently about basic economic indicators, we are unlikely to make genuine progress toward sustainable development.

Governing the Future

It has been said that for the first time in evolutionary history, human beings have achieved a greater measure of influence over the future of their planet than evolution itself. If this is so, we have no alternative but to decide what kind of future we want. One possibility is to continue on our present course of human development. A growing world consensus holds, however, that this course cannot be sustained without triggering catastrophic changes in the Earth's natural systems. A 1992 report of the National Academy of Sciences and the Royal Society of London opened with a dire warning: "If current predictions of population growth prove accurate and patterns of human activity on the planet remain unchanged, science and technology may not be able to prevent either irreversible degradation of the environment or continued poverty for much of the world." [79] Yet most environmental experts believe we have time to preserve our essential life support systems if we act with sufficient foresight in the next few decades.

Doing so will demand far more international cooperation and "governance" than we now have. [80] The challenges we face are ultimately human and political: meeting basic human needs, limiting population growth, restricting consumption of nonrenewable resources, building a sense of world community, and negotiating mutually beneficial agreements among nations. These goals can be achieved only with a much longer time horizon than we are accustomed to in democratic societies. Political leadership is therefore essential. Democracies in the twentieth century proved capable of sustaining national and international efforts to defeat enemies in war and to contain them for decades in peacetime. Sustainable development will be the challenge of the twenty-first century.

Suggested Web Sites

Institute for the Analysis of Global Security (www.iags.org/saf.html)
International Institute for Sustainable Development (www.iisd.org)
NatureServe: A Network Connecting Science with Conservation (www.natureserve.org)
Pew Center on Global Climate Change (www.pewclimate.org)
Sustainable Measures (www.sustainablemeasures.com)
World Business Council for Sustainable Development (www.wbcsd .ch/templates/TemplateWBCSD5/layout.asp?MenuID=1)
World Wide Web Virtual Library on Sustainable Development (www .ulb.ac.be/ceese/meta/sustain.htm)
World Wildlife Fund (WWF) (www.panda.org)

Notes

1. The landmark *Millennium Ecosystem Assessment,* issued March 30, 2005, concluded that "approximately 60 percent of the ecosystem services that support life on Earth . . . are being degraded or used unsustainably." The assessment was conducted by 1,300 experts from 95 countries. See www.maweb.org for details.
2. World Commission on Environment and Development, *Our Common Future* (Oxford, U.K.: Oxford University Press, 1987), 43.
3. Documents relating to the World Summit on Sustainable Development can be found at www.johannesburgsummit.org. See also Gary Gardner, "The Challenge of Johannesburg: Creating a More Secure World," in *State of the World 2002,* ed. Christopher Flavin et al. (Washington, D.C.: Worldwatch Institute, 2002); and James Gustave Speth, "Perspectives on the Johannesburg Summit," *Environment* 45 (January–February 2003): 24–29.
4. See also Robert C. Paehlke, "Sustainability," in *Environmental Governance Reconsidered,* ed. Robert F. Durant, Daniel J. Fiorino, and Rosemary O'Leary (Cambridge: MIT Press, 2004), 35–67; John C. Dernbach, ed., *Stumbling Toward Sustainability* (Washington, D.C.: Environmental Law Institute, 2002); and Keekok Lee, Alan

Holland, and Desmond McNeill, *Global Sustainable Development in the 21st Century* (Edinburgh, U.K.: Edinburgh University Press, 2000).

5. For a discussion of the corresponding three generations of public policy responses, sometimes described in terms of three "environmental epochs," see Daniel A. Mazmanian and Michael E. Kraft, eds., *Toward Sustainable Communities: Transition and Transformations in Environmental Policy* (Cambridge: MIT Press, 1999).

6. *Choosing a Sustainable Future: The Report of the National Commission on the Environment* (Washington, D.C.: Island Press, 1993), xi.

7. President's Council on Sustainable Development, *Sustainable America* and *Sustainable Development: A New Consensus* (Washington, D.C.: U.S. Government Printing Office, 1996); *Building on Consensus: A Progress Report on Sustainable America* (Washington, D.C.: President's Council on Sustainable Development, 1997).

8. Mazmanian and Kraft, *Toward Sustainable Communities,* contains case studies of local and regional sustainable development initiatives.

9. Gary C. Bryner, "The United States: 'Sorry—Not Our Problem,' " in *Implementing Sustainable Development: Strategies and Initiatives in High Consumption Societies,* ed. William M. Lafferty and James Meadowcroft (Oxford, U.K.: Oxford University Press, 2000), 273–302.

10. Bush's environmental philosophy can be found at www.whitehouse.gov/infocus/environment.

11. Daniel C. Esty, Mark Levy, Tanja Srebotnjak, and Alexander de Sherbinin, *2005 Environmental Sustainability Index: Benchmarking National Environmental Stewardship* (New Haven: Yale Center for Environmental Law & Policy, 2005), available online at www.yale.edu/esi. States are ranked on the basis of twenty-one indicators reflecting seventy-six underlying variables.

12. Lizette Alvarez, "Blair Outlines Plans to Slash Emissions over 50 Years," *New York Times,* February 25, 2003.

13. See, for example, Kenneth Chang, "As Earth Warms, the Hottest Issue Is Energy," *New York Times,* Science Times, November 4, 2003; Associated Press, "Carbon Dioxide in Air Rises at Faster Rate, Scientists Say," March 21, 2004, www.nytimes.com; Andrew C. Revkin, "Global Warming Is Expected to Raise Hurricane Intensity," *New York Times,* September 30, 2004; Revkin, "U.S. and 7 Countries Weigh New Findings on Arctic Climate," *New York Times,* November 24, 2004; Larry Rohter, "Antarctica, Warming, Looks Ever More Vulnerable," *New York Times,* January 25, 2005; Erik Stokstad, "Defrosting the Carbon Freezer of the North," *Science* 304 (June 11, 2004): 1618–1620.

14. "This Year Was the 2nd Hottest, Confirming a Trend, UN Says," *New York Times,* December 19, 2001; William K. Stevens, "1998 and 1999 Warmest Years Ever Recorded," *New York Times,* December 19, 1999; Associated Press, "Hot Spot in 2003? The Earth, U.N. Says," December 17, 2003, www.nytimes.com; Kevin Gray, "4th-Hottest Year on Record: 2004," *Minneapolis Star Tribune,* December 16, 2004.

15. Philip P. Pan, "Scientists Issue Dire Prediction on Warming," *Washington Post,* January 22, 2001; "Report Warns of Disaster from Global Warming," *New York Times,* January 22, 2001. The text of the report can be found in Intergovernmental Panel on Climate Change, *Climate Change 2001: The Scientific Basis,* ed. John T. Houghton et al. (Cambridge, U.K.: Cambridge University Press, 2001).

16. David G. Victor, *Climate Change: Debating America's Policy Options* (New York: Council on Foreign Relations, 2004), 11.

17. Larry Rohter, "U.S. Waters Down Global Commitment to Curb Greenhouse Gases," *New York Times,* December 19, 2004.

18. Eileen Claussen, "Climate Change Solutions: A Science and Policy Agenda," December 6, 2004, www.pewclimate.org/presss_room/speech_transcripts/climatechange.cfm, February 28, 2005.

19. The Bush administration is spending about $1.2 billion annually on energy efficiency, renewable energy, and energy conservation technologies. See "Department of Energy FY2006 Congressional Budget Request: Budget Highlights," February 2005, www .mbe.doe.gov/budget/06budget/Content/Highlights/06_highlights.pdf.

20. Katherine Q. Seelye, "McCain and Lieberman Offer Bill to Require Cuts in Gases," *New York Times*, January 9, 2003; Eric Pianin, "Fight Ahead on Emissions, McCain, Lieberman Plan Push for Greenhouse Gas Limits, *Washington Post*, January 7, 2003; Pianin, "Senate Rejects Mandatory Cap on Greenhouse Gas Emissions," *Washington Post*, October 31, 2003; Andrew C. Revkin, "Election Over, McCain Criticizes Bush on Climate Change," *New York Times*, November 16, 2004.

21. For one such scenario, see Victor, *Climate Change*, especially pp. 103–114. See also Stuart E. Eizenstat and David B. Sandalow, "The Years after Tomorrow," *New York Times*, July 5, 2004; and Mark Landler, "Mixed Feelings as Treaty on Greenhouse Gases Takes Effect," *New York Times*, Business Section, February 16, 2005.

22. For a summary, see Pew Center for Global Climate Change, "Learning from State Action on Climate Change," December 2004, www.pewclimate.org/policy_center/policy_reports_and_analysis/states/index.cfm. See also Danny Hakim, "California Backs Plan for Big Cut in Car Emissions," *New York Times*, September 25, 2004; and Eli Sanders, "Rebuffing Bush, 132 Mayors Embrace Kyoto Rules," *New York Times*, May 14, 2005.

23. See, for example, Niles Eldredge, "The Sixth Extinction," at www.actionbioscience .org/newfrontiers/eldredge2.html.

24. World Wildlife Fund for Nature, *Living Planet Report 2004*, October 2004, www .panda.org/downloads/general/lpr2004.pdf.

25. Andrew C. Revkin, "Warming Is Found to Disrupt Species," *New York Times*, January 2, 2004; James Gorman, "Scientists Predict Widespread Extinction by Global Warming," *New York Times*, January 8, 2004.

26. B. A. Stein, L. S. Kutner, and J. S. Adams, eds., *Precious Heritage: The Status of Biodiversity in the United States* (Oxford, U.K.: Oxford University Press, 2000). See also Stein, "A Fragile Cornucopia: Assessing the Status of U.S. Biodiversity," *Environment* (September 2001): 10–22.

27. Stein, "A Fragile Cornucopia," 13–15. Detailed information can be found on Nature-Serve: An On-line Encyclopedia of Life, www.natureserve.org.

28. U.S. Fish and Wildlife Service, "Threatened and Endangered Animals and Plants," http://endangered.fws.gov/wildlife.html#species.

29. Michael Grunwald, "Bush Seeks to Curb Endangered Species Suits," *Washington Post*, April 12, 2001; Jenifer 8. Lee, "Money Gone, U.S. Suspends Designations of Habitats," *New York Times*, May 29, 2003; "Saving Species: Landmark Law Turns 30," *Minneapolis Star Tribune*, December 28, 2003.

30. Jennifer 8. Lee, "Clear Skies No More for Millions in U.S.," *New York Times*, April 13, 2004; Associated Press, "EPA Designates 474 Counties as Failing Air Quality Standards," April 15, 2004, www.nytimes.com; Michael Janofsky, "Many Counties Failing Fine-Particle Air Rules," *New York Times*, December 18, 2004.

31. Katherine Q. Seelye, "Study Sees 6,000 Deaths from Power Plants," *New York Times*, April 18, 2002.

32. EPA News Release, "Diesel Retrofit Grants and Clean Diesel Campaign Announced," February 23, 2005.

33. See, for example, Jennifer 8. Lee, "U.S. Proposes Easing Rules on Emissions of Mercury," *New York Times*, December 3, 2003; Michael Janofsky, "Inspector General Says E.P.A. Rule Aids Polluters," *New York Times*, October 1, 2004; Felicity Barringer, "E.P.A. Accused of a Predetermined Finding on Mercury," *New York Times*, February 4, 2005; and Shankar Vedantam, "New EPA Mercury Rule Omits Conflicting Data," *Washington Post*, March 22, 2005. According to the latter article, the EPA ignored a study by the Harvard Center for Risk Analysis that projected health benefits from

regulating mercury that were 100 times higher than those based on data used in issuing the rule.

34. Natural Resources Defense Council, "Clear Skies Would Let Plants Pollute More, Study Concludes," January 13, 2005, www.nrdc.org/bushrecord/articles/br_1857.asp.

35. Michael Janofsky, "Climate Debate Threatens Republican Clean-Air Bill," *New York Times,* January 27, 2005.

36. Douglas Jehl, "EPA Delays Further Rules of Clinton Era," *New York Times,* July 17, 2001; Associated Press, "E.P.A. Opposes Plan on Runoff Protection," December 21, 2002, www.nytimes.com; Christopher Marquis, "Bush Administration Rolls Back Clinton Rules for Wetlands," *New York Times,* January 15, 2002; Douglas Jehl, "U.S. Plan Could Ease Limits on Wetlands Development," *New York Times,* January 11, 2003.

37. White House press release, "President Bush Announces Wetlands Initiative on Earth Day," April 22, 2004, www.whitehouse.gov/news/releases/2004/04/20040422-4.html. See also Elisabeth Bumiller, "Bush Promotes Wetlands Plan to Counter Kerry's Attack," *New York Times,* April 24, 2004.

38. Stephen Kinzer, "Bush Panel Will Study Great Lakes Cleanup," *New York Times,* May 19, 2004; Cornelia Dean, "Bush Forms Panel to Coordinate Ocean Policy," *New York Times,* December 18, 2004.

39. Matthew L. Wald, "Energy Department Recommends Yucca Mountain for Nuclear Waste Burial," *New York Times,* February 15, 2002; Alison Mitchell, "Senate Approves Nuclear Waste Site in Nevada Mountain," *New York Times,* July 10, 2002.

40. Katharine Q. Seelye, "Bush Proposing to Shift Burden of Toxic Cleanups to Taxpayers," *Washington Post,* February 24, 2002; Eric Pianin, "Superfund Faces Struggle for Room in the Budget," *Washington Post,* September 14, 2003; Felicity Barringer, "Polluted Sites Could Face Shortage of Cleanup Money," *New York Times,* August 16, 2004.

41. Michael Janofsky, "Changes May Be Needed in Superfund, Chief Says," *New York Times,* December 5, 2004.

42. U.S. Environmental Protection Agency, "People, Places, and Partnerships: A Progress Report on Community-Based Environmental Protection" (Washington, D.C.: EPA, Office of the Administrator, July 1997). See also Mazmanian and Kraft, *Toward Sustainable Communities*; and Kent E. Portney, *Taking Sustainable Cities Seriously* (Cambridge: MIT Press, 2003).

43. Will Rogers, "It's Easy Being Green," *New York Times,* November 20, 2004.

44. William A. Shutkin, *The Land That Could Be: Environmentalism and Democracy in the Twenty-First Century* (Cambridge: MIT Press, 2000).

45. For more detail, see Evan J. Ringquist, "Environmental Justice," in *Environmental Governance Reconsidered,* ed. Durant, Fiorino, and O'Leary, 255–287.

46. Alan Cowell, "Blair Calls on United States to Cooperate with Rest of the World," *New York Times,* January 27, 2005.

47. See Richard Benedick, *Ozone Diplomacy* (Cambridge: Harvard University Press, 1991); and, more generally, Lynton K. Caldwell, *International Environmental Policy,* 3rd ed. (Durham, N.C.: Duke University Press, 1996).

48. See Regina S. Axelrod, David Leonard Downie, and Norman J. Vig, eds., *The Global Environment: Institutions, Law and Policy,* 2nd ed. (Washington, D.C.: CQ Press, 2005).

49. Paul G. Harris, ed., *The Environment, International Relations, and U.S. Foreign Policy* (Washington, D.C.: Georgetown University Press, 2001).

50. "America, the Indifferent," *New York Times,* December 23, 2004.

51. James Gustave Speth, *Red Sky at Morning* (New Haven: Yale University Press, 2004); and Speth, ed., *Worlds Apart: Globalization and the Environment* (Washington, D.C.: Island Press, 2003).

52. See, for example, Elizabeth C. Economy, *The River Runs Black: The Environmental Challenge to China's Future* (Ithaca, N.Y.: Cornell University Press, 2004).

53. Daniel C. Esty, "Economic Integration and Environmental Protection," in Axelrod, Downie, and Vig, *Global Environment*, 155.

54. See, for example, Norman Myers, *Ultimate Security* (New York: Norton, 1993); Thomas F. Homer-Dixon, *Environment, Scarcity, and Violence* (Princeton: Princeton University Press, 1999); T. F. Homer-Dixon and Jessica Blitt, eds., *Ecoviolence* (Lanham, Md.: Rowman and Littlefield, 1998); Worldwatch Institute, *State of the World 2005: Redefining Global Security* (New York: Norton, 2005). For a useful chronology of academic and official studies of environment-security links, see Ken Conca, Alexander Carius, and Geoffrey D. Dabelko, "Building Peace through Environmental Cooperation," in the latter volume.

55. The study was leaked to the press in early 2004. See, for example, David Stipp, "Climate Collapse: the Pentagon's Weather Nightmare," *Fortune,* January 26, 2004 (full text available online at http://sierratimes.com/04/02/09/ar_weather.htm); Mark Townsend and Paul Harris, "Now the Pentagon Tells Bush: Climate Change Will Destroy Us," *The Observer* (London), February 24, 2004.

56. See Institute for the Analysis of Global Security, "Open Letter to the American People," www.iags.org/saf.html; and Thomas L. Friedman, "Geo-Greening by Example," *New York Times,* March 27, 2005.

57. David A. King, "Climate Change Science: Adapt, Mitigate, or Ignore?," *Science* (January 9, 2004): 176.

58. Norman J. Vig and Michael G. Faure, eds., *Green Giants? Environmental Policies of the United States and the European Union* (Cambridge: MIT Press, 2004).

59. See, for example, Durant, Fiorino, and O'Leary, *Environmental Governance Reconsidered*; Winston Harrington, Richard D. Morgenstern, and Thomas Sterner, eds., *Choosing Environmental Policy: Comparing Instruments and Outcomes in the United States and Europe* (Washington, D.C.: Resources for the Future, 2004); and Michael T. Hatch, ed., *Environmental Policymaking: Assessing the Use of Alternative Policy Instruments* (Albany: State University of New York Press, 2005). For somewhat more skeptical views, see Andrew Jordan, Rüdiger K. W. Wurzel, and Anthony R. Zito, eds., *"New" Instruments of Environmental Governance? National Experiences and Prospects* (London: Frank Cass, 2003); and Theo de Bruijn and Vicki Norberg-Bohm, eds., *Industrial Transformation: Environmental Policy Innovation in The United States and Europe* (Cambridge: MIT Press, 2005).

60. See, for example, J. Clarence Davies and Jan Mazurek, *Pollution Control in the United States: Evaluating the System* (Washington, D.C.: Resources for the Future, 1998).

61. Ken Geiser, "Pollution Prevention," in *Environmental Governance Reconsidered,* ed. Durant, Fiorino, and O'Leary, 427–454. See also Lester R. Brown, *Eco-Economy: Building an Economy for the Earth* (New York: Norton, 2001); Paul Hawken, Amory Lovins, and L. Hunter Lovins, *Natural Capitalism: Creating the Next Industrial Revolution* (Boston: Little, Brown, 1999); Joel S. Hirschhorn and Kirsten U. Oldenburg, *Prosperity without Pollution* (New York: Van Nostrand Reinhold, 1991); and Stephen Schmidheiney, *Changing Course: A Global Business Perspective on Development and Environment* (Cambridge: MIT Press, 1992).

62. Rio Declaration on Environment and Development, Principle 15. It is found in different versions in treaties including the Framework Convention on Climate Change, the Biosafety Protocol, and the Stockholm Convention on Persistent Organic Pollutants. See also Global Development Research Center, "Wingspread Statement on the Precautionary Principle," www.gdrc.org/u-gov/precaution-3.html.

63. For a summary, see Theofanis Christoforou, "The Precautionary Principle, Risk Assessment, and the Comparative Role of Science in the European Community and the U.S. Legal Systems," in *Green Giants?* ed. Vig and Faure, 17–51.

64. Cass R. Sunstein, *Laws of Fear: Beyond the Precautionary Principle* (Cambridge, U.K.: Cambridge University Press, 2005); Jonathan B. Wiener and Michael D. Rogers, "Comparing Precaution in the US and Europe," *Journal of Risk Research* 5 (2002):

317–349. Compare Joel A. Tickner, ed., *Precaution, Environmental Science and Preventive Public Policy* (Washington, D.C.: Island Press, 2002).

65. See Rüdiger Wurzel et al., "From High Regulatory State to Social and Ecological Market Economy? 'New' Environmental Policy Instruments in Germany," in *"New" Instruments of Environmental Governance?* ed. Jordan et al., 123–127; and Michael Kohlhaas and Bettina Meyer, "Ecological Tax Reform in Germany: Economic and Political Analysis of an Evolving Policy," in *The Use of Alternative Policy Instruments for Environmental Protection,* ed. Hatch, 125–150.

66. See chaps. 2, 6, 7 and 8 in Harrington, Morgenstern, and Sterner, *Choosing Environmental Policy.*

67. James P. Lester, "A New Federalism? Environmental Policy in the States," in *Environmental Policy in the 1990s,* 3rd ed., Norman J. Vig and Michael E. Kraft, eds. (Washington, D.C.: CQ Press, 1994).

68. See especially National Academy of Public Administration (NAPA), *Resolving the Paradox of Environmental Protection: An Agenda for Congress, EPA and the States* (Washington, D.C.: NAPA, 1997); and DeWitt John, *Civic Environmentalism: Alternatives to Regulation in States and Communities* (Washington, D.C.: CQ Press, 1994).

69. Terry Davies et al., *Reforming Permitting* (Washington, D.C.: Resources for the Future, 2001), 8.

70. Denise Scheberle, "Devolution," and DeWitt John, "Civic Environmentalism," in *Environmental Governance Reconsidered,* ed. Durant, Fiorino, and O'Leary; Mazmanian and Kraft, *Toward Sustainable Communities;* and Michael E. Kraft and Denise Scheberle, "Environmental Federalism at Decade's End: New Approaches and Strategies," *Publius* 28 (winter 1998): 131–146.

71. See Alfred A. Marcus, Donald A. Geffen, and Ken Sexton, *Reinventing Environmental Regulation: Lessons from Project XL* (Washington, D.C.: Resources for the Future, 2002).

72. For an excellent discussion of the pros and cons of devolution, see Scheberle, "Devolution."

73. Tomas M. Koontz et al., *Collaborative Environmental Management: What Roles for Government?* (Washington, D.C.: Resources for the Future, 2004).

74. See Timothy Beatley, *Habitat Conservation Planning: Endangered Species and Urban Growth* (Austin: University of Texas Press, 1994); Reed F. Noss and Allen Y. Cooperrider, *Saving Nature's Legacy: Protecting and Restoring Biodiversity* (Washington, D.C.: Island Press, 1994).

75. Koontz et al., *Collaborative Environmental Management,* chap. 4. See also John, "Civic Environmentalism," for a discussion of the conditions under which collaborative processes are likely to work or to fail.

76. See, for example, the Environmental Sustainability Index cited in note 11; Paehlke, "Sustainability"; Portney, *Taking Sustainable Cities Seriously;* and Robert W. Kates, Thomas M. Parris, and Anthony A. Leiserowitz, "What Is Sustainable Development?," *Environment* 47 (April 2005): 8–21. For other sources, see www .sustainablemeasures.com and www.iisd.org/ic/info/ss9504.htm.

77. See National Research Council, *Nature's Numbers: Expanding the National Income Accounts to Include the Environment* (Washington, D.C.: National Academy of Sciences, 1999); Robert Repetto, "Earth in the Balance Sheet: Incorporating Natural Resources in National Income Accounts," *Environment* 34 (September 1992): 12–20, 43–45; and Herman E. Daly and John B. Cobb Jr., *For the Common Good* (Boston: Beacon, 1989), 62–84.

78. See note 11.

79. Quoted in Lester Brown, "A New Era Unfolds," *State of the World 1993,* ed. Lester Brown et al. (New York: Norton, 1993), 3.

80. See Axelrod, Downie, and Vig, *Global Environment;* Speth, *Red Sky at Morning;* and Hilary French, "Reshaping Global Governance," in *State of the World 2002,* ed. Christopher Flavin et al. (Washington, D.C.: Worldwatch Institute, 2002), 174–198.

Appendix 1 Major Federal Laws on the Environment, 1969–2004

Legislation	Implementing Agency	Key Provisions
		Nixon Administration
National Environmental Policy Act of 1969, PL 91–190	All federal agencies	Declared a national policy to "encourage productive and enjoyable harmony between man and his environment"; required environmental impact statements; created Council on Environmental Quality.
Resources Recovery Act of 1970, PL 91–512	Health, Education, and Welfare Department (later Environmental Protection Agency)	Set up a program of demonstration and construction grants for innovative solid waste management systems; provided state and local agencies with technical and financial assistance in developing resource recovery and waste disposal systems.
Clean Air Act Amendments of 1970, PL 91–604	Environmental Protection Agency (EPA)	Required administrator to set national primary and secondary air quality standards and certain emissions limits; required states to develop implementation plans by specific dates; required reductions in automobile emissions.
Federal Water Pollution Control Act (Clean Water Act) Amendments of 1972, PL 92–500	EPA	Set national water quality goals; established pollutant discharge permit system; increased federal grants to states to construct waste treatment plants.
Federal Environmental Pesticides Control Act of 1972 (amended the Federal Insecticide, Fungicide, and Rodenticide Act [FIFRA] of 1947), PL 92–516	EPA	Required registration of all pesticides in U.S. commerce; allowed administrator to cancel or suspend registration under specified circumstances.
Marine Protection Act of 1972, PL 92–532	EPA	Regulated dumping of waste materials into the oceans and coastal waters.

(Continued on next page)

Appendix 1 *(Continued)*

Legislation	Implementing Agency	Key Provisions
Coastal Zone Management Act of 1972, PL 92-583	Office of Coastal Zone Management, Commerce Department	Authorized federal grants to the states to develop coastal zone management plans under federal guidelines.
Endangered Species Act of 1973, PL 93-205	Fish and Wildlife Service, Interior Department	Broadened federal authority to protect all "threatened" as well as "endangered" species; authorized grant program to assist state programs; required coordination among all federal agencies.
Ford Administration		
Safe Drinking Water Act of 1974, PL 93-523	EPA	Authorized federal government to set standards to safeguard the quality of public drinking water supplies and to regulate state programs for protecting underground water sources.
Toxic Substances Control Act of 1976, PL 94-469	EPA	Authorized premarket testing of chemical substances; allowed the EPA to ban or regulate the manufacture, sale, or use of any chemical presenting an "unreasonable risk of injury to health or environment"; prohibited most uses of PCBs.
Federal Land Policy and Management Act of 1976, PL 94-579	Bureau of Land Management, Interior Department	Gave Bureau of Land Management authority to manage public lands for long-term benefits; officially ended policy of conveying public lands into private ownership.
Resource Conservation and Recovery Act of 1976, PL 94-580	EPA	Required the EPA to set regulations for hazardous waste treatment, storage, transportation, and disposal; provided assistance for state hazardous waste programs under federal guidelines.
National Forest Management Act of 1976, PL 94-588	U.S. Forest Service, Agriculture Department	Gave statutory permanence to national forest lands and set new standards for their management; restricted timber harvesting to protect soil and watersheds; limited clear-cutting.

Carter Administration

Legislation	Administering agency	Description
Surface Mining Control and Reclamation Act of 1977, PL 95–87	Interior Department	Established environmental controls over strip mining; limited mining on farmland, alluvial valleys, and slopes; required restoration of land to original contours.
Clean Air Act Amendments of 1977, PL 95–95	EPA	Amended and extended Clean Air Act; postponed deadlines for compliance with auto emissions and air quality standards; set new standards for "prevention of significant deterioration" in clean air areas.
Clean Water Act Amendments of 1977, PL 95–217	EPA	Extended deadlines for industry and cities to meet treatment standards; set national standards for industrial pretreatment of wastes; increased funding for sewage treatment construction grants and gave states flexibility in determining spending priorities.
Public Utility Regulatory Policies Act of 1978, PL 95–617	Energy Department, states	Provided for Energy Department and Federal Energy Regulatory Commission regulation of electric and natural gas utilities and crude oil transportation systems in order to promote energy conservation and efficiency; allowed small cogeneration and renewable energy projects to sell power to utilities.
Alaska National Interest Lands Conservation Act of 1980, PL 96–487	Interior Department, Agriculture Department	Protected 102 million acres of Alaskan land as national wilderness, wildlife refuges, and parks.
Comprehensive Environmental Response, Compensation, and Liability Act of 1980 (CERCLA), PL 96–510	EPA	Authorized federal government to respond to hazardous waste emergencies and to clean up chemical dump sites; created $1.6 billion "Superfund"; established liability for cleanup costs.

Reagan Administration

Legislation	Administering agency	Description
Nuclear Waste Policy Act of 1982, PL 97–425; Nuclear Waste Policy Amendments Act of 1987, PL 100–203	Energy Department	Established a national plan for the permanent disposal of high-level nuclear waste; authorized the Energy Department to site, obtain a license for, construct, and operate geologic repositories for spent fuel from commercial nuclear power plants. Amendments in 1987 specified Yucca Mountain, Nevada, as the sole national site to be studied.

(Continued on next page)

Appendix 1 (*Continued*)

Legislation	Implementing Agency	Key Provisions
Resource Conservation and Recovery Act Amendments of 1984, PL 98-616	EPA	Revised and strengthened EPA procedures for regulating hazardous waste facilities; authorized grants to states for solid and hazardous waste management; prohibited land disposal of certain hazardous liquid wastes; required states to consider recycling in comprehensive solid waste plans.
Food Security Act of 1985 (also called the farm bill), PL 99-198. Renewed in 1990, 1996, and 2002.	Agriculture Department	Limited federal program benefits for producers of commodities on highly erodible land or converted wetlands; established a conservation reserve program; authorized Agriculture Department technical assistance for subsurface water quality preservation; revised and extended the Soil and Water Conservation Act (1977) programs through the year 2008. The 1996 renewal of the farm bill authorized $56 billion over seven years for a variety of farm and forestry programs. These include an Environmental Quality Incentives Program to provide assistance and incentive payments to farmers, especially those facing serious threats to soil, water, grazing lands, wetlands, and wildlife habitat. Spending was increased substantially in 2002.
Safe Drinking Water Act of 1986, PL 99-339	EPA	Reauthorized the Safe Drinking Water Act of 1974 and revised EPA safe drinking water programs, including grants to states for drinking water standards enforcement and groundwater protection programs; accelerated EPA schedule for setting standards for maximum contaminant levels of eighty-three toxic pollutants.
Superfund Amendments and Reauthorization Act of 1986 (SARA), PL 99-499	EPA	Provided $8.5 billion through 1991 to clean up the nation's most dangerous abandoned chemical waste dumps; set strict standards and timetables for cleaning up such sites; required that industry provide local communities with information on hazardous chemicals used or emitted.
Clean Water Act Amendments of 1987, PL 100-4	EPA	Amended the Federal Water Pollution Control Act of 1972; extended and revised EPA water pollution control programs, including grants to states for construction of wastewater treatment facilities and implementation of mandated nonpoint-source pollution management plans; expanded EPA enforcement authority; established a national estuary program.

Global Climate Protection Act of 1987, PL 100–204	State Department	Authorized the State Department to develop an approach to the problems of global climate change; created an intergovernmental task force to develop U.S. strategy for dealing with the threat posed by global warming.
Ocean Dumping Act of 1988, PL 100–688	EPA	Amended the Marine Protection, Research, and Sanctuaries Act of 1972 to end all ocean disposal of sewage sludge and industrial waste by December 31, 1991; revised EPA regulation of ocean dumping by establishing dumping fees, permit requirements, and civil penalties for violations.

G.H.W. Bush Administration

Oil Pollution Act of 1990, PL 101–380	Transportation Department, Commerce Department	Sharply increased liability limits for oil spill cleanup costs and damages; required double hulls on oil tankers and barges by 2015; required federal government to direct cleanups of major spills; required increased contingency planning and preparedness for spills; preserved states' rights to adopt more stringent liability laws and to create state oil spill compensation funds.
Pollution Prevention Act of 1990, PL 101–508	EPA	Established Office of Pollution Prevention in the EPA to coordinate agency efforts at source reduction; created voluntary program to improve lighting efficiency; stated waste minimization was to be primary means of hazardous waste management; mandated source reduction and recycling report to accompany annual toxics release inventory under SARA in order to promote voluntary industry reduction of hazardous waste.
Clean Air Act Amendments of 1990, PL 101–549	EPA	Amended the Clean Air Act of 1970 by setting new requirements and deadlines of three to twenty years for major urban areas to meet federal clean air standards; imposed new, stricter emissions standards for motor vehicles and mandated cleaner fuels; required reduction in emission of sulfur dioxide and nitrogen oxides by power plants to limit acid deposition and created a market system of emissions allowances; required regulation to set emissions limits for all major sources of toxic or hazardous air pollutants and listed 189 chemicals to be regulated; prohibited the use of CFCs by the year 2000 and set phase-out of other ozone-depleting chemicals.

(Continued on next page)

Appendix 1 (*Continued*)

Legislation	Implementing Agency	Key Provisions
Intermodal Surface Transportation Efficiency Act of 1991 (ISTEA, also called the highway bill), PL 102–240	Transportation Department	Authorized $151 billion over six years for transportation, including $31 billion for mass transit; required statewide and metropolitan long-term transportation planning; authorized states and communities to use transportation funds for public transit that reduces air pollution and energy use consistent with Clean Air Act of 1990; required community planners to analyze land use and energy implications of transportation projects they review.
Energy Policy Act of 1992, PL 102–486	Energy Department	Comprehensive energy act designed to reduce U.S. dependency on imported oil. Mandated restructuring of the electric utility industry to promote competition; encouraged energy conservation and efficiency; promoted renewable energy and alternative fuels for cars; eased licensing requirements for nuclear power plants; authorized extensive energy research and development.
The Omnibus Water Act of 1992, PL 102–575	Interior Department	Authorized completion of major water projects in the West; revised the Central Valley Project in California to allow transfer of water rights to urban areas and to encourage conservation through a tiered pricing system that allocates water more flexibly and efficiency; mandated extensive wildlife and environmental protection, mitigation, and restoration programs.

Clinton Administration

Food Quality Protection Act of 1996, PL 104–170	EPA	A major revision of FIFRA that adopted a new approach to regulating pesticides used on food, fiber, and other crops by requiring EPA to consider the diversity of ways in which people are exposed to such chemicals. Created a uniform "reasonable risk" health standard for both raw and processed foods that replaced the requirements of the 1958 Delaney Clause of the Food, Drug, and Cosmetic Act that barred the sale of processed food containing even trace amounts of chemicals found to cause cancer; required the EPA to take extra steps to protect children by establishing an additional tenfold margin of safety in setting acceptable risk standards.

| Safe Drinking Water Act Amendments of 1996, PL 104–182 | EPA | Granted local water systems greater flexibility to focus on the most serious public health risks; authorized $7.6 billion through 2003 for state–administered loan and grant funds to help localities with the cost of compliance; created a "right–to–know" provision requiring large water systems to provide their customers with annual reports on the safety of local water supplies, including information on contaminants found in drinking water and their health effects. Small water systems are eligible for waivers from costly regulations. |
| Transportation Equity Act for the 21st Century (also called ISTEA II or TEA 21), PL 105–178 | Transportation Department | Authorized a six–year, $218 billion program that increased by 40 percent spending to improve the nation's highways and mass transit systems; provided $41 billion for mass transit programs, with over $29 billion coming from the Highway Trust Fund; provided $592 million for research and development on new highway technologies, including transportation–related environmental issues; provided $148 million for a scenic byways program and $270 million for building and maintaining trails; continued support for improvement of bicycle paths. |

G. W. Bush Administration

| The Small Business Liability Relief and Brownfields Revitalization Act of 2002, PL 107–118 | EPA | Amended CERCLA (Superfund) to provide liability protection for prospective purchasers of brownfields and small business owners who contributed to waste sites; authorized increased funding for state and local programs that assess and clean up such abandoned or underused industrial or commercial sites. |
| The Healthy Forests Restoration Act of 2003, PL 108–148 | Agriculture Department, Interior Department | Intended to reduce the risks of forest fires on federal lands by authorizing the cutting of timber in selected areas managed by the Forest Service and the Bureau of Land Management. Sought to protect communities, watersheds, and certain other lands from the effects of catastrophic wildfires. Directed the Secretary of Agriculture and the Secretary of the Interior to plan and conduct hazardous fuel reduction programs on federal lands within their jurisdictions. |

Note: For an update on legislative developments, consult *CQ Weekly* or other professional news sources, or Congressional Quarterly's annual *Almanac*, which summarizes key legislation enacted by Congress and describes the major issues and leading policy actors.

Appendix 2   Budgets of Selected Environmental and Natural Resource
Agencies, 1980–2004 (in billions of dollars)

Agency	1980	1985	1990	1995	2000	2004
Environmental Protection Agency operating budget[a]	1.269	1.340	1.901	2.471	2.480	4.402
	2.540	2.079	2.522	2.903	2.684	4.402
Interior Department total budget	4.678	5.016	6.681	7.519	8.394	10.467
	9.359	7.779	8.862	8.834	9.084	10.467
Selected Agencies						
Bureau of Land Management	0.919	0.800	1.226	1.180	1.616	1.893
	1.840	1.241	1.627	1.386	1.749	1.893
Fish and Wildlife Service	0.435	0.586	1.133	1.278	1.498	1.308
	0.872	0.909	1.503	1.502	1.621	1.308
National Park Service	0.531	1.005	1.275	1.453	2.071	2.259
	1.064	1.561	1.691	1.707	2.241	2.259
Forest Service	2.250	2.116	3.473	3.613	3.728	4.940
	4.505	3.285	4.607	4.245	4.035	4.940

Sources: Office of Management and Budget, *Budget of the United States Government,* fiscal years 1982, 1987, 1992, 1997, 2002, 2006 (Washington, D.C.: U.S. Government Printing Office, 1981, 1986, 1991, 1996, 2001, 2005).

Note: The upper figure for each agency represents budget authority in nominal dollars. Actual budget outlays differ only slightly from these amounts. The lower figure represents budget authority in constant 2004 dollars. These adjustments use the gross domestic product implicit price deflator as calculated by the Bureau of Economic Analysis, Department of Commerce, and reported in the 2004 *Economic Report of the President* (Washington, D.C.: U.S. Government Printing Office, 2004). Data for 2002 to 2004 are taken from the bureau's update of the price deflator issued on January 28, 2005.

[a] The EPA operating budget, which supplies funds for most of the agency's research, regulation, and enforcement programs, is the most meaningful figure. The other two major elements of the total EPA budget historically have been sewage treatment construction or water infrastructure grants (now called state and tribal assistance grants) and Superfund allocations, both of which are excluded from this table. The operating budget is defined here as the remaining amount. The EPA and the White House define the agency's operating budget differently. They do not exclude all of these amounts and thus arrive at a higher figure. The president's proposed fiscal 2006 budget reported an EPA operating budget of $4.325 billion for 2004.

The total EPA budget for fiscal 2004 was $8.366 billion, of which $1.26 billion was allocated for Superfund and $2.7 billion for the assistance grants. The total EPA budget was significantly higher in 2004 than it was in 2002 and 2003 ($7.8 and $7.9 billion, respectively). The trend may not continue. President Bush's 2006 budget proposal calls for a steadily decreasing EPA budget through 2010, when it is projected to be $7.189 billion. For consistency, all figures in the table are taken from the president's budgets for the respective years, except for 2004, where the figures come from *CQ Weekly,* November 27, 2004, pp. 2795 and 2806, in a special report on congressional action on fiscal 2005 appropriations. Final 2004 budget figures should be close to these amounts.

Appendix 3   Employees in Selected Federal Agencies and Departments, 1980, 1990, 2000, and 2005

Agency/Department	Personnel[a]			
	1980	1990	2000	2005
Environmental Protection Agency	12,891	16,513	17,416	17,738
(excluding Superfund-related employees)[b]	NA	13,185	14,205	14,453
Bureau of Land Management	9,655	8,753	9,328	11,065
Fish and Wildlife Service	7,672	7,124	7,011	7,875
National Park Service	13,934	17,781	18,418	18,914
Forest Service	40,606	40,991	33,426	37,247

Sources: U.S. Senate Committee on Governmental Affairs, "Organization of Federal Executive Departments and Agencies," January 1, 1980, and January 1, 1990; and Office of Management and Budget, *Budget of the United States Government,* FY 1982, 1992, 2002, and 2006 (Washington, D.C.: U.S. Government Printing Office, 1981, 1991, 2001, and 2005).

[a] Personnel totals represent full-time equivalent employment, reflecting both permanent and temporary employees. Data for 2000 are based on the fiscal 2002 proposed budget submitted to Congress by the Bush administration in early 2001, and data for 2005 are taken from the administration's proposed fiscal 2006 budget submitted to Congress in February 2005. Because of organizational changes within departments and agencies, the data presented here are not necessarily an accurate record of agency personnel growth or decline over time. The information is presented chiefly to provide an indicator of approximate agency size during different time periods. The gains in employment at the Bureau of Land Management and the Forest Service may reflect approval of the 2003 Healthy Forests initiative.

[b] The Superfund program was created only in late 1980.

Appendix 4   Federal Spending on Natural Resources and the Environment, Selected Fiscal Years, 1980–2004 (in billions of dollars)

Budget item	1980	1988	1996	2000	2004
Water resources	4.085	4.295	4.175	4.803	5.632
	8.180	6.141	4.814	5.198	5.632
Conservation and land management	1.572	3.062	5.980	6.604	10.692
	3.148	4.378	6.896	7.147	10.692
Recreational resources	1.373	1.234	2.111	2.737	2.988
	2.749	1.764	2.434	2.962	2.988
Pollution control and abatement	4.672	4.932	6.433	7.490	8.557
	9.355	7.052	7.418	8.106	8.557
Other natural resources	1.395	1.852	2.814	3.397	4.853
	2.793	2.648	3.245	3.676	4.853
Total	13.097	15.375	21.513	25.031	32.722
	26.225	21.983	24.807	27.090	32.722

Source: Office of Management and Budget, *Historical Tables, Budget of the United States Government Fiscal Year 2006* (Washington, D.C.: U.S. Government Printing Office, 2005), 82–84.

Note: Data are provided for eight-year intervals until 1996, and for four-year intervals thereafter to focus on recent trends. The upper figure for each item represents budget authority in nominal dollars. Actual budget outlays differ only slightly from these amounts. Figures for 1980 are provided to indicate pre–Reagan administration spending bases. The lower figure represents budget authority in constant 2004 dollars. These adjustments use the gross domestic product implicit price deflator as calculated by the Bureau of Economic Analysis, Department of Commerce, and reported in the 2004 *Economic Report of the President* (Washington, D.C.: U.S. Government Printing Office, 2004). Data for 2002 to 2004 are taken from the Bureau's update of the price deflator issued on January 28, 2005. The natural resources and environment function in the federal budget reported in this table does not include environmental cleanup programs within the Departments of Defense and Energy, which are substantial.

Author Citations Index

Subject Index

Tables, figures, and boxes are indicated by *t, f,* and *b,* respectively.